Images of Women
in American Popular Culture

Images of *Women* in American Popular Culture

ANGELA G. DORENKAMP
Associate Professor of English
ASSUMPTION COLLEGE

JOHN F. McCLYMER
Professor of History
ASSUMPTION COLLEGE

MARY M. MOYNIHAN
Assistant Professor of Sociology
ASSUMPTION COLLEGE

ARLENE C. VADUM
Associate Professor of Psychology
ASSUMPTION COLLEGE

HARCOURT BRACE JOVANOVICH, PUBLISHERS
*San Diego   New York   Chicago   Atlanta   Washington, D.C.
London   Sydney   Toronto*

Cover and illustrations by courtesy of the Dover Pictorial Archive Series, Dover Publications Inc.

Copyright © 1985 by Harcourt Brace Jovanovich, Inc.

Requests for permission to make copies of any part of the work should be mailed to: Permissions, Harcourt Brace Jovanovich, Publishers, Orlando, Florida 32887.

ISBN: 0-15-540600-0
Library of Congress Catalog Card Number: 84-81747
Printed in the United States of America

To the countless women whose experiences inspired this book

Preface

LONG BEFORE IT BECAME A BOOK, this anthology was a large, untidy pile of stories, advertising copy, poems, magazine articles, best-sellers, advice literature, marriage manuals, political manifestos, and newspaper columns. What tied this diverse mass of material together was the fact that it all dealt with the way representatives of American popular culture have portrayed women over the past two centuries. We had collected these readings for our interdisciplinary course in women's studies, which we developed and taught under a grant from the National Endowment for the Humanities.

From this rich store, we have selected about a hundred pieces for this volume. Some of these documents, like the 1848 Seneca Falls *Declaration of Rights and Sentiments* and Betty Friedan's "The Problem That Has No Name," are well known. Others, like Fanny Fern's witty and barbed social commentary on mid-nineteenth century American mores, ought to be. We have included some selections, like a 1908 *Harper's Bazaar* article called "How to Get Plump," not for any intrinsic merits of their own, but for the attitudes they exemplify.

We have avoided tying the selections to a particular feminist perspective. Instead, we have assembled readings that have important implications for all feminists, for women's studies scholars, and for students of popular culture. We looked for classic statements of dominant beliefs about women, searched out some areas of female experience these beliefs affect, and selected readings that recapture the flavor of the debates they inspired. In addition, we have included some selections from women's diaries, letters, memoirs, and fiction to illustrate the effects of popular images on private lives. As a result, our choices reflect a wide range of viewpoints, from unregenerate male supremacy to radical feminism.

As we tested these readings in the classroom with our students, we realized that using evidence from popular publications to illuminate basic themes in women's studies affords a number of benefits. Most beneficial, perhaps, is the accessibility of the materials themselves. Because such publications by nature appeal to a wide and varied audience, they usually have a high level of readability; even the older selections engage the attention of contemporary students. The mass media generally reflect the accepted wisdom about women—their nature, place, and roles—so students come to recognize not only the power of such widely disseminated images in the shaping of social expectations, but the difficulty that dissenters like Elizabeth Cady Stanton, Charlotte Perkins Gilman, Betty Friedan, and Shulamith Firestone faced in trying to change them.

Because we want students to draw their own conclusions, we have kept the editorial matter to a minimum. Headnotes sketch the historical, literary, and social contexts for individual documents, identifying authors and describing the media in which the materials first appeared, but they do not interpret the documents, which we have reprinted intact whenever possible. This text both invites and requires students and teachers to construe and construct, to make connections, to analyze and interpret. We have organized our materials thematically rather than chronologically so that users can hear the echoes and reprises of certain ideas over time.

Chapter 1 considers woman's nature through comments—from Charles D. Meigs, the nineteenth-century physician whose *Woman: Her Diseases and Remedies* epitomized what Barbara Welter called the "cult of true womanhood," to Carol Gilligan, the contemporary psychologist whose theories of female moral development are at the cutting edge of current scholarship. Chapter 2, on cultural definitions of woman's "place," includes Elise Johnson McDougald's 1925 essay on the black woman's "double task" of overcoming both racism and sexism, as well as a commentary on Genesis from the 1895 *Woman's Bible*. Next, in Chapter 3, come materials on images of women as sexual objects, from Nora Ephron's article on breasts to Gloria Steinem's editorial on Linda Lovelace's *Ordeal*. In Chapter 4, documents illustrating cultural ideals for women as "sweethearts and wives" range from an 1841 short story of that name to a modern marriage manual from the Detroit archdiocese of the Roman Catholic church.

Chapter 5 discusses motherhood, from the traditional mother of McGuffey's *Eclectic Readers* to the Native American mother of Zitkala-Ša's memoir. Selections on images of women who work, both inside and outside the home, make up Chapter 6. Some, like the 1980 article from *Essence* and the 1908 account of "Stenography in New York City," deal with what society now often considers woman's work; others, like the nineteenth-century "Feminine Waiters at Hotels" and the recent report on women coal miners, deal with the entry of women into previously male domains. Chapter 7, on sisterhood, contains materials on women's friendships, loyalties, and loves. They include letters from Emily Dickinson to a childhood friend, Susan Glaspell's classic one-act play, *Trifles*, and the Boston Women's Health Collective's "In Amerika They Call Us Dykes." The last chapter concentrates on organized efforts to change those images that distort, even as they define, women. Here we present debates on suffrage and the Equal Rights Amendment. Here, too, we offer to students writings by the militants of Seneca Falls and La Raza, along with the visions of Gilman and Firestone.

The logic of this organization proceeds from popular perceptions about what women are like physically, morally, and socially (Chapters 1–3), to pronouncements about their "proper" roles and duties (4–6), to women's prospects for gaining control over their own destinies (7–8). Not everyone who uses the book will want to follow this order. We have taken considerable care to make the individual selections and chapters independent of each other. Instructors can assign the readings in any sequence they wish or can combine the readings with other, more theoretical treatises or with American history or literature, sociology, or psychology texts. Likewise, students can satisfy their curiosity about topics toward the back of the book by reading ahead.

No collection can include everything, but we have made our anthology as inclusive as the constraints of size and cost allowed. We hope that you will share your suggestions for additions and deletions with us. And we will be especially grateful if you will take the time to share with us your experiences using this text.

Acknowledgments

This book grew out of our work together on an interdisciplinary course in women's studies. Neither the course nor the book would have been possible without an institutional grant from the National Endowment for the Humanities (#ED-20030). The Assumption College Faculty Development Fund also provided much-needed assistance.

Many of our colleagues at Assumption College gave moral and scholarly support that lightened our task at critical points. We also benefited from the services of some unusually dedicated and effective student assistants: Janice A. Pothier, Jessie M. Rodrique, JoAnn Robichaud, Keith A. Bruso, Nancy E. Legere, Ann C. Brady, Sheila Waldron, and Ann Gillerlane. We are indebted, too, to Ellen McSweeney for her conscientious handling of many difficult tasks associated with the gathering of permissions.

Librarians at Assumption College and elsewhere served us in countless ways. We particularly wish to thank Priscilla Gonneville of Assumption College, Nancy Burkett of the American Antiquarian Society, Virginia Quinn and Penny Johnson of the Worcester Public Library, and Lucy Fisher West, college archivist at Bryn Mawr. Their expertise made the locating and reproducing of materials far easier and more pleasant.

Many people offered us good advice. They include our NEH consultants, D'Ann Campbell of the University of Indiana and Margo Culley of the University of Massachusetts at Amherst; our editors, Drake Bush, Gene Carter Lettau, Ellen Aleksic, and Eleanor Garner; and the designer, Merilyn Britt.

Others who helped with the project merit our special thanks as well. They include Konstantina Lukes, Eleanor Hawley, Robert Moynihan, and Neil Rankin, and the reviewers, Professors Janet Sharistanian of the University of Kansas, Lawrence; Deborah Rosenfelt of San Francisco State University; and Bonnie Zimmerman of San Diego State University. To them, and to others who read all or parts of this book and tried to save us from various gaffes, we extend the traditional exoneration for whatever errors may remain.

Most of all, we want to thank the students who, for three years now, have patiently borne with us as we offered them the various readings that make up this book. Their good humor and fair-mindedness made them ideal first readers. Their enthusiasm for the subject has been a constant inspiration. We hope they can be proud of this book.

Contents

xi

THREE

Woman as Object   125

FOUR

Sweethearts and Wives   173

FIVE

Mothers *229*

SIX

Workers *285*

SEVEN

Sisters *341*

EIGHT

Struggles and Visions   405

Images of Women
in American Popular Culture

ONE

Woman's Nature

IN 1960 GOOD HOUSEKEEPING magazine
published an article entitled "How to
Know When You're Really Feminine."
Its author, Leonard Robinson, wrote the
article to correct popular misconcep-
tions about femininity that he understood to be causing needless confusion
and self-doubt in women. He promised
his readers "one clear, infallible formula" for judging their femininity,
based on a single, "deep and permanent"
trait possessed by every woman.

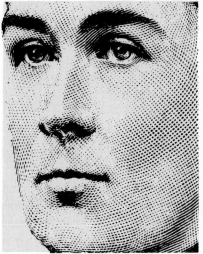

Robinson found specialists in agreement that woman's psychology is firmly
anchored in her biology; more specifically, that her psychology stems from
"the fact that nature has made her . . .
'womb-centered'." Her "womb-centeredness" assures a woman's devotion to
husband and family, they agreed, and "gives her the unique psychological trait
which is the very core of her femininity"—"essential feminine altruism." "For
the true woman," that is, the woman manifesting this trait, "children and

husband come first, *way before self,* for that is how her altruism expresses itself." According to one expert, "If this basic altruism is undeveloped in a woman, it doesn't matter what else she has. A bust measurement of 40, fearlessness in childbirth, and all the perfumes of Arabia won't make her truly feminine." And conversely, when essential feminine altruism motivates her behavior, any woman can be certain that she is genuinely feminine.

The article, purporting to unlock the secret of femininity, is by no means unique. Throughout the past two centuries, the period encompassed by the readings, people have debated the question of woman's nature perennially, and no dearth of experts, often male, like Robinson, have advised women on what they really are like, and on the criteria for "true femininity." Likewise, a large and responsive female audience, concerned about their femininity, and eager to meet accepted standards of womanliness, has sought such counsel. Traditionally, the clergy, using the authority of scripture, has been a potent force in defining "woman's nature." And because of their special understanding of woman's biology, physicians have acquired expert status in describing women as well. More recently, psychologists and others trained in the scientific analysis of human behavior have joined their ranks.

The *Good Housekeeping* article asserted that femininity springs from being "womb-centered." But, depending on the historical epoch and the "trait" being considered, experts have used every conceivable physical distinction between the sexes to explain woman's "true" intellectual, emotional, or social qualities. They have focused on differences in the size and functioning of women's brains compared to men's, the greater sensitivity and complexity of their nervous systems, the appearance and functioning of their external genitals, their internal reproductive organs, the passivity of ova compared to sperm, and differences between the sex chromosomes, hormones, and muscular development of women and men, as explanations of woman's behavior.

Although woman's nature is presumably unchanging, being based on her biology, popular views of it show remarkable variability over time. Major shifts in imagery have occurred even from one decade to the next, and certain ideas have dropped out, only to recur later. During the colonial period, women and men worked together in the home, and women were represented in the major trades. But the early nineteenth century movement of the workplace out of the home led, by midcentury, to a new concept of the home and of woman, its guardian. When "home" began to be thought of, not as a bustling center of familial livelihood, but instead as a tranquil island of purity and love in an increasingly urbanized and industrialized society, a narrow and restrictive view of woman, uncharacteristic of colonial times, developed along with it. Only toward the end of the century did a new image of woman emerge, along with greater educational and work opportunities for many women, and expanded demands by women for their rights. These developments culminated in the early twentieth century "flapper," with her unparalleled, and heretofore "masculine," new freedoms.

While some of the reforming zeal of the 1920s was lost in the ensuing decades, the image of woman as capable and autonomous persisted. During the second world war women took over formerly "male jobs" in unprecedented numbers. They had done so during the first world war as well. But, ironically, the end of WW II signaled the appearance of the most restrictive and exclusively domestic feminine ideal of the century. Indeed, a major thrust of the current woman's movement has been to undo the image of woman that developed during the 1950s.

Despite such variation, the notion of a fixed feminine nature has persisted and been used to draw conclusions about woman's biologically ordained roles or, in more popular terms, her "proper sphere." The experts quoted in the *Good Housekeeping* article concluded that woman's "womb-centeredness" ensures her commitment to husband and family and her service to others. A century earlier an editorial in *Harper's New Monthly Magazine* (1854), warning against women assuming public functions, argued: "Her flaccid muscles, tender skin, highly nervous organization, and aptitude for internal injury, decide the question of offices involving hard bodily labor; while the predominance of instinct over reason, and of feeling over intellect, as a rule, unfits her for judicial or legislative command. Her power is essentially a silent and unseen moral influence; her functions are those of wife and mother." Such cases illustrate how arguments about woman's nature have been used to woman's disadvantage, to close off avenues of achievement and satisfaction to her by arguing that various "feminine" attributes unsuit her to particular activities and occupations.

In addition, society has often devalued the assumed characteristics of women and has given men title to many of the most respected traits. Sometimes the devaluation is subtle indeed. "Essential feminine altruism," the "deep and permanent" standard of femininity cited in the *Good Housekeeping* article, required that the true woman always place the needs of her husband and children before her own—"*way before*" her own. Although such unerring self-sacrifice is one criterion for sainthood as well as femininity, nonetheless there is a depreciation of women implied in this definition. The husband and children are assumed to be worthy and important; the self-sacrificing woman is not. As this example points out all too well, to strive to be "feminine" or "womanly" has meant to attempt to match impossible standards of perfection, and, at the same time, to be moved to accept a decidedly negative self-image.

Though women are praised for enthusiastically conforming to popular ideals of femininity, to embrace these cultural definitions commonly has meant to sacrifice the fulfillment of certain fundamental human needs—such as the need for self-expression, autonomy, and self-regard—in order to avoid the loss of satisfaction of other, equally basic, needs. For to not live up to accepted standards means to court rejection and even declassification as unnatural or unwomanly. And for women, who have been indoctrinated from early childhood in the view that their identity rests in their relationships with others, and that their "niceness" and interpersonal sensitivity are their great powers and their most estimable qualities, this is a particularly dreadful prospect. In the readings, women speak of their efforts to live with the ideal images of femininity and of their attempts to reconcile the fact of their womanhood, with their sometimes seemingly incompatible human desires for autonomy, self-respect, and creativity.

Despite the power of the cultural images in shaping women's experience, complete and unquestioning acceptance of the popular views has never existed. As the readings document, throughout the past two centuries, some women and men have been able to transcend cultural perceptions and prescriptions and have risked the almost inevitable public censure to experiment with change or to tamper with cherished beliefs. Some have spoken from personal pain or from witnessing the suffering of others, some from unrelenting pride, some from anger, some from seeing that they or others have been forgotten or misrepresented in the popular white, middle and upper-class imagery. And because of their courage, women today have a different legacy and new power to transcend restrictive and untenable definitions of their nature. In the words of the early twentieth century sociologist, Elsie Clews Parsons:

> To be declassified is very painful to most persons and so the charge of unwomanliness has ever been a kind of whip against the would-be woman rebel. Not until she fully understands how arbitrary it is will she cease to feel its crack.*

---

*As quoted in Rosalind Rosenberg, *Beyond Separate Spheres: The Roots of Modern Feminism*, New Haven: Yale University Press, 1982, 172.

CHIMAERA*; OR MODERN WOMAN

Ferdinand Lundberg and Marynia F. Farnham, M.D.

Advice literature for women has been a flourishing industry for at least the past two centuries. At first the experts were clergymen and physicians. Later they were joined, but not displaced, by home economists, efficiency experts, dieticians, psychologists, and a host of others. One of the most popular and influential advice books of this century was *Modern Woman: The Lost Sex* (1947) by Ferdinand Lundberg, a journalist and financial expert, and Dr. Marynia Farnham, a psychoanalyst.

In the late 1940s and early '50s, popular women's magazines were all spouting ideas from the pages of Lundberg and Farnham's book. Modern woman had become lost, a problem to herself and others, they asserted, because she had forsaken her femininity in a search for an independence unsuited to her nature. So persuasive was this message that in Betty Friedan's view, it was instrumental in recasting feminine ideals for the 1950s. Friedan called the image they promoted, which focused on fulfillment through domesticity and motherhood, "the feminine mystique."

In the following excerpt from *Modern Woman: The Lost Sex,* Lundberg and Farnham describe woman's nature as an unsolved problem. The remainder of their book attempted to supply solutions based on psychoanalytic theory and Dr. Farnham's clinical experiences with women.

. . .Women, if we turn to the poets, philosophers and prophets, have always been something of an enigma. No trust whatever is to be placed in them, according to nodding Homer, who believed there was "no fouler fiend than a woman when her mind is bent to evil." Aristophanes thought there was nothing worse in the world than a woman, unless some other woman. To Aristotle she was "an inferior man," to Virgil "fickle and changeful," to Milton a "fair defect," to Pope "the best reserv'd of God" but nevertheless invariably "at heart a rake," to the scientific Francis Galton "capricious and coy" and far less straightforward than a man, to Whitman the very gate of the human soul, to Nietzsche the "second mistake of God," etc. "Woman, at best, is bad," said Thomas Dekker, seventeenth century English playwright. George Wilkins, a contemporary, said that they were "in churches, saints; abroad, angels; at home, devils." Nathaniel Field, who wrote at about the same time, believed them to be "torturous as Hell, insatiate as the grave," and John Webster, another playwright of the day, summarized it all: "Woman to man is either a god or a wolf." Shakespeare, who probably saw more deeply into

*Chimaera: In Greek mythology, a fire-breathing monster, usually pictured as having the head of a lion, the body of a goat, and the tail of a serpent.

women (and men, too) than anyone else, either before or since, finally throws up his hands with a despairing, "Who is't can read a woman?" Lest too much be made of such remarks, which could be extended ad infinitum, we must say the poets and philosophers have been no less confused and contradictory respecting the male, alternately self-abasing and self-apostrophizing.

Anthropologists, carrying the inquiry a bit farther afield, have found that in nearly all primitive cultures women are considered a fearsome mystery. A primitive man no more wants a woman to cross his path at certain inauspicious periods of the month than certain Americans want a black cat to at any time. In both instances, a powerful bad medicine is thought to be generated, blighting to hopeful endeavors.

This book, however, does not deal with women as a general historical or evolutionary riddle, which they unquestionably are, but as a specific one produced by our own times. For in our times women have become, in sober truth, a riddle within a riddle. Men, too, may be a problem; one must concede this, if only out of deference to the bedeviled female who has had to cope with a man who was. And, by way of placing our subject matter in more precise perspective (and at the same time showing our awareness of male misdoings), we may casually remark that Hitler was not a woman, nor was Mussolini, Al Capone, Dillinger, Lord Haw Haw or Judas Iscariot. We have not forgotten that there is an extensive historical rogues' gallery of males. But, focusing even more precisely, men usually become problems whenever women do, because anything that affects women very much soon affects everyone. Biographers will one day, we hope, come to understand that their true subject is hardly the man (or woman) they have chosen to scrutinize, and not his or her mistress or lover, but the mother or her substitute. Men, standing before the bar of historical judgment, might often well begin their defense with the words: "I had a mother. . . . "

Women in general are a more complicated question than men, as a few of the poets have sensed, for they are more complicated organisms. They are endowed with a complicated reproductive system (with which the male genito-urinary system compares in complexity not at all), a more elaborate nervous system and an infinitely complex psychology revolving about the reproductive function. Women, therefore, cannot be regarded as any more similar to men than a spiral is to a straight line.

Each sex represents an organic tracing of reality. But in one instance the tracing is simple (relatively), in the other complex and even devious. Because of their unchallengeably greater physiological and psychological complexity and because this fact of greater complexity has not yet begun to be taken into systematic social account (although the psychiatrists are grappling with it and are beginning to see a great light), women are the ones about whom debate rages, among themselves as well as among men. . . .

SEXUAL PECULIARITIES
Charles D. Meigs, M.D.

Charles D. Meigs, M. D. (1792–1869) was a professor of midwifery and the diseases of women and children at Jefferson Medical College in Philadelphia from 1841 to 1861, and he also maintained a large and lucrative private practice. This prestige helped produce a large audience for his book. Although ostensibly written for his medical students, Meigs' *Woman: Her Diseases and Remedies* became something of a best seller and went through several editions.

At the heart of the book is Meigs' forceful summing up of what polite society of his day thought woman's nature was. So successfully did Meigs capture these beliefs that when historian Barbara Welter wrote her classic essay on "The Cult of True Womanhood," it was to Meigs' text that she turned again and again for evidence. "True womanhood," a phrase Meigs never used himself, consisted in a series of moral virtues and social characteristics—piety, purity, submissiveness, and domesticity—which Meigs and other spokespeople for "respectable" society imputed to woman's physical and moral natures. Thus, the chastity which men struggled to acquire supposedly came naturally to women. And woman's proper sphere of influence was reflected in her body structure. To Meigs, for example, woman's head appeared "almost too small for intellect, but just big enough for love."

Popular writers of the day favored the self-consciously literary style, filled with classical references, that Meigs used. Whatever difficulty this style may occasion is offset by the importance of Meigs' ideas both at the time and later.

. . .The female is naturally prone to be religious. Hers is a pious mind. Her confiding nature leads her more readily than men to accept the proffered grace of the Gospel. If an undevout astronomer is mad, what shall we say of an irreligious woman? See how the temples of the Christian worship are filled with women. They flock thither with their young children, and endeavor to implant in their souls the seeds of virtue and piety, to be reared in that pure soil and by their watchful nurture, into plants that shall blossom like the immortal amaranth among the stars. See, then, what and how great is the influence that women exert on the morals of society, of whole nations, of the whole world! Wherever there is a true civilization, woman reigns in society. It is not until she comes to sit beside him, in view of all the people, that man ceases to be barbarous, or semi-barbarous, brutal, and ignorant.

She spreads abroad the light of civilization and improvement as soon as she issues from the prison of the Harem or Zenana, to live with him in the world. Who made us human? Whose were the hands that led us to kneel down, and whose the lips that taught our infant voices the earliest invocations to Heaven? Is it not so, that after the world and fortune have done their best, or their worst by us, we, in late years, and early, forget not those pious mothers, who so steadfastly strove to bias our young minds in favor of whatsoever is true, whatsoever is pure, whatsoever is of good report!! How can we forget the rewards we received at her hands for all our good, and her gentle, and

SEXUAL PECULIARITIES From *Woman: Her Diseases and Remedies. A Series of Lectures to His Class*, Philadelphia: Blanchard & Lea, 1859, 4th ed., revised and enlarged. Abridged, 62–67.

sometimes tearful reprovings of our evil inclinations and practices? She was not only our teacher and pattern, but our companion and playfellow, for, of a truth, she was of a childlike temper—and that was the secret of the bond that united us to her so long and so closely. . . .

The male is less versatile than the woman. His mission is more adventurous and dangerous. *He* enters on the path of ambition, that dark and dangerous, or broad and shining road.

He pursues the devious track of politics with a resolute will; reaching ever onwards to the possession of fame and patronage, and rank and wealth, and power.

She sits at home to adorn the tent or the cottage with wreaths of flowers, or to guide the tendrils that give shade to his bower. She plies the busy loom—and the sweet sounds of her singing—how often have I listened as they accompany the hum and buzz of her wheel, as she gracefully advances and retires by turns, forming the threads about to be woven into garments for her husband or child! Her nimble fingers, all day long, ply the shining needle, to fashion the robe for her spouse—or to arrange the more elegant embellishments of her person, that they may engage his admiration, and augment the flame of his love. For woman, man's love is the moving spring of all her actions. This is at the foundation even of her vanity. Lais herself is said to have sacrificed even her rage for wealth, at times, to the gratification of her vanity; and though the lioness tearing a ram to pieces, which was sculptured upon her tomb, was the emblem of her insatiable avarice, yet Lais lived more for love than for gain.

What say you of the fortitude of woman? She bears the evils of life without repining or complaining against the providence of God. Is she evil entreated, prevented, injured? That which sets a man on fire with an insane rage, kindles in her bosom, perhaps, only a virtuous feeling of indignation. She bears the greatest crosses. How beautifully does Shakspeare say so in the words,

> "She never told her love,
> But let Concealment, like a worm i' the bud,
> Feed on her damask cheek;
> And sate, like Patience on a monument,
> Smiling at grief."

She dies a willing martyr for religion, for country—for her children.

Who can number the Lucretias and Portias? How many are like unto the charming Roland? Think of the calm features of Charlotte Corday! Did you read of the deeds and the death of La Puçelle?

Women possess a peculiar trait—modesty, which is one of the most charming of their attributes; springing probably from their natural timidity and sense of dependence, of which it is the ideal in expression. All rude, boisterous, and immodest speech or action unsexes and disgraces woman. Hence, modesty is one of the strongest of her attractions; and she sometimes, perhaps, affects to possess it for the purpose of riveting her chains on the conqueror man. . . .

The attribute of modesty certainly lends the most powerful aid to the other charms of a woman. It is one of the qualities given to her in order to be a strong fence for her children, for it binds her to the domestic altar—her children could not but endure damage and loss, should she leave them at home to plunge into the torrent of public affairs, or mingle freely with the distracting world! Her modesty, gentleness, and timidity, assimilate her to the characters of children, whose best playfellow, nurse, and instructress she is. Come out from the world, and be separate from it, is peculiarly a command for her.

There is in the Museo Pio-Clementino, at Rome, an antique statue, which the learned Visconti asserts to be a statue of Modesty, and which, as I am informed, is among the most beautiful of the works of ancient art now remaining in the world. It is completely clothed from head to foot, and veiled. It seems to me that such a work is proof enough of the ancient admiration of the quality in question; for the artist who could produce, and the people who could appreciate, such an exquisite specimen of taste and right feeling, must have had a keen perception of the charm.

By her physical form and proportion, she is still more trenchantly divided from the male. Look at two statues, male and female. Take the Venus de Medici as the consummate exposition—the very eidolon of the female form, just as Praxiteles in the greatest verve, fervor, and enthusiasm of his genius, and he alone of all mankind, could conceive the idea of the Queen of the Loves.

Compare her with the Apollo of the Belvidere—she has a head almost too small for intellect, but just big enough for love. His magnificent forehead, calm as heaven, and almost as high as it, rises above those eyes that are following the shaft he has sped with his clanging silver bow.

> "The front of Jove himself,
> An eye like Mars, to threaten and command;
> A station, like a feathered Mercury, new-lighted on
> Some heaven-kissing hill."

Her thorax seems built as the sanctuary of that beautiful bosom, whence is destined to flow the sweet nutriment of the winged boy.

Man's vast chest is for breathing, for eloquence and command. From its capacious stores of oxygen he draws the elements of the most strenuous, the most protracted exertions. He breathes deep, that he may ascend the highest hills and the sharpest crags in pursuit of his game or his prey, and that his loud harmonious voice may command his armies in the midst of the conflict, or sway the forum with its tones. Like Virgil's wild horse, he is equal to the longest career—nothing can stay him in his race.

See his loins how they are narrowed down, as they approach the hips, that he may balance himself, as it were, on the point of an inverted cone, prompt for the quickest motion. His pelvis contains no variable organs, requiring ample space for extraordinary developments; but its depth and solidity afford origin and insertion to the powerful muscles by whose immense strength he can act well in the wild, rude, and adventurous life to which he is ordained.

The cone, on the other hand, is reversed in the female. The apex is above, and the base at the hips. It is within that bony cell that are hidden those miraculous organs that out of nothing can evolve the wondrous work of reproduction. The pelvis is broad and shallow, light in substance, its excavation ample, and its pubic arch round or Roman; while his is Gothic or lanceolate. From under this arch a child could not go; the other gives it easy utterance. His organisms are permanent—hers are mutable. The uterus—no bigger than a thumb—comes in gestation to be twelve inches long and nine in width. Its invisible vessels and nerves come to be great cords and tubes, and its undiscoverable muscles acquire a force to rend itself in pieces in its rage, or, what seems still more miraculous, to expel a full-grown infant from its cavity, against the enormous resistance of flesh and bone. She is a germiparous and vitelliferous creature. She—the female—possesses that strange compound or concrete which you call stroma, ovarian *stroma,* of which I already have spoken, but must again speak. Now, that stroma lives by the common blood it receives out of a common endangium, and yet it has a nerve which enables it to convert that blood into vitellus or yelk. The perpetuation of races and germs depends on the elimination of that matter. There is no animal germ without it—so that an organ so small, so unobvious, is endowed with the vast responsibility of keeping up the living scheme of the world—with its moralities—its lives—its actions—its trial—which, were it to cease, there would be left no flowers to bloom, no insects to sport in the evening beam, no choral song of birds, no lowing of cattle, no bleating of flocks, nor voices of men to thank and praise and acknowledge the Author of every good and every perfect gift.

Think, gentlemen, of such great power—and ask your own judgments whether such an organ can be of little influence in the constitution of the woman; whether *she* was not made in order that *it* should be made, and whether it may not on occasion become a disturbing radiator in her economy, and how much so. You will answer yes, if you know that her ovary is her sex—and that she is peculiar because of, and in order that she might have this great, this dominant organ planted within the recesses of her body.

Men cannot suffer the same pains as women. *What* do you call the pain of parturition? There is no name for it but *Agony.*

Why does she love her child more than its father does? Why, he grew to her! He was perhaps an acinus cast out of her stroma, and after drawing his blood from her own blood, he drank life at the living well of her bosom, and character from her monitions and example. What were Cornelia's jewels! Who was Washington's mother!

A young lady after a very severe and dangerous labor, while still languid and pale, was asked this question: Mary, shall we have some verses from you, now that the baby is born? "Yes," and the impromptu was the following:—

MY LITTLE IDA.

I've a wee thing to love—an infant new-born,
With cheeks like a rose, and breath fresh as the morn,
And methought when she first op'd her bright beaming eyes,
That *twin* stars had fall'n in my bed from the skies.

Her hands although idle, no mischief have done,
Her feet are too tiny in sin's path to run,
No word e'er escaped her of slander or guile,
Her lips close as they open, *always* with a smile.

At night, when she makes her soft pillow my breast,
How calm, how unbroken, how peaceful my rest!
For I know that pure angels whom no eye can see,
To guard my sweet babe, then approach near to me.

> I have gaz'd with delight on the lovely and fair,
> On locks dark as midnight and bright golden hair,
> But beauty to me was a something unknown,
> Till I looked on my first-born and called her my own.

What do we owe her?—life, peace, liberty, social order. *She* built up this great frame of society in civilization. . . .

Christianity is propagated by her domestic influence. The loom is her work, and the tapestried walls are of her imagining. Were it not for her, we were this day clothed in sheep skins and goat skins, and should lie down in dens and caves. It is for her that the looms of Cashmere, the silks of China, the gauzes of Hindustan, the mousselines of Lyons, the laces of Belgium and England are formed; the carpets of Ispahan and Dresden, Cornelius's blazing chandelier, all the riches displayed by Levy and Bailey are for her. Everything that man is and hath, except his brute force and brutal inclinations, are of her and for her. . . .

SPEECH AT AKRON WOMEN'S RIGHTS CONVENTION, 1851

Sojourner Truth

Sojourner Truth epitomized just about everything that an ideal antebellum woman was not supposed to be: She was tall and gaunt; she was physically powerful; she was black and illiterate. She was a speaker who never appeared demure, reserved, or submissive.

Because of her power some of her opponents could deny that she was indeed a woman. It was just too much of a challenge to their belief that women, regardless of color, ought to be domestic, submissive, and frail. A rumor started that Sojourner Truth was a "Negro man" who spoke on women's rights. The rumor was so widespread that at one of her appearances, it is said, Truth bared her breasts to prove she was a woman.

Born a slave around 1797, Truth received the name "Isabella" from her master. In 1827, when mandatory emancipation was proclaimed for slaves in New York, Isabella reunited with two of her children and moved to New York City. After early work as a missionary, she lived quietly doing domestic work and raising her children. In 1843, she rejected her slave name, took the name Sojourner Truth, and began to travel and preach again. Truth was a charismatic speaker, and her reputation as an abolitionist and preacher grew during the 1840s and '50s.

In this famous speech to the Women's Rights Convention in Akron, Ohio, in 1851, Sojourner Truth's constant refrain, "And a'n't I a woman?" questioned the many romanticized images of women that prevented them from gaining the right to vote.

. . .The tumult subsided at once, and every eye was fixed on this almost Amazon form, which stood nearly six feet high, head erect, and eyes piercing the upper air like one in a dream. At her first word there was a profound hush. She spoke in deep tones, which, though not loud, reached every ear in the

SPEECH AT AKRON WOMEN'S RIGHTS CONVENTION   From Susan B. Anthony, Elizabeth Cady Stanton, and Matilda Joslyn Gage, *History of Woman Suffrage*, Vol. I, New York, Fowler & Wells, 1881, 116.

house, and away through the throng at the doors and windows.

"Wall, chilern, whar dar is so much racket dar must be somethin' out o' kilter. I tink dat 'twixt de niggers of de Souf and de womin at de Norf, all talkin' 'bout rights, de white men will be in a fix pretty soon. But what's all dis here talkin' 'bout?

"Dat man ober dar say dat womin needs to be helped into carriages, and lifted ober ditches, and to hab de best place everywhar. Nobody eber helps me into carriages, or ober mud-puddles, or gibs me any best place!" And raising herself to her full height, and her voice to a pitch like rolling thunder, she asked, "And a'n't I a woman? Look at me! Look at my arm! (and she bared her right arm to the shoulder, showing her tremendous muscular power). I have ploughed, and planted, and gathered into barns, and no man could head me! And a'n't I a woman? I could work as much and eat as much as a man—when I could get it—and bear de lash as well! And a'n't I a woman? I have borne thirteen chilern, and seen 'em mos' all sold off to slavery, and when I cried out with my mother's grief, none but Jesus heard me! And a'n't I a woman?

"Den dey talks 'bout dis ting in de head; what dis dey call it?" ("Intellect," whispered some one near.) "Dat's it, honey. What's dat got to do wid womin's rights or nigger's rights? If my cup won't hold but a pint, and yourn holds a quart, wouldn't ye be mean not to let me have my little half-measure full?" And she pointed her significant finger, and sent a keen glance at the minister who had made the argument. The cheering was long and loud.

"Den dat little man in black dar, he say women can't have as much rights as men, 'cause Christ wan't a woman! Whar did your Christ come from?" Rolling thunder couldn't have stilled that crowd, as did those deep, wonderful tones, as she stood there with outstretched arms and eyes of fire. Raising her voice still louder, she repeated, "Whar did your Christ come from? From God and a woman! Man had nothin' to do wid Him." Oh, what a rebuke that was to that little man.

Turning again to another objector, she took up the defense of Mother Eve. I can not follow her through it all. It was pointed, and witty, and solemn; eliciting at almost every sentence deafening applause; and she ended by asserting: "If de fust woman God ever made was strong enough to turn de world upside down all alone, dese women togedder (and she glanced her eye over the platform) ought to be able to turn it back, and get it right side up again! And now dey is asking to do it, de men better let 'em." Long-continued cheering greeted this. " 'Bleeged to ye for hearin' on me, and now ole Sojourner han't got nothin' more to say." . . .

DEADLIER THAN THE MALE

Marya Mannes

The well-known verse from the nursery rhyme, "When she was good, she was very, very good, but when she was bad, she was horrid," aptly captures the age-old view of woman as angel or devil. Besides showing that images of women as temptress-destroyer persist in contemporary society, in the following selection Marya Mannes points to a seeming paradox. It's not just the "bad girls" who can be absolutely horrid, says Mannes, "good girls" too can be "deadlier than the male."

Marya Mannes is a poet, essayist, and playwright. She has written stories and articles for many national magazines, and she has been a feature editor for *Vogue* and *Glamour*. Mannes wrote this article for her column in *McCall's*, a popular women's magazine with a circulation of almost five million by the late 1950s. As her byline *Let's Face It* indicates, Mannes prides herself on telling it like it is.

 In a recent film, *The Tenth Victim*, the opening scene shows a nightclub stripper who kills a male customer by firing shots from her ballistic bra.

A cosmetic ad consists of a sungilded female torso clad only in a gold-mail cartridge belt stuffed with lipstick bullets.

In the new Modesty Blaise film, the girl spy resorts to whatever lethally aggressive techniques serve her dubious missions.

Yet these feral females are not really new. Ian Fleming introduced us to a few dillies, among them the unforgettable Pussy Galore; and whether in Shmersch or Thrush or U.N.C.L.E. or whatever combination of initials spells a gadget-ridden underground organization dedicated to good or evil, you'll find some holster-slung, brass-knuckled, karate-belted, whiplashing, trigger-happy girl who is now, it would seem, heightening the public pulse and boosting box-office receipts.

Why? Well, a number of answers could be hazarded, ranging from light to serious. The easiest would be to file it under Fad, or Kick, or the Scene. Okay, so we've had James Bond with his concealed arsenals and deadly footwork— let's have Jane Bond, and take her clothes off. The sight of someone with flamboyantly female attributes not only technically equipped for homicide but itching to commit it is, to say the least, arresting. But it's just a fad, and next year we'll have kid killers (which, alas, is no gimmick).

If you start digging a little deeper, you can come up with considerable legendary and some historical precedent for the warrior female. In the Homeric poems, the Amazons appeared as a horde of warrior women who strove against men and with whom conflict was dangerous even for the bravest of heroes.

Whether the Amazons actually existed or not, historical reality among other societies has proved time and again that, given the social premise based on social need, women can become not only as psychically aggressive but as

DEADLIER THAN THE MALE   From *McCall's*, November 1966, 30. Reprinted by permission.

proficient as men in the hunt and the kill, whether for food, for land, for honor or for vengeance.

A decade ago, Erich Neumann wrote in *The Great Mother:* "There is no such thing as sexual fitness or unfitness for this or that task. We find inactive men and warrior women just as we find inactive women and warrior men, and the relation of the group to the powers may be the affair either of men or women."

You don't have to go back very far for evidence: to wit, the women partisans in World War II, the underground agents, the militiawomen of Cuba and—for that matter—the gang girls of the big American cities, who, police will attest, are often even more viciously aggressive than the boys. As life gets tougher, you might say, women get rougher.

But there's still more to this business of the armed and lethal female, and it isn't very pretty. With the wide-open society we now have, where everything can be read by anybody, there must be few people left who have not learned at least superficially about sadistic-masochistic tendencies present, either latently or openly, in a great many men and women. The literature (if that is the word) for this audience has become widely distributed and lucrative, and you don't have to go farther than the nearest city newsstand to find comic books and magazines in which naked women (leather booted and belted, weapon slung) are either inflicting pain on others or themselves being subjected to it. This brew of sex and sadism is one of the poisons in our social blood, for in equating cruelty, harm and aggression with pleasure, it has already contributed—I feel sure—to the growing brutality and callousness of our population and the distortion of sexual values in the young.

But maybe we take this new phenomenon too clinically. If it isn't a fad or a perversion, maybe the female-fighter concept is merely the tacit acknowledgment by men (for they still write the scripts and produce the pictures) that the jig is up. Woman *has* usurped their power; woman *is* the aggressor; woman *has* become the ascendant sex. So let's show her in all the trappings of aggression and let her do the dirty work of hunting and killing. The burden of maintaining such virile postures has become too exhausting for men, so let the girls take over.

In all seriousness, this is happening in far less conspicuous ways in a great many homes. A lot of men, who have grown tired of making decisions, voluntarily abdicate them to their wives, whether in the choice of cars, books, vacations, companions or their own clothes. The wife then becomes a sociological statistic in the overall percentage of female-dominated households and a chapter in another book on Matriarchy in the U.S.A. Although this condition is generally deplored by conventional thinkers, the fact that women enjoy this decision making and that the national economy thrives on it is one of the little ironies.

An even greater irony is that men aren't yet aware of the real nature of female aggression. It is not the arms in her holster but arms around his neck that make her a killer. It is not the spirited, independent, competent companion who threatens his masculinity; it is the little woman taught, from the age of eight, how to hunt and snare him and, from eighteen onward, how to tame and settle him, so that by the time he is thirty, his freedom has disappeared along with his manhood. She is the consumer sex symbol, with wet lips and shining tresses, who permits nothing to enter her pretty head except the strategies of capture. She is also the product of certain successful women writers who on the one hand instruct her how to massage the male ego and on the other reduce man to an accessory.

Even more deadly is the "weak" woman, whose compliancy and helplessness appeal to the protective male, unaware—until too late—that she has committed the ultimate aggression on his spirit: possession. The more she clings, the less he can loosen her hold. This kind of female has throttled the life out of men far more than any gun-girded Amazon of masculine nightmares—or movies.

A man should fear equally another form of weapon carrier: the needler. She may be the model housewife and oh, so feminine, but she needles her mate in a subtle variety of deadly ways. He sits down to read the paper after a grueling day, and she says, "Dear, don't you think you should see the doctor about always being tired?" Or, "Haven't you asked for that raise *yet?*" Or, "Bob is so handy with tools. It must be a joy for Marge to have him around." Or, after a party where he had a lot of fun, "Well, you certainly acted the clown, didn't you?" The poor fellow is so riddled with punctures that he ends by ceasing to feel—or, if you will, to live.

But then, you could never make a popular thriller out of that, could you?

THE PSYCHOPATHOLOGY OF FEMINISM
Ferdinand Lundberg and Marynia F. Farnham, M.D.

Modern Woman: The Lost Sex was published in 1947, just after WW II ended. It argued that only by full involvement in domesticity and motherhood could women avoid marital difficulties, prevent emotional disturbance in their children, and find personal and sexual happiness. Newsreels of the day featured Dr. Farnham urging "Rosie the Riveter" to get out of the work force, where she could not be truly feminine, and back into the home.

In the following excerpt from the book, Lundberg and Farnham examine the psychological disturbance they believed to be at the core of feminists' demands for equality. Using Mary Wollstonecraft, author of *A Vindication of the Rights of Women* (1792) as a case study, they argue that feminist ambitions and attitudes derive from unresolved, albeit unconscious, oedipal conflicts. The woman who fails to find satisfaction in "feminine pursuits" is, in their view, deeply neurotic and not the victim of an unjust social system, as feminists had contended.

Imlay, who is referred to in the excerpt, was Mary Wollstonecraft's lover.

That Mary Wollstonecraft was an extreme neurotic of a compulsive type there can be no doubt. Out of her illness arose the ideology of feminism, which was to express the feelings of so many women in years to come.

THE PSYCHOPATHOLOGY OF FEMINISM   From *Modern Woman: The Lost Sex* by Ferdinand Lundberg and Marynia F. Farnham, M.D. Copyright 1947 by Ferdinand Lundberg and Marynia F. Farnham. Reprinted by permission of Harper & Row, Publishers, Inc. Pp. 159–62.

Consciously, as a strictly moral character, Mary was out to do only good. Feminism, too, was dedicated—on the surface—only to good works, to bringing the lives of women somewhat nearer to ideal perfection. Unconsciously, however, Mary and the feminists wanted to do injury. Mary had a real grievance, but it was against her parents; the same was true of later feminists. These parents had been the agents of a vicious society (as exemplified by the childhood household) vis-a-vis the growing child. To Mary, all men were oppressors of women. All women were long-suffering, all the cards in the deck stacked against them—they were muscularly weaker and smaller than the male, inflicted with menstruation, pregnancy, childbirth, child tending and were denied the marvelous sphere of carefree action of the male (as for sober example, on the battlefield, an enlarged playing field). All men had always, without exception, beaten women black an blue, humiliated them, degraded them, as her father had done to her and her mother. And all women had, like her mother, accepted such humiliation without a whimper. It was a notion that the feminists never tired of elaborating upon. The first line, for example, in the *History of Woman Suffrage* (1889), by Susan B. Anthony, Elizabeth Cady Stanton and Matilda Gage, militant American feminists, reads: "The prolonged slavery of woman is the darkest page in human history."

In retaliation Mary wanted women to turn on men and injure them. The worst humiliation she could think of for them, however, the crowning ignominy, was to make them acknowledge the "equality" of women, their identity with men. Mary could visualize nothing worse, for while hating and condeming them she had too much need of them. Men, in her distorted view, could never be regarded as inferior to women. Men were never, in her view, overcome by women. It was women who were overcome by men. Underneath her aggressive writings, Mary was a masochist like her mother, as indeed all the leading feminist theorists were in fact. Aggressively Mary flung herself at men, only to be repeatedly repulsed. For her actions invited repulse. Overeager for what she desired—a man the precise opposite of her father, but measured against his remembered silhouette—Mary discerned what she sought where it did not exist and then took the initiative, committing the unpardonable sexual blunder of depriving the male of the initiative. The feminists were always doing this, thereby either driving men away from them or capturing psychologically impaired males.

By behaving as she did Mary indicated, as we know from clinical practice, that she was unconsciously seeking to deprive the male of his power, to castrate him. Unconsciously she probably wished to emulate the heroine of Greek drama, Electra, and kill her father, but this desire, although powerful, was powerfully deflected as untenable. It came out only in her round scolding of all men. The feminists have ever since symbolically slain their fathers by verbally consigning all men to perdition as monsters.

What Mary wanted, underneath all the confusion of her mind, was brought out in the stress of her tortured pursuit of Imlay when in a letter she expressed the desire to go with him to America, settle on a farm, and bear six children. She was ready, in emotional extremity, to repeat her mother's role, and unquestionably she would even have endured Imlay's blows—gladly—if only he had married her. Mary was ready to settle for anything, and therein further revealed her neuroticism. Women down through history have, as a rule, not bowed so low before the male as the arch-feminist, Mary Wollstonecraft, bowed before Imlay.

Mary was emotionally forced to strive for power (until capitulating on any terms) vis-a-vis Imlay or any other man. This striving came out in her rushing talk and her professed familiarity with every idea that might be broached. It also came out in the way she forced herself on men and in the way she sought to hold Imlay to a bargain that had not been made. Not to strive for power, for mastery, made Mary feel helpless, then afraid and anxious, then utterly hostile and unhappy. Mastery made her feel less helpless; it was a defense against anxiety that, actually, revolved about her deep doubt of her power as a woman. This power was hopelessly compromised by her male strivings. The happiness she felt during the first stage of her affair with Imlay undoubtedly derived in large measure from the feelings of mastery it gave her. She had suddenly, we may surmise, glimpsed the possibility of establishing mastery as a woman. We can only guess at the state of her libidinal organization, but Imlay was unquestionably a versatile lover, had enchanted her sexually. Very probably he had been the instrument for lifting her sexual inhibitions.

Feminism did not select its underlying ideas from Mary's letters to Imlay. If it had done so it would have been the opposite of what it was. In either event, it would have been drawing from a poisoned source. Only deeply disturbed women—disturbed by the nature of their childhood upbringing in the shattered home and the constricted circumstances they encountered in adult life—could have drawn what they supposed was pure wisdom from A Vindication.

As we have seen, A Vindication prescribed "equality" in all things between the sexes. Equality was the political catchword of the day; it would resolve everything, especially if joined with Reason and Liberty. In sober fact, however, whatever else men and women may be in relation to each other, they are not equal, identical. They are similar in species, different individually, and always complementary. In relation to each other what is crucial is not their similarity but their difference. Havelock Ellis, himself not a little infected with the feminist virus, tried to resolve the confusion caused by the easy use of the word "equality" by substituting for it the term "equivalence," meaning equality of value. But Ellis' well-intentioned efforts were hardly appreciated, and Ellis entirely missed the point of what the feminists were actually aiming for, which was definitely not justice. It was, as Mary Wollstonecraft flatly said (and as many repeated after her), simply masculinity. And a female who attempts to achieve masculinity is psychically ill in the same way as a male who attempts to achieve femininity.

Once it is understood that Mary and her feminist successors,—including such eccentric arabesques as George Sand, who lived out the feminist neurosis in all its details—sought to achieve masculinity, that is, the impossible, then everything else falls into place. . . .

WHAT EVERY WOMAN SHOULD KNOW ABOUT KINSEY

By 1953, Albert Kinsey, of the Institute for Sexual Research of the University of Indiana, had earned a reputation as "America's number one sex expert." Sales of the Kinsey report on male sexuality had been staggering. And *Cosmopolitan* magazine described the forthcoming report on female sexuality as "the most feverishly awaited, most widely speculated on, most sensationally publicized book in history." Although *Cosmopolitan* noted that "Those who anticipated a lurid, all-revealing peek into the boudoirs of American women will be greatly disappointed," its findings and interpretations, sometimes presented in a dry statistical format, were nevertheless shocking.

Kinsey seemed to be arguing against premarital chastity. According to the report, the best predictor of sexual satisfaction in marriage was the incidence of orgasm before marriage. He reported too that the frequency of masturbation, lesbianism, and adultery were much higher than generally realized. And Kinsey's findings discredited the popular myth of female passionlessness. Physiologically, he said, male and female sexual responses differed little. Lack of responsiveness in women was due therefore to lack of interest in or information about what was physically or psychologically arousing to them, or to fear, guilt, and aversion to sexuality resulting from societal conditioning.

This article from *Look*, a popular family magazine of the 1950s, presents the startling facts that its author believed "every woman should know about Kinsey."

 Waves of magazine and newspaper writers journeyed hundreds of miles in recent weeks to a University of Indiana basement to peek at guarded galley proofs of a book composed of statistical tables and the turgid prose beloved among sociologists. Some of the writers had clamored for the privilege; all were bound by written agreement to accept restrictions they ordinarily would have spurned. It was a press agent's dream of a journalistic mountain going to an author Mohammed, and the man who achieved it was a 59-year-old zoologist who made his academic reputation by measuring gall wasps. While Dr. Alfred Charles Kinsey's scientific fervor about gall wasps never heated the public imagination, his subsequent investigations did. Publication of his *Sexual Behavior in the Human Male* in 1948 (at least 250,000 copies sold) excited a taste for stronger stuff. This was reflected in the journalistic invasion of the University campus for a prepublication look at the long-awaited *Sexual Behavior in the Human Female,* scheduled for September 14 release by W. B. Saunders Company, Philadelphia, at $8 a copy.

Dr. Kinsey promised the public some "surprises" in the new book, and his words may be accepted as the understatement of 1953. Among items of significance, in his opinion, were some indications regarding the effect of premarital sex experience on conjugal success and some conclusions drawn from thousands of inscriptions collected from the walls of public toilets. While Dr. Kinsey lays no claim to the discovery of sex, he opens himself to inference that the world was groping in the dark until he and his associates tackled the problem. Not even Freud knew the answers. "What we in science knew about the physiologic aspects of sexual response when we began this study 15 years ago," said Dr. Kinsey, "was about the equivalent of what was known of the nature of the digestive system in the Middle Ages."

Writers who visited the institute learned that the finds for *Sexual Behavior in the Human Female* were based on the stories of 5,940 women. Swallowing any notions of delicacy they might have had, the subjects told all to Dr. Kinsey and his assistants. There are references to babes of a few months and a report of the love life of a woman of 90. To check their records for accuracy, the staff went out on the town, visiting bars, dances and swimming pools. There they observed people "making socio-sexual approaches." In the quaint language of sociology, that means making passes. What kind of picture does the report draw of the American woman's sex life, or at least that part of it represented by the 5,940 who bared their souls to the Kinsey researchers?

Fifty per cent of the married women among them were not virgin when they wed. Three per cent had their first experience before they were 15; 20 per cent between their 16th and 21st birthdays. Most of them (53 per cent) had confined their relations to a single man, but 34 per cent had been intimate with two to five men and 13 per cent with six or more. Forty-six per cent confined their experience to the men they later married. The Kinsey report takes issue with the frequently uttered warnings that only woe can come of such surrender of virtue. As a matter of fact, the report says, 69 per cent of the still unmarried women in the non-virgin category had no regret whatever. Twelve per cent expressed "minor" regret. And 77 per cent of the married women who had premarital experience saw no reason to regret. The report's statistics on marital infidelity will cause some eyebrow raising. According to the report, 26 per cent of the married women had strayed from the connubial bed by the time they were 40 years old. Of them, 41 per cent restricted their philandering to a single male, but 40 per cent were unfaithful with two to five men, 19 per cent with more than five and 3 per cent with more than 20. Among those who remained true to their marriage vows, 83 per cent assured Kinsey they had no intention of committing infidelities at any time in the future, but Kinsey found the other 17 per cent not opposed to the idea. Some of the unfaithful, according to the report, had succumbed to some respected friend as a matter of accommodation, not because the act gave them any pleasure.

The Kinsey investigation also collected data on the number of times a week married couples have sexual relations. Fourteen per cent of the teen-age wives among the 5,940 set a figure of more than seven times a week, and some of them admitted to or boasted of 28 times a week. The group averages were listed as 2.8 times a week for teen-age wives, 2.2 times for those 30, 1.5 for the 40-year-olds, once a week for women 50 and once in 12 days for those 60. Kinsey attributes the decline in frequency to the male. Women, according to his study, show no aging of their sexual capacities until late life. But he points out that the male's loss of interest may be limited to his wife, whose inhibitions and lack of response in the early years of marriage dulled the edge of male desire.

In assessing his report, the doctor conceded his data did not represent a large enough sampling of women of little education, of rural groups and some other segments of the population. He confined his generalizations to the 5,940 women used as case histories, but said the findings might not be "too far from the actuality" for women with high-school and college backgrounds. For those with an old-fashioned desire to keep womanhood on a pedestal, the new Kinsey report will bring one small word of cheer. Women, he found, are much less interested than men in pornography or erotic art. In his researches, the doctor heard of few pornographic publications or movies designed specifically for women. Arrests of women for window peeping are exceedingly rare, he learned, and only 25 per cent of the art and writing copied from the walls of public toilets for women was unmistakably sexual in subject matter. On the "men's" side, it was 86 per cent.

Dr. Kinsey said he was impelled to undertake his studies of sex behavior by his University of Indiana students. What they wanted was the real dope on sex—"information not biased by moral, philosophic or social considerations." If that was so, the doctor has given it to them with both barrels in his two books. In reply to critics who challenge his methods and aims, he points out that the scientists who first sought to explore the nature of matter suffered similar condemnation.

His researches have led him to the conclusion that it is time to change the laws to conform to the realities of human behavior. "As long as you have unenforceable laws," Dr. Kinsey said, "you will have ineffective police departments throughout the country." The doctor pointed out that man's mammalian origin cannot be escaped though, up to a point, his brain gives him a choice not available to lower mammals. But when aroused to response, man loses his control and behaves like the other mammals, according to Kinsey. "Down the course of the years, man has liked to think of himself as a unique creation," the doctor said. "He is not, you know."

STATISTICS ON FEMALE HEALTH
Catharine Beecher

Catharine Beecher (1800–1878), eldest daughter of the celebrated Beecher family, was a teacher, director of a school, busy lecturer, best selling author, and an ardent reformer. Although she was an unmarried career woman herself, she wrote several authoritative manuals for women on a variety of subjects, from domestic management to care of the body.

Beecher was convinced that, compared to her mother's generation and to women in Europe, the current generation of American women was weak and unhealthy. Among the practices she blamed for women's declining health were "pernicious customs of dress." Popular fashions, she believed, compressed and weighed down delicate organs, and alternately overheated or exposed the body in unhealthy ways. Inadequate exercise, poor ventilation, and improper hygiene and nutrition also contributed to women's poor health. Finally, she noted, the drudgery of home life left housewives of the day with little or no time free from care to enjoy pure air and social activities and so their sensitive nervous systems rebelled. Upper class women, suffered not from these stresses, but from the "want of some worthy object in life, or from excesses in seeking amusement." In

STATISTICS ON FEMALE HEALTH   From *Letters to the People on Health and Happiness*, New York: Harper & Bros., 1856. Abridged, 121–30.

both cases, she asserted that women needed a proper balance of work and pleasure, which they could achieve through adequate training in domestic management.

Beecher's special interest in women's health reflected, in part, her own life experiences. Both she and her sister, Harriet Beecher Stowe, had suffered for years from physical problems, and Catharine had spent a great deal of time taking cures in various health establishments. In the following excerpt from her book, *Letters to the People on Health and Happiness,* Beecher presents the results of a survey she conducted among her friends, family and acquaintances.

During my extensive tours in all portions of the Free States, I was brought into most intimate communion, not only with my widely-diffused circle of relatives, but with very many of my former pupils who had become wives and mothers. From such, I learned the secret domestic history both of those I visited and of many of their intimate friends. And oh! what heartaches were the result of these years of quiet observation of the experience of my sex in domestic life. How many young hearts have revealed the fact, that what they had been trained to imagine the highest earthly felicity, was but the beginning of care, disappointment, and sorrow, and often led to the extremity of mental and physical suffering. Why was it that I was so often told that "young girls little imagined what was before them when they entered married life?" Why did I so often find those united to the most congenial and most devoted husbands expressing the hope that their daughters would never marry? For years these were my quiet, painful conjectures.

But the more I traveled, and the more I resided in health establishments, the more the conviction was pressed on my attention that there was a terrible decay of female health all over the land, and that this evil was bringing with it an incredible extent of individual, domestic, and social suffering, that was increasing in a most alarming ratio. At last, certain developments led me to take decided measures to obtain some reliable statistics on the subject. During my travels the last year I have sought all practicable methods of obtaining information, and finally adopted this course with most of the married ladies whom I met, either on my journeys or at the various health establishments at which I stopped.

I requested each lady first to write the *initials* of *ten* of the married ladies with whom she was best acquainted in her place of residence. Then she was requested to write at each name, her impressions as to the health of each lady. In this way, during the past year, I obtained statistics from about two hundred different places in almost all the Free States. . . .

As to the terms used in these statements, in all cases there was a previous statement made as to the sense in which they were to be employed.

A "perfectly healthy" or "a vigorous and healthy woman" is one of whom there are *specimens* remaining in almost every place; such as used to *abound* when all worked, and *worked in pure air.*

Such a woman is one who can through the whole day be actively employed on her feet in all kinds of domestic duties without injury, and constantly and habitually has a feeling of perfect health and perfect freedom from pain. Not that she never has a fit of sickness, or takes a cold that interrupts the feeling of health, but that these are out of her ordinary experience.

A woman is marked "well" who usually has good health, but can not bear exposures, or long and great fatigue, without consequent illness.

A woman is marked "delicate" who, though she may be about and attend to most of her domestic employments, has a frail constitution that either has been undermined by ill health, or which easily and frequently yields to fatigue, or exposure, or excitement. . . .

MOST RELIABLE STATISTICS.

Milwaukee, Wis.   Mrs. A. frequent sick headaches. Mrs. B. very feeble. Mrs. S. well, except chills. Mrs. L. poor health constantly. Mrs. D. subject to frequent headaches. Mrs. B. very poor health. Mrs. C. consumption. Mrs. A. pelvic displacements and weakness. Mrs. H. pelvic disorders and a cough. Mrs. B. always sick. Do not know one perfectly healthy woman in the place.

Essex, Vt.   Mrs. S. very feeble. Mrs. D. slender and delicate. Mrs. S. feeble. Mrs. S. not well. Mrs. G. quite feeble. Mrs. C. quite feeble. Mrs. B. quite feeble. Mrs. S. quite slender. Mrs. B. quite feeble. Mrs. F. very feeble. Knows but one perfectly healthy woman in town.

Peru, N. Y.   Mrs. C. not healthy. Mrs. H. not healthy. Mrs. E. healthy. Mrs. B. pretty well. Mrs. K. delicate. Mrs. B. not strong and healthy. Mrs. S. healthy and vigorous. Mrs. L. pretty well. Mrs. L. pretty well.

Canton, Penn.   Mrs. R. feeble. Mrs. B. bad headaches. Mrs. D. bad headaches. Mrs. V. feeble. Mrs. S. erysipelas. Mrs. K. headaches, but tolerably well. Mrs. R. miserably sick and nervous. Mrs. G. poor health. Mrs. L. invalid. Mrs. G. invalid.

Oberlin, Ohio   Mrs. A. usually well, but subject to neuralgia. Mrs. D. poor health. Mrs. K. well, but subject to nervous headaches. Mrs. M. poor health. Mrs. C. not in good health. Mrs. P. not in good health. Mrs. P. delicate. Mrs. F. not in good health. Mrs. F. not in good health.

Wilmington, Del.   Mrs.——, scrofula. Mrs. B. in good health. Mrs. D. delicate. Mrs. H. delicate. Mrs. S. healthy. Mrs. P. healthy. Mrs. G. delicate. Mrs. O. delicate. Mrs. T. very delicate. Mrs. S. headaches.

New Bedford, Mass.   Mrs. B. pelvic diseases, and every way out of order. Mrs. J. W. pelvic disorders. Mrs. W. B. well, except in one respect. Mrs. C. sickly. Mrs. C. rather delicate. Mrs. P. not healthy. Mrs. C. unwell at times. Mrs. L. delicate. Mrs. B subject to spasms. Mrs. H. very feeble. Can not think of but one perfectly healthy woman in the place.

Paxton, Vt.   Mrs. T. diseased in liver and back. Mrs. H. stomach and back diseased. Mrs. W. sickly. Mrs. S. very delicate. Mrs. C. sick headaches, sickly. Mrs. W. bilious complaints. Mrs. T. very delicate. Mrs. T. liver complaint. Mrs. C. bilious sometimes, well most of the time. Do not know a perfectly healthy woman in the place. Many of these are the wives of wealthy farmers, who *overwork* when there is no need of it.

Crown Point, N. Y.   Mrs. H. bronchitis. Mrs. K. very delicate. Mrs. A. very delicate. Mrs. A. diseased in back and stomach. Mrs. S. consumption. Mrs. A.

dropsy. Mrs. M. delicate. Mrs. M. G. delicate. Mrs. P. delicate. Mrs. C. consumption. Do not know one perfectly healthy woman in the place. . . .

[Additional statistics are given here. . . .]

I will now add my own personal observation. First, in my own family connection: I have nine married sisters and sisters-in-law, all of them either delicate or invalids, except two. I have fourteen married female cousins, and not one of them but is either delicate, often ailing, or an invalid. In my wide circle of friends and acquaintance all over the land out of my family circle, the same impression is made. In Boston I can not remember but one married female friend who is perfectly healthy. In Hartford, Conn., I can think of only one. In New Haven, but one. In Brooklyn, N. Y., but one. In New York city, but one. In Cincinnati, but one. In Buffalo, Cleveland, Chicago, Milwaukee, Detroit, those whom I have visited are either delicate or invalids. I am not able to recall, in my immense circle of friends and acquaintance all over the Union, so many as *ten* married ladies born in this century and country, who are perfectly sound, healthy, and vigorous. Not that I believe there are not more than this among the friends with whom I have associated, but among all whom I can bring to mind of whose health I have any accurate knowledge, I can not find this number of entirely sound and healthy women.

Another thing has greatly added to the impression of my own observations, and that is the manner in which my inquiries have been met. In a majority of cases, when I have asked for the number of perfectly healthy women in a given place, the first impulsive answer has been "not one." In other cases, when the reply has been more favorable, and I have asked for specifics, the result has always been such as to diminish the number calculated, rather than to increase it. With a few exceptions the persons I have asked, who had not directed their thoughts to the subject, and took a favorable view of it, have expressed surprise at the painful result obtained in their own immediate circle.

But the thing which has pained and surprised me the most is the result of inquiries among the country-towns and industrial classes in our country. I had supposed that there would be a great contrast between the statements gained from persons from such places, and those furnished from the wealthy circles, and especially from cities. But such has not been the case. It will be seen that the larger portion of the accounts inserted in the preceding pages are from country-towns, while a large portion of the worst accounts were taken from the industrial classes. . . .

REST

S. Weir Mitchell

S. Weir Mitchell (1829–1914), novelist and poet, medical researcher and distinguished physician, was a specialist in the nervous disorders of women. Some of his patients suffered from nervous exhaustion; others were diagnosed as hysteric. Most had been treated by many doctors before him, for gastric, spinal, or uterine troubles, and his work with such difficult cases had earned him an international reputation. The most fashionable women sought Mitchell's services, and he was the toast of Philadelphia society.

His treatment, known as the "rest cure," consisted of isolation and rest; excessive feeding with dietary supplements; and "passive exercise," that is, massage and electrical stimulation of the body. Mitchell had discovered during the Civil War that rest could cure battle fatigue. He believed that running a household, caring for children, nursing sick relatives, or getting a college education could produce similar fatigue in women, and also could be helped with rest. Because his patients frequently had digestive problems, were underweight and anaemic, and sometimes were addicted to drugs and opiates, he put them on the special diet. The massage and electrical stimulation were needed to prevent the debilitating effects of total bed rest.

The rest cure also had a "moral," or psychological, aspect. Mitchell believed that the treatment would not be successful unless the patient cooperated in fighting the disease. And such cooperation was sometimes difficult to acquire. "For the most entire capacity to make a household wretched," wrote Mitchell, "there is no more complete human receipt" [recipe] "than a silly woman who is to a high degree nervous and feeble, and who craves pity and power." In his view, to get such women to obey his behavioral prescriptions, the doctor had to inspire complete confidence even to the point of promoting child-like acquiescence.

. . . Whether we shall ask a patient to walk or to take rest is a question which turns up for answer almost every day in practice. Most often we incline to insist on exercise, and are led to do so from a belief that women walk too little, and that to move about a good deal every day is good for everybody. I think we are as often wrong as right. A good brisk daily walk is for well folks a tonic, breaks down old tissues, and creates a wholesome demand for food. The same is true for some sick people. The habit of horse exercise or a long walk every day is needed to cure or to aid in the cure of disordered stomach and costive bowels, but if all exertion gives rise only to increase of trouble, to extreme sense of fatigue, to nausea, what shall we do? And suppose that tonics do not help to make exertion easy, and that the great tonic of change of air fails us, shall we still persist? And here lies the trouble: there are women who mimic fatigue, who indulge themselves in rest on the least pretence, who have no symptoms so truly honest that we need care to regard them. These are they who spoil their own nervous systems as they spoil their children, when they have them, by yielding to the least desire and teaching them to dwell on little pains. For such people there is no help but to insist on self-control and on daily use of the limbs. They must be told to exert themselves, and made to do so if

REST   From *Fat and Blood: And How to Make Them*, Philadelphia: J. B. Lippincott & Co., 1877, 37–44.

that can be. If they are young this is easy enough. If they have grown to middle life, and made long habits of self-indulgence, the struggle is always useless. But few, however, among these women are free from some defect of blood or tissue, either original or having come on as a result of years of indolence and attention to aches and ailments which should never have had given to them more than a passing thought, and which certainly should not have been made an excuse for the sofa or the bed.

Sometimes the question is easy to settle. If you find a woman who is in good state as to color and flesh, and who is always able to do what it pleases her to do, and who is tired by what does not please her, that is a woman to order out of bed and to control with a firm and steady will. That is a woman who is to be made to walk, with no regard to her aches, and to be made to persist until exertion ceases to give rise to the mimicry of fatigue. In such cases the man who can insure belief in his opinions and obedience to his decrees secures very often most brilliant and sometimes easy success; and it is in such cases that women who are in all other ways capable doctors fail, because they do not obtain the needed control over those of their own sex. There are still other cases in which the same mischievous tendencies to repose, to endless tire, to hysterical symptoms, and to emotional displays have grown out of defects of nutrition so distinct that no man ought to think for them of mere exertion as a sole means of cure. The time comes for that, but it should not come until entire rest has been used, with other means, to fit them for making use of their muscles. Nothing upsets these cases like overexertion, and the attempt to make them walk usually ends in some mischievous emotional display, and in creating a new reason for thinking that they cannot walk. As to the two sets of cases just sketched, no one need hesitate; the one must walk, the other should not until we have bettered her nutritive state. She may be able to drag herself about, but no good will be done by making her do so. But between these two classes lies the larger number of such cases, giving us every kind of real and imagined symptom, and dreadfully well fitted to puzzle the most competent physician. As a rule, no harm is done by rest, even in such people as give us doubts about whether it is or is not well for them to exert themselves. There are plenty of these women who are just well enough to make it likely that if they had motive enough for exertion to cause them to forget themselves they would find it useful. In the doubt I am rather given to insisting on rest, but the rest I like for them is not at all their notion of rest. To lie abed half the day, and sew a little and read a little, and be interesting and excite sympathy, is all very well, but when they are bidden to stay in bed a month, and neither to read, write, nor sew, and to have one nurse,—who is not a relative,—then rest becomes for some women a rather bitter medicine, and they are glad enough to accept the order to rise and go about when the doctor issues a mandate which has become pleasantly welcome and eagerly looked for. I do not think it easy to make a mistake in this matter unless the woman takes with morbid delight to the system of enforced rest, and unless the doctor is a person of feeble will. I have never met myself with any serious trouble about getting out of bed any woman for whom I thought rest needful, but it has happened to others, and the man who resolves to send any nervous woman to bed must be quite sure that she will obey him when the time comes for her to get up.

I have, of course, made use of every grade of rest for my patients, from insisting upon repose on a lounge for some hours a day up to entire rest in bed. In carrying out my general plan of treatment it is my habit to ask the patient to remain in bed from six weeks to two months. At first, and in some cases for four or five weeks, I do not permit the patient to sit up or to sew or write or read. The only action allowed is that needed to clean the teeth. In some instances I have not permitted the patient to turn over without aid, and this I have done because sometimes I think no motion desirable, and because sometimes the moral influence of absolute repose is of use. In such cases I arrange to have the bowels and water passed while lying down, and the patient is lifted on to a lounge at bedtime and sponged, and then lifted back again into the newly-made bed. In all cases of weakness, treated by rest, I insist on the patient being fed by the nurse, and, when well enough to sit up in bed, I insist that the meats shall be cut up, so as to make it easier for the patient to feed herself.

In many cases I allow the patient to sit up in order to obey the calls of nature, but I am always careful to have the bowels kept reasonably free from costiveness, knowing well how such a state and the efforts it gives rise to enfeeble a sick person.

Usually, after a fortnight I permit the patient to be read to,—one to three hours a day,—but I am daily amazed to see how kindly nervous and anæmic women take to this absolute rest, and how little they complain of its monotony. In fact, the use of massage and the battery, with the frequent comings of the nurse with food and the doctor's visits, seem so to fill up the day as to make the treatment less tiresome than might be supposed. And, besides this, the sense of comfort which is apt to come about the fifth or sixth day,—the feeling of ease, and the ready capacity to digest food, and the growing hope of final cure, fed as it is by present relief,—all conspire to make most patients contented and tractable.

The moral uses of enforced rest are readily estimated. From a restless life of irregular hours, and probably endless drugging, from hurtful sympathy and over-zealous care, the patient passes to an atmosphere of quiet, to order and control, to the system and care of a thorough nurse, to an absence of drugs, and to simple diet. The result is always at first, whatever it may be afterwards, a sense of relief, and a remarkable and often a quite abrupt disappearance of many of the nervous symptoms with which we are all of us only too sadly familiar.

All the moral uses of rest and isolation and change of habits are not obtained by merely insisting on the physical conditions needed to effect these ends. If the physician has the force of character required to secure the confidence and respect of his patients he has also much more in his power, and should have the tact to seize the proper occasions to direct the thoughts of his patients to the lapse from duties to others, and to the selfishness which a life of invalidism is apt to bring about. Such moral medication belongs to the higher sphere of the doctor's duties, and if he means to cure his patient permanently, he cannot afford to neglect them. Above all, let him be careful that the masseuse and the nurse do not talk of the patient's ills, and let him by degrees teach the sick person how very essential it is to speak of her aches and pains to no one but himself. . . .

THE YELLOW WALLPAPER

Charlotte Perkins (Stetson) Gilman

For much of her adult life, Charlotte Perkins Gilman (1860–1935) earned her living by travelling all over the country lecturing. She wrote poetry and short stories, and for seven years she was sole writer and editor of *The Forerunner*, a magazine devoted to women and social change. Her famous novel, *Herland*, about a utopian society of women, was published in installments in the magazine. She wrote several nonfiction books as well. The most famous, *Women and Economics* (1898), analyzed the damage done to women by confining them to the domestic sphere. It advocated financial independence and jobs outside the home for women, as well as communal living arrangements with cooperative kitchens and nurseries staffed by experts.

In her personal life too, Gilman fought against the confinement of domesticity. After struggling with indecision, she married Charles Stetson at the age of twenty-four. Although seemingly happily married, after the birth of her daughter a year later, Gilman lapsed into a deep depression. Unable to cope with domestic and maternal duties, she set out to visit friends in California. She felt better almost immediately, and her symptoms came back only as she approached home.

Upon her return she was seen by S. Weir Mitchell. He diagnosed her problem as hysteria and administered "the rest cure." After a month of what she described as an "agreeable treatment," she was sent home with the prescription: "Live as domestic a life as possible. Have your child with you all the time. Lie down an hour after each meal. Have but two hours' intellectual life a day. And never touch pen, brush or pencil as long as you live." She later reported that this prescription almost drove her mad. Realizing that her choice was between staying with her husband and going mad, or leaving and staying sane, she left, taking her daughter with her. Later she divorced Stetson, and when he married her best friend, she gave up her daughter to the care of Stetson and his new wife. Gilman was criticized as unnatural for these decisions.

In 1900, Gilman married George Houghton Gilman, her cousin. And, in 1935 she committed suicide rather than face a slow and painful death from breast cancer.

"The Yellow Wallpaper" was published in *The New England Magazine* in 1892.

It is very seldom that mere ordinary people like John and myself secure ancestral halls for the summer.

A colonial mansion, a hereditary estate, I would say a haunted house, and reach the height of romantic felicity—but that would be asking too much of fate!

Still I will proudly declare that there is something queer about it.

Else, why should it be let so cheaply? And why have stood so long untenanted?

John laughs at me, of course, but one expects that in marriage.

John is practical in the extreme. He has no patience with faith, an intense horror of superstition, and he scoffs openly at any talk of things not to be felt and seen and put down in figures.

John is a physician, and *perhaps*—(I would not say it to a living soul, of course, but this is dead paper and a great relief to my mind—) *perhaps* that is one reason I do not get well faster.

THE YELLOW WALLPAPER   From *The New England Magazine*, January 1892, 647–56.

You see he does not believe I am sick!

And what can one do?

If a physician of high standing, and one's own husband, assures friends and relatives that there is really nothing the matter with one but temporary nervous depression—a slight hysterical tendency—what is one to do?

My brother is also a physician, and also of high standing, and he says the same thing.

So I take phosphates or phosphites—whichever it is, and tonics, and journeys, and air, and exercise, and am absolutely forbidden to "work" until I am well again.

Personally, I disagree with their ideas.

Personally, I believe that congenial work, with excitement and change, would do me good.

But what is one to do?

I did write for a while in spite of them; but it *does* exhaust me a good deal—having to be so sly about it, or else meet with heavy opposition.

I sometimes fancy that in my condition if I had less opposition and more society and stimulus—but John says the very worst thing I can do is to think about my condition, and I confess it always makes me feel bad.

So I will let it alone and talk about the house.

The most beautiful place! It is quite alone, standing well back from the road, quite three miles from the village. It makes me think of English places that you read about, for there are hedges and walls and gates that lock, and lots of separate little houses for the gardeners and people.

There is a *delicious* garden! I never saw such a garden—large and shady, full of box-bordered paths, and lined with long grape-covered arbors with seats under them.

There were greenhouses, too, but they are all broken now.

There was some legal trouble, I believe, something about the heirs and coheirs; anyhow, the place has been empty for years.

That spoils my ghostliness, I am afraid, but I don't care—there is something strange about the house—I can feel it.

I even said so to John one moonlight evening, but he said what I felt was a *draught,* and shut the window.

I get unreasonably angry with John sometimes. I'm sure I never used to be so sensitive. I think it is due to this nervous condition.

But John says if I feel so, I shall neglect proper self-control; so I take pains to control myself—before him, at least, and that makes me very tired.

I don't like our room a bit. I wanted one downstairs that opened on the piazza and had roses all over the window, and such pretty old-fashioned chintz hangings! but John would not hear of it.

He said there was only one window and not room for two beds, and no near room for him if he took another.

He is very careful and loving, and hardly lets me stir without special direction.

I have a schedule prescription for each hour in the day; he takes all care from me, and so I feel basely ungrateful not to value it more.

He said we came here solely on my account, that I was to have perfect rest and all the air I could get. "Your exercise depends on your strength, my dear," said he, "and your food somewhat on your appetite; but air you can absorb all the time." So we took the nursery at the top of the house.

It is a big, airy room, the whole floor nearly, with windows that look all ways, and air and sunshine galore. It was nursery first and then playroom and gymnasium, I should judge; for the windows are barred for little children, and there are rings and things in the walls.

The paint and paper look as if a boys' school had used it. It is stripped off—the paper—in great patches all around the head of my bed, about as far as I can reach, and in a great place on the other side of the room low down. I never saw a worse paper in my life.

One of those sprawling flamboyant patterns committing every artistic sin.

It is dull enough to confuse the eye in following, pronounced enough to constantly irritate and provoke study, and when you follow the lame uncertain curves for a little distance they suddenly commit suicide—plunge off at outrageous angles, destroy themselves in unheard of contradictions.

The color is repellant, almost revolting; a smouldering unclean yellow, strangely faded by the slow-turning sunlight.

It is a dull yet lurid orange in some places, a sickly sulphur tint in others.

No wonder the children hated it! I should hate it myself if I had to live in this room long.

There comes John, and I must put this away,—he hates to have me write a word.

◇◇◇

We have been here two weeks, and I haven't felt like writing before, since that first day.

I am sitting by the window now, up in this atrocious nursery, and there is nothing to hinder my writing as much as I please, save lack of strength.

John is away all day, and even some nights when his cases are serious.

I am glad my case is not serious!

But these nervous troubles are dreadfully depressing.

John does not know how much I really suffer. He knows there is no *reason* to suffer, and that satisfies him.

Of course it is only nervousness. It does weigh on me so not to do my duty in any way!

I meant to be such a help to John, such a real rest and comfort, and here I am a comparative burden already!

Nobody would believe what an effort it is to do what little I am able,—to dress and entertain, and order things.

It is fortunate Mary is so good with the baby. Such a dear baby!

And yet I *cannot* be with him, it makes me so nervous.

I suppose John never was nervous in his life. He laughs at me so about this wall-paper!

At first he meant to repaper the room, but afterwards he said that I was letting it get the better of me, and that nothing was worse for a nervous patient than to give way to such fancies.

He said that after the wall-paper was changed it would be the heavy bedstead, and then the barred windows, and then that gate at the head of the stairs, and so on.

"You know the place is doing you good," he said, "and really, dear, I don't care to renovate the house just for a three months' rental."

"Then do let us go downstairs," I said, "there are such pretty rooms there."

Then he took me in his arms and called me a blessed little goose, and said he would go down cellar, if I wished, and have it whitewashed into the bargain.

But he is right enough about the beds and windows and things.

It is an airy and comfortable room as any one need wish, and, of course, I would not be so silly as to make him uncomfortable just for a whim.

I'm really getting quite fond of the big room, all but that horrid paper.

Out of one window I can see the garden, those mysterious deep-shaded arbors, the riotous old-fashioned flowers, and bushes and gnarly trees.

Out of another I get a lovely view of the bay and a little private wharf belonging to the estate. There is a beautiful shaded lane that runs down there from the house. I always fancy I see people walking in these numerous paths and arbors, but John has cautioned me not to give way to fancy in the least. He says that with my imaginative power and habit of story-making, a nervous weakness like mine is sure to lead to all manner of excited fancies, and that I ought to use my will and good sense to check the tendency. So I try.

I think sometimes that if I were only well enough to write a little it would relieve the press of ideas and rest me.

But I find I get pretty tired when I try.

It is so discouraging not to have any advice and companionship about my work. When I get really well, John says we will ask Cousin Henry and Julia down for a long visit; but he says he would as soon put fireworks in my pillow-case as to let me have those stimulating people about now.

I wish I could get well faster.

But I must not think about that. This paper looks to me as if it *knew* what a vicious influence it had!

There is a recurrent spot where the pattern lolls like a broken neck and two bulbous eyes stare at you upside down.

I get positively angry with the impertinence of it and the everlastingness. Up and down and sideways they crawl, and those absurd, unblinking eyes are everywhere. There is one place where two breaths didn't match, and the eyes go all up and down the line, one a little higher than the other.

I never saw so much expression in an inanimate thing before, and we all know how much expression they have! I used to lie awake as a child and get more entertainment and terror out of blank walls and plain furniture than most children could find in a toy-store.

I remember what a kindly wink the knobs of our big, old bureau used to have, and there was one chair that always seemed like a strong friend.

I used to feel that if any of the other things looked too fierce I could always hop into that chair and be safe.

The furniture in this room is no worse than inharmonious, however, for we had to bring it all from downstairs. I suppose when this was used as a playroom they had to take the nursery things out, and no wonder! I never saw such ravages as the children have made here.

The wall-paper, as I said before, is torn off in spots, and it sticketh closer than a brother—they must have had perseverance as well as hatred.

Then the floor is scratched and gouged and splintered, the plaster itelf is dug out here and there, and this great heavy bed which is all we found in the room, looks as if it had been through the wars.

"But I don't mind it a bit—only the paper.

There comes John's sister. Such a dear girl as she is, and so careful of me! I must not let her find me writing.

She is a perfect and enthusiastic housekeeper, and hopes for no better profession. I verily believe she thinks it is the writing which made me sick!

But I can write when she is out, and see her a long way off from these windows.

There is one that commands the road, a lovely shaded winding road, and one that just looks off over the country. A lovely country, too, full of great elms and velvet meadows.

This wallpaper has a kind of subpattern in a different shade, a particularly irritating one, for you can only see it in certain lights, and not clearly then.

But in the places where it isn't faded and where the sun is just so—I can see a strange, provoking, formless sort of figure, that seems to skulk about behind that silly and conspicuous front design.

There's sister on the stairs!

◇◇◇

Well, the Fourth of July is over! The people are all gone and I am tired out. John thought it might do me good to see a little company, so we just had mother and Nellie and the children down for a week.

Of course I didn't do a thing. Jennie sees to everything now.

But it tired me all the same.

John says if I don't pick up faster he shall send me to Weir Mitchell in the fall.

But I don't want to go there at all. I had a friend who was in his hands once, and she says he is just like John and my brother, only more so!

Besides, it is such an undertaking to go so far.

I don't feel as if it was worth while to turn my hand over for anything, and I'm getting dreadfully fretful and querulous.

I cry at nothing, and cry most of the time.

Of course I don't when John is here, or anybody else, but when I am alone.

And I am alone a good deal just now. John is kept in town very often by serious cases, and Jennie is good and lets me alone when I want her to.

So I walk a little in the garden or down that lovely lane, sit on the porch under the roses, and lie down up here a good deal.

I'm getting really fond of the room in spite of the wallpaper. Perhaps *because* of the wallpaper.

It dwells in my mind so!

I lie here on this great immovable bed—it is nailed down, I believe—and follow that pattern about by the hour. It it [sic] as good as gymnastics, I assure you. I start, we'll say, at the bottom, down in the corner over there where it has nos [sic] been touched, and I determine for the thousandth time that I *will* follow that pointless pattern to some sort of a conclusion.

I know a little of the principle of design, and I know this thing was not arranged on any laws of radiation, or alternation, or repetition, or symmetry, or anything else that I ever heard of.

It is repeated, of course, by the breadths, but not otherwise.

Looked at in one way each breadth stands alone, the bloated curves and flourishes—a kind of "debased Romanesque" with *delirium tremens*—go waddling up and down in isolated columns of fatuity.

But, on the other hand, they connect diagonally, and the sprawling outlines run off in great slanting waves of optic horror, like a lot of wallowing seaweeds in full chase.

The whole thing goes horizontally, too, at least it seems so, and I exhaust myself in trying to distinguish the order of its going in that direction.

They have used a horizontal breadth for a frieze, and that adds wonderfully to the confusion.

There is one end of the room where it is almost intact, and there, when the crosslights fade and the low sun shines directly upon it, I can almost fancy radiation after all,—the interminable grotesque seem to form around a common centre and rush off in headlong plunges of equal distraction.

It makes me tired to follow it. I will take a nap I guess.

◇◇◇

I don't know why I should write this.

I don't want to.

I don't feel able.

And I know John would think it absurd. But I *must* say what I feel and think in some way—it is such a relief!

But the effort is getting to be greater than the relief.

Half the time now I am awfully lazy, and lie down ever so much.

John says I mustn't lose my strength, and has me take cod liver oil and lots of tonics and things, to say nothing of ale and wine and rare meat.

Dear John! He loves me very dearly, and hates to have me sick. I tried to have a real earnest reasonable talk with him the other day, and tell him how I wish he would let me go and make a visit to Cousin Henry and Julia.

But he said I wasn't able to go, nor able to stand it after I got there; and I did not make out a very good case for myself, for I was crying before I had finished.

It is getting to be a great effort for me to think straight. Just this nervous weakness I suppose.

And dear John gathered me up in his arms, and just carried me upstairs and laid me on the bed, and sat by me and read to me till it tired my head.

He said I was his darling and his comfort and all he had, and that I must take care of myself for his sake, and keep well.

He says no one but myself can help me out of it, that I must use my will and self-control and not let any silly fancies run away with me.

There's one comfort, the baby is well and happy, and does not have to occupy this nursery with the horrid wallpaper.

If we had not used it, that blessed child would have! What a fortunate escape! Why, I wouldn't have a child of mine, an impressionable little thing, live in such a room for worlds.

I never thought of it before, but it is lucky that John kept me here after all, I can stand it so much easier than a baby, you see.

Of course I never mention it to them any more—I am too wise,—but I keep watch of it all the same.

There are things in that paper that nobody knows but me, or ever will.

Behind that outside pattern the dim shapes get clearer every day.

It is always the same shape, only very numerous.

And it is like a woman stooping down and creeping about behind that pattern. I don't like it a bit. I wonder—I begin to think—I wish John would take me away from here!

❖❖❖

It is so hard to talk with John about my case because he is so wise, and because he loves me so.

But I tried it last night.

It was moonlight. The moon shines in all around just as the sun does.

I hate to see it sometimes, it creeps so slowly, and always comes in by one window or another.

John was asleep and I hated to waken him, so I kept still and watched the moonlight on that undulating wallpaper till I felt creepy.

The faint figure behind seemed to shake the pattern, just as if she wanted to get out.

I got up softly and went to feel and see if the paper *did* move, and when I came back John was awake.

"What is it, little girl?" he said. "Don't go walking about like that—you'll get cold."

I thought it was a good time to talk, so I told him that I really was not gaining here, and that I wished he would take me away.

"Why, darling!" said he, "our lease will be up in three weeks, and I can't see how to leave before.

"The repairs are not done at home, and I cannot possibly leave town just now. Of course if you were in any danger, I could and would, but you really are better, dear, whether you can see it or not. I am a doctor, dear, and I know. You are gaining flesh and color, your appetite is better, I feel really much easier about you."

"I don't weigh a bit more," said I, "nor as much; and my appetite may be better in the evening when you are here, but it is worse in the morning when you are away!"

"Bless her little heart!" said he with a big hug, "she shall be as sick as she pleases! But now let's improve the shining hours by going to sleep, and talk about it in the morning!"

"And you won't go away?" I asked gloomily.

"Why, how can I, dear? It is only three weeks more and then we will take a nice little trip of a few days while Jennie is getting the house ready. Really dear you are better!"

"Better in body perhaps—" I began, and stopped short, for he sat up straight and looked at me with such a stern, reproachful look that I could not say another word.

"My darling," said he, "I beg of you, for my sake and for our child's sake, as well as for your own, that you will never for one instant let that idea enter your mind! There is nothing so dangerous, so fascinating, to a temperament like yours. It is a false and foolish fancy. Can you not trust me as a physician when I tell you so?"

So of course I said no more on that score, and we went to sleep before long.

He thought I was asleep first, but I wasn't, and lay there for hours trying to decide whether that front pattern and the back pattern really did move together or separately.

❖❖❖

On a pattern like this, by daylight, there is a lack of sequence, a defiance of law, that is a constant irritant to a normal mind.

The color is hideous enough, and unreliable enough, and infuriating enough, but the pattern is torturing.

You think you have mastered it, but just as you get well underway in following, it turns a back-somersault and there you are. It slaps you in the face, knocks you down, and tramples upon you. It is like a bad dream.

The outside pattern is a florid arabesque, reminding one of a fungus. If you can imagine a toadstool in joints, an interminable string of toadstools, budding and sprouting in endless convolutions—why, that is something like it.

That is, sometimes!

There is one marked peculiarity about this paper, a thing nobody seems to notice but myself, and that is that it changes as the light changes.

When the sun shoots in through the east window—I always watch for that first long, straight ray—it changes so quickly that I never can quite believe it.

That is why I watch it always.

By moonlight—the moon shines in all night when there is a moon—I wouldn't know it was the same paper.

At night in any kind of light, in twilight, candlelight, lamplight, and worst of all by moonlight, it becomes bars! The outside pattern I mean, and the woman behind it is as plain as can be.

I didn't realize for a long time what the thing was that showed behind, that dim sub-pattern, but now I am quite sure it is a woman.

By daylight she is subdued, quiet. I fancy it is the pattern that keeps her so still. It is so puzzling. It keeps me quiet by the hour.

I lie down ever so much now. John says it is good for me, and to sleep all I can.

Indeed he started the habit by making me lie down for an hour after each meal.

It is a very bad habit I am convinced, for you see I don't sleep.

And that cultivates deceit, for I don't tell them I'm awake—O no!

The fact is I am getting a little afraid of John.

He seems very queer sometimes, and even Jennie has an inexplicable look.

It strikes me occasionally, just as a scientific hypothesis,—that perhaps it is the paper!

I have watched John when he did not know I was looking, and come into the room suddenly on the most innocent excuses, and I've caught him several times *looking at the paper!* And Jennie too. I caught Jennie with her hand on it once.

She didn't know I was in the room, and when I asked her in a quiet, a very quiet voice, with the most restrained manner possible, what she was doing with the paper—she turned around as if she had been caught stealing, and looked quite angry—asked me why I should frighten her so!

Then she said that the paper stained everything it touched, that she had found yellow smooches on all my clothes and John's, and she wished we would be more careful!

Did not that sound innocent? But I know she was studying that pattern, and I am determined that nobody shall find it out but myself!

❖❖❖

Life is very much more exciting now than it used to be. You see I have something more to expect, to look forward to, to watch. I really do eat better, and am more quiet than I was.

John is so pleased to see me improve! He laughed a little the other day, and said I seemed to be flourishing in spite of my wall-paper.

I turned it off with a laugh. I had no intention of telling him it was *because* of the wall-paper—he would make fun of me. He might even want to take me away.

I don't want to leave now until I have found it out. There is a week more, and I think that will be enough.

❖❖❖

I'm feeling ever so much better! I don't sleep much at night, for it is so interesting to watch developments; but I sleep a good deal in the daytime.

In the daytime it is tiresome and perplexing.

There are always new shoots on the fungus, and new shades of yellow all over it. I cannot keep count of them, though I have tried conscientiously.

It is the strangest yellow, that wall-paper! It makes me think of all the yellow things I ever saw—not beautiful ones like buttercups, but old foul, bad yellow things.

But there is something else about that paper—the smell! I noticed it the moment we came into the room, but with so much air and sun it was not bad. Now we have had a week of fog and rain, and whether the windows are open or not, the smell is here.

It creeps all over the house.

I find it hovering in the dining-room, skulking in the parlor, hiding in the hall, lying in wait for me on the stairs.

It gets into my hair.

Even when I go to ride, if I turn my head suddenly and surprise it—there is that smell!

Such a peculiar odor, too! I have spent hours in trying to analyze it, to find what it smelled like.

It is not bad—at first, and very gentle, but quite the subtlest, most enduring odor I ever met.

In this damp weather it is awful, I wake up in the night and find it hanging over me.

It used to disturb me at first. I thought seriously of burning the house—to reach the smell.

But now I am used to it. The only thing I can think of that it is like is the *color* of the paper! A yellow smell.

There is a very funny mark on this wall, low down, near the mopboard. A streak that runs round the room. It goes behind every piece of furniture, except the bed, a long, straight, even *smooch*, as if it had been rubbed over and over.

I wonder how it was done and who did it, and what they did it for. Round and round and round—round and round and round—it makes me dizzy!

❖❖❖

I really have discovered something at last.

Through watching so much at night, when it changes so, I have finally found out.

The front pattern *does* move—and no wonder! The woman behind shakes it!

Sometimes I think there are a great many women behind, and sometimes only one, and she crawls around fast, and her crawling shakes it all over.

Then in the very bright spots she keeps still, and in the very shady spots she just takes hold of the bars and shakes them hard.

And she is all the time trying to climb through. But nobody could climb through that pattern—it strangles so; I think that is why it has so many heads.

They get through, and then the pattern strangles them off and turns them upside down, and makes their eyes white!

If those heads were covered or taken off it would not be half so bad.

◇◇◇

I think that woman gets out in the daytime!

And I'll tell you why—privately—I've seen her!

I can see her out of every one of my windows!

It is the same woman, I know, for she is always creeping, and most women do not creep by daylight.

I see her in that long shaded lane, creeping up and down. I see her in those dark grape arbors, creeping all around the garden.

I see her on that long road under the trees, creeping along, and when a carriage comes she hides under the blackberry vines.

I don't blame her a bit. It must be very humiliating to be caught creeping by daylight!

I always lock the door when I creep by daylight. I can't do it at night, for I know John would suspect something at once.

And John is so queer now, that I don't want to irritate him. I wish he would take another room! Besides, I don't want anybody to get that woman out at night but myself.

I often wonder if I could see her out of all the windows at once.

But, turn as fast as I can, I can only see out of one at one time.

And though I always see her, she *may* be able to creep faster than I can turn!

I have watched her sometimes away off in the open country, creeping as fast as a cloud shadow in a high wind.

If only that top pattern could be gotten off from the under one! I mean to try it, little by little.

I have found out another funny thing, but I shan't tell it this time! It does not do to trust people too much.

There are only two more days to get this paper off, and I believe John is beginning to notice. I don't like the look in his eyes.

And I heard him ask Jennie a lot of professional questions about me. She had a very good report to give.

She said I slept a good deal in the daytime.

John knows I don't sleep very well at night, for all I'm so quiet!

He asked me all sorts of questions, too, and pretended to be very loving and kind.

As if I couldn't see through him!

Still, I don't wonder he acts so, sleeping under this paper for three months.

It only interests me, but I feel sure John and Jennie are secretly affected by it.

◆◆◆

Hurrah! This is the last day, but it is enough. John to stay in town over night, and won't be out until this evening.

Jennie wanted to sleep with me—the sly thing! but I told her I should undoubtedly rest better for a night all alone.

That was clever, for really I wasn't alone a bit! As soon as it was moonlight and that poor thing began to crawl and shake the pattern, I got up and ran to help her.

I pulled and she shook, I shook and she pulled, and before morning we had peeled off yards of that paper.

A strip about as high as my head and half around the room.

And then when the sun came and that awful pattern began to laugh at me, I declared I would finish it to-day!

We go away to-morrow, and they are moving all my furniture down again to leave things as they were before.

Jennie looked at the wall in amazement, but I told her merrily that I did it out of pure spite at the vicious thing.

She laughed and said she wouldn't mind doing it herself, but I must not get tired.

How she betrayed herself that time!

But I am here, and no person touches this paper but me,—not *alive!*

She tried to get me out of the room—it was too patent! But I said it was so quiet and empty and clean now that I believed I would lie down again and sleep all I could; and not to wake me even for dinner—I would call when I woke.

So now she is gone, and the servants are gone, and the things are gone, and there is nothing left but that great bedstead nailed down, with the canvas mattress we found on it.

We shall sleep downstairs to-night, and take the boat home to-morrow.

I quite enjoy the room, now it is bare again.

How those children did tear about here!

This bedstead is fairly gnawed!

But I must get to work.

I have locked the door and thrown the key down into the front path.

I don't want to go out, and I don't want to have anybody come in, till John comes.

I want to astonish him.

I've got a rope up here that even Jennie did not find. If that woman does get out, and tries to get away, I can tie her!

But I forgot I could not reach far without anything to stand on!

This bed will *not* move!

I tried to lift and push it until I was lame, and then I got so angry I bit off a little piece at one corner—but it hurt my teeth.

Then I peeled off all the paper I could reach standing on the floor. It sticks horribly and the pattern just enjoys it! All those strangled heads and bulbous eyes and waddling fungus growths just shriek with derision!

I am getting angry enough to do something desperate. To jump out of the window would be admirable exercise, but the bars are too strong even to try.

Besides I wouldn't do it. Of course not. I know well enough that a step like that is improper and might be misconstrued.

I don't like to *look* out of the windows even—there are so many of those creeping women, and they creep so fast.

I wonder if they all come out of that wall-paper as I did?

But I am securely fastened now by my well-hidden rope—you don't get *me* out in the road there!

I suppose I shall have to get back behind the pattern when it comes night, and that is hard!

It is so pleasant to be out in this great room and creep around as I please!

I don't want to go outside. I won't, even if Jennie asks me to.

For outside you have to creep on the ground, and everything is green instead of yellow.

But here I can creep smoothly on the floor, and my shoulder just fits in that long smooch around the wall, so I cannot lose my way.

Why there's John at the door!

It is no use, young man, you can't open it!

How he does call and pound!

Now he's crying for an axe.

It would be a shame to break down that beautiful door!

"John dear!" said I in the gentlest voice, "the key is down by the front steps, under a plaintain leaf!"

That silenced him for a few moments.

Then he said—very quietly indeed, "Open the door, my darling!"

"I can't," said I. "The key is down by the front door under a plantain leaf!"

And then I said it again, several times, very gently and slowly, and said it so often that he had to go and see, and he got it of course, and came in. He stopped short by the door.

"What is the matter?" he cried. "For God's sake, what are you doing!"

I kept on creeping just the same, but I looked at him over my shoulder.

"I've got out at last," said I, "in spite of you and Jane? And I've pulled off most of the paper, so you can't put me back!"

Now why should that man have fainted? But he did, and right across my path by the wall, so that I had to creep over him every time!

THE WELL OF LONELINESS
Radclyffe Hall

The Well of Loneliness, an early twentieth century novel about lesbianism, created shock waves. When the book was published in England in 1928, the *Times of London* and other newspapers regarded it as having literary merit, and being an important psychological and sociological study. But some of the popular press saw it as obscene, and it was finally banned in England (*New York Times*, 1943). In 1929, when the book appeared in the United States, the Society for the Suppression of Vice began censorship proceedings against it. Although the charge was dismissed, customs officials nevertheless refused to permit its entry into the country on the grounds of obscenity. It was finally cleared and its sales of over 20,000 copies made it a best seller for 1929.

In addition to *The Well of Loneliness*, Radclyffe Hall (1856–1943) wrote other novels including the prize winning *Adam's Breed*. She also wrote short stories and poetry. However, because of the furor caused by her first book, none of her later works focused on lesbianism.

Millions of women encountered lesbianism in literature for the first time reading *The Well of Loneliness*. In her autobiography, *I Know Why the Caged Bird Sings* (1970), Maya Angelou confessed that reading it as a teenager led her to question her own heterosexuality, to seek a liaison with a young man as a critical test, and to end up pregnant as a result. Although *The Well of Loneliness* was a radical analysis for its day, it has been criticized of late for its defensive and outmoded portrayal of lesbianism.

Some background is needed to appreciate the excerpt. Sir Philip had wanted a son, and when a daughter was born, he named her Stephen. Stephen was encouraged in a variety of pursuits (riding, hunting) that were commonly regarded as "masculine," and she was not discouraged from dressing up and playing at being a boy (Nelson) as a child. As she grew up, Sir Philip sensed his daughter's differentness and accepted her in a way that Anna, her mother, never could. In the passage below, Martin, a young male friend of Stephen's, goes to meet her at the stables at Morton, the family estate, where she is with the stableman Williams and her horse Raftery. He then professes his love for her.

. . . People gossiped a little because of the freedom allowed Martin and Stephen by her parents; but on the whole they gossiped quite kindly, with a great deal of smiling and nodding of heads. After all the girl was just like other girls— they almost ceased to resent her. Meanwhile Martin continued to stay on in Upton, held fast by the charm and the strangeness of Stephen—her very strangeness it was that allured him, yet all the while he must think of their friendship, not even admitting that strangeness. He deluded himself with these thoughts of friendship, but Sir Philip and Anna were not deluded. They looked at each other almost shyly at first, then Anna grew bold, and she said to her husband:

'Is it possible the child is falling in love with Martin? Of course he's in love with her. Oh, my dear, it would make me so awfully happy—' And her heart went out in affection to Stephen, as it had not done since the girl was a baby.

Her hopes would go flying ahead of events; she would start making plans for her daughter's future. Martin must give up his orchards and forests and buy Tenley Court that was now in the market; it had several large farms and some excellent pasture, quite enough to keep any man happy and busy. Then Anna would suddenly grow very thoughtful; Tenley Court was also possessed of fine nurseries, big, bright, sunny rooms facing south, with their bathroom, there were bars to the windows—it was all there and ready.

Sir Philip shook his head and warned Anna to go slowly, but he could not quite keep the great joy from his eyes, nor the hope from his heart. Had he been mistaken? Perhaps after all he had been mistaken—the hope thudded ceaselessly now in his heart.

◇◇◇

Came a day when winter must give place to spring, when the daffodils marched across the whole country from Castle Morton Common to Ross and beyond, pitching camps by the side of the river. When the hornbeam made patches of green in the hedges, and the hawthorn broke out into small, budding bundles; when the old cedar tree on the lawn at Morton grew reddish pink tips to its elegant fingers; when the wild cherry trees on the sides of the hills were industriously putting forth both leaves and blossoms; when Martin looked into his heart and saw Stephen—saw her suddenly there as a woman.

Friendship! He marvelled now at his folly, at his blindness, his coldness of body and spirit. He had offered this girl the cold husks of his friendship, insulting her youth, her womanhood, her beauty—for he saw her now with the eyes of a lover. To a man such as he was, sensitive, restrained, love came as a blinding revelation. He knew little about women, and the little he did know was restricted to episodes that he thought best forgotten. On the whole he had led a fairly chaste life—less from scruple than because he was fastidious by nature. But now he was very deeply in love, and those years of restraint took their toll of poor Martin, so that he trembled before his own passion, amazed at its strength, not a little disconcerted. And being by habit a quiet, reserved creature, he must quite lose his head and become the reverse. So impatient was he that he rushed off to Morton very early one morning to look for Stephen, tracking her down in the end of the stables, where he found her talking to Williams and Raftery.

He said: 'Never mind about Raftery, Stephen—let's go into the garden, I've got something to tell you.' And she thought that he must have had bad news from home, because of his voice and his curious pallor.

She went with him and they walked on in silence for a while, then Martin stood still, and began to talk quickly; he was saying amazing, incredible things: 'Stephen, my dear—I do utterly love you.' He was holding out his arms, while she shrank back bewildered: 'I love you, I'm deeply in love with you, Stephen—look at me, don't you understand me, belovèd? I want you to marry me—you do love me, don't you?' And then, as though she had suddenly struck him, he flinched: 'Good God! What's the matter, Stephen?'

She was staring at him in a kind of dumb horror, staring at his eyes that were clouded by desire, while gradually over her colourless face there was spreading an expression of the deepest repulsion—terror and repulsion he saw on her face, and something else too, a look as of outrage. He could not believe this thing that he saw, this insult to all that he felt to be sacred; for a moment he in his turn, must stare, then he came a step nearer, still unable to believe. But at that she wheeled round and fled from him wildly, fled back to the house that had always protected; without so much as a word she left him, nor did she once pause in her flight to look back. Yet even in this moment of headlong panic, the girl was conscious of something like amazement, amazement at herself, and she gasped as she ran: 'It's Martin—Martin—' And again: 'It's Martin!'

He stood perfectly still until the trees hid her. He felt stunned, incapable of understanding. All that he knew was that he must get away, away from Stephen, away from Morton, away from the thoughts that would follow after. In less than two hours he was motoring to London; in less than two weeks he was standing on the deck of the steamer that would carry him back to his forests that lay somewhere beyond the horizon.

◈◈◈

No one questioned at Morton; they spoke very little. Even Anna forbore to question her daughter, checked by something that she saw in the girl's pale face.

But alone with her husband she gave way to her misgivings, to her deep disappointment: 'It's heartbreaking, Philip. What's happened? They seemed so devoted to each other. Will you ask the child? Surely one of us ought to—'

Sir Philip said quietly: 'I think Stephen will tell me.' And with that Anna had perforce to be content.

Very silently Stephen now went about Morton, and her eyes looked bewildered and deeply unhappy. At night she would lie awake thinking of Martin, missing him, mourning him as though he were dead. But she could not accept this death without question, without feeling that she was in some way blameworthy. What was she, what manner of curious creature, to have been so repelled by a lover like Martin? Yet she had been repelled, and even her pity for the man could not wipe out that stronger feeling. She had driven him away because something within her was intolerant of that new aspect of Martin.

Oh, but she mourned his good, honest friendship; he had taken that from her, the thing she most needed—but perhaps after all it had never existed except as a cloak for this other emotion. And then, lying there in the thickening darkness, she would shrink from what might be waiting in the future, for all that had just happened might happen again—there were other men in the world beside Martin. Fool, never to have visualized this thing before, never to have faced the possibility of it; now she understood her resentment of men when their voices grew soft and insinuating. Yes, and now she knew to the full the meaning of fear, and Martin it was, who had taught her its meaning—her friend—the man she had utterly trusted had pulled the scales from her eyes and revealed it. Fear, stark fear, and the shame of such fear—that was the legacy left her by Martin. And yet he had made her so happy at first, she had felt so contented, so natural with him; but that was because they had been like two men, companions, sharing each other's interests. And at this thought her bitterness would all but flow over; it was cruel, it was cowardly of him to have deceived her, when all the time he had only been waiting for the chance to force this other thing on her.

But what was she? Her thoughts, slipping back to her childhood, would find many things in her past that perplexed her. She had never been quite like the other children, she had always been lonely and discontented, she had always been trying to be someone else—that was why she had dressed herself up as young Nelson. Remembering those days she would think of her father, and would wonder if now, as then, he could help her. Supposing she should ask him to explain about Martin? Her father was wise, and had infinite patience— yet somehow she instinctively dreaded to ask him. Alone—it was terrible to feel so much alone—to feel oneself different from other people. At one time she had rather enjoyed this distinction—she had rather enjoyed dressing up as a young Nelson. Yet had she enjoyed it? Or had it been done as some sort of inadequate, childish protest? But if so against what had she been protesting when she strutted about the house, masquerading? In those days she had wanted to be a boy—had that been the meaning of the pitiful young Nelson? And what about now? She had wanted Martin to treat her as a man, had expected it of him. . . . The questions to which she could find no answers would pile themselves up and up in the darkness; oppressing, stifling by sheer weight of numbers, until she would feel them getting her under; 'I don't know—oh, God, I don't know!' she would mutter, tossing as though to fling off those questions.

Then one night towards dawn she could bear it no longer; her dread must give place to her need of consolation. She would ask her father to explain her to herself; she would tell him her deep desolation over Martin. She would say: 'Is there anything strange about me, Father, that I should have felt as I did about Martin?' And then she would try to explain very calmly what it was she had felt, the intensity of it. She would try to make him understand her suspicion that this feeling of hers was a thing fundamental, much more than merely not being in love; much, much more than not wanting to marry Martin. She would tell him why she found herself so utterly bewildered; tell him how she had loved Martin's strong, young body, and his honest brown face, and his slow thoughtful eyes, and his careless walk—all these things she had loved. Then suddenly terror and deep repugnance because of that unforeseen change in Martin, the change that had turned the friend into the lover—in reality it had been no more than that, the friend had turned lover and had wanted from her what she could not give him, or indeed any man, because of that deep repugnance. Yet there should have been nothing repugnant about Martin, nor was she a child to have felt such terror. She had known certain facts about life for some time and they had not repelled her in other people—not until they had been brought home to herself had these facts both terrified and repelled her. . . .

SEX IN EDUCATION
Edward H. Clarke, M.D.

In the 1860s, women were increasingly demanding entry into the already crowded medical profession and there was a growing feminist sentiment that female practitioners exclusively should treat women's unique physical problems. In response to such pressures, medical experts were claiming that women shouldn't train as doctors, first, because they didn't have the intellectual aptitude and, second, because they couldn't perform their medical duties responsibly at certain points in their menstrual cycles. Yet when male peers bodily removed female medical students from classes in Philadelphia, Dr. Edward Clarke, one time professor and member of the board of Harvard Medical School, deplored the incident, arguing that women had every right to enter medicine, provided that they could demonstrate their fitness for it.

Because of his liberal views, Clarke was invited in 1872 to address the New England Women's Club in Boston on the subject of the relation of sex to education. Club members expected a defense of women in higher education. Instead, Clarke stunned his audience by concluding that higher education was destroying the health and reproductive capacities of young women. Just when energy was most needed to develop their reproductive systems, he asserted, women were depleting their energy supplies by building up their brains.

A year later Clarke expanded his ideas into a book, *Sex in Education; or, A Fair Chance for the Girls*, from which this excerpt is taken. The book was immensely popular. The first edition was sold out in a week, and it went through seventeen editions in thirteen years. Despite widespread criticism of his work, Clarke's ideas continued to shape popular views and educational practices for years to come.

. . . Miss D——— entered Vassar College at the age of fourteen. Up to that age, she had been a healthy girl, judged by the standard of American girls. Her parents were apparently strong enough to yield her a fair dower of force. The catamenial function first showed signs of activity in her Sophomore Year, when she was fifteen years old. Its appearance at this age* is confirmatory evidence of the normal state of her health at that period of her college career. Its commencement was normal, without pain or excess. She performed all her college duties regularly and steadily. She studied, recited, stood at the blackboard, walked, and went through her gymnastic exercises, from the beginning to the end of the term, just as boys do. Her account of her regimen there was so nearly that of a boy's regimen, that it would puzzle a physiologist to determine, from the account alone, whether the subject of it was male or female. She was an average scholar, who maintained a fair position in her class, not one of the anxious sort, that are ambitious of leading all the rest. Her first warning was fainting away, while exercising in the gymnasium, at a time when she should have been comparatively quiet, both mentally and physically. This warning was repeated several times, under the same circumstances. Finally she was compelled to renounce gymnastic exercises altogether. In her Junior Year, the

---

*It appears, from the researches of Mr. Whitehead on this point, that an examination of four thousand cases gave fifteen years six and three-quarter months as the average age in England for the appearance of the catamenia—Whitehead, *on Abortion, & c.*

SEX IN EDUCATION   From *Sex in Education: or, A Fair Chance for the Girls*, Boston: James R. Osgood and Co., 1873, 79–85.

organism's periodical function began to be performed with pain, moderate at first, but more and more severe with each returning month. When between seventeen and eighteen years old, dysmenorrhœa was established as the order of that function. Coincident with the appearance of pain, there was a diminution of excretion; and, as the former increased, the latter became more marked. In other respects she was well; and, in all respects, she appeared to be well to her companions and to the faculty of the college. She graduated before nineteen, with fair honors and a poor physique. The year succeeding her graduation was one of steadily-advancing invalidism. She was tortured for two or three days out of every month; and, for two or three days after each season of torture, was weak and miserable, so that about one sixth or fifth of her time was consumed in this way. The excretion from the blood, which had been gradually lessening, after a time substantially stopped, though a periodical effort to keep it up was made. She now suffered from what is called amenorrhœa. At the same time she became pale, hysterical, nervous in the ordinary sense, and almost constantly complained of headache. Physicians were applied to for aid: drugs were administered; travelling, with consequent change of air and scene, was undertaken; and all with little apparent avail. After this experience, she was brought to Boston for advice, when the writer first saw her, and learned all these details. She presented no evidence of local uterine congestion, inflammation, ulceration, or displacement. The evidence was altogether in favor of an arrest of the development of the reproductive apparatus, at a stage when the development was nearly complete. Confirmatory proof of such an arrest was found in examining her breast, where the milliner had supplied the organs Nature should have grown. It is unnecessary for our present purpose to detail what treatment was advised. It is sufficient to say, that she probably never will become physically what she would have been had her education being physiologically guided.

This case needs very little comment: its teachings are obvious. Miss D——— went to college in good physical condition. During the four years of her college life, her parents and the college faculty required her to get what is popularly called an education. Nature required her, during the same period, to build and put in working-order a large and complicated reproductive mechanism, a matter that is popularly ignored,—shoved out of sight like a disgrace. She naturally obeyed the requirements of the faculty, which she could see, rather than the requirements of the mechanism within her, that she could not see. Subjected to the college regimen, she worked four years in getting a liberal education. Her way of work was sustained and continuous, and out of harmony with the rhythmical periodicity of the female organization. The stream of vital and constructive force evolved within her was turned steadily to the brain, and away from the ovaries and their accessories. The result of this sort of education was, that these last-mentioned organs, deprived of sufficient opportunity and nutriment, first began to perform their functions with pain, a warning of error that was unheeded; then, to cease to grow;* next, to set up once a month a grumbling torture that made life miserable; and, lastly, the

---

*The arrest of development of the uterus, in connection with amenorrhœa, is sometimes very marked. In the New-York Medical Journal for June, 1873, three such cases are recorded, that came under the eye of those excellent observers, Dr. E. R. Peaslee and Dr. T. G. Thomas. In one of these cases, the uterine cavity measured

brain and the whole nervous sytem, disturbed, in obedience to the law, that, if one member suffers, all the members suffer, became neuralgic and hysterical. And so Miss D——— spent the few years next succeeding her graduation in conflict with dysmenorrhœa, headache, neuralgia, and hysteria. Her parents marvelled at her ill-health; and she furnished another text for the often-repeated sermon on the delicacy of American girls. . . .

DIARY EXCERPTS (1870, 1871)
M. Carey Thomas

When Bryn Mawr, a women's college under Quaker auspices, opened in 1885, M. Carey Thomas (1857–1935) was hired as its first dean, a post she held for several years. She was Bryn Mawr's president from 1894 to 1922, the first fourteen years serving also as dean. Under her direction the college came to be recognized as one of the country's leading academic institutions. In addition to her work at Bryn Mawr, Thomas was instrumental in getting Johns Hopkins Medical School to admit women at a time when less respected schools would not consider it. She earned a reputation as a distinguished leader in higher education and as an activist for women's rights.

Although her father believed that higher education was not necessary for women given their future domestic lives, somehow Thomas never accepted such views of woman's place. Perhaps she was influenced more by the Quaker belief in the spiritual equality of the sexes, which was also a part of her background. Or, perhaps her family's insistence that the girls have the same freedoms as the boys had a greater influence on her. At any rate, she never married, but instead actively sought a career.

She persuaded her father, against his better judgment, to allow her to enter Cornell University, where she earned the AB degree in 1877. Then she attended graduate classes at the University of Leipzig. Later she transferred to the University of Zurich because, unlike Leipzig, it granted the Ph.D. degree to women. After obtaining her doctorate in English there in 1882, she was hired by Bryn Mawr College.

The first selection from M. Carey Thomas' journal was written when she was thirteen. She was called Minnie at that time. Her journal entry of November 25th read, in part: "Have come across such a glorious book called 'Boys Play Book of Science' am going to read it through and see if whether ain't some experiments Bess and I can try." The second selection from the journal was written three months after the first. The spelling and punctuation here appear in the original.

 **SEVENTH DAY 26th [NOVEMBER 26, 1870]** Set a mouse trap last night in case Bess & I might want to get his skeleton   caught him but he was'nt dead   neither Julie nor Netty would kill him so I heroicly dropped the trap in to a pail of water & rushed out of the room. Then took my slippers into mothers room who is lots better & is sitting up & *sewed sewed sewed*   Oh the monotony of worstered! Laurie aint worth half this bother. "But there are moments when the gush of feeling hath its sway" & in one of

---

one and a half inches; in another, one and seven-eighths inches; and, in a third, one and a quarter inches. Recollecting that the normal measurement is from two and a half to three inches, it appears that the arrest of development in these cases occurred when the uterus was half or less than half grown. Liberal education should avoid such errors.

ose moments I escaped to refresh myself by looking over my cabnet. Pretty on I heard some one calling "Min" & knew it must be Bess 'cause no one se ever calls me Min   Well first we roasted some chestnuts And proceeded to the more important duty of getting to skeleton of a mouse. The poor little fellow being drowned by this time we took our victim out in the yard   bared our glittering knives & commenced operations but the horrid little mouse's fur was so soft that we couldn't make a hole in [it] & besides it made us sick & our hands trembled so we could'nt do a thing but concluding that it was *feminine* nonsense we made a hole & squeezed his insides out   it was the most disgusting thing I ever did. We then took off his skin   it came of[f] elegantly just like a glove & then holding it by the tail we chased poor Julie all around   she was so afraid of it. Just as if it was any worse than a chicken & finaly put it on the fire to boil to Julie's great disgust   when it had boiled some we took it again and picked all the meat of[f] it & saved its tongue & eyes to look through the microscope & then the mouse looked like a real skeleton   we then put it out the window to bleach & then as Bess had to go I walked down with her   Was'nt it funny she had been thinking about experiments too & so we planned together & are going to spend our money in instruments instead of candy & then we will invite our friends to see our experiments. I think I'd almost rather be a chemical fellow than a doctor. When I got [home] I found that Netty had thrown away our tongue & eyes & worst of all woe woe is me that our skeleton that had taken us 3 mortal hours to get had fallen out of the window & smashed   oh my we are unfortunate   Oh Science! why wilt thou not protect thy votaries? In the afternoon lolled around learnt Greek & sewed everlasting slippers. Bess said when she told her father about our getting the mouse he looked grave and said "Bessie Bessie thee is loosing all thy *feminine* traits"   I [am] afraid I have'nt got any to loose for I greatly prefer cutting up mice to sewing worsted.

FIRST DAY FEB. 26th [1871] I have at length come to the conclusion that it will be more interesting to me when, as an old dried up woman with aid of spectacles I descipher these scrawls to read what I thought than what I did & accordingly I am going to commit my reflections to paper trusting to kind fortune to keep them from careless eyes.

An english man Joseph Beck was here to dinner the other day & he dont blieve in the Education of women. Neither does Cousin Frank King & my such a disgusson as they had. Mother of course was for. They said that they did'nt see any good of a womans learning Latin or Greek it did'n't make them any more entertaining to their *husbands*. A woman had plenty of other things to do sewing cooking taking care of children dressing & flirting. "What noble elevating things for a whole life time to be occupied with", In fact they talked as if the whole end & aim of a womans life was to get *married* & when she attained that *greatest state* of *earthly bliss* it was her duty to amuse her husband & to learn nothing   never to execise the powers of her mind so that he might have the *exquisite* pleasure of knowing more than his wife   of course they talked the usual cant of woman being to *high* to *exalted* to do anything & sit up in perfect ignorance with folded hands & let men worship at her shrine meaning in other words like all the rest of such high faluting stuff that woman ought to be *mere dolls* for men to be amused with to kiss fondle pet &, love maybe, but as for associating with them on terms of equality, they would'nt think of such a thing. Now I don't mean to say the these two men believed this but these were the principles they upheld. I got perfectly enraged how *unjust*-how *narrow minded*-how *utterly uncomprehensible* to deny that women ought to be educated & worse than all to deny that they have equal powers of mind. If I ever live & grow up my *one* aim & consentated purpose *shall* be & is to show that a woman *can learn can reason can* compete with men in the grand fields of literature & science & conjecture that opens before the 19 century that a woman can be a woman & a *true* one with out having all her time engrossed by dress & society-that the woman who has fought all the battles of olden time over again whilesst reading the spirited pages of Homer Vergil Herroditus who has sympathised in the longings after something beyond mere daily exhistance found in the works of Socrates, Plato & Eschelus, who has reasoned out all the great laws which govern the universe with Newton, Cirago, Gallileo who has mourned with Dante reasoned & speculated with Shiller Goethe & Jean Paul been carried away by Carlyle "mildly enchanted by Emerson" who has idealised with Milton & emerged with strengthen intelect from the intricate labyrinth of Geometry Trigonometry & Calculous is not any less like what God really intended a woman to be than the trifling ballroom butterfly than the ignorant [rag] doll baby which *they* admire. My firm fixed purpose (for Puncheon, I heard him lecture on Eliga yesterday says that unless you have one you will never *do* or *be* anything) is to have a througher knowledge of French Latin Greek & German & then to read & study carefully all the principle authors especially the old german metaphyseans & to go high in mathamatics for even if they aint any "practical" use they stregnth the mind & I think I would like to take some science for my espesiallity & then my greatest hope & ambition is too be an author an essayist an historian to write hearty earnest true books that may do their part towards elevating the human race towards inducing some at least to let the money bags on which they are wasting such a wealth of hope & desire & intellect drop from their hands & aim at something higher than merely providing for our miserable earthly exhistance to look higher then the miserable [silly] disappointments of every day life & not to live on in utter forgetfulness of God & their duty to their fellow men. In the words of Longfellow I would like when to.

"When departing leave behind me
Footprints on the sands of time
Footprints that perhaps another sailing on lifes dreary main
A folorn a shiprecked brother seeing may take heart again"
It seems to me that that is a purpose worth striving after. Oh may it
not be *only* a purpose.
"I wait for the *future* the birds cannot sing it.
Not one as he sits on the tree
The bells cannot ring it. But long years
On bring it. Such as *I wish it*"

ADDRESS TO THE STUDENTS AT THE OPENING OF THE ACADEMIC YEAR 1899-1900

M. Carey Thomas

In 1885, no colleges open to women could compare in academic excellence to the best men's colleges. M. Carey Thomas decided to correct this situation and to discredit theories of women's intellectual inferiority by making Bryn Mawr's entrance examinations tougher than those of the best male colleges and its academic standards second to none. Bryn Mawr was to produce an elite group of women, all Phi Beta Kappa quality, who, by their outstanding scholarship and excellent breeding, would inspire others to similar achievements. Bryn Mawr did not require domestic service of students as most colleges did, and Thomas actively discouraged students from thinking that it was woman's destiny to marry and have children.

Thomas admitted that, because of Dr. Clarke's ideas, she was never quite sure how the experiment at Bryn Mawr would turn out. She claimed too that many Philadelphia girls were discouraged from coming to Bryn Mawr by Dr. S. Weir Mitchell, who maintained that no young woman could get an advanced degree and remain healthy.

The following is a speech by M. Carey Thomas given at Bryn Mawr in 1899.

It is always my custom to welcome the students at the beginning of each academic year. I regretted very much that I was compelled to be absent on the first day, the opening of the fifteenth year of the college, but I was, I think, well employed in assisting to welcome the new President of Wellesley College. Indeed the speechmaking at Wellesley was so interesting in many ways that I shall refer to it again in a few moments and shall make some of the views on women's education there put forth the text of what I wish to speak to you about after I have given out the necessary announcements. . . .

In our little community of students we have . . . all grades represented, from Freshmen (I might almost say from even sub-Freshmen, so many scores are living at our gates) to the Faculty. This year for the first time we can begin to test the experiment of older and younger students, graduates and seniors and juniors and freshmen living together in each of our halls of residence in nearly equal proportions, instead of being massed in halls by classes. Hall association rather than class association, or rather hall association combined with class association, will, I believe, give us a far wider college culture. After all to know well sixty-five fellow students of different ages is itself to know the college world. Angles should rub off, awkwardness should disappear, the younger classmen should learn the scholarly point of view of older students, and insensibly be affected by their atmosphere, while older students learn how to influence younger students and especially graduate students how to keep in touch with them; and so in this mutual association will, we hope, be fashioned and perfected the type of Bryn Mawr women which will, we hope, become as well known and universally admired a type as the Oxford and Cambridge man or as the graduate of the great English public schools. No such type can possibly be created except by a residence college and unless carefully divided like Oxford and Cambridge into resident halls a very large college loses the power to mould its students in external ways. There used to be, but at present we might almost say there is not a type of Harvard man, and it is much lamented by old Harvard men and Harvard professors. Princeton still preserves a type, but the Cornell, Hopkins, Columbia, University of Pennsylvania, Michigan men are as different as the homes from which they come or as the homes or boarding houses in which they live, and this great lack is so strongly felt that there is a great modern movement in men's education to return to the dormitory system. President Eliot in his address of welcome to President Hazard said that as men's colleges in this country had failed as schools of manners it was left to women's colleges to lead the way in showing how youth of both sexes could be taken by the hundred and be given the bearing and manners of gentlemen and gentlewomen. He then proceeded to say that manners as such were of vastly more importance to women than men. Whether this is true or not, and in the old fashioned matrimonial market which President Eliot was probably referring to, where a man exchanges dollars for a woman's social charm, it is true, it is certainly true that for both men and women success of every kind in after life depends greatly on gentle breeding. Doctors, lawyers, teachers, philanthropists, social leaders, everything in life in which men and women are associated together is aided or retarded by good breeding. Such breeding can best be learned at home, but in a large community like this there will always be those whose student homes are better schools of manners than the homes of other students, and living together as we do the highest standards should prevail. We all have an opportunity to correct provincialisms, uncouth pronunciations, to get rid of expressions that no person of culture could possibly use. . . .

I am so infinitely proud of the standard of good conduct here wherever I go I am met by unknown friends that you the students of the college have made for me. Your system of self government is the fullest system known; it preceded all other self government systems in colleges in this country. Bryn Mawr is the only college in the world where a student has never been disciplined for offences of conduct apart from the strictly academic offences of unfairness in examinations. I appeal to the student body assembled to maintain this standard, to raise it higher. I sometimes wonder if you know how people regard the Bryn Mawr standards and how [much] lies in your hands by some rough hoyden horse play or brutal practical joking. Manners do, as President Eliot says, matter immensely and if the Bryn Mawr woman could add to scholarship and character gentle breeding and could join high standards of behavior and usages of culture and gentle observances to high standards of scholarship we should have the type we are seeking to create.

President Carter of Williams in answering to the toast "The ideal New England college", said that he wondered sometimes if the ideal women's college in flooding with the light of learning the women within its walls could also look after the sweetness, whether sweet sixteen at entering would be sweet sixteen at graduation. Emphatically no. Sweet sixteen has the charm of childhood and ignorance that will shortly be relegated to the harems of the east.

President Eliot also said (you see that there were many doctrinaire utterances about women, for when do men gathered together on the platform of a women's college resist the attempt to shove, usually out of its path, the resistless force they see before them, which we call the higher education of women) President Eliot said that the president and faculty of a women's college had no guide from the past, that the great tradition of learning existing from the time of the Egyptians to the present existed only for men and that this vast body of inherited tradition was of no service in women's education, that women's colleges simply imitated men when they used the same educational methods instead of inventing new ones of their own and that furthermore it would indeed be strange if women's intellects were not at least as unlike men's as their bodies. This is the old argument of the rural deans over again who came up from all the country villages of England to vote against Oxford and Cambridge giving women the same degrees as men when they had done the same work and would not be worthy of a serious reply had it not been thrown deliberately by the president of one of the greatest of American universities as a gauntlet in the face of an immense audience, most of whom were directly interested in the education of women students. It only shows us that as progressive as one may be in education or other things there may be in our minds some dark spot of mediaevalism, and clearly in President Eliot's other-wise luminous intelligence women's education is this dark spot. He might as well have told the president of Wellesley to invent a new Christian religion for Wellesley and new symphonies or operas, a new Beethoven and Wagner, new statues and pictures, a new Phidias and a new Titian, new tennis, new golf, a new way to swim, skate and run, new food, and new drink. It would be easier to do all this than to create for women a new science of geography, a new Greek Tragedies, new Chemistry, new philosophies, in short, a new intellectual heavens and earth. President Taylor of Vassar in talking over this remark afterward said to me—and I think he would not object to my quoting it to you, as he told me he had often said it, that during all the years he had been educating women he had been trying to find some difference between their intellects and men's and that whenever he thought he could put his finger on a difference he found that the accuracy of his observation was overturned by future classes of students. He thought he had found but one difference, a difference of habit of life, the difference implied by women's willingness to work more hours over a difficult problem or a difficult passage of translation, whereas a man would see that a change of occupation was the proper thing and would return to attack the difficult subject after several hours of relaxation and fresh air, a woman would pore over it until she had lost her power of thinking freshly. This he accounted for by the different conditions of women's life and the fact that a woman's work in the household is never finished. I think that I may add one more difference to that suggested by President Taylor; it is this: as yet college women are not as ready to accept criticism, they are not used to the take and give of life. They have been more sheltered, less criticised and more praised. Often in teaching women professors have to be more careful then in teaching men, as honest criticism depresses students unduly.

   Professor Palmer, of Harvard, whose remarks are always sane and to the point, said in answering the toast "The Ideal College Woman", as having married Wellesley's former president and holding the post, as he said, of husband of the college, that if the difference between the minds of men and women is so great, it is strange that under the free elective system women did not overwhelmingly elect certain courses: French and German, for example, instead of Greek and Latin, Art and Music instead of Mathematics, and that undoubtedly if the difference existed it ought to manifest itself in this way. In point of fact you will find by comparing the favourite studies at men's and women's colleges that the same waves of interest seem to sweep over both. In certain periods of the years modern languages are given the preference over classical languages. In certain other years History and Political Economy draw the most students. Furthermore it is strange if the intellectual training for men is not fit for women that we see in women's as in men's students [sic] such a steady growth in intellectual honesty, in clear thinking, in reasonableness, in scientific habit of thinking.

When I was in Aix-les-Bains this summer taking the cure for sciatica, my books gave out and as I could not do serious reading during a great deal of the time I had to supply myself with the only available literature, modern French novels. In reading these novels I was very much struck with the different type of women the Anglo-Saxon race has evolved by the wider opportunities given to women of the Anglo-Saxon race. Much of the interest and tragedy of these novels turned on the doubt and distrust felt by the French husband of his wife, of his fear that she was deceiving him and that her love for him had stopped. Instead of asking her a frank question and receiving a frank reply the whole miserable drama of suspicion and jealousy and watching and spying unfolded itself. He did not ask her a question because he knew that she would deceive him. Thus, however unworthy of love and confidence women are men will love them and it is correspondingly true of women's love for men. The world is made so and the happiness of the home depends upon love and confidence between men and women. I thought as I read these novels how impossible it would be for such relations to exist between the collegebred woman and her husband. I should like to read to you a poem written by a great writer of English prose as embodying this new type of woman which we are, I hope, moulding and fashioning at Bryn Mawr College. I will close by reading Stevenson's verses: "To my Wife":

"Trusty, dusky, vivid, true,
With eyes of gold and bramble-dew,
Steel-true and blade-straight,
The great artificer
Made my mate.

"Honour, anger, valour, fire;
A love that life could never tire,
   Death quench or evil stir,
The mighty master
   Gave to her.

"Teacher, tender, comrade, wife,
A fellow-farer true through life,
   Heart-whole and soul-free
The august father
   Gave to me."

WOMEN MAKE BIG GAINS IN MARATHON
Neil Amdur

The first Olympic Marathon for women was approved in 1983. This victory was the final outcome of a long fight by women athletes. In 1967, for example, when Kathy Switzer tried to run in the Boston Marathon (she had entered under her initials and had a private physical), the codirector of the marathon tried to rip off her numbers during the race. She finished anyhow, but was suspended by the Amateur Athletic Union for fraudulent entry. In 1979, the American College of Sports Medicine paved the way for women's participation in Olympic marathons by recommending that they be allowed to run nationally and internationally in events longer than 1500 meters.

The same year as the Boston Marathon admitted women, Congress passed Title IX. This law specifies that "No person shall on the basis of sex be excluded from participation in, be denied the benefits of, or be subjected to discrimination under any educational program or activity receiving federal financial assistance." Given the past barriers to their participation in sports, we can only wonder what advances for women will come from complete implementation of this law at all educational levels.

Neil Amdur's article, from the *New York Times*, documents the tremendous progress women have made in the Boston Marathon since 1974.

Ten hours after she had shattered the women's world record in the marathon, Joan Benoit was still on her feet dancing at a post-marathon party in Boston early yesterday morning.

"Don't you have to be up for a morning TV show?" Fred Lebow, the race director of the New York City Marathon, asked the 25-year-old Miss Benoit, glancing at his watch and realizing it was 12:30 A.M.

"I don't plan on going to sleep at all," Miss Benoit replied, sounding as confident about her durability as she had been en route to breaking the world record by 2 minutes 47 seconds in the Boston Marathon Monday.

Miss Benoit's time was a remarkable 2 hours 22 minutes 42 seconds. Eleven years ago, Nina Kuscsik, the first official Boston women's champion, won in 3:08:58. "I thought she might do 2:23 or 2:24," Miss Kuscsik said yesterday from her home in Huntington, L. I., reflecting on Miss Benoit's performance. "But I couldn't bring myself to figure out what kind of splits Joanie needed to run that fast."

TIMES ARE FASTER   The improvement by American women in the marathon in recent years has been extraordinary. In 1978, for example, only 18 women finished under 2:50 during the entire year; by 1981, the figure was 62.

In Monday's Boston race, according to Honeywell computations, 60 women broke 3 hours, and 552 of the 652 starters finished under 4 hours, including 2 over 60 years of age. The average time for the women was 3:20:58.

Faster times have not necessarily been confined to world-class racers. Between 1978 and 1982, according to the National Running Data Center in

Tucson, Ariz., the 50th fastest time by American women has improved each year, from 2:57:34 in 1978 to 2:48:57 last year.

Equally as interesting is the increased participation in marathons by women. In 1975, according the center, 433 different women ran an estimated 600 marathons. In 1980 the total number of marathon performances was 10,002.

"We gave up doing it after 1980 because the list got so long," Ken Young, the co-director of the center, said yesterday from Tucson.

LOOKING TOWARD 2:20 Young said Miss Benoit's performance may have also established world standards for 10 miles (51:38), half-marathon (1:08:23) and 20 miles (1:46:44) if official splits that were announced were actually recorded and documented during the race.

Asked to project when the next marathon frontier, 2:20, might be reached by women, Young said: "My wife, Jennifer, thinks it'll be done this year. I don't think it will be done until 1986 or 1987."

Allison Roe's post-race comment that she could see Greg Meyer and other male leaders longer during Monday's race than anytime she could remember was another indication of how the gap is closing. Mrs. Roe, a co-holder of the old record at 2:25:29, dropped out at 17 miles. According to friends, she had menstrual cramps.

Mrs. Kuscsik, who is chairman of the women's long distance running committee of The Athletics Congress, credits the improvement among the women to a "bigger base from where the iceberg can get larger."

COLLEGIATE PROGRAMS CITED The proliferation of collegiate track programs for women during the last five years has been especially important, Mrs. Kuscsik believes.

"We're seeing a different breed of women now," she said, referring to the 20-to-29 age group, which has become the prime marathon group for women. "I was there as a pioneer years ago, but what you're seeing now are women who are coming into the marathon with considerably more track experience. I don't know what the optimum age is now."

Today's marathoners may also be better athletes than their predecessors. Miss Benoit is an accomplished cross-country skier, and Mrs. Roe, who may run in the Rome Marathon this weekend, has competed in triathlons, which involve endurance swimming, cycling and marathoning.

Bill Squires, a prominent long-distance running coach, believes all marathoners must also compete in track events in order to succeed in the marathon. Squires, who currently coaches Meyer, the Boston champion this year at 2:09, says marathons are no longer enough.

"They've got to go to mecca," said Squires, meaning the world-class track events. "They've got to be able to run on the track and against the roadies as well."

Miss Benoit demonstrated her versatility last winter. She lost a thrilling 3,000-meter indoor race in the final stride to Patti Sue Plumer of Stanford during the United States Olympic Invitational track meet at the Byrne Meadowlands Arena. The times were 8:53:54 to 8:53:55.

Mrs. Kuscsik, 44 years old, finished Monday's 26-mile-385-yard race in 3:17:24. Her time was not fast enough to qualify for next spring's United

States Olympic Trials, but 27 other women in Boston joined Miss Benoit in bettering the qualifying time of 2:51:16 for the women's trials.

The 2:51:16 was selected as the qualifying time by The Athletics Congress because it represented the 100th fastest time by a female American marathoner in 1982.

The question of whether Miss Benoit, off Monday's record-setting race, should be exempted from next year's Olympic Trials to concentrate on the Olympics is likely to be debated in the coming months. Mrs. Kuscsik said no formal discussions had been held on the subject, but exemptions and the possibility of holding one of the three places on the Olympic team for a decision by the long-distance running committee might be reviewed.

In her postrace interview, Miss Benoit said she planned no further marathons until the trials. Some coaches, athletes and officials feel that the trial dates for men (May 26 in Buffalo) and women (May 13 in Olympia, Wash.) do not provide sufficient recovery time for an August marathon in Los Angeles.

But the approval of the first Olympic marathon for women unquestionably has focused greater attention on the event. For years, the longest distance event for women at an Olympics was the 1,500-meter run.

Marathon Improvement

The best recorded each year by American women in the marathon

NAME	YEAR	TIME
Jacqueline Hansen	1974	2:43:55
Jacqueline Hansen	1975	2:38:19
Miki Gorman	1976	2:39:11
Kim Merritt	1977	2:37:57
Julie Brown	1978	2:36:23
Joan Benoit	1979	2:35:15
Patti Catalano	1980	2:29:33
Patti Catalano	1981	2:27:52
Joan Benoit	1982	2:26:11
Joan Benoit	1983	2:22:42

Source: National Running Data Center, Tucson, Ariz.
The New York Times/April 20, 1983

THE NATURAL SUPERIORITY OF WOMEN
Ashley Montagu

A physical anthropologist by training, Ashley Montagu is a prolific writer, popularizer of science, and a student of human behavior. He has written scores of books and articles on a variety of topics, from the concept of race, to anatomy and physiology, to the meaning of love. Much of his work is designed to debunk various "highly popular and erroneous ideas and practices."

In 1952, Montagu's *Saturday Review* article on the natural superiority of women, reprinted here, attracted widespread public attention. In it Montagu questions the "myth of female inferiority." Mixed in with quite conventional notions are some highly provocative ones. For example, contrary to the Freudian premise that women are incomplete men, Montagu argues that, chromosomally, men are incomplete women. In place of female "penis envy," Montagu sees unconscious male "womb and breast envy." And, rather than seeing woman as delicate and vulnerable, he offers evidence of her superior resistance to physical and psychological stress.

The stir caused by the publication of this article inspired Montagu to express his ideas in book form. With the book's publication in 1953, Montagu became a popular celebrity who appeared frequently on television.

And now for the evidence which proves the superiority of woman to man. But first, one word in explanation of the use of the word "superiority." The word is used in its common sense as being of better quality than, or of higher nature or character. Let us begin at the very beginning. What about the structure of the sexes? Does one show any superiority over the other? The answer is a resounding "Yes!" And I should like this "Yes" to resound all over the world, for no one has made anything of this key fact which lies at the base of all the differences between the sexes and the superiority of the female to the male. I refer to the chromosomal structure of the sexes. The chromosomes, those small cellular bodies which contain the hereditary particles, the genes, which so substantially influence one's development and fate as an organism, provide us with our basic facts.

In the sex cells there are twenty-four chromosomes, but only one of these is a sex chromosome. There are two kinds of sex chromosomes, X and Y. Half the sperm cells carry X and half carry Y chromosomes. All the female ova are made up of X-chromosomes. When an X-bearing sperm fertilizes an ovum the offspring is always female. When a Y-bearing chromosome fertilizes an ovum the offspring is always male. And this is what makes the difference between the sexes. So what? Well, the sad fact is that the Y-chromosome is but an iota, the merest bit, of a remnant of an X-chromosome; it is a crippled X-chromosome. The X-chromosomes are fully developed structures; the Y-chromosome is the merest comma. It is as if in the evolution of sex a particle one day broke away from an X-chromosome, and thereafter in relation to X-chromosomes could

THE NATURAL SUPERIORITY OF WOMEN   From *The Saturday Review* Magazine, March 1, 1952, 9. © 1952, Saturday Review Magazine Co. Reprinted by permission.

produce only an incomplete female—the creature we now call the male! It is to this original chromosomal deficiency that all the various troubles to which the male falls heir can be traced.

In the first place the chromosomal deficiency of the male determines his incapacity to have babies. This has always been a sore point with men, though consciously they would be the last to admit it, although in some primitive societies, as among the Australian aborigines, it is the male who conceives a child by dreaming it, and then telling his wife. In this way a child is eventually born to them, the wife being merely the incubator who hatches the egg placed there through the grace of her husband.

The fact that men cannot have babies and suckle them nor remain in association with their children as closely as the wife has an enormous effect upon their subsequent psychological development. Omitting altogether from consideration the psychologic influences exercised by the differences in the hormonal secretions of the sexes, one can safely say that the mother-child relationship confers enormous benefits upon the mother which are not nearly so substantively operative in the necessary absence of such a relationship between father and child. The maternalizing influences of being a mother in addition to the fact of being a woman has from the very beginning of the human species—about a million years ago—made the female the more humane of the sexes. The love of a mother for her child is the basic patent and the model for *all* human relationships. Indeed, to the extent to which men approximate in their relationships with their fellow men to the love of the mother for her child, to that extent do they move more closely to the attainment of perfect human relations. The mother-child relationship is a dependent-interdependent one. The interstimulation between mother and child is something which the father misses, and to that extent suffers from the want of. In short, the female in the mother-child relationship has the advantage of having to be more considerate, more self-sacrificing, more cooperative, and more altruistic than usually falls to the lot of the male.

The female thus acquires, in addition to whatever natural biological advantages she starts with, a competence in social understanding which is usually denied the male. This, I take it, is one of the reasons why women are usually so much more able to perceive the nuances and pick up the subliminal signs in human behavior which almost invariably pass men by. It was, I believe, George Jean Nathan who called woman's intuition merely man's transparency. With all due deference to Mr. Nathan and sympathy for his lot as a mere male, I would suggest that man's opacity would be nearer the mark. It is because women have had to be so unselfish and forbearing and self-sacrificing and maternal that they possess a deeper understanding than men of what it is to be human. What is so frequently termed feminine indecision, the inability of women to make up their minds, is in fact an inverse reflection of the trigger-thinking of men. Every salesgirl prefers the male customer because women take time to think about what they are buying, and the male usually hasn't the sense enough to do so. Women don't think in terms of "Yes" or "No." Life isn't as simple as all that—except to males. Men tend to think in terms of the all-or-none principle, in terms of black and white. Women are more ready to make adjustments, to consider the alternative possibilities, and see the other colors and gradations in the range between black and white.

By comparison with the deep involvement of women in living, men appear to be only superficially so. Compare the love of a male for a female with the love of the female for the male. It is the difference between a rivulet and a great deep ocean. Women love the human race; men are, on the whole, hostile to it. Men act as if they haven't been adequately loved, as if they had been frustrated and rendered hostile, and becoming aggressive they say that aggressiveness is natural and women are inferior in this respect because they tend to be gentle and unaggressive! But it is precisely in this capacity to love and unaggressiveness that the superiority of women to men is demonstrated, for whether it be natural to be loving and cooperative or not, so far as the human species is concerned, its evolutionary destiny, its very survival is more closely tied to this capacity for love and cooperation than with any other. So that unless men learn from women how to be more loving and cooperative they will go on making the kind of mess of the world which they have so effectively achieved thus far.

And this is, of course, where women can realize their power for good in the world, and make their greatest gains. *It is the function of women to teach men how to be human.* Women must not permit themselves to be deviated from this function by those who tell them that their place is in the home in subservient relation to man. It is, indeed, in the home that the foundations of the kind of world in which we live are laid, and in this sense it will always remain true that the hand that rocks the cradle is the hand that rules the world. And it is in this sense that women must assume the job of making men who will know how to make a world fit for human beings to live in. The greatest single step forward in this direction will be made when women consciously assume this task— the task of teaching their children to be like themselves, loving and cooperative. . . .

ARE WOMEN MORE MORAL THAN MEN?:
An Interview

Martha Saxton with *Psychologist Carol Gilligan*

In Lawrence Kohlberg's widely accepted theory of moral development, a person reaches the highest level of moral reasoning when using "universal principles of justice, of the reciprocity of human rights and of respect for the dignity of human beings as individual persons." Carol Gilligan, an associate professor of education at Harvard, was troubled by the fact that women rarely scored at the highest stage in Kohlberg's scheme and by the widespread interpretation of this finding as indicating a lack of maturity in their moral reasoning. In Gilligan's view, an equally likely possibility was that the women's scores reflected, not their deficiency, but rather the failure of Kohlberg's theory to incorporate the full range of human experience. This led to her own study of the conflicts expressed by women involved in real life moral decisions. The results, reported in her book *In A Different Voice* (1983), revealed a distinctive morality based on the value of human relatedness.

Ms magazine named Carol Gilligan Woman of the Year for 1983. The editors' rationale was: "Gilligan's work has created a new appreciation for a previously uncatalogued female sensibility, as well as possibilities for new understanding between the genders. But her contributions go beyond these. Because we live in a world where our survival may depend on our sense of connection, Gilligan's work has implications for a rather different kind of future—one in which humanity takes its cues not from Big Brother, but from sisters, mothers and daughters."

Ms published the interview with Gilligan, reprinted here, in 1981. Martha Saxton has herself written a book on morality.

Martha Saxton: How did you begin your work on women and morality?
Carol Gilligan: In the spring of 1975, Mary Belenky, a friend and graduate student at the time, and I began a study of the decision-making process of twenty-nine women who were considering abortions. The women, who were diverse in age, social class, and ethnic background, were interviewed at the time they were pregnant and then at the end of the following year. The first question we asked was: "How did you get pregnant?"—a question that some of the teenagers found enormously amusing—and "how have you been think-ing about it so far?" But the question did communicate our interest in the women's view of the situation. Rather than ask them to resolve a hypothetical moral problem, such as Kohlberg's famous dilemma: "Should Hans steal medicine for his ailing wife if he is too poor to pay for it?"—I had them describe which conflicts were moral problems for them. This shift was critical to the discovery of a different mode of moral thought—one that was more appropriate to women.

Saxton: How was this different from previous studies of women and morality?
Gilligan: In talking about morality, nobody talked about women except as a problem. They didn't fit anyone's data, so they were ignored. Erik Erikson studied the lives of men like Gandhi to trace the development of a capacity to care, and Lawrence Kohlberg derived his six stages of moral development from

ARE WOMEN MORE MORAL THAN MEN?   From *Ms.* Magazine, December 1981, 63–64, 66. Copyright © 1981 by Martha Saxton. Reprinted by permission.

a research sample that only included males. And in his scheme, women rarely scored higher than stage three. It is striking now that nobody—neither men nor women—noticed or saw as significant the repeated exclusion of women from the critical theory-building studies of psychological research. It is also ironic that nobody thought of looking at women's lives in order to discover how people develop the capacity to take care.

Saxton: How did the women you studied see morality?

Gilligan: What is distinctive is that they thought morality is connected to responsibility in relationships, and they always assume a connection between self and others, whereas men tend to look at moral issues in terms of the rights of individuals to noninterference. For the women in my studies, the abortion decision was a moral one, because it was framed in the context of relationships and hinged on issues of responsibility. And their means of sustaining relationships and of being responsible was through taking care.

Saxton: You have defined three stages in the maturing of this morality. Could you describe them?

Gilligan: The word "stage" is somewhat problematic in that it implies a hierarchy that does not fully characterize people's changing experiences and thinking. Time is important, so there *is* a linear dimension to the process, but development is often characterized by coming back around the same insight from different perspectives and in terms of different experiences. An eleven-year-old girl knows that she can't know if her decision to go to camp is the right one, because she can never know how it would have been if she hadn't gone. Often, women have to struggle to come back to that insight—that you have to live with uncertainty.

But there were three distinct ways in which women talked about care. The conflicts in their thinking and the shifts over time suggested how one position turns into the other, how the focus of women's thinking about care shifts from the self to the other and then from the other to the relationship.

The women who felt alone in the world, helpless and uncared for, spoke of the need to care for themselves in order simply to survive. Often they saw a baby as someone who would care for them; their pregnancies were often part of a search for connection. When the women criticized their own position, they called it "selfish" and opposed to what they saw as the "responsible" choice, which would have been to remain alone. For example, one teenager spoke of her wish to have a baby in order "not to feel lonely and stuff," but then realized how much responsibility it takes to raise a child. She concluded that having the baby would be selfish and that having an abortion would be responsible, since if she couldn't take care of herself, how could she take care of a child? Another teenager thought that having an abortion was selfish because she wanted to finish school, and that having the baby would be responsible since the pregnancy was, in her eyes, her fault. The moral choice— what you *should* do—was opposed to the "selfish" choice—what you *wanted* to do.

This equation of wants with selfishness sets up a complicated dynamic in women's psychology, leading them to consider what they want as wrong. But the pregnancy, demonstrating the connection between self and other, often led women to see that if they did not take care of themselves, they would hurt others, and that in hurting others, they also hurt themselves. This realization led several teenagers to start taking better care of themselves, to stop drinking or taking drugs, to go back to school so that someday they would be able to care for a child. The decision to have an abortion often signaled the beginning of a more responsible way of acting, toward others and toward themselves, and there were some dramatic improvements after a period of struggle in the lives of these teenagers in the course of the following year.

But the equation of goodness with self-sacrifice seems to override this insight. The image of the "good woman" is part of a morality in which caring for others is responsible and caring for oneself selfish. This conventional definition of feminine goodness has enormous power in women's lives, since it carries with it the threat that if a woman responds to her own needs rather than to those of others, she will be abandoned. Several women reported that their husbands or lovers said that they would leave them if they decided to have the child. Often, in the face of this threat, the women felt that they had no choice.

Saxton: Were any of the women glad to have had the abortion?

Gilligan: Yes, but this fact had to be concealed by the woman who saw herself as good only if she was acting on another's behalf. For a woman to say, as some did, "I don't want this child; it wouldn't be fair to the child or to me," is to risk being considered a selfish and bad woman. Faced with this accusation, women either disguise their own needs, or they begin to talk about the truth—what is really going on in their own lives and in society. Until a woman, in any relationship, can give up saying that she has no needs and desires or that they are not important and that all she wants to do is what the other person wants, she is bound to be resentful and there are bound to be problems in a relationship. She must recognize that strategies of evasion and disguise, though often undertaken in the interest of sustaining relationships, can, on the contrary, erode care and lead to feeling angry, betrayed, and hurt. When women include themselves among the people for whom they see it as moral to care, it seems not only fair and just, but also strengthens their relationships.

When women separate care from self-sacrifice, they begin to live openly with conflict and ambiguity, since there is no longer clearly a "right" solution to problems that arise in relationships. The classical Freudian formulation of egoism versus altruism is itself called into question because of its failure to recognize the connection between other and self. Yet the centrality of this connection in women's definitions of self leads them to be described as having weak ego boundaries, no sense of self, as lacking autonomy, as not being adult.

Saxton: How do men differ in this regard?

Gilligan: Most men seem to develop greater emphasis on separation and autonomy in their definitions of self. My work is not addressed to the issue of sex differences *per se*, but rather aims to show that what has been characterized as "women's logic," a supposedly irrational, illogical, and underdeveloped form of thought, actually has a clear logic and rationality, is closely in touch with reality, and reflects certain central facts about the lives of both sexes. While the ethic of care has a long history and has been articulated by members of both sexes, the importance of separation and autonomy in men's lives often leads them to focus the discussion of morality around issues of justice, fairness, rules, and rights, while women discuss sustaining relationships through care.

Saxton: In a relationship between a man and a woman, how do these two ways of thinking work together?

Gilligan: They can inform one another or lead to serious problems in communications. If we envision these points of view, one of responsibilities and the other of rights, as sharing a moral vocabulary but attaching different meanings to the words, the possibilities for misunderstanding and mistranslation are clear. In a marriage of pure types, what a man will see as care and respect, a woman may experience as neglect. What she sees as care and concern, he may see as interference with his autonomy. A woman who sees herself as loving may discover that her man views her as manipulative, castrating, and out to control. Women consider the failure to respond as a serious moral problem. A man who sees himself as caring may be surprised to find that his woman finds him cold and unresponsive. Then, if you place this dialogue in a social context, where the man has more power and where his way of thinking is defined as more mature, he will tend not to listen to what the woman says and she to decide that something is wrong with her. Jean Baker Miller [in *The Psychology of Women*] has pointed out that what have been regarded as women's weaknesses are better conceived of as human strengths. Let's ask how women come to know what they know about relationships, how they develop the capacity to care and sustain connections.

Saxton: Nancy Chodorow [in *The Reproduction of Mothering*] suggests that if we change our child-raising practices, girls can learn to separate more. But is separation such a good thing?

Gilligan: Chodorow also suggests that a change in child-rearing practices might lead to a greater sense of connection in men. As for separation, the other side of separation is alienation, the isolation and loneliness vividly described in the literature on mid-life crises in men. People who are unconnected are in danger at all stages of life, not only in childhood but also in adolescence, adulthood, and old age. Their survival is literally at risk.

Saxton: Why are so many more women frightened of becoming disconnected than most men? Why is aloneness so much more threatening?

Gilligan: You could say that it's because they are more in touch with reality. But it may also be because the feeling of connection is embedded in woman's primary sense of self, while male identity, as Chodorow points out, is contingent on a primary separation from the mother. Masculinity is defined through that separation, and the image of smothering mothering reflects men's fears that if others get too close, they will lose their sense of themselves. In contrast, women tend to fear that separation will lead to isolation, that the ending of a relationship will mean the loss of their sense of themselves.

Saxton: Has your work on women's development changed your teaching?

Gilligan: I have included it in my course on human development, which does represent a change, since much of what is taught in courses on human development is based on studies of males.

In looking at child development, for instance, I draw on the activities and games of girls, and consider inclusion and exclusion, who feels what, who's my friend, who's not my friend, and the time girls spend talking about what different people want and think. These are games through which children acquire factual knowledge of human relationships. This is the knowledge that gives people the power to help or hurt. How the power is used makes this a moral question. In talking about adolescents and their moral philosophies, their passion for equality, justice, and exposing hypocrisy, I also talk about their moral psychologies, the intensity of their concern about care and relationships and who is being hurt.

Saxton: And after adolescence?

Gilligan: Afterward comes the discovery that there is a disparity between the ideal and the real, the recognition that life is unfair and that hurt may be unavoidable. One woman described a situation where a man wanted to marry her and she didn't want to marry him. There was no way of not hurting, and she struggled to retain her ideal of care in the face of the realization that she had caused hurt. If women don't recognize this dilemma as something real in their lives, then they will tend either to abandon the effort to care as untenable or conclude that they are selfish and wrong. The vulnerability of women to the accusation of selfishness has been a recurrent observation in my work and creates a serious problem for women—beginning in adolescence—by impeding their recognition of their own needs as real and legitimate.

Saxton: How do you see an optimal fusing of the men's and women's views?

Gilligan: To fuse is to live with conflict, to see that there is more than one way, to give up the search for justification, to become more responsive to others and to oneself—in other words, to be mature. Women say that they don't have a clear rule for moral decisions in the sense of a Categorical Imperative or Golden Rule, but they do have a sense of how you make a moral decision. That is, to pay attention to everything, to see and to know as much as you can about yourself and others and the situation so that you can try to anticipate the consequences of action and act in a way that is not likely to cause suffering and hurt.

Saxton: In my work, a study of the changing concepts of morality and women from the seventeenth century to the present, it seems clear that much more of life is in the moral domain for women than for men. For example, women entered politics as abolitionists, temperance workers, or suffragists—and women's suffrage was very often argued on moral grounds. Historically, they chose professions such as teaching, nursing, and social work, which are nurturing and therefore morally justified.

Gilligan: That is also my impression, and I think it is because women define morality as a problem of responsibility in relationships, and since life is lived in relationships, all action takes place in a moral context and has moral implications. Larry Kohlberg and I observed that women place morality and self together and men separate them.

Saxton: Do you think that this morality of care will get women anywhere, or leave them politically powerless, as they have always been?

Gilligan: I think it is essential for everyone politically. If power is not used to take care of the world, it may well be destroyed. But if you are asking, how do you gain power if you care about other people, that is a complicated question in a competitive and hierarchical system. On the other hand, if you gain power by abandoning care and severing connections, what really is the point? If women have access to another way of thinking about relationships that is more cooperative and less hierarchical, then they know something that is very important for everybody. If they bring such knowledge into positions of social power, they may bring about important social change.

Saxton: It doesn't seem to me that women have changed the system as often as they have been changed by it.

Gilligan: If change isn't happening, it's very understandable, because women are very vulnerable, they don't have much power, and it's very hard to change anything, ever.

Saxton: How would you define morality now, as opposed to the way you defined it ten years ago?

Gilligan: Ten years ago, I thought in terms of the work of Piaget and Kohlberg on the development of the idea of justice. Now I see morality as reflecting two themes that are woven into the cycle of life: inequality and interdependence. These experiences are universal, and they give rise to the ethics of justice and care, the ideals of human relationships—that everyone will be treated with equal respect and that no one will be left alone or hurt.

TWO

Woman's Place

JUST AS SOME MEDICAL AUTHORITIES and other experts have used theories of woman's nature to justify the restriction of women to home and hearth, other experts have used theories about the needs of society to accomplish the same end. Indeed, many experts fuse ideas of the natural and social order, so that separating out the rationales being used to defend conventional ideas is frequently impossible. Charles Meigs, whose lectures to his medical students summed up mid-nineteenth century ideas on women, defended the notion that there was but one true calling for women, on the grounds that only in filling her prescribed social role could a woman fulfill herself.

"Let Mary be brought up to her trade," he wrote in *Woman: Her Diseases and Remedies* (1859). "What is that? It is taking care of a family—wisely, happily, elegantly, with a good temper; to do that, let her learn the world and the ways of it—not too much though. . . ." He continued, "Mr. Clay, Mr.

Webster, Colonel Benton, and Mr. Calhoun will take care of the politics; General Scott and General Taylor will take care of the soldiers; let the daughters take care of the children, and learn to be bright at the breakfast table, elegant at dinner, enchanting as pourers out of tea, and the ornaments and grace of the saloon."

Some mid-twentieth century experts, like those quoted in *Good Housekeeping*, agreed that a woman's "womb-centeredness" assured her "essential feminine altruism," that is, a life of service to husband and children. Yet not every proponent of tradition rests the case on woman's supposedly innate characteristics. Many, from Catharine Beecher to Marabel Morgan, are willing to concede that women are not naturally domestic or deferential. In fact, Morgan openly acknowledges how difficult women find it to conform to their traditional roles. Nonetheless, she and many other commentators insist that the well-being of society in general, and of children in particular, requires that women devote themselves to domestic duties.

While sharing the view that woman's place is defined by social custom, the readings in this chapter differ on whether they express acceptance or rejection of the traditional ideas. Some defend the legitimacy of the status quo on the grounds that conventional arrangements best meet the needs not only of society but of women as well. Others, written by women and men who refuse to accept the idea that for women "that's all there is," challenge the social conventions and the theories that support them. Whether basing their ideas on their observations of others or on personal experience, these writers argue for women's emancipation from the sacrifice of self and the lived-for-others life that marriage brings. They argue, too, for the right of women to exercise their productive powers beyond the confines of the home, through expanded political, educational, and employment opportunities.

On the theory that knowledge provides the power that leads to change, some of the readings attempt to make visible aspects of culture that promote unthinking acceptance of the customary status and roles of women and of their identification as "natural." Some poke fun at the social conventions that define the relations between the sexes; some suggest radical reinterpretations of cherished beliefs. Others argue that language itself, the basic tool of thought and communication, has been so shaped by male-dominated conventions (e.g., use of "he" for person or "man" for humanity) that it helps perpetuate women's powerlessness.

Combined with courage and determination, such passionate critiques have resulted in social change. Over the years women have achieved advances in status under the law. In many states in pre-Civil War America, for example, a married woman was denied the right to make contracts, to keep her own income and property, and even to have custody over her children in the event of legal separation or the death of her spouse, if contrary to his wishes. Today these discriminatory laws no longer exist. And women now have educational and occupational options unheard of in Meigs' day. And, perhaps for the first time, a considerable portion of the population currently believes that women's ideal roles are not exclusively domestic ones and that women legitimately belong in positions of influence.

But, although the nineteenth century ideas we began with may be antique, Americans have cherished them over the years. And, like antiques, which we may store away and almost forget for a time, sooner or later we rediscover them, dust them off, polish them up, and once more make them the focus of attention. The events of the past two centuries reveal that society abandons the idea of home life as the preferred vocation for women only out of necessity and reactivates it again whenever the particular military or economic crisis that weakened its influence is resolved. Even today many women still receive encouragement to get an education only so they will have "something to fall back on." Many people see the career woman as merely "marking time" until the right man comes along. The childless woman continues to be an object of pity. And housework and child-care are still, for the most part, female responsibilities; even in the most liberated of modern households, women typically must reconcile jobs and domestic responsibilities in ways men do not have to.

But in domestic matters as well, the years have made a difference. The dictum, "a woman's place is in the home," with all the powerlessness and restriction that exclusive domesticity implies, no longer has the force it once had. Medical authority as a rationale for the dictum has eroded, and women have demonstrated their competence in positions outside the home. Moreover, because of the growing recognition of its arbitrariness, the dictum no longer evokes the pious acceptance it once did. In fact, the dictum itself is now the source of feminist humor, as women continue to expand the definition of their proper place. A recently popular t-shirt, defying tradition and calling for women's liberation and empowerment, reads

> A WOMAN'S PLACE IS IN THE HOUSE . . .
> AND THE SENATE.

HOW THE AMERICANS UNDERSTAND THE EQUALITY OF THE SEXES

Alexis de Tocqueville

Alexis de Tocqueville is by far the most celebrated of the many foreign visitors who recorded their impressions of the new republic, and his *Democracy in America* (published in two volumes: 1835, 1840) became a best-seller in the United States as well as in France. Americans are still fond of quoting his largely laudatory opinions of their society and politics, and even manage occasionally to ponder his famous warning about the potential tyranny of the majority.

de Tocqueville and his companion, Gustave Beaumont, spent nine months in 1831-32 touring the United States and preparing a report on America's new penitentiary system for the French government. His interest in things American went far beyond prisons, however, and he spent much of his time trying to gauge the success of America's experiment in self-government. His views of American women are less well-known, but they were highly influential in the decades before the Civil War.

Near the conclusion of his second volume, de Tocqueville attributed the greatest share of the credit for the success of American democracy to the character of American women. And he praised Americans for resolving the apparent paradox of proclaiming equality as their highest ideal while restricting women to the home and hearth. His explanation of why the restricted roles of women did not contradict the nation's democratic ethos provided a ready rationale for many conservative social commentators. The logic of his argument, especially his premises, merits special attention since his conclusions proved so popular.

I have shown how democracy destroys or modifies the different inequalities which originate in society: but is this all? or does it not ultimately affect that great inequality of man and woman which has seemed, up to the present day, to be eternally based in human nature? I believe that the social changes which bring nearer to the same level the father and son, the master and servant, and superiors and inferiors generally speaking, will raise woman and make her more and more the equal of man. But here, more than ever, I feel the necessity of making myself clearly understood; for there is no subject on which the coarse and lawless fancies of our age have taken a freer range.

There are people in Europe who, confounding together the different characteristics of the sexes, would make of man and woman beings not only equal but alike. They would give to both the same functions, impose on both the same duties, and grant to both the same rights: they would mix them in all

HOW THE AMERICANS UNDERSTAND . . . From *Democracy in America: Part the Second, The Social Influence of Democracy,* Translated by Henry Reeve, Esq., New York: J. & H. G. Langley, 1840, 224–27.

things—their occupations, their pleasures, their business. It may readily be conceived, that by thus attempting to make one sex equal to the other, both are degraded; and from so preposterous a medley of the works of nature, nothing could ever result but weak men and disorderly women.

It is not thus that the Americans understand that species of democratic equality which may be established between the sexes. They admit, that as nature has appointed such wide differences between the physical and moral constitutions of man and woman, her manifest design was to give a distinct employment to their various faculties; and they hold that improvement does not consist in making beings so dissimilar do pretty nearly the same things, but in getting each of them to fulfil their respective tasks in the best possible manner. The Americans have applied to the sexes the great principle of political economy which governs the manufactures of our age, by carefully dividing the duties of man from those of woman, in order that the great work of society may be the better carried on.

In no country has such constant care been taken as in America to trace two clearly distinct lines of action for the two sexes, and to make them keep pace one with the other, but in two pathways which are always different. American women never manage the outward concerns of the family, or conduct a business, or take a part in political life; nor are they, on the other hand, ever compelled to perform the rough labor of the fields, or to make any of those laborious exertions which demand the exertion of physical strength. No families are so poor as to form an exception to this rule. If on the one hand an American woman cannot escape from the quiet circle of domestic employments, on the other hand she is never forced to go beyond it. Hence it is that the women of America, who often exhibit a masculine strength of understanding and a manly energy, generally preserve great delicacy of personal appearance and always retain the manners of women, although they sometimes show that they have the hearts and minds of men.

Nor have the Americans ever supposed that one consequence of democratic principles is the subversion of marital power, or the confusion of the natural authorities in families. They hold that every association must have a head in order to accomplish its object, and that the natural head of the conjugal association is man. They do not therefore deny him the right of directing his partner; and they maintain, that in the smaller association of husband and wife, as well as in the great social community, the object of democracy is to regulate and legalize the powers which are necessary, not to subvert all power.

This opinion is not peculiar to one sex, and contested by the other: I never observed that the women of America consider conjugal authority as a fortunate usurpation of their rights, nor that they thought themselves degraded by submitting to it. It appeared to me, on the contrary, that they attach a sort of pride to the voluntary surrender of their own will, and make it their boast to bend themselves to the yoke, not to shake it off. Such at least is the feeling expressed by the most virtuous of their sex; the others are silent; and in the United States it is not the practice for a guilty wife to clamour for the rights of woman, while she is trampling on her holiest duties.

It has often been remarked that in Europe a certain degree of contempt lurks even in the flattery which men lavish upon women: although a European frequently affects to be the slave of woman, it may be seen that he never sincerely thinks her his equal. In the United States men seldom compliment women, but they daily show how much they esteem them. They constantly display an entire confidence in the understanding of a wife, and a profound respect for her freedom; they have decided that her mind is just as fitted as that of a man to discover the plain truth, and her heart as firm to embrace it; and they have never sought to place her virtue, any more than his, under the shelter of prejudice, ignorance, and fear.

It would seem that in Europe, where man so easily submits to the despotic sway of women, they are nevertheless curtailed of some of the greatest qualities of the human species, and considered as seductive but imperfect beings; and (what may well provoke astonishment) women ultimately look upon themselves in the same light, and almost consider it as a privilege that they are entitled to show themselves futile, feeble, and timid. The women of America claim no such privileges.

Again, it may be said, that in our morals we have reserved strange immunities to man; so that there is, as it were, one virtue for his use, and another for the guidance of his partner; and that, according to the opinion of the public, the very same act may be punished alternately as a crime or only as a fault. The Americans know not this iniquitous division of duties and rights; among them the seducer is as much dishonoured as his victim.

It is true that the Americans rarely lavish upon women those eager attentions which are commonly paid them in Europe; but their conduct to women always implies that they suppose them to be virtuous and refined; and such is the respect entertained for the moral freedom of the sex, that in the presence of a woman the most guarded language is used, lest her ear should be offended by an expression. In America a young unmarried woman may, alone and without fear, undertake a long journey.

The legislators of the United States, who have mitigated almost all the penalties of criminal law, still make rape a capital offence, and no crime, is visited with more inexorable severity by public opinion. This may be accounted for; as the Americans can conceive nothing more precious than a woman's honour, and nothing which ought so much to be respected as her independence, they hold that no punishment is too severe for the man who deprives her of them against her will. In France, where the same offence is visited with far milder penalties, it is frequently difficult to get a verdict from a jury against the prisoner. Is this a consequence of contempt of decency or contempt of woman? I cannot but believe that it is a contempt of one and of the other.

Thus the Americans do not think that man and woman have either the duty or the right to perform the same offices, but they show an equal regard for both their respective parts; and though their lot is different, they consider both of them as beings of equal value. They do not give to the courage of woman the same form or the same direction as to that of man; but they never doubt her courage: and if they hold that man and his partner ought not always to exercise their intellect and understanding in the same manner, they at least believe the understanding of the one to be as sound as that of the other, and her intellect to be as clear. Thus, then, while they have allowed the social inferior-

woman to subsist, they have done all they could to raise her morally and
ctually to the level of man; and in this respect they appear to me to have
excellently understood the true principle of democratic improvement.

As for myself, I do not hesitate to avow, that, although the women of the
United States are confined within the narrow circle of domestic life, and their
situation is in some respects one of extreme dependance, I have nowhere seen
women occupying a loftier position; and if I were asked, now that I am
drawing to the close of this work, in which I have spoken of so many
important things done by the Americans, to what the singular prosperity and
growing strength of that people ought mainly to be attributed, I should
reply—to the superiority of their women.

SOBER HUSBANDS
WOMEN AND MONEY
MRS. WEASEL'S HUSBAND

Fanny Fern

Sara Payson Willis Parton (1811-1872), better known as Fanny Fern, was a nationally
known columnist and best-selling author of the mid-nineteenth century. The first
collection of her periodical pieces, *Fern Leaves from Fanny's Port-Folio* (1853), sold
80,000 copies in the first year after its publication, a number comparable to a sale of
800,000 today. A Second Series, from which the following selections are taken, was
published the next year.

Fanny Fern's work, which included novels as well as children's books, combines the
sentimental tradition in literature with the journalistic tradition of humorous commentary. Her columns, ranging in subject matter from critiques of manners and fashion to
the injustices suffered by married women, provide a kind of social history of her time,
especially in regard to the status of women. She makes fun of male pomposity, argues
for intellectual equality, condemns excessive housework, and points out the double
standards, all in a lively and colloquial style.

Fanny Fern was born in Portland, Maine, but her family moved to Boston soon after
her birth. She was educated there and at Catharine Beecher's Seminary in Hartford. At
the age of 26, she married and had three daughters before she was widowed. Unable to
support herself and her children, she married again in 1849, but this marriage ended in
divorce. She tried to support her family by taking work as a teacher and as a seamstress,
then began writing pieces for Boston papers. Her success was instantaneous, and after
the publication of her collected pieces, Robert Bonner recruited her to write for the *New
York Ledger* at the then unheard of sum of $100 a week. In 1856, she married the
biographer and journalist James Parton, who was eleven years younger than she was.
She stayed with him, and with the *Ledger*, until her death.

SOBER HUSBANDS . . . From *Fern Leaves from Fanny's Port-folio, Second Series,* Buffalo: Miller, Orton and
Mulligan, 1854, 192–93, 247–48, 187–88.

SOBER HUSBANDS

"If your husband looks grave, let him alone; don't disturb or annoy him."

 Oh, pshaw! were I married, the soberer my husband looked, the more fun I'd rattle about his ears. *Do n't disturb him!* I guess so! I'd salt his coffee—and pepper his tea— and sugar his beef-steak—and tread on his toes—and hide his newspaper—and sew up his pockets—and put pins in his slippers—and dip his cigars in water,—and I would n't stop for the great Mogul, till I had shortened his long face to my liking. Certainly, he'd "get vexed;" there would n't be any fun in teasing him if he did n't; and that would give his melancholy blood a good, healthful start; and his eyes would snap and sparkle, and he'd say, "Fanny, WILL you be quiet or not?" and I should laugh, and pull his whiskers, and say decidedly, "*Not!*" and then I should tell him he had n't the slightest idea how handsome he looked when he was vexed, and then he would pretend not to hear the compliment—but would pull up his dickey, and take a sly peep in the glass (for all that!) and then he'd begin to grow amiable, and get off his stilts, and be just as agreeable all the rest of the evening *as if he was n't my husband;* and all because I didn't follow that stupid bit of advice "to let him alone." Just as if *I* did n't know! Just imagine ME, Fanny, sitting down on a cricket in the corner, with my forefinger in my mouth, looking out the sides of my eyes, and waiting till that man got ready to speak to me! You can see at once it would be—be—. Well, the amount of it is, *I should n't do it!*

WOMEN AND MONEY

"A wife should n't ask her husband for money at meal-times."—*Exchange.*

By no manner of means; *nor at any other time;* because, it is to be hoped, he will be gentlemanly enough to spare her that humiliating necessity. Let him hand her his porte-monnaie every morning, with *carte-blanche* to help herself. The consequence would be, she would lose all desire for the contents, and hand it back, half the time without abstracting a single *sou.*

It's astonishing men have no more diplomacy about such matters. *I* should like to be a husband! There *are* wives whom I verily believe might be trusted to make way with a ten dollar bill without risk to the connubial donor! I'm not speaking of those doll-baby libels upon womanhood, whose chief ambition is to be walking advertisements for the dressmaker; but a rational, refined, sensible woman, who knows how to look like a lady upon small means; who would both love and respect a man less for requiring an account of every copper; but who, at the same time, would willingly wear a hat or garment that is "out of date," rather than involve a noble, generous-hearted husband in unnecessary expenditures.

I repeat it—"It *is n't every man who has a call to be a husband.*" Half the married men should have their "licenses" taken away, and the same number of judicious bachelors put in their places. I think the attention of the representatives should be called to this. They can't expect to come down to town and peep under all the ladies' bonnets the way they do, and have all the newspapers free gratis, and two dollars a day besides, without "paying their way!

t's none of *my* business, but I question whether their wives, whom they left home, stringing dried apples, know how spruce they look in their new hats and coats, or how facetious they grow with their landlady's daughter; or how many of them pass themselves off for bachelors, to verdant spinsters. Nothing truer than that little couplet of *Shakspeare's*—

> "When the cat's away
> The mice *will* play."

MRS. WEASEL'S HUSBAND

> "A woman, a dog, and a walnut tree,
> The more they are beaten the better they be."

"Any man who believes that, had better step into my shoes," said little Mr. Weasel. "I suppose I'm what you call 'the head of the family,' but I should n't know it if somebody did n't tell me of it. Heigho! who'd have thought it five and twenty years ago? Did n't I stifle a tremendous strong penchant for Diana Dix, (never smoked, I remember, for four hours after it,) because I had my private suspicions she'd hold the reins in spite of my teeth, and so I offered myself to little Susey Snow, (mistake in her name, by the way.) You might have spanned her round the waist, or lifted her with one hand. She never looked anybody in the face when they spoke to her, and her voice was as soft as——my brains! I declare, it's unaccountable how deceitful female nature is! Never was so taken in in my life; she's a regular Vesuvius crater! Her will? (don't mention it!) Try to pry up the Alps with a cambric needle! If she'd only fly into a passion, I think I could venture to pluck up a little spirit; but that cool, determined, never-say-die look! would turn Cayenne pepper to oil. It wilts *me* right down, like a cabbage leaf. I 'd as lief face a loaded cannon! I wish I could go out evenings; but she won't let me. Tom Jones asked me yesterday why I was n't at Faneuil Hall the night before. I told him I had the bronchitis. He saw through it! Sent me a pair of reins the next day,—'said to be a certain cure!' Ah! it's very well for *him* to laugh, but it's no joke to me. I suppose it's time to feed that baby; Mrs. Weasel will be home pretty soon, from the 'Woman's Rights Convention.' No, I won't, either; I'll give it some paregoric, and run up garret and smoke one cigar. I feel as though I *could n't look a humming-bird in the eye! very* nice! What a fool I am to be ordered round by a little blue-eyed woman, three feet high! I'm a very good looking fellow, and I won't stand it! Is n't that little Weasel as much her baby as it is mine? Certainly."

"M-r. W-e-a-s-e-l!"

"Hem,—my—dear—(oh! that eye of hers!)—you see, my dear, (there, I won't do it again, Mrs. Weasel.) How's 'the Convention,' dear? Carried the day, I hope?—made one of your smart speeches, hey? 'Tis n't every man owns such a chain-lightning wife;—look out for your rights, dear; (deuce knows *I* dare not!")

TWENTY YEARS AT HULL HOUSE
Jane Addams

Jane Addams (1860-1935) was the most famous and most admired woman in the United States during the first third of this century. She was also, in the opinion of contemporaries like philosopher John Dewey, one of the most gifted members, male or female, of her generation. *Twenty Years at Hull House,* the first volume of her autobiography, recounts her struggles to find appropriate outlets for her great talent.

Addams discovered that the America of the 1880s had no place for intelligent, ambitious women other than missionary work. And she virtually invented a whole new type of career, a secularized mission to the urban poor called settlement work. The dedicated young women (and young men) who flocked to the settlements in turn invented a whole series of new career opportunities for themselves ranging from factory and housing inspection to social casework.

This excerpt from *Twenty Years at Hull House* candidly confronts the feelings of frustration and inadequacy the women of Addams' generation experienced when they sought to find a way, outside of marriage and motherhood, of engaging in meaningful work.

. . . "It is true that there is nothing after disease, indigence and a sense of guilt, so fatal to health and to life itself as the want of a proper outlet for active faculties." I have seen young girls suffer and grow sensibly lowered in vitality in the first years after they leave school. In our attempt then to give a girl pleasure and freedom from care we succeed, for the most part, in making her pitifully miserable. She finds "life" so different from what she expected it to be. She is besotted with innocent little ambitions, and does not understand this apparent waste of herself, this elaborate preparation, if no work is provided for her. There is a heritage of noble obligation which young people accept and long to perpetuate. The desire for action, the wish to right wrong and alleviate suffering haunts them daily. Society smiles at it indulgently instead of making it of value to itself. The wrong to them begins even farther back, when we restrain the first childish desires for "doing good" and tell them that they must wait until they are older and better fitted. We intimate that social obligation begins at a fixed date, forgetting that it begins with birth itself. We treat them as children who, with strong-growing limbs, are allowed to use their legs but not their arms, or whose legs are daily carefully exercised that after a while their arms may be put to high use. We do this in spite of the protest of the best educators, Locke and Pestalozzi. We are fortunate in the meantime if their unused members do not weaken and disappear. They do sometimes. There are a few girls who, by the time they are "educated," forget their old childish desires to help the world and to play with poor little girls "who haven't play things." Parents are often inconsistent: they deliberately expose their daughters to knowledge of the distress in the world; they send them to hear mission-

TWENTY YEARS AT HULL HOUSE   From *Twenty Years at Hull House* by Jane Addams. Reprinted with permission of Macmillan Publishing Company. Copyright 1910 by Macmillan Publishing Co., Inc., renewed 1938 by James W. Linn. New American Library, Signet, New York, 1961. Pp. 93–95.

ary addresses on famines in India and China; they accompany them to lectures on the suffering in Siberia; they agitate together over the forgotten region of East London. In addition to this, from babyhood the altruistic tendencies of these daughters are persistently cultivated. They are taught to be self-forgetting and self-sacrificing, to consider the good of the whole before the good of the ego. But when all this information and culture show results, when the daughter comes back from college and begins to recognize her social claim to the "submerged tenth," and to evince a disposition to fulfill it, the family claim is strenuously asserted; she is told that she is unjustified, ill-advised in her efforts. If she persists, the family too often are injured and unhappy unless the efforts are called missionary and the religious zeal of the family carry them over their sense of abuse. When this zeal does not exist, the result is perplexing. It is a curious violation of what we would fain believe a fundamental law—that the final return of the deed is upon the head of the doer. The deed is that of exclusiveness and caution, but the return, instead of falling upon the head of the exclusive and cautious, falls upon a young head full of generous and unselfish plans. The girl loses something vital out of her life to which she is entitled. She is restricted and unhappy; her elders, meanwhile, are unconscious of the situation and we have all the elements of a tragedy.

We have in America a fast-growing number of cultivated young people who have no recognized outlet for their active faculties. They hear constantly of the great social maladjustment, but no way is provided for them to change it, and their uselessness hangs about them heavily. Huxley declares that the sense of usefulness [sic] is the severest shock which the human system can sustain, and that if persistently sustained, it results in atrophy of function. These young people have had advantages of college, of European travel, and of economic study, but they are sustaining this shock of inaction. They have pet phrases, and they tell you that the things that make us all alike are stronger than the things that make us different. They say that all men are united by needs and sympathies far more permanent and radical than anything that temporarily divides them and sets them in opposition to each other. If they affect art, they say that the decay in artistic expression is due to the decay in ethics, that art when shut away from the human interests and from the great mass of humanity is self-destructive. They tell their elders with all the bitterness of youth that if they expect success from them in business or politics or in whatever lines their ambition for them has run, they must let them consult all of humanity; that they must let them find out what the people want and how they want it. It is only the stronger young people, however, who formulate this. Many of them dissipate their energies in so-called enjoyment. Others not content with that, go on studying and go back to college for their second degrees; not that they are especially fond of study, but because they want something definite to do, and their powers have been trained in the direction of mental accumulation. Many are buried beneath this mental accumulation which lowered vitality and discontent. Walter Besant says they have had the vision that Peter had when he saw the great sheet let down from heaven, wherein was neither clean nor unclean. He calls it the sense of humanity. It is not philanthropy nor benevolence, but a thing fuller and wider than either of these.

This young life, so sincere in its emotion and good phrase and yet so undirected, seems to me as pitiful as the other great mass of destitute lives. One is supplementary to the other, and some method of communication can surely be devised. Mr. Barnett, who urged the first Settlement—Toynbee Hall, in East London—recognized this need of outlet for the young men of Oxford and Cambridge, and hoped that the Settlement would supply the communication. It is easy to see why the Settlement movement originated in England, where the years of education are more constrained and definite than they are here, where class distinctions are more rigid. The necessity of it was greater there, but we are fast feeling the pressure of the need and meeting the necessity for Settlements in America. Our young people feel nervously the need of putting theory into action, and respond quickly to the Settlement form of activity. . . .

THE DOUBLE TASK

Elise Johnson McDougald

The 1920's witnessed a "Harlem Renaissance" in which black poets, musicians, and other artists turned a Jewish and Italian neighborhood into the cultural capital of black America. The attractions of Harlem for ambitious young blacks were many. Here they could find newspapers and magazines devoted to their lives. Here was a black theater which, under the leadership of Noble Sissle and Eubie Blake, was starting to crack into the previously all-white world of Broadway. Here were nightclubs, like the famous Cotton Club, where young musicians, like Duke Ellington, were creating a new American music, jazz. Here also were some opportunities, however limited, to achieve economic success. Harlem, in short, became a true mecca.

By the mid-1920s white Americans had begun to discover Harlem too. More important, ideas of racial equality began—for the first time in a generation—to find influential white spokespeople. The following essay, written by a black social worker, is part of that white discovery. It appeared in a special issue of the *Survey Graphic,* a magazine devoted to social questions on Harlem. McDougald sought to explain to these newly sympathetic whites what it was like to be a black woman in the 1920s, facing the "double task" of overcoming racism and sexism.

 Throughout the long years of history, woman has been the weather-vane, the indicator, showing in which direction the wind of destiny blows. Her status and development have augured now calm and stability, now swift currents of progress. What then is to be said of the Negro woman today?

In Harlem, more than anywhere else, the Negro woman is free from the cruder handicaps of primitive household hardships and the grosser forms of sex and race subjugation. Here she has considerable opportunity to measure her powers in the intellectual and industrial fields of the great city. Here the questions naturally arise: "What are her problems?" and "How is she solving them?"

THE DOUBLE TASK   From *Survey Graphic,* March 1925, 689–91.

To answer these questions, one must have in mind not any one Negro woman, but rather a colorful pageant of individuals, each differently endowed. Like the red and yellow of the tiger-lily, the skin of one is brilliant against the star-lit darkness of a racial sister. From grace to strength, they vary in infinite degree, with traces of the race's history left in physical and mental outline on each. With a discerning mind, one catches the multiform charm, beauty and character of Negro women; and grasps the fact that their problem cannot be thought of in mass.

Because only a few have caught this vision, the attitude of mind of most New Yorkers causes the Negro woman serious difficulty. She is conscious that what is left of chivalry is not directed toward her. She realizes that the ideals of beauty, built up in the fine arts, exclude her almost entirely. Instead, the grotesque Aunt Jemimas of the street-car advertisements proclaim only an ability to serve, without grace or loveliness. Not does the drama catch her finest spirit. She is most often used to provoke the mirthless laugh of ridicule; or to portray feminine viciousness or vulgarity not peculiar to Negroes. This is the shadow over her. To a race naturally sunny comes the twilight of self-doubt and a sense of personal inferiority. It cannot be denied that these are potent and detrimental influences, though not generally recognized because they are in the realm of the mental and spiritual. More apparent are the economic handicaps which follow her recent entrance into industry. It is conceded that she has special difficulties because of the poor working conditions and low wages of her men. It is not surprising that only the determined women forge ahead to results other than mere survival. The few who do prove their mettle stimulate one to a closer study of how this achievement is won in Harlem.

Better to visualize the Negro woman at her job, our vision of a host of individuals must once more resolve itself into groups on the basis of activity. First, comes a very small leisure group—the wives and daughters of men who are in business, in the professions and in a few well-paid personal service occupations. Second, a most active and progressive group, the women in business and the professions. Third, the many women in the trades and industry. Fourth, a group weighty in numbers struggling on in domestic service, with an even less fortunate fringe of casual workers, fluctuating with the economic temper of the times.

The first is a pleasing group to see. It is picked for outward beauty by Negro men with much the same feeling as other Americans of the same economic class. Keeping their women free to preside over the family, these women are affected by the problems of every wife and mother, but touched only faintly by their race's hardships. They do share acutely in the prevailing difficulty of finding competent household help. Negro wives find Negro maids unwilling generally to work in their own neighborhoods, for various reasons. They do not wish to work where there is a possibility of acquaintances coming into contact with them while they serve and they still harbor the misconception that Negroes of any station are unable to pay as much as persons of the other race. It is in these homes of comparative ease that we find the polite activities of social exclusiveness. The luxuries of well-appointed homes, modest motors, tennis, golf and country clubs, trips to Europe and California, make for social standing. The problem confronting the refined Negro family is to know others of the same achievement. The search for kindred spirits gradually grows less difficult; in the past it led to the custom of visiting all the large cities in order to know similar groups of cultured Negro people.

A spirit of stress and struggle characterizes the second two groups. These women of business, profession and trade are the hub of the wheel of progress. Their burden is twofold. Many are wives and mothers whose husbands are insufficiently paid, or who have succumbed to social maladjustment and have abandoned their families. An appalling number are widows. They face the great problem of leaving home each day and at the same time trying to rear children in their spare time—this too in neighborhoods where rents are large; standards of dress and recreation high and costly, and social danger on the increase.

The great commercial life of New York City is only slightly touched by the Negro woman of our second group. Negro business men offer her most of their work, but their number is limited. Outside of this field, custom is once more against her and competition is keen for all. However, Negro girls are training and some are holding exceptional jobs. One of the professors in a New York college has had a young colored woman as secretary for the past three years. Another holds the head clerical position in an organization where reliable handling of detail and a sense of business ethics are essential. For four years she has steadily advanced. Quietly these women prove their worth, so that when a vacancy exists and there is a call, it is difficult to find even one competent colored secretary who is not employed. As a result of opportunity in clerical work in the educational system of New York City a number have qualified for such positions, one being appointed within the year to the office work of a high school. In other departments the civil service in New York City is no longer free from discrimination. The casual personal interview, that tenacious and retrogressive practice introduced in the Federal administration during the World War has spread and often nullifies the Negro woman's success in written tests. The successful young woman just cited above was three times "turned down" as undesirable on the basis of the personal interview. In the great mercantile houses, the many young Negro girls who might be well suited to salesmanship are barred from all but the menial positions. Even so, one Negro woman, beginning as a uniformed maid, has pulled herself up to the position of "head of stock."

Again, the telephone and insurance companies which receive considerable patronage from Negroes deny them proportionate employment. Fortunately, this is an era of changing customs. There is hope that a less selfish racial attitude will prevail. It is a heartening fact that there is an increasing number of Americans who will lend a hand in the game fight of the worthy.

In the less crowded professional vocations, the outlook is more cheerful. In these fields, the Negro woman is dependent largely upon herself and her own race for work. In the legal, dental, medical and nursing professions, successful women practitioners have usually worked their way through college and are "managing" on the small fees that can be received from an underpaid public. Social conditions in America are hardest upon the Negro because he is lowest in the economic scale. This gives rise to a demand for trained college women in the profession of social work. It has met with a response from young college women, anxious to devote their education and lives to the needs of the submerged classes. In New York City, some fifty-odd women are engaged in social work, other than nursing. In the latter profession there are over two hundred and fifty. Much of the social work has been pioneer in nature: the pay has been small with little possibility of advancement. For even in work among Negroes, the better paying positions are reserved for whites. The Negro college woman is doing her bit in this field at a sacrifice, along such lines as these: in the correctional departments of the city, as probation officers, investigators, and police women; as Big Sisters attached to the Childrens' Court; as field workers and visitors for relief organizations and missions; as secretaries for travelers-aid and mission societies; as visiting teachers and vocational guides for the schools of the city; and, in the many branches of public health nursing, in schools, organizations devoted to preventive and educational medicine, in hospitals and in private nursing.

In New York City, nearly three hundred Negro women share the good conditions in the teaching profession. They measure up to the high pedagogical requirements of the city and state law and are increasingly, leaders in the community. Here too the Negro woman finds evidence of the white workers' fear of competition. The need for teachers is still so strong that little friction exists. When it does seem to be imminent, it is smoothed away, as it recently was at a meeting of school principals. From the floor, a discussion began with: "What are we going to do about this problem of the increasing number of Negro teachers coming into our schools?" It ended promptly through the suggestion of another principal: "Send all you get and don't want over to my school. I have two now and I'll match their work to any two of your best whom you name." One might go on to such interesting and more unusual professions as journalism, chiropody, bacteriology, pharmacy, etc., and find that, though the number in any one may be small, the Negro woman is creditably represented in practically every one. According to individual ability she is meeting with success.

Closing the door on the home anxieties, the woman engaged in trades and in industry faces equally serious difficulty in competition in the open working field. Custom is against her in all but a few trade and industrial occupations. She has, however been established long in the dressmaking trade among the helpers and finishers, and more recently among the drapers and fitters in some of the best establishments. Several Negro women are themselves proprietors of shops in the country's greatest fashion district. Each of them has, against great odds, convinced skeptical employers of her business value; and, at the same time, has educated fellow workers of other races, doing much to show the oneness of interest of all workers. In millinery, power sewing-machine operating on cloth, straw and leather, there are few Negro women. The laissez-faire attitude of practically all trade unions makes the Negro woman an unwilling menace to the cause of labor.

In trade cookery, the Negro woman's talent and past experience is recognized. Her problem here is to find employers who will let her work her way to managerial positions, in tea-rooms, candy shops and institutions. One such employer became convinced that the managing cook, a young colored graduate of Pratt Institute, would continue to build up a business that had been failing. She offered her a partnership. As in the cases of a number of such women, her barrier was lack of capital. No matter how highly trained, nor how much speed and business acumen has been acquired, the Negro's credit is held in doubt. An exception in this matter of capital will serve to prove the rule. Thirty years ago, a young Negro girl began learning all branches of the fur trade. She is now in business for herself, employing three women of her race and one Jewish man. She has made fur experts of still another half-dozen colored girls. Such instances as these justify the prediction that the foothold gained in the trade world will, year by year, become more secure.

Because of the limited fields for workers in this group, many of the unsuccessful drift into the fourth social grade, the domestic and casual workers. These drifters increase the difficulties of the Negro woman suited to housework. New standards of household management are forming and the problem of the Negro woman is to meet these new business-like ideals. The constant influx of workers unfamiliar with household conditions in New York keeps the situation one of turmoil. The Negro woman, moreover, is revolting against residential domestic service. It is a last stand in her fight to maintain a semblance of family life. For this reason, principally, the number of day or casual workers is on the increase. Happiness is almost impossible under the strain of these conditions. Health and morale suffer, but how else can her children, loose all afternoon, be gathered together at night-fall? Through it all she manages to give satisfactory service and the Negro woman is sought after for this unpopular work largely because her honesty, loyalty and cleanliness have stood the test of time. Through her drudgery, the women of other groups find leisure time for progress. This is one of her contributions to America.

It is apparent from what has been said, that even in New York City, Negro women are of a race which is free neither economically, socially nor spiritually. Like women in general, but more particularly like those of other oppressed minorities, the Negro woman has been forced to submit to over-powering conditions. Pressure has been exerted upon her, both from without and within her group. Her emotional and sex life is a reflex of her economic station. The women of the working class will react, emotionally and sexually, similarly to the working-class women of other races. The Negro woman does not maintain any moral standard which may be assigned chiefly to qualities of race, any more than a white woman does. Yet she has been singled out and advertised as having lower sex standards. Superficial critics who have had contact only with the lower grades of Negro women, claim that they are more immoral than other groups of women. This I deny. This is the sort of criticism which predicates of one race, to its detriment, that which is common to all races. Sex irregularities are not a matter of race, but of socio-economic conditions. Research shows that most of the African tribes from which the Negro sprang have strict codes for sex relations. There is no proof of inherent weakness in the ethnic group.

Gradually overcoming the habitual limits imposed upon her by slave masters, she increasingly seeks legal sanction for the consummation and dissolution of sex contracts. Contrary to popular belief, illegitimacy among Negroes is cause for shame and grief. When economic, social and biological forces about unwed motherhood, the reaction is much the same as in racial groups. Secrecy is maintained if possible. Generally the even the mother, claims that the illegitimate child is her own. sylum is seldom sought. Schooled in this kind of suffering in ery, Negro women often temper scorn with sympathy for weakness. Stigma does fall upon the unmarried mother, but perhaps in this matter the Negroes' attitude is nearer the modern enlightened ideal for the social treatment of the unfortunate. May this not be considered another contribution to America?

With all these forces at work, true sex equality has not been approximated. The ratio of opportunity in the sex, social, economic and political spheres is about that which exists between white men and women. In the large, I would say that the Negro woman is the cultural equal of her man because she is generally kept in school longer. Negro boys, like white boys, are usually put to work to subsidize the family income. The growing economic independence of Negro working women is causing her to rebel against the domineering family attitude of the cruder working-class Negro man. The masses of Negro men are engaged in menial occupations throughout the working day. Their baffled and suppressed desires to determine their economic life are manifested in over-bearing domination at home. Working mothers are unable to instill different ideals in their sons. Conditions change slowly. Nevertheless, education and opportunity are modifying the spirit of the younger Negro men. Trained in modern schools of thought, they begin to show a wholesome attitude of fellowship and freedom for their women. The challenge to young Negro womanhood is to see clearly this trend and grasp the proferred comradeship with sincerity. In this matter of sex equality, Negro women have contributed few outstanding militants. Their feminist efforts are directed chiefly toward the realization of the equality of the races, the sex struggle assuming a subordinate place.

Obsessed with difficulties that might well compel individualism, the Negro woman has engaged in a considerable amount of organized action to meet group needs. She has evolved a federation of her clubs, embracing between eight and ten thousand women, throughout the state of New York. Its chief function is to crystallize programs, prevent duplication of effort, and to sustain a member organization whose cause might otherwise fail. It is now firmly established, and is about to strive for conspicuous goals. In New York City, one association makes child welfare its name and special concern. Others, like the Utility Club, Utopia Neighborhood, Debutante's League, Sempre Fidelius, etc., raise money for old folks' homes, a shelter for delinquent girls and fresh air camps for children. The Colored Branch of the Y. W. C. A. and the womens' organizations in the many churches, as well as in the beneficial lodges and associations, care for the needs of their members.

On the other hand, the educational welfare of the coming generation, has become the chief concern of the national sororities of Negro college women. The first to be organized in the country, Alpha Kappa Alpha, has a systematized and continuous program of educational and vocational guidance for students of the high schools and colleges. The work of Lambda Chapter, which covers New York City and its suburbs, is outstanding. Its recent campaign gathered together nearly one hundred and fifty such students at a meeting to gain inspiration from the life-stories of successful Negro women in eight fields of endeavor. From the trained nurse, who began in the same schools as they, these girls drank in the tale of her rise to the executive position in the Harlem Health Information Bureau. A commercial artist showed how real talent h overcome the color line. The graduate physician was a living example modern opportunities in the newer fields of medicine open to women. The vocations as outlets for the creative instinct became attractive under the persuasion of the musician, the dressmaker and the decorator. Similarly, Alpha Beta Chapter of the national Delta Sigma Theta Sorority recently devoted a week to work along similar lines. In such ways as these are the progressive and privileged groups of Negro women expressing their community and race consciousness.

We find the Negro woman, figuratively, struck in the face daily by contempt from the world about her. Within her soul, she knows little of peace and happiness. Through it all, she is courageously standing erect, developing within herself the moral strength to rise above and conquer false attitudes. She is maintaining her natural beauty and charm and improving her mind and opportunity. She is measuring up to the needs and demands of her family, community and race, and radiating from Harlem a hope that is cherished by her sisters in less propitious circumstances throughout the land. The wind of the race's destiny stirs more briskly because of her striving.

DEADLIER THAN THE MALE

John C. Ewers

John C. Ewers' portraits of Plains Indian women warriors of the nineteenth century stand in stark contrast to the "true woman" image of the encroaching white society of the time. Although his survey does not negate the fact that the lot of many Indian women included "women's work" around the camp or village, the tribes about which he writes appear to accept individual differences among women. While most women fulfilled the more traditional roles, others found their place as warriors and hunters.

Ewers, an ethnologist and thirty-year student of Plains Indian history, held the position of museum director of the Smithsonian Institute in 1965. He wrote this article for *American Heritage* at a time when white scholars were attempting to portray American Indians to the general public more sensitively than in the past.

When I first met Elk Hollering in the Water on the Blackfeet Reservation in Montana in 1941, she was a frail little old lady in her middle seventies. She was short and she was spare. I doubt if she ever weighed as many as one hundred pounds. Nothing about her appearance would remind one of artists' conceptions of the legendary Amazons. Nevertheless, Elk Hollering in the Water was a combat veteran in her own right, a fighting member of the most aggressive tribe of the upper Missouri. As a lively teen-ager she had accompanied her stalwart husband, Bear Chief, on raids against enemy tribes. And she had won honors by "taking things from the enemy."

DEADLIER THAN THE MALE   © 1965 American Heritage Publishing Co., Inc. Reprinted by permission from *American Heritage* (June/July 1965). Pp. 10–13.

Aged men of her tribe, men who had journeyed on many war excursions against the Crows, Crees, Assiniboins, Flatheads, and Sioux, readily acknowledged Elk Hollering in the Water's claim. Furthermore, they assured me that womanly participation in what we commonly regard as the man's game of war was not considered abnormal conduct in the days of intertribal conflict on the upper Missouri prior to the middle 1880's. Young childless women sometimes joined their husbands on fatiguing and dangerous horse-stealing raids upon distant enemy villages in preference to remaining at home praying and worrying about the safety of their mates. Sometimes small war parties travelled two or three hundred miles before their scouts located an enemy camp. Usually the women cooked for the entire party and performed other menial tasks during the outward journey. But they also took active parts in the dawn attacks on enemy camps and helped to drive the stolen horses homeward. Sometimes the fleeing raiders were overtaken by angry enemy warriors bent upon recapturing their pilfered livestock. Then the horse thieves, female and male, had to fight for their lives as well as for their newly acquired property.

Women warriors also appeared among the Crows, south of the Yellowstone. The Crows were a small tribe, but they were wealthier in horses than any other Indians on the upper Missouri. They fought valiantly to protect their herds from frequent raids by the Blackfeet from the north and the mighty Sioux from the east. To protect themselves from extermination by those more powerful tribes, the Crows made alliances with the white men.

Some thirty years ago or more an aged Crow woman, Pretty Shield, told Frank Bird Linderman of a brave Crow girl who aided General Crook against the Sioux and Cheyenne under Crazy Horse in the historic Battle of the Rosebud on June 17, 1876, only a week prior to the Custer debacle on the Little Big Horn. The Other Magpie was her name. She was wild and she was pretty. But she had no man of her own. When some 175 Crow warriors rode off to join Three Stars (General Crook) in his campaign against the hostile Sioux and Cheyenne, The Other Magpie went along. She had recently lost a brother at the hands of the Sioux, and she was eager for revenge. In the Battle of the Rosebud, the Crow scouts bore the brunt of the hostile Indian attack. Many of these scouts carried improved .50 caliber breech-loading rifles. But The Other Magpie's only weapons were her belt knife and a long, thin willow coup stick. Yet she counted coup on a live Sioux warrior and later took his scalp—one of only eleven scalps taken by the Crows in the day's bitter fighting.

Pretty Shield remembered the return of the Crows from that battle. She saw The Other Magpie proudly carrying a bright feather tied to the end of her coup stick to symbolize her recent achievement. And she saw her cut the Sioux scalp she had taken into several pieces and give them to the men so that they would have more scalps to dance with.

The greatest of all the women warriors among the upper Missouri tribes lived among the Crows in the middle of the nineteenth century. Rudolph Kurz, a romantic young Swiss artist who had journeyed into the wilderness to draw primitive Indians, met her at Fort Union near the mouth of the Yellowstone on October 27, 1851. He confided to his journal for that day, "In the afternoon the famous Absaroka amazon arrived. Mr. Denig [the factor in charge of the trading post] called me to his office that I might have an opportunity to see her. She looked neither savage nor warlike. On the contrary, as I entered the room, she sat with her hands in her lap, folded, as when one prays. She is about 46 years old; appears modest in manner and good natured rather than quick to quarrel." Kurz was so awed by this woman and so delighted to receive as a present a scalp she had taken in battle that he neglected to draw her portrait. Unfortunately, no likeness of this remarkable woman has been preserved. But Edwin T. Denig wrote a short biographical sketch of Woman Chief, as she was known to the Indians. He had known her for twelve years prior to her untimely death in 1854.

Woman Chief was not a Crow Indian by birth. She was a Gros Ventre girl who, at the age of about ten, was captured by the Crows. The Crow family that adopted her soon found that she showed little interest in helping the women with their domestic tasks. She preferred to shoot birds with a bow and arrow, to guard the family horses, and to ride horseback fast and fearlessly. Later she learned to shoot a gun accurately, and she became the equal if not the superior of any of the young men in hunting on foot or on horseback.

She grew taller and stronger than most women. She could carry a deer or bighorn home from the hunt on her back. She could kill four or five buffalo in a single chase, butcher them, and load them on pack horses without assistance. Yet, despite her prowess in men's activities, she always dressed like a woman. Although she was rather good-looking, she didn't attract the fancy of young men. After her foster father died she took charge of his lodge and family, acting as both father and mother to his children.

Her first war experience was gained in a defensive action outside the white-men's trading post in the Crow country. A Blackfoot war party approached the post and called upon the traders and Crows to come out and parley. This young woman alone had the nerve to answer their invitation. And when the treacherous enemy charged upon her, she killed one and wounded two others before running to safety in the traders' fort. This deed of daring marked her as a woman of unusual courage in the eyes of the Crows. They composed songs in her honor telling of her bravery, and sang them in their camps.

A year later she led her first war party against the Blackfeet; seventy horses were stolen. She succeeded in killing and scalping one Blackfoot and in capturing the gun of another. Her continued success as a war leader won her greater and greater honors among the Crows until she gained a place in the council of chiefs of the tribe, ranking third in a band of 160 lodges. Thereafter she was known as Woman Chief. This was a station and a title never before known among Crow women.

In the summer of 1854, twenty years after Woman Chief had begun to acquire a reputation as a warrior, she sought to try her skill as a peacemaker. She proposed a visit to the Gros Ventres, the tribe of her birth, to negotiate a peace between them and her adopted tribe, the Crows. Her friends, both Indian and white, sought to dissuade her from this bold undertaking. They well knew that the Gros Ventres looked upon her as a leader of their enemies. But Woman Chief persisted. In company with four Crows she travelled north of the Missouri, where she met a large party of Gros Ventres en route home from a visit to the trading post of Fort Union. She approached them boldly, talked to them in their own language, and smoked with them. While she journeyed with them to the main Gros Ventre camp, some of the party turned upon her and her four Crow comrades and coldly shot them down.

Weasel Tail, a Blood Indian who was over eighty years of age when I met him some twenty-odd years ago, told me that he was the son of very poor parents. In his late teens and early twenties he repeatedly joined horse-raiding expeditions in the hope of bettering both his economic status and his social prestige in his tribe. His wife, Throwing Down, used to go along with him during the early years of their marriage and before their first child was born. Weasel Tail explained, "She told me she loved me, and if I was to be killed she wanted to be killed with me. My wife was in five battles with me. She carried a six-shooter and knew how to use it. Once she stole a horse, a saddlebag filled with ammunition, and a war club from the enemy."

Weasel Tail told me the story of Running Eagle, most famous of all Blackfoot women warriors, who was killed in action about the time of Weasel Tail's birth in 1860. He had known several older men who had been members of war parties under Running Eagle's leadership, and they often had talked about her. One of these men was White Grass, who later became a prominent band chief among the Piegans, a Blackfoot tribe.

Running Eagle was a large, strong woman. When she was still young, her husband was killed in a fight with the Crows. Seeking some way to avenge his death, Running Eagle prayed to the sun, and thought she heard the sun answer, "I will give you great power in war. But if you give yourself to any other man you will be killed."

In a short time Running Eagle became a successful leader of sizable war parties. When on the warpath, she wore men's leggings, a peculiar loin cloth doubled over like a diaper, and a woman's dress. Although men who went to war under her leadership respected her highly, she was never proud. She insisted upon cooking for the men of her party, and she also mended their worn moccasins. When one young brave complained that it was not proper for a Blackfoot war leader to have to mend moccasins, she replied, "I am a woman. You men don't know how to sew."

One winter White Grass joined an expedition of about thirty men under Running Eagle's leadership, bound southward to the Crow country beyond the Yellowstone. They had not gone far before one of the younger men began to grumble because the leader was a woman. Running Eagle heard him and said, "You are right. I am only a woman." Then she sang her sacred war song, "All of you bachelors, try your best." The dissenter was so impressed by her manner that he decided to stay with the party to observe how this woman behaved.

When they reached the Yellowstone River, Running Eagle sang another song, "I should like to marry a buffalo bull, to have a two-year-old heifer for a sister, and to have a fall calf." Then she told her companions, "My brothers, I shall leave camp tonight. Tomorrow morning you must follow my footsteps in the snow."

So saying, she picked up her gun and walked off alone into the darkness. At daybreak she sighted a buffalo herd. She crawled toward it and shot first a large fat bull, then a two-year-old heifer, and then a fall calf. When the others overtook her they found her sitting down, quietly cleaning her gun. As they approached she told them calmly, "See, I have killed my husband, my two-year-old sister, and my baby."

After she had helped the men cut up the buffalo, Running Eagle ordered four men to scout ahead, saying, "I'm afraid the Nez Percés may be near here." Two days later the scouts returned and reported that they had seen no enemy signs. But not long after the party resumed its journey they discovered a Nez Percé encampment in the Yellowstone River bottom. Unfortunately, a Nez Percé horseman saw them at the same time. While he summoned the men of his camp, the Piegans hastily retreated and dug foxholes for protection against a Nez Percé attack. Running Eagle dug her hole a little in advance of her companions. From her pouch she took her war medicine—two feathers attached to a flat disk of brass—and tied it in her hair. Then she sang her war song.

When the Nez Percés charged, Running Eagle killed the first man to come within range. Then she cried out, "Brothers, I got the first one. You lie still. I shall keep killing them." Inspired by their leader's courage and calmness under fire, the doughty Piegans repulsed the Nez Percé attack, killing a number of the enemy. As the Nez Percés withdrew to care for their dead and wounded, Running Eagle howled like a wolf and shouted, "Now we are going to quit fighting." She led her happy warriors home without a casualty.

Toward spring of the following year, young White Grass again joined a war party led by Running Eagle. On the Sun River they sighted a camp of Flatheads who had crossed the Rockies to hunt buffalo on the plains. Running Eagle confided to her followers, "Last night I dreamed that some horses were given to me. Tonight we shall find them in the Flathead camp."

Shortly before daybreak the Piegans silently approached the tepees of the sleeping Flatheads. Running Eagle swiftly gave her orders: "Brothers, catch the horses you can rope outside the camp. I am no good with a rope. I'll go into the camp and see what's there." She sang her war song and prayed to the sun. "Sun, I am not a man. But you gave me this power to do what I desired." Then she walked quietly into the enemy camp, quickly cut loose five prize horses picketed near their owners' tepees, and led them away. Meanwhile, the men of her party roped a goodly number of the loose horses. When Running Eagle returned, the party was ready to make a fast getaway. She then told her comrades, "I'll take the lead. I am only a woman. I'm not as strong as you men. Keep any of those who may fall asleep on their horses from falling behind." For two days and two nights they rode without stopping to sleep. After the party reached their home camp, Running Eagle gave a bay and a roan to her eldest brother and a horse to each of her other relatives.

Running Eagle led several successful raids upon the Flatheads before those Indians learned that a woman had been a principal cause of their misfortunes. Then they set a trap for her by posting night guards to look out for any strange woman in their camp. The next time Running Eagle walked into the enemy village, the guard accosted her and asked her name. Running Eagle could not understand the Flathead tongue. As she hastily backed away, the Flathead sentry lifted his gun and shot and killed her. Some of the old Blackfoot Indians claimed that Running Eagle lost her life because she had broken her promise to the sun. She had fallen in love with a handsome young member of her war party, and she had not resisted his advances. . . .

THE PROBLEM THAT HAS NO NAME

Betty Friedan

Betty Friedan's book, *The Feminine Mystique*, became an instant best seller in 1963 and is now considered a classic of the modern feminist movement. It launched Friedan's career as indefatigable spokesperson for equal rights and the women's movement. Friedan graduated from Smith College in 1942, studied psychology at the University of California/Berkeley, and married Carl Friedan in 1947. In 1957 she sent a questionnaire to her Smith College classmates and the answers they gave led to the writing of *The Feminine Mystique*, the introductory chapter of which is reprinted here.

Friedan's book questioned the myth of natural domesticity, or the feminine mystique; she found too many suburban housewives suffering from "the problem that has no name," the "strange dissatisfied voice" repeating "Is this all there is?" Women's maladjustment to the feminine mystique, she argued, indicated the need for change in the social role rather than in the woman herself.

In 1966, along with several other women, Friedan founded NOW, the National Organization for Women. In addition to *The Feminine Mystique*, she is the author of *It Changed My Life* (1976) and *The Second Stage* (1981).

The problem lay buried, unspoken, for many years in the minds of American women. It was a strange stirring, a sense of dissatisfaction, a yearning that women suffered in the middle of the twentieth century in the United States. Each suburban wife struggled with it alone. As she made the beds, shopped for groceries, matched slipcover material, ate peanut butter sandwiches with her children, chauffeured Cub Scouts and Brownies, lay beside her husband at night—she was afraid to ask even of herself the silent question—"Is this all?"

For over fifteen years there was no word of this yearning in the millions of words written about women, for women, in all the columns, books and articles by experts telling women their role was to seek fulfillment as wives and mothers. Over and over women heard in voices of tradition and of Freudian sophistication that they could desire no greater destiny than to glory in their own femininity. Experts told them how to catch a man and keep him, how to breastfeed children and handle their toilet training, how to cope with sibling rivalry and adolescent rebellion; how to buy a dishwasher, bake bread, cook gourmet snails, and build a swimming pool with their own hands; how to dress, look, and act more feminine and make marriage more exciting; how to keep their husbands from dying young and their sons from growing into delinquents. They were taught to pity the neurotic, unfeminine, unhappy women who wanted to be poets or physicists or presidents. They learned that truly feminine women do not want careers, higher education, political rights— the independence and the opportunities that the old-fashioned feminists fought for. Some women, in their forties and fifties, still remembered painfully giving up those dreams, but most of the younger women no longer even thought

---

THE PROBLEM THAT HAS NO NAME   Reprinted from *The Feminine Mystique* by Betty Friedan, New York: W. W. Norton and Company, Inc., 1963, by permission of the publisher. Copyright © 1974, 1963 by Betty Friedan, 13–29.

about them. A thousand expert voices applauded their femininity, their adjust-ment, their new maturity. All they had to do was devote their lives from earliest girlhood to finding a husband and bearing children.

By the end of the nineteen-fifties, the average marriage age of women in America dropped to 20, and was still dropping, into the teens. Fourteen million girls were engaged by 17. The proportion of women attending college in comparison with men dropping from 47 per cent in 1920 to 35 per cent in 1958. A century earlier, women had fought for higher education; now girls went to college to get a husband. By the mid-fifties, 60 per cent dropped out of college to marry, or because they were afraid too much education would be a marriage bar. Colleges built dormitories for "married students," but the stu-dents were almost always the husbands. A new degree was instituted for the wives—"Ph.T." (Putting Husband Through).

Then American girls began getting married in high school. And the women's magazines, deploring the unhappy statistics about these young marriages, urged that courses on marriage, and marriage counselors, be installed in the high schools. Girls started going steady at twelve and thirteen, in junior high. Manufacturers put out brassieres with false bosoms of foam rubber for little girls of ten. And an advertisement for a child's dress, sizes 3—6x, in the *New York Times* in the fall of 1960, said: "She Too Can Join the Man-Trap Set."

By the end of the fifties, the United States birthrate was overtaking India's. The birth-control movement, renamed Planned Parenthood, was asked to find a method whereby women who had been advised that a third or fourth baby would be born dead or defective might have it anyhow. Statisticians were especially astounded at the fantastic increase in the number of babies among college women. Where once they had two children, now they had four, five, six. Women who had once wanted careers were now making careers out of having babies. So rejoiced *Life* magazine in a 1956 paean to the movement of American women back to the home.

In a New York hospital, a woman had a nervous breakdown when she found she could not breastfeed her baby. In other hospitals, women dying of cancer refused a drug which research had proved might save their lives: its side effects were said to be unfeminine. "If I have only one life, let me live it as a blonde," a larger-than-life-sized picture of a pretty, vacuous woman pro-claimed from newspaper, magazine, and drugstore ads. And across America, three out of every ten women dyed their hair blonde. They ate a chalk called Metrecal, instead of food, to shrink to the size of the thin young models. Department-store buyers reported that American women, since 1939, had become three and four sizes smaller. "Women are out to fit the clothes, instead of vice-versa," one buyer said.

Interior decorators were designing kitchens with mosaic murals and original paintings, for kitchens were once again the center of women's lives. Home sewing became a million-dollar industry. Many women no longer left their homes, except to shop, chauffeur their children, or attend a social engagement with their husbands. Girls were growing up in America without ever having jobs outside the home. In the late fifties, a sociological phenomenon was suddenly remarked: a third of American women now worked, but most were no longer young and very few were pursuing careers. They were married women who held part-time jobs, selling or secretarial, to put their husbands through school, their sons through college, or to help pay the mortgage. Or they were widows supporting families. Fewer and fewer women were entering professional work. The shortages in the nursing, social work, and teaching professions caused crises in almost every American city. Concerned over the Soviet Union's lead in the space race, scientists noted that America's greatest source of unused brain-power was women. But girls would not study physics: it was "unfeminine." A girl refused a science fellowship at Johns Hopkins to take a job in a real-estate office. All she wanted, she said, was what every other American girl wanted—to get married, have four children and live in a nice house in a nice suburb.

The suburban housewife—she was the dream image of the young American women and the envy, it was said, of women all over the world. The American housewife—freed by science and labor-saving appliances from the drudgery, the dangers of childbirth and the illnesses of her grandmother. She was healthy, beautiful, educated, concerned only about her husband, her children, her home. She had found true feminine fulfillment. As a housewife and mother, she was respected as a full and equal partner to man in his world. She was free to choose automobiles, clothes, appliances, supermarkets; she had everything that women ever dreamed of.

In the fifteen years after World War II, this mystique of feminine fulfillment became the cherished and self-perpetuating core of contemporary American culture. Millions of women lived their lives in the image of those pretty pictures of the American suburban housewife, kissing their husbands goodbye in front of the picture window, depositing their stationwagonsful of children at school, and smiling as they ran the new electric waxer over the spotless kitchen floor. They baked their own bread, sewed their own and their children's clothes, kept their new washing machines and dryers running all day. They changed the sheets on the beds twice a week instead of once, took the rug-hooking class in adult education, and pitied their poor frustrated mothers, who had dreamed of having a career. Their only dream was to be perfect wives and mothers; their highest ambition to have five children and a beautiful house, their only fight to get and keep their husbands. They had no thought for the unfeminine problems of the world outside the home; they wanted the men to make the major decisions. They gloried in their role as women, and wrote proudly on the census blank: "Occupation: housewife."

For over fifteen years, the words written for women, and the words women used when they talked to each other, while their husbands sat on the other side of the room and talked shop or politics or septic tanks, were about problems with their children, or how to keep their husbands happy, or improve their children's school, or cook chicken or make slipcovers. Nobody argued whether women were inferior or superior to men; they were simply different. Words like "emancipation" and "career" sounded strange and embarrassing; no one had used them for years. When a Frenchwoman named Simone de Beauvoir wrote a book called *The Second Sex*, an American critic commented that she obviously "didn't know what life was all about," and besides, she was talking about French women. The "woman problem" in America no longer existed.

If a woman had a problem in the 1950's and 1960's, she knew that something must be wrong with her marriage, or with herself. Other women were satisfied with their lives, she thought. What kind of a woman was she if she did not feel this mysterious fulfillment waxing the kitchen floor? She was so ashamed to admit her dissatisfaction that she never knew how many other women shared it. If she tried to tell her husband, he didn't understand what she was talking about. She did not really understand it herself. For over fifteen years women in America found it harder to talk about this problem than about sex. Even the psychoanalysts had no name for it. When a woman went to a psychiatrist for help, as many women did, she would say, "I'm so ashamed," or "I must be hopelessly neurotic." "I don't know what's wrong with women today," a suburban psychiatrist said uneasily. "I only know something is wrong because most of my patients happen to be women. And their problem isn't sexual." Most women with this problem did not go to see a psychoanalyst, however. "There's nothing wrong really," they kept telling themselves. "There isn't any problem."

But on an April morning in 1959, I heard a mother of four, having coffee with four other mothers in a suburban development fifteen miles from New York, say in a tone of quiet desperation, "the problem." And the others knew, without words, that she was not talking about a problem with her husband, or her children, or her home. Suddenly they realized they all shared the same problem, the problem that has no name. They began, hesitantly, to talk about it. Later, after they had picked up their children at nursery school and taken them home to nap, two of the women cried, in sheer relief, just to know they were not alone.

Gradually I came to realize that the problem that has no name was shared by countless women in America. As a magazine writer I often interviewed women about problems with their children, or their marriages, or their houses, or their communities. But after a while I began to recognize the telltale signs of this other problem. I saw the same signs in suburban ranch houses and split-levels on Long Island and in New Jersey and Westchester County; in colonial houses in a small Massachusetts town; on patios in Memphis; in suburban and city apartments; in living rooms in the Midwest. Sometimes I sensed the problem, not as a reporter, but as a suburban housewife, for during this time I was also bringing up my own three children in Rockland County, New York. I heard echoes of the problem in college dormitories and semi-private maternity wards, at PTA meetings and luncheons of the League of Women Voters, at suburban cocktail parties, in station wagons waiting for trains, and in snatches of conversation overheard at Schrafft's. The groping words I heard from other women, on quiet afternoons when children were at school or on quiet evenings when husbands worked late, I think I understood first as a woman long before I understood their larger social and psychological implications.

Just what was this problem that has no name? What were the words women used when they tried to express it? Sometimes a woman would say "I feel empty somehow . . . incomplete." Or she would say, "I feel as if I don't exist." Sometimes she blotted out the feeling with a tranquilizer. Sometimes she thought the problem was with her husband, or her children, or that what she really needed was to redecorate her house, or move to a better neighborhood, or have an affair, or another baby. Sometimes, she went to a doctor with symptoms she could hardly describe: "A tired feeling . . . I get so angry with the children it scares me . . . I feel like crying without any reason." (A Cleveland doctor called it "the housewife's syndrome.") A number of women told me about great bleeding blisters that break out on their hands and arms. "I call it the housewife's blight," said a family doctor in Pennsylvania. "I see it so often lately in these young women with four, five and six children who bury themselves in their dishpans. But it isn't caused by detergent and it isn't cured by cortisone."

Sometimes a woman would tell me that the feeling gets so strong she runs out of the house and walks through the streets. Or she stays inside her house and cries. Or her children tell her a joke, and she doesn't laugh because she doesn't hear it. I talked to women who had spent years on the analyst's couch, working out their "adjustment to the feminine role," their blocks to "fulfillment as a wife and mother." But the desperate tone in these women's voices, and the look in their eyes, was the same as the tone and the look of other women, who were sure they had no problem, even though they did have a strange feeling of desperation.

A mother of four who left college at nineteen to get married told me:

> I've tried everything women are supposed to do—hobbies, gardening, pickling, canning, being very social with my neighbors, joining committees, running PTA teas. I can do it all, and I like it, but it doesn't leave you anything to think about—any feeling of who you are. I never had any career ambitions. All I wanted was to get married and have four children. I love the kids and Bob and my home. There's no problem you can even put a name to. But I'm desperate. I begin to feel I have no personality. I'm a server of food and putter-on of pants and a bedmaker, somebody who can be called on when you want something. But who am I?

A twenty-three-year-old mother in blue jeans said:

> I ask myself why I'm so dissatisfied. I've got my health, fine children, a lovely new home, enough money. My husband has a real future as an electronics engineer. He doesn't have any of these feelings. He says maybe I need a vacation, let's go to New York for a weekend. But that isn't it. I always had this idea we should do everything together. I can't sit down and read a book alone. If the children are napping and I have one hour to myself I just walk through the house waiting for them to wake up. I don't make a move until I know where the rest of the crowd is going. It's as if ever since you were a little girl, there's always been somebody or something that will take care of your life: your parents, or college, or falling in love, or having a child, or moving to a new house. Then you wake up one morning and there's nothing to look forward to.

A young wife in a Long Island development said:

> I seem to sleep so much. I don't know why I should be so tired. This house isn't nearly so hard to clean as the cold-water flat we had when I was working. The children are at school all day. It's not the work. I just don't feel alive.

In 1960, the problem that has no name burst like a boil through the image of the happy American housewife. In the television commercials the pretty housewives still beamed over their foaming dishpans and *Time's* cover story on "The Suburban Wife, an American Phenomenon" protested: "Having too good a time . . . to believe that they should be unhappy." But the actual unhappiness of the American housewife was suddenly being reported—from the *New York Times* and *Newsweek* to *Good Housekeeping* and CBS Television ("The

Trapped Housewife"), although almost everybody who talked about it found some superficial reason to dismiss it. It was attributed to incompetent appliance repairmen *(New York Times),* or the distances children must be chauffeured in the suburbs *(Time),* or too much PTA *(Redbook).* Some said it was the old problem—education: more and more women had education, which naturally made them unhappy in their role as housewives. "The road from Freud to Frigidaire, from Sophocles to Spock, has turned out to be a bumpy one," reported the *New York Times* (June 28, 1960). "Many young women—certainly not all—whose education plunged them into a world of ideas feel stifled in their homes. They find their routine lives out of joint with their training. Like shut-ins, they feel left out. In the last year, the problem of the educated housewife has provided the meat of dozens of speeches made by troubled presidents of women's colleges who maintain, in the face of complaints, that sixteen years of academic training is realistic preparation for wifehood and motherhood."

There was much sympathy for the educated housewife. ("Like a two-headed schizophrenic . . . once she wrote a paper on the Graveyard poets; now she writes notes to the milkman. Once she determined the boiling point of sulphuric acid; now she determines her boiling point with the overdue repairman. . . . The housewife often is reduced to screams and tears. . . . No one, it seems, is appreciative, least of all herself, of the kind of person she becomes in the process of turning from poetess into shrew.")

Home economists suggested more realistic preparation for housewives, such as high-school workshops in home appliances. College educators suggested more discussion groups on home management and the family, to prepare women for the adjustment to domestic life. A spate of articles appeared in the mass magazines offering "Fifty-eight Ways to Make Your Marriage More Exciting." No month went by without a new book by a psychiatrist or sexologist offering technical advice on finding greater fulfillment through sex.

A male humorist joked in *Harper's Bazaar* (July, 1960) that the problem could be solved by taking away woman's right to vote. ("In the pre-19th Amendment era, the American woman was placid, sheltered and sure of her role in American society. She left all the political decisions to her husband and he, in turn, left all the family decisions to her. Today a woman has to make both the family *and* the political decisions, and it's too much for her.")

A number of educators suggested seriously that women no longer be admitted to the four-year colleges and universities: in the growing college crisis, the education which girls could not use as housewives was more urgently needed than ever by boys to do the work of the atomic age.

The problem was also dismissed with drastic solutions no one could take seriously. (A woman writer proposed in *Harper's* that women be drafted for compulsory service as nurses' aides and baby-sitters.) And it was smoothed over with the age-old panaceas: "love is their answer," "the only answer is inner help," "the secret of completeness—children," "a private means of intellectual fulfillment," "to cure this toothache of the spirit—the simple formula of handing one's self and one's will over to God."[1]

---

[1] See the Seventy-fifth Anniversary Issue of *Good Housekeeping,* May, 1960, "The Gift of Self," a symposium by Margaret Mead, Jessamyn West, et al.

The problem was dismissed by telling the housewife she doesn't realize how lucky she is—her own boss, no time clock, no junior executive gunning for her job. What if she isn't happy—does she think men are happy in this world? Does she really, secretly, still want to be a man? Doesn't she know yet how lucky she is to be a woman?

The problem was also, and finally, dismissed by shrugging that there are no solutions: this is what being a woman means, and what is wrong with American women that they can't accept their role gracefully? As *Newsweek* put it (March 7, 1960):

> She is dissatisfied with a lot that women of other lands can only dream of. Her discontent is deep, pervasive, and impervious to the superficial remedies which are offered at every hand. . . . An army of professional explorers have already charted the major sources of trouble. . . . From the beginning of time, the female cycle has defined and confined woman's role. As Freud was credited with saying: "Anatomy is destiny." Though no group of women has ever pushed these natural restrictions as far as the American wife, it seems that she still cannot accept them with good grace. . . . A young mother with a beautiful family, charm, talent and brains is apt to dismiss her role apologetically. "What do I do?" you hear her say. "Why nothing. I'm just a housewife." A good education, it seems, has given this paragon among women an understanding of the value of everything except her own worth . . .

And so she must accept the fact that "American women's unhappiness is merely the most recently won of women's rights," and adjust and say with the happy housewife found by *Newsweek*: "We ought to salute the wonderful freedom we all have and be proud of our lives today. I have had college and I've worked, but being a housewife is the most rewarding and satisfying role. . . . My mother was never included in my father's business affairs . . . she couldn't get out of the house and away from us children. But I am an equal to my husband; I can go along with him on business trips and to social business affairs."

The alternative offered was a choice that few women would contemplate. In the sympathetic words of the *New York Times:* "All admit to being deeply frustrated at times by the lack of privacy, the physical burden, the routine of family life, the confinement of it. However, none would give up her home and family if she had the choice to make again." *Redbook* commented: "Few women would want to thumb their noses at husbands, children and community and go off on their own. Those who do may be talented individuals, but they rarely are successful women."

The year American women's discontent boiled over, it was also reported (*Look*) that the more than 21,000,000 American women who are single, widowed, or divorced do not cease even after fifty their frenzied, desperate search for a man. And the search begins early—for seventy per cent of all American women now marry before they are twenty-four. A pretty twenty-five-year-old secretary took thirty-five different jobs in six months in the futile hope of finding a husband. Women were moving from one political club to another, taking evening courses in accounting or sailing, learning to play golf or ski, joining a number of churches in succession, going to bars alone, in their ceaseless search for a man.

Of the growing thousands of women currently getting private psychiatric help in the United States, the married ones were reported dissatisfied with their marriages, the unmarried ones suffering from anxiety and, finally, depression. Strangely, a number of psychiatrists stated that, in their experience, unmarried women patients were happier than married ones. So the door of all those pretty suburban houses opened a crack to permit a glimpse of uncounted thousands of American housewives who suffered alone from a problem that suddenly everyone was talking about, and beginning to take for granted, as one of those unreal problems in American life that can never be solved—like the hydrogen bomb. By 1962 the plight of the trapped American housewife had become a national parlor game. Whole issues of magazines, newspaper columns, books learned and frivolous, educational conferences and television panels were devoted to the problem.

Even so, most men, and some women, still did not know that this problem was real. But those who had faced it honestly knew that all the superficial remedies, the sympathetic advice, the scolding words and the cheering words were somehow drowning the problem in unreality. A bitter laugh was beginning to be heard from American women. They were admired, envied, pitied, theorized over until they were sick of it, offered drastic solutions or silly choices that no one could take seriously. They got all kinds of advice from the growing armies of marriage and child-guidance counselors, psychotherapists, and armchair psychologists, on how to adjust to their role as housewives. No other road to fulfillment was offered to American women in the middle of the twentieth century. Most adjusted to their role and suffered or ignored the problem that has no name. It can be less painful for a woman, not to hear the strange, dissatisfied voice stirring within her.

It is no longer possible to ignore that voice, to dismiss the desperation of so many American women. This is not what being a woman means, no matter what the experts say. For human suffering there is a reason; perhaps the reason has not been found because the right questions have not been asked, or pressed far enough. I do not accept the answer that there is no problem because American women have luxuries that women in other times and lands never dreamed of; part of the strange newness of the problem is that it cannot be understood in terms of the age-old material problems of man: poverty, sickness, hunger, cold. The women who suffer this problem have a hunger that food cannot fill. It persists in women whose husbands are struggling internes and law clerks, or prosperous doctors and lawyers; in wives of workers and executives who make $5,000 a year or $50,000. It is not caused by lack of material advantages; it may not even be felt by women preoccupied with desperate problems of hunger, poverty or illness. And women who think it will be solved by more money, a bigger house, a second car, moving to a better suburb, often discover it gets worse.

It is no longer possible today to blame the problem on loss of femininity: to say that education and independence and equality with men have made American women unfeminine. I have heard so many women try to deny this dissatisfied voice within themselves because it does not fit the pretty picture of femininity the experts have given them. I think, in fact, that this is the first clue to the mystery: the problem cannot be understood in the generally accepted terms by which scientists have studied women, doctors have treated them, counselors have advised them, and writers have written about them. Women who suffer this problem, in whom this voice is stirring, have lived their whole lives in the pursuit of feminine fulfillment. They are not career women (although career women may have other problems); they are women whose greatest ambition has been marriage and children. For the oldest of these women, these daughters of the American middle class, no other dream was possible. The ones in their forties and fifties who once had other dreams gave them up and threw themselves joyously into life as housewives. For the youngest, the new wives and mothers, this was the only dream. They are the ones who quit high school and college to marry, or marked time in some job in which they had no real interest until they married. These women are very "feminine" in the usual sense, and yet they still suffer the problem.

Are the women who finished college, the women who once had dreams beyond housewifery, the ones who suffer the most? According to the experts they are, but listen to these four women:

> My days are all busy, and dull, too. All I ever do is mess around. I get up at eight—I make breakfast, so I do the dishes, have lunch, do some more dishes, and some laundry and cleaning in the afternoon. Then it's supper dishes and I get to sit down a few minutes, before the children have to be sent to bed. . . . That's all there is to my day. It's just like any other wife's day. Humdrum. The biggest time, I am chasing kids.

> Ye Gods, what do I do with my time? Well, I get up at six. I get my son dressed and then give him breakfast. After that I wash dishes and bathe and feed the baby. Then I get lunch and while the children nap, I sew or mend or iron and do all the other things I can't get done before noon. Then I cook supper for the family and my husband watches TV while I do the dishes. After I get the children to bed, I set my hair and then I go to bed.

> The problem is always being the children's mommy, or the minister's wife and never being myself.

> A film made of any typical morning in my house would look like an old Marx Brothers' comedy. I wash the dishes, rush the older children off to school, dash out in the yard to cultivate the chrysanthemums, run back in to make a phone call about a committee meeting, help the youngest child build a blockhouse, spend fifteen minutes skimming the newspapers so I can be well-informed, then scamper down to the washing machines where my thrice-weekly laundry includes enough clothes to keep a primitive village going for an entire year. By noon I'm ready for a padded cell. Very little of what I've done has been really necessary or important. Outside pressures lash me through the day. Yet I look upon myself as one of the more relaxed housewives in the neighborhood. Many of my friends are even more frantic. In the past sixty years we have come full circle and the American housewife is once again trapped in a squirrel cage. If the cage is now a modern plate-glass-and-broadloom ranch house or a convenient modern apartment, the situation is no less painful than when her grandmother sat over an embroidery hoop in her gilt-and-plush parlor and muttered angrily about women's rights.

The first two women never went to college. They live in developments in Levittown, New Jersey, and Tacoma, Washington, and were interviewed by a team of sociologists studying workingmen's wives.[2] The third, a minister's

---

[2]Lee Rainwater, Richard P. Coleman, and Gerald Handel, *Workingman's Wife*, New York, 1959.

wife, wrote on the fifteenth reunion questionnaire of her college that she never had any career ambitions, but wishes now she had.[3] The fourth, who has a Ph.D. in anthropology, is today a Nebraska housewife with three children.[4] Their words seem to indicate that housewives of all educational levels suffer the same feeling of desperation.

The fact is that no one today is muttering angrily about "women's rights," even though more and more women have gone to college. In a recent study of all the classes that have graduated from Barnard College,[5] a significant minority of earlier graduates blamed their education for making them want "rights," later classes blamed their education for giving them career dreams, but recent graduates blamed the college for making them feel it was not enough simply to be a housewife and mother; they did not want to feel guilty if they did not read books or take part in community activities. But if education is not the cause of the problem, the fact that education somehow festers in these women may be a clue.

If the secret of feminine fulfillment is having children, never have so many women, with the freedom to choose, had so many children, in so few years, so willingly. If the answer is love, never have women searched for love with such determination. And yet there is a growing suspicion that the problem may not be sexual, though it must somehow be related to sex. I have heard from many doctors evidence of new sexual problems between man and wife—sexual hunger in wives so great their husbands cannot satisfy it. "We have made women a sex creature," said a psychiatrist at the Margaret Sanger marriage counseling clinic. "She has no identity except as a wife and mother. She does not know who she is herself. She waits all day for her husband to come home at night to make her feel alive. And now it is the husband who is not interested. It is terrible for the women, to lie there, night after night, waiting for her husband to make her feel alive." Why is there such a market for books and articles offering sexual advice? The kind of sexual orgasm which Kinsey found in statistical plenitude in the recent generations of American women does not seem to make this problem go away.

On the contrary, new neuroses are being seen among women—and problems as yet unnamed as neuroses—which Freud and his followers did not predict, with physical symptoms, anxieties, and defense mechanisms equal to those caused by sexual repression. And strange new problems are being reported in the growing generations of children whose mothers were always there, driving them around, helping them with their homework—an inability to endure pain or discipline or pursue any self-sustained goal of any sort, a devastating boredom with life. Educators are increasingly uneasy about the dependence, the lack of self-reliance, of the boys and girls who are entering college today. "We fight a continual battle to make our students assume manhood," said a Columbia dean.

---

[3]Betty Friedan, "If One Generation Can Ever Tell Another," *Smith Alumnae Quarterly*, Northampton, Mass., Winter, 1961. I first became aware of "the problem that has no name" and its possible relationship to what I finally called "the feminine mystique" in 1957, when I prepared an intensive questionnaire and conducted a survey of my own Smith College classmates fifteen years after graduation. This questionnaire was later used by alumnae classes of Radcliffe and other women's colleges with similar results.

[4]Jhan and June Robbins, "Why Young Mothers Feel Trapped," *Redbook*, September, 1960.

[5]Marian Freda Poverman, "Alumnae on Parade," *Barnard Alumnae Magazine*, July, 1957.

A White House conference was held on the physical and muscular deterioration of American children: were they being over-nurtured? Sociologists noted the astounding organization of suburban children's lives: the lessons, parties, entertainments, play and study groups organized for them. A surburban housewife in Portland, Oregon, wondered why the children "need" Brownies and Boy Scouts out here. "This is not the slums. The kids out here have the great outdoors. I think people are so bored, they organize the children, and then try to hook everyone else on it. And the poor kids have no time left just to lie on their beds and daydream."

Can the problem that has no name be somehow related to the domestic routine of the housewife? When a woman tries to put the problem into words, she often merely describes the daily life she leads. What is there in this recital of comfortable domestic detail that could possibly cause such a feeling of desperation? Is she trapped simply by the enormous demands of her role as modern housewife: wife, mistress, mother, nurse, consumer, cook, chauffeur; expert on interior decoration, child care, appliance repair, furniture refinishing, nutrition, and education? Her day is fragmented as she rushes from dishwasher to washing machine to telephone to dryer to station wagon to supermarket, and delivers Johnny to the Little League field, takes Janey to dancing class, gets the lawnmower fixed and meets the 6:45. She can never spend more than 15 minutes on any one thing; she has no time to read books, only magazines; even if she had time, she has lost the power to concentrate. At the end of the day, she is so terribly tired that sometimes her husband has to take over and put the children to bed.

[Thus] terrible tiredness took so many women to doctors in the 1950's that one decided to investigate it. He found, surprisingly, that his patients suffering from "housewife's fatigue" slept more than an adult needed to sleep—as much as ten hours a day—and that the actual energy they expended on housework did not tax their capacity. The real problem must be something else, he decided—perhaps boredom. Some doctors told their women patients they must get out of the house for a day, treat themselves to a movie in town. Others prescribed tranquilizers. Many suburban housewives were taking tranquilizers like cough drops. "You wake up in the morning, and you feel as if there's no point in going on another day like this. So you take a tranquilizer because it makes you not care so much that it's pointless."

It is easy to see the concrete details that trap the suburban housewife, the continual demands on her time. But the chains that bind her in her trap are chains in her own mind and spirit. They are chains made up of mistaken ideas and misinterpreted facts, of incomplete truths and unreal choices. They are not easily seen and not easily shaken off.

How can any woman see the whole truth within the bounds of her own life? How can she believe that voice inside herself, when it denies the conventional, accepted truths by which she has been living? And yet the women I have talked to, who are finally listening to that inner voice, seem in some incredible way to be groping through to a truth that has defied the experts.

I think the experts in a great many fields have been holding pieces of that truth under their microscopes for a long time without realizing it. I found pieces of it in certain new research and theoretical developments in psychological, social and biological science whose implications for women seem never to have been examined. I found many clues by talking to suburban doctors, gynecologists, obstetricians, child-guidance clinicians, pediatricians, high-school guidance counselors, college professors, marriage counselors, psychiatrists and ministers—questioning them not on their theories, but on their actual experience in treating American women. I became aware of a growing body of evidence, much of which has not been reported publicly because it does not fit current modes of thought about women—evidence which throws into question the standards of feminine normality, feminine adjustment, feminine fulfillment, and feminine maturity by which most women are still trying to live.

I began to see in a strange new light the American return to early marriage and the large families that are causing the population explosion; the recent movement to natural childbirth and breastfeeding; suburban conformity, and the new neuroses, character pathologies and sexual problems being reported by the doctors. I began to see new dimensions to old problems that have long been taken for granted among women: menstrual difficulties, sexual frigidity, promiscuity, pregnancy fears, childbirth depression, the high incidence of emotional breakdown and suicide among women in their twenties and thirties, the menopause crises, the so-called passivity and immaturity of American men, the discrepancy between women's tested intellectual abilities in childhood and their adult achievement, the changing incidence of adult sexual orgasm in American women, and persistent problems in psychotherapy and in women's education.

If I am right, the problem that has no name stirring in the minds of so many American women today is not a matter of loss of femininity or too much education, or the demands of domesticity. It is far more important than anyone recognizes. It is the key to these other new and old problems which have been torturing women and their husbands and children, and puzzling their doctors and educators for years. It may well be the key to our future as a nation and a culture. We can no longer ignore that voice within women that says: "I want something more than my husband and my children and my home."

THE TOTAL WOMAN
Marabel Morgan

Marabel Morgan's *The Total Woman* (1973) was one of the best selling nonfiction books of the mid-1970s; and the Total Woman seminar classes in which women learned the "secrets" of making their "marriage come alive" enrolled tens of thousands. The secrets were the "four A's." Women should "accept, admire, adapt (to), and appreciate" their husbands. Like the book, the seminar considered each one in turn. Each session culminated in an "assignment," a list of specific instructions on how to behave which the participants were to put into practice as soon as they got home. They reported the outcomes in class the next day.

Marabel Morgan was a former beauty queen who married straight out of college and immediately settled into a fulltime career as a wife (her husband was an attorney), homemaker, mother. After a few years, Morgan found that although there was nothing wrong with her marriage, the "sizzle" had gone out of it. One way or another, she determined, she was going to get that "sizzle" back. Her book addressed the longing for romance, for sexual fulfillment, and for a sense of self worth, of middle class house-wives, like herself. And it promised answers! The answers combined religious injunctions about wives subordinating themselves to their husbands with "pop" psychology techniques for fostering communication. These, plus a no-holds-barred attitude towards sex in marriage, made the "Total Woman" message a heady brew.

Some of my friends have asked why I want to tell all this. I realize that much of it sounds like something out of a slick magazine, and in a sense it is. The only reason I can share it at all is that my life has changed for the better. If another woman can learn and profit from my mistakes, why not pass it on?

This book is not intended to be the ultimate authority on marriage. Far from it. I don't pretend to have an automatic, ready-to-wear answer for every marriage problem. I do believe it is possible, however, for almost any wife to have her husband absolutely adore her in just a few weeks' time. She can revive romance, reestablish communication, break down barriers, and put sizzle back into her marriage. It really is up to her. She has the power.

If, through reading and applying these principles, you become a Total Woman, with your husband more in love with you than ever before, my efforts in writing this book will have been rewarded.

ASSIGNMENT

MAN ALIVE

1.   Accept your husband just as he is. Write out two lists—one of his faults and one of his virtues. Take a long, hard look at his faults and then throw the list away; don't ever dwell on them again. Only think about his virtues. Carry that list with you and refer to it when you are mad, sad, or glad.

2.   Admire your husband every day. Refer to his virtue list if you need a place

to start. Say something nice about his body today. Put his tattered ego back together with compliments.

3. Adapt to his way of life. Accept his friends, food, and life-style as your own. Ask him to write the six most important changes he'd like to see take place at your house. Read the list in private, react in private, and then set out to accomplish these changes with a smile. Be a "Yes, let's!" woman some time of every day.

4. Appreciate all he does for you. Sincerely tell him "Thank you" with your attitudes, actions, and words. Give him your undivided attention, and try not to make any telephone calls after he comes home, especially after 8:00 P. M.

SUPER SEX

Sex is an hour in bed at ten o'clock; super sex is the climax of an atmosphere that has been carefully set all day. Your attitude during your husband's first four waking minutes in the morning sets the tone for his entire day. The atmosphere for love in the evening can be set by you even before breakfast. Give him a kiss first thing tomorrow morning. Rub his back as he's waking up. Whisper in his ear. Slip into the bathroom to clear a few cobwebs before he wakes.

Remember, he can stand almost anything but boredom. The same night-gown month after month is not too exciting to any man. Treat him and yourself to some snazzy new ones. Have you ever looked so sexy in the morning that your husband called in late to the office? At least you can make him wish he could stay home.

One wife changes the sheets every few days while her husband is dressing for work. As she sprays the sheets with cologne, she purrs, "Honey, hurry home tonight." It gives him incentive for the whole day. If you expect great sex tonight, it should definitely start in the morning, with words. That's basic. Sex 201.

Edna St. Vincent Millay wrote, " 'Tis not love's going hurts my days, but that it went in little ways." Marriage is but a basketful of those little things.

Tomorrow morning as your husband leaves for work, stand at the door and wave until he's out of sight. That's his last memory of you, in the open doorway. Make him want to hurry home.

In class recently, one cute girl I'll call Janet told how she had anxiously anticipated her husband's coming home one day. At four o'clock she called his office somewhat nervously and said, "Honey, I'm eagerly waiting for you to come home. I just crave your body."

Jack said, with great consternation, "Ummmmmmph."

"Is there someone there with you, darling?" she asked.

"Ummhum," came the same reply.

"Well, I'll see you soon, darling," she said.

"Ummhum," was his final utterance.

And they both hung up.

Five minutes later the phone rang. It was Jack. In unbelief he said, "Would you please repeat slowly what you said five minutes ago?"

The sequel to the story was almost as amusing. Janet called her girl friend, Barbara, to tell what had happened. Barbara couldn't wait to try it on her husband, Pete. She called his office number and when the male voice answered, she said, "Darling, I wanted to call to say that I just crave your body. Hurry home!"

The voice on the other end demanded, "Who is this?" Realizing that another man, not her husband, had answered the phone, Barbara quickly hung up, absolutely mortified.

That night when her husband came in the door, he said, "Wait until I tell you about Ron's phone call today. You'll never believe it!" (She never told him, by the way, who the anonymous caller had been.)

So when you call your husband's office, first be sure you've got the right man! Then keep it short, just long enough to let him know that you're ready and willing. It may be the greatest news he has heard all day.

LUNCHEON SPECIAL

If you pack your husband's lunch in the morning, try tucking in a surprise love note. Mail a beautiful card to his office (marked PERSONAL) that would brighten up his day. Or appear in person. I know of one woman who arrived at her husband's office at lunch hour with a picnic basket. Behind locked doors they spent the longest lunch hour the boss had taken in months. The secretaries are still talking about that one!

Arrange your day's activities so that you'll be totally and eagerly prepared as he walks in the door. A psychiatrist told me, "Lots of men would be less preoccupied with work—or other women—if their wives made coming home the most exciting part of the day."

I find that after a hard day at the office, most husbands don't usually arrange flowers and light the candles in the bedroom. At least mine doesn't, but he appreciates my efforts. And it's my privilege to do it.

Set an atmosphere of romance tonight. Set your table with cloth, flowers, and silver. Prepare his favorite dinner for him. Eat by candlelight; you'll light his candle!

Make up your mind to be available for him. Schedule your day so you won't start projects at nine o'clock. The number-one killer of love is fatigue, but you won't be exhausted if you're using your $25,000 plan. You'll have the energy to be a passionate lover.

Next, be sure the outside of your "house" is prepared. Bubble your troubles away at five o'clock. Of course, you'll be shaven, perfumed, and seductive in an utterly lovely outfit. Perhaps you're thinking, "Since I'm forty pounds overweight, I don't feel very seductive in my baby-doll pajamas." That's all right, he chose you because he loves you. Concentrate on your good points and he will, too. He won't be able to take his eyes off you. Best of all, he'll know how much you care.

Prepare now for making love tonight. This is part of our class assignment. In fact by the second week, the women are to be prepared for sexual intercourse every night for a week. When I gave the homework in one class, a woman muttered audibly, "What's she think I am, a sex maniac?"

Another gal told a Total Woman teacher, "I tried to follow the assignment this past week, but I couldn't keep up—I was only ready for sex six nights; Monday night I was just too tired." The teacher gave her a B—, but her husband gave her an A!

One Fort Lauderdale housewife told how she diligently prepared for love for seven straight nights, "whatever, whenever, and wherever," and it was her husband who couldn't take it. "I don't know what's happened to you, honey," he said with a weak grin, "but I love it!"

COMPANION, NOT COMPETITION

Sex can restore a bad mood or disagreement. One wife felt she had been wronged by her husband. Her pride took over and she refused to give in until he changed. The Bible advises, ". . . let not the sun go down upon your wrath." Watch that no bitterness or resentment takes root in you for it causes deep trouble.

Nip it in the bud. Don't let your grudge carry over to the next day. There is no place for resentment in a good marriage. Part of his problem may be his need for your sexual love. Talk it out and change your attitude. Often that's all it takes.

Love never makes demands. Love is unconditional acceptance of him and his feelings. He does not need competition at home; he's had that all day at work. He needs your companionship and compliments instead.

A mature couple does not demand perfection. They do not chase false goals, which can only end in disillusionment. They are willing to work together for each other's good, which produces a happy sexual adjustment.

Don't deprive your husband of intercourse when he acts like a bear. He may be tired when he comes home tonight. He needs to be pampered, loved, and restored. Fill up his tummy with food; soothe away his frustrations with sex. Lovemaking comforts a man. It can comfort you too.

In speaking to a men's service club recently, I told them some of the class assignments for super sex. The reason for the homework, I explained, was that sex comforts a man. The reaction of the men was completely unexpected. These sophisticated businessmen spontaneously shouted, pounded the tables, picked up their spoons, and clanged their water glasses!

Lovemaking is an art you can develop to any degree, according to *How to Be a Happily Married Mistress*. You can become a Rembrandt in your sexual art. Or, you can stay at the paint-by-numbers stage. One husband, by the way, felt his wife was more like Grandma Moses because she always wore a flannel granny gown. The benefits in your becoming a Rembrandt just cannot be overemphasized. You can begin now to be a budding artist. Tonight is your night for super sex. Prepare, anticipate, relax, and enjoy!

ASSIGNMENT
SEX 201

1.   Be an atmosphere adjuster in the morning. Set the tone for love. Be pleasant to look at, be with, and talk to. Walk your husband to the car each morning and wave until he's out of sight.

2.   Once this week call him at work an hour before quitting time, to say, "I wanted you to know that I just crave your body!" or some other appropriate tender term. Then take your bubble bath shortly before he comes home.

3.   Thrill him at the front door in your costume. A frilly new nighty and heels will probably do the trick as a starter. Variety is the spice of sex.

4.   Be prepared mentally and physically for intercourse every night this week. Be sure your attitude matches your costume. Be the seducer, rather than the seducee.

5.   If you feel your situation involves a deeper problem, either psychological or physiological, seek professional help.

COMMENTS ON GENESIS
Elizabeth Cady Stanton and The Revising Committee

Elizabeth Cady Stanton (1815-1902), together with Lucretia Mott, organized the first women's rights convention at Seneca Falls, New York in 1848, and she drafted its famous Declaration of Sentiments. Beginning in 1868, with her longtime friend Susan B. Anthony as publisher, until 1872, Stanton edited *The Revolution,* a radical weekly paper devoted to issues related to the woman question. She was instrumental also in getting the woman suffrage amendment introduced into Congress for the first time in 1878. It was reintroduced at every succeeding Congress until the vote was attained in 1920. In addition to these projects and her other writing and lecturing, Stanton was the mother of seven children. She began work on *The Woman's Bible* just before her eightieth birthday in 1895, and Part I was published later that year.

"The Old Testament," she wrote, "makes woman a mere after-thought in creation; the author of evil; cursed in her maternity; a subject in marriage; and all female life, animal and human, unclean. The Church in all ages has taught these doctrines and acted on them, claiming divine authority therefor." *The Woman's Bible* challenged "the injustices to women contained in the Scriptures or their interpretations." To this end, a Revising Committee of eight women organized to comment on the Old and New Testament passages referring to women and on those passages where women were conspicuous by their absence. Some women agreed to serve but withdrew their names later fearing to associate themselves with such a radical project.

According to Stanton, when Part I of *The Woman's Bible* was published, some New York newspapers devoted an entire page to it, including pictures of members of the Revising Committee and their critics. And newspapers all over the country and abroad quoted and reviewed it. The clergy called it "the work of women, and the devil." Several editions were published and an expanded Revising Committee worked on Part II, published in 1898.

The comments on Genesis below were written by Stanton; Ellen Battelle Dietrick, a like-minded Bostonian who had herself published articles on dress reform and woman suffrage; and Lillie Devereux Blake, author of a feminist novel and short stories, and a leader in the woman suffrage movement.

> *Genesis i: 26, 27, 28.*
> 26 ¶ And God said, Let us make man in our image, after our likeness: and let them have dominion over the fish of the sea, and over the fowl of the air, and over the cattle, and over all the earth, and over every creeping thing that creepeth upon the earth.
> 27 So God created·man in his *own* image, in the image of God created he him; male and female created he them.

COMMENTS ON GENESIS   From *The Woman's Bible, Part I,* New York: European Publishing Company, 1895, 14–19.

28 And God blessed them, and God said unto them, Be fruitful, and multiply, and replenish the earth, and subdue it; and have dominion over the fish of the sea, and over the fowl of the air, and over every living thing that moveth upon the earth.

Here is the sacred historian's first account of the advent of woman; a simultaneous creation of both sexes, in the image of God. It is evident from the language that there was consultation in the Godhead, and that the masculine and feminine elements were equally represented. Scott in his commentaries says, "this consultation of the Gods is the origin of the doctrine of the trinity." But instead of three male personages, as generally represented, a Heavenly Father, Mother, and Son would seem more rational.

The first step in the elevation of woman to her true position, as an equal factor in human progress, is the cultivation of the religious sentiment in regard to her dignity and equality, the recognition by the rising generation of an ideal Heavenly Mother, to whom their prayers should be addressed, as well as to a Father.

If language has any meaning, we have in these texts a plain declaration of the existence of the feminine element in the Godhead, equal in power and glory with the masculine. The Heavenly Mother and Father! "God created man in his *own image, male and female.*" Thus Scripture, as well as science and philosophy, declares the eternity and equality of sex—the philosophical fact, without which there could have been no perpetuation of creation, no growth or development in the animal, vegetable, or mineral kingdoms, no awakening nor progressing in the world of thought. The masculine and feminine elements, exactly equal and balancing each other, are as essential to the maintenance of the equilibrium of the universe as positive and negative electricity, the centripetal and centrifugal forces, the laws of attraction which bind together all we know of this planet whereon we dwell and of the system in which we revolve.

In the great work of creation the crowning glory was realized, when man and woman were evolved on the sixth day, the masculine and feminine forces in the image of God, that must have existed eternally, in all forms of matter and mind. All the persons in the Godhead are represented in the Elohim the divine plurality taking counsel in regard to this last and highest form of life. Who were the members of this high council, and were they a duality or a trinity? Verse 27 declares the image of God male and female. How then is it possible to make woman an afterthought? We find in verses 5-16 the pronoun "he" used. Should it not in harmony with verse 26 be "they," a dual pronoun? We may attribute this to the same cause as the use of "his" in verse II instead of "it." The fruit tree yielding fruit after "his" kind instead of after "its" kind. The paucity of a language may give rise to many misunderstandings.

The above texts plainly show the simultaneous creation of man and woman, and their equal importance in the development of the race. All those theories based on the assumption that man was prior in the creation, have no foundation in Scripture.

As to woman's subjection, on which both the canon and the civil law delight to dwell, it is important to note that equal dominion is given to woman over every living thing, but not one word is said giving man dominion over woman.

Here is the first title deed to this green earth giving alike to the sons and daughters of God. No lesson of woman's subjection can be fairly drawn from the first chapter of the Old Testament.   E. C. S.

The most important thing for a woman to note, in reading Genesis, is that that portion which is now divided into "the first three chapters" (there was no such division until about five centuries ago), contains two entirely separate, and very contradictory, stories of creation, written by two different, but equally anonymous, authors. No Christian theologian of to-day, with any pretensions to scholarship, claims that Genesis was written by Moses. As was long ago pointed out, the Bible itself declares that all the books the Jews originally possessed were burned in the destruction of Jerusalem, about 588 B. C., at the time the people were taken to Babylonia as slaves to the Assyrians, (see II Esdras, ch. xiv, v. 21, Apocrypha). Not until about 247 B. C. (some theologians say 226 and others 169 B. C.) is there any record of a collection of literature in the re-built Jerusalem, and, then, the anonymous writer of II Maccabees briefly mentions that some Nehemiah "gathered together the acts of the kings and the prophets and those of David" when "founding a library" for use in Jerusalem. But the earliest mention anywhere in the Bible of a book that might have corresponded to Genesis is made by an apocryphal writer, who says that *Ezra* wrote "all that hath been done in the world since the beginning," after the Jews returned from Babylon, under his leadership, about 450 B. C. (see II Esdras, ch. xiv, v. 22, of the Apocrypha).

When it is remembered that the Jewish books were written on rolls of leather, without much attention to vowel points and with no division into verses or chapters, by uncritical copyists, who altered passages greatly, and did not always even pretend to understand what they were copying, then the reader of Genesis begins to put herself in position to understand how it can be contradictory. Great as were the liberties which the Jews took with Genesis, those of the English translators, however, greatly surpassed them.

The first chapter of Genesis, for instance, in Hebrew, tells us, in verses one and two, "As to origin, created the gods (Elohim) these skies (or air or clouds) and this earth. . . And a wind moved upon the face of the waters." Here we have the opening of a polytheistic fable of creation, but, so strongly convinced were the English translators that the ancient Hebrews must have been originally monotheistic that they rendered the above, as follows: "In the beginning God created the heaven and the earth. . . . And the spirit of God (!) moved upon the face of the waters."

It is now generally conceded that some one (nobody pretends to know who) at some time (nobody pretends to know exactly when), copied two creation myths on the same leather roll, one immediately following the other. About one hundred years ago, it was discovered by Dr. Astruc, of France, that from Genesis ch. i, v. I to Genesis ch. ii, v. 4, is given one complete account of creation, by an author who always used the term "the gods" (*Elohim*), in speaking of the fashioning of the universe, mentioning it altogether thirty-four times, while, in Genesis ch. ii, v. 4, to the end of chapter iii, we have a totally different narrative, by an author of unmistakably different style, who uses the term "Iahveh of the gods" twenty times, but "Elohim" only three times. The first author, evidently, attributes creation to a council of gods, acting in concert, and seems never to have heard of Iahveh. The second attributes creation to Iahveh, a tribal god of ancient Israel, but represents Iahveh as one of two or more gods, conferring with them (in Genesis ch. xiii, v. 22) as to the danger of man's acquiring immortality.

Modern theologians have, for convenience sake, entitled these two fables, respectively, the Elohistic and the Iahoistic stories. They differ, not only in the point I have mentioned above, but in the order of the "creative acts;" in regard to the mutual attitude of man and woman, and in regard to human freedom from prohibitions imposed by deity. In order to exhibit their striking contradictions, I will place them in parallel columns:

ELOHISTIC.

Order of Creation:
First—Water.
Second—Land.
Third—Vegetation.
Fourth—Animals.
Fifth—Mankind; male and female.

In this story male and female man are created simultaneously, both alike, in the image of the gods, *after* all animals have been called into existence.

Here, joint dominion over the earth is given to woman and man, without limit or prohibition.

Everything, without exception, is pronounced "very good."

Man and woman are told that "every plant bearing seed upon the face of the earth and *every tree*. . . . "To you it shall be for meat." They are thus given perfect freedom.

Man and woman are given special dominion over all the animals—"every creeping thing that creepeth upon the earth."

IAHOISTIC.

Order of Creation:
First—Land.
Second—Water.
Third—Male Man, only.
Fourth—Vegetation.
Fifth—Animals.
Sixth—Woman.

In this story male man is sculptured out of clay, *before* any animals are created, and *before* female man has been constructed.

Here, woman is punished with subjection to man for breaking a prohibitory law.

There is a tree of evil, whose fruit, is said by Iahveh to cause sudden death, but which does not do so, as Adam lived 930 years after eating it.

Man is told there is *one tree* of which he must not eat, "for in the day thou eatest thereof, thou shalt surely die."

An animal, a "creeping thing," is given dominion over man and woman, and proves himself more truthful than Iahveh Elohim. (Compare Genesis chapter ii, verse 17, with chapter iii, verses 4 and 22.)

Now as it is manifest that both of these stories cannot be true; intelligent women, who feel bound to give the preference to either, may decide according to their own judgment of which is more worthy of an intelligent woman's acceptance. Paul's rule is a good one in this dilemma, "Prove all things: hold fast to that which is good." My own opinion is that the second story was manipulated by some Jew, in an endeavor to give "heavenly authority" for requiring a woman to obey the man she married. In a work which I am now

completing, I give some facts concerning ancient Israelitish history, which will
be of peculiar interest to those who wish to understand the origin of woman's
subjection.   E. B. D.

Many orientalists and students of theology have maintained that the consultation of the Gods here described is proof that the Hebrews were in early
days polytheists—Scott's supposition that this is the origin of the Trinity has
no foundation in fact, as the beginning of that conception is to be found in the
earliest of all known religious nature worship. The acknowledgment of the
dual principal, masculine and feminine, is much more probably the explanation of the expressions here used.

In the detailed description of creation we find a gradually ascending series.
Creeping things, "great sea monsters," (chap. I, v. 21, literal translation).
"Every bird of wing," cattle and living things of the earth, the fish of the sea
and the "birds of the heavens," then man, and last and crowning glory of the
whole, woman.

It cannot be maintained that woman was inferior to man even if, as asserted
in chapter ii, she was created after him without at once admitting that man is
inferior to the creeping things, because created after them.   L. D. B.

YOU ARE WHAT YOU SAY
Robin Lakoff

Language is a potent force shaping attitudes toward women, including the beliefs and
feelings of women toward themselves. In the following essay Robin Lakoff examines
how the terms used to refer to women—"women of all ages are 'girls' "—and the kinds
of "women's language" they are taught to speak, both reflect and contribute to
women's devaluation and powerlessness in contemporary society.

The essay appeared in Ms., the first national magazine owned and managed by
women. Lakoff is a professor of linguistics at the University of California, and author of
Language and Woman's Place (1975).

"Women's language" is that pleasant (dainty?), euphemistic, never-aggressive
way of talking we learned as little girls. Cultural bias was built into the
language we were allowed to speak, the subjects we were allowed to speak
about, and the ways we were spoken of. Having learned our linguistic lesson
well, we go out in the world, only to discover that we are communicative
cripples—damned if we do, and damned if we don't.

If we refuse to talk "like a lady," we are ridiculed and criticized for being
unfeminine. ("She thinks like a man" is, at best, a left-handed compliment.) If
we do learn all the fuzzy-headed, unassertive language of our sex, we are

YOU ARE WHAT YOU SAY   From Ms., July 1974, 65–67. Reprinted by permission.

ridiculed for being unable to think clearly, unable to take part in a serious discussion, and therefore unfit to hold a position of power.

It doesn't take much of this for a woman to begin feeling she deserves such treatment because of inadequacies in her own intelligence and education.

"Women's language" shows up in all levels of English. For example, women are encouraged and allowed to make far more precise discriminations in naming colors than men do. Words like *mauve, beige, ecru, aquamarine, lavender,* and so on, are unremarkable in a woman's active vocabulary, but largely absent from that of most men. I know of no evidence suggesting that women actually *see* a wider range of colors than men do. It is simply that fine discriminations of this sort are relevant to women's vocabularies, but not to men's; to men, who control most of the interesting affairs of the world, such distinctions are trivial—irrelevant.

In the area of syntax, we find similar gender-related peculiarities of speech. There is one construction, in particular, that women use conversationally far more than men: the tag-question. A tag is midway between an outright statement and a yes-no question; it is less assertive than the former, but more confident than the latter.

A *flat statement* indicates confidence in the speaker's knowledge and is fairly certain to be believed; a *question* indicates a lack of knowledge on some point and implies that the gap in the speaker's knowledge can and will be remedied by an answer. For example, if, at a Little League game, I have had my glasses off, I can legitimately ask someone else: "Was the player out at third?" A *tag question,* being intermediate between statement and question, is used when the speaker is stating a claim, but lacks full confidence in the truth of that claim. So if I say, "Is Joan here?" I will probably not be surprised if my respondent answers "no"; but if I say, "Joan is here, isn't she?" instead, chances are I am already biased in favor of a positive answer, wanting only confirmation. I still want a response, but I have enough knowledge (or think I have) to predict that response. A tag question, then, might be thought of as a statement that doesn't demand to be believed by anyone but the speaker, a way of giving leeway, of not forcing the addressee to go along with the views of the speaker.

Another common use of the tag-question is in small talk when the speaker is trying to elicit conversation: "Sure is hot here, isn't it?"

But in discussing personal feelings or opinions, only the speaker normally has any way of knowing the correct answer. Sentences such as "I have a headache, don't I?" are clearly ridiculous. But there are other examples where it is the speaker's opinions, rather than perceptions, for which corroboration is sought, as in "The situation in Southeast Asia is terrible, isn't it?"

While there are, of course, other possible interpretations of a sentence like this, one possibility is that the speaker has a particular answer in mind—"yes" or "no"—but is reluctant to state it baldly. This sort of tag question is much more apt to be used by women than by men in conversation. Why is this the case?

The tag question allows a speaker to avoid commitment, and thereby avoid conflict with the addressee. The problem is that, by so doing, speakers may also give the impression of not really being sure of themselves, or looking to the addressee for confirmation of their views. This uncertainty is reinforced in more subliminal ways, too. There is a peculiar sentence intonation-pattern, used almost exclusively by women, as far as I know, which changes a declarative answer into a question. The effect of using the rising inflection typical of a yes-no question is to imply that the speaker is seeking confirmation, even though the speaker is clearly the only one who has the requisite information, which is why the question was put to her in the first place:

(Q) When will dinner be ready?

(A) Oh . . . around six o'clock . . . ?

It is as though the second speaker were saying, "Six o'clock—if that's okay with you, if you agree." The person being addressed is put in the position of having to provide confirmation. One likely consequence of this sort of speech-pattern in a woman is that, often unbeknownst to herself, the speaker builds a reputation of tentativeness, and others will refrain from taking her seriously or trusting her with any real responsibilities, since she "can't make up her mind," and "isn't sure of herself."

Such idiosyncrasies may explain why women's language sounds much more "polite" than men's. It is polite to leave a decision open, not impose your mind, or views, or claims, on anyone else. So a tag-question is a kind of polite statement, in that it does not force agreement or belief on the addressee. In the same way a request is a polite command, in that it does not force obedience on the addressee, but rather suggests something be done as a favor to the speaker. A clearly stated order implies a threat of certain consequences if it is not followed, and—even more impolite—implies that the speaker is in a superior position and able to enforce the order. By couching wishes in the form of a request, on the other hand, a speaker implies that if the request is not carried out, only the speaker will suffer; noncompliance cannot harm the addressee. So the decision is really left up to addressee. The distinction becomes clear in these examples:

Close the door.

Please close the door.

Will you close the door?

Will you please close the door?

Won't you close the door?

In the same ways as words and speech patterns used *by* women undermine her image, those used *to describe* women make matters even worse. Often a word may be used of both men and women (and perhaps of things as well); but when it is applied to women, it assumes a special meaning that, by implication rather than outright assertion, is derogatory to women as a group.

The use of euphemisms has this effect. A euphemism is a substitute for a word that has acquired a bad connotation by association with something unpleasant or embarrassing. But almost as soon as the new word comes into common usage, it takes on the same old bad connotations, since feelings about the things or people referred to are not altered by a change of name; thus new euphemisms must be constantly found.

There is one euphemism for *woman* still very much alive. The word, of course is *lady*. *Lady* has a masculine counterpart, namely *gentleman*, occasionally shortened to *gent*. But for some reason *lady* is very much commoner than *gent(leman)*.

The decision to use *lady* rather than *woman*, or vice versa, may considerably alter the sense of a sentence, as the following examples show:

(a) A woman (lady) I know is a dean at Berkeley.

(b) A woman (lady) I know makes amazing things out of shoelaces and old boxes.

The use of *lady* in (a) imparts a frivolous, or nonserious, tone to the sentence: the matter under discussion is not one of great moment. Similarly, in (b), using *lady* here would suggest that the speaker considered the "amazing things" not to be serious art, but merely a hobby or an aberration. If *woman* is used, she might be a serious sculptor. To say *lady doctor* is very condescending, since no one ever says *gentleman doctor* or even *man doctor*. For example, mention in the San Francisco *Chronicle* of January 31, 1972, of Madalyn Murray O'Hair as the *lady atheist* reduces her position to that of scatter-brained eccentric. Even *woman atheist* is scarcely defensible: sex is irrelevant to her philosophical position.

Many women argue that, on the other hand, *lady* carries with it overtones recalling the age of chivalry: conferring exalted stature on the person so referred to. This makes the term seem polite at first, but we must also remember that these implications are perilous: they suggest that a "lady" is helpless, and cannot do things by herself.

Lady can also be used to infer frivolousness, as in titles of organizations. Those that have a serious purpose (not merely that of enabling "the ladies" to spend time with one another) cannot use the word *lady* in their titles, but less serious ones may. Compare the *Ladies' Auxiliary* of a men's group, or the *Thursday Evening Ladies' Browning and Garden Society* with *Ladies' Liberation* or *Ladies' Strike for Peace*.

What is curious about this split is that *lady* is in origin a euphemism—a substitute that puts a better face on something people find uncomfortable—for *woman*. What kind of euphemism is it that subtly denigrates the people to whom it refers? Perhaps *lady* functions as a euphemism for *woman* because it does not contain the sexual implications present in *woman:* it is not "embarrassing" in that way. If this is so, we may expect that, in the future, *lady* will replace woman as the primary word for the human female, since *woman* will have become too blatantly sexual. That this distinction is already made in some contexts at least is shown in the following examples, where you can try replacing *woman* with *lady*:

(a) She's only twelve, but she's already a woman.

(b) After ten years in jail, Harry wanted to find a woman.

(c) She's my woman, see, so don't mess around with her.

Another common substitute for *woman* is *girl*. One seldom hears a man past the age of adolescence referred to as a boy, save in expressions like "going out with the boys," which are meant to suggest an air of adolescent frivolity and irresponsibility. But women of all ages are "girls": one can have a man—not a boy—Friday, but only a girl—never a woman or even a lady—Friday; women have girlfriends, but men do not—in a nonsexual sense—have boyfriends. It may be that this use of *girl* is euphemistic in the same way the use of *lady* is: in stressing the idea of immaturity, it removes the sexual connotations lurking in *woman*. *Girl* brings to mind irresponsibility: you don't send a girl to do a woman's errand (or even, for that matter, a boy's errand). She is a person who is both too immature and too far from real life to be entrusted with responsibilities or with decisions of any serious or important nature.

Now let's take a pair of words which, in terms of the possible relationships in an earlier society, were simple male-female equivalents, analogous to *bull: cow*. Suppose we find that, for independent reasons, society has changed in such a way that the original meanings now are irrelevant. Yet the words have not been discarded, but have acquired new meanings, metaphorically related to their original senses. But suppose these new metaphorical uses are no longer parallel to each other. By seeing where the parallelism breaks down, we discover something about the different roles played by men and women in this culture. One good example of such a divergence through time is found in the pair, *master: mistress*. Once used with reference to one's power over servants, these words have become unusable today in their original master-servant sense as the relationship has become less prevalent in our society. But the words are still common.

Unless used with reference to animals, *master* now generally refers to a man who has acquired consummate ability in some field, normally nonsexual. But its feminine counterpart cannot be used this way. It is practically restricted to its sexual sense of "paramour." We start out with two terms, both roughly paraphrasable as "one who has power over another." But the masculine form, once one person is no longer able to have absolute power over another, becomes usable metaphorically in the sense of "having power over *something*." *Master* requires as its object only the name of some activity, something inanimate and abstract. But *mistress* requires a masculine noun in the possessive to precede it. One cannot say: "Rhonda is a mistress." One must be *someone's* mistress. A man is defined by what he does, a woman by her sexuality, that is, in terms of one particular aspect of her relationship to men. It is one thing to be an *old master* like Hans Holbein, and another to be an *old mistress*.

The same is true of the words *spinster* and *bachelor*—gender words for "one who is not married." The resemblance ends with the definition. While *bachelor* is a neuter term, often used as a compliment, *spinster* normally is used pejoratively, with connotations of prissiness, fussiness, and so on. To be a bachelor implies that one has the choice of marrying or not, and this is what makes the idea of a bachelor existence attractive, in the popular literature. He has been pursued and has successfully eluded his pursuers. But a spinster is one who has not been pursued, or at least not seriously. She is old, unwanted goods. The metaphorical connotations of *bachelor* generally suggest sexual freedom; of *spinster*, puritanism or celibacy.

These examples could be multiplied. It is generally considered a *faux pas*, in society, to congratulate a woman on her engagement, while it is correct to congratulate her fiancé. Why is this? The reason seems to be that it is impolite to remind people of things that may be uncomfortable to them. To congratulate a woman on her engagement is really to say, "Thank goodness! You had a close call!" For the man, on the other hand, there was no such danger. His choosing to marry is viewed as a good thing, but not something essential.

The linguistic double standard holds throughout the life of the relationship. After marriage, bachelor and spinster become man and wife, not man and woman. The woman whose husband dies remains "John's widow"; John, however, is never "Mary's widower."

Finally, why is it that salesclerks and others are so quick to call women customers "dear," "honey," and other terms of endearment they really have no business using? A male customer would never put up with it. But women, like children, are supposed to enjoy these endearments, rather than being offended by them.

In more ways than one, it's time to speak up.

A PURPOSE FOR MODERN WOMAN

Adlai Stevenson

Adlai Stevenson was the keeper of the flame of New Deal liberalism during the Eisenhower years. A former governor of Illinois, he was the Democratic presidential nominee in both 1952 and 1956. And he was still the first choice of the party's most liberal wing, that associated with former first lady Eleanor Roosevelt, in 1960 when the Democrats turned instead to John Kennedy. Stevenson served as U.S. Ambassador to the United Nations in the Kennedy administration. The speech reprinted here was given by the leading liberal of the day, speaking at Smith, one of the leading women's colleges, on what young women should do with their education—and with their lives. Stevenson's essential conservatism on women's issues is unmistakable. And so is the complete absence of feminist ideas in the political debates of the 1950s.

One can measure the impact of the contemporary women's movement by comparing this speech with another commencement address, also given at Smith, that of Adrienne Rich, which follows Stevenson's speech here.

I think there is much you can do about our crisis in the humble role of housewife.

The peoples of the West are still struggling with the problems of a free society and just now are in dire trouble. For to create a free society is at all times a precarious and audacious experiment. Its bedrock is the concept of man as an end in himself. But violent pressures are constantly battering away at this concept, reducing man once again to subordinate status, limiting his range of choice, abrogating his responsibility and returning him to his primitive status of anonymity in the social group. I think you can be more helpful in identifying, isolating and combatting these pressures, this virus, than you perhaps realize.

Let me put it this way: individualism has promoted technological advance, technology promoted increased specialization, and specialization promoted an ever closer economic interdependence between specialties.

As the old order disintegrated into this confederation of narrow specialties, each pulling in the direction of its particular interest, the individual person tended to become absorbed literally by his particular function in society.

A PURPOSE FOR MODERN WOMAN   From *Woman's Home Companion*, September 1955, 29–31. Reprinted by permission of Adalai Stevenson III.

Having sacrificed wholeness of mind and breadth of outlook to the demands of their specialties, individuals no longer responded to social stimuli as total human beings; rather they reacted in partial ways as members of an economic class or industry or profession whose concern was with some limited self-interest.

Thus this typical Western man, or typical Western husband, operates well in the realm of means, as the Romans did before him. But outside his specialty, in the realm of ends, he is apt to operate poorly or not at all. And this neglect of the cultivation of more mature values can only mean that his life, and the life of the society he determines, will lack valid purpose, however busy and even profitable it may be.

And here's where you come in: to restore valid, meaningful purpose to life in your home; to beware of instinctive group reaction to the forces which play upon you and yours, to watch for and arrest the constant gravitational pulls to which we are all exposed—your workaday husband especially—in our special-ized, fragmented society, that tend to widen the breach between reason and emotion, between means and ends.

And let me also remind you that you will live, most of you, in an environ-ment in which "facts," the data of the senses, are glorified, and values—judgments—are assigned inferior status as mere "matters of opinion." It is an environment in which art is often regarded as an adornment of civilization rather than a vital element of it, while philosophy is not only neglected but deemed faintly disreputable because "it never gets you anywhere." Even reli-gion, you will find, commands a lot of earnest allegiance that is more verbal than real, more formal than felt.

You may be hitched to one of these creatures we call "Western man" and I think part of your job is to keep him Western, to keep him truly purposeful, to keep him whole. In short—while I have had very little experience as a wife or mother—I think one of the biggest jobs for many of you will be to frustrate the crushing and corrupting effects of specialization, to integrate means and ends, to develop that balanced tension of mind and spirit which can be properly called "integrity."

This assignment for you, as wives and mothers, has great advantages. In the first place, it is home work—you can do it in the living-room with a baby in your lap or in the kitchen with a can opener in your hand. If you're really clever, maybe you can even practice your saving arts on that unsuspecting man while he's watching television!

And, secondly, it is important work worthy of you, whoever you are, or your education, whatever it is, because we will defeat totalitarian, authoritarian ideas only by better ideas; we will frustrate the evils of vocational specializa-tion only by the virtues of intellectual generalization. Since Western rational-ism and Eastern spiritualism met in Athens and that mighty creative fire broke out, collectivism in various forms has collided with individualism time and again. This twentieth-century collision, this "crisis" we are forever talking about, will be won at last not on the battlefield but in the head and heart.

So you see, I have some rather large notions about you and what you have to do to rescue us wretched slaves of specialization and group thinking from further shrinkage and contraction of mind and spirit. But you will have to be alert or you may get caught yourself—even in the kitchen or the nursery—by the steady pressures with which you will be surrounded.

And now that I have dared to suggest what you should do about your husbands and friends, I am, recklessly, going to even make some suggestions about your children as well.

In the last 50 years, so much of our thinking has been in terms of institutional reform—reform of the economic system, social security, the use and misuse of government, international co-operation, et cetera. All this thinking has been necessary and salutary but somewhere along the line, the men and women whose personalities and potentialities will largely determine the spirit of such institutions have been lost to sight. Worse than that, we have even evolved theories that the paramount aim of education and character formation is to produce citizens who are "well adjusted" to their institutional environment, citizens who can fit painlessly into the social pattern.

While I am not in favor of maladjustment, I view this cultivation of neutrality, this breeding of mental neuters, this hostility to eccentricity and controversy, with grave misgiving. One looks back with dismay at the possibility of a Shakespeare perfectly adjusted to bourgeois life in Stratford, a Wesley contentedly administering a county parish, George Washington going to London to receive a barony from George III, or Abraham Lincoln prospering in Springfield with nary a concern for the preservation of the crumbling union.

In this decisive century it seems to me that we need not just "well-adjusted," "well-balanced" personalities, not just better groupers and conformers (to casually coin a couple of words) but more idiosyncratic, unpredictable characters (that rugged frontier word "ornery" occurs to me); people who take open eyes and open minds out with them into the society which they will share and help to transform. In short, we need all kinds of people, not just one standard variety.

But before any of you gallant girls swear any mighty oaths about fighting the shriveling corruptions and conformations of mind and spirit, before you adopt any rebellious resolutions for the future, make no mistake about it: it is much easier to get yourself and yours adjusted and to accept the conditioning which so many social pressures will bring to bear upon you. After all, tribal conformity and archaic dictatorship could not have lasted so long if they did not accord comfortably with basic human needs and desires. The modern dictators are reviving a very ancient and encrusted way of life. Hitler discovered this. The Fascists knew it. The Communists are busy brainwashing, all over Asia. And what they are washing out is precisely independence of judgment and the moral courage with which to back such judgments. And there are, alas, some leaders in our country who certainly have a brainwashing glint in their eye when they meet with an unfamiliar idea.

Women, especially educated women, have a unique opportunity to influence us, man and boy, and to play a direct part in the unfolding drama of our free society. But I am told that nowadays the young wife or mother is short of time for such subtle arts, that things are not what they used to be; that once immersed in the very pressing and particular problems of domesticity, many women feel frustrated and far apart from the great issues and stirring debates for which their education has given them understanding and relish. Once they read Baudelaire. Now it is the Consumers' Guide. Once they wrote poetry. Now it's the laundry list. Once they discussed art and philosophy until late in the night. Now they are so tired they fall asleep as soon as the dishes are finished. There is, often, a sense of contraction, of closing horizons and lost opportunities. They had hoped to play their part in the crisis of the age. But what they do is wash the diapers. (Or do they any longer?)

Now I hope I have not painted too depressing a view of your future, for the fact is that Western marriage and motherhood are yet another instance of the emergence of individual freedom in our Western society. Their basis is the recognition in women as well as men of the primacy of personality and individuality. I have just returned from sub-Sahara Africa where the illiteracy of the African mother is a formidable obstacle to the education and advancement of her child and where polygamy and female labor are still the dominant system.

The point is that whether we talk of Africa, Islam or Asia, women "never had it so good" as you do. And in spite of the difficulties of domesticity, you have a way to participate actively in the crisis in addition to keeping yourself and those about you straight on the difference between means and ends, mind and spirit, reason and emotion—not to mention keeping your man straight on the differences between Botticelli and Chianti.

In brief, if one of the chief needs in these restless times is for a new quality of mind and heart, who is nearer to the care of this need, the cultivation of this quality, than parents, especially mothers, who educate and form the new generation?

So, add to all of your concerns for Western man, your very special responsibility for Western children. In a family based upon mutual respect, tolerance and understanding affection, the new generation of children—the citizens of tomorrow—stand their best chance of growing up to recognize the fundamental principle of free society—the uniqueness and value and wholeness of each individual human being. For this recognition requires discipline and training. The first instinct of all our untutored egos is to smash and grab, to treat the boy next door as a means, not an end, when you pinch his air rifle, or deny the uniqueness of your small sister's personality when you punch her in the stomach and snatch her lollipop.

Perhaps this is merely to say that the basis of any tolerable society—from the small society of the family up to the great society of the state—depends upon its members learning to love. By that I do not mean sentimentality or possessive emotion. I mean the steady recognition of others' uniqueness and a sustained intention to seek their good. In this, freedom and charity go hand in hand, and they both have to be learned. Where better than in the home? And by whom better than the parents, especially the mother?

In short, far from the vocation of marriage and motherhood leading you away from the great issues of our day, it brings you back to their very center and places upon you an infinitely deeper and more intimate responsibility than that borne by the majority of those who hit the headlines and make the news and live in such a turmoil of great issues that they end by being totally unable to distinguish which issues are really great.

In modern America the home is not the boundary of a woman's life. There are outside activities aplenty. But even more important is the fact, surely, that what you have learned and can learn will fit you for the primary task of making homes and whole human beings in whom the rational values of freedom, tolerance, charity and free inquiry can take root.

I hope you'll not be content to wring your hands, feed your family and just echo all the group, the tribal ritual refrains. I hope you'll keep everlastingly at the job of seeing life steady and seeing it whole. And you can help others—husbands, children, friends—to do so too. You may, indeed you must, help to integrate a world that has been falling into bloody pieces. History's pendulum has swung dangerously far away from the individual and you may, indeed you must, help to restore it to the vital center of its arc.

Long ago at the origins of our way of life it was written of a valiant woman in the Book of Proverbs: "Strength and beauty are her clothing; and she shall laugh in the latter day. She hath opened her mouth to wisdom and the law of clemency is on her tongue; she hath looked well to the paths of her house and hath not eaten her bread idle. Her children rose up and called her blessed; her husband, and he praised her."

I could wish you no better vocation than that. I could wish a free society no better hope for the future. And I could wish you no greater riches and rewards.

COMMENCEMENT ADDRESS AT SMITH COLLEGE, 1979
Adrienne Rich

On the surface the graduates of Smith College to whom Rich delivered this commencement address were very much like those to whom Stevenson spoke a quarter of a century earlier. The "Smithies" were, after all, still women of privilege, even though all were not white and affluent. And Rich noted that all had received an elite education that would expose them to the temptation to join male-centered institutions as "tokens." The graduates could be co-opted, that is, into thinking of themselves as insiders.

But, Rich argued, that, in actuality, they, like all women, were outsiders because all lived in a world where men defined and controlled the most basic institutions, from language to the family, from the economy to the sciences. Rich called on Smith women to use their privileged educations to help all women redefine this man's world. In doing so, she sketched out a much different vision for the graduates of Smith than that envisioned by Stevenson.

Rich is one of America's most distinguished and influential poets as well as an essayist of considerable renown. Her books include: *Diving Into the Wreck* (1973), *The Dream Of A Common Language* (1978), and *Of Woman Born: Motherhood As Experience and Institution* (1976).

I have been very much moved that you, the class of 1979, chose me for your commencement speaker. It is important to me to be here, in part because Smith is one of the original colleges for women, but also because she has chosen to continue identifying herself as a women's college. We are at a point in history where this fact has enormous potential, even if that potential is as yet unrealized. The possibilities for the future education of women that haunt these buildings and grounds are enormous, when we think of what an independent women's college might be: a college dedicated both to teaching women what women need to know, and, by the same token, to changing the landscape of knowledge itself. The germ of those possibilities lies symbolically in The Sophia Smith Collection, an archive much in need of expansion and increase, but which by its very existence makes the statement that women's lives and work are valued here, and that our foresisters, buried and diminished in male-centered scholarship, are a living presence, necessary and precious to us.

Suppose we were to ask ourselves, simply: What does a woman need to know, to become a self-conscious, self-defining human being? Doesn't she need a knowledge of her own history; of her much-politicized female body; of the creative genius of women of the past—the skills and crafts and techniques and visions possessed by women in other times and cultures, and how they have been rendered anonymous, censored, interrupted, devalued? Doesn't she, as one of that majority who are still denied equal rights as citizens, enslaved as sexual prey, unpaid or underpaid as workers, withheld from her own power—doesn't she need an analysis of her condition, a knowledge of the women thinkers of the past who have reflected on it, a knowledge too of women's world-wide individual rebellions and organized movements against economic and social injustice, and how these have been fragmented and silenced? Doesn't she need to know how seemingly natural states of being, like heterosexuality, like motherhood, have been enforced and institutionalized to deprive her of power? Without such education, women have lived and continued to live in ignorance of our collective context, vulnerable to the projections of men's fantasies about us as they appear in art, in literature, in the sciences, in the media, in the so-called humanistic studies. I suggest that not anatomy, but enforced ignorance, has been a crucial key to our powerlessness.

There is—and I say this with sorrow—there is no women's college today which is providing young women with the education they need for survival as whole persons in a world which denies women wholeness—that knowledge which, in the words of Coleridge, "returns again as power." The existence of Women's Studies courses offers at least some kind of lifeline: but even Women's Studies can amount simply to compensatory history; too often they fail to challenge the intellectual and political structures that must be challenged if women as a group are ever to come into collective, non-exclusionary freedom. The belief that established science and scholarship—which have so relentlessly excluded women from their making—are "objective" and "value free" and that feminist studies are "unscholarly," "biased," and "ideological" dies hard. Yet the fact is that all science, and all scholarship, and all art, are ideological; there is no neutrality in culture. And the ideology of the education you have just spent four years acquiring in a women's college, has been largely, if not entirely, the ideology of white male supremacy, a construct of male subjectivity. The silences, the empty spaces, the language itself, with its excision of the female, the methods of discourse, tell us as much as the content, once we learn to watch for what is left out, to listen for the unspoken, to study the patterns of established science and scholarship with an outsider's eye. One of the dangers of a privileged education for women is that we may lose the eye of the outsider, and come to believe that those patterns hold for humanity, for the universal, and that they include us.

And so I want to talk today about privilege, and about tokenism, and about power. Everything I can say to you on this subject comes hard-won, from the lips of a woman privileged by class and skin-color, a father's favorite daughter, educated at Radcliffe, then casually referred to as the Harvard "Annex." Much of the first four decades of my life was spent in a continuous tension between the world the Fathers taught me to see, and had rewarded me for seeing, and the flashes of insight that came through the eye of the outsider. Gradually those flashes of insight, which at times could seem like brushes with madness, began to demand that I struggle to connect them with each other, to insist that I take them seriously. It was only when I could finally affirm the outsider's eye as the source of a legitimate and coherent vision, that I began to be able to do the work I truly wanted to do, live the kind of life I truly wanted to live, instead of carrying out the assignments I had been given as a privileged woman and a token.

For women, all privilege is relative. Some of you were not born with class or skin-color privilege; but you all have the privilege of education, even if it is an education which has largely denied you knowledge of yourselves as women. You have, to begin with, the privilege of literacy; and it is well for us to remember that, in an age of increasing illiteracy, sixty per cent of the world's illiterates are women. Between 1960 and 1970, according to a UNESCO report, the number of illiterate men in the world rose by 8 million; while the number of illiterate women rose by 40 million. And the number of illiterate women is increasing. Beyond literacy, you have the privilege of training and tools which can allow you to go beyond the content of your education and re-educate yourselves—to debrief yourselves, we might call it, of the false messages of your education in this culture, the messages telling you that women have not really cared about power or learning or creative opportunities, because of a psychobiological need to serve men and produce children; that only a few atypical women have been exceptions to this rule; the messages telling you that woman's experience is neither normative, nor central, to human experience. You have the training and the tools to do independent research, to evaluate data, to criticize, and to express in language and visual forms what you discover. This is a privilege, yes; but only if you do not give up in exchange for it the deep knowledge of the unprivileged, the knowledge that, as a woman, you have historically been viewed and still are viewed as existing, not in your own right, but in the service of men. And only if you refuse to give up your capacity to think like a woman; even though in the graduate schools and professions to which many of you will be going, you will be praised and rewarded for "thinking like a man."

The word "power" is highly charged for women. It has been so long associated, for us, with the use of force, with rape, with the stockpiling of weapons, with the ruthless accrual of wealth and the hoarding of resources, with the power that acts only in its own interest, despising and exploiting the powerless—including women and children. The effects of this kind of power are all around us; even literally in the water we drink and the air we breathe, in the form of carcinogens and radioactive wastes. But for a long time now, feminists have been talking about redefining power; about that meaning of power which returns to the root: *posse, potere, pouvoir*—to be able, to have the potential, to possess and use one's energy of creation: *transforming power*. An early objection to feminism—in both the 19th and 20th centuries—was that it would make women behave like men—ruthlessly, exploitatively, oppressively. In fact, radical feminism looks to a transformation of human relationships and structures in which power, instead of a thing to be hoarded by a few, would be released to and from within the many, shared in the form of knowledge, expertise, decision-making, access to tools, as well as in the basic forms of food and shelter and health care and literacy. Feminists—and many non-feminists—are, and rightly so, still concerned with what power would mean in such a society, and with the relative differences in power among women as a group here and now. Which brings me to a third meaning of power where women are concerned: the false power which masculine society offers to a few women, on condition that they use it to maintain things as they are, and that they essentially "think like men." This is the meaning of female tokenism: that power withheld from the vast majority of women is offered to a few, so that it may appear that any truly qualified woman can gain access to leadership, recognition and reward; hence, that justice based on merit actually prevails. The token woman is encouraged to see herself as different from most other women; as exceptionally talented and deserving; and to separate herself from the wider female condition; and she is perceived by "ordinary" women as separate also: perhaps even as stronger than themselves.

Because you are, within the limits of all women's ultimate outsiderhood, a privileged group of women, it is extremely important for your future sanity that you understand the way tokenism functions. Its most immediate contradiction is that, while it seems to offer the individual token woman a means to realize her creativity, to influence the course of events, it also, by exacting of her certain kinds of behavior and style, acts to blur her outsider's eye, which could be her real source of power and vision. Losing her outsider's vision, she loses the insight which both binds her to other women and affirms her in herself. Tokenism essentially demands that the token deny her identification with women as a group, especially with women less privileged than she: if she is a lesbian, that she deny her relationships with individual women; that she perpetuate rules and structures and criteria and methodologies which have functioned to exclude women, that she renounce or leave undeveloped the critical perspective of her female consciousness. Women unlike herself—poor women, women of color, waitresses, secretaries, housewives in the supermarket, prostitutes, old women—become invisible to her; they may represent too acutely what she has escaped or wished to flee.

Jill Conway tells me that ever-increasing numbers of you are going on from Smith to medical and law schools. The news, on the face of it, is good: that, thanks to the feminist struggle of the past decade, more doors into these two powerful professions are open to women. I would like to believe that any profession would be better for having more women practicing it, and that any woman practicing law or medicine would use her knowledge and skill to work to transform the realm of health care and the interpretations of the law, to make them responsive to the needs of all those—women, people of color, children, the aged, the dispossessed—for whom they function today as repressive controls. I would like to believe this, but it will not happen *even* if fifty per cent of the members of these professions are women, unless those women refuse to be made into token insiders, unless they zealously preserve the outsider's view and the outsider's consciousness.

For no woman is really an insider in the institutions fathered by masculine consciousness. When we allow ourselves to believe we are, we lose touch with parts of ourselves defined as unacceptable by that consciousness; with the vital toughness and visionary strength of the angry grandmothers, the shamanesses, the fierce market-women of the Ibo, the marriage-resisting women silk-workers of pre-revolutionary China, the millions of widows, midwives and women healers tortured and burned as witches for three centuries in Europe, the Beguines of the 12th century, who formed independent women's orders outside the domination of the Church, the women of the Paris Commune who marched on Versailles, the uneducated housewives of the Women's Cooperative Guild in England who memorized poetry over the washtub and organized against their oppression as mothers, the women thinkers discredited as "strident," "shrill," "crazy," or "deviant," whose courage to be heretical, to speak their truths, we so badly need to draw upon in our own lives. I believe that every woman's soul is haunted by the spirits of earlier women who fought for their unmet needs and those of their children and their tribes and their peoples, who refused to accept the prescriptions of a male church and state, who took risks and resisted as women today—like Inez Garcia, Yvonne Wanrow, Joan Little, Cassandra Peten—are fighting their rapists and batterers. Those spirts dwell in us, trying to speak to us; but we can choose to be deaf; and tokenism, the myth of the "special" woman, the unmothered Athena sprung from her father's brow, can deafen us to their voices.

In this decade now ending, as more women are entering the professions (though still suffering sexual harassment in the workplace, though still, if they have children, carrying two full-time jobs, though still vastly outnumbered by men in upper-level and decision-making jobs), we need most profoundly to remember that early insight of the feminist movement as it evolved in the late sixties: *that no woman is liberated until we all are liberated.* The media flood us with messages to the contrary: telling us that we live in an era when "alternate life-styles" are freely accepted, when "marriage contracts" and "the new intimacy" are revolutionizing heterosexual relationships: that shared parenting and the "new fatherhood" will change the world. And we live in a society leeched upon by the "personal growth" and "human potential" industry, by the delusion that individual self-fulfillment can be found in thirteen weeks or a weekend, that the alienation and injustice experienced by women, by Black and Third World people, by the poor, in a world ruled by white males, in a society which fails to meet the most basic needs, and which is slowly poisoning itself, can be mitigated or solved by Transcendental Meditation. Perhaps the most succinct expression of this message I have seen is the appearance of a magazine for women called "SELF." The insistence of the feminist movement, that each woman's selfhood is precious, that the feminine ethic of self-denial and self-sacrifice must give way to a true woman-identification, which would affirm our connectedness with all women, is perverted into a commercially profitable and politically debilitating narcissism. It is important for each of you, toward whom many of these messages are especially directed, that you discriminate clearly between "liberated life-style" and feminist struggle, and that you make a conscious choice.

It's a cliché of Commencement speeches that the speaker ends with a peroration telling the new graduates that however badly past generations have behaved, their generation must save the world. I would rather say to you, women of the Class of 1979: try to be worthy of your foresisters, learn from your history, look for inspiration to your ancestresses. If this history has been poorly taught to you, if you do not know it, then use your educational privilege to learn it. Learn how some women of privilege have compromised the greater liberation of women, how others have risked their privileges to further it; learn how brilliant and successful women have failed to create a more just and caring society, precisely because they have tried to do so on terms that the powerful men around them would accept and tolerate. Learn to be worthy of the women of every class, culture, and historical age who did otherwise, who spoke boldly when women were jeered and physically harassed for speaking in public: who—like Anne Hutchinson, Mary Wollstonecraft, the Grimke sisters, Abbey Kelley, Ida B. Wells Barnett, Susan B. Anthony, Lillian Smith, Fannie Lou Hamer—broke taboos: who resisted slavery—their own and other people's. To become a token woman—whether you win the Nobel Prize or merely get tenure at the cost of denying your sisters—is to become something less than a man indeed, since men are loyal at least to their own world-view, their laws of brotherhood and male self-interest. I am not suggesting that you imitate male loyalties; with the philosopher Mary Daly, I believe that the bonding of women must be utterly different, and for an utterly different end: not the misering of resources and power, but the release, in each other, of the yet unexplored resources and transformative power of women, so long despised, confined, and wasted. Get all the knowledge and skill you can, in whatever professions you enter; but remember that most of your education must be self-education, in learning the things women need to know, and in calling up the voices we need to hear within ourselves.

I am going to end by reading a short poem of mine; it is called "Power":*

POWER

Living in the earth-deposits of our history

Today a backhoe divulged out of a crumbling flank of earth
one bottle   amber   perfect   a hundred-year-old
cure for fever   or melancholy   a tonic
for living on this earth   in the winters of this climate

Today I was reading about Marie Curie:
she must have known she suffered   from radiation sickness
her body bombarded for years   by the element
she had purified
It seems she denied to the end
the source of the cataracts on her eyes
the cracked and suppurating skin   of her finger-ends
till she could no longer hold   a test-tube or a pencil

She died   a famous woman   denying
her wounds
denying
her wounds   came   from the same source as her power

Adrienne Rich

THREE

Woman as Object

"TODAY'S STANDARD OF womanhood is contained in three words, health, youth, and daintiness." So ran a 1925 advertisement which went on to warn women that "the charm of feminine immaculacy is continually threatened by the results of fatigue and listlessness, a general letting down of physical tone." Happily, women could stave off this threat by regular douching with "Lysol." They would particularly prize, according to the ad copy, its "gentle, deodorant qualities," as well as its "soothing" and "lubricating" effects.

Messages of just this sort have long inundated women. You have only to turn on the radio or pick up a magazine to appreciate just how ubiquitous they are. Most follow the pattern illustrated in the "Lysol" ad. They hold up some image of female perfection (such as "daintiness"). They then insinuate that the reader (or listener or viewer) herself falls somewhat short of perfection. This failing not only jeopardizes her chances for happiness but also calls into question her femininity. Immediate steps to correct the situation are clearly required, steps which involve using whatever product or service the advertisement happens to be promoting.

Advertisers, of course, are hardly the only ones to traffic in the insecurities women feel about their appearance. Experts of all sorts, often male, usually self-appointed, have long made careers out of telling women how to lose (or gain) weight, how to dress for success (whether success means a promotion or a proposal), how—in a phrase—to please men.

The simple truth is that we live in a culture in which women are, to a very considerable extent, defined as physical objects rather than as persons. Men are not entirely immune to the same process, of course. But, men have traditionally had less at stake when it came to measuring up to cultural ideals. And the ideals themselves are more attainable. Little boys, for example, are urged to grow up to be "big and strong," a goal actually within the reach of most. Little girls, however, learn that they have to be pretty when they grow up. Most, in the nature of things, will turn out to be rather ordinary looking instead. In addition, boys are taught to think of their bodies primarily in terms of what they will enable them to do. Girls, in contrast, are taught to think of theirs in terms of how boys will regard them. The boy who is not handsome, as a result, is scarcely a tragic figure; the girl who is not beautiful, on the other hand, is.

Being beautiful means, as a practical matter, being able to attract men. And, it turns out, not only do individual tastes vary, but general notions of beauty also change. The charms our grandfathers most prized leave their grandsons cold. In today's society, for example, beauty is linked to slenderness. In earlier decades, as some of the documents included here will demonstrate, the ideal beauty was "plump." Her arms were well-rounded as were her other, less visible, charms. The fashions of the day emphasized the hips and buttocks, something the bustle took to a grotesque extreme.

So far are women from desiring to appear "plump" today that a 1983 survey, of some 33,000 readers of *Glamour,* found that most of those whose weight was "normal" for their height ("normal" here was defined according to standards worked out by Metropolitan Life Insurance Company in 1959) nonetheless thought of themselves as needing to lose weight. So, for that matter, did a substantial minority of those readers whose weights were below the 1959 Metropolitan standards for their height. One need look no farther for proof of the power of popular images to affect the way people regard themselves.

The slender woman born into a society which glorified plumpness, no less than the plump woman born into a world which worships slenderness, faced the injunction that she remake herself to conform to the dominant taste. And it is this underlying consistency which unifies the disparate documents collected here. Fashions in beauty changed, but the individual woman's obligation to "improve" upon nature remained constant. Throughout the whole of the century and a half these documents cover, that is, women were urged to think of themselves as a sort of sculpture. They were to chip away at their imperfections until they achieved the ideal.

Few can expect to attain perfection. And even those who come close to embodying the ideals of the day can expect only the most fleeting surcease from self-doubt. This is because perfection includes, as the "Lysol" ad reminded the women of 1925, a quality—youth—which necessarily disappears after a brief time. Women suffer, in philosopher Susan Sontag's phrase, from a "double standard of aging." Men do not have to be young to be thought attractive. Lines in their faces can connote character, not simply age; the gray at their temples can suggest the coming of wisdom; even the thinning of their hair can hint at intellectual depths.

Not so for women. Lines, gray hair, and all the other physical signs of youth's passing, simply mean—for women—that they are growing old. And age means the end of allure.

It does not, on the other hand, mean the end of sexuality. Although present-day cultural patterns identify sexiness with youthfulness, women's sexual drives—unlike men's—do not diminish with age.

This dissonance between culture and biology signifies how little say women have historically had in determining the sexual rules of the game. Instead they have had to play by male rules. And rule number one has been that women exist to satisfy male needs and desires. Hence a dominant motif in our culture's images of female sexuality has been subservience. Anthropologist Erving Goffman's classic study of how women and men are most commonly posed in magazine ads, for example, disclosed that women are commonly shown as leaning, or even hanging, on men while men are almost never portrayed as physically dependent on women.* The ads, in short, are reenforcements of the culture's basic message to women: You must learn to see yourselves as men see you. You must learn to regard yourselves as objects rather than as persons.

Goffman's work reminds us that images of women as sexual objects are by no means limited to the explicitly pornographic. There we find merely the most blatant examples. But we can also find this same objectification of women in television's fondness for "jiggle," in fashion magazines' fascination with sado-masochist themes, and in rock videos where women often figure merely as projections of male fantasies. If pornography in fact consists of the reduction of people to the status of objects, then we need to recognize this more subtle pornography of everyday life.

The documents collected in this chapter range from popular exercise routines of the 1840s and 1980s to suggestions for office workers on how to cultivate a winning smile. We have not attempted to catalog all the different ideals of female beauty and sexuality over the years, itself a major task. But we do hope we have illustrated that they are social creations, ones over which women have traditionally had very little control. Similarly, we have not tried to survey all of the sources of those images we do include. Instead we have included enough material to give one a context for making sense of the mind-numbingly vast number of images of female attractiveness and sexuality our culture provides.

---

* *Gender Advertisements*, New York: Harper & Row, 1979.

HEALTH AND BEAUTY

"The first and greatest sign of health in woman is beauty." So wrote William J. Cromie in 1914. Cromie was a physical education instructor at the University of Pennsylvania and author of an "Eight Minutes' Common-Sense Exercise For the Nervous Woman" plan which, he claimed, would prevent fat from accumulating "upon the neck, abdomen, and hips." A woman could thus preserve "the symmetrical contour" of those parts of her body. Fashions in exercise, like fashions in female beauty, have changed over the years as a comparison of the following two documents will demonstrate. But, similarities over time are just as striking. Primary among these is the equation of health and beauty for women.

Godey's Lady's Book, source of our first document, was the first major woman's magazine. Previously, as Godey's own name suggests, collections of fashionable dress patterns, recipes, homemaking tips, and decorous fiction—the staples of woman's magazines in the nineteenth century—had been published as books, suitable as Christmas or birthday presents. Godey's brought these elements together in magazine form and wrought a publishing revolution.

Family Circle, source of our second document, also pioneered a new type of magazine, one geared to the busy middle-class housewife (rather than the upper-class lady of leisure who had read Godey's) and published cheaply enough to be sold at supermarket checkout counters.

I have stated that the effect of exercise is, by frequent contraction of the fibres, to brace the muscles and render them stronger, and generally to give more strength to the organs.

Nothing evidently can be more suitable to the organization of woman. Her tissues are soft and flexible; exercise renders them more firm and resisting: her fibres are thin and weak; exercise increases their size and strength: they are moistened with oils and juices; exercise diminishes the superabundant humidity.

In regard to strength in general, it may be observed that, in the present state of society, we have less need of it than the people of ancient times. Muscular strength is a kind of superiority no longer in such favor, and the aim of gymnastics is consequently nothing more than to endow the body with all the strength, vigor, and activity, compatible with health, without injury to the development of the intellectual faculties.

Moreover, the education which is suited to the male, is not calculated to render the female amiable and useful in society.

The constitution of women, indeed, bears only moderate exercise. Their feeble arms cannot support severe and long-continued labor. It renders them

HEALTH AND BEAUTY   From Godey's Lady's Book, (August, 1848), pp. 111–12.

meagre, and deforms the organs, by compressing and destroying the cellular substance which contributes to the beauty of their outlines, and of their complexion. The graces accommodate themselves little to labor, perspiration, and sun-burning.

We must not, however, conclude from this, that females should be kept in a state of continual repose, or that the delicacy of their organization prevents their taking exercise.

It is a fact that labor, even the most excessive, is not so much to be feared as absolute idleness. The state of want which forces some women of the lowest class to perform labors that seem reserved for men, deprives them only of some attractions. Excessive indolence, on the contrary, destroys at once health, and that which women value more than health, though it never can subsist without it, namely, beauty.

The more robust state of health in females brought up in the country, is attributable to the exercise they enjoy. Their movements are active and firm; their appetite is good, and their complexion florid; they are alert and gay; they know neither pain nor lassitude, although they are in action without cessation under all kinds of weather. It is exercise which gives them vigor, health, and happiness—exercise to which they are so frequently subjected, even in infancy and youth.

We observe, also, that in a family where there are several sisters of similar constitution, the one who from circumstances has been accustomed to regular and daily exercise, almost always possesses more strength and vigor.

Mothers and teachers, therefore, instead of fearing that their children should fatigue themselves by exertion in active sports, should subject them early to it. They will thus give them more than merely life and instruction; they will confer on them health and strength.

We now proceed to give illustrations of these exercises, or *extension motions*. These three figures are intended to show one variety of these exercises.

One. The forearms are bent upon the arms upward and toward the body, having the elbows depressed, the shut hands touching on the little finger sides, and the knuckles upward, the latter being raised as high as the chin, and at the distance of about a foot before it.

Two. While the arms are thrown forcibly backward, the forearms are as much as possible bent upon the arms, and the palmar sides of the wrists are turned forward and outward.

These two motions are to be repeatedly and rather quickly performed.

A modification of the same movements is performed as a separate extension motion, but may be given in continuation, with the numbers following these as words of command.

Three. The arms are extended at full length in front, on a level with the shoulders, the palms of the hands in contact.

Four. Thus extended, and the palms retaining their vertical position, the arms are thrown forcibly backward, so that the backs of the hands may approach each other as nearly as possible.

We now come to what is termed *"Exercise with the Rod."* Here are three llustrations.

The rod for this purpose should be light, smooth, inflexible, and need not be more than three or four feet in length.

First Exercises. The rod is first grasped near the extremities by the two hands, the thumbs being inward.

Without changing the position of the hands on the rod, it is then brought to a vertical position: the right hand being uppermost holds it above the head, the left is against the lower part of the body.

By an opposite movement, the right is lowered and the left raised.

This change is executed repeatedly and quickly.

Second Exercise. From the first position of the rod, it is raised over the head; and, in doing so, the closer the hands are, the better will be the effect upon the shoulder.

It is afterwards carried behind the back, holding so firmly that no change takes place in the position of the hands.

This movement is then reversed, to bring it back over the head to the first position.

SECRETS TO WEIGHT LOSS AND VITALITY FROM THE GOLDEN DOOR—THE WORLD'S MOST EXPENSIVE BEAUTY SPA

Maxine Lewis

EXERCISE FOR VITALITY AND FIGURE-FIRMING

"If you want an exciting life, you need energy. Exercise has a measurable effect on body tone—on physical function and on the mind, as well. It both relaxes you and gives you more vitality."

So says Deborah Szekely Mazzanti, founder and director of the Golden Door and its lower-cost family-spa counterpart, Rancho La Puerta, just across the border in Tecate, Mexico. Deborah serves on both the President's Council on Physical Fitness and Sports, and the board of trustees of the Menninger Foundation. Knowing the importance of mind *and* body to our well-being, she believes in vigorous exercise—"going out and getting your heart pumping"—but also that periods of high activity (or hard work) should alternate with quiet tasks and relaxation.

THE 30/10 AND 10/30 PLANS. When and how you get your exercise is important. The Golden Door recommends two exercise plans:

For *early-day vitality* (for homemakers especially): 30 minutes of vigorous exercise in the morning to keep you energetic till afternoon; 10 minutes exercise in the late afternoon to revive you.

For *tension relief* (for office workers, business people): 10 minutes vigorous exercise in the morning to get you going; 30 minutes exercise at the end of the day to relieve accumulated tensions.

MORNING STRETCH. For everyone, Deborah Mazzanti advises a warmup stretch on awakening. Start it in bed and continue for two minutes after you get up.

Lie on back, yawn loudly, take a deep breath and bring arms way up over head.

Stretch, holding breath; point toes down and reach with hands as far as you can—and then a little farther. Exhale, bringing arms down to your sides. Repeat three times.

Lie on back, bend knees, clasp ankles. Roll up to sitting position, then down again onto back. Repeat once.

Stand, feet together. As you inhale, rise on toes and stretch arms overhead. Reach higher. Exhale and relax to heels. Breathing deeply, raise arms overhead, stretch; bend to right side, bend to left side. Bending knees, bend backward and forward. Stretch legs apart. Raise arms overhead; bend to right, bend to left. Bending knees, bend backward, bend forward. Relax and repeat.

SECRETS TO WEIGHT LOSS AND VITALITY FROM THE GOLDEN DOOR   Reprinted from the March issue of Family Circle Magazine. © 1976 The Family Circle, Inc. Pp. 88, 164.

MORNING JOG-WALK. The exercise program at the Golden Door begins before breakfast with a 7:30 A.M. jog-walk. This means you walk a little, jog a little, then walk a little as your endurance permits. (Rope-skipping is a good at-home substitute.)

BODY CONTROL. Your exercise is more valuable if your body is in good alignment. Here are three pointers to keeping good posture while you go about your daily tasks:

Draw body up, squeeze buttocks tightly together to align pelvis.

Pretend you have a cube of gelatin on each shoulder; when you walk, don't let it jiggle.

Imagine a spotlight shining straight out from your chest—keep it pointed straight ahead.

WHOLE-BODY EXERCISES. These are intended to help achieve perfect form and coordinate mind and body. They are vigorous, working the muscle of the heart as well as other muscles, and are done at alternating speed intervals—fast/slow/medium/fast. At the Door they are done in a group to music, with the leader improvising and the class following. A towel, hoop or ball held between the hands helps stretch the upper torso. Exercises can be done standing, sitting or lying down, whatever gets you moving.

Stand with feet apart, swing sideways and down, stretching towel between arms; swing back, left, right.

Bend one knee and stretch towel overhead; shift weight from left to right.

Lean forward, shifting weight from left to right, and beat floor with towel.

Sit, stretching towel, and swing from side to side.

Place feet against middle of towel and roll forward and backward on buttocks.

Sit on floor and "walk" with buttocks, polishing the floor with your seat.

Note: Music makes the exercises easier.

SPOT REDUCERS. Emphasis is on tummy, hips and thighs

◆◆◆

Start with 10 times each; increase 5 times a day to 30.
Hips. Lie on floor, back flat, arms outstretched. Bend both knees and lock ankles. Bring knees up to chest as far as possible; roll to the right, then to the left. Try to keep shoulders flat, and remember to bring knees to chest between each roll.
Waist and hips. Lie on floor, back flat. Separate legs and bend knees. Keep shoulders down and bring knees to the right, kneecaps touching floor; then lower knees down to the left side. Be sure legs and feet are far apart and that you work with resistance in legs.
Stomach. Lie on floor, back flat, with arms and hands tucked under your lower back and buttocks. Put legs together and bend knees. Bring knees to chest, then

straighten legs and extend them overhead. Bend knees back to chest, then bring bent legs down to touch toes to the floor.

SPECIAL LEG EXERCISES   *Starting Position:* Lie on right side, resting head in right hand with right knee bent. Left leg is behind right leg with the left leg stretched straight and left heel tipped up. Place the left hand on floor in front of the body.
1. Slowly lift left leg, keeping left hip forward and left heel tipped. Lower left leg slowly to floor.
2. Lift left leg as high as possible. Then bring the left leg forward, touching the toe to the ground and keeping the heel raised. Lift left leg high again, then lower to starting position.
3. Bring left hip slightly forward and touch the left knee on the floor in front, with the left lower leg perpendicular to the floor. Bring the left hip slightly back as you stretch the left leg straight toward the ceiling.
4. Bend left leg and tip the ankle as you place the left knee on the floor slightly behind the right knee. Bring left hip back as you stretch the left leg straight toward the ceiling. *Repeat all leg exercises with right leg.*

❖❖❖

Golden Door rules: When exercising on your back, never lift legs without also raising head. And when doing a stand-up exercise, never bend forward until you've stretched to both sides. These are back savers.

❖❖❖

IN-WATER EXERCISES. Besides keeping you cool, exercising in water speeds muscle-toning, saves sore muscles and makes you feel more graceful. Anything is fine, from familiar calisthenics to water sports such as volleyball. Swimming itself is a champion all-round exercise.

RELAXATION. The Door program also includes passive activities such as yoga, nude sunbathing, water-spray baths, Japanese body-walk massage and a morning meditation. Each guest room has a contemplation corner and a moon-watching loggia. Opening oneself to serenity is one of the functions of a stay at the Golden Door. Even the plantings are designed for "aroma therapy"—the scent of pines, fragrant shrubs, trees and flowers encourage you to breathe deeply and find pleasure in being alive.

HOW TO GET PLUMP

We live in a culture where the dominant ideal of beauty emphasizes, even exalts, the slender. Diet books, for example, invariably claim a substantial share of the best-seller listings; and, as the preceding document illustrates, much of the current interest in exercise is due to its role in weight control. We are, to a considerable extent, a nation of calorie counters and weight watchers.

This fascination with the slender is a relatively recent phenomenon, one dating back to the second decade of this century but no further. The preceding ideal of the beautiful is aptly conveyed in the title of the following document, "How to Get Plump." *Harper's Bazar*, then as now, was a magazine devoted to high fashion. Its editors could accurately think of themselves as arbiters of style. And thinness was anything but stylish in 1908. Those beyond the call of fashion, "those who do not consider beauty of sufficient importance to warrant an expenditure of time and effort," were warned that slenderness was also unhealthy.

So, just as the woman of today whose body weight exceeds the culturally decreed maximum is expected to dedicate herself to losing weight, the too slender woman of 1908 was urged to *work* at getting plump. It is worthwhile to look at the definition of "normal" weights given in the article. The "normal" woman of 1908 would be considered overweight today. And, it goes without saying, the models who grace *Harper's* or *Vogue's* pages today would have been thought scrawny then. Indeed they would have been put on a rigid diet until they had gained twenty, thirty, or even forty pounds.

Those who are too thin do not take the same interest in trying to reach the ideal proportion between height and weight as do those who are too fat, although there is every reason why they should. The woman of five feet seven whose scale balances at ninety-seven, or even one hundred and seven, should be as anxious to increase her weight as her friend of the same height who weighs one hundred and eighty is to decrease hers. One is travelling as rapidly away from her own highest standard of good looks as the other, and both should take an equally vital interest in its restoration. The ways and means to attain this should appeal as much to one as to the other, and both should take an equally vital interest in its restoration. The ways and means to attain this should appeal as much to one as to the other, and both should look upon the result as well worth the self-sacrifice and petty warfare against inclination entailed in its accomplishment. They must approach their objective point from opposite directions, but the point is the same, standing for increased beauty and health as well.

She who has lost weight rapidly from some acute disease can usually gain it back just as rapidly, and she who is suffering from some chronic illness and on that account cannot eat or digest the food which she has eaten, must necessarily take treatment for the fundamental cause of her illness from her physician before she considers the resulting thinness. It is those who are well and yet thin, who look upon themselves as the victims of an unhappy fate and refer with bitter resentment to their supposedly responsible parents or grandparents, who must be won away from their habit of looking upon their fate as inevitable. They must be taught that their condition is curable and that it must be struggled against instead of being accepted and made the best of. If their ancestors have persevered in using up too much force and taking in too little force-making fuel, they do not need to do the same. Inherited conditions are all too frequently the result of inherited bad habits, and this is one of them. One who thinks twice about the life of tireless energy forced upon the farmer's wife does not need an explanation for the characteristic "wiry thinness" inherited from generation to generation in the farm towns. A life of steady hard work upon one's feet is certainly not fat-producing, but it is generally possible to take life a little more easily and to select foods that will make it less exhausting. Moreover, the intensely active person, especially in town, is generally indulging herself in unnecessary nervous activity, throwing her valuable strength away recklessly, and living on her nerves, which were not intended for that purpose.

Even those who do not consider beauty of sufficient importance to warrant an expenditure of time and effort in its cultivation must realize that their thinness indicates very plainly that they are using up in some way all the fuel that they are taking into their bodies and that, consequently, no reserve is being laid aside for an emergency. If the time comes, and it surely will, when they are forced to endure an unusual strain, either nervous or physical, they will find themselves sadly in need of this reserve force; for *fat is force* and *stored-up fat is stored-up force*. They may even be drawing daily upon the foods intended for the renewal of tissues after using up those intended for the production of energy. In that case the crisis will arrive more quickly. When it comes they call it nervous exhaustion or something similar, and do not appreciate the fact that extreme thinness should have warned them of the approaching danger, and that a normal amount of surplus fat might have carried them through the crisis. An abnormal amount of fat makes its possessor uncomfortable, and its pressure upon the vital organs is felt in time to give the danger signal, so that the fact that it is bad for the health as well as the looks is brought home to its possessor much more quickly than the dangers of a lack of necessary fat are brought home to those who are too thin. Those who are too thin are *dangerously* comfortable until the nervous tension snaps.

On the side of looks there is much to be said, a great deal, in fact, that is so apparent that there is no necessity of putting it into words. Thinness, up to a certain point, is now the fashion, but it is a thinness that does not include angles and hollows. The possibilities of ruffles and pads make those with troubles of this kind feel infinitely superior to their sisters who cannot resort to artificial helps so easily, but, after all, the consciousness of these concealed helps is humiliating at the best. Moreover, the face cannot be doctored in this way, and as age creeps on the wrinkles increase much more easily and rapidly when one is thin; the skin loses its flexibility when deprived of the needed fat and oil. Those who allow this to happen are soon numbered among those who look ten years older than they really are, a most unhappy point for any woman to reach.

Physicians, moreover, say that ninety-five per cent. of these supposedly hopeless cases can be cured, and those who are struggling with the difficulties of reducing flesh laugh scornfully at the comparative difficulties which their friends must undergo to accomplish it. To the unprejudiced observer the path of the would-be fat person lies along much pleasanter ways than that of her unfortunate sister, although it is probably true that temperance in expenditure of energy is a difficult habit to form after a lifetime of reckless waste of that highly valuable commodity. Certainly little sympathy will be forthcoming for those living on the attractive diet recommended.

Both those who are too thin and those who are too fat have the same objective point in view—a perfect balance between the revenues of the body, consisting of food and air, and its expenditure, consisting of heat and energy. Those who are too fat must decrease the food and increase the energy, and those who are too thin must increase the food and decrease the energy; it is important that as much attention should be given to the decreasing quality as to the increasing.

Food is taken into the body for two purposes: first, to renew the tissues of the body, and second, to be used as fuel to form heat and energy for the activities of the body. Certain foods are primarily for one function and certain others are primarily for the other functions. Every normal person must have both, but the proportions may be varied according to special needs. The person who is too thin must, as a usual thing, have more of all kinds, but since her object is to increase fat she must take foods that do that, primarily, in large quantities. Fats, oils, sugars, and starches are the foods that contribute most largely to the production of fat, and it will usually be found that these are not the favorite articles of the person who is too thin. In most cases her reformation will consist more in kind than in quantity. These foods produce fat, and fat in its combination produces heat and energy, so that fat in reserve means force in reserve. The tissue-making foods will assist in making energy if there are not enough pure fats, but that is dangerous capital to borrow from. The conclusion is that fats must be taken into the system in excess of the supply needed for making energy, and that the thin person who wishes to maintain this excess must also economize on its expenditure.

The normal weights to be maintained are as follows:

Five feet 1 inch, 120 pounds; 5 feet 2 inches, 126 pounds; 5 feet 3 inches, 133 pounds; 5 feet 4 inches. 136 pounds; 5 feet 5 inches, 142 pounds; 5 feet 6 inches, 145 pounds; 5 feet 7 inches, 149 pounds; 5 feet 8 inches, 155 pounds; 5 feet 9 inches, 162 pounds.

In order to economize on the expenditure of energy it is necessary to learn how to take things easily. Even from the standpoint of accomplishment it is not always the person who rushes about his duties nervously, putting fully as much nervous activity into his work as calm, cool thought, who accomplishes the most in the end. Even when the energy is well directed it may be recklessly wasted in consideration of the time required for rest later on. One should learn how to move quietly and moderately about duties or pleasures without rush or hurry. When we are children we are constantly being restrained by our parents and told to stop and walk instead of running from place to place. Some people are never broken of the habit, and they are usually thin. If possible, one shoud sleep at least eight hours or nine hours out of the twenty-four, with as many naps between as possible. One should cultivate the habit of laziness, stopping at any and all times to relax the tensely drawn nerves and doing everything leisurely and without worry. Moderate exercise should be taken in the open air so that the appetite will be increased, the muscles hardened, the circulation increased, and the nerves relaxed, but this exercise should not be violent and should never reach the point of exhaustion. No nervous energy should be expended during it.

With our activities carefully economized we must study the subject of the foods required to form the needed fat. The thin person must indulge herself in exactly the foods forbidden the friend who is rigorously following a diet for flesh reduction. In her case we call it indulgence because it includes the foods usually looked upon as luxuries. If she does not enjoy the sweets recommended for her diet she will receive little sympathy from the majority of mankind.

The fat-producing foods are principally milk, cream, eggs, butter, olive oil; the sweets—sugar, honey, sweet desserts, jams, sweet fruits; the starchy vegetables—potatoes, pease, beans, corn, beets; wheat bread, rye, cereals of all kinds, rice, sago, etc. Of the fruits, peaches, grapes, bananas, prunes, and figs are especially recommended. The only foods cut out of a thin person's diet are the condiments—pickles, pepper, mustard, curry, salt, etc.; the acids, including acid fruits, the vinegar in salad dressing, etc.; and the stimulants, tea and coffee. It must not be forgotten that although the tissue-making foods, such as meats, fish, etc., are not fat-producing, they are required for their own especial functions. Some of the green vegetables and fruits are not fat-producing, but they are needed for other purposes. The fat-producing foods should be indulged in principally, but not to the exclusion of others.

The thin person should eat frequently and heartily. It is a good thing to take milk and eggs between meals as well as at meals. Milk made up partly of rich cream is, of course, much more fattening than thin milk. When heated very hot, but not to the boiling point, it is more effective than when taken cold. One can beat up an egg in it when taking it between meals or take the egg raw. A glass of hot milk is very good taken just before going to bed and also just after waking in the morning. The glass taken in the morning is especially good for a nervous stomach. It will frequently start the day right for those who find the morning a trying part of the day. Two quarts of milk and six eggs are not too much taken during the day. Cream should be poured generously over cereals and puddings and coffee, if the coffee is a necessity. Chocolate or milk is better for one who is thin than coffee, but if coffee is taken it should be made in the French way, largely of hot milk with some additional cream. Chocolate is both nourishing and fattening. Cream sauces will make vegetables and meats fattening when they would not be otherwise.

A quarter of a pound of butter should be consumed during the day. It is almost the best fattener there is. It should be spread thickly on bread. Olive oil is very pure and very effective. A salad dressing for a thin person should be made almost entirely of oil. A tablespoonful of pure oil taken after meals will help the good work along. Cod-liver oil is effective, but harder to take.

Cereals, rice, and potatoes are very good, indeed, and the cereals and rice are also very nourishing. Eggs are the very essence of food and the yolks contain a large percentage of fat. A box of pure candy or sweet chocolate for consumption at odd moments should be looked upon as a pleasant duty under these circumstances instead of a forbidden luxury. Sugar is pure energy.

When meat is eaten it should be both rare and fat. Salmon is the most fattening of all the fish.

Beer, ale, stout, and port are warranted to produce fat for those who do not want it, and may be relied upon to assist those who are thin if taken regularly.

A characteristic day's menu appropriate for one who is trying to gain weight is as follows:

At rising.—One glass hot milk.

Breakfast, at eight o'clock.—Sweet fruit, cereal with cream and sugar; two soft-boiled eggs; bread with thick layer of butter, jam, or honey; cup of chocolate or glass of milk.

At eleven.—Glass of milk; bread and butter.

Luncheon, at one o'clock.—Creamed fish; baked potatoes with butter; pease; pudding made of sago and eggs; glass of milk.

At four o'clock.—Glass of milk with egg beaten up in it; cake.

Dinner, at seven o'clock.—Cream soup; fat rare beefsteak; mashed potatoes; beans; creamed asparagus; beet salad, French dressing; rice pudding.

Bedtime.—Glass of hot milk; raw egg.

She who wishes to get fat should drink water or milk or both with her meals. Drinking water is said to make one eat more.

FOODS THAT FIGHT CELLULITE and TAKE-HOME SPA TREATMENT

So far are the women of today from wanting to be plump that even those who are already slender worry about "that ugly dimply, 'cottage cheese' fat called cellulite." Feeding these concerns, even as they promise to relieve them, are whole legions of beauty and health experts. The following excerpts, from a *Family Circle* article on the anti-cellulite program at the exclusive Sonoma Mission Inn Spa in California, detail some of the steps women unable to go to spas can undertake in their own homes.

FOODS THAT FIGHT CELLULITE

Nutrition Director Toni Christensen believes that the foods you eat are a contributing factor to whether or not you develop cellulite. She suggests these 10 guidelines to help combat those dreaded ripples.

1. Reduce consumption of meats, poultry, and fish to about 3-4 ounces per portion. Try substituting lentils, lima beans, chickpeas or soybeans in combination with vegetables for a meat course.

2. Make fruits and fresh and steamed vegetables the foods that provide you with the majority of your calories during the day.

3. Cut down on processed foods, especially those with added sugar and salt.

FOODS THAT FIGHT CELLULITE   TAKE HOME SPA TREATMENT   Reprinted from the March 29, 1983 issue of Family Circle Magazine. © 1983 The Family Circle, Inc. Pp. 30, 32.

4. Get acquainted with low-salt cheeses such as: Jarlsberg, Gouda, Swiss, Gruyere, Emmenthaler, Tilsit and Muenster. Try about 2 ounces of these at lunch.

5. Include more raw and unsalted nuts in your diet. (Almonds, cashews, peanuts, filberts, pecans, walnuts, etc.) A 2-ounce portion of any of these could be used at lunch instead of cheese.

6. Include whole grains in your daily meals. For example: whole grain bread, brown rice, oatmeal or whole grain pasta. Also eat baked potatoes in their skin but without topping.

7. Make sure you get two tablespoons of cold-pressed oils (olive or sesame, for example) daily.

8. Watch your vitamin intake. A daily multi-vitamin is probably a good idea.

9. Stress slows down food digestion. If possible, take 10-15 minutes before a meal to slowly sip a glass of water and relax.

10. When you can't exercise, try to make lunch, not dinner, your heavy meal of the day. You need the time to digest your food properly.

TAKE-HOME SPA TREATMENT

According to Spa Director Eva Jensch, cellulite is a mixture of fat, fluids and toxic wastes that accumulate in the layer of connective tissue between muscles and skin. It usually settles around the thighs, hips and arms and, at times, even at the knees and ankles. To get rid of it, you must work on releasing the toxins as well as toning the fat deposits. One way the experts at the Spa do this is with twice-a-week herbal wrap treatments. The treatments, which combine heat, massage and herbal therapy, stimulate circulation and help excrete toxins. With just a few changes, here's how you can do the treatment at home.

1. Dip a bath-sized towel in a tub of steaming water scented with herbs. The spa recommends the following mix: Use a teaspoon each of peppermint (an aromatic stimulant), lavender (a stimulant), orange peel (a mild antiseptic), comfrey (a toner), rose petal (a slightly astringent moisturizer), camomile (a relaxant), and yarrow (an astringent), tied tightly in a cheesecloth bag. Most herb and spice shops carry these ingredients and they can be purchased in small quantities. Also, check mail-order catalogs that carry potpourri products.

2. Wring out the towel and wrap yourself in it. Cover warm wet towel with a few dry ones to prevent a chill when the wet towel cools down.

3. Lie down and relax for about 10 minutes or until you begin to feel cold and chilled.

4. Remove towels. Scrub yourself down with a wet loofah to help stimulate circulation. (An easy way to do this is while you're in the tub or shower.)

TIP: No time to wrap? Massage cellulite prone areas for five to ten minutes with a wet loofah while you are soaking in an herb-filled warm bath.

MARCH, 1937 ENTRY, *THE DIARY OF ANAIS NIN*

There is perhaps no more evocative description of a young woman's dawning awareness of herself as an object which must, if she is to find romance, strike men as desirable
than this entry in Anais Nin's diary. Here we encounter first the young child, oblivious
to her own image, who, when she looks into a mirror, sees only the historical characters
her imagination has conjured up or the blue bow so meticulously tied for her by her
godmother. This Anais, at age six or ten or twelve, had not yet learned to wonder how
she appears to others, especially to males, because she had nothing at stake. But, by age
fifteen, she knows that her future depends on how she looks "in the eyes and faces of the
boys who dance with her . . ." and not on her talent as a writer.

In fact, the opposite proved to be true. Nin (1903-1977), a leading figure in Parisian
artistic circles in the 1930's and later, did achieve fame as a writer. Most of her celebrity
in the United States derives from her erotica, particularly *Delta of Venus* (1969), and
from her *Diary*. She also wrote a number of other novels, most notably *A Spy in the
House of Love* (1954), as well as short stories, essays, and poetry.

I cannot remember what I saw in the mirror as a child. Perhaps a child never
looks at a mirror. Perhaps a child, like a cat, is so much inside of himself that
he does not see himself in the mirror. He sees a child. The child does not
remember what he looks like. Later I remembered what I looked like. But
when I look at photographs of myself one, two, three, four, five years old, I do
not recognize myself. The child is *one*. At one with himself. Never outside of
himself. I can remember what I did but not the reflection of what I did. No
reflections. Six years old. Seven years old. Eight years old. Nine. Ten. Eleven.
No images. No Reflections. Feelings. I can feel what I felt about my father's
white mice, the horror they inspired in me, the revolting odor, the taste of a
burnt omelette my father made for us while my mother was sick and expecting
Joaquin in Berlin. The feel of the beach in Barcelona, the feel of the balcony
there, the fear of death and the writing of a testament, the feelings in church, in
the street. Sounds in the Spanish courtyard, singing, a memory of a gaiety
which was to haunt me all my life, totally absent from America. The face of the
maid Ramona, the music in the streets, children dancing on the sidewalks.
Voices. The appearance of others, the long black mustache of Granados, the
embrace of the nuns, drowning me in veils as they leaned over. No picture in
the mind's eye of what I wore. The long black stockings of Spanish children I
saw in a photograph. I do remember my passion for penny "surprise" packages, the passion for surprise. Yet at the age of six the perfection of the blue
bow on my hair, shaped like a butterfly, preoccupied me, since I insisted that
my godmother tie it because she tied it better than anyone else. I must have
seen this bow in the mirror then. I do not remember whether I saw this bow,
the little girl in the very short white-lace-edged dress, or again a photograph
taken in Havana where all my cousins and I stood in a row according to our
heights, all wearing enormous ribbons and short white dresses. In the mirror
there never was a child. The first mirror had a frame of white wood. In it there
is no Anaïs Nin, but Marie Antoinette with a white lace cap, a long black dress,

MARCH 1937 ENTRY   From *The Diary of Anais Nin, 1934–1939*, Volume II, copyright © 1967 by Anais Nin.
Reprinted by permission of Harcourt Brace Jovanovich, Inc. Pp. 180–182.

standing on a pile of chairs, the chariot, riding to her beheading. No Anaïs Nin. An actress playing all the parts of characters in French history. I am Charlotte Corday plunging a knife into the tyrant Marat. I am, of course, Joan of Arc. At fourteen, the portrayal of a Joan burning at the stake was my brother's favorite horror story.

The first mirror in which the self appears is very large, it is inlaid inside of a brown wood wall in the room of a brownstone house. Next to it the window pours down so strong a light that the rest of the room is not reflected in the mirror. The image of the girl who approaches it is brought into luminous relief. Against a foggy darkness, the girl of fifteen stands with frightened eyes. She is looking at her dress, a dress of shiny worn blue serge, which was fixed up for her out of an old one belonging to a cousin. It does not fit her. It is meager. It looks poor. The girl is looking at the worn shiny dark-blue serge dress with shame. It is the day she has been told in school that she is gifted for writing. They had come purposely into the class to tell her. In spite of being a foreigner, in spite of having to use the dictionary, she had written the best essay in the class. She who was always quiet and who did not wish to be noticed, was told to come up the aisle and speak to the English teacher before everyone, to hear the compliment. And the joy, the dazzling joy which had first struck her was instantly killed by the awareness of the dress. I did not want to get up, to be noticed. I was ashamed of this meager dress with a shine on it, its worn air, its orphan air, its hand-me-down air.

There is another mirror framed in brown wood. The girl is looking at the new dress which transfigures her. What an extraordinary change. She leans over very close to look at the humid eyes, the humid mouth, the moisture and luminousness brought about by the change of dress. She walks up very slowly to the mirror, very slowly, as if she did not want to frighten reflections away. Several times, at fifteen, she walks very slowly towards the mirror. Every girl of fifteen has put the same question to a mirror: "Am I beautiful?" The face is masklike. It does not smile. It does not want to charm the mirror, or deceive the mirror, or flirt with it and gain a false answer. The girl is in a trance. She does not want to frighten the reflection away herself. Someone has said she is very pale. She approaches the mirror and stands very still like a statue. Immobile. Waxy. She never makes a gesture. Surprised. Somnambulistic? She only moves to become someone else, impersonating Sarah Bernhardt, Mélisande, *La Dame aux Camélias*, Madame Bovary, Thaïs. She is never Anaïs Nin who goes to school, and grows vegetables and flowers in her backyard. She is immobile, haunting, like a figure moving in a dream. She is decomposed before the mirror into a hundred personages, recomposed into paleness and immobility. Silence. She is watching for an expression which will betray the spirit. You can never catch the face alive, laughing, or loving. At sixteen she is looking at the mirror with her hair up for the first time. There is always the question. The mirror is not going to answer it. She will have to look for the answer in the eyes and faces of the boys who dance with her, men later, and above all the painters.

A FEW WORDS ABOUT BREASTS
Nora Ephron

"I suppose that for most girls, breasts, brassieres, that entire thing, has more trauma, more to do with the coming of adolescence, with becoming a woman, than anything else." So wrote Nora Ephron, a well-known essayist, novelist, and screenwriter. The reason for breasts' importance, she continued, is ". . . you could see breasts." The "you" in that sentence includes everyone, but most especially it is boys that Ephron was referring to. *They* were especially likely to define female sexual allure in terms of cup sizes, Ephron noted. And they were even more apt to do so in the 1950s, she argued, for that was the decade of Jane Russell, cashmere sweaters, and—be it added—*Playboy* and its first Playmate, Marilyn Monroe.

There is some irony in the fact that this essay first appeared in *Esquire*, a "magazine for men." In the days before *Playboy* it was the most widely circulated of the many magazines which featured "cheesecake" photos and which thereby did so much to diffuse the stereotype of the buxom starlet as the epitome of female beauty. *Esquire,* however, had largely ceased running such pictures by the time Ephron started writing for it.

 I have to begin with a few words about androgyny. In grammar school, in the fifth and sixth grades, we were all tyrannized by a rigid set of rules that supposedly determined whether we were boys or girls. The episode in *Huckleberry Finn* where Huck is disguised as a girl and gives himself away by the way he threads a needle and catches a ball—that kind of thing. We learned that the way you sat, crossed your legs, held a cigarette, and looked at your nails—the way you did these things instinctively was absolute proof of your sex. Now obviously most children did not take this literally, but I did. I thought that just one slip, just one incorrect cross of my legs or flick of an imaginary cigarette ash would turn me from whatever I was into the other thing; that would be all it took, really. Even though I was outwardly a girl and had many of the trappings generally associated with girldom—a girl's name, for example, and dresses, my own telephone, an autograph book—I spent the early years of my adolescence absolutely certain that I might at any point gum it up. I did not feel at all like a girl. I was boyish. I was athletic, ambitious, outspoken, competitive, noisy, rambunctious. I had scabs on my knees and my socks slid into my loafers and I could throw a football. I wanted desperately not to be that way, not to be a mixture of both things, but instead just one, a girl, a definite indisputable girl. As soft and as pink as a nursery. And nothing would do that for me, I felt, but breasts.

I was about six months younger than everyone else in my class, and so for about six months after it began, for six months after my friends had begun to develop (that was the word we used, develop), I was not particularly worried. I would sit in the bathtub and look down at my breasts and know that any day now, they would start growing like everyone else's. They didn't. "I want to buy a bra," I said to my mother one night. "What for?" she said. My mother was really hateful about bras, and by the time my third sister had gotten to the point where she was ready to want one, my mother had worked the whole business into a comedy routine. "Why not use a Band-Aid instead?" she would say. It was a source of great pride to my mother that she had never even had to wear a brassiere until she had her fourth child, and then only because her gynecologist made her. It was incomprehensible to me that anyone could ever be proud of something like that. It was the 1950s, for God's sake. Jane Russell. Cashmere sweaters. Couldn't my mother see that? *"I am too old to wear an undershirt."* Screaming. Weeping. Shouting. "Then don't wear an undershirt," said my mother. "But I want to buy a bra." "What for?"

I suppose that for most girls, breasts, brassieres, that entire thing, has more trauma, more to do with the coming of adolescence, with becoming a woman, than anything else. Certainly more than getting your period, although that, too, was traumatic, symbolic. But you could see breasts; they were there; they were visible. Whereas a girl could claim to have her period for months before she actually got it and nobody would ever know the difference. Which is exactly what I did. All you had to do was make a great fuss over having enough nickels for the Kotex machine and walk around clutching your stomach and moaning for three to five days a month about The Curse and you could convince anybody. There is a school of thought somewhere in the women's lib/women's mag/gynecology establishment that claims that menstrual cramps are purely psychological, and I lean toward it. Not that I didn't have them finally. Agonizing cramps, heating-pad cramps, go-down-to-the-school-nurse-and-lie-on-the-cot cramps. But, unlike any pain I had ever suffered, I adored the pain of cramps, welcomed it, wallowed in it, bragged about it. "I can't go. I have cramps." "I can't do that. I have cramps." And most of all, gigglingly, blushingly: "I can't swim. I have cramps." Nobody ever used the hard-core word. Menstruation. God, what an awful word. Never that. "I have cramps."

The morning I first got my period, I went into my mother's bedroom to tell her. And my mother, my utterly-hateful-about-bras mother, burst into tears. It was really a lovely moment, and I remember it so clearly not just because it was one of the two times I ever saw my mother cry on my account (the other was when I was caught being a six-year-old kleptomaniac), but also because the incident did not mean to me what it meant to her. Her little girl, her firstborn, had finally become a woman. That was what she was crying about. My reaction to the event, however, was that I might well be a woman in some scientific, textbook sense (and could at least stop faking every month and stop wasting all those nickels). But in another sense—in a visible sense—I was as androgynous and as liable to tip over into boyhood as ever.

I started with a 28 AA bra. I don't think they made them any smaller in those days, although I gather that now you can buy bras for five-year-olds that don't have any cups whatsoever in them; trainer bras they are called. My first brassiere came from Robinson's Department Store in Beverly Hills. I went there alone, shaking, positive they would look me over and smile and tell me to come back next year. An actual fitter took me into the dressing room and stood over me while I took off my blouse and tried the first one on. The little puffs stood out on my chest. "Lean over," said the fitter. (To this day, I am not sure what fitters in bra departments do except to tell you to lean over.) I leaned over, with the fleeting hope that my breasts would miraculously fall out of my body and into the puffs. Nothing.

"Don't worry about it," said my friend Libby some months later, when things had not improved. "You'll get them after you're married."

"What are you talking about?" I said.

"When you get married," Libby explained, "your husband will touch your breasts and rub them and kiss them and they'll grow."

That was the killer. Necking I could deal with. Intercourse I could deal with. But it had never crossed my mind that a man was going to touch my breasts, that breasts had something to do with all that, petting, my God, they never mentioned petting in my little sex manual about the fertilization of the ovum. I became dizzy. For I knew instantly—as naïve as I had been only a moment before—that only part of what she was saying was true: the touching, rubbing, kissing part, not the growing part. And I knew that no one would ever want to marry me. I had no breasts. I would never have breasts.

My best friend in school was Diana Raskob. She lived a block from me in a house full of wonders. English muffins, for instance. The Raskobs were the first people in Beverly Hills to have English muffins for breakfast. They also had an apricot tree in the back, and a badminton court, and a subscription to *Seventeen* magazine, and hundreds of games, like Sorry and Parcheesi and Treasure Hunt and Anagrams. Diana and I spent three or four afternoons a week in their den reading and playing and eating. Diana's mother's kitchen was full of the most colossal assortment of junk food I have ever been exposed to. My house was full of apples and peaches and milk and homemade chocolate-chip cookies—which were nice, and good for you, but-not-right-before-dinner-or-you'll-spoil-your-appetite. Diana's house had nothing in it that was good for you, and what's more, you could stuff it in right up until dinner and nobody cared. Bar-B-Q potato chips (they were the first in them, too), giant bottles of ginger ale, fresh popcorn with melted butter, hot fudge sauce on Baskin-Robbins jamoca ice cream, powdered-sugar doughnuts from Van de Kamp's. Diana and I had been best friends since we were seven; we were about equally popular in school (which is to say, not particularly), we had about the same success with boys (extremely intermittent), and we looked much the same. Dark. Tall. Gangly.

It is September, just before school begins. I am eleven years old, about to enter the seventh grade, and Diana and I have not seen each other all summer. I have been to camp and she has been somewhere like Banff with her parents. We are meeting, as we often do, on the street midway between our two houses, and we will walk back to Diana's and eat junk and talk about what has happened to each of us that summer. I am walking down Walden Drive in my jeans and my father's shirt hanging out and my old red loafers with the socks falling into them and coming toward me is . . . I take a deep breath . . . a young woman. Diana. Her hair is curled and she has a waist and hips and a bust and she is wearing a straight skirt, an article of clothing I have been repeatedly told I will be unable to wear until I have the hips to hold it up. My jaw drops, and suddenly I am crying hysterically, can't catch my breath sobbing. My best friend has betrayed me. She has gone ahead without me and done it. She has shaped up.

Here are some things I did to help:

Bought a Mark Eden Bust Developer.

Slept on my back for four years.

Splashed cold water on them every night because some French actress said in *Life* magazine that that was what *she* did for her perfect bustline.

Ultimately, I resigned myself to a bad toss and began to wear padded bras. I think about them now, think about all those years in high school I went around in them, my three padded bras, every single one of them with different-sized breasts. Each time I changed bras I changed sizes: one week nice perky but not too obtrusive breasts, the next medium-sized slightly pointy ones, the next week knockers, true knockers; all the time, whatever size I was, carrying around this rubberized appendage on my chest that occasionally crashed into a wall and was poked inward and had to be poked outward—I think about all that and wonder how anyone kept a straight face through it. My parents, who normally had no restraints about needling me—why did they say nothing as they watched my chest go up and down? My friends, who would periodically inspect my breasts for signs of growth and reassure me—why didn't they at least counsel consistency?

And the bathing suits. I die when I think about the bathing suits. That was the era when you could lay an uninhabited bathing suit on the beach and someone would make a pass at it. I would put one on, an absurd swimsuit with its enormous bust built into it, the bones from the suit stabbing me in the rib cage and leaving little red welts on my body, and there I would be, my chest plunging straight downward absolutely vertically from my collarbone to the top of my suit and then suddenly, wham, out came all that padding and material and wiring absolutely horizontally.

Buster Klepper was the first boy who ever touched them. He was my boyfriend my senior year of high school. There is a picture of him in my high-school yearbook that makes him look quite attractive in a Jewish, horn-rimmed-glasses sort of way, but the picture does not show the pimples, which were air-brushed out, or the dumbness. Well, that isn't really fair. He wasn't dumb. He just wasn't terribly bright. His mother refused to accept it, refused to accept the relentlessly average report cards, refused to deal with her son's inevitable destiny in some junior college or other. "He was tested," she would say to me, apropos of nothing, "and it came out a hundred and forty-five. That's near-genius." Had the word "underachiever" been coined, she probably would have lobbed that one at me, too. Anyway, Buster was really very sweet—which is, I know, damning with faint praise, but there it is. I was the editor of the front page of the high-school newspaper and he was editor of the back page; we had to work together, side by side, in the print shop, and that was how it started. On our first date, we went to see *April Love,* starring Pat Boone. Then we started going together. Buster had a green coupe, a 1950 Ford with an engine he had hand-chromed until it shone, dazzled, reflected the image of anyone who looked into it, anyone usually being Buster polishing it or the gas-station attendants he constantly asked to check the oil in order for them to be overwhelmed by the sparkle on the valves. The car also had a boot stretched over the back seat for reasons I never undersood; hanging from the rearview mirror, as was the custom, was a pair of angora dice. A previous girl friend named Solange, who was famous throughout Beverly Hills High School for having no pigment in her right eyebrow, had knitted them for him. Buster and I would ride around town, the two of us seated to the left of the steering wheel. I would shift gears. It was nice.

There was necking. Terrific necking. First in the car, overlooking Los Angeles from what is now the Trousdale Estates. Then on the bed of his parents' cabana at Ocean House. Incredibly wonderful, frustrating necking, I loved it, really, but no further than necking, please don't, please, because there I was absolutely terrified of the general implications of going-a-step-further with a near-dummy and also terrified of his finding out there was next to nothing there (which he knew, of course; he wasn't that dumb).

I broke up with him at one point. I think we were apart for about two weeks. At the end of that time, I drove down to see a friend at a boarding school in Palos Verdes Estates and a disc jockey played "April Love" on the radio four times during the trip. I took it as a sign. I drove straight back to Griffith Park to a golf tournament Buster was playing in (he was the sixth-seeded teen-age golf player in Southern California) and presented myself back to him on the green of the 18th hole. It was all very dramatic. That night we went to a drive-in and I let him get his hand under my protuberances and onto my breasts. He really didn't seem to mind at all.

"Do you want to marry my son?" the woman asked me.

"Yes," I said.

I was nineteen years old, a virgin, going with this woman's son, this big strange woman who was married to a Lutheran minister in New Hampshire and pretended she was gentile and had this son, by her first husband, this total fool of a son who ran the hero-sandwich concession at Harvard Business School and whom for one moment one December in New Hampshire I said—as much out of politeness as anything else—that I wanted to marry.

"Fine," she said. "Now, here's what you do. Always make sure you're on top of him so you won't seem so small. My bust is very large, you see, so I always lie on my back to make it look smaller, but you'll have to be on top most of the time."

I nodded. "Thank you," I said.

"I have a book for you to read," she went on. "Take it with you when you leave. Keep it." She went to the bookshelf, found it, and gave it to me. It was a book on frigidity.

"Thank you," I said.

That is a true story. Everything in this article is a true story, but I feel I have to point out that that story in particular is true. It happened on December 30, 1960. I think about it often. When it first happened, I naturally assumed that the woman's son, my boyfriend, was responsible. I invented a scenario where he had had a little heart-to-heart with his mother and had confessed that his only objection to me was that my breasts were small; his mother then took it upon herself to help out. Now I think I was wrong about the incident. The mother was acting on her own, I think: that was her way of being cruel and competitive under the guise of being helpful and maternal. You have small breasts, she was saying; therefore you will never make him as happy as I have. Or you have small breasts; therefore you will doubtless have sexual problems. Or you have small breasts; therefore you are less woman than I am. She was, as it happens, only the first of what seems to me to be a never-ending string of women who have made competitive remarks to me about breast size. "I would love to wear a dress like that," my friend Emily says to me, "but my bust is too big." Like that. Why do women say these things to me? Do I attract these remarks the way other women attract married men or alcoholics or homosexuals? This summer, for example. I am at a party in East Hampton and I am introduced to a woman from Washington. She is a minor celebrity, very pretty and Southern and blond and outspoken, and I am flattered because she has read something I have written. We are talking animatedly, we have been talking no more than five minutes, when a man comes up to join us. "Look at the two of us," the woman says to the man, indicating me and her. "The two of us together couldn't fill an A cup." Why does she say that? It isn't even true, dammit, so why? Is she even more addled than I am on this subject? Does she honestly believe there is something wrong with her size breasts, which, it seems to me, now that I look hard at them, are just right? Do I unconsciously bring out competitiveness in women? In that form? What did I do to deserve it?

As for men.

There were men who minded and let me know that they minded. There were men who did not mind. In any case, *I* always minded.

And even now, now that I have been countlessly reassured that my figure is a good one, now that I am grown-up enough to understand that most of my feelings have very little to do with the reality of my shape, I am nonetheless obsessed by breasts. I cannot help it. I grew up in the terrible fifties—with rigid stereotypical sex roles, the insistence that men be men and dress like men and women be women and dress like women, the intolerance of androgyny—and I cannot shake it, cannot shake my feelings of inadequacy. Well, that time is gone, right? All those exaggerated examples of breast worship are gone, right? Those women were freaks, right? I know all that. And yet here I am, stuck with the psychological remains of it all, stuck with my own peculiar version of breast worship. You probably think I am crazy to go on like this: here I have set out to write a confession that is meant to hit you with the shock of recognition, and instead you are sitting there thinking I am thoroughly warped. Well, what can I tell you? If I had had them, I would have been a completely different person. I honestly believe that.

After I went into therapy, a process that made it possible for me to tell total strangers at cocktail parties that breasts were the hang-up of my life, I was often told that I was insane to have been bothered by my condition. I was also frequently told, by close friends, that I was extremely boring on the subject. And my girl friends, the ones with nice big breasts, would go on endlessly about how their lives had been far more miserable than mine. Their bra straps were snapped in class. They couldn't sleep on their stomachs. They were stared at whenever the word "mountain" cropped up in geography. And *Evangeline*, good God what they went through every time someone had to stand up and recite the Prologue to Longfellow's *Evangeline*: ". . . stand like druids of eld . . ./ With beards that rest on their bosoms." It was much worse for them, they tell me. They had a terrible time of it, they assure me. I don't know how lucky I was, they say.

I have thought about their remarks, tried to put myself in their place, considered their point of view. I think they are full of shit.

THE CULTURE OF ROMANCE

Shulamith Firestone

Cultural pressures on women to conform to stereotypical definitions of beauty and femininity have not lessened in this century despite the efforts of feminists and other critics. This is the message of radical feminist Shulamith Firestone who argued that the prevalence of erotic imagery in contemporary America has led both men and women to become ever more conscious of appearance, their own and that of every prospective partner. We all, she continued, have sacrificed our *selves* for our *images*. Men fancy themselves so many James Bonds. Women too become whatever image manipulators in Hollywood or Madison Avenue dictate.

Firestone's deeper point is that only a radical feminist revolution can lead to a social order in which this tyranny of images is overthrown. What such an order would be like is described in another selection from *The Dialectic of Sex* reprinted in Chapter 8. *The Dialectic of Sex* was one of the most widely read and discussed feminist works of the early 1970's.

These are some of the major components of the cultural apparatus, romanticism, which, with the weakening of "natural" limitations on women, keep sex oppression going strong. The political uses of romanticism over the centuries became increasingly complex. Operating subtly or blatantly, on every cultural level, romanticism is now—in this time of greatest threat to the male power role—amplified by new techniques of communication so all-pervasive that men get entangled in their own line. How does this amplification work?

With the cultural portrayal of the smallest details of existence (e.g., deodorizing one's underarms), the distance between one's experience and one's perceptions of it becomes enlarged by a vast interpretive network; If our direct experience contradicts its interpretation by this ubiquitous cultural network, the experience must be denied. This process, of course, does not apply only to women. The pervasion of image has so deeply altered our very relationships to ourselves that even men have become objects—if never *erotic* objects. Images become extensions of oneself; it gets hard to distinguish the real person from his latest image, if indeed, the Person Underneath hasn't evaporated altogether. Arnie, the kid who sat in back of you in the sixth grade, picking his nose and cracking jokes, the one who had a crook in his left shoulder, is lost under successive layers of adopted images: the High School Comedian, the Campus Rebel, James Bond, the Salem Springtime Lover, and so on, each image hitting new highs of sophistication until the person himself doesn't know who he is. Moreover, he deals with others through this image-extension (Boy-Image meets Girl-Image and consummates Image-Romance). Even if a woman could get beneath this intricate image facade—and it would take months, even years, of a painful, almost therapeutic relationship—she would be met not with gratitude that she had (painfully) loved the man for his real self, but with

---

THE CULTURE OF ROMANCE   From *The Dialectic of Sex* (New York: William Morrow Publishers, 1970; Bantam edition, 1971). Excerpts from pp. 152–155 of *The Dialectic of Sex* by Shulamith Firestone. By permission of William Morrow & Company.

shocked repulsion and terror that she had found him out. What he wants instead is The Pepsi-Cola Girl, to smile pleasantly to his Johnny Walker Red in front of a ski-lodge fire.

But, while this reification affects both men and women alike, in the case of women it is profoundly complicated by the forms of sexploitation I have described. Woman is not only an Image, she is the Image of Sex Appeal. The stereotyping of women expands: now there is no longer the excuse of ignorance. Every woman is constantly and explicitly informed on how to "improve" what nature gave her, where to buy the products to do it with, and how to count the calories she should never have eaten—indeed, the "ugly" woman is now so nearly extinct even she is fast becoming "exotic." The competition becomes frantic, because everyone is now plugged into the same circuit. The current beauty ideal becomes all-pervasive ("Blondes have more fun . . .").

And eroticism becomes erotomania. Stimulated to the limit, it has reached an epidemic level unequalled in history. From every magazine cover, film screen, TV tube, subway sign, jump breasts, legs, shoulders, thighs. Men walk about in a state of constant sexual excitement. Even with the best of intentions, it is difficult to focus on anything else. This bombardment of the senses, in turn, escalates sexual provocation still further: ordinary means of arousal have lost all effect. Clothing becomes more provocative; hemlines climb, bras are shed. See-through materials become ordinary. But in all this barrage of erotic stimuli, men themselves are seldom portrayed as erotic objects. Women's eroticism, as well as men's, becomes increasingly directed toward women.

One of the internal contradictions of this highly effective propaganda system is to expose to men as well as women the stereotyping process women undergo. Though the idea was to better acquaint women with their feminine role, men who turn on the TV are also treated to the latest in tummy-control, false eyelashes, and floor waxes (Does she . . . or doesn't she?). Such a crosscurrent of sexual tease and exposé would be enough to make man hate women, if he didn't already.

Thus the extension of romanticism through modern media enormously magnified its effects. If before culture maintained male supremacy through Eroticism, Sex Privatization, and the Beauty Ideal, these cultural processes are now almost too effectively carried out: the media are guilty of "overkill." The regeneration of the women's movement at this moment in history may be due to a backfiring, an internal contradiction of our modern cultural indoctrination system. For in its amplification of sex indoctrination, the media have unconsciously exposed the degradation of "femininity."

In conclusion, I want to add a note about the special difficulties of attacking the sex class system through its means of cultural indoctrination. Sex objects *are* beautiful. An attack on them can be confused with an attack on beauty itself. Feminists need not get so pious in their efforts that they feel they must flatly deny the beauty of the face on the cover of *Vogue*. For this is not the point. The real question is: is the face beautiful in a *human* way—does it allow for growth and flux and decay, does it express negative as well as positive emotions, does it fall apart without artificial props—or does it falsely imitate the very different beauty of an *inanimate* object, like wood trying to be metal?

To attack eroticism creates similar problems. Eroticism is *exciting*. No one wants to get rid of it. Life would be a drab and routine affair without at least that spark. That's just the point. Why has all joy and excitement been concentrated, driven into one narrow, difficult-to-find alley of human experience, and all the rest laid waste? When we demand the elimination of eroticism, we mean not the elimination of sexual joy and excitement but its rediffusion over—there's plenty to go around, it increases with use—the spectrum of our lives.

CONFESSIONS: "HE *MADE* ME DO IT!"

Susan Brownmiller

Susan Brownmiller, a journalist and free-lance writer, wrote *Against Our Will* "because I am a woman who changed her mind about rape" and because she thought it crucial that others, especially other women, also come to see through the "myths" about rape she had once believed. The myths were: "ALL WOMEN WANT TO BE RAPED"; "NO WOMAN CAN BE RAPED AGAINST HER WILL"; "SHE WAS ASKING FOR IT"; and "IF YOU'RE GOING TO BE RAPED, YOU MIGHT AS WELL RELAX AND ENJOY IT."

Against Our Will, a Book-of-the-Month Club selection, was an immediate best seller. It played a role in changing popular ideas about rape and rapists which underlay legal reforms of the 1970's (removing a husband's immunity from prosecution for raping his wife, for example), and it helped inspire campaigns against violent pornography. Brownmiller played an active role in these campaigns. She also published a best selling analysis of cultural definitions of femininity (1984).

In the excerpt printed below Brownmiller examines one of the vehicles through which myths about rape have long been promulgated, the "confession" magazines.

 Who takes romance-confession magazines seriously? Certainly not the editors who edit them, and certainly not any literary critic or chronicler of the culture. Nor have the sociologists and psychologists shown interest, for that matter. Fredric Wertham's *Seduction of the Innocent*, the famous study of cultural violence and its effect on children, raised the comic book to serious and controversial status, but no one has examined the romance, confession and movie magazine industry for its cumulative effect on impressionable young women.* Who takes the magazines seriously? Only the several million girls

---

*"Comic books," Dr. Werthham wrote in 1954, "create sex fears of all kinds. . . . A Western with a picture of Tom Mix on the cover has in one story no less than *sixteen consecutive* pictures of a girl tied up with ropes, her hands of course tied behind her back! She is shown in all kinds of poses, each more sexually suggestive than the other, and her facial expression shows that she seems to enjoy this treatment. Psychiatrically speaking, this is nothing but the masturbation fantasy of a sadist, and it has a corresponding effect on boys. For girls, and those boys who identify themselves with the girl, it may become the starting-point for masochistic fantasies."

and women who read them each month, women who are, for the most part, from the lower economic classes, with high-school educations or less, women who, statistics show, are the most frequent victims of forcible rape.

Between one dozen and fifteen confession magazines are carried on the newsstands, and each sells a minimum of one-quarter of a million copies. Confession-magazine addicts usually read more than one magazine a month and as many as nine readers may share one copy, passing it from hand to hand until it is in tatters. This multiple readership is generally acknowledged to be higher than for any other magazine genre. In the South and the Southwest, where the magazines have a wide audience, the readership is estimated to be 40 percent black. More than ten million girls and women form the faithful market for the confessions but occasional readership may be twice that number. According to one sales survey, magazines with cover lines pertaining to brute force ("HE MADE ME DO IT!") sell best.*

The confession magazines I purchased during one expedition to my corner store were dated February or March, 1972. Each featured a tale of rape, a near-rape or a rape fantasy. Taken *in toto* they promulgated a philosophy of submission in which the female victim was often to blame, whereas the men in her life—husband, boyfriend or rapist—emerged as persons of complex emotion deserving of sympathy. In strict adherence to the confession formula, the rape functioned as a positive catalyst for the heroine in her never-ending quest for a new boyfriend or an improved relationship with a husband. Here are brief synopses.

"I WAS THE VICTIM OF A SEX GANG" (*True Life Confessions*, March). The blurb reads, *"I was out for kicks and nobody was going to stop me! That's how I got caught by the toughest gang of guys around."* Conceited Dory is bored by steady Perry, who tells her, "You talk too much. Guys don't like girls who are too quick with the wisecracks." On a dare Dory walks into the clubhouse of a gang of toughs and is nearly gang-raped. When she comes to after "blacking out," a stern policeman is bending over her. The gang is packed off to a reform school, but Dory confesses, "Actually I felt a little guilty." In the last paragraph Dory tells us, "I learned a lesson that I hope other girls will remember. When you ask for trouble—as I did—you can be sure you'll get it. And I'm grateful that I got out of it without being assaulted, that my sharp tongue and know-it-all attitude didn't wreck my life as it could so easily have done." Her virginity saved, she goes back to faithful Perry and "grows up."

"SEX CREEPS ALWAYS PICK ON GIRLS LIKE ME" (*Modern Love*, March). The blurb reads, *"It happens too often to be just accidental."* Susan is disturbed by exhibitionists who expose themselves. She joins an encounter group and re-

---

*I speak from firsthand knowledge of the field, once having worked as an assistant editor for a group of confessions. The house I worked for also published a group of men's magazines, and we divided our editorial time accordingly. In contrast to the confessions—woeful tales of girls gone wrong—the men's magazines marketed a formula of blood and guts—superman triumphs over dangerous animals and luscious women. The cover art for both sets of magazines was revealing. The female confessions invariably pictured a young woman peeking out from a thicket of one-line blurbs implying guilt and/or distress. Covers for the men's magazines alternately depicted (a) an evil doctor, often in Nazi uniform, about to jab a hypodermic needle into a girl who was bound and gagged while a hero figure manfully strode to the rescue, or (b) a jungle animal, often a black panther, clawing at a prostrate, hysterical blonde while a white hunter in khakis rushed to the rescue. This cover, my boss informed me, was meant to symbolize interracial rape.

veals her problem. The leader, a psychologist, suggests that Susan sends out signals to the men because deep down she is afraid of sex. Susan suddenly understands that unconsciously she had been staring at the men. She starts a new relationship with Chuck, one of the young men in her group.

"I THOUGHT NOBODY HAD RAPE DREAMS LIKE MINE" (*Real Confessions*, February). Betty Jo has daydreams of rape and coincidentally doesn't want to get pregnant. Husband Jack, a big guy, is a gentle lover. "I was disappointed by his tenderness," Betty Jo says. "I wanted to be overwhelmed by brute force." They consult a minister who tells them that Betty Jo's fantasies are normal. He recommends that they consult a doctor, who assures them, "Rape is a very common fantasy that women have, and that's why it turns up so often in movies and books. Most women who have these fantasies don't really want to be raped, not in the sense of being mistreated or hurt. They like being dominated and overwhelmed by a man." Thus reassured, Jack 'fesses up: "I have a few sex dreams of my own. Like—what it's like to make love to a woman whose [sic] fighting you every inch of the way. . . . The idea of forcing a woman turns me on. I don't mean beating her up, just showing her it's all gotta be my way, no matter what she wants." Betty Jo and Jack decide to practice "rape games" at home. The first time Jack tries, Betty Jo protests that she isn't wearing her diaphragm—she could get pregnant! Jack persists with "brute force." Betty Jo tells us, "I didn't have any choice. I had to submit and be overwhelmed by his absolute strength and masculinity. It left me free, somehow, in a way I never felt before, to experience all the thrills I could only dream about till then." In the last paragraph she reports they now have two kids.

"I MADE HIM DO IT . . . TO ME!" (*True Confessions*, February). The blurb reads, "*What kind of girl gets raped? What kind of man is a rapist? Right away you think you know the answers. But after you read this story, you may find you're wrong.*" Helen, a shy girl from Indiana, goes to a singles bar in New York where she meets Danny, an ex-marine "with a nice-looking face and large brown eyes." She is too prim and proper for Danny's tastes, and he ignores her. Crushed, she leaves the bar, "knowing that I should really take a taxi since no New York street is safe for a girl alone after dark." A few evenings later she returns to the bar, determined not to let Danny get away. She is very flirtatious and Danny accompanies her to her studio apartment for a cup of coffee. They kiss—but suddenly it gets more serious: "Danny, I—" "Shut up." Then, "A strangled sound broke from my throat as he forced himself upon me." Danny rapes her and leaves. Bleeding and in pain, Helen staggers to her feet and calls a girlfriend. The girlfriend wants to call the police, but Helen refuses. She will not go to a hospital, either. A young intern who lives in the friend's building is called in. He tells Helen she'll be "okay" after a few days of bed rest. Helen's friend still wants to call the police, but Helen is adamant. It is her fault! "What other girl would be such a fool? What other girl would invite a total stranger into her apartment in the middle of the night, let him start to make love to her and expect him to stop?" A few days later a remorseful Danny sends Helen $50 "for the doctor's bill." Next he calls her on the telephone, apologizes and says he has sworn off alcohol for good. Helen and Danny are dating now: "We seem to be helping each other through a bad time—a bad time that is slowly getting better."

"I GAVE UP THE MAN I LOVED TO KEEP A RAPIST'S CHILD" (*True Romance*, February). Karen is raped by an escapee from the state mental hospital. Her family is afraid the town "will jeer," so Karen's mother tells the newspapers that *she* was the victim. But Karen discovers she is pregnant. Despite a law that allows abortion, Karen decides to bear and keep the rapist's child, who is born retarded. Boyfriend Neal rejects her but new boyfriend Mark steps into the breach. The blurb: *"Does a woman ever forget her helpless little first-born?"*

"RAPED WHILE PREGNANT!—AND I CAN'T TELL MY HUSBAND!" (*Personal Romances*, March). The blurb reads, *"It can only end in more terrible violence if I identify my attacker."* Cathy, a pregnant teacher's aide, is raped in her classroom. She miscarries that evening. Cathy decides not to tell the sheriff or husband Burt about the rape because the town will jeer and because Burt has always said he'd kill any man who attacked her. By coincidence, Cathy's friend Janice is also raped—and murdered—that same night in a neighboring county. The sheriff picks up a supect for Janice's murder, but the suspect offers an unusual alibi. It was not Janice whom he raped, but Cathy. In this curious story, Cathy is finally convinced to admit her rape and identify her attacker *in order to save him* from the false and more serious charge of murdering Janice. There is much talk in this story about how "unmanned" Burt feels by Cathy's rape. Burt gets in a good sock at Cathy's rapist in the county jail, and the sheriff's wife says approvingly, "I'm glad he got to him, Cathy. It's the only way he could get some of that poison out and feel like a man again."

"DADDY, WHY DOES MOMMY CALL YOU A RAPIST?" (*True Love*, February). A child-rapist is at large and Midge's mother begins to suspect Midge's father because she has not slept with him for years and "it ain't natural for a man to go without . . ." Midge's mother is wrong about her husband, of course, and in the last paragraph it looks like the family sex life is beginning to improve.

I intended to limit my random sampling to one sweep of the magazine rack, but a few weeks later while I was buying my newspaper at the corner store I noticed that the March *Real Confessions* had just come in. I already had February in my possession, but a particularly provocative title caught my eye. The plot was the same story of an uppity girl getting her comeuppance from a gang of boys that I had read in the March *True Life Confessions*, "I WAS THE VICTIM OF A SEX GANG." The blurb on this new one, though, was a trifle more explicit: *"I knew I was partly to blame, too—because I tried too hard to change everybody's life."* But the title spoke volumes! It read: "GANG-RAPED BY 7 BOYS— BECAUSE I LED THEIR GIRLS INTO A WOMEN'S LIB CLUB."

LINDA LOVELACE'S "ORDEAL"

Gloria Steinem

Pornography is doubtless the most blatant instance of the reduction of women to the status of objects. So it is not surprising that feminists have launched major campaigns against it. And, given the fact that pornography has become more openly available as a result of a series of Supreme Court decisions upholding individual rights of free speech and artistic expression, it is also not surprising that civil libertarians—usually otherwise quite sympathetic to feminist causes—have criticized these campaigns as potential threats to the first amendment.

Linda Lovelace's autobiographical account of her career as a pornographic film performer touched off the following exchange between Gloria Steinem, editor and co-founder of *Ms.,* and Aryeh Neier, a law professor at New York University, director of the NYU Institute for the Humanities, and an editor of *The Nation* magazine. Lovelace starred in "Deep Throat," probably the most successful—and certainly the most celebrated—hardcore movie ever made. The film made Lovelace, for a brief period, a kind of media celebrity. She appeared on television talk shows, was interviewed by *Playboy* (with the inevitable pictorial); and, through it all, radiated happiness about her career as a pornographic film star. Seeing "Deep Throat," she said, could be therapeutic for the sexually inhibited.

A decade later, Lovelace published *Ordeal* in which she claimed that she had been forced to make the movie and to engage in a host of other degrading sexual activities by her psychotic husband who threatened to kill her if she did not do as she was told. Her story raises several key questions about pornography. Is pornography linked to rape and other violent crimes against women? Are the women who perform in these films victims? Or are most, if not all, simply women who have chosen this as a financially rewarding line of work?

Remember "Deep Throat"? It was the porn movie that made porn movies chic; the stag film that took only $40,000 and a few days to make in 1972, and ended the decade with an estimated gross income of $600 million from the film itself, plus the subindustry of sequels, cassettes, T-shirts, bumper stickers, and sexual aids that it inspired. In fact, so many media men gave it their amused or heartfelt approval that "Deep Throat" entered our language and our consciousness, whether or not we ever saw the film itself. From the serious Watergate journalists of the Washington *Post* (who immortalized the movie by bestowing its title on their top-secret news source) to the sleazy pornocrats of *Screw* magazine—a range that may be, on a scale of male supremacy, the distance from *A* to *B*—such strange bedfellows turned this cheap feature into a national and international profit-center and dirty joke.

At the heart of this joke was Linda Lovelace (née Linda Boreman) whose innocent face offered moviegoers the titillating thought that even the girl-next-door might be the object of pornstyle sex.

Using Linda had been the idea of Gerry Damiano, the director-writer of "Deep Throat." "The most amazing thing about Linda, the truly amazing thing," she remembers his saying enthusiastically to Lou Peraino, who bank-

LINDA LOVELACE'S "ORDEAL" From: *Ms.* Magazine, May, 1980, 72 +. Reprinted by permission.

rolled the movie, "is that she still looks sweet and innocent." Nonetheless, Peraino (recently arrested by the FBI as an alleged figure in organized crime activities in the illicit film industry) complained that Linda wasn't the "blonde with big boobs" that he had wanted for his first porn flick, and he continued to complain, even after she was ordered to service him sexually.

In fact, watching Linda perform as a prostitute had given Damiano the idea for "Deep Throat" in the first place. He had been at a party where men were the beneficiaries of the sexual sword-swallower trick Linda had been taught by her husband and keeper, Chuck Traynor. By relaxing her throat muscles, she could receive the full-length plunge of a penis without choking; a desperate survival technique for her, but a constant source of novelty and amusement for clients. Thus creatively inspired, Damiano had thought up a movie gimmick; one perhaps second only to Freud's elimination of the clitoris and invention of the vaginal orgasm. He would tell the story of a woman whose clitoris is in her throat, and therefore is constantly eager for oral sex with men.

Though Damiano's physiological fiction about *one* woman was far less ambitious than Freud's distortion of *all* women, his porn movie had a whammo audio-visual impact; a teaching device that Freudian theory had lacked.

Literally millions of women seem to have been taken to "Deep Throat" by their boyfriends or husbands (not to mention prostitutes by pimps) so that each one might learn what a woman could do to please a man *if she really wanted to.*

If she were really a spoilsport, she might identify with the woman onscreen and realize her humiliation, danger, and pain, but the smiling, happy face of Linda Lovelace could serve to cut off empathy, too. *She's there because she wants to be. Who is forcing her?*

Eight years later, Linda has told us the humiliating and painful answer in *Ordeal,* her autobiography, but it's important to understand how difficult it was (and probably still is, in the case of other victims) to know the truth.

At the height of the movie's popularity, for instance, Nora Ephron wrote an essay about going to see "Deep Throat." She was determined not to react like those "crazy feminists carrying on, criticizing nonpolitical films in political terms." Nonetheless, she sat terrified through such scenes as one in which a hollow glass dildo is inserted in Linda Lovelace, filled with Coca-Cola, which was then drunk through a surgical straw. ("All I could think about," she confessed, "was what would happen if the glass broke.") Feeling humiliated and angry (and told by her male friends that she is "overreacting" and that the Coca-Cola scene is "hilarious"), she uses her license as a writer to get a telephone interview with Linda Lovelace. "I totally enjoyed myself making the movie," she is told, "I don't have any inhibitions about sex. I just hope that everybody who goes to see the film . . . loses some of their inhibitions."

So Nora wrote an article that assumed Linda to be a happy and willing porn queen who was enjoying "$250 a week . . . and a piece of the profits." And she accepted her own reaction as a "puritanical feminist who lost her sense of humor at a skin flick."

What she did not know (how could any interviewer know?) was that Linda would later list these and other answers as having been dictated by Chuck Traynor for just such journalistic occasions; that he punished her for betraying any unacceptable emotion (when, for instance, one of five men to whom she was delivered in a motel room for a gang-bang refused to pay because she cried); in fact, that she had been beaten and raped so severely and regularly that she suffered rectal damage and permanent injury to the blood vessels in her legs.

What Nora did not know was that Linda would also write of her three escape attempts, and her three forcible returns to this life of sexual servitude: first by the betrayal of another prostitute; then by her own mother who had been charmed into telling Chuck Traynor Linda's whereabouts by his protestation of being both sorry and relatively innocent; and finally by Linda's fear for the lives of two friends who had sheltered her after hearing that she had been made to do a sex film with a dog, and outside whose home Traynor had parked a van that contained, Linda believed, his collection of hand grenades and a machine gun.

Even now, all of these and other facts about Traynor must be read with the word "alleged" in front of them; for they come from Linda's account of more than two years of fear, sadism, and forced prostitution. Traynor has been quoted as calling these charges "so ridiculous I can't take them seriously." He has also been quoted as saying that "when I first dated her she was so shy, it shocked her to be seen nude by a man . . . *I created Linda Lovelace.*"

Linda's account of being "created" includes guns being put to her head, turning tricks while being watched through a peephole to make sure she couldn't escape, and having a garden hose jammed up her rectum and turned on if she refused to offer such amusements as exposing herself in restaurants and to passing drivers on the highway.

Ordeal is a very difficult book to read—and must have been more difficult still to write. But Linda says she wanted to purge forever the idea that she had become "Linda Lovelace" voluntarily.

Was profit a motive? Certainly she badly needs money for herself, her three-year-old son, imminently expected baby, and her husband, a childhood friend named Larry Marchiano, whose work as a TV cable installer has been jeopardized by Linda's past. Recently, they have been living on partial welfare. But Linda points out that she has refused offers of more than $3 million to do another movie like "Deep Throat." (For that filming eight years ago, Linda was paid $1,200; a sum that, like her fees for tricks, she never saw.) "I wouldn't do any of that again," she says, "even if I could get fifty million dollars."

Another motive for publishing *Ordeal* becomes clear when she talks about receiving a postcard from a young woman coerced into prostitution, who said she got the courage to escape after seeing a television program in which Linda was interviewed. "Women have to be given the courage to try to escape, and to know that you *can* get your self-respect back," she says. "It meant the whole world to me to get that postcard."

Ironically, her own hope of escape returned when, thanks to the surprising success of "Deep Throat," she could have contact with other people occasionally; with a world that she says had been denied to her, even in the form of listening to the radio or reading newspapers. Nonetheless, she sees many women used in porn now as being in even more danger than she was. "I thank God today that they weren't making snuff movies back then. . . . Women are being beaten to death, and the people who are making [these movies] are getting away with murder and making money on it."

She says she escaped by feigning trustworthiness for 10 minutes, then a little longer each time until, six months later, she was left unguarded during rehearsals for a stage version of "Linda Lovelace." Even then, she spent weeks hiding out in hotels alone, convinced she might be beaten or killed for her fourth try, but feeling stronger this time for having only her own life to worry about. It took a long period of hiding, with help and disguises supplied by a sympathetic secretary from the newly successful Linda Lovelace Enterprises—and no help from police who said they could do nothing to protect her "until the man with the gun is in the room with you"—but the fear finally dwindled into a nagging terror of running into Traynor at all, and a lawsuit against her for breach of contract.

When she finally did see Traynor in a restaurant, he was with a new porn star: Marilyn Chambers, the model who appeared in "Behind the Green Door."

And then suddenly, she got word through a lawyer that Traynor was willing to sign divorce papers. The threats and entreaties to return just stopped.

Free of hiding and disguises at last, she tried to turn her created identity into real acting by doing "Linda Lovelace for President," a comedy with no explicit sex, but discovered that producers who offered her roles always expected nudity in return. She went to a Cannes Film Festival, but was depressed by her very acceptance among celebrities she had respected. "I had been in a disgusting film with disgusting people . . . what were they doing watching a movie like that in the first place?"

Now that she was giving her own answers to questions and trying to explain her years of coercion, she discovered that reporters were reluctant to rush into print. Her story was depressing: not glamorous or titillating at all. Because she had been passed around like a sexual trading coin, sometimes to men who were famous, there was also fear of lawsuits.

Only in 1978 when she was believed by Mike McGrady, a respected newspaper reporter on Long Island where she had moved with her new husband, did her story begin the long process of reaching the public. Even with the benefit of McGrady as collaborator, plus an 11-hour lie-detector test by the former chief polygraphist of the New York District Attorney's office—a test that included great detail and brutal cross-questioning—several major publishers still turned down the manuscript. It was finally believed and accepted by Lyle Stuart, a maverick in the world of books who often takes on sensational or controversial subjects.

One wonders: Would a male political prisoner or a hostage telling a similar story have been so disbelieved? *Ordeal* attacks the myth of female masochism that insists women enjoy pain and seek domination, but prostitution and pornography may be the last bastions to fall. When asked why she didn't escape earlier, Linda wrote: "I can understand why some people have such trouble accepting the truth. When I was younger, when I heard about a woman being raped, my secret feeling was that could never happen to me. I would never *permit* it to happen. Now I realize that can be about as meaningful as saying I won't permit an avalanche."

Perhaps the unknown victims of sexual servitude—the young blondes of the

Minnesota Pipeline, "seasoned" by pimps and set up in Times Square; the welfare mothers pressured into legal prostitution in Nevada; the "exotic" dancers imported for porn films and topless bars—will be the next voiceless, much-blamed women to speak out and begin placing the blame where it belongs. Now, they are just as disbelieved as rape victims and battered women were a few years ago.

Because of her book, Linda is sitting quiet and soft-spoken on TV's Phil Donahue Show. Under her slacks, she wears surgical stockings to protect the veins that were damaged by the beatings in which she curled up, fetuslike, to protect her stomach and breasts from kicks and blows; this she says under Donahue's questioning. Probably, she will need surgery after her baby is born. The silicone injected in her breasts by a doctor (who, like many other professionals to whom she was taken, was paid by Linda's sexual services) has shifted painfully, and drastic surgery may be necessary there, too.

Yet Donahue, usually an insightful interviewer, is asking her psychological questions about her background: How did she get along with her parents? What did they tell her about sex? Didn't her fate have something to do with the fact that she had been pregnant when she was 19, and had given birth to a baby that Linda's mother put up for adoption?

Some of the women in the audience take up this line of questioning, too. *They* had been poor. *They* had strict and authoritarian parents; yet *they* didn't end up as part of the pornographic underground. The air is thick with the virtue of self-congratulation. Donahue talks on about the tragedy of teenage pregnancy, and what parents can do to keep their children from a Linda-like fate.

Because Traynor had a marriage ceremony performed somewhere along the way (Linda says this was to make sure she couldn't testify against him on drug charges), she has to nod when he is referred to as "your husband." On her own, however, she refers to him as "Mr. Traynor."

Linda listens patiently to doubts and objections, but she never gives up trying to make the audience understand. If another woman had met a man of violence and sadism who "got off on pain" as Linda has described in her book, *she might have ended up exactly the same way.* No, she never loved him—he was the object of her hatred and terror. Yes, he was very nice, very gentlemanly when they first met. They had no sexual relationship at all. He had just offered an apartment as a refuge from her strict childlike regime at home. *And then he did a 180-degree turn.* She became, she says quietly, a prisoner. A prisoner of immediate violence and the fear of much more.

She describes being so isolated and controlled that she was not allowed to speak in public or to go to the bathroom without Traynor's permission. *There was no choice. It could happen to anyone.* She says this simply, over and over again, and to many women in the audience, the point finally comes through. But to some, it never does. Donahue continues to ask questions about her childhood, her background. What attracted her to this fate? How can we raise our daughters to avoid it?

No one asks how we can stop raising men who fit Linda's terrified description of Chuck Traynor. Or the millions of men who went to "Deep Throat" and laughed. Or the millions more who assume that violence and aggression are a natural part of sex.

A woman in the audience asks if this isn't an issue for feminism. Linda says yes, she has heard there are antipornography groups, she is getting in touch with Susan Brownmiller.

But it's clear that this is a new hope and connection.

For women who want to support Linda now, and save others who are still in the life against their will, this may also be the greatest sadness. At no time during those months of suffering and dreams of escape, not even during the years of silence that followed, was Linda aware of any signal from the world around her that strong women as a group—or feminists, or something called the Women's Movement—might be there to help her. Surely, a victim of anti-Semitism might go to the Jewish community for help, or a victim of racism might look to the civil rights movements. But feminist groups haven't yet grown strong enough to be a public presence in the world of pornography, prostitution, and gynocide, or even the world of welfare and the working poor that Linda then joined. Even now, her help and her identity come only from sympathetic men: from McGrady who believed her life story (and wrote it in well-intentioned, journalistic style, but not her gentle speech pattern); from her husband who loses jobs in defense of her honor; from the male God of her obedient Catholic girlhood to whom she prayed as a sexual prisoner and prays now in her daily routine as mother and homemaker.

Even her feelings of betrayal are attached only to her father. During her long lie-detector test, the only time she cried and completely broke down was over an innocuous mention of his name. "I was watching that movie 'Hard Core,' " she explained, "where George C. Scott searches and searches for his daughter.

"Why didn't my father come looking for me? He saw 'Deep Throat.' He should've known. . . . He should've done something. Anything!"

After all, who among us had mothers with the power to rescue us, to *do something*? We don't even expect it—not even of ourselves. What price do we pay with our own imitative powerlessness? Demeter rescued her daughter from the King of the Underworld who had abducted and raped her: she was a strong and raging mother who turned the earth to winter in anger at her daughter's fate. Could a mother now rescue her daughter from the underworld of pornography? Not even Hollywood can fantasize such a plot.

But Linda has begun to uncover her own rage, at least when talking about her fear for other women as pornography becomes even more violent. "Next," she says, as if to herself, "they're going to be selling women's skins by the side of the road."

And women have at least begun to bond together to rescue each other; to be powerful sisters. There are centers for battered women, for instance, with publicized phone numbers for the victims, and private shelter locations so they cannot be followed. It's a system that might also work for some of the unwilling victims of prostitution and pornography. If it existed—and if women knew help was there.

In the meantime, Linda takes time out from cleaning her tiny house on Long Island ("I clean twice a day," she says proudly) to do interviews, to send out a message of hope and strength to other women who are living in sexual servitude right now. She keeps answering questions, most of them from male interviewers who are far less sympathetic than Donahue.

How could she write such a book for her son to read? ("I've already explained to him," she says firmly, "that some people hurt Mommy—a long time ago.") How can her husband stand to have a wife with such a sexual past? ("It wasn't sexual. I never experienced any sexual pleasure, not one orgasm, nothing. I learned how to fake pleasure so I wouldn't get punished for doing a bad job.") And the most popular doubt of all: *If she really wanted to, why couldn't she have escaped sooner?*

Linda explains as best she can, but as I watch her, I come to believe the question should be a different one. *How could she have the courage to escape at all?*

Inside the kind patience with which she answers these questions—the result of long years of training to be a "good girl" that may make victims of us all—there is some core of strength and stubbornness that is itself the answer. She *will* make people understand. She will *not* give up.

In the microcosm of this one woman is the familiar miracle; the way in which women survive—and fight back.

And a fight there must be.

Since "Deep Throat," a whole new genre of pornography has developed. Added to all the familiar varieties of rape, there is now an ambition to rape the throat. Porn novels treat this theme endlessly. Real-life victims of suffocation may be on the increase; so some emergency-room doctors believe. And then there is "snuff": not even the dignity of a word like "murder" is accorded to these victims. There is also "chicken porn," which specializes in the very young.

As for Chuck Traynor himself, he is still the husband and manager of Marilyn Chambers. They are said to be living in London.

Larry Fields, a columnist for the Philadelphia *Daily News,* remembers interviewing them both for his column a few years ago when Marilyn was performing a song-and-dance act in a local nightclub. Traynor bragged that he had taught Linda Lovelace everything she knew, but that "Marilyn's got what Linda never had. Talent."

While Traynor was answering questions on Marilyn's behalf, she asked him for permission to go to the bathroom. Permission was refused. "Not right now," Fields remembers his saying to her. And when she objected that she was about to appear onstage: "Just sit there and shut up."

When Fields also objected, Traynor was adamant. "I don't tell you how to write your column," he said angrily. "Don't tell me how to treat my broads."

LINDA LOVELACE'S "ORDEAL":
MEMOIRS OF A WOMAN'S DISPLEASURE

Aryeh Neier

 *Ordeal*, by Linda Lovelace (with Mike McGrady), as everyone must know by now, is the quondam porn actress's account of how she was forced into her trade by her brute of a husband. Not surprisingly, given its sensational subject, the book quickly established itself on the best-seller lists. More surprisingly, it has made Lovelace a heroine to a segment of the feminist movement. She gets star billing in demonstrations sponsored by Women Against Pornography. A leading feminist crusader against pornography, Andrea Dworkin, lauds her "courage." And she is celebrated in the pages of *Ms.*, where Gloria Steinem proclaims, "She *will* make people understand. She will *not* give up. In the microcosm of this one woman is the familiar miracle; the way in which women survive—and fight back."

If Lovelace's tale of woe is true—and I have no reason to doubt that it is—she certainly deserves sympathy. But why do feminists like Steinem see her as a "microcosm" of all women, as a symbol of women's determination to fight back, as a heroine of our time? Is it because they believe that many or most of the women who perform in pornographic movies and live shows or pose for pornographic photographs are coerced the way Lovelace says she was coerced? If so, where is the evidence for this belief? And if they have no evidence but believe it to be so because it fits their ideology, what is the significance of this new development in feminist thought?

In pondering these questions, I find it helpful to consider Lovelace's story against the backdrop of the shifting fashions in the way society regards women who sell their bodies or whose bodies are sold by others. These fashions are reflected in the literature of the last three centuries. Whether because of the intrinsic importance of the subject, or because of its salacious possibilities, or because the stories of such women lend themselves to the narrative and dramatic arts, fallen women are among the most popular characters in all literature. Moreover, some of these fictional women have seemed to burst out of the pages of literature, becoming emblematic figures for social reformers of their times, much as Lovelace has been taken up as a representative figure by some feminists.

First place, chronologically and in some other ways too, belongs to Daniel Defoe's heroines Moll Flanders and Roxana. They use their bodies to surmount desperate circumstances. In Moll's case, it is a life of "service," which is the best she can expect as the abandoned daughter of a woman "transported to the plantations" as punishment for theft; with Roxana, it is a life of penury, the usual fate of a woman with five children abandoned after eight years of marriage by a wastrel of a husband. The only path to a good life for such

---

LINDA LOVELACE'S "ORDEAL": MEMOIRS ...   From *The Nation*, 231: 137, 154–156 (Aug. 16-23, 1980) by Aryeh Neier, Copyright 1980 Nation Magazine.

women in eighteenth-century England, Defoe informs us through Moll and Roxana, whose tales are told autobiographically, is to exploit their bodies. But Moll and Roxana are not tragic heroines. They are resolute and resourceful women who do what they must. In today's cliché, they would be called survivors. Neither seems to take much pleasure in the sexual side of her adventures; they derive satisfaction primarily from their material success, especially Roxana who, like Samuel Pepys, periodically calculates the advances in her net worth.

Far from condemning his heroines for exploiting their bodies, Defoe employs their stories to condemn the way men treat women, which makes it necessary for them to resort to prostitution to achieve economic independence. Many of the lines Defoe gives his women suggest his feminist sympathies, as when Roxana tells a suitor that she thinks "a woman was a free agent as well as a man, and was born free, and, could she manage herself suitably, might enjoy that liberty to as much purpose as the men do"; when she asserts, "that the very nature of the marriage-contract was, in short, nothing but giving up liberty, estate, authority, and everything to the man, and the woman was indeed a mere woman ever after—that is to say, a slave," and when she says, "that while a woman was single, she was a masculine in her politic capacity; that she had then the full command of what she had, and the full direction of what she did . . . that she was controlled by none, because accountable to none, and was in subjection to none."

Nineteenth-century novelists paint a different picture. Typically, their prostitute-heroines are virtuous women coerced into their trade by brutal men. They almost never control their own destinies like Moll and Roxana. Nancy in *Oliver Twist,* though her career is only described obliquely because of the prudish conventions of England in the 1830s, is one of the earliest of these tragic heroines. Dickens tells us that she was led into her way of life "step by step, deeper and deeper down into an abyss of crime and misery whence there was no escape." Like many prostitutes with hearts of gold in nineteenth-century fiction, she breaks with her evil associates and, shortly thereafter, dies an untimely death, murdered by Bill Sikes. Esther Gobseck, the virtuous prostitute in Honoré de Balzac's *Splendeurs et misères des courtisanes,* commits suicide moments before she can be informed that she has inherited seven million francs from a rich relative. Marguerite Gautier of Alexandre Dumas's *La dame aux camélias* dies of tuberculosis. Fleur-de-Marie, abducted from her aristocratic family, plied with liquor and sold into prostitution in Eugène Sue's *Les Mystères de Paris* ("undoubtedly the most popular novel of the 19th century," according to Peter Brooks), succumbs to a mysterious illness shortly after breaking with her way of life to enter a convent. Edmond de Goncourt's *La Fille Élisa* dies in a prison hospital, demented by the institution's system of enforced silence. And Maggie, the pathetic heroine of Stephen Crane's *Maggie: A Girl of the Streets,* drowns herself. (Even the century's most notable literary example of a nonvirtuous prostitute, Emile Zola's Nana, meets an early death—of smallpox: the pustules disfiguring her once beautiful face symbolize her inner corruption.) Death redeems these heroines from woman's worst fate: the violation of her body.

As the nineteenth century drew to a close, a few authors discarded the convention of the prostitute-victim and replaced her with heroines who had more in common with Moll and Roxana. Theodore Dreiser's turn-of-the-century novel *Sister Carrie* was at first thought so shocking that its original publisher all but scuttled the first edition. Since the book is not sexually explicit (even by the standard of its day) the scandal apparently lay in the narrative. Carrie, an attractive young woman from a small town in Wisconsin, goes to Chicago to live with her married sister and to earn her living. Discouraged by the miserable opportunities her time provides to working women, she readily gives up sweat-shop labor and moves in with a traveling salesman she met on the train to Chicago. The arrangement is a triumph for the salesman but Carrie thinks she ought to feel guilty. ("'Oh,' thought Drouet, 'how delicious is my conquest.' 'Ah,' thought Carrie, with mournful misgivings, 'what is it I have lost.'") Yet her delight in the finery the salesman provides for her quickly overcomes any sense of remorse.

While her salesman is out on the road, Carrie develops a relationship with Hurstwood, an older man of higher social standing. His interest in her, like the salesman's, is in making a conquest. Her interest in him is that he appears able to help her live more luxuriously than the salesman. Hurstwood abandons his family and his job and steals from his employer to run off with her. After installing her in an apartment in New York City, things go bad for him. Desperate for money, Carrie uses her good looks to get a job as a chorus girl and becomes a hit on the stage. Resentful of having to share her earnings with the man who gave up everything to run off with her—by this time Hurstwood is down and out—Carrie abandons him. At the end of the book, he dies a pauper's death while she reigns as the toast of New York.

What was shocking about *Sister Carrie* was its heroine's failure to come to a bad end. Dreiser did not kill Carrie off—whether by murder, suicide, a mysterious disease, or a broken heart—to punish her for exploiting her looks to advance herself. She is not so degraded by promiscuity that she must die to achieve redemption. We leave her in control of her own life while Hurstwood, the man who made a fool of himself for an amorous conquest, dies tragically.

Even more shocking in its time was George Bernard Shaw's early play *Mrs. Warren's Profession*. Like Carrie, Moll and Roxana, Mrs. Warren's choice is dictated by the denial of economic opportunities to women. But also like them, she pursues her career not with a sense of victimization but with a sense of triumph. As she explains her choice of a profession to her daughter, "If you have a turn for music, or the stage, or newspaper writing: that's different. But neither Liz [her sister] nor I had a turn for such things: all we had was our appearance and our turn for pleasing men. Do you think we were such fools as to let other people trade in our good looks by employing us as shopgirls, or barmaids, or waitresses, when we could trade in them ourselves and get all the profits instead of starvation wages? Not likely."

Shaw set out to challenge nineteenth-century thinking about prostitutes. As he wrote subsequently in a preface, "*Mrs. Warren's Profession* was written in 1894 to draw attention to the truth that prostitution is caused not by female depravity and male licentiousness, but simply by underpaying, undervaluing and overworking women so shamefully that the poorest of them are forced to resort to prostitution to keep body and soul together." Yet by itself, the exposition of that view would not have caused a great scandal. As it was, it took eight years until *Mrs. Warren's Profession* could be staged in London and a year longer before it could be performed in New York City. When it finally opened in New York, the police raided it and arrested the producer and the members of the company.

Mrs. Warren's Profession is even less sexually explicit than *Sister Carrie*. In deference to the censors, even the word to describe the profession of Mrs. Warren is never mentioned. What was shocking about the play, apparently, is that Mrs. Warren does not suffer for her sins; she enjoys herself. Convention demanded, as Shaw wrote in the preface, that prostitutes "shall, at the end of the play, die of consumption to the sympathetic tears of the whole audience, or step into the next room to commit suicide, or at least be turned out by their protectors, passed on to be 'redeemed' by old and faithful lovers." Mrs. Warren does not die because Shaw, an ardent feminist, did not think her reason for existence disappeared simply because she had sullied her body sexually.

Linda Lovelace's story fits the convention against which Shaw rebelled nearly a century ago. While she hasn't died, she reports that she has endured such misery and physical debilitation that even nineteenth-century censors might concede that she has suffered enough. As a further sign of her redemption, *Ordeal* concludes with an epilogue in which Lovelace tells us, "Today, after finishing this, I'm going to clean my house. I've borrowed a vacuum cleaner for the afternoon and the thought of doing that gives me a great deal of pleasure. I'm a cleanliness nut, and if my little house isn't spotless, I get very upset." In *Ms.*, Steinem vouchsafes that "Linda takes time out from cleaning her tiny house on Long Island ('I clean twice a day,' she says proudly) to do interviews, to send out a message of hope and strength to other women who are living in sexual servitude right now." In further certifying Lovelace's virtue, Steinem asks. "How can her husband stand to have a wife with such a sexual past?" and quotes Lovelace's answer approvingly: "It wasn't sexual. I never experienced any sexual pleasure, not one orgasm."

In celebrating Lovelace's preservation of her virtue through nonenjoyment and her redemption through suffering and housework, feminists like Steinem contradict feminists like Shaw. To Shaw, Mrs. Warren's sexuality did not define her; it was merely her profession. To Steinem, Lovelace's sexuality is everything; the "miracle" is that she survives despite the violation of her body. In a curious way, Steinem's perception of Lovelace resembles that of the producers of *Deep Throat:* she is solely a sexual object.

Lovelace is a great prize. *Deep Throat* is probably the most popular pornographic work ever. Steinem estimates that it grossed $600 million. While that sounds preternaturally high—nearly half again as much as *Star Wars,* the movie usually regarded as the all-time champion—unquestionably it earned a lot. *Deep Throat* symbolizes the pornography industry and enhances Lovelace's credibility as a representative of all women depicted in pornography. If she was terrorized to make her perform in *Deep Throat,* it becomes easier to believe that the practice is pervasive in the industry than if the same complaint were made by a performer in some obscure film. To my knowledge, there is no evidence that what used to be called "white slavery" is widely practiced in the United States today, though thanks to *Ordeal* and its feminist enthusiasts, the idea (if not the name) is being revived.

The assumption that many of the women who perform in pornographic movies are coerced as Lovelace was serves a double purpose. First, and most obviously, it supplies the elusive link between pornography and actual harm to women; pornography becomes merely another manifestation of rape, appearing to justify censorship. Second, and perhaps more important, it answers a question that seems to nag feminists who campaign against pornography: Are they condemning the women who take part in it? Those who believe in the sisterhood of all women prefer to limit their attacks on pornographers to the males in the business. This is difficult, unless Lovelace's ordeal is considered representative of the ordeals experienced by many or most other women taking part in pornography.

In assuming that women take part in pornography only because they are physically coerced, these feminists align themselves with the pervasive nineteenth-century belief that women are mere pawns manipulated by men. Perhaps they also repudiate as outdated the views of those like Defoe and Shaw who would not censure the prostitute because they believed that her choice of a career reflected a reasonable response to her restricted economic opportunities. Other paths to economic independence are no longer completely closed to women. But that hardly means that every woman has an alternative. Some start selling their bodies when they are too young to earn their livings any other way, among them runaways forced out by families less tolerant of sexual activity by their daughters than their sons. Women who start selling their bodies when they are older may also find few alternatives if they lack skills. And, even where alternatives are available, some women still choose pornography or prostitution. Thirty years ago, Simone de Beauvoir wrote, "As a matter of fact, the prostitute would often have been able to make a living in other ways. But if the way she has chosen does not seem to her to be the worst, that does not prove that vice is in her blood; it rather condemns a society in which this occupation is still one of those which seem the least repellent to many women. It is often asked: why does she choose it? The question is rather: why has she not chosen it?"

Those who see Lovelace as a representative figure seem to contradict de Beauvoir and to deny that women choose to take part in pornography and prostitution. The fault is exclusively male. It is not sufficient to blame men for consuming pornography and prostitution. They must also be excoriated as the subjugators of the women without whom these industries could not exist. No doubt males have much to answer for, but it is not clear that the feminist cause is advanced by insisting that any woman who exploits her body is not responsible for her own life. Lovelace may well be the victim she is portrayed as in *Ordeal*. But for women generally (as for men), Emma Goldman's advice still seems sound: "A true conception of the relation of the sexes will not admit of conqueror and conquered."

NAKED AUTHOR

Mike McGrady, Lovelace's co-author and the object of praise by Steinem and other feminists for helping her tell her story, is identified on the dust jacket of *Ordeal* as "the chief catalyst" of *Naked Came the Stranger*. For those who may have forgotten, *Naked* was a very popular porn novel published in 1969. It was also a hoax. Purportedly the work of "Penelope Ashe," identified on its dust jacket as "a demure Long Island housewife," it was actually written by twenty-five reporters and editors of *Newsday*, a leading Long Island newspaper. McGrady enlisted his colleagues in this enterprise with a memorandum inviting them to become co-authors of a best-selling novel that would have "an unremitting emphasis on sex."

Naked became the best seller McGrady anticipated. According to *The New York Times*, it sold 20,000 hardcover copies within two weeks of publication and the paperback rights were sold for $127,500—when that was a very large sum. *The Times*, which headed its account "Does Sex Sell? Ask Penelope Ashe," also reported that "twenty producers and directors are competing for the movie rights."

The theme of *Naked* is similar to Lovelace's *Deep Throat*. A woman craves sexual satisfaction. Her search leads to sexual relations with a large number of men. Both works try to be funny, their labored humor deriving from the assortment of male types enjoying sex with their heroines and the settings of the encounters. Like *Ordeal*, *Naked* was issued by Lyle Stuart, Inc., publishers of the sensational.

MORE THAN SKIN DEEP

Helen Whitcomb and Rosalind Lang

"More Than Skin Deep" is a chapter from a widely used textbook for secretarial students. The text, *Charm*, was designed to complement the student's training in shorthand, typing, and other office skills. The text simply took it for granted that all secretarial students would be women. And it accepted as well the notion that bosses (presumed to be men) could rightfully expect more from their "girls" than accurate filing or error-free typing. The "girl" who wished to get ahead would give bosses what they wanted.

We surround the word girl with quotation marks because we want you to notice how unself-consciously Whitcomb and Lang used this diminutive. For them, writing in the 1960s, the word conveyed no overt connotations of female inferiority or dependency. Still, the question remains: Were those connotations present regardless of the authors' intentions? And, if they were, did they perhaps play a role in limiting the opportunities available to women? Would a boss, for example, entrust a "girl" with a "man's job"?

How much joy do you find in life? Hopefully, a large amount, for your facial expressions will be taken as an indication of whether or not you're nice to know. Facial expressions and general appearance are the first clues a stranger has to go on in deciding what type of person you are. Some girls have beauty but little or no charm. Good looks won't guarantee social success. They must be accompanied by facial expressions that reveal warmth and friendliness. How emotionally flat we feel when confronted with Miss Deadpan. She may

MORE THAN SKIN DEEP   From: *Charm: The Career Girl's Guide To Business And Personal Success* (New York: Gregg Division of McGraw-Hill Book Co., 1964) 127–33. Reprinted by permission.

be the most beautiful girl in Oshkosh, and may have a heart of gold down there somewhere, but unless her face shows her kindly disposition her plus qualities are lost.

Attractive facial expressions add a shine that can make a plain girl stand out from the crowd. A lively smile and sparkling eyes will attract attention, and a face that mirrors a warm and kindly personality has a vivacious quality far more desirable than mere beauty.

Let the face you show the world advertise you as someone who is nice to know. Too much reserve detracts from charm. Once you really understand Miss Deadpan, you may become bosom pals; but often you haven't the time or the opportunity to dig beneath a cold exterior. Especially in the brief encounters of busy offices, the ability to project your feelings instantly with features, gestures, and movements is all important.

The girl who wants more expressive features can easily teach them to be more responsive. Just watch a movie or TV play and note how the actors express their feelings. A fascinating study can be made by turning off the sound while watching a TV play. Through actions alone you can often get the gist of the story. A good actor is an astute student of human nature. He knows that a smile comes from the eyes as well as the mouth. Some of the most intense feelings can be vividly portrayed without uttering a word.

Notice the difference between an accomplished actor and a ham—the actor is an artist who uses facial expressions and gestures with restraint. His movements are subtle, not flamboyant. Unnatural theatrical expressions and gestures only smack of affectation. Features should express *sincere* feelings or they make you look false or comic.

CULTIVATE A SMILE   An easy, natural smile is the most important facial expression anyone can have. When you have made a happy smile a habit, you have a beauty asset that will keep your face pleasant and youthful no matter how many gray hairs the years bring. Just as good posture is a matter of good habits, a cheerful expression is often merely a habit of remembering to smile. Although we may feel quite pleased with our world, we are sometimes just so naturally lazy that we allow our faces to remain blank. How much prettier is the girl who lets her pleasant feelings light up her face!

Conversely, when your spirits are low, do your best not to advertise it by your expression. This only spreads your gloom, and can often increase it. Unhappy expressions are too costly to tolerate; if they become habits, they can actually distort features.

Teach yourself to smile easily and often. It's amazing how a sincere smile can charm others. No need to tell you that a smile is contagious. Perhaps you can promote an epidemic!

LET YOUR EYES SPARKLE   When you enjoy something, show it. Let your eyes radiate your delight. A sparkle in the eyes is something you can develop if it doesn't already come naturally. Many people forget to use their eyes in expressing themselves, but eyes can dramatize feelings with great effectiveness and subtlety. Let the sparkle in your eyes proclaim you as someone who's fun to be with.

THINK HAPPY Trying to cultivate a smile has many benefits. Not only does it look pretty, but you are forced to develop a pleasant mood to back it up. Otherwise the smile quickly fades—or gives itself away as being merely mechanical.

The easiest way to promote a good mood is to allow nothing but pleasant, kindly thoughts to lodge in your mind, which, granted, is far from easy. It's all too human to take a certain pleasure from telling someone off mentally or secretly spotting another's flaws to enjoy the feeling of superiority. But what wasteful thoughts they are! Worse yet, they are sure to show—if not in our faces, in our actions. If we criticize, our disapproval can't help but leak through and do damage we did not intend.

The brain—marvel though it is—is unable to give primary attention to more than one thing at a time. Only one thought can be supreme. Fill your mind with a pleasant thought and the disagreeable one must fade out. Actually, you can build yourself a protective armor of happiness if you resolve not to give room to useless gripes, grievances, envy, and similar destructive negative thoughts. The disturbing trifles of life will stay in their proper perspective. The rude salesgirl, the man who shoved the door in your face, the thoughtless remark your boss made—these will be less likely to upset you or disrupt your poise and self-control.

Search for happiness in everything you do. What ideas of your own can you add to these?

Make other people happy. Take a few moments each morning—perhaps while you're churning up enough energy to climb out of bed, or while traveling to school or office—to analyze the day for opportunities to be gracious and kind. Go out of your way to be especially thoughtful today.

Use your senses to the fullest in your search for beauty. Develop the artist's eye for appreciating the beautiful lacy design of leafless tree branches or the pattern of city streets. Notice the lovely fragrance of springtime blossoms, the aroma of morning toast and coffee, the sounds of the city at evening when the workaday noises give way to nighttime glamour. There's beauty of some sort all round you if you can learn to appreciate it.

Let yourself be inspired by those you admire most. Cultivate their acquaintance, for some of their greatness will surely rub off on you.

Ruthlessly weed out any strangling self-pity. A certain masochistic pleasure can be derived from picturing ourselves as "poor little me." Sometimes we tend to flaunt our difficulties almost proudly, and often we use them as excuses for inertia and lack of effort. All of us have limitations of some sort. It's how we surmount these limitations that reveals our strength and character.

Learn to accept others as they are and don't compare yourself with them. Concentrate instead on making the most of what you have.

Try to bring out the charm in others. Charm is merely your effect on others. If you can help them to feel more clever and important—to bring out the best in themselves—you will be cherished dearly.

Try to become deeply interested in someone or something. Perhaps it can be a hobby, an organization, charity work at the local orphanage, a little theater group—or you-know-who. Love and enthusiasm are the greatest beautifiers.

Don't criticize. Don'even let yourself think criticism. Such unpleasant thoughts are merely a waste of the precious energy you wish to devote to beautifying thoughts—to understanding, tolerance, forgiveness, sympathy, friendship, love, and appreciation. Margery Wilson in her wonderfully wise book, *The Woman You Want to Be,** offered this advice to those who wish to develop charm. "Your job is to keep yourself so saturated with beauty that you cannot help expressing it under all conditions, and continue to express it without hope of reward.

"The practice of this . . . is, in the last analysis, the sternest economy of emotion, time, and happiness. When the expression of loveliness fills you as completely as that, the reward is much greater than any return you could dare to plan or wish for."

LISTEN WITH YOUR FACE   Some of the most successful conversationalists are the best listeners. Your face can often say more than words in encouraging a speaker. Let your features and expressions respond to his words and reflect his feelings. Show that you are concentrating on what he is saying by letting your eyes follow his. Blink occasionally to avoid staring. Nod slightly when you agree with a particular point. Even without saying a word, you will seem to speak volumes with great eloquence and understanding.

MIX WITH MODERATION   Any recipe for developing facial vivaciousness should include the caution "don't overdo it." Excessive mugging, screaming enthusiasm, and clownish behavior are childish. Any facial expressions you adopt must be an outgrowth of *your* personality. The too-cute wrinkling of the nose or the affected sidelong glance can be deadly if practiced by the wrong type. In everything you do, you want to express the mature warmth and kindness of a poised, cultivated young woman.

CHECK YOUR UNCONSCIOUS EXPRESSIONS   Many people are unaware that they possess unpleasant facial expressions that give a wrong impression. Check yourself frequently for a day or two to be sure none of these bad habits have crept into your expressions.

A frown while concentrating—gives the impression you're a sour apple.

Overuse of eyebrows to add intensity to speech—looks artificial, pulls the face apart.

Raised eyebrows—can seem superior or haughty.

Too wide a smile—can look insincere.

Too mild a smile—can seem halfhearted, lacking in warmth and spirit.

Biting, pursing, or licking your lips—betrays nervousness.

Become conscious of your face and how much it can say, and use it well to project the pleasant, friendly thoughts that mean so much to your charm.

FOLLOW-UP

1 For one whole day see how many *sincere* compliments you can pay.

---

*Published by J. B. Lippincott Company, Philadelphia, 1942.

2 Act out the following situations, remembering to use your eyes as well as your mouth to reveal your feelings. Talk aloud and make up the dialogue as you go along.

    a You are greeting a good friend you haven't seen in some time.

    b Someone has just surprised you with an unexpected gift.

    c You are showing a friend a little baby robin that fell from its nest.

    d You are describing something beautiful you have recently seen or heard.

3 Demonstrate different expressions by acting pleased, angry, surprised, pained, sympathetic, humorously aloof, disappointed, impressed to a "Wow!" degree, and so on. Add your own ideas to the list.

FOUR

Sweethearts and Wives

LOVE AND MARRIAGE may go together like a horse and carriage, as the popular song asserts, but the ride has not always been smooth, especially for women. "In America," de Tocqueville wrote in the widely-read *Democracy in America* (1835), "the independence of woman is irrecoverably lost in the bonds of matrimony." The French observer viewed this as a necessary loss, but the 1848 *Declaration of Sentiments* issued at Seneca Falls indicated that some women, at least, thought otherwise.

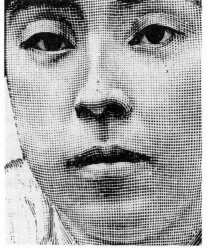

The *Declaration* inveighed against the fact that a married woman had no right to property, not even to her own wages; that she was required to promise obedience to her husband, who became her master; that she was forced into dependence; and that in cases of separation or divorce, the husband was given custody of children as well as property. "He has made her, if married," one article stated, "in the eye of the law, civilly dead."

When they married, women exchanged the rule and name of their fathers for the rule and name of their husbands. (It is still common for the father of the bride to "give her away.") In the rural economy of the early Republic, however, work site and home site were the same, so the division of labor was not totally gender-linked. But the integration of the family into the market economy of the nineteenth century changed the family from a unit of production to one of consumption. Husbands went off to factories and offices, leaving wives behind to do the work of the house. For a great majority of women, marriage became the only vocation open to them.

Magazines and advice books assured women that they would find total fulfillment in housework and childcare. As "angels in the house," they maintained for their husbands a refuge from the public world. By reinforcing ideals of female domesticity, submissiveness, conformity, and sexual purity, often on religious grounds, popular publications attempted to hold the line against changing values. Courtship became the main activity of the marriage market, and women learned to alter their own preferences and even their personalities in order to shape themselves to potential suitors.

Scarlett O'Hara, the spirited and independent heroine of Margaret Mitchell's best-seller of 1936, *Gone With the Wind,* got tired of "being unnatural" in order to find a husband. "I'm tired of saying, 'How wonderful you are!' to fool men who haven't got one-half the sense I've got, and I'm tired of pretending I don't know anything, so men can tell me things and feel important while they're doing it," she complained. Until recently, even the entrance of women into higher education had not substantially affected this charade. Hollywood films of the 1930s and 1940s, in fact, often presented the college campus as a place where women went to pursue the M.R.S. degree.

As the practical aims of marriage combined with the growing ideal of romantic love, weddings became formal public events. By the twentieth century, businesses specializing in wedding products and services had been established. Bride magazines proliferated, offering guidance on everything from the most fashionable patterns of china and silverware to the kinds of canapés to serve at the reception. The trappings of the event often overshadowed the seriousness of the commitment.

Wedding customs reflected the influence of romantic love, which was itself in part an expression of the freedom to choose one's mate. But love did not quite conquer all. It did not, for example, conquer differences in social and economic class. Alliances with the poor, many of them immigrants, were discouraged on the grounds that they might weaken the race and lead to lower moral standards. The question the popular radio soap opera of the 1940s, *Our Gal Sunday,* posed—Could a girl from a small mining town in the West find happiness married to a titled Englishman?—reflected this class bias.

Married women who took work into their homes or who worked outside did so out of economic necessity, but they remained responsible for domestic tasks as well. The current paradigm of the "superwoman," who holds a full-time job in addition to performing all domestic chores, is not a contemporary phenomenon. Working wives, however, were indicative of their husbands' inability to support them, and the ideal for middle and upper class marriages as well as for members of some ethnic groups was that wives should not work outside the home. Thorstein Veblen described women of the leisure class as displayers of wealth and idleness, both of which served to verify their husbands' social and economic status. Charlotte Perkins Gilman saw dependent wives as combinations of housemaids and prostitutes. "The transient trade we think evil," she wrote in *Women and Economics* (1898), "the bargain for life we think good."

The experiences of Black women differed markedly from those of their white middle class sisters, not only because they suffered the effects of racism, but because, as slaves, they had been perceived primarily as workers. In spite of the popular stereotypes of the domestic Mammy and Aunt Jemima, most women slaves were fieldworkers; their domestic lives in the slave quarters were in many ways a respite from the oppression of owners and overseers. After Emancipation, Black women entered domestic service in great numbers, making it possible for white women of leisure to avoid such chores.

The social pressure to marry was so intense that women who chose not to commit themselves to men were considered unfortunate or deviant. Unmarried women—called spinsters or old maids—were allowed into the domestic hierarchy to do women's work in the homes of relatives. Others entered teaching, a profession which did not accept married females, or religious orders. At the turn of the century, approximately four times as many women as men were in religious orders in the Boston area.

Even within the constraints of marriage, many women led active and productive lives as members of female networks, providing volunteer services to their communities and mutual support in times of need. In light of the circumscribed roles they were expected to play, married women such as Elizabeth Cady Stanton, Angelina Grimké, Harriet Beecher Stowe, Edith Wharton, and Eleanor Roosevelt were extraordinary indeed, in spite of their class advantages.

Extant marriage contracts from the nineteenth century indicate that egalitarian marriages were possible, although rare. The more recent popularity of such formal agreements, however, is based more on the recognition that marriage is not always permanent and on the acceptance of serial marriage. As life spans have lengthened, married people have found it more difficult to maintain certain commitments, and divorce, once a scandal of no small proportion, has become common. During the 60 years from 1867 to 1927, the rate of divorce increased 2000%. At the same time, as women outlived men, the number of widows increased. These divorced and widowed women have often found themselves the victims of the dependent role which they accepted in their marriages. Today they are called "displaced homemakers," women who, without husbands, have been left with little or no means of self-support.

For women, marriage has meant the acceptance of a double standard. Women were destined for one occupation; men for many. Women were fit for domestic work; men were not. Independence was a negative quality in women, a positive one in men. Wives were expected to be pure and faithful, but husbands were expected to have "sown their wild oats" and to have minor—or major—dalliances.

The popular image of the happy housewife may not be as pervasive now as it has been at other times, but it seems to hover below the surface of events, ready to be resurrected in times of social or economic necessity. Love and marriage still go together like a horse and carriage, perhaps, but more and more women are learning to drive.

WHY DON'T THE MEN PROPOSE?

T. H. Bayly

From its beginning in the 1830s, *Godey's Lady's Book* was the arbiter of taste and fashion for white middle class women. Its famous editor, Sarah Josepha Hale, wielded the power of her office with care and discretion. Although she never fully supported the movement for women's rights, she did campaign for higher education for women, against tight corsets, and for the admission of women to the health professions. She also succeeded in keeping the Civil War out of the magazine.

Along with the moral tales, the articles of advice covering everything from food to furbelows, and the fashion plates, Hale included some poetry, usually uplifting or inspirational. The following poem, however, pokes gentle fun at the lengths to which some young women would go in order to elicit a proposal of marriage. The persona of the poem addresses her complaint to her mother, whom she considers her chief advisor in this campaign.

> Why don't the men propose, mamma?
>   Why don't the men propose?
> Each seems coming to a point,
>   And then away he goes!
> It is no fault of yours, mamma,
>   That every body knows;
> You fete the finest men in town,
>   Yet, oh! they won't propose!
>
> I'm sure I've done my best, mamma,
>   To make a proper match;
> For coronets and eldest sons
>   I'm ever on the watch;
> I've hopes when some distingue beau
>   A glance upon me throws:
> And though he'll dance, and smile, and flirt,
>   Alas! he won't propose!
>
> I've tried to win by languishing
>   And dressing like a blue;
> I've bought big books, and talk'd of them
>   As if I'd read them through!
> With hair cropp'd like a man, I've felt
>   The heads of all the beaux;
> But Spurzheim could not touch their hearts,
>   And oh! they won't propose.

WHY DON'T THE MEN PROPOSE?   From *Godey's Lady's Book*, February 1835, pp. 85.

I threw aside the books, and thought
　　That ignorance was bliss;
I felt convinced that men preferred
　　A simple sort of Miss;
And so I lisp'd out naught beyond
　　Plain "yeses" or plain "noes,"
And wore a sweet unmeaning smile;
　　Yet, oh, they won't propose!

Last night, at Lady Ramble's rout,
　　I heard Sir Harry Gale
Exclaim, "Now I propose again;"
　　I started, turning pale;
I really thought my time was come,
　　I blush'd like any rose;
But oh! I found 'twas only at
　　Escarte he'd propose!

And what is to be done, mamma?
　　Oh, what is to be done?
I really have no time to lose,
　　For I am thirty-one;
At balls I am too often left
　　Where spinsters sit in rows;
Why won't the men propose, mamma?
Why *won't* the men propose?

A TREE GROWS IN BROOKLYN

Betty Smith

Born in Brooklyn, Betty Smith (1896-1972) left school after the eighth grade and worked at various factory and clerical jobs. After moving to the midwest, she attended the University of Michigan as a special student, won an Avery Hopwood Prize for drama, married, and had two daughters. She was primarily a playwright before she wrote her first novel, *A Tree Grows in Brooklyn*. Based on her own life and her mother's recollections, Smith's autobiographical work was an instant best seller and was subsequently made into a film and a Broadway musical.

A Tree Grows in Brooklyn is the story of Francie Nolan's childhood and adolescence in the Brooklyn slums during the early part of the twentieth century. Although the sufferings and the joys of the Nolans are sentimentalized, the concrete details of their lives ring true. In the following excerpt, Francie is sixteen and working as a teletype operator when she meets Lee, a soldier on leave. Lee tells her he is engaged, but asks Francie to pretend she is his "best girl." He waits for her the next day after work, and they go dancing. When they leave the dance, Francie is faced with a choice between her values as a "good" girl and her own needs and desires.

A TREE GROWS IN BROOKLYN   Harper & Row, Popular Library Edition, 1956, pp. 401–407. First Edition, Harper & Row, 1943 from Chapters LII and LIII, pp. 410–419, in *A Tree Grows in Brooklyn* by Betty Smith. Copyright 1943 by Betty Smith. Reprinted by permission of Harper & Row Publishers, Inc.

They walked down the stairs slowly, the song following them. As they reached the street, they waited until the song died away.

> . . . Pray each night for me,
> Till we meet again.

"Let it be our song," he whispered, "and think of me every time you hear it."

As they walked, it started to rain and they had to run and find shelter in the doorway of a vacant store. They stood in the protected and dark doorway, held each other's hand and watched the rain falling.

"People always think that happiness is a faraway thing," thought Francie, "something complicated and hard to get. Yet, what little things can make it up; a place of shelter when it rains—a cup of strong hot coffee when you're blue; for a man, a cigarette for contentment; a book to read when you're alone—just to be with someone you love. Those things make happiness."

"I'm leaving early in the morning."

"Not for France?" Suddenly she was jolted out of her happiness.

"No, for home. My mother wants me for a day or two before . . . "

"Oh!"

"I love you, Francie."

"But you're engaged. That's the first thing you ever told me."

"Engaged," he said bitterly. "Everybody's engaged. Everybody in a small town is engaged or married or in trouble. There's nothing else to do in a small town.

"You go to school. You start walking home with a girl—maybe for no other reason than that she lives out your way. You grow up. She invites you to parties at her home. You go to other parties—people ask you to bring her along; you're expected to take her home. Soon no one else takes her out. Everybody thinks she's your girl and then . . . well, if you don't take her around, you feel like a heel. And then, because there's nothing else to do, you marry. And it works out all right if she's a decent girl (and most of the time she is) and you're a half-way decent fellow. No great passion but a kind of affectionate contentment. And then children came along and you give them the great love you kind of miss in each other. And the children gain in the long run.

"Yes, I'm engaged all right. But it isn't the same between her and me as it is between you and me."

"But you're going to marry her?"

He waited a long time before he answered.

"No."

She was happy again.

"Say it, Francie," he whispered. "Say it."

She said, "I love you, Lee."

"Francie . . . " there was urgency in his voice, "I may not come back from over there and I'm afraid . . . afraid. I might die . . . die, never having had anything . . . never . . . Francie, *can't* we be together for a little while?"

"We are together," said Francie innocently.

"I mean in a room . . . alone . . . Just till morning when I leave?"

"I . . . couldn't."

"Don't you *want* to?"

"Yes," she answered honestly.

"Then why. . . ."

"I'm only sixteen," she confessed bravely. "I've never been with . . . anybody. I wouldn't know how."

"That makes no difference."

"And I've never been away from home overnight. My mother would worry."

"You could tell her you spent the night with a girl friend."

"She knows I have no girl friend."

"You could think of some excuse . . . tomorrow."

"I wouldn't need to think of an excuse. I'd tell her the truth."

"You *would*?" he asked in astonishment.

"I love you. I wouldn't be ashamed . . . afterwards if I stayed with you. I'd be proud and happy and I wouldn't want to lie about it."

"I had no way of knowing, no way of knowing," he whispered as if to himself.

"*You* wouldn't want it to be something . . . sneaky, would you?"

"Francie, forgive me. I shouldn't have asked. I had no way of knowing."

"Knowing?" asked Francie, puzzled.

He put his arms around her and held her tightly. She saw that he was crying.

"Francie, I'm afraid . . . so afraid. I'm afraid that if I go away I'll lose you . . . never see you again. Tell me not to go home and I'll stay. We'll have tomorrow and the next day. We'll eat together and walk around or sit in a park or ride on top of a bus and just talk and be with each other. Tell me not to go."

"I guess you have to go. I guess that it's right that you see your mother once more before. . . . I don't know. But I guess it's right."

"Francie, will you marry me when the war's over—*if* I come back?"

"*When* you come back, I'll marry you."

"Will you, Francie? . . . please, will you?"

"Yes."

"Say it again."

"I'll marry you when you come back, Lee."

"And, Francie, we'll live in Brooklyn."

"We'll live wherever you want to live."

"We'll live in Brooklyn, then."

"Only if *you* want to, Lee."

"And will you write to me every day? *Every* day?"

"Every day," she promised.

"And will you write to me tonight when you get home and tell me how much you love me so that the letter will be waiting for me when I get home?" She promised. "Will you promise never to let anyone kiss you? Never to go out with anyone? To wait for me . . . no matter how long? And if I don't come back, never to *want* to marry anyone else?"

She promised.

And he asked for her whole life as simply as he'd ask for a date. And she promised away her whole life as simply as she'd offer a hand in greeting or farewell.

It stopped raining after a while and the stars came out. She wrote that night as she had promised—a long letter in which she poured out all her love and repeated the promises she had given.

She left a little earlier for work to have time to mail the letter from the Thirty-fourth Street post office. The clerk at the window assured her that it would reach its destination that afternoon. That was Wednesday.

She looked for but tried not to expect a letter Thursday night. There hadn't been time—unless he, too, wrote immediately after they had parted. But of course, he had to pack maybe—get up early to make his train. (It never occurred to her that *she* had managed to find time.) There was no letter Thursday night.

Friday, she had to work straight through—a sixteen hour shift—because the company was short-handed on account of an influenza epidemic. When she got home a little before two in the morning, there was a letter propped against the sugar bowl on the kitchen table. She ripped it open eagerly.

"Dear Miss Nolan:"

Her happiness died. It couldn't be from Lee because he'd write, "Dear Francie." She turned the page and looked at the signature. "Elizabeth Rhynor (Mrs.)" Oh! His mother. Or a sister-in-law. Maybe he was sick and couldn't write. Maybe there was an army rule that men about to go overseas couldn't write letters. He had asked someone to write for him. Of course. That was it. She started to read the letter.

"Lee told me all about you. I want to thank you for being so nice and friendly to him while he was in New York. He arrived home Wednesday afternoon but had to leave for camp the next week. He was home only a day and a half. We had a very quiet wedding, just the families and a few friends. . ."

Francie put the letter down. "I've been working sixteen hours in a row," she thought, "and I'm tired. I've read thousands of messages today and no words make sense right now. Anyhow, I got into bad reading habits at the Bureau—reading a column at a glance and seeing only one word in it. First I'll wash the sleep out of my eyes, have some coffee, and read the letter again. This time I'll read it right."

While the coffee heated, she splashed cold water on her face thinking that when she came to the part of the letter that said "wedding" she'd go on reading and the next words would be; "Lee was the best man. I married his brother you know."

Katie lying awake in her bed heard Francie moving about in the kitchen. She lay tense . . . waiting. And she wondered what it was she waited for.

Francie read the letter again.

". . . wedding, just the families and a few friends. Lee asked me to write and explain why he hadn't answered your letter. Again thank you for entertaining him so nicely while he was in your city. Yours truly, Elizabeth Rhynor (Mrs.)"

There was a postscript.

"I read the letter you sent Lee. It was mean of him to pretend to be in love with you and I told him so. He said to tell you he's dreadfully sorry. E.R."

Francie was trembling violently. Her teeth made little biting sounds. "Mama," she moaned. *"Mama!"*

Katie heard the story. "It's come at last," she thought, "the time when you can no longer stand between your children and heartache. When there wasn't enough food in the house you pretended that you weren't hungry so they could have more. In the cold of a winter's night you got up and put your blanket on their bed so they wouldn't be cold. You'd kill anyone who tried to harm them—I tried my best to kill that man in the hallway. Then one sunny day, they walk out in all innocence and they walk right into the grief that you'd give your life to spare them."

Francie gave her the letter. She read it slowly and as she read, she thought she knew how it was. Here was a man of twenty-two who evidently (to use one of Sissy's phrases) had been around. Here was a girl sixteen years old; six years younger than he. A girl—in spite of bright-red lipstick and grown-up clothes and a lot of knowledge picked up here and there—who was yet tremulously innocent; a girl who had come face to face with some of the evil of the world and most of its hardships, and yet had remained curiously untouched by the world. Yes, she could understand her appeal for him.

Well, what could she say? That he was no good or at best just a weak man who was easily susceptible to whoever he was with? No, she couldn't be so cruel as to say that. Besides the girl wouldn't believe her anyhow.

"Say something," demanded Francie. "Why don't you say something?"

"What can I say?"

"Say that I'm young—that I'll get over it. Go ahead and say it. Go ahead and lie."

"I know that's what people say—you'll get over it. I'd say it, too. But I know it's not true. Oh, you'll be happy again, never fear. But you won't forget. Everytime you fall in love it will be because something in the man reminds you of *him*."

"Mother. . . ."

Mother! Katie remembered. She had called her own mother "mama" until the day she had told her that she was going to marry Johnny. She had said, "Mother, I'm going to marry . . . " She had never said "mama" after that. She had finished growing up when she stopped calling her mother "mama." Now Francie . . .

"Mother, he asked me to be with him for the night. Should I have gone?"

Katie's mind darted around looking for words.

"Don't make up a lie, Mother. Tell me the truth."

Katie couldn't find the right words.

"I promise you that I'll never go with a man without being married first—if I ever marry. And if I feel that I must—without being married, I'll tell you first. That's a solemn promise. So you can tell me the truth without worrying that I'll go wrong if I know it."

"There are two truths," said Katie finally.

"As a mother, I say it would have been a terrible thing for a girl to sleep with a stranger—a man she had known less than forty-eight hours. Horrible things might have happened to you. Your whole life might have been ruined. As your mother, I tell you the truth.

"But as a woman . . . " she hesitated. "I will tell you the truth as a woman. It would have been a very beautiful thing. Because there is only once that you love that way."

Francie thought, "I should have gone with him then. I'll never love anyone as much again. I wanted to go and I didn't go and now I don't want him that way anymore because *she* owns him now. But I wanted to and I didn't and now it's too late." She put her head down on the table and wept.

COMING OF AGE IN MISSISSIPPI
Anne Moody

Anne Moody was an activist in the Civil Rights struggles of the 1950s and 1960s. As a student at Tougaloo College, she worked with the National Association for the Advancement of Colored People (NAACP), the Congress of Racial Equality (CORE), and the Student Non-violent Coordinating Committee (SNCC) on various projects. She participated, for example, in an action to integrate the Woolworth lunch counter in Jackson, Mississippi.

When Moody's autobiography was published in 1969, it received high praise, especially for its powerful account of her gradual move toward militancy. But it is also a book about "coming of age" in other ways. The following excerpt recounts Moody's experience with her first boyfriend when she was 20 years old and a student at Natchez Junior College.

That second year at Natchez, I discovered that I had changed. The year before almost every boy on campus had tried to make it with me, especially the basketball boys, and I had turned them down one after the other. Now I found myself wondering whether I should have been so rude to them. When I saw girls and boys sneaking kisses out under the trees, I got curious. Sometimes I wished I had a boyfriend. I was twenty years old and I had never been kissed, not even a smack on the lips. I wanted to know how it felt.

There was a new basketball player on campus named Keemp, whom all the girls and boys were talking about. He was tall—six feet five—and slim. Besides being tall, he had a "cool" about him that most girls liked. So they all went around talking about how handsome he was. It was early October and we hadn't started practicing yet, so I didn't know whether he was a good player or not, but I certainly didn't think his looks were anything special. He looked just like my daddy without a mustache and I never thought Daddy was handsome. I used to see Keemp walking around on campus and wondered what was it that all the girls saw in him. Then too he made me wonder what all the women had seen in my daddy when he was young.

COMING OF AGE IN MISSISSIPPI Dell Books, 1969, 229–33.

Excerpt from *Coming of Age in Mississippi* by Anne Moody. Copyright © 1968 by Anne Moody. A Dial Press book, reprinted by permission of Doubleday & Company, Inc., Pp. 229–33.

One Sunday after church, I was leaving chapel when Keemp walked up to me and said, "So you are Anne Moody, huh?"

"Yes. Why?" I asked, and kept walking.

"I heard a lot of talk about you," he said, walking beside me. "Where are you going now?"

"To the dorm," I answered.

"If you'll slow down, I'll walk you over there," he said coolly.

For the first time in my life I slowed down for a boy. I was a little surprised at myself.

As we walked together, Keemp didn't try to force the conversation. He hardly said anything and whenever he did it was like a brother to a sister. When we got to the dorm he asked if he could walk me to dinner. I again surprised myself by answering yes.

Because Natchez College was so small, most of the relationships between girls and boys were a public thing. Everybody knew everybody else's business. The students were all shocked when I started going with Keemp, especially the sophomore boys who had tried to make it with me the year before. A couple of the guys who had tried hardest came up and bluntly asked me what did I see in Keemp or what did Keemp have to offer me that they didn't. I was a little surprised at the girls' reaction. Most of them seemed glad that I had finally decided to join the club. So much so that they started giving me all kinds of advice about how to handle men.

When Keemp started playing basketball, I really began to like him. He had the longest limbs I had ever seen. As he moved down the basketball court, he was so light he looked like he was flying. He could just walk up to the goal and dunk the ball with ease. Through basketball, he became the most popular boy on campus.

Keemp tried to kiss me many times but I wouldn't let him. I always told him that I had a headache or something. When we traveled to play other teams, all the other boys and their girls on the team kissed around on the bus. Keemp, the best player on the team, sat beside me begging me to kiss him. Everyone else on the bus knew that Keemp wasn't getting anywhere with me, and most of the boys began to tease him.

There were a couple of girls on the team who were having spasms over Keemp. One of them sat in the seat behind us and late at night she would start clawing on the seat like a big cat. When Keemp started answering her clawing, I went to one of my friends, seeking advice on how to kiss. She told me that I didn't have to do anything but part my lips to Keemp and he would do the rest. For the next two months I thought of how I would part my lips. Then one night I dreamt that Keemp and I were kissing around nude on the back seat of the bus and just as we were about to have intercourse, I woke up screaming. I was so frightened by the dream, I began to think that if I kissed Keemp it might lead to something else. The mere thought of getting sexually involved caused me all kinds of anxieties. But I had a tremendous guilt about treating Keemp the way I did when another girl would have treated him better, so I made up my mind to quit him and let that clawing girl have him.

One night in November, when we were playing Philander Smith College in Little Rock, Arkansas, I decided that this would be the night I would quit Keemp. Since the game was one of our biggest, I decided to wait and tell him after it was over. I knew we would lose if he wasn't at his best.

Keemp shot forty-some points during that game. He played better than I had ever seen him play. Just about every time he raised his arms, it was two points for us. When the game was over, the rest of the boys hugged him down to the floor, then picked him up and declared him "King of Basketball." As I watched him play and then saw how everyone loved him, it suddenly dawned upon me that he was a terrific person and that I was a fool to be thinking about quitting him.

When the boys let him go, he walked up to me smiling. Without saying a word, he put his arms around my shoulders and walked me to the bus. As he touched me, a warm current ran through my body.

As I sat on the bus beside Keemp that night, a feeling I had never known before came over me. He held my hands, and it seemed like every hormone in my body reacted. Neither one of us said a word. As the bus was coming to a stop, Keemp leaned over and gently placed his lips on mine. They were like a magnet slowly pulling my lips apart. Once my mouth was open his tongue explored areas that had never been touched by anything but a toothbrush. I completely forgot where I was until one of the boys sitting near us started banging on the basketball and yelling.

"Jesus! Y'aaaall! It finally happened! Keemp done did it!"

The bus had stopped. The lights were on and everybody was looking at us. Keemp wouldn't stop. He pretended that he didn't even hear the yelling, that we weren't on a bus surrounded by spectators. I tried to pull away but I was so weak I couldn't control myself, so I just gave in to his kisses.

Didn't anyone on the bus say one word or stir, not even Mrs. Evans. No one made a move to get off the bus until Keemp and I did. When Keemp finished kissing me, I saw that he had lipstick all over his mouth. My first reaction was to wipe it off real quick before anyone could see it. Keemp just smiled as I wiped it off. When I finished, he took me by the hand, pulled me up out of the seat, buried my head in his shoulder and we walked off the bus.

I was very embarrassed about the fact that my first kiss had been such a public thing. But I didn't regret the kiss at all. Once we were back on campus, Keemp and I greeted each other with a kiss every time we met.

We never did hide behind trees or posts to sneak kisses like the other students. When Mrs. Evans blinked the lights for the girls to come in, I'd give Keemp a smack on the lips right in front of her. Soon most of the other girls started smacking kisses on their boyfriends in front of Mrs. Evans too. Finally, one day Mrs. Evans called me in for a "conference" and accused me of leading the kissing game on campus.

During the first six months of our relationship I was happier than I had ever been. Keemp turned me on to so much that I made the first straight-A average that had been made at Natchez in many years. Studying was a cinch and everything else seemed so easy. But that spring when the basketball season was all over and the excitement of traveling was gone and boys and girls began swarming all over each other like bees, I slowly began to drift away from the whole scene. I had gotten tired of being part of "the club." There was something about the way couples were relaxing into relationships and making them everything that bothered me. I didn't want to get all wrapped up in Keemp the way some of the other girls did with their boyfriends. My relation with him had gradually become a brother-sister thing. He could tell I was moving away from him, so he got himself a girl in the city. I wasn't even jealous and I didn't say anything. I just didn't care. I knew I would be leaving him behind next year and figured he'd have somebody else. I pretended that I didn't know he had another girl and went on being friends with him. He was the best friend I had had since Lola, and I told him everything.

SWEETHEARTS AND WIVES

T. S. Arthur

Author of over 100 didactic books and tales, T. S. Arthur (1809-1885) is best known for his *Ten Nights in a Barroom* (1854), a favorite text of temperance orators. A prolific and successful writer, he also established his own magazine, *Arthur's Home Gazette,* in 1850. "Sweethearts and Wives," a story which appeared in *Godey's Lady's Book,* describes and prescribes the roles of married men and women. In defining the terms of his title, Arthur reinforces the observations of Alexis de Tocqueville, who, on his visit to the United States in 1831-1832, noted the differences between unmarried and married women.

"When you come to deal with the sober realities of a married life, Agnes, you will, I fear, find less of sunshine than you fondly hope for."

"Aunt Mildred, how can you talk so! Surely, you ought to have more regard for William Fairfield's true character, than to insinuate, as you evidently intend to do, that he will not be the same to me after we are married, than he now is."

"Sweethearts and wives, are, somehow or other, looked at with different eyes, Agnes."

"Aunt Mildred, you will offend me if you talk so!"

"You are willing to be offended, because I speak the truth. I had hoped more from the good sense of my niece"—Aunt Mildred said, in a tone of rather more seriousness than that in which she had, at first, spoken.

"But, Aunt Mildred," said her niece, looking into her face, while the moisture gathered in her eyes, "How can I bear to hear you talk so! Do I not know that William Fairfield loves me, as he loves his own life, and that he would sooner die than give me a moment's pain?"

"You must not be offended at me when I speak what I feel to be the truth, my dear child. I have lived longer, and have seen more of the world than you have. It is not, then, let me tell you, according to the nature of men to love any one as they love their own lives, nor to prefer death to giving pain to those they do love. This is all romance, Agnes, and the sooner you get it out of your head, the better. It will take itself out, if you don't, mark my word for it!"

"But Aunt, William has said so to me himself," urged the blushing maiden,

---

SWEETHEARTS AND WIVES   From *Godey's Lady's Book,* December, 1841, pp. 264–69.

"and I am sure, by his very manner, and the tone of his voice, that he was in earnest. Surely, *he* would not deceive me!"

"I have no idea, Agnes, that William meant to deceive you; I believe him to be above wilful deception. But, in the warmth of a first, ardent affection, he is carried out of himself, and led to mistake his real feelings."

"O Aunt, you will kill me if you talk so! If I thought that William did not love me as deeply as he says that he does, I would never see him again. I never can and never will be satisfied with any thing but a love that will sacrifice all for me. *I* will give such a pure, fervent love—nothing less than a like return can make me happy."

"You do not know yourself my child. You offer more than you will be able to give, and ask more than you ever can receive. None of us are perfect; all of us are selfish. You are, in a certain degree, selfish, so is William. And in just so far as this selfish principle comes into activity, will both of you expect to receive more from the other, than you are willing to give. Then will come secret pains."

"Indeed, indeed, Aunt Mildred, you frighten me! I fear some sad experience of your own has made you doubt every one—doubt even the possibility of being happy here."

A shadow flitted across Aunt Mildred's benevolent face, but it was gone in an instant; "I have not lived thus long in the world," she said, "without having learned many of its painful secrets; and one of these is that young love's promise is never realized. I have known many as full of the romance of love as you, and yet, all have been disappointed."

"And I know a good many, too, aunt, whose marriage promise has utterly failed. But, then, how could it have been otherwise; where there was no character or principle in the husband? I have built my happiness on a safer foundation. No one, I am sure, can breathe ought against William Fairfield."

"He is, if I judge him rightly, Agnes, a young man of a good heart, and sound principles. Indeed, I know of no one to whom I had rather commit the happiness of my niece."

"Thank you, my dear aunt, for that admission! And do not trouble yourself; I shall be as happy as I expect."

"But not in the way you expect, my child."

"You deal in riddles, aunt," said the now laughing girl, kissing fondly the cheek of her who had been from early years to her, a mother and friend; and then danced lightly from the room, humming a pleasant ditty.

That evening her lover came as usual. It need not be denied that Aunt Mildred's warning had made some impression upon her mind, notwithstanding her effort to throw it off. And as this impression was of a somewhat sombre cast, a slight shadow was thrown upon her countenance.

"You do not seem as lively as usual," William said, half an hour, perhaps, after he had come in.

"Don't I? Well, the fact is, Aunt Mildred has been saying something to me, that, if I could believe there was any truth in it, would make me feel gloomy enough."

"Indeed! And what is that, Agnes?"

"Why, she says," replied the simple-hearted maiden looking him in the face, "that you will not love me after we are married, as you do now."

"She is right there, dear Agnes! for I will love you a thousand times more"; the lover responded fervently, kissing at the same time the glowing cheek of his affianced bride.

Agnes did not reply; but her heart seemed too large for her bosom.

"And you did not believe it?"

"O no, no, not for a moment!" said the warm-hearted girl.

Three weeks after saw them in a new relation, that of husband and wife.

"You do not love me less, I know," said the young wife a month after the happy day of their marriage, leaning her head back upon her husband's bosom, and looking up into his face with eyes beaming with love's own peculiar brightness.

"I love you more and more, every hour, my dear Agnes," replied the fond husband, touching his lips to her's, and smoothing with his fingers the dark hair that covered her brow of snowy whiteness.

"How happy we shall be, dear husband!"

"I shall be happy, I know. But I have sometimes feared, that I might not be able to make you always feel happy."

"Only love me, dear husband, and that is all I ask."

"If my love for you will make you happy, then, no shadow can ever fall upon your heart."

"Love me, as you now do, and no shadow, I know, will ever darken it."

Our fond lovers are now united; and, as the honey moon is over, it becomes necessary for them to come down from their romance, and enter upon the sober duties of a married life. Aunt Mildred, though a very sensible woman, had not acted with her usual good sense towards her niece. She had thoroughly accomplished her in every thing but what she most needed, to make her competent to fill the place of wife and mother. She had not failed to warn her of the coming sober realities of married life, but had, alas! neglected to prepare her to encounter them aright.

It was not long, therefore, before her husband began to experience little annoyances, in consequence of her want of domestic knowledge; and what was worse, from her distaste for the practical duties required of every wife. She seemed to have looked forward to the married state, as one that was to elevate her to a higher degree of happiness, and yet bring with it no cares nor duties. When, therefore, repeated irregularities in household economy occurred, and were felt by the husband as annoyances, he could not help thinking, sometimes, that the wife he so dearly loved, was not as thoughtful of his comfort, as he was of her's. Such thoughts will always produce corresponding feelings, and these latter cannot exist without in some way showing themselves. In the case of William Fairfield, they were exhibited in the form of a reserve, sometimes, that, while it existed, was exceedingly painful to his young wife. Besides this cause, fruitful in domestic disquietude, there was another that too frequently intrudes itself upon the first few years of marriage, a desire to lead, rather than to be led by the husband, in little things,—a habit of expecting him to consult, in all things, the will and tastes of the wife even at the sacrifice, sometimes, of duty and judgment. In fact, the wife, unconscious that in the marriage relation the husband should be looked to as of some consequence and consideration, as possessing claims upon her will to be guided by his understanding,—still imagines that all the power and peculiar influence which she possessed over him in the sweetheart-state, must of right continue. From this false view, induced by the self-sacrificing devotion of the lover, much unhappiness flows when the sweetheart becomes the wife.

We will now look in upon our young couple, and see how they get along during their first and most trying year—most trying usually, to all new married pairs.

Fairfield installed his wife mistress of a neatly furnished house, and both settled themselves down in it, brimfull of present pleasure, and delightful anticipations. The two servants managed things pretty well for the first few weeks, but after that, many irregularities became apparent. The meals were often an hour beyond the usual and set time, and were frequently very badly cooked. The sweeping and dusting were carelessly done, and the furniture, from want of attention, began to look a little dingy, much to the annoyance of Mrs. Fairfield. Still, it did not occur to her, that she was wrong in leaving every thing to her servants. It never came into her thoughts that her mind should be the governing one of her household, in *all things*, great and small, as much as was her husband's the governing mind in his business. The idea, that she was to take pleasure in exemption from domestic duties, and not in the performance of them, was fully entertained by her, and this her husband soon perceived, and it pained him much, for he saw that in this false idea was an active germ of future disquietude.

Punctual, almost, some would say, to a fault, he felt much the want of regularity, which was daily growing worse instead of better. Too frequently he was kept from his store in the morning, half an hour later than business required him to be there, in consequence of breakfast not being ready. Whenever this happened, he usually hurried away without the parting kiss which young wives most usually expect, for he did not feel like giving it. Sometimes Agnes would claim the token of love, but she felt that it was coldly given, and its price was a gush of tears, as soon as he had passed from her sight.

But the evening usually compensated for the disquietude of the day. Then, no duties unperformed vexed the feelings of either. Agnes sung, and played sweetly, and had, besides these accomplishments a mind well stored, and a taste highly cultivated. Home was to each a little paradise and they felt how happy they were in each other. Gradually, however, the shadows, too frequently cast over their feelings, passed not off entirely, even when all duties and cares were laid aside.

"Why does not Agnes think!" Fairfield would sometimes exclaim internally. "Surely, she cannot but perceive that these things annoy me very much. I spare no toil or pains to make her happy, and, surely, she ought to be willing to assume some cares and duties for my sake!"

"I fear he does not love me!" the young wife would often say, bursting into tears, as she closed her chamber door after her, and sat down to weep in abandonment of feelings after her husband had gone out to his business. "What would I not do to retain the love once given me so freely! But he is, I fear, disappointed in me. O I would rather die than lose the pure love he once lavished upon me!"

Notwithstanding William Fairfield would often suffer his feelings to be disturbed, in consequence of the irregularities which appertained to his household economy, he more frequently endeavoured to palliate the cause of these, and tried to feel willing to bear any thing unpleasant for the sake of his wife.

"If it is irksome to her to attend to domestic affairs," he would say to himself on these occasions, "why, it would be selfish in me to wish to confine her to them merely for my own comfort."

Such reasonings, however, did not long exercise an influence over him. They soon proved to be powerless. And he would again give way mentally to regrets and censure. One day, perhaps six months after their marriage, Fairfield, much pressed and perplexed with business, left his store at the usual hour for dinner. On his way home, his mind was still intent upon business affairs, and he walked faster than usual, anxious to get back as soon as possible, as his presence was needed. Much to his disappointment, he found the cloth not even laid for dinner.

"It isn't dinner time, surely?" Agnes said, as he came into the parlor, where she was practising a new piece on the piano.

"Indeed then, it is," he replied in a tone of disappointment.

"Why, I'm sure it can't be two o'clock," responded Agnes, getting up and examining a time-piece on the mantel, that struck the hour regularly. "It is, as I live! Why how swiftly the time has passed, I had no idea that it was so late." Then ringing the bell, she directed the cook to get dinner immediately.

"It won't be done for half an hour," the cook replied carelessly.

"Half an hour! that is too bad!" Fairfield said, impatiently.

"Indeed, Sally, you must be more punctual," said Mrs. Fairfield, her cheek colouring, for she always felt distressed when her husband was moved to displeasure.

"I've got it as quick as I could," Sally replied, tartly, gliding off to the kitchen.

An oppressive silence followed the withdrawal of the cook.

"Why don't she go down and hurry the dinner?" the husband could not help saying, after some fifteen minutes had elapsed, and there was no reappearance of Sally, for the purpose of arranging the table. "If I were to leave every thing in my store to clerks and porters, my business would soon run into disorder."

After awhile, Mrs. Fairfield rung the bell again, and on Sally's appearance said, "Why don't you set the table?"

Sally did not reply, but jerked out the table, threw on the cloth, and then made the dishes rattle upon it, grumbling all the while in an under tone. Fairfield was irritated, and his wife much annoyed. He dared not trust himself to speak, and she was distressed at his moody silence.

It was near three o'clock when the meal was ready, but neither had any appetite for it. After swallowing a few mouthfuls, Fairfield hurried away to his store, and got there just too late to meet an important customer, who he knew was in town, and had been expecting all the morning. Mrs. Fairfield, who had been left sitting at the table, got up instantly and retired to her chamber, to spend the afternoon in weeping. She knew that her husband blamed her, but this she could not help feeling to be unreasonable.

"How could I help it?" she asked herself, as a fresh gush of tears streamed down her cheeks, "am I not dependent upon worthless servants? Surely, he don't expect me to go into the kitchen! If he does, he is much mistaken!" This last sentence was uttered in a calm, and somewhat indignant tone.

That evening, the supper passed off in moody silence. Fairfield, though disposed, when he came in, to lay aside, if possible, his vexed and unpleasant feelings, found a cloud upon his wife's face, and this created a positive indisposition on his part, to say even the first kind word that was to bring about a reaction. She felt that he blamed her, and she thought unjustly, and this prevented her from speaking in her usual kind and affectionate tone.

Evening passed away, and they retired for the night, still oppressed and gloomy, and each still disposed to blame the other. The morning found them in a much calmer frame of mind, and the husband's affectionate tones restored the light to Agnes' countenance. After conversing freely at the breakfast table, Fairfield said, just before rising, "I wish, Agnes, you would try to have dinner on the table punctually at two; my business requires all my attention just now, and a little delay is often a serious disadvantage to me."

The face of Agnes coloured deeply, and for a few moments she was too much disturbed to speak. At last she said, "I know you blame me, William. But how can I help it? Sally will have her own way. I can't go into the kitchen myself and do the cooking."

"But, then, Agnes, you know you could keep an eye over Sally, and when you see she is likely to be behindhand, hurry her on a little."

"Yes, and I might be at it everlastingly," Agnes responded, rather warmly. "If I have got to be at the heels of servants all the while, I might as well give up at once."

"But, Agnes, how do other ladies get along with their domestics?"

"I don't know any that get along better than I do. They have to put up with them, and we will have to do the same."

William Fairfield felt that it would be useless to urge the matter further on his young wife, and so did not reply. But he felt a good deal discouraged as he left the house, and hurried along to his store. Agnes saw that his manner towards her was altered after what she had said, and she was equally troubled with himself. Dinner happened to be in good time this day, and, as William Fairfield ignorantly supposed it was in consequence of more attention having been given to the operations of the cook, by his wife, he felt relieved, and pleased. His kind manner—so kind, when it was genuine—made the heart of Agnes leap again. She was once more happy.

But this pleasant sunshine was not of long continuance. Causes of unpleasant feeling, other than those relating to the domestic arrangements of the family, were in existence. For the first few months, the tastes and preferences of Agnes were consulted by her husband, in every thing. But now he began to feel that she exacted too much, and considered him too little. She evidently preferred, in all things, her own will, to his; and expected him, as a matter of course, always to yield to her inclinations. This began to annoy him, and its impropriety to force itself upon his thoughts. He also began to yield to her with less apparent willingness. This was, of course, perceived, and thought to be an evidence of declining affection, and its discovery was a new source of pain to the heart of Agnes. Visions of estrangement, and entire loss of affection, began to flit before her mental vision, and many hours were passed in tears, when no eye but that of the Invisible was upon her. Still, she never seemed to imagine the true cause. No more attention was given to domestic affairs, and when the kind manner of her husband would return, after a temporary reserve, she would be as wilful, and as exacting as ever. If he proposed a call on some friend, during the evening, it was almost sure that she not only preferred going somewhere else, but expressed her wish to go there. In this wish, her husband generally acquiesced, thus denying himself to gratify her. Instead of trying to become assimilated to his tastes, or at least, of endeavouring to tolerate them, she generally expressed a difference, where any existed; and not content with this, looked for him to enter into her gratifications. Even in walking along the street, instead of leaving him to choose the right way, she would object as he turned into this street, wishing to go by another—or to crossing here or there; thus, constantly checking him, and annoying him. So uniformly was this the case, that they never walked out, without his having to yield to her will in such unimportant matters, some half dozen times. It was so little a thing to feel annoyed at, that he would chide himself for his foolishness; but it was no use, upon every recurrence of the same thing, the same feelings would return. At last, he got so, that when she checked him, he would slightly resist. But she was so thoughtless and wilful, as to, as uniformly, pull against him, saying, "No, this is the best way, I want to go this way."

Then, as she seemed so much determined on having her own will, he would not resist. But he condemned in his mind her conduct, distinctly. With all this she would be full of expressions and tokens of love, would tell him how dear he was to her, and how she could not live without him. Sometimes, while thus lavishing upon him acts of affection, and words of love, he would ask almost involuntarily, "If she so really loved me, would it not lead her to do more for my comfort, to consult my wishes more. Love, it is said, speaks plainer in actions than words. I fear she is too selfish, too much disposed to seek for happiness away from, instead of in, her duties."

It was impossible for such thoughts to be passing in the mind of a husband, without the wife perceiving in some way, that all within was not as her fond heart could wish it. And Agnes always saw something in the manner of her husband that pained her; something that sent the blood coldly about her heart; yet, she seemed utterly ignorant of the true cause.

This evident unconsciousness, was also a source of trouble to William Fairfield. He saw that she was pained, even at times distressed, by his manner, and yet, he felt that he could not tell her the cause of that manner. She would not, he feared, understand him. Indeed, when he came to think of one source of disquietude, her consultation of her own, instead of his wishes, it seemed to him so selfish, that he should want her to look to, and be guided by him, that he could not entertain the idea of breathing it to her, for a moment. Notwithstanding this, however, he was none the less annoyed by it; nor did his judgment condemn it the less a wrong in his wife.

Fortunately for them, one source of trouble was for a time removed. Agnes obtained a much better cook, and things under her arrangement, went on like clock work. But she remained only a few months. The next obtained by Mrs. Fairfield, was one of those creatures that seem made to try the patience of even the best and most attentive housekeepers. Under her administration, all the irregularities which characterised the culinary department of the family, while Sally was cook, were not only renewed, but increased tenfold.

Fairfield lost all command over his patience, and now and then exhibited traits of no very amiable character. This added to his wife's distress of mind, but did not cause her to reflect as she should have done. The reader must not suppose that the discord which reigned too frequently in this family, or its effects, were at all perceptible to the friends and casual visitors of the young couple. All upon the surface presented to the world, was smooth and beautiful. Often the remark was made, in speaking of them.—"What a happy union! How well they have both done!" And they did, really love one another, but had not yet learned to accommodate themselves to each other's peculiarities. Fairfield was to blame, as well as Agnes. He should have been open and candid towards her, and have explained to her rationally, calmly, and affectionately, her duty; but he shrunk from this for fear of wounding her, thus wounding her a thousand times more acutely, in permitting her to go on in actions and omissions the natural results of which, were exceedingly painful to the heart of a young and loving wife.

One evening they started out to take a walk, neither of them feeling as happy as once they did, when, as lover and maiden, they had strolled along under the soft light of a quiet moon. Fairfield was silent, and Agnes but little inclined to talk, and each was too much occupied in mind with the other's peculiarities and faults. It so happened that, as the husband made a movement to turn down a certain street, as they were going home, that the wife objected and held back. The husband persevered, and the wife continued to resist; when, finding that he was not at all disposed to yield, she let go, saying, "Well, I am going this way, you can go that, if you would rather."

Surprised, yet irritated, and too much under the influence of the latter feeling to pause a moment for reflection, Fairfield, without replying, kept on, and Agnes, repenting her wilfulness, but too proud to pause, went another direction. Both arrived at home nearly at the same moment; and both had experienced in the five minutes since they parted, an age of misery. Neither of them spoke as they entered the house together. Agnes went up to her chamber, and her husband seated himself in the parlour below. In about half an hour, the excitement of the young wife's feelings began to subside, and with this calmer mood, came a distinct perception that she had done wrong; and with this consciousness, arose the determination to tell the husband so, as soon as he came up stairs. But the time continued to wear away, and yet he came not. Wearied and anxious, she laid herself across the bed and fell asleep.

In the mean time, Fairfield sat in the parlour, an agitated and miserable man. An open rupture had at last occurred, and he was reasoning himself into the determination not to suffer it to be healed until there was a full explanation and understanding between them. He also felt much anger towards the affectionate, but thoughtless and wilful, girl who had cast her lot in life with his, who had, in the confidence of a trusting maiden, committed her happiness to his keeping. Thus he sat, hour after hour, brooding over the incidents of the past year, and extracting accusation after accusation against her.

Startled by a painful dream, Agnes awoke about midnight, and rousing herself up, looked around in alarm for her husband. When she recovered her bewildered senses, the scene of the evening previous came up vividly before her mind.

"Where is he?" she asked herself, in a husky whisper.

Then catching up the light she hurried down stairs. The sound of her hastening feet startled her husband, who instantly thought, truly, that she had fallen asleep, and had just awakened; and now, in surprise and fear at his absence, had come to seek him. This thought at once modified and tendered his feelings towards her.

"O William! William!" she exclaimed, springing forward towards him, "can you, will you forgive me!"

Then sinking into his arms, she buried her head in his bosom, and lay trembling and sobbing like a frightened child.

After this excitement had, in a degree, subsided, Fairfield bent down, and kissing her cheek, whispered—"All is forgiven, dear Agnes! But let us now try so to understand each other, that no further cause for unhappiness may exist. We have not been happy during the past year, the first of our marriage—and yet, we love each other, and desire to make each other happy. Something must, then, be wrong in both of us. Now, let us lay aside all reserves, and be open, honest, and candid with each other. Do you tell me wherein I pain you, and I will tell you the same in frankness, but yet in affection. Will you do this, Agnes?"

"O I have nothing to complain of, dear husband! You have always been good and kind to me!"

"My own conscience does not acquit me in this, Agnes; neither, I am sure, can your heart. Speak out plainly, then, I will love you the better for it."

But Agnes could not speak; she only continued to hide her face in his bosom, and weep.

Gradually, however, she grew calm, and by degrees, her husband, who felt the necessity for a perfect understanding at that particular time, got her into a state of mind to converse. He then, as she would not bring a word against him, reluctantly entered upon his complaints against her, in regard to her want of due attention to the concerns of her household. This roused her up a little.

"Surely," she said "William, you do not wish to see your wife a drudge?"

"Not by any means, Agnes. But, then, I wish to see her engaged in the steady performance of every duty required by her station; because I know that only by doing so, can she render herself and family truly happy. No station, my dear wife, is exempt from its cares and its duties; if these are faithfully and willingly assumed, peace of mind will follow; if neglected, pain. As the mistress of a family, the comfort of others is placed in your hands, and, particularly, that of your husband. If you put aside your care and responsibility, and refer them to hired servants, you are in the neglect of plain and important duties; and one of the consequences which follows is, that your domestic arrangements are disturbed, and your family subjected to many annoyances. Suppose, for instance, during the past year, instead of trusting every thing to your cook, you had yourself had a careful eye, every day, over her department—had superintended the cooking so far as to know that dinner went on in time, and was properly served up at the exact hour, do you not perceive that the care which this would have subjected you to, would have been happiness compared with the feelings you have experienced in seeing me, almost daily, annoyed by the irregularities which I saw you could correct, and blamed you for not correcting?"

Agnes heaved a long, deep sigh, but made no answer.

"I speak thus plain," continued the husband, "because I think it best for our happiness that I should do so. Your error lies in a false idea which you have entertained, that your happiness was to come somewhere from out of your domestic duties, instead of in the performance of them—that they were not part of a wife's obligations, but something that she could put aside if she were able to hire enough servants. I cannot, thus, delegate my business duties to any one; without my governing mind and constant attention, every thing would soon be in disorder, and an utter failure, instead of prosperity, be the result of my efforts. By my carefulness and constant devotion to business, I am enabled to provide you with every comfort; surely, then, you should be willing also to give careful attention to your department, that I may feel home to be a pleasant place. Under this view, my dear Agnes, do you conceive that I am ungenerous or unkind in wishing to see you take upon yourself more cares, and to perform more domestic duties?"

"Oh, no—no—no, dear husband!" said his wife, twining her arms around his neck, and kissing his cheek fondly. "I see very plainly how wrong I have been, and how false the views were that I have entertained. Hereafter I will strive to find my delight in what I now perceive, plainly, to be my duties. And if, at any time, I grow weary or think them irksome, I will say to myself—'I am but trying to make my husband happy, and his home a home indeed.' Only keep an unclouded brow, William—only love me, and I ask nothing more."

"I have always loved you tenderly, Agnes, although you sometimes tried me sorely."

"I know I have, my dear husband. And now, if there is any thing else, speak out plainly; I would know my faults, that I may correct them. It will be true charity for you to do so now."

"I believe it will, Agnes," he said, touching his lips to hers; "and if I pain you, remember it is only that you may be freed from a greater and lasting pain. Do not think me selfish in what I am about to say, or that I desire to rule over you tyrannically. In the wise order of Providence, there is a distinct and important difference in the relation of the sexes; and, particularly, in that which a man and his wife bear to each other. He is stronger, and his mind is a form receptive of more wisdom; she is weaker, and her mind is a form receptive of more affection. Thus they are radically different. As husband and wife, his wisdom becomes, as it were, joined to her affection, and her affection to his wisdom; thus they mutually act and react upon each other, and in just so far as each acts in a true position, do they become one, and happy in the marriage union. But if the wife attempt to guide or to force his understanding, then discord will occur, in the very nature of things; for only in just so far as her will is united with his understanding, can they, or will they act in harmony. Now one fault which you have, Agnes, is a disposition to have little things your own way, even in opposition to my expressed or implied preference. Whenever you do this, I feel as if you were unwilling to be influenced at all by me—as if you wished to be understanding and will both; thus making me a mere cypher. No man can or ought to bear this, without feeling that it is wrong. Do you understand me, Agnes?"

"I think I understand you perfectly, William. And what is better, you will say I see my fault distinctly, and will try my best to correct it. I did not think, before, that I was so selfish and wilful as I now perceive myself to be. You will forgive me the past, dear husband, will you not?"

"All—all is forgiven" he said, earnestly, again kissing her tear-moistened cheek. "And now let us begin life anew, each trying to make the other happy."

It was near morning when they retired to rest, but the few hours given to slumber were sweet and refreshing. Every thing wore a different aspect. The shadow that had begun to settle upon the brow of Mrs. Fairfield, quickly disappeared; for her husband, always meeting with order and an affectionate and constant consideration of his wishes, repaid, a hundred fold, her kind care, in increasing and manifested love. Fatigue often followed her now constant attention to her household duties; but when thus fatigued, she remembered that he, too, devoted himself day by day to business and care for her sake; and, also, that though wearied, it was from a devotion to her husband and family.

It was, perhaps, a year after, that, in a conversation with Aunt Mildred, she ventured an allusion to her first year of painful trial, and to contrast it with her present happiness. After she had done speaking, her Aunt said, smiling—"You will now acknowledge, I suppose, Agnes, that there is a very great difference between a sweetheart and a wife."

"And yet I would sooner be a wife than a sweetheart, a thousand times," responded Agnes, the tears of delight starting to her eyes.

"No doubt," Aunt Mildred said, with her usual gentle tone and quiet smile.

ME AND MINE

Helen Sekaquaptewa, as told to Louise Udall

Louise Udall got to know Helen Sekaquaptewa when they did church work together among the Maricopa Indians. On their way to and from the reservation southwest of Phoenix, Sekaquaptewa told Udall stories about her life. Udall not only suggested that her friend record these accounts, but she also served as the recorder.

Helen and Emory Sekaquaptewa decided to marry in a Hopi ceremony in order to please their families. In the following abridgement, Sekaquaptewa describes the preparations for the wedding and the roles which men and women of the community play in those preparations. Halfway through the Hopi rites, however, Helen and Emory, who had learned the ways of the white world, decided to get married "legally."

The home of the bridegroom is the center of activity in a Hopi wedding. When a couple decides to marry, the father of the groom takes over. He furnishes everything—cotton for the weaving and food to feed the workers during the time the weaving is in progress. Each household keeps a supply of cotton on hand against the time when a son may marry.

In Emory's case there was a problem. His parents had separated years before and his mother had remarried and lived in Oraibi. . . .

Emory's mother wanted us to come to her home in Oraibi, but Emory had been away at school so many years that it wasn't really home to him. As he grew older he had lived in Bacabi, with his cousin Susie and her husband, who

---

ME AND MINE   University of Arizona Press, 1969. By permission of Louise Udall, *Me and Mine: The Life Story of Helen Sekaquaptewa as Told to Louise Udall*, Tucson: The University of Arizona Press, copyright 1969, abridged, pp. 153–66.

was his godfather, during the summers that he was home, helping in whatever way he could. Susie invited us to come to her home, and Emory's uncle and cousins all helped put in for the cotton and food and were the hosts for us.

After we decided to get married, I spent every minute that I could grinding in preparation for feeding the wedding guests. Women and girls of my relatives who wanted to help started grinding too. When my sister Verlie walked with me to Bacabi to Susie's house, I carried a big pan full of fine white cornmeal. I never left Susie's house for the entire period (about a month) and was under her watchful care, even slept with her the first three nights.

As a bride I was considered sacred the first few days, being in a room with the shades on the windows, talking to no one. All this time I was steadily grinding corn which was brought in by Emory's kinswomen. . . .

The fourth day is the actual wedding day. Everyone of the relatives is up when the cock crows, to participate in the marriage ritual, the hair washing. Suds are made from the tuber of the yucca root, pounded into a pulp, put into two basins of water, and worked with the hands until the pan is filled with foamy suds.

Two pans were placed side by side on the floor, where Susie and my sister Verlie prepared the suds. Usually the mothers of the bride and groom do this. Susie and Verlie acted for our mothers. While Susie washed my hair, Verlie washed Emory's. Then each took a strand of hair and twisted them together hard and tight as a symbol of acceptance of the new in-law into the clan (family) and also to bind the marriage contract, as they said, "Now you are united, never to go apart."

Next Emory was taken outside and stripped to the waist by the women of my family. Each had brought her small container of water which she poured over his shoulders as he knelt over a tub. They splashed the water over him with their hands. It was still dark, so they could not see him; they put a blanket around him, and he came back into the house to get warm from that icy bath.

Now, with our hair still wet and hanging loose, Emory and I walked together to the eastern edge of the village and once more faced the rising sun, and with bowed heads we prayed in silence for a long time; for a good life together, for children, and to be together all of our lives and never stray from each other.

After my hair was dry on this day, they combed it up like a married woman, never to be worn in maiden style again. Married women parted their hair from the center in the front to the nape of the neck. Each side was folded over the hand until it reached nearly to the ear where it was bound with a cord made from hair and a little yarn, leaving a soft puff at the ends. The hair in front of the ears was cut into sideburns about two inches long.

The making of the robes begins on the morning of the nuptial hair washing. The father or uncle of the groom (in our case Susie's father) took a bag of cotton and, passing through the village, stopped at each house. He was expected, and each housewife opened her door and extended a plaque to receive some cotton (everyone was required to wash his hands before touching the cotton). Immediately all hands went to work cleaning the cotton of seeds, burrs, and little sticks. It was all cleaned that same day. . . .

All the men in the village worked to spin this cotton into thread in one day. Food was obtained and prepared to feed the whole village. Ten or fifteen sheep were required. If the host didn't have sheep of his own, he bought them. One or two might be donated by someone. Wood had to brought in for the cooking and to heat the kivas. . . .

In the meantime the women were getting the food and tables ready. My relatives and myself were served earlier so we could be free to serve the community dinner. However, the bride did not serve but mingled with the other women. They teased me as all made merry and had a happy time. The men were served at the tables in Susie's house and neighboring houses as needed, and then the women and children of the village ate. Whatever food was left, especially the stew, was divided among the people.

The weaving took about two weeks, and it began a few days after the spinning was finished. One sheep was butchered this time, and the other foods were made ready for the first day of the weaving. At dawn and before breakfast the three special looms used in wedding weaving were brought out from their storage place to the kiva (one kiva) where they were untied and spread out on the floor. Two or three men at a time worked at the long and tedious job of stringing each loom, rolling the warp back and forth to each other, over the notches close together on the two end poles.

The bridal clothing consisted of a robe six by eight feet, a second one about four by six feet to cover the shoulders, and a girdle about ten inches wide and eight feet long, which is tied around the waist. The moccasins had leggings made of white buckskin. Then there is the reed roll, which is a sort of suitcase in which to wrap and carry extra gifts. Emory gathered the reeds from the edge of the wash, cut them into uniform lengths and tied them together with cord like a bamboo window blind.

The threaded looms were hung from loops in the ceiling beams and fastened to loops on the floor and stretched tight, and the weaving began, the best weavers taking turns during the day. The belt is braided rather than woven.

At noon, food was brought to the kiva by relatives. After dinner a man took his place at each loom and worked until evening. The host did not weave all the time, but he stayed with them at all times. In the evening each man carried the loom he had worked on to Susie's house, where I received them and put them away in a back room for safekeeping. The men sat down to eat of piki and beans and leftover food from dinner and somviki, which is tamales made from finely ground blue corn, sweetened and wrapped in corn husks, and tied with yucca strips and then boiled, and made by the bride every evening. As the weavers left after supper, I gave each of them a few tamales on top of a folded piki. Each morning the weaving continued. Only one man could work on each loom at a time, but the best weavers came and took turns during the day. Other men came, bringing their spinning or knitting, or just sat and visited and listened as the older men retold the traditional stories. Sometimes they all sang together.

About halfway through the rites, our consciences troubled us, because we felt the Hopi way was not quite right. We decided to get a license and be married legally. Emory told his folks what we wanted to do. He made application to the agency at Keams Canyon, and a marriage license was obtained by mail from Holbrook, the nearest county seat. It took about a week. In the afternoon that the license came, I went to my father's house in Hotevilla; Emory went with me. I just walked in and told my father that I was going to be married by license that night and had come to get my clothes. I could feel the disapproval of my father and my sister as I gathered the things I was going to wear. I just could not stay there and get dressed. I took my clothes and went to one of the school teachers, and she let me dress in her house.

I was married in a white batiste dress, which was my pride and joy. I had earned the money and bought the material and made the dress in domestic art class in the Phoenix school. It had lace insertion set in bow knots around the gathered skirt, on the flared sleeves, and on the collar. My teacher had entered it in the State Fair, and I got second prize on it. I wore it once to a party and then decided it was too nice to wear and put it away in a box. . . .

We were married in the evening on February 14, 1919, in the living room of the home of Mr. Anderson, principal of the school in Hotevilla, by Reverend Dirkson of the Mennonite Mission. Emory's people, including some of his cousins, came to the ceremony. The teachers served some refreshments and gave us some little presents and a room where we could spend the night. In the morning they served a wedding breakfast, and then we went back to finish the tribal wedding rites at Bacabi.

Emory was working at the school and had to be on the job, so he wasn't able to participate in the weaving during the daytime. The activity died down after the first few days anyway, the weavers carrying on until everything was done. I helped with the grinding and cooking until the outfit was completed.

When the weaving was finished the men took the robes from the looms and brought them into the house to be tried on. A border of sixteen running stitches in red was embroidered in the two corners, suggesting a limit of sixteen children, the most a person should have, and four stitches in each of the other two corners in orange, suggesting a minimum number of children. The white moccasins with leggings in one piece were finished just in time to be put on with the rest of the outfit. It was by then evening; food was placed before the guests and everyone ate again. (Hopis do not invite you to eat. They set the food before you, and the food invites.)

The next morning before sunup, Susie led the others in clothing me, first washing my hair. Everyone admired the bride, and I was now ready to go back to my father's house. A line of white cornmeal was sprinkled on the ground, pointing the way. There was a lot of snow on the ground, so they wrapped rags over my white moccasins so I wouldn't get them wet or muddy. Emory's people went with me out of the village and over the little hill back to my home in Hotevilla. Emory did not go with me this time. How I wished that my own dear mother could be there to meet me. The sun was just coming up when we got to my father's house. Verlie opened the door, and my father thanked them for the beautiful bridal apparel that would make his daughter eligible to enter the world of the hereafter. Thus ends the wedding ritual. . . .

The groom may follow the bride to her home as soon as he likes. Some go right away, some wait a long time before claiming their brides. Emory came over after a few days and stayed a couple of nights, but I could see that the tension and hostility was hard on him; too many children, too little room, not even a room to ourselves. After my going through all that ceremony just to please my family, my sister was still so hostile that I felt neither wanted nor welcome.

One day, about a month after we were married, when no one was at home, I felt that I could not stand it another minute. I gathered and packed my belongings, as many as I could carry, returning later for the rest of them, and went to the house where Emory lived near the school. He was at his work teaching shop when I got there. I cleaned up the house and had a meal cooked when he came home, and we were real happy. Soon afterward I got a job teaching beginners in the school. It was hard to get teachers there because it was so isolated.

WOMEN ARE NO GIVE-AWAYS
Abigail Van Buren

Abigail Van Buren (b. 1918) is the author of the nationally syndicated column, "Dear Abby." She and her sister, Ann Landers, are probably the most widely read advice columnists of our time. In addition to her daily column, Van Buren has written for popular magazines, lectured extensively, and won numerous awards.

Although Van Buren advises readers on a wide range of topics from birth to death, she also belongs to the tradition of journalists who provided "advice to the lovelorn." Such newspaper features have reflected the society's changing mores, especially in the area of relationships between men and women. In her response to the following letter, Van Buren associates a traditional wedding practice with the historical view of women as property and indicates that change is in the wind.

Dear Abby: I am a 58-year-old woman. When I was a young girl, I attended a formal wedding and was greatly enraged when I heard the minister ask, "Who gives this woman . . . ?"

The question still arouses my anger and I am amazed that more women are not insulted by this question—asked publicly yet!

Only the woman herself has the right to "give" herself to anyone, any time, for any reason.

I've finally begun to express defiantly my indignation when a bride-to-be tells me she is going to be "given away" by her father or stepfather. Of course, I am a "nut" to even suggest that a woman belongs to no one but herself and is not an inanimate object to be "given away."

Thanks for listening.—Margaret Jonas in San Francisco

Dear Margaret: The original marriage vows were written during Biblical times when a woman was considered "chattel"—a piece of property owned by her father. He had the right to "give" her to her husband, who then regarded her as his property.

However, in recent years, many couples have requested that that portion of the marriage ceremony be omitted for the reason you cited.

WOMEN ARE NO . . .   *The Evening Gazette*, Worcester, MA, Oct. 12, 1983. Taken from the Dear Abby column. Copyright, 1983, Universal Press Syndicate. Reprinted with permission. All rights reserved, p. 68.

THE BRIDAL VEIL

Alice Cary

Alice Cary (1820-1871) was one of the most popular poets of the mid-nineteenth century. Born in Ohio, she moved to New York to make her living by writing and was later joined there by her sister, Phoebe, also a writer. The two established a literary salon which met at their home regularly for fifteen years.

  Cary, a strong supporter of abolition and of women's rights, was the first president of the women's club now known as Sorosis. Her poems, novels, sketches, and short stories, which were published in *Harper's,* the *Atlantic,* and *Putnam's* as well as in book form, reflected her belief in the values of marriage and motherhood, but with some qualifications. The persona of "The Bridal Veil," for instance, asks her husband to remember that she has "wings flattened down and hid under my veil."

We're married, they say, and you think you have won me,—
Well, take this white veil from my head, and look on me:
Here's matter to vex you, and matter to grieve you,
Here's doubt to distrust you, and faith to believe you,—
I am all as you see, common earth, common dew;
Be wary, and mould me to roses, not rue!

Ah! shake out the filmy thing, fold after fold,
And see if you have me to keep and to hold,—
Look close on my heart—see the worst of its sinning—
It is not yours to-day for the yesterday's winning—
The past is not mine—I am too proud to borrow—
You must grow to new heights if I love you to-morrow.

We're married! I'm plighted to hold up your praises,
As the turf at your feet does its handful of daisies;
That way lies my honor,—my pathway of pride,
But, mark you, if greener grass grow either side,
I shall know it, and keeping in body with you,
Shall walk in my spirit with feet on the dew!

We're married! Oh, pray that our love do not fail!
I have wings flattened down and hid under my veil:
They are subtle as light—you can never undo them,
And swift in their flight—you can never pursue them,
And spite of all clasping, and spite of all bands,
I can slip like a shadow, a dream, from your hands.

Nay, call me not cruel, and fear not to take me,
I am yours for my lifetime, to be what you make me,—
To wear my white veil for a sign, or a cover,
As you shall be proven my lord, or my lover;
A cover for peace that is dead, or a token
Of bliss that can never be written or spoken.

THE BRIDAL VEIL From *Ballads, Lyrics, and Hymns,* Boston: Houghton, Mifflin and Co., 1865, 143–44.

YOUR MARRIAGE

John F. DeYonker, D.O. and Rev. Thomas E. Tobin, C.SS.R.

Your Marriage is the program of premarital counselling which the Roman Catholic church offered to couples in the Archdiocese of Detroit. This and similar manuals were used by thousands of men and women who turned to their priests, rabbis, and ministers for advice and instruction on marriage. "A Checklist for Husbands and Wives" summarizes the ideas which informed that instruction.

A CHECKLIST FOR HUSBANDS AND WIVES

Self-evaluation is always a useful means to encourage better performance.

At regular intervals it would be a good idea to read over this checklist.

Instead of scattering your efforts on many different points select one or two matters in which you will make determined efforts to improve. From time to time change the points for improvement.

To help communication and to better your marriage it might be a good idea to ask your partner to go over the list with you.

I. THE HUSBAND

AS A MAN DO I

Assume my role as leader, breadwinner, protector, teacher?

Follow high moral principles?

Recognize that marriage restricts the freedom I had as a single man?

Treat other women as I expect other men to treat my wife or daughter?

Fulfill the responsibilities of my job and strive to get ahead by study and hard work?

Keep myself neat and well-groomed so that my wife can be proud of me?

Make religion important in my life by learning more about it and practicing it better?

Improve myself intellectually by serious reading?

Better myself socially by becoming a good conversationalist?

Take an active part in community activities?

YOUR MARRIAGE   Reprinted from *Your Marriage*, Liguori Publications, One Liguori Drive, Liguori, Missouri 63057. Used with permission. All rights reserved.

AS A HUSBAND DO I

Show my wife signs of affection and tell her very often that I love her?

Remember wedding anniversaries, birthdays, Mothers' Day, Valentine Day and special days of importance in my marriage?

Notice and make favorable comments on new dresses, hair-dos, and other personal things?

Inform my wife of the family's complete financial picture, salary, debts, insurance, etc.?

Show appreciation for her cooking, baking and housekeeping?

Give her the money she needs for the house as well as some money that she can use for herself?

Try to work out a budget with her?

Put some meaning into my kiss on leaving and returning home?

Make my wife and family happy and not afraid to see me come home?

Make sex an act of love?

Provide for her and the children in case of my death?

Treat her relatives and friends kindly and graciously?

Discuss frustrations and differences in an adult fashion with understanding, calmness and intelligence?

Consult her and take her into my confidence?

Have enough humility and love to seek professional help if our marriage needs it?

Tell or joke about our personal secrets and intimacies?

Readily forgive her human mistakes?

Make sarcastic remarks or act in a grouchy way?

Help her in household tasks? Feeding the baby? Changing diapers? Washing dishes?

Thoughtlessly tease too much?

Show leadership in religious practices, family prayers and devotions?

Act as a good host to her relatives and friends?

Gamble with money needed for the welfare of the family?

Drink excessively and cause unnecessary worry and trouble?

Misinterpret her attention to detail as nagging?

Date my wife by taking her out to dinner, shows, dances, etc.?

II. THE WIFE

AS A WOMAN DO I

Remember my dignity as a woman and the tremendous power of love that I have to give?

Realize that I am guide, comforter, teacher, nurse, bookkeeper, judge, spirtual director, mother confessor, cook, seamstress, housekeeper, buyer, banker and entertainer?

Strive to develop my personality and live according to high principles?

Show respect to my husband especially in front of the children?

Take pride in my work and strive to do it well?

Fix my husband's breakfast? He likes it and it gives me a good start on the day.

Patiently wait until he does his chores? Do I spoil him by doing them myself?

Keep myself neat and well-groomed especially when he returns home from work?

Spiritually set a good example by avoiding vulgarity and cattiness, and by promoting family prayer and reading?

Read good books and magazines, speak grammatically, make efforts to improve myself, keep interested in current events and sports if my husband is interested?

AS A WIFE DO I

Recognize that my role is to complete rather than compete?

Give signs of affection and love to my husband and willingly accept his signs of affection?

Show an interest in his work and the people with whom he works?

Act charitably and give subtle hints of approaching special days or anniversaries and not wait for him to forget?

Make favorable comments on his appearance and try to improve it by proper maintenance of his clothing and gifts of suitable clothing?

Try to save a little toward a nest egg for the future?

Kiss him when he leaves and returns from work?

Do little things for him to keep alive the fires of love?

Search for his virtues rather than his faults?

Belittle or frustrate his ambitions rather than give the necessary encouragement?

Respect his confidences and not reveal his faults and the intimacies of love?

Try to maintain a cheerful atmosphere in the home?

Stoop to using sex as a weapon to be given if he is a good boy and to be denied if he is a bad boy?

Discuss frustrations and differences in an adult fashion?

Treat his relatives and friends courteously and respectfully?

Consult him in matters of importance about personal matters and points which concern the children and come to a common decision?

Seek professional guidance if needed?

Avoid all types of open and subtle nagging?

Help him in his business or employment if necessary?

Thank him for many big and little things:

  his dependability as a good and steady provider

  help with household chores in time of sickness or a crowded schedule

  his interest in my welfare

  his willing acceptance of errands

  care of the children so that I can have some free time

  a comfortable home with work-saving appliances

  tolerance of my whims

  phone calls when detained

  little kindnesses, courtesies, and signs of affection

See the spiritual value of even routine duties in marriage?

Try to economize and manage the household according to income?

Lie to cover up mistakes?

Understand that male thoughtlessness is not intentional? Insist on giving my husband detailed accounts of events in which he has no interest?

Leave him alone when he is tired or grouchy?

Have a snappy comeback to sting him whenever he says anything displeasing?

Show generosity in making sacrifices for him?

THE DREAM OF AN HOUR

Kate Chopin

Kate Chopin (1851-1904) was born in St. Louis and moved to New Orleans after her marriage to a Creole cotton broker. After her husband's death from swamp fever in 1883, Chopin returned to St. Louis with her six children and began to write. Her stories, which appeared in the leading popular magazines of the time, including *Harper's* and the *Atlantic Monthly,* were collected in *Bayou Folk* (1894) and *A Night in Acadia* (1897). Chopin also wrote three novels, the last of which, *The Awakening,* is probably the best known.

"The Dream of an Hour," which first appeared in *Vogue* magazine, is a brief but pointed story about the conflict between marriage and autonomy. Its surprise ending, a technique which was especially popular at the time, underscores the common tendency to interpret women's lives in patriarchal terms.

Knowing that Mrs. Mallard was afflicted with a heart trouble, great care was taken to break to her as gently as possible the news of her husband's death.

It was her sister Josephine who told her, in broken sentences; veiled hints that revealed in half concealing. Her husband's friend Richards was there, too, near her. It was he who had been in the newspaper office when intelligence of the railroad disaster was received, with Brently Mallard's name leading the list of "killed." He had only taken the time to assure himself of its truth by a second telegram, and had hastened to forestall any less careful, less tender friend in bearing the sad message.

She did not hear the story as many women have heard the same, with a paralyzed inability to accept its significance. She wept at once, with sudden, wild abandonment, in her sister's arms. When the storm of grief had spent itself she went away to her room alone. She would have no one follow her.

There stood, facing the open window, a comfortable, roomy armchair. Into this she sank, pressed down by a physical exhaustion that haunted her body and seemed to reach into her soul.

She could see in the open square before her house the tops of trees that were all aquiver with the new spring life. The delicious breath of rain was in the air. In the street below a peddler was crying his wares. The notes of a distant song which some one was singing reached her faintly, and countless sparrows were twittering in the eaves.

There were patches of blue sky showing here and there through the clouds that had met and piled one above the other in the west facing her window.

She sat with her head thrown back upon the cushion of the chair, quite motionless, except when a sob came up into her throat and shook her, as a child who has cried itself to sleep continues to sob in its dreams.

She was young, with a fair, calm face, whose lines bespoke repression and even a certain strength. But now there was a dull stare in her eyes, whose gaze was fixed away off yonder on one of those patches of blue sky. It was not a glance of reflection, but rather indicated a suspension of intelligent thought.

There was something coming to her and she was waiting for it, fearfully. What was it? She did not know; it was too subtle and elusive to name. But she felt it, creeping out of the sky, reaching toward her through the sounds, the scents, the color that filled the air.

Now her bosom rose and fell tumultuously. She was beginning to recognize this thing that was approaching to possess her, and she was striving to beat it back with her will—as powerless as her two white slender hands would have been.

When she abandoned herself a little whispered word escaped her slightly parted lips. She said it over and over under her breath: "free, free, free!" The vacant stare and the look of terror that had followed it went from her eyes. They stayed keen and bright. Her pulses beat fast, and the coursing blood warmed and relaxed every inch of her body.

She did not stop to ask if it were or were not a monstrous joy that held her. A clear and exalted perception enabled her to dismiss the suggestion as trivial.

She knew that she would weep again when she saw the kind, tender hands folded in death; the face that had never looked save with love upon her, fixed and gray and dead. But she saw beyond that bitter moment a long procession of years to come that would belong to her absolutely. And she opened and spread her arms out to them in welcome.

There would be no one to live for her during those coming years; she would live for herself. There would be no powerful will bending hers in that blind persistence with which men and women believe they have a right to impose a private will upon a fellow-creature. A kind intention or a cruel intention made the act seem no less a crime as she looked upon it in that brief moment of illumination.

And yet she had loved him—sometimes. Often she had not. What did it matter! What could love, the unsolved mystery, count for in face of this possession of self-assertion which she suddenly recognized as the strongest impulse of her being!

"Free! Body and soul free!" she kept whispering.

Josephine was kneeling before the closed door with her lips to the keyhole, imploring for admission. "Louise, open the door! I beg; open the door—you will make yourself ill. What are you doing, Louise? For heaven's sake open the door."

"Go away. I am not making myself ill." No; she was drinking in a very elixir of life through that open window.

Her fancy was running riot along those days ahead of her. Spring days, and summer days, and all sorts of days that would be her own. She breathed a quick prayer that life might be long. It was only yesterday she had thought with a shudder that life might be long.

She arose at length and opened the door to her sister's importunities. There was a feverish triumph in her eyes, and she carried herself unwittingly like a goddess of Victory. She clasped her sister's waist, and together they descended the stairs. Richards stood waiting for them at the bottom.

Some one was opening the front door with a latchkey. It was Brently Mallard who entered, a little travel-stained, composedly carrying his grip-sack and umbrella. He had been far from the scene of accident, and did not even know there had been one. He stood amazed at Josephine's piercing cry; at Richards' quick motion to screen him from the view of his wife.

But Richards was too late.

When the doctors came they said she had died of heart disease—of joy that kills.

EVALUATING THE SEXUAL REVOLUTION
Linda Wolfe

Cosmopolitan magazine (circulation 1,500,000) is designed to appeal to an audience of attractive, intelligent, and aware women between the ages of 18 and 35. Under the editorship of Helen Gurley Brown, the magazine promulgated the image of "That Cosmopolitan Girl," a sophisticated and sexually liberated woman. In a 1976 advertisement for the magazine, the text accompanying the photograph of a woman reads: "My favorite magazine says you can do a little 'social lying' and still keep your integrity . . . just be sure you keep the facts straight in your *heart*. I love that magazine. I guess you could say I'm That COSMOPOLITAN girl."

When the magazine conducted its survey of sexual attitudes and practices among its readers, it placed itself in a long line of such studies, a line which includes the Kinsey and Hite Reports. The *Cosmo Report* did boast the largest number of respondents, but since they were all ostensibly readers of the magazine, they could be expected to agree or sympathize with the publication's editorial support of the sexual revolution of the 1960s and 1970s. It is therefore somewhat surprising that the results of that revolution appear to be mixed, even for That *Cosmopolitan* Girl.

MAJOR FINDINGS:
Forty-nine percent of the respondents felt that the sexual revolution had had a good effect on the lives of most women. Fifty-three percent felt that it had caused sex to be too casual or made it hard for them to find acceptable reasons to say no to a man sexually. (The figures add to more than 100 percent because 2 percent of the women straddled both sides of the question.)

As a group, the *Cosmo* women are perhaps the most sexually experienced women in western history. They tend to start their erotic lives young, have sex with a considerable number of partners, and practice a considerable variety of sexual techniques. They are comfortable about acknowledging masturbation and sexual fantasy, and the great majority of them believe that good sex is possible without love. These women have apparently reaped the sexual fruits planted by idealistic social reformers throughout the eighteenth, nineteenth and early twentieth centuries. But as the figures above show, by no means all the *Cosmo* women are happy about the harvest.

EVALUATING THE SEXUAL REVOLUTION   From *The Cosmo Report*, New York: Arbor House, 1981, pp. 301–05.

More than half of them are disappointed in or disillusioned with the sexual revolution.

Why? Is their dissatisfaction simply a result of the usual human tendency to disparage whatever exists and long for the greener grass of whatever does not? Or are there, in fact, real and serious flaws in the sexual revolution, at least as it affects women? The *Cosmo* women who were dissatisfied with the sexual revolution seemed to feel there were. Many believed that, like the heirs to political revolutions, they had been betrayed. They had participated in the overthrow of one tyranny only to see another installed in its place. A 24-year-old schoolteacher from Pennsylvania was typical of this group:

> The sexual revolution is in reality a big sad joke that we women mindlessly allowed to be played on us. What we did when we freed ourselves physically was free men to live out their wildest fantasies of promiscuity and irresponsibility. Men never wanted to form commitments, but in the past they had to in order to obtain sex. Now that we women are no longer afraid of one-night stands, men don't have to commit themselves. Before the revolution, life offered the average women half a glass with which to slake her thirst. Now she's being doused with a fire hose.

Similarly, a 24-year-old aeronautics worker from Florida wrote:

> I have to say that the sexual revolution has made sex worse for me, not better. Yes, the men I meet know how to kiss, suck, touch and fondle, They know how to make me come. But they do it to satisfy their own egos, not because they want to give me pleasure. They don't really care about me, about women, just about sex and their egos. In the past a man used to have to offer a relationship in order to get sex. Tat for tit. But now, since so many women give sex so freely, the men offer nothing—and we women must accept this, even if we don't like it. Throughout the centuries, women have gotten the short end of the stick. We're still getting it. Only now it's a different stick.

The feeling that sexual freedom had benefited men more than women was the predominant underlying complaint against the sexual revolution. The dissatisfied women did not register this complaint out of a Victorian sensibility; they did not argue that sex was not as physically pleasurable to women as it was to men. Rather, they tended to feel that what women wanted from enjoyable sex was not what men wanted from it.

What women wanted, said the critics of the sexual revolution, was not necessarily love. Three-fourths of the *Cosmo* women, including a large number of those who disliked the sexual revolution, believed that good sex was possible without love. What they wanted, *needed,* said the critics, was some form of committed ongoing interchange, and men did not. They believed, for example, that men, unlike women, thoroughly enjoyed one-night stands.

I wonder about this distinction. If it were true, why would so many millions of men continue to opt, today, for living-together arrangements and even marriage? (Despite the sexual revolution and divorce rate, the latest census shows no decline in the American marriage rate.) Some men may have one-night stands—isolated sexual encounters after which they never call again—not so much because they like casual sex as because they decide, after an evening with a particular woman, that they don't care to pursue further intimacy with *her*. What woman doesn't have a friend who complained about having sex with some man who never called her again and then learned, six months or a year later, that he was about to marry someone else—thereby throwing cold water on her theory that he was a devotee of casual sex?

Of course, there *are* men who never form commitments, who never have sex with the same woman twice if they can help it. And although I suspect they are rarer than some imagine, to the woman who has been unable to link up with a lover willing to form an ongoing relationship with her, the sexual revolution can seem empty indeed. A 23-year-old from New York City writes:

> I'm always surprised when I hear from a man after we've spent the night in bed. You can't count on it. That's the way men are. And we women, myself included, have made fools of ourselves by going along with the sexual revolution. We've made it possible for them to have sex with us at the drop of a hat, and never feel enough responsibility to call up the next day and see how we are, or even *if* we are. There are nights I say goodbye to a lover to whom I've just given the greatest ecstasies in bed, and I think to myself, Here I am in my dangerous Greenwich Village apartment, with its fire escapes and dingy staircases. Maybe someone will break in and rape me during the night. Or kill me. Will this guy I'm saying goodbye to ever wonder about me in the morning? Will he wonder enough to call and discover I don't answer the phone? Will he notify the police? Probably not. That's the sexual revolution for you.

Some women who were dissatisfied with the sexual revolution felt that a great deal of what they said and did sexually was insincere. They pretended to enjoyments they did not actually feel. A 22-year-old from Maine was typical:

> I feel 40, I've had so many lovers. I usually go to bed with men on the first date. All the guys I meet expect this. If you don't do it, you run the very high risk of never seeing them again. I try to convince myself I enjoy sex with a total, or semi-total, stranger. I do it because the guys I meet are convinced that they do. But I really detest it. Why can't things be the way they used to be before this sexual revolution? Why can't a woman get to know and like a guy first, and then have intercourse with him?

And a 19-year old from Oregon who pretends to an enjoyment of sadomasochistic sex with her lover, but who has never had an orgasm during this kind of sex, writes:

> My feelings about the sexual revolution are that it is moving too fast. People are too free about sex. But you have to act like you like it or you'll be sitting home all alone.

Those who approve of and admire the sexual revolution do not feel they have been insincere about their pleasures. And, usually, they are women who have had, at least from time to time, ongoing committed relationships with men. A 22-year-old woman from Oregon, whose route to orgasm was described in Chapter Five, is typical: Although she had some ten lovers during college, many of whom were one-night stands, she praises the sexual revolution because it enabled her to experiment with men until she found the one she has now, a man she is planning to marry at the end of the year:

> My earlier sexual experiences, while not very good, helped me over some insecurities and feelings of unattractiveness, and paved the way for me to enjoy my present boyfriend. I am all for the sexual revolution. There are

some problems connected with it, but for the most part it seems to mature people faster and help them not to have fears about sexual feelings. Life seems a lot more natural this way.

The contrast between the feelings of this Oregon woman and those of the Oregon woman whose letter precedes hers suggests an all-important . . . if not surprising . . . fact about the sexual revolution: It is different things to different people. To one woman, the revolution may be in her having had premarital sex with one or two lovers. To another, it may be in her having had a dozen. To one woman, it means she can comfortably discuss with her husband the sexual techniques most likely to bring her to orgasm. To another it's that the men who call her expect her to accompany them to orgies. There has been a sexual revolution, but when people say they are for it or against it, they are often speaking about very different phenomena.

So it is not enough to know that a woman approves of the sexual revolution for Reason X, or disapproves of it for Reason Y. For her reasons to be meaningful, one needs to know what experiences shaped her reasoning. Is her sexual revolution the same as yours or mine?

CAN A WOMAN BE LIBERATED AND MARRIED?

Caryl Rivers

Caryl Rivers (b. 1937) is the author of *Aphrodite at Midcentury: Growing up Female and Catholic in Postwar America* (1973) and co-author, with Rosalind Barnett and Grace Baruch, of *Beyond Sugar and Spice: How Girls and Women Develop Competence* (1979). Her work has also appeared in *Glamour, McCall's,* and *Ms.*

In this account of her own and her husband's accommodations to the demands of marriage, parenthood, and career, Rivers attempts to answer the question of her title according to certain criteria. Her conclusion—"You can't have it all, all the time"—suggests the need for compromise, even in a family which can afford the cost of child care and other services, services which often reduce the need for compromise.

I can remember the exact moment when I was sure I was part of a "liberated" marriage. We were driving along a city street, my husband Alan at the wheel and the two kids, Steven, 8, and Alyssa, 5, in the back seat. Alyssa was clutching a grimy but beloved doll and tugging at the doll's equally grimy and shopworn dress. The overworked threads gave out and the sleeve pulled off. Alyssa looked at the sleeve and then, ignoring me, handed it to my husband and said, "Will you sew it for me, Daddy?"

He didn't sew the dress. He can't sew. I didn't sew the dress. I can't sew either. We gave it to his mother. She's the only one around who isn't all thumbs with a needle. But it was clear that my daughter's question indicated that her

---

CAN A WOMAN BE LIBERATED AND MARRIED? From *New York Times Magazine*, November 2, 1975. Copyright © by The New York Times Company. Reprinted by permission, 18–20, 24, 27–28, 31–32, 35.

mind is—for the time being at least—free of a model of the universe in which the things men do and the things women do are separate spheres, solitary planets that orbit in their own paths, never touching. Since both my husband and I are writers, I suppose she assumes that what grown-ups do is sit in hot stuffy rooms and type a lot, now and then looking up to let out a string of cuss words. It may be the reason she says she would like to stay a kid for a long, long time.

I wonder sometimes if, by the time she grows up, society will be on its way to shattering the old sex-role stereotypes that have made so many men and women so miserable. I see young women today who were raised with one set of assumptions about woman's place and then confronted by the women's movement with a whole new life-style. Since I teach at the college level, I see a dogged professionalism growing among a great many women students. There is also a growing leeriness about any kind of permanent relationship with men. They prize their new-found freedom and are loath to give it up. The prospect of marriage and children seems terrifying—permanent bondage. I respect their seriousness and their need to achieve on their own. And yet, I wonder if some of them will end up like too many men, who sacrificed their emotional lives and wound up with a pension check, a gold watch and nobody who gives a damn.

Can a woman be both liberated and married? And a parent? Can a man? That is a question that is being asked often these days. I think the answer is yes, although one tends to hear more about the failures than the successes—the divorce rate, the runaway wives, the women in consciousness-raising groups who have their consciousnesses lifted right up and out of marriage. I know couples who are splitting up from too much change, too fast. Many of my contemporaries had a decade of very traditional marriages before the women's movement prompted them to try changing their lives. The life they had expected to be heaven when they were 20 turned out to be a source of frustration at 30. Now they are trying to change their way of life and are asking their husbands to adjust to women who are different—often exactly opposite—from the sweet young things they used to be. That sort of wrenching change is what tears marriages apart.

I also know couples who are trying to achieve a balance, as my husband and I are doing. It's easier for us because we started out with a set of expectations that weren't so far apart. He knew that I wanted to be a reporter as much as he wanted to be. We both knew we wanted children. I'm convinced that a liberated marriage, like ours, isn't just luck or a gift of Providence. It has a lot to do with what the bride and the bridegroom think they are at the outset and what they want to be.

I guess I would define a "liberated" marriage as one in which there is a rough parity of both the dirtwork and the glory—and, life being what it is, there is always more of the former. Everyone's solutions are different; ours is a sort of haphazard taking of turns. We have no formal contract about who will do what and when; we are not comfortable with rhetoric and don't really use the word "liberated" very much.

For a number of years, my husband worked full time and his income was the major one; my part-time income bought the extras. Recently I've been the one to work full time, with his income being supplemental. A rough breakdown of the work would probably go this way: Child care, about equal. He handles food shopping, most lunches, the car pool, trash, the dog and miscellaneous tidying. I am in charge of breakfast and dinner, vacuuming, the wash and the ponytail. We both wash dishes. All these chores shift when necessary, the way an outfield shifts over for left-handed hitters. My husband is totally unthreatened by being spotted with a dish towel in his hand. We have no household help, but we do have a baby sitter, a neighbor who comes over when the kids get home from school. She has four kids of her own. Things around the house are rarely dull.

We had always planned to have a family and neither of us has ever regretted that decision. The family unit is an emotional center of gravity in our lives. The kids, while they are a lot of work and a lot of worry, are also a constant source of delight—more than I had expected. They break me up constantly. My son, at the family Passover celebration, was asked the ritual question: "Why is this night different from all other nights?" He deadpanned, "Because on all other nights we eat spaghetti." My daughter announced the other day, out of the blue, "I wish my head was flat, like Frankenstein's, so I could carry things on it." In hindsight, my own upbringing was preparation for a liberated marriage.

I think, with some puzzlement now and then, of a line that Sylvia Plath wrote: "Every woman adores a fascist/the boot in the face, the brute." That rang false to me when I read it; only a masochist could adore a boot in the face. But then, I have known so many women schooled in masochism. I consider myself a feminist. I've written about women's issues, and I think I understand the twinges, the force, the maddening inconsistencies of the movement. One thing I have never really felt is the rage. I have been angry, resentful, just plain mad—but I have never owned the rage, particularly the sort that is unleashed against men. That kind of fury cannot, I suspect, be fired by proxy. It bears directly on something that has happened *to you*. The well of rage is personal, and why, I wondered, was it lacking in me? I grew up in the fifties, that queen of repressive decades, under the shadow of Anatomy Is Destiny.

Many women of my generation wore hobbles on their souls as crippling as the strips of cloth wrapped around the feet of Chinese girl babies to give them a "delicate" walk. Matina Horner, the psychologist who is now president of Radcliffe, discovered the hobbles in her studies of women's fear of success. For many women, particularly bright ones, to succeed in any intellectual task was also to fail as a woman. Those who broke free did not forget the feel of the hobbles. I never knew them. Many women look on men as despots, oppressors, owners of power, brutes. I cannot. I come from a line of liberated men.

There was a picture in my parents' house of my grandfather, my mother's father. I never knew him. He died before I was born. In his picture he seemed the very prototype of the Victorian paterfamilias, with his strong jaw and black full mustache. He raised his children to be hardy, self-reliant and ambitious—and one of them was a girl.

My mother was talking about him recently, and she said she had just realized how unusual it was that her father raised her like a boy. She was a tomboy, free to race and run and skin her knees. Chores were equally shared; she was not banished to the kitchen while her brothers did "men's work." Her father emphasized to her the need to be financially independent, and at one point offered to set her up in business. She chose to go to law school instead.

My mother met my father in law school. Those were the heady, vigorous years of the thirties, and the momentum of the suffrage movement had not yet waned. Women in the thirties breathed freer air than did my contemporaries. In the fifties, we were rebels without a cause; it was a dull toothache of a decade.

I had no strong sense, growing up, that my family was much different from others (although my mother practiced law until I was 5, when she went to join my father at a Navy base in Alabama). My father seemed nicer, funnier, than most fathers, but otherwise I did not perceive him as being that different. I did notice that he was more deeply involved in my life than other girls' fathers were involved in theirs. Those fathers seemed distant—loving, perhaps, but drifting like a cloud, miles above. The father of one of my friends always seemed to be sitting in a chair, smoking a cigar and reading a newspaper, cut off from our lives.

For my father, sports was the thread that bound our activities together. I was a baseball fanatic, and every year he and I went to Griffith Stadium to see Harry Truman or Dwight Eisenhower throw out the first ball.

When I started to play Catholic Youth Organization basketball in the seventh grade, I inherited a ready-made coach: my father. He had once played semipro basketball, and we had strategy sessions around the dining-room table. When the salt shakers would no longer suffice, the whole family would repair to the living room, where my father would assign positions to my mother, my brother and me, and we would run through a play. He taught me how to use my hips and elbows so the referee wouldn't see, and thanks to him, I was the only girl in the league who could execute a jump shot. (The jump shot was considered, I suppose, too strenuous or too unladylike for girls. This was tommyrot to my father, who knew that ladies didn't win ball games. You had to be aggressive if you wanted to be a good basketball player, he said.)

Basketball was serious business at our house. So what if it was only the C.Y.O. girls' team. It did not occur to me that whether or not we beat Blessed Sacrament was not of cosmic concern to everyone. I did notice that there were only a few fathers who went to the girls' games but a lot when the boys played. My father could not live out any fantasies through me. Clearly, I would never be a future Bob Cousy or Sammy Baugh. But our postgame session could not have been more serious if we had been talking about the Knicks or the Celtics instead of the St. Michael's varsity. My father never in any way gave me the impression that what I accomplished was less than it might have been because I was a girl. He was as proud as I of the little cluster of trophies resting on top of the TV set.

Later, when I abandoned basketball for tulle ballgowns with matching pumps and little dabs of perfume behind the ears, the trophies stayed on the TV. At first, I had wanted to pack them away, sure that my boyfriends would think me an Amazon with huge thighs, but my father argued that I had won them, and they ought to stay. He was right, of course. To pack away the trophies would have been betrayal of the rankest order—betrayal of my own past, my accomplishment.

Those were the days when women were supposed to be seen but not heard. In an article for The Ladies' Home Journal in 1954, Marlene Dietrich wrote that women should be like moons, floating about the male sun, shining in reflected glory. (The title of the article was "How to Be Loved.") I tried and inevitably flubbed. I was a lousy moon. I tried to lose prettily at tennis. I never lost that instinct for the jugular, developed in those C.Y.O. games. I won arguments with swains about admitting Red China to the U.N. I got good marks. Finally, I faced it. My mother and father had not produced a moon; they taught me to shine on my own.

Lacking a proper indoctrination in the national mores, I was a bit slow to sense all the nuances. I was truly puzzled by the male contempt for women that was so openly expressed around me. Men used the word for the female sexual organ as a term of utter scorn, and it was hatred, as much as lust, that dripped through the words of the guy who would mutter on a corner, "I'd like to——you, babe!" There was also a female contempt for men that was muted, indirect but had no less a sting.

I wonder how many men realize how deep and bitter runs the contempt of women. Barred so often from the arena, where the lights are hot and a man's performance is on display, women have the power of the people in the bleachers. They can criticize, ridicule and demand, safe in the knowledge that the stamina the arena demands will not be asked of them. Their weapon is not the Bronx cheer—that is too direct—but the well-timed laugh, the curl of a lip. If a man could listen in while his sex—or he himself—was being discussed by a group of "traditional, subservient" women, it would chill his blood. I have heard such discussions in which men were reduced to buffoons and incompetents by women who were supposed to love them—and hold them in awe. It is the power of the weak, never openly displayed because there is too much to lose.

I was astonished by all this, because contempt was something I had to learn about outside my own home. My mother and my father were equals in their house. If, as the years passed, their marriage was not the paradise that M.-G.-M. said marriage should be, it *was* rooted in the sort of loyalty and trust that can exist only between people of like weight and power. Never, in the entire time I was growing up, did I hear my father put my mother down. Never did I hear her mock him. I grew up believing that is how things were between men and women.

It may seem insignificant—or cute—to see ponytailed moppets out there playing shortstop in Little League. But consider. The women those girls will grow up to be will not be inclined to laugh at men when they fail, to mock them when their best turns out to be not good enough. They will have known what it feels like to take a third strike swinging or to bobble a grounder. Contempt will only vanish when women have a chance to play all the games now owned by men.

I always wanted to play—ever since I was a kid. I wanted to be where things were happening, not on the sidelines. When Alan and I were married, two years out of grad school, our careers had begun to progress at an even, steady rate. We worked on a small paper in New York State, then went on to jobs reporting politics and urban affairs, he in Baltimore and I in Washington. I must confess that I half-believed his work was more "serious" than mine because he was a man. I was happy, for a time, with the fact that I had been allowed into a man's game.

The real changes for us came with the birth of our first child. They had nothing to do with religion. Alan and I had agreed that the children would be raised in the Jewish religion and I would follow my own unorthodox brand of Catholicism. But with Steven's birth, we faced the problem of work roles. Now the responsibility for bringing home the bacon was Alan's. I was determined to continue my career by freelancing, but it was as if a large rock had been placed on the scale of our professional lives—on his side. I accepted the curtailments on my freedom. I did not get upset when he called at 11 and said he was going to have a drink with the other reporters. I know how one likes to talk shop after a hard day. But I had no one to talk shop with. If he called and said he had to miss dinner, I said, "Sure," because I knew about deadlines. But if I was working on a story, there was no one to call and say, "I won't be home," because the baby sitter had deadlines of her own. Sometimes I thought I was living vicariously through my husband's experiences. He was the one in the middle of things and I was on the periphery. I learned a new sensation—the "invisible woman" effect. There were times when we went to parties that people came up eagerly to speak to him and looked through me as if I didn't exist.

I became a hoarder of time. My work time was severely rationed. I would rarely ask Alan to give up something he had scheduled to baby-sit while I worked. In my mind I had assigned us places—he was first and I was way behind. I resented this, often. I resented the fact that he simply accepted this, as if it were the way of the world. He never said my work was not important. He was always careful to praise what I had done. But I had the feeling that his work was capital I important and mine was little i important.

When he designed a news show for public television and served as its anchorman and news editor, his working day ran from 9 A.M. to 9 P.M. or after. I was home alone night after night with the children. I kept active professionally but it was a great juggling act, calling the baby sitter, making sure Steven had clean underpants and that the meat for dinner was out of the freezer. My husband was exhausted when he came home at night. The 60-hour-plus week left him so frayed it took him half the weekend to get back to normal. I knew how important the idea of the show was to him.

At the same time I grew restive about the strain his work put on both of us, how it was beginning to isolate him from the family that was so important to both of us. He would remark, often, that he was missing seeing his daughter grow from an infant into a little girl. This was one of the major factors in his decision to leave television for a magazine job with more reasonable hours. If he had followed the traditional upwardly mobile success pattern, he would have gone on to "bigger" jobs that would have eaten up more and more of his time. Increasingly, I would have had to assume more and more of the burden of the household and the kids. I suspect that my resentment would have grown like a malevolent weed. He would have been too busy to see it growing. It could well have choked the life out of our relationship.

If the women's movement has had an impact on our personal balance, I guess it is because I felt more able to articulate my frustrations and he was able to understand that they were common to a great many women. He has been very considerate about trying to understand the things that were bugging me, to understand my need to be serious about my work, and I have tried not to get on a soapbox with movement speeches. We have the usual yelling matches now and then, but they are usually less intense than our disagreements over more cosmic issues, such as whether or not pouring the water from the dog's dish in the kitchen sink is a sanitary practice. I say the dog germs will gurgle down the sink and disappear and he sees rabies microbes dancing on the silverware.

I have to admit, too, that despite the limits on my freedom in the time I spent at home, the lack of economic pressure gave me the chance to experiment, to start off on roads that might lead nowhere. My first book, about growing up as a Catholic in America, was the result of one of those experiments. I would never have written it if I had been hiking after some politician on the trail of a headline.

I no longer feel that there is an inequality in our professional lives. Sure, I made sacrifices, but so has he. At different periods of our lives, we have both subsidized each other's work with time and money, and I have learned a simple truth that I should have known: You can't have it all, all of the time. Many of the men of my generation thought they could, so they tied themselves to the conveyor belt, thinking that women would manage their emotions. They wound up with a vacuum where part of their lives should have been. My husband and I don't want that to happen to us. So perhaps I will not climb every mountain and ford every stream (a cliché, but my daughter has played "The Sound of Music" to the point where the sight of whiskers on kittens makes me want to throw up) but I am damned sure I will get to a lot of them. My husband will climb back on the merry-go-round but he will know when to get off. There will be areas in which we can't compete with the people who work 16 hours a day, who eat, live and breathe only for work. So be it. As the children grow older, some of the old demands they make on us will dwindle, but the parents of teen-agers assure me that some dandy new ones will arise.

I hear some young people talking of the "division of child-care tasks" and it sounds very clean and scientific, something a computer could manage. It is not like that. As a reporter in urban America in the sixties and seventies, my husband got acclimated to the front lines. A black militant once tried to run him over, he patrolled the streets of New York with the Jewish Defense League, and he got hit with a tomato meant for Teddy Kennedy when the whites of Boston got upset over busing. He was accustomed to danger, tension, confusion and chaos—and then came the real test of his mettle: home.

This year, when he got a book contract, we pulled the big switch. He is now working at home, writing. Mornings he also takes care of Alyssa before she goes off to kindergarten. I work full time, teaching at Boston University. Here, in terms of a "division of childcare tasks," are a few highlights from an actual day in the life of a liberated man:

Somewhere between 6:30 and 7 we struggle out of bed and try to shuffle everybody in and out of one bathroom. Alan makes the bed and I wrestle with the ponytail. I cook bacon and he makes bologna sandwiches. He takes Steven, a third-grader, to school and I get Alyssa in the right coat and shoes for rain or shine. We hop in the car, because Alan will drive me to the university where I have a morning course. The traffic at the entrance to the Sumner Tunnel is its usual incredible snarl. Alyssa announces, brightly, "We are all going to play puppet hands!"

Alan moans, audibly. I groan. Puppet hands is a game she invented all by herself. In it, she turns her left hand into Cowey and her right hand into Horsey. The two of them converse in a screechy falsetto that would drive a saint to screaming heresy. But it doesn't stop there. My right hand is Frog and my left hand is Phyllis Frog. Alan's right hand is Fishy and his left hand is Elephant. Elephant is a morose sort, but Fishy has been too engaging for his own good. So Alyssa chants, in a sort of nagging chirp, "Fishy, where are you? Fishy? Fishy? Fiiiisssssshhhhyyyyyy!" until her father relents and Fishy speaks.

Through the tunnel, up Storrow Drive, Alyssa does puppet hands. My teeth are on edge. Alan drops me off at B.U. Alyssa waves good-by and I hear her saying, "Fishy, Fishy, want to hear me sing?" Alan's knuckles, where he grips the wheel, are turning white.

When he and Alyssa arrive home, Alan goes up to the attic-office to work. He has been at the typewriter for half an hour when peculiar sounds, accompanied by a peculiar smell, drift up the stairs. He goes down and discovers that the sounds are being made by Jane, the medium-sized family dog—loyal, dumb and cowardly—who is having an attack of diarrhea on the living-room rug. He drags Jane into the kitchen and starts to swab her off when Alyssa wanders in, wrinkles her nose and says, "I think I have to throw up." He hustles her out of the kitchen. Eventually, he gets back to work.

Next comes lunch time and the kindergarten car pool. After the noon car-pool run, there is a precious two and a half hours for work on the book. Then it is time to pick up Steven. Steven's cronies, Joey, Jonathan, Chris and Michael, ride along. Third-grade conversation—and particularly humor—is cheerfully and relentlessly anal. Punch lines involving excrement produce gales of laughter. Alan drives home, attempting to block out the punching, cackling and assorted animal sounds from the back seat.

Up in his office, he types vigorously for 12 minutes and eight seconds before he becomes aware of eyes boring into his back. It is Deanna, aged 3, our neighbor's daughter.

"Awan," she says. "Can I kiss Jane? Does Jane have jorms?" (Her version of germs.)

"You can kiss Jane. She hasn't got germs. Just don't kiss her on the mouth."

"Will I get a cold if I kiss Jane, Awan? Does Jane have jorms?"

"No jorms. I mean germs."

"Do you have jorms, Awan?"

"No."

"Does Alyssa have jorms?"

"No."

"Does Alyssa have jorms?"

"No. NOBODY HAS JORMS!"

Steven and Joey come charging in. There is a wounded pigeon on the lawn. Alan hollers at the kids not to touch the pigeon. Pigeons are filthy, plague-carrying birds. He calls the dog officer and waits on the lawn to make sure the pigeon doesn't hobble into the street and get run over, which would upset the children. The dog officer comes and takes the pigeon. Alan goes back to the typewriter. Nothing will come. The muse has vanished. The phone rings. It is I, his loving wife. "Are you having a nice day, dear?"

◈◈◈

My husband is, I think, one of a growing breed of free men who have not been stamped out of a mold like a chocolate bunny, who can dry a dish or wipe a runny nose without an attack of castration anxiety. I have known too many men struggling honestly with the new ambitions and hopes of women to think the liberated man is a rare species. But there are men—a great many, I suppose—who cannot function in anything but the old way, who must see women as satellites to sustain their own egos. I have known women married to such men: when the women began to grow in their own self-estimation, the marriages broke up.

I know other women who are sticking with marriages where there is a great deal of tension about sex roles and division of chores. They stay because they value the relationships and hope things will work out. Sometimes women are afraid to speak out. Other times they bark demands, forgetting that a marriage is not the U.A.W. bargaining table. Some marriages ought to fail, for the sanity of both parties. It is easy to say, in ringing tones, that a woman ought to up and leave any man who isn't liberated. But the formula that works for one person could be deadly for another.

I am optimistic, however, for the future of liberated marriage. I think it makes good sense. It is easier than the old model, because it allows both parties more options. I think it must be tough to be a man, looking ahead year after year after year to driving a cab or teaching high-school civics or selling insurance, with no prospects of climbing off the treadmill, even for a while. Is that really much better than the plight of the woman who looks ahead and sees an Everest of dirty dishes and unmade beds?

I have a feeling that the men and women of my daughter's generation will be dealing with their expectations earlier and in a more rational way than most of us did. My husband is always saying to Alyssa, "Girls can be doctors" or "Girls can be pilots" or "Girls can be anything they want." He will transmit to her the message my father (and my mother) beamed to me: You are a person of worth, of value, and it is your right to achieve and grow. My husband accorded me that right freely; I did not have to wrest it from him. If I am a free woman, and I believe I am, it is due in no small measure to the fact that I have lived with—and loved and been nurtured by—free men.

FOG AT THE SCENE OF THE CRIME

Richard Cohen

When Vernon E. Jordan, Jr., president of the National Urban League, was shot and wounded in 1980, media reports of the incident identified his companion as a "white divorcée." The fact that Martha Coleman, a white woman, had been out at night with a black man added a racial element to the pejorative image.

Divorced women have long suffered from the stereotyping which ascribes to them sexually promiscuous behavior and generally loose morals. As journalist Richard Cohen points out in the following article, there is no term used for men which parallels that of "divorcée" for women. Such linguistic double standards serve to reinforce the stereotype.

Many years ago, when I worked in the insurance biz, I asked my boss why divorced women were charged higher rates for auto insurance than married or single women. The man, an executive in our company, said that divorced women were what he called "moral risks" although he could not explain—nor was he asked—how the same legal process had left their former husbands either morally unchanged or changed in a way that did not affect their driving.

Quite a lot has changed since then, but not, it appears, our attitude towards divorced women. One of them—a four-time loser—was present at the shooting of Vernon E. Jordan Jr., the president of the National Urban League. Her name is Martha C. Coleman and she was initially described in a ton of newspapers as a "white divorcee." It is as if no more need be said.

Of course, there is a lot more to be said than that. She is a woman with a job—supervisor at the International Harvester truck plant in Fort Wayne, Ind. She is on the board of the local chapter of the Urban League. She helped set up the dinner where Jordan spoke. She could have been called a civil rights activist, an organizer, a factory supervisor—all the things she is other than a four-time divorcee. It was as if nothing else really mattered.

Across the board, people said things they should not have. The President, apparently relying on the same information as everyone else, called the Jordan shooting an "assassination attempt." The FBI said it was a "conspiracy" and the local cops gave their version of events. It was, they said, a "domestic" matter, which is what some cops are wont to call any crime where a woman is in the vicinity. In this case, the woman was more than just in the vicinity. She was a witness to the actual event, and an important event it was. A major civil rights leader had been shot. The nation was already tense and edgy after the Miami riots. People wanted to know who shot Jordan and why and it was natural for people to want to know more about the woman who was with him. In that context, her four divorces were fair game—grist for the media mill.

But the term "divorcee" is not just a statement of marital status. It is

FOG AT THE SCENE OF THE CRIME   Washington Post Company, June 16, 1980, © 1980, The Boston Globe Newspaper Company/Washington Post Writer's Group, reprinted with permission, 14.

something more. It's code, newspaper code, if you like, like ruddy for drunk or jolly for fat. In this case, it's a statement about morals. "Divorcee" means she ain't got none—a satisfying enough explanation for those offended by a white woman being with a black man.

Now you may want pause here and figure out if this is more insulting to Jordan than to Coleman, or you may want to simply ask what this all has to do with the shooting. It doesn't. Things would not have been materially different had Coleman been married three times or twice or once or never at all. All you really need for a sordid situation is a man and a woman and put them together alone late at night. It matters not at all then the race of either party or, for that matter, their marital status.

But in the popular imagination logic plays no part. It is as if the divorce MUST somehow be linked to the shooting. It is as if these divorces are moral lapses and that one moral lapse must lead to another. In the insurance industry, they thought it would lead to auto accidents and in the crimestopper biz the thinking appears to be that it would connect, somehow, to a shooting.

But this is a standard we apply only to women. We never refer to men by their marital status or the number of times they are married. I, for one, have no idea if Jordan himself was ever married before and I have never yet seen a man described in the newspapers as a "white divorce." It is a description that would fit, among others, Ronald Reagan.

The reason for this is that divorce, marriage—all that stuff—is about sex and when men are concerned there are thought to be more important things. There is what they do and what they believe and who they are—titles and that sort of thing. With women, though, sex is thought to be the whole story, almost all you need to know, as if the "essential" truth of a woman's character is the answer to the old question, "Does She or Doesn't She?"

It's almost always the wrong question. It tells you nothing of importance, is never asked of a man, and, in the case of Martha Coleman, is entirely beside the point. There's only one question that mattered and it has nothing to do with her divorces. It had to do, instead, with the shooting.

What did she know?

THE OLD MAID OF THE PERIOD

Fanny Fern

The stereotype of the single woman—usually called an old maid or a spinster—was that of a woman unable to attract a man for reasons of appearance, taste, or disposition. Often, she became a dependent in the house of a relative and filled the role of servant, caring for the children, nursing the sick, and performing other domestic tasks in exchange for her keep. Considered sexless, such women were often the object of pity and ridicule.

Fanny Fern finds that Women's Rights has succeeded in challenging the stereotype. The modern old maid, she says, is as good as the modern young maid: sociable, intelligent, fashionable, resourceful, and independent. As exemplars of this type, she mentions Phoebe and Alice Cary, the well known writers who lived independently and never married.

 She don't shuffle round in "skimpt" raiment, and awkward shoes, and cotton gloves, with horn side-combs fastening six hairs to her temples; nor has she a sharp nose, and angular jaw, and hollow cheeks, and only two front teeth. She don't read "Law's Serious Call," or keep a cat, or a snuff-box, or go to bed at dark, save on vestry-meeting nights, nor scowl at little children, or gather catnip, or apply a broomstick to astonished dogs.

Not a bit of it. The modern "old maid" is round and jolly, and has her full complement of hair and teeth, and two dimples in her cheek, and has a laugh as musical as a bobolink's song. She wears pretty, nicely fitting dresses too, and cunning little ornaments around her plump throat, and becoming bits of color in her hair, and at her breast, in the shape of little knots and bows; and her waist is shapely, and her hands have sparkling rings, and no knuckles; and her foot is cunning, and is prisoned in a bewildering boot; and she goes to concerts and parties and suppers and lectures and matinees, and she don't go alone either; and she lives in a nice house, earned by herself, and gives jolly little teas in it. She don't care whether she is married or not, nor need she. She can afford to wait, as men often do, till they have "seen life," and when their bones are full of aches, and their blood tamed down to water, and they have done going out, and want somebody to swear at and to nurse them—then marry!

Ah! the modern old maid has her eye-teeth cut. She takes care of herself, instead of her sister's nine children, through mumps, and measles, and croup, and chicken-pox, and lung fever and leprosy, and what not.

She don't work that way for no wages and bare toleration, day and night. No, sir! If she has no money, she teaches, or she lectures, or she writes books or poems, or she is a book-keeper, or she sets types, or she does anything but hang on to the skirts of somebody's else husband, and she feels well and independent in consequence, and holds up her head with the best, and asks no favors, and *"Woman's Rights"* has done it!

THE OLD MAID OF THE PERIOD   From *Ginger-Snaps*. New York: Carleton, Publisher, 1870, 146–48.

That awful bugbear, "Woman's Rights"! which small-souled men, and, I am sorry to say, narrow *women* too, burlesque and ridicule, and wont believe in, till the Juggernaut of Progress knocks them down and rides over them, because they will neither climb up on it, nor get out of the way.

The fact is, the *Modern* Old Maid is as good as the Modern Young Maid, and a great deal better, to those who have outgrown bread and butter. She has sense as well as freshness, and conversation and repartee as well as dimples and curves.

She carries a dainty parasol, and a natty little umbrella, and wears killing bonnets, and has live poets and sages and philosophers in her train, and knows how to use her eyes, and don't care if she never sees a cat, and couldn't tell a snuff-box from a patent reaper, and has a bank-book and dividends: yes, sir! and her name is Phœbe or Alice; and Woman's Rights has done it.

MARVIN V. MARVIN

Michelle Triola Marvin's suit for property-division and support from film star Lee Marvin was probably the most widely publicized of the "palimony" cases. Triola had lived with Marvin, who was still married, for seven years. When their relationship ended, she sought the kind of compensation traditionally granted to wives in cases of divorce.

The commentary which follows the legal summary of this case notes the substantial increase in the number of unmarried couples who are living together and suggests that the courts will have to accommodate these "quasi-marriages." Until the legal system is prepared to do that, however, unmarried couples are advised to draw up written contracts governing the disposition of property when and if their relationships end.

18 Cal. 3d 660, 134 Cal. Rptr. 815
557 Pac. 2d 106 (1976)

This milestone case has been widely noted in the press and elsewhere. Because of the long and illuminating opinion of the California Supreme Court, and because the decision has been extensively cited and quoted in other jurisdictions, the case deserves special attention.

Michele Triola and screen actor Lee Marvin lived together for seven years without marrying. During this period Marvin accumulated $3.6 million, mostly as a motion picture actor. Before the couple separated, Ms. Triola legally changed her name to Marvin. When they broke up, she sued Marvin for half the property he acquired while they were living together, and asked for support. She asserted that, relying on Marvin's oral promise to share the property with her, she had given up a promising career as a singer to become his companion and housekeeper. He defended on the ground that because of

MARVIN V. MARVIN *Separation Agreements and Ante-Nuptial Contracts.* Cumulative Supplement. Rev. Ed. New York: Matthew Bender. Copyright © 1984 by Matthew Bender & Co., Inc., and reprinted with permission from *Separation Agreements and Ante-Nuptial Contracts.* 95–9, 95–13.

the "immoral" character of the relationship, the alleged agreement was unenforceable as against California public policy.

The lower court agreed with Marvin. While conceding that not all property agreements between cohabitants were invalid, the court pointed out that in this case Ms. Triola had known that Marvin was a married man; and that the alleged contract was therefore founded on an adulterous relationship. Whatever services Ms. Triola may have rendered to Marvin as "companion, homemaker, housekeeper and cook," said the court, did not constitute a contribution to the acquisition of property entitling her to share in it. The court dismissed the complaint.

The Supreme Court of California disagreed. It reversed and remanded. In ruling that oral agreements between unwed couples to share equally in the property acquired by them during their cohabitation were enforceable, the Supreme Court made the following points:

1. The provisions of the divorce statutes do not govern the distribution of property acquired during a nonmarital relationship; such property remains subject solely to judicial decision.

2. The courts should enforce express contracts between non-marital partners unless founded on the consideration of "meretricious" sexual services.

3. In the absence of an express contract, the courts should inquire into the conduct of the parties to determine whether the conduct indicates a contract implied in law or fact, or a partnership agreement, or a joint venture.

4. "The courts may also employ the doctrine of quantum meruit or equitable remedies such as constructive or resulting trusts when warranted by the facts of the case."

5. "Adults who voluntarily live together and engage in sexual relations are nonetheless as competent as any other persons to contract respecting their earnings and property rights. Of course they cannot lawfully contract to pay for the performance of sexual service . . . but they may agree to pool their earnings and to hold all property acquired during the relationship in accord with the law covering community property; conversely they may agree that each partner's earnings and the property acquired from those earnings remain the separate property of the earning partner."

6. "The argument that granting remedies to non-marital partners would discourage marriage must fail."

7. "Although we recognize the well-established public policy to foster and promote the institution of marriage . . . the perpetuation of judicial rules which result in an inequitable distribution of property accumulated during a non-marital relationship is neither a just nor effective way of carrying out that policy."

8. The acceptance of Marvin's defense "would invalidate all agreements between non-marital partners, a result no one favors."

9. ". . . to the extent that denial of relief 'punishes' one partner, it necessarily rewards the other by permitting him to retain a disproportionate amount of

the property. Concepts of 'guilt' thus cannot justify an unequal division of property between two equally 'guilty' persons."

10.   Where neither party claims the status of actual or putative spouse, an action for the nullity of a marriage cannot serve as a device for adjudicating contract and property rights arising from the non-marital relationship. In such a case the woman may correctly choose to assert her rights by means of an ordinary civil action.

11.   Where an alleged contract between a man and a woman who lived together did not require the man to divorce his wife nor reward him for so doing, it was not invalid as an agreement to encourage divorce. Such ground for asserting the invalidity of the contract would not apply in any event if the marriage in question was beyond redemption.

Pursuant to the remand, the case was retried, without a jury. The trial lasted more than 11 weeks; upward of 60 witnesses testified. In a decision handed down on April 18, 1979, Judge Marshall found that no contract express or implied had subsisted between the parties; but under the general doctrine of equitable remedies he awarded Ms. Triola $104,000 to enable her to "return from her status as companion to a motion picture star to a separate, independent but perhaps more prosaic existence," and so that she would have "the economic means to reeducate herself and to learn new employable skills". The Judge indicated that he based the amount on the maximum sum, i.e. $1,000 per week that she had earned as a singer over a two-year period.

In August, 1981, the California Court of Appeals, Second District, reversed the trial court, holding that the lower court's findings of fact and conclusions in support of the rehabilitative award to the plaintiff were beyond the issues as framed in the pleadings. The plaintiff had asked in her amended complaint that the defendant, with whom she lived in a non-marital relationship for seven years, be ordered to pay her a reasonable sum per month for support and maintenance. Nevertheless, the trial court's detailed findings of fact precluded it from granting the requested relief, for it found specifically that: (1) the defendant never had any obligation to pay support or maintenance; (2) the plaintiff suffered no damage from the relationship or its termination; (3) the plaintiff actually benefitted socially and economically from the parties' cohabitation; (4) a confidential and fiduciary relationship never existed between the parties with respect to property; (5) the defendant was not unjustly enriched by services which the plaintiff performed for him or them; and (6) the defendant never acquired property or money from the plaintiff by any unlawful act.

The rehabilitative award apparently was based on language in the Supreme Court's decision to the effect that additional equitable remedies may well evolve to protect the expectations of the parties in a non-marital relationship where existing remedies prove inadequate.

However, the court's findings in support of the award merely established the plaintiff's need and the defendant's ability to respond to it. In the view of the California Court of Appeals, Second District, this rationale was not sufficient to sustain the award which, being non-consensual in nature, must be supported by some recognized underlying obligation in law or in equity. Although a court of equity has broad powers, it may not create totally new substantive rights under the guise of doing equity (Marvin v. Marvin 7 FLR 2661).

COMMENT

1.   Cohabitation without marriage is, and for sometime has been, a reality. According to the report of the U.S. Bureau of Census, the number of unmarried persons living together increased from 1,386,622 in 1960 to 1,988,930 in 1970—a rise of nearly 50 percent. No statistics are available for the period from 1970 to date, but it has been estimated that the 1980 figure may run as high as 3 million. Clearly, quasi-marriages are not a passing phenomenon. They have led to litigation, and will lead to more.

2.   It is idle to argue that judicial recognition of the rights of unmarried couples, regardless of the *nature* of those rights, and regardless of the character of the relationship, means sanctioning "legal concubinage." It is equally idle to deny that recognition means the validation of a status partly akin to that of common-law spouses. Only fifteen jurisdictions in the United States countenance common-law marriages. Superficially, this poses a dilemma. But the dilemma dissolves in part if the crucial distinction between *marital* property rights and *non-marital* ones is noted. (See Property Rights of Non-Marital Partners in Meretricious Cohabitation, 13 New Engl. L. Rev. 453, 457 [1978]). The dilemma persists only where questions of support arise.

3.   The imprecise and inconsistent use of terms in judicial opinions has tended to obscure the basic distinction. Sometimes *all* forms of cohabitation without marriage, no matter how settled and enduring, have been branded illicit and meretricious; at other times only casual affairs have earned the invidious adjectives. Nor have the courts taken the trouble to define "illicit" and "meretricious" with any degree of exactness. (According to *Webster's Collegiate Dictionary* "illicit" means "unlawful;" and "meretricious" means "of or relating to a prostitute" or "tawdrily attractive" or "based on pretense or insincerity.") It would lessen confusion and provide clearer guidance if the courts—and commentators—(a) abandoned the use of the term "illicit and meretricious cohabitation" altogether; (b) used the term "illicit relationship" to describe alliances that were frivolous, intermittent and fleeting; and (c) used the term "living together without marriage" to denote stable, serious relationships.

4.   The courts should—and in due course doubtless will—come to view living together without marriage as a *unique* relationship, and develop a set of equity guidelines particularly suited to it, instead of trying to drag in inappropriate traditional doctrines to buttress their decisions.

5.   Until then, contractual arrangements offer the safest course for unmarried couples. Agreements between them pertaining to money or property will be given legal effect if they do not explicitly hinge on the "illicit" relationship. Should the agreements be oral or in writing? In writing, by all means. Oral bargains invite fraud, present difficulties of proof, entail needless expenditure of judicial time and effort.

6.   However, if one is to judge by the cases, unmarried spouses, with their disdain of social conventions and legal formalities, are not disposed to set down on paper their understanding (if any) as to their property rights. In every case mentioned in this commentary in which the plaintiff alleged a contract, the contract was an oral one.

7.   As for the element of "intent," judges have said that it must govern in property-division cases in the absence of contract. This assumes, of course, that there lurks in every case an element of *mutual* intent awaiting discovery by the judge. The assumption is fallacious. The man usually has his ideas and expectations about ownership, and the woman has hers, and they are hardly apt to coincide.

8.   Attorneys will be well advised to point out to their quasi-marital clients the hazards of informality, and to stress the benefits of a written agreement.

FIVE

Mothers

OF ALL THE IMAGES of women, that of woman as mother is the most central and, perhaps, the most ambivalent. During the earliest ages of human history, the Great Goddess or Great Mother was part of the mythos of almost all cultures. Representing the mystery of life, of decay as well as fecundity, she also appeared under the aegis of The Terrible Mother. Although images of mothers and motherhood vary from culture to culture, they often contain within themselves these dual elements of generation and corruption. Their cultural relativity derives from those economic, social, and political forces which affect the balance between these perceptions.

Such forces were at work in the change from an agricultural to an industrialized economy which occurred in the United States during the early nineteenth century. In a rural economy, most people worked at home, so a more equitable division of family responsibilities was possible. Puritan advice on childrearing, for example, emphasized the father's responsibility for shaping the character of his offspring. When men went to work in mills and factories, however, their homes became havens, and the women who presided there became "angels in the house." By the 1800s, the division between public and private spheres, between male and female realms, had been drawn, and the "Mystique of Motherhood," which the emerging middle class fostered, became the expression of an ideal.

This ideal, shaped by the sentimentalization of women in general and of mothers in particular, was based on the belief that women possessed certain "feminine" qualities—that they were by nature warm, gentle, sensitive, nurturing, moral, self-sacrificing, patient, and enduring. Such worthy surrogates for absent fathers received certain rewards: their status was deemed sacred; they were deferred to in their own sphere; they were considered the heart of the family's refuge; and they were allowed a certain amount of power over the activities of the household, especially those involving children.

Children, of course, were the primary responsibility of mothers. Serving as models, mothers instructed the young in moral perfection and thus shaped the character of the next generation. Nineteenth century commentators, emphasizing this awesome responsibility, maintained that the health of the Republic itself depended on mothers. Although removed from public life, then, women ostensibly controlled, through their sons and daughters, the future of the public as well as the private sphere.

Many elements of nineteenth century society supported and enlarged the ideal. The "mother-women" whom Kate Chopin describes in *The Awakening* (1899) are the ideal's exemplars, but similar portraits appeared in the popular periodical literature of the last century, especially in the publications designed to appeal to women. Religious leaders, taking their texts from the Old and New Testaments, praised the valiant woman and gratefully encouraged her active participation in their congregations. The authors of sentimental novels, most of them women, focused on the hearth and home; although their heroines were not usually mothers, they often had mothers or surrogates who reflected the ideal. In *Uncle Tom's Cabin*, Harriet Beecher Stowe imposed the middle class ideal on the slave mother, Eliza, who risks life and limb for her child. Even Fanny Fern, who directed her pointed wit at the target of male supremacy, wrote about mothers with great sentimentality and little humor.

Although the Mystique of Motherhood was most compelling during the nineteenth century, it has persisted into the twentieth, especially in the popular advice literature designed for middle and upper class women. In their bestseller of 1947, *Modern Woman: The Lost Sex*, social analyst Ferdinand Lundberg and psychoanalyst Marynia Farnham maintained that it is a woman's role as mother which validates her: "If a woman does not have children, she asks ingenuously"—and "ingenuously" is an important word here—"what is everything all about for her?" The acceptance and availability of birth control and abortion, of course, eventually made it possible for women not only to choose the number of children they wanted to have, but to choose not to be mothers at all.

Whether we consider the nineteenth century conception of the ideal mother or the modern version, it is clear that both describe a role which no human being could play without serious difficulty. The "true woman" may have believed that her *raison d'être* was motherhood, but real mothers often asked: "Is this all there is?" Such questioning can be found in the private writing of women; in their literary works, where they speak through imagined characters; and in their public pronouncements.

When Charlotte Perkins Gilman (1860-1935), one of the most influential thinkers of her time, gave up her daughter to be reared by the child's father and his second wife, she was accused of being "unnatural" and of giving up her child in order to obtain her freedom. Her own life was difficult at that time, and she wanted her daughter to grow up in a more stable environment. Similar concerns prompted Jane Cannary Hickock, better known as Calamity Jane, to give up her daughter to be reared by friends. Jane's life was nomadic and adventurous, unfit, she thought, for a child.

Some women resisted the total selflessness which the ideal required. In *The Awakening,* Edna Pontellier's attitude toward her children is affectionate but unprotective; she misses them from time to time when they are away visiting their grandparents, but she is also relieved to be free of the responsibility for their care. Edna states her position clearly when she says to a friend: "I would give up the unessential; I would give my money, I would give my life for my children; but I wouldn't give myself." It is not surprising that hostile reviewers of the novel described Edna as an unfit mother.

Mothers who behaved in this way were considered deviant, and they often suffered feelings of guilt and failure. The heavy psychological toll of the Mystique of Motherhood is evident, not only in the "mom" who seeks some kind of power within the confines of the home, where guilt often becomes her means of social control, but in those women who subscribed to the ideal, tried to live up to it, and perceived themselves to be failures. Experts, of course, warned that the failure of mothers to live up to the ideal would have dire effects on their children. Indeed, Lundberg and Farnham connect the Holocaust to the behavior of Adolph Hitler's mother. It is only in the very recent past, in fact, that psychologists have begun to look beyond the behavior or attitudes of the mother for the causes of disturbance in children.

If anatomy is destiny, that destiny has been altered by the social and economic requirements of the time. The institution of motherhood is a social creation molded as much by economic and political forces as by biology, so it is subject to change. As a result, images of mothers during the last two centuries are often complex and even contradictory. In addition, the dominant image was often modified, varied, reduced, or rejected by some ethnic and racial groups. Still, it is difficult to comprehend the enormity of the enterprise which socialized, trained and educated millions of women—no matter what their skills and abilities, their talents and accomplishments, or their preferences—to fill this one role. In *Women and Economics,* Charlotte Gilman said that the role of mothers was "To bear and rear the majestic race to which they can never fully belong! To live vicariously forever, through their sons, the daughters being only another vicarious link. What a supreme and magnificent martyrdom." For many women, motherhood was martyrdom; but for many others, it was a demanding but happy experience which they lived with courage and strength, often against enormous physical and psychological odds. That so many did so and survived is the wonder.

THE AWAKENING
Kate Chopin

Kate O'Flaherty Chopin, the mother of six children, began to write seriously after her husband's death. By the mid-1890s, she was well-known for her stories and sketches, many of them, like *Bayou Folk* (1894), drawn from her life in Louisiana. When *The Awakening* was published in 1899, however, it was met with a storm of criticism because its theme involved female sexuality and adultery.

Critics called Chopin's novel a "Creole Bovary" and "an essentially vulgar story." One commented that the protagonist, Edna Pontellier, "fails to perceive that the relation of a mother to her children is far more important than the gratification of a passion which experience has taught her is, by its very nature, evanescent. . . ."

In the novel, Edna, a Presbyterian from Kentucky, has been transplanted by marriage into a Catholic Creole culture where women are comfortable about sexuality while fulfilling traditional roles. Edna, however, was not a mother-woman; she could not find total fulfillment in taking care of her family. "I would give up my life for my children," she tells her friend Adèle Ratignolle, "but I wouldn't give up myself."

It would have been a difficult matter for Mr. Pontellier to define to his own satisfaction or any one else's wherein his wife failed in her duty toward their children. It was something which he felt rather than perceived, and he never voiced the feeling without subsequent regret and ample atonement.

If one of the little Pontellier boys took a tumble whilst at play, he was not apt to rush crying to his mother's arms for comfort; he would more likely pick himself up, wipe the water out of his eyes and the sand out of his mouth, and go on playing. Tots as they were, they pulled together and stood their ground in childish battles with doubled fists and uplifted voices, which usually prevailed against the other mother-tots. The quadroon nurse was looked upon as a huge encumbrance, only good to button up waists and panties and to brush and part hair; since it seemed to be a law of society that hair must be parted and brushed.

In short, Mrs. Pontellier was not a mother-woman. The mother-women seemed to prevail that summer at Grand Isle. It was easy to know them, fluttering about with extended, protecting wings when any harm, real or imaginary, threatened their precious brood. They were women who idolized their children, worshiped their husbands, and esteemed it a holy privilege to efface themselves as individuals and grow wings as ministering angels.

Many of them were delicious in the rôle; one of them was the embodiment

---

THE AWAKENING   From *The Awakening*, Chicago: Herbert S. Stone, 1899, pp. 19–20.

of every womanly grace and charm. If her husband did not adore her, he was a brute, deserving of death by slow torture. Her name was Adèle Ratignolle. There are no words to describe her save the old ones that have served so often to picture the bygone heroine of romance and the fair lady of our dreams. There was nothing subtle or hidden about her charms; her beauty was all there, flaming and apparent: the spun-gold hair that comb nor confining pin could restrain; the blue eyes that were like nothing but sapphires; two lips that pouted, that were so red one could only think of cherries or some other delicious crimson fruit in looking at them. She was growing a little stout, but it did not seem to detract an iota from the grace of every step, pose, gesture. One would not have wanted her white neck a mite less full or her beautiful arms more slender. Never were hands more exquisite than hers, and it was a joy to look at them when she threaded her needle or adjusted her gold thimble to her taper middle finger as she sewed away on the little night-drawers or fashioned a bodice or a bib.

MY MOTHER'S GRAVE

Many of the stories which appeared in McGuffey's *Eclectic Readers* reflected the popular sentimentality of the time. "My Mother's Grave" mines the sentimental potential of motherhood by addressing what is for many children their deepest fear— the loss of a parent, especially a mother. Such a loss was not unusual in the nineteenth century, when the chances of a parent dying while a child was still young were much greater than they are today. Children were particularly likely to lose their mothers because of the comparatively high number of deaths in childbirth and because women often had their last child in their forties, and so often did not live to see that child fully grown. Reading this story, then, must have been more powerful for children in 1866, when it appeared in the *Fourth Reader,* than it is for children today.

1. It was thirteen years since my mother's death, when, after a long absence from my native village, I stood beside the sacred mound beneath which I had seen her buried. Since that mournful period, a great change had come over me. My childish years had passed away, and with them my youthful character. The world was altered, too; and as I stood at my mother's grave, I could hardly realize that I was the same thoughtless, happy creature, whose cheeks she so often kissed in an excess of tenderness.

2. But the varied events of thirteen years had not effaced the remembrance of that mother's smile. It seemed as if I had seen her but yesterday—as if the blessed sound of her well-remembered voice was in my ear. The gay dreams of my infancy and childhood were brought back so distinctly to my mind that, had it not been for one bitter recollection, the tears I shed would have been gentle and refreshing.

MY MOTHER'S GRAVE   From W. H. McGuffey, *Fourth Reader. Eclectic Series,* 1866, pp. 253–55.

3. The circumstance may seem a trifling one, but the thought of it now pains my heart; and I relate it, that those children who have parents to love them may learn to value them as they ought. My mother had been ill a long time, and I had become so accustomed to her pale face and weak voice, that I was not frightened at them, as children usually are. At first, it is true, I sobbed violently; but when, day after day, I returned from school, and found her the same, I began to believe she would always be spared to me; but they told me she would die.

4. One day when I had lost my place in the class, I came home discouraged and fretful. I went to my mother's chamber. She was paler than usual, but she met me with the same affectionate smile that always welcomed my return. Alas! when I look back through the lapse of thirteen years, I think my heart must have been stone not to have been melted by it. She requested me to go downstairs and bring her a glass of water. I pettishly asked her why she did not call a domestic to do it. With a look of mild reproach, which I shall never forget if I live to be a hundred years old, she said, "Will not my daughter bring a glass of water for her poor, sick mother?"

5. I went and brought her the water, but I did not do it kindly. Instead of smiling, and kissing her as I had been wont to do, I set the glass down very quickly, and left the room. After playing a short time, I went to bed without bidding my mother good night; but when alone in my room, in darkness and silence, I remembered how pale she looked, and how her voice trembled when she said, "Will not my daughter bring a glass of water for her poor, sick mother?" I could not sleep. I stole into her chamber to ask forgiveness. She had sunk into an easy slumber, and they told me I must not waken her.

6. I did not tell anyone what troubled me, but stole back to my bed, resolved to rise early in the morning and tell her how sorry I was for my conduct. The sun was shining brightly when I awoke, and, hurrying on my clothes, I hastened to my mother's chamber. She was dead! She never spoke more—never smiled upon me again; and when I touched the hand that used to rest upon my head in blessing, it was so cold that it made me start.

7. I bowed down by her side, and sobbed in the bitterness of my heart. I then wished that I might die, and be buried with her; and, old as I now am, I would give worlds, were they mine to give, could my mother but have lived to tell me she forgave my childish ingratitude. But I can not call her back; and when I stand by her grave, and whenever I think of her manifold kindness, the memory of that reproachful look she gave me will bite like a serpent and sting like an adder.

MODERN WOMAN: THE LOST SEX

Ferdinand Lundberg and Marynia Farnham

The portrait of modern motherhood which Lundberg and Farnham presented in their popular advice book emphasized the responsibility of mothers for the neuroses of their children. The following passage, which is from a section entitled "The Slaughter of the Innocents," classifies mothers into five types, four of which are destructive. It is only the "fully maternal mother" who produces well-adjusted children.

MOTHER AND CHILD

 The spawning ground of most neurosis in Western civilization is the home. The basis for it is laid in childhood, although it emerges strongly later, usually from late adolescence until middle age, provoked by circumstances and conditions encountered in life. And as we have pointed out, the principal agent in laying the groundwork for it is the mother. Many women classified as housewives and mothers are just as disturbed as were the feminists, and for the same general reasons. There are mothers, for example, who, although not neurotic, feel dissatisfied with the life they are leading. The home offers them few energy outlets. The work they do in it does not bring them prestige. Others, neurotic by reason of their own childhood upbringing and the failure of life to provide them with satisfactory outlets, suffer from the same general affliction as the feminists—penis-envy. It is more repressed than it was in the feminists, but it is at work in the psychic depths.

The feminists, turning their backs on a feminine life, lived out, expressed, their penis-envy, and obtained great satisfaction thereby. The neurotically disturbed women who find themselves mothers and housewives, however, have *consciously* accepted the feminine way of life, are not aware that deep within them they suffer from the same general affliction as the feminists. For they were reared in homes greatly resembling those of the feminists, and they were subject to the same cultural influences. They could not escape.

Unlike the feminists, they have made sure of libidinal outlets in their lives. But they have increasingly foregone ego outlets, and have been unable at the same time to utilize their libidinal opportunities. Many of them, even though not neurotic, cannot help but feel passed by, inferior, put upon by society's denial of ego outlets for them. When they are neurotic they feel the lack even more. To a certain extent a woman can derive great ego satisfaction from playing a fully feminine role, but there are dangers in it both to herself and to her children. Too many women today are forced to derive their entire ego-support from their children, which they do at the expense of the children, to the danger of society. A child can never be an adult plaything and turn out well.

MODERN WOMAN: THE LOST SEX   Harper & Row, New York, 1947, 303–305, From *Modern Woman: The Lost Sex* by Ferdinand Lundberg and Marynia F. Farnham, M.D. Copyright 1947 by Ferdinand Lundberg and Marynia F. Farnham. Reprinted by permission of Harper & Row, Publishers, Inc.

The mothers of neurotics and of persons with marked neurotic character traits, with very few exceptions break down into four broad categories, each susceptible of further breakdown until one reaches the great personal complexity of individuals. These categories, in each of which the mother carries out the pattern of her own upbringing and of the culture around her, are as follows:

1. The rejecting mother, who in various degrees from extreme to subtle, apes society around her and rejects the child. She ordinarily has no more than one, or at most two.

2. The oversolicitous or overprotective mother, who underneath closely resembles the rejecting mother but whose entire activity represents a conscious denial of her unconscious rejection.

3. The dominating mother, who is also very often a strict disciplinarian. This type obtains release for her misdirected ego-drives at the expense of the child. Denied other opportunities for self-realization, she makes her children her pawns, usually requires of them stellar performance in all their undertakings.

4. The over-affectionate mother, who makes up for her essentially libidinal disappointments through her children. Her damage is greatest with her sons, whom she often converts into "sissies"—that is, into passive-feminine or passive-homosexual males.

There is, on the other hand, the fully maternal mother, who fortunately accounts for perhaps 50 per cent or more of the births because she has more children than the other types. She does not reject her children, attempt to overprotect them out of her guilty anxiety, dominate them or convert them into lap dogs. She merely loves her children.

It is the first three types who produce the delinquents, the difficult behavior-problem children, some substantial percentage of criminals and persons who, although moving in socially approved channels, are a trouble to themselves, to close associates and often to society. Along with the over-affectionate mother, they also produce a large percentage of the confirmed alcoholics. Since somewhere around 40 to 50 per cent of the mothers are in the first three categories, the wide damage they do is obvious and warrants fuller discussion.

COMMON WOMEN

Philip Wylie

Philip Wylie (1902-1971), born in Beverly, Massachusetts, was the son of a writer and a Presbyterian minister. After three years at Princeton, he became a staff writer for *The New Yorker*. The prolific author of novels, short stories, screen plays, and social commentaries, he is chiefly remembered today as the man who coined the term "Momism."

"Common Women" was the most controversial chapter in the most controversial book of 1942, *Generation of Vipers*. In iconoclastic style, Wylie swept the first of the mythical American triumvirate—motherhood, the flag, and apple pie—off its pedestal. In another chapter, "A Specimen American Myth," he inveighed against the contemporary distortion of the story of Cinderella. Originally designed to indicate that virtue can be found in the most humble trappings, the tale had come to mean that women were destined to find handsome and affluent Prince Charmings. Wylie maintains that this myth is related to the idea that the experience of childbirth entitled women to be released from other responsibilities, ". . . in spite of the fact that modern medical practice is able to turn most childbearing into no more of a hardship than, say, a few months of benign tumor plus a couple of hours in a dental chair."

MOM IS THE END PRODUCT OF SHE.

She is Cinderella, the creature I discussed earlier, the shining-haired, the starry-eyed, the ruby-lipped virgo aeternis, of which there is presumably one, and only one, or a one-and-only for each male, whose dream is fixed upon her deflowerment and subsequent perpetual possession. This act is a sacrament in all churches and a civil affair in our society. The collective aspects of marriage are thus largely compressed into the rituals and social perquisites of one day. Unless some element of mayhem or intention of divorce subsequently obtrudes, a sort of privacy engulfs the union and all further developments are deemed to be the business of each separate pair, including the transition of Cinderella into mom, which, if it occasions any shock, only adds to the huge, invisible burthen every man carries with him into eternity. It is the weight of this bundle which, incidentally, squeezes out of him the wish for death, his last positive biological resource.

Mom is an American creation. Her elaboration was necessary because she was launched as Cinderella. Past generations of men have accorded to their mothers, as a rule, only such honors as they earned by meritorious action in their individual daily lives. Filial *duty* was recognized by many sorts of civilizations and loyalty to it has been highly regarded among most peoples. But I cannot think, offhand, of any civilization except ours in which an entire division of living men has been used, during wartime, or at any time, to spell out the word "mom" on a drill field, or to perform any equivalent act.

The adoration of motherhood has even been made the basis of a religious cult, but the mother so worshipped achieved maternity without change in her

---

COMMON WOMEN   From *Generation of Vipers*, Holt, Rinehart and Winston. New York, 1942, 184–204. From *Generation of Vipers* by Philip Wylie. Copyright 1942, © 1970 by Philip Wylie. Reprinted by permission of Holt, Rinehart and Winston, Publishers.

virgin status—a distinction worthy of contemplation in itself—and she thus in no way resembled mom.

Hitherto, in fact, man has shown a considerable qui vive to the dangers which arise from momism and freely perceived that his "old wives" were often vixens, dragons, and Xanthippes. Classical literature makes a constant point of it. Shakespeare dwelt on it. Man has also kept before his mind an awareness that, even in the most lambent mother love, there is always a chance some extraneous current will blow up a change, and the thing will become a consuming furnace. The spectacle of the female devouring her young in the firm belief that it is for their own good is too old in man's legends to be overlooked by any but the most flimsily constructed society.

Freud has made a fierce and a wondrous catalogue of examples of mother-love-in-action which traces its origin to an incestuous perversion of a normal instinct. That description is, of course, sound. Unfortunately, Americans, who are the most prissy people on earth, have been unable to benefit from Freud's wisdom because they can *prove* that they do not, by and large, sleep with their mothers. That is their interpretation of Freud. Moreover, no matter how many times they repeat the Scriptures, they cannot get the true sense of the passage about lusting in one's heart—especially when they are mothers thinking about their sons, or vice versa.

Meanwhile, megaloid momworship has got completely out of hand. Our land, subjectively mapped, would have more silver cords and apron strings crisscrossing it than railroads and telephone wires. Mom is everywhere and everything and damned near everybody, and from her depends all the rest of the U.S. Disguised as good old mom, dear old mom, sweet old mom, your loving mom, and so on, she is the bride at every funeral and the corpse at every wedding. Men live for her and die for her, dote upon her and whisper her name as they pass away, and I believe she has now achieved, in the hierarchy of miscellaneous articles, a spot next to the Bible and the Flag, being reckoned part of both in a way. She may therefore soon be granted by the House of Representatives the especial supreme and extraordinary right of sitting on top of both when she chooses, which, God knows, she does. At any rate, if no such bill is under consideration, the presentation of one would cause little debate among the solons. These sages take cracks at their native land and make jokes about Holy Writ, but nobody among them—no great man or brave—from the first day of the first congressional meeting to the present ever stood in our halls of state and pronounced the one indubitably most-needed American verity: "Gentlemen, mom is a jerk."

Mom is something new in the world of men. Hitherto, mom has been so busy raising a large family, keeping house, doing the chores, and fabricating everything in every home except the floor and the walls that she was rarely a problem to her family or to her equally busy friends, and never one to herself. Usually, until very recently, mom folded up and died of hard work somewhere in the middle of her life. Old ladies were scarce and those who managed to get old did so by making remarkable inner adjustments and by virtue of a fabulous horniness of body, so that they lent to old age not only dignity but metal.

Nowadays, with nothing to do, and all the tens of thousands of men I wrote about in a preceding chapter to maintain her, every clattering prickamette in the republic survives for an incredible number of years, to stamp and jibber in the midst of man, a noisy neuter by natural default or a scientific gelding sustained by science, all tongue and teat and razzmatazz. The machine has deprived her of social usefulness; time has stripped away her biological possibilities and poured her hide full of liquid soap; and man has sealed his own soul beneath the clamorous cordillera by handing her the checkbook and going to work in the service of her caprices.

These caprices are of a menopausal nature at best—hot flashes, rage, infantilism, weeping, sentimentality, peculiar appetite, and all the ragged reticule of tricks, wooings, wiles, suborned fornications, slobby onanisms, indulgences, crotchets, superstitions, phlegms, debilities, vapors, butterflies-in-the-belly, plaints, connivings, cries, malingerings, deceptions, visions, hallucinations, needlings and wheedlings, which pop out of every personality in the act of abandoning itself and humanity. At worst—i.e., the finis—this salaginous mess tapers off into senility, which is man's caricature of himself by reversed ontogeny. But behind this vast aurora of pitiable weakness is mom, the brass-breasted Baal, or mom, the thin and enfeebled martyr whose very urine, nevertheless, will etch glass.

Satan, we are told, finds work for idle hands to do. There is no mistaking the accuracy of this proverb. Millions of men have heaped up riches and made a conquest of idleness so as to discover what it is that Satan puts them up to. Not one has failed to find out. But never before has a great nation of brave and dreaming men absent-mindedly created a huge class of idle, middle-aged women. Satan himself has been taxed to dig up enterprises enough for them. But the field is so rich, so profligate, so perfectly to his taste, that his first effort, obviously, has been to make it self-enlarging and self-perpetuating. This he has done by whispering into the ears of girls that the only way they can cushion the shock destined to follow the rude disillusionment over the fact that they are not really Cinderella is to institute momworship. Since he had already infested both male and female with the love of worldly goods, a single step accomplished the entire triumph: he taught the gals to teach their men that dowry went the other way, that it was a weekly contribution, and that any male worthy of a Cinderella would have to work like a piston after getting one, so as to be worthy, also, of all the moms in the world.

The road to hell is spiral, a mere bend in the strait and narrow, but a persistent one. This was the given torque, and most men are up to their necks in it now. The devil whispered. The pretty girl then blindfolded her man so he would not see that she was turning from a butterfly into a caterpillar. She told him, too, that although caterpillars ate every damned leaf in sight, they were moms, hence sacred. Finally, having him sightless and whirling, she snitched his checkbook. Man was a party to the deception because he wanted to be fooled about Cinderella, because he was glad to have a convenient explanation of mom, and also because there burned within him a dim ideal which had to do with proper behavior, getting along, and, especially, making his mark. Mom had already shaken him out of that notion of being a surveyor in the Andes which had bloomed in him when he was nine years old, so there was nothing left to do, anyway, but to take a stockroom job in the hairpin factory and try to work up to the vice-presidency. Thus the women of America raped the men, not sexually, unfortunately, but morally, since neuters come hard by morals.

I pass over the obvious reference to the deadliness of the female of the species, excepting only to note that perhaps, having a creative physical part in the universe, she falls more easily than man into the contraposite role of spiritual saboteur.

Mom got herself out of the nursery and the kitchen. She then got out of the house. She did not get out of the church, but, instead, got the stern stuff out of *it,* padded the guild room, and moved in more solidly than ever before. No longer either hesitant or reverent, because there was no cause for either attitude after her purge, she swung the church by the tail as she swung everything else. In a preliminary test of strength, she also got herself the vote and, although politics never interested her (unless she was exceptionally naïve, a hairy foghorn, or a size forty scorpion), the damage she forthwith did to society was so enormous and so rapid that even the best men lost track of things. Mom's first gracious presence at the ballot-box was roughly concomitant with the start toward a new all-time low in political scurviness, hoodlumism, gangsterism, labor strife, monopolistic thuggery, moral degeneration, civic corruption, smuggling, bribery, theft, murder, homosexuality, drunkenness, financial depression, chaos and war. Note that.

The degenerating era, however, marked new highs in the production of junk. Note that, also.

Mom, however, is a great little guy. Pulling pants onto her by these words, let us look at mom.

She is a middle-aged puffin with an eye like a hawk that has just seen a rabbit twitch far below. She is about twenty-five pounds overweight, with no sprint, but sharp heels and a hard backhand which she does not regard as a foul but a womanly defense. In a thousand of her there is not sex appeal enough to budge a hermit ten paces off a rock ledge. She none the less spends several hundred dollars a year on permanents and transformations, pomades, cleansers, rouges, lipsticks, and the like—and fools nobody except herself. If a man kisses her with any earnestness, it is time for mom to feel for her pocketbook, and this occasionally does happen.

She smokes thirty cigarettes a day, chews gum, and consumes tons of bonbons and petits fours. The shortening in the latter, stripped from pigs, sheep and cattle, shortens mom. She plays bridge with the stupid voracity of a hammerhead shark, which cannot see what it is trying to gobble but never stops snapping its jaws and roiling the waves with its tail. She drinks moderately, which is to say, two or three cocktails before dinner every night and a brandy and a couple of highballs afterward. She doesn't count the two cocktails she takes before lunch when she lunches out, which is every day she can. On Saturday nights, at the club or in the juke joint, she loses count of her drinks and is liable to get a little tiddly, which is to say, shot or blind. But it is her man who worries about where to acquire the money while she worries only about how to spend it, so he has the ulcers and colitis and she has the guts of a bear; she can get pretty stiff before she topples.

Her sports are all spectator sports.

She was graduated from high school or a "finishing" school or even a college in her distant past and made up for the unhappiness of compulsory education by sloughing all that she learned so completely that she could not pass the final examinations of a fifth grader. She reads the fiction in three women's magazines each month and occasionally skims through an article, which usually angers her so that she gets other moms to skim through it, and then they have a session on the subject over a canister of spiked coffee in order to damn the magazine, the editors, the author, and the silly girls who run about these days. She reads two or three motion-picture fan magazines also, and goes to the movies about two nights a week. If a picture does not coincide precisely with her attitude of the moment, she converses through all of it and so whiles away the time. She does not appear to be lecherous toward the moving photographs as men do, but that is because she is a realist and a little shy on imagination. However, if she gets to Hollywood and encounters the flesh-and-blood article known as a male star, she and her sister moms will run forward in a mob, wearing a joint expression that must make God rue his invention of bisexuality, and tear the man's clothes from his body, yea, verily, down to his B.V.D.'s.

Mom is organization-minded. Organizations, she has happily discovered, are intimidating to all men, not just to mere men. They frighten politicians to sniveling servility and they terrify pastors; they bother bank presidents and they pulverize school boards. Mom has many such organizations, the real purpose of which is to compel an abject compliance of her environs to her personal desires. With these associations and committees she has double parking ignored, for example. With them she drives out of the town and the state, if possible, all young harlots and all proprietors of places where "questionable" young women (though why they are called that—being of all women the least in question) could possibly foregather, not because she competes with such creatures but because she contrasts so unfavorably with them. With her clubs (a solid term!) she causes bus lines to run where they are convenient for her rather than for workers, plants flowers in sordid spots that would do better with sanitation, snaps independent men out of office and replaces them with clammy castrates, throws prodigious fairs and parties for charity and gives the proceeds, usually about eight dollars, to the janitor to buy the committee some beer for its headache on the morning after, and builds clubhouses for the entertainment of soldiers where she succeeds in persuading thousands of them that they are momsick and would rather talk to her than take Betty into the shrubs. All this, of course, is considered social service, charity, care of the poor, civic reform, patriotism and self-sacrifice.

As an interesting sidelight, clubs afford mom an infinite opportunity for nosing into other people's business. Nosing is not a mere psychological ornament of her; it is a basic necessity. Only by nosing can she uncover all incipient revolutions against her dominion and so warn and assemble her co-cannibals.

Knowing nothing about medicine, art, science, religion, law, sanitation, civics, hygiene, psychology, morals, history, geography, poetry, literature, or any other topic except the all-consuming one of momism, she seldom has any especial interest in *what*, exactly, she is doing as a member of any of these endless organizations, so long as it is *something*.

I, who grew up as a "motherless" minister's son and hence was smothered in multimomism for a decade and a half, had an unusual opportunity to observe the phenomenon at zero range. Also, as a man stirring about in the cesspool of my society, I have been foolhardy enough to try, on occasion, to steer moms into useful work. For example, owing to the fact that there was no pasteurization law in Miami and hundreds of people were flecking the pavement with tubercular sputum, while scores, including my own wife, lay sick and miserable with undulant fever, I got a gaggle of these creatures behind a move toward a pasteurization law, only to find, within a few weeks, that there was a large, alarmed, and earnest committee at work in my wake to *prevent* the passage of any such law. This falange, fanned by the milk dealers, who would not even deliver the stuff if they could get their money without, had undone even that one small crusade because it had uncovered a quack doctor, unknown and unheard-of, who had printed the incandescent notion that cancer, the big boogie of the moms, was caused by the pasteurization of milk!

In the paragraph above I have given, I know, the golden tip for which any moms able to read this volume have been searching all the long way. I had no mother: therefore, all my bitterness and—especially—this cruel and wanton attack of moms for which, they will doubtless think, I should be shot or locked up. Well, let them make the most of that. All mothers are not such a ravening purulence as they, and mine was not. Mine, I can show, felt much as I do about the thundering third sex, as do all good women, of whom there are still a few. But I have researched the moms, to the beady brains behind their beady eyes and to the stones in the center of their fat hearts. I am immune to their devotion because I have already had enough. Learning the hard way, I have found out that it is that same devotion which, at the altar, splits the lamb from his nave to his chaps. And none of the moms, at least, will believe that I am a lamb. Let them mark time on that.

In churches, the true purpose of organized momhood is to unseat bishops, snatch the frocks off prelates, change rectors just for variety, cross-jet community gossip, take the customary organizational kudos out of the pot each for each, bestow and receive titles, and short-circuit one another.

Mom also has patriotism. If a war comes, this may even turn into a genuine feeling and the departure of her son may be her means to grace in old age. Often, however, the going of her son is only an occasion for more show. She has, in that case, no deep respect for him. What he has permitted her to do to him has rendered him unworthy of consideration—and she has shown him none since puberty. She does not miss him—only his varletry—but over that she can weep interminably. I have seen the unmistakable evidence in a blue star mom of envy of a gold star mom; and I have a firsthand account by a woman of unimpeachable integrity, of the doings of a shipload of these supermoms-of-the-gold-star, en route at government expense to France to visit the graves of their sons, which I forbear to set down here, because it is a document of such naked awfulness that, by publishing it, I would be inciting to riot, and the printed thing might even rouse the dead soldiers and set them tramping like Dunsany's idol all the way from Flanders to hunt and haunt their archenemy progenitrices—who loved them—to death.

But, peace or war, the moms have another kind of patriotism that, in the department of the human spirit, is identical to commercialized vice, because it captures a good thing and doles it out for the coin of unctuous pride—at the expense of deceased ancestors rather than young female offspring. By becoming a Daughter of this historic war or that, a woman makes herself into a sort of madam who fills the coffers of her ego with the prestige that has accrued to the doings of others. A frantic emptiness of those coffers provides the impulse for the act. There are, of course, other means of filling them, but they are difficult, and mom never does anything that is difficult—either the moving of a piano or the breaking of a nasty habit.

Some legionnaires accept, in a similar way, accolade due their associates only. But legionnaires learned a little wisdom, since they still can function in ways that have some resemblance to normality. Furthermore, competition with the legions from the new war will probably make veritable sages out of thousands.

But mom never meets competition. Like Hitler, she betrays the people who would give her a battle before she brings up her troops. Her whole personal life, so far as outward expression is concerned, is, in consequence, a mopping-up action. Traitors are shot, yellow stars are slapped on those beneath notice, the good-looking men and boys are rounded up and beaten or sucked into pliability, a new slave population continually goes to work at making more munitions for momism, and mom herself sticks up her head, or maybe the periscope of the woman next door, to find some new region that needs taking over. This technique pervades all she does.

In the matter of her affiliation of herself with the Daughters of some war the Hitler analogue especially holds, because these sororities of the sword often constitute her Party—her shirtism. Ancestor worship, like all other forms of religion, contained an instinctual reason and developed rituals thought to be germane to the reason. People sedulously followed those rituals, which were basically intended to remind them that they, too, were going to be ancestors someday and would have to labor for personal merit in order to be worthy of veneration. But mom's reverence for her bold forebears lacks even a ritualistic significance, and so instructs her in nothing. She is peremptory about historical truth, mandates, custom, fact, and point. She brushes aside the ideals and concepts for which her forebears perished fighting, as if they were the crumbs of melba toast. Instead, she attributes to the noble dead her own immediate and selfish attitudes. She "knows full well what they would have thought and done," and in that whole-cloth trumpery she goes busting on her way.

Thus the long-vanished warriors who liberated this land from one George in order to make another its first president guide mom divinely as she barges along the badgering boulevard of her life, relaying fiats from the grave on birth control, rayon, vitamins, the power trust, and a hundred other items of which the dead had no knowledge. To some degree most people, these days, are guilty of this absurd procedure. There has been more nonsense printed lately detailing what Jefferson would say about matters he never dreamed of than a sensible man can endure. (I do not have any idea, for instance, and I am sure nobody has any idea, what Jefferson would think about the giddy bungle of interstate truck commerce; but people, columnists especially, will tell you.)

Mom, however, does not merely quote Thomas Jefferson on modern topics: she *is* Thomas Jefferson. This removes her twice from sanity. Mom wraps herself in the mantle of every canny man and coward who has drilled with a musket on this continent and reproduced a line that zigzagged down to mom. In that cloak, together with the other miters, rings, scepters, and power symbols which she has swiped, she has become the American pope.

People are feebly aware of this situation and it has been pointed out at one time or another that the phrase "Mother knows best" has practically worn out the staircase to private hell. Most decriers of matriarchy, however, are men of middle age, like me.

Young men whose natures are attuned to a female image with more feelings than mom possesses and different purposes from those of our synthetic archetype of Cinderella-the-go-getter bounce anxiously away from their first few brutal contacts with modern young women, frightened to find their shining hair is vulcanized, their agate eyes are embedded in cement, and their ruby lips casehardened into pliers for the bending males like wire. These young men, fresh-startled by learning that She is a chrome-plated afreet, but not able to discern that the condition is mom's unconscious preparation of somebody's sister for a place in the gynecocracy—are, again, presented with a soft and shimmering resting place, the bosom of mom.

Perseus was carefully *not* told that the Gorgons had blonde back hair and faces on the other side, like Janus, which, instead of turning him to stone, would have produced orgasms in him. Thus informed he would have failed to slay Medusa and bring back her head. He might have been congealed—but he might not. Our young men are screened from a knowledge of this duality also, but they are told only about the blonde side. When they glimpse the other, and find their blood running cold and their limbs becoming like concrete, they carom off, instanter, to mom. Consequently, no Gorgons are ever clearly seen, let alone slain, in our society. Mom dishes out her sweetness to all fugitives, and it turns them not to stone, but to slime.

"Her boy," having been "protected" by her love, and carefully, even shudderingly, shielded from his logical development through his barbaric period, or childhood (so that he has either to become a barbarian as a man or else to spend most of his energy denying the barbarism that howls in his brain—an autonomous remnant of the youth he was forbidden), is cushioned against any major step in his progress toward maturity. Mom steals from the generation of women behind her (which she has, as a still further defense, also sterilized of integrity and courage) that part of her boy's personality which should have become the love of a female contemporary. Mom transmutes it into sentimentality for herself.

The process has given rise to the mother-problem, and the mother-in-law problem, and mom has occasionally been caught tipping the bat, but she has contrived even then to make the thing an American joke in order to hide what it really is—as invidious a spiritual parasitism as any in the book. With her captive son or sons in a state of automatic adoration of herself (and just enough dubiety of their wives to keep them limp or querulous at home), mom has ushered in the new form of American marriage: eternal ricochet. The oppositeness of the sexes provides enough of that without mom's doubling of the dose and loading of the dice, but mom does it—for mom. Her policy of protection, from the beginning, was not love of her boy but of herself, and as she found returns coming in from the disoriented young boy in smiles, pats, presents, praise, kisses, and all manner of childish representations of the real business, she moved on to possession.

Possession of the physical person of a man is slavery; possession of the spirit of a man is slavery also, because his body obeys his spirit and his spirit obeys its possessor. Mom's boy will be allowed to have his psychobiological struggle with dad: to reach the day when he stands, emotionally, toe-to-toe with his father and wins the slugging-out. That contest is as unavoidable as the ripening of an apple. It may last only a second—in which a young man says, "I will," and an older man says, "You will not," and the younger man does. And it is a struggle no youth can engage in, but only a youth who has reached full manhood. But if it occurs prematurely, as under mom's ruinous aegis it usually does, it leads to more serfdom for the boy. He is too young for independence.

Thus the sixteen-year-old who tells his indignant dad that he, not dad, is going to have the car that night and takes it—while mom looks on, dewy-eyed and anxious—has sold his soul to mom and made himself into a lifelong sucking-egg. His father, already well up the creek, loses in this process the stick with which he had been trying to paddle. It is here that mom has thrust her oar into the very guts of man—and while she has made him think she is operating a gondola through the tunnels of love, and even believes it herself, she is actually taking tickets for the one-way ferry ride across the Styx.

As men grow older, they tend to become more like women, and vice versa. Even physically, their characteristics swap; men's voices rise, their breasts grow, and their chins recede; women develop bass voices and mustaches. This is another complementary, or opposite, turn of nature. It is meant to reconcile sexuality and provide a fountainhead of wisdom uncompromised by it, in the persons of those individuals who are hardy enough and lucky enough to survive to old age in a natural environment. But survival, as I have said, no longer depends on any sort of natural selection, excepting a great basic one which our brains are intended to deal with, and which, if allowed to go brainlessly on, will have to reduce our species to savagery in order to get back to a level on which instinct itself can rule effectively.

The mealy look of men today is the result of momism and so is the pinched and baffled fury in the eyes of womankind. I said a while ago that I had been a motherless minister's son and implied that I had been mauled by every type of mom produced in this nation. I pointed out that the situation was one on which the moms would try to fix their pincers. I did not bother to prod at any misgivings they might feel about what the rude minister's boy, trained in snoopery by the example of the moms, might have found out about the matriarchy and its motivations through hanging around sewing clubrooms, hiding in heavy draperies, and holing up in choir lofts. Rather, I let any moms and adherents of momism who may be reading this slug along in the happy belief that, whether or not *I* knew it, they had got me off base.

Now, really.

Some of the doting ones, ready to write off all I have said if I will only make up and shove myself back into the groove for them, are now about to be clipped—but good. For, by a second contumelious revelation, I have caught onto all of middle-aged, middle-class, earth-owning Mrs. America that I happened to miss in the portieres. Hold your seats, ladies. I have been a *clerk* in a *department store*. Not merely that, but I have been a clerk behind the dress goods remnant counter. And not only that, but I have served and observed the matriarchy from the vantage point during *sales*. If there is a woman still on her feet and not laughing, nab her, because that will mark her as a ringleader in this horrid business.

Much of the psychological material which got me studying this matter of moms came into my possession as I watched the flower-hatted goddesses battle over fabric. I have seen the rich and the poor, the well-dressed and the shabby, the educated and the unlettered, tear into the stacked remnants day after day, shoving and harassing, trampling each other's feet, knocking hats, coiffures and glasses awry, cackling, screaming, bellowing, and giving the elbow, without any differential of behavior no matter how you sliced them. I have watched them deliberately drive quiet clerks out of their heads and their jobs and heard them whoop over the success of the stratagem. I have seen them cheat and steal and lie and rage and whip and harry and stampede—not just a few times but week after week, and not just a few women but thousands and thousands and thousands, from everywhere. I know the magnitude of their rationalizing ability down to the last pale tint and I know the blackguard rapacity of them down to the last pennyworth.

I have, as a matter of confidential fact, twice beheld the extraordinary spectacle occasioned by two different pairs of rich and world-famous women who managed, in the morass the moms make of the remnant counter by ten o'clock each morning, to get hold of opposite ends of the same three and a half yards of Liberty crepe or dotted swiss and who found out that the object under scrutiny was also being considered by another. This I hold to be the Supreme Evidence.

In both cases both women were "merely looking," but immediately they sensed possible antagonism for what *might* be a purchase (though the statistics ran about five thousand to one against *that*) they began to struggle with the state most insufferable to momism: competition.

First, perhaps, a lifting of a lorgnette; then a cold stare; next, a reproachful glance at the clerk, and a refined but snappy little jerk designed to yank free the far end of the goods. Riposte: a fierce clutch and a facial response in kind. Next, the buttery attempt—the so-called "social" smile—like a valentine laced around an ice pick, and a few words, "I *beg* your pardon—but I—er—am *looking* at—this remnant." The wise clerk will now begin to search for the floorwalker and, in general, canvass his resources. (I should say, of course, that while I have seen only four renowned women engaged in this contretemps I have seen dozens of less distinguished moms hit the same jackpot.) The upper-class rejoinder to the foregoing gambit is, of course, "I'm quite sorry, but *I* happened to notice that *I* selected *this* piece quite some time before *you* picked up the *end* of it." At this point a hard yank is, of course, optional. But usually there come two simultaneous jerks which loosen hair, knock both hats askew, and set the costume jewelry clattering. The women now start toward each other, down the remnant, hand over hand. Bystanders are buffeted. All dress goods that cover the rope of cloth are flung about. The dialogue takes a turn to "I'll have to ask you to be good enough to let go of *my* material!" It rises in register to a near-scream. Upper lips begin to sweat. Chests heave. Elbows swing up to the ready.

Both women are now yelling at once and the tonal quality is like the sound of fingernails drawn along slates. They punctuate their words with loud cries of "Manager!" and begin to jostle each other. Peripheral moms, punched by accident in the aggression, now take up with each other a contagion of brawls and bickerings. The principals, meanwhile, have met knuckle to knuckle in the middle of the fabric and are yowling in each other's faces. Toward this the floorwalker or section manager moves cautiously. The thing has an almost invariable denouement. One woman stalks out of the store and closes her account by mail, only to open it within a matter of days. The other trium- phantly purchases the draggled cloth, charges it, signs for it, bears it away, and has the truck pick it up the following afternoon.

I have been a clerk. Clerks are wallpaper to mom, and it has never occurred to her that she needs to hide her spurting soul from them. Clerks see moms in the raw—with their husbands, sons, daughters, nieces, nephews, gigolos, and companion viragoes. That anybody such as I, an articulate man with a memory like a tombstone, should be standing behind a counter conducting an inadvertent espionage on the moms has never entered their brawling brains. But there I was—and I was there, too, in the church, and at the manse. And I have hung around hospitals a lot—and insane asylums.

It can be pointed out—and has, indeed, been pointed out before, though not, so far as I know, by any chap who has had such diverse and intimate contacts with the moms as I—that they are taking over the male functions and interpreting those functions in female terms. When the mothers built up their pyramid of perquisite and required reverence in order to get at the checkbook, and so took over the schools (into which they have put gelding moms), churches, stores, and mass production (which included, of course, the railroads, boats, and airplanes and, through advertising, the radio and the magazines), they donned the breeches of Uncle Sam. To this inversion I shall refer again. Note it.

I have explained how the moms turned Cinderellaism to their advantage and I have explained that women possess some eighty per cent of the nation's money (the crystal form of its energy) and I need only allude, I think, to the statistical reviews which show that the women are the spenders, wherefore the controlling consumers of nearly all we make with our machines. The steel puddler in Pittsburgh may not think of himself as a feminine tool, but he is really only getting a Chevrolet ready for mom to drive through a garden wall. I should round out this picture of America existing for mom with one or two more details, such as annual increase in the depth of padding in vehicles over the past thirty years due to the fact that a fat rump is more easily irritated than a lean one, and the final essential detail of mom's main subjective preoccupation, which is listening to the radio. The radio is mom's soul; a detail, indeed.

It is also a book in itself, and one I would prefer to have my reader write after he has learned a little of the art of catching overtones as a trained ear, such as mine, catches them. But there must be a note on it.

The radio has made sentimentality the twentieth century Plymouth Rock. As a discipline, I have forced myself to sit a whole morning listening to the soap operas, along with twenty million moms who were busy sweeping dust under carpets while planning to drown their progeny in honey or bash in their heads. This filthy and indecent abomination, this trash with which, until lately, only moron servant girls could dull their credulous minds in the tawdry privacy of their cubicles, is now the national saga. Team after team of feeble-minded Annies and Davids crawl from the loud-speaker into the front rooms of America. The characters are impossible, their adventures would make a saint spew, their morals are lower than those of ghouls, their habits are uncleanly, their humor is the substance that starts whole races grinding bayonets, they have no manners, no sense, no goals, no worthy ambitions, no hope, no faith, no information, no values related to reality, and no estimate of truth. They merely sob and snicker—as they cheat each other.

Babies die every hour on the hour to jerk so many hundred gallons of tears. Cinderella kidnaps the Prince and then mortgages the palace to hire herself a gigolo. The most oafish cluck the radio executives can find, with a voice like a damp pillow—a mother-lover of the most degraded sort—is given to America as the ideal young husband. His wife, with a tin voice and a heart of corrosive sublimate, alternately stands at his side to abet some spiritual swindle or leaves him with a rival for as much time as is needed to titillate mom without scaring her.

The radio is mom's final tool, for it stamps everybody who listens with the matriarchal brand—its superstitions, prejudices, devotional rules, taboos, musts, and all other qualifications needful to its maintenance. Just as Goebbels has revealed what can be done with such a mass-stamping of the public psyche in his nation, so our land is a living representation of the same fact worked out in matriarchal sentimentality, goo, slop, hidden cruelty, and the foreshadow of national death.

That alone is sinister enough, but the process is still more vicious, because it fills in every crack and cranny of mom's time and mind—and pop's also, since he has long ago yielded the dial-privilege to his female; so that a whole nation of people lives in eternal fugue and never has to deal for one second with itself or its own problems. Any interior sign of worry, wonder, speculation, anxiety, apprehension—or even a stirring of an enfeebled will to plan sanely—can be annihilated by an electrical click whereby the populace puts itself in the place, the untenable place—of somebody called Myrt, for Christ's sake—and never has even to try to *be* itself alone in the presence of this real world.

This is Nirvana at last. It is also entropy. For here the spirit of man, absorbed, disoriented, confused, identified with ten thousand spurious personalities and motives, has utterly lost itself. By this means is man altogether lost. The radio, in very truth, sells soap. We could confine it to music, intelligent discourse, and news—all other uses being dangerous—but mom will not let us. Rather than study herself and her environment with the necessary honesty, she will fight for this poisoned syrup to the last. Rather than take up her democratic responsibility in this mighty and tottering republic, she will bring it crashing down simply to maintain to the final rumble of ruin her personal feudalism. Once, sentimentalism was piecework, or cost the price of a movie or a book; now it is mass produced and not merely free, but almost compulsory.

I give you mom. I give you the destroying mother. I give you her justice— from which we have never removed the eye bandage. I give you the angel—and point to the sword in her hand. I give you death—the hundred million deaths that are muttered under Yggdrasill's ash. I give you Medusa and Stheno and Euryale. I give you the harpies and the witches, and the Fates. I give you the woman in pants, and the new religion: she-popery. I give you Pandora. I give you Proserpine, the Queen of Hell. The five-and-ten-cent-store Lilith, the mother of Cain, the black widow who is poisonous and eats her mate, and I designate at the bottom of your program the grand finale of all the soap operas: the mother of America's Cinderella.

We must face the dynasty of the dames at once, deprive them of our pocketbooks when they waste the substance in them, and take back our dreams which, without the perfidious materialism of mom, were shaping up a new and braver world. We must drive roads to Rio and to Moscow and stop spending all our strength in the manufacture of girdles: it is time that mom's sag became known to the desperate public; we must plunge into our psyches and find out there, each for each, scientifically, about immortality and miracles. To do such deeds, we will first have to make the conquest of momism, which grew up from male default.

Our society is too much an institution built to appease the rapacity of loving mothers. If that condition is an ineluctable experiment of nature, then we are the victims of a failure. But I do not think it is. Even while the regiments spell out "mom" on the parade grounds, I think mom's grip can be broken by private integrity. Even though, indeed, it is the moms who have made this war.

For, when the young men come back from the war, what then will they feel concerning mom and her works?

EVERYDAY USE
Alice Walker

Alice Walker was born in Eatonton, Georgia, in 1944, attended Spelman College, and graduated from Sarah Lawrence College. During the 1960s, she worked on voter registration in Jackson, Mississippi. Her published works include five books of fiction, three books of poetry, a children's biography of Langston Hughes, and an edition of the selected works of Zora Neale Hurston. In 1982, her novel *The Color Purple* won both the National Book Award and the Pulitzer Prize for fiction.

Walker's work illuminates the lives of ordinary people and underscores the importance of family life. "In the black family," she says, "love, cohesion, support, and concern are crucial since the racist society constantly acts to destroy the black individual, the black family unit, the black child. In America black people have only themselves and each other."

In "Everyday Use," which was included in the *Best American Short Stories of 1973,* Walker writes about a mother who must decide which of her daughters will have the family quilts: Dee, who wants the quilts to hang on her wall as evidence of her "heritage"; or Maggie, who would put the quilts to "everyday use." The mother's choice reflects her own values, as well as her sensitivity to both daughters, even though she must deny one.

 I will wait for her in the yard that Maggie and I made so clean and wavy yesterday afternoon. A yard like this is more comfortable than most people know. It is not just a yard. It is like an extended living room. When the hard clay is swept clean as a floor and the fine sand around the edges lined with tiny, irregular grooves, anyone can come and sit and look up into the elm tree and wait for the breezes that never come inside the house.

Maggie will be nervous until after her sister goes: she will stand hopelessly in corners, homely and ashamed of the burn scars down her arms and legs, eying

---

EVERY DAY USE From *In Love and Trouble*, Harcourt, Brace Jovanovich, Inc., New York, 1974, 47–59. Copyright © 1973 by Alice Walker. Reprinted from her volume *In Love & Trouble* by permission of Harcourt Brace Jovanovich, Inc.

her sister with a mixture of envy and awe. She thinks her sister has held life always in the palm of one hand, that "no" is a word the world never learned to say to her.

You've no doubt seen those TV shows where the child who has "made it" is confronted, as a surprise, by his own mother and father, tottering in weakly from backstage. (A pleasant surprise, of course: what would they do if parent and child came on the show only to curse out and insult each other?) On TV mother and child embrace and smile into each other's faces. Sometimes the mother and father weep, the child wraps them in his arms and leans across the table to tell how he would not have made it without their help. I have seen these programs.

Sometimes I dream a dream in which Dee and I are suddenly brought together on a TV program of this sort. Out of a dark and soft-seated limousine I am ushered into a bright room filled with many people. There I meet a smiling, gray, sporty man like Johnny Carson who shakes my hand and tells me what a fine girl I have. Then we are on the stage and Dee is embracing me with tears in her eyes. She pins on my dress a large orchid, even though she has told me once that she thinks orchids are tacky flowers.

In real life I am a large big-boned woman with rough, man-working hands. In the winter I wear flannel nightgowns to bed and overalls during the day. I can kill and clean a hog as mercilessly as a man. My fat keeps me hot in zero weather. I can work outside all day, breaking ice to get water for washing; I can eat pork liver cooked over the open fire minutes after it comes steaming from the hog. One winter I knocked a bull calf straight in the brain between the eyes with a sledgehammer and had the meat hung up to chill before nightfall. But of course all this does not show on television. I am the way my daughter would want me to be; a hundred pounds lighter, my skin like an uncooked barley pancake. My hair glistens in the hot bright lights. Johnny Carson has much to do to keep up with my quick and witty tongue.

But that is a mistake. I know even before I wake up. Who ever knew a Johnson with a quick tongue? Who can even imagine me looking a strange white man in the eye? It seems to me I have talked to them always with one foot raised in flight, with my head turned in whichever way is farthest from them. Dee, though. She would always look anyone in the eye. Hesitation was no part of her nature.

"How do I look, Mama?" Maggie says, showing just enough of her thin body enveloped in pink skirt and red blouse for me to know she's there almost hidden by the door.

"Come out into the yard," I say.

Have you ever seen a lame animal, perhaps a dog run over by some careless person rich enough to own a car, sidle up to someone who is ignorant enough to be kind to him? That is the way my Maggie walks. She has been like this, chin on chest, eyes on ground, feet in shuffle, ever since the fire that burned the other house to the ground.

Dee is lighter than Maggie, with nicer hair and a fuller figure. She's a woman now, though sometimes I forget. How long ago was it that the other house burned? Ten, twelve years? Sometimes I can still hear the flames and feel Maggie's arms sticking to me, her hair smoking and her dress falling off her in little black papery flakes. Her eyes seemed stretched open, blazed open by the flames reflected in them. And Dee. I see her standing off under the sweetgum tree she used to dig gum out of; a look of concentration on her face as she watched the last dingy gray board of the house fall in toward the red-hot brick chimney. Why don't you do a dance around the ashes? I'd wanted to ask her. She had hated the house that much.

I used to think she hated Maggie too. But that was before we raised the money, the church and me, to send her to Augusta to school. She used to read to us without pity; forcing words, lies, other folks' habits, whole lives upon us two, sitting trapped and ignorant underneath her voice. She washed us in a river of make-believe, burned us with a lot of knowledge we didn't necessarily need to know. Pressed us to her with the serious way she read, to shove us away, like dimwits, at just the moment we seemed about to understand.

Dee wanted nice things. A yellow organdy dress to wear to her graduation from high school; black pumps to match a green suit she'd made from an old suit somebody gave me. She was determined to stare down any disaster in her efforts. Her eyelids would not flicker for minutes at a time. Often I fought off the temptation to shake her. At sixteen she had a style of her own: and knew what style was.

I never had an education myself. After second grade the school was closed down. Don't ask me why: in 1927 colored asked fewer questions than they do now. Sometimes Maggie reads to me. She stumbles along good-naturedly but can't see well. She knows she is not bright. Like good looks and money, quickness passed her by. She will marry John Thomas (who has mossy teeth in an earnest face), and then I'll be free to sit here and I guess just sing church songs to myself. Although I never was a good singer. Never could carry a tune. I was always better at a man's job. I used to love to milk till I was hooked in the side in '49. Cows are soothing and slow and don't bother you, unless you try to milk them the wrong way.

I have deliberately turned my back on the house. It is three rooms, just like the one that burned, except the roof is tin; they don't make shingle roofs anymore. There are no real windows, just some holes cut in the sides, like the portholes in a ship, but not round and not square, with rawhide holding the shutters up on the outside. This house is in a pasture too, like the other one. No doubt when Dee sees it she will want to tear it down. She wrote me once that no matter where we "choose" to live, she will manage to come see us. But she will never bring her friends. Maggie and I thought about this and Maggie asked me, "Mama, when did Dee ever *have* any friends?"

She had a few. Furtive boys in pink shirts hanging about on washday after school. Nervous girls who never laughed. Impressed with her, they worshiped the well-turned phrase, the cute shape, the scalding humor that erupted like bubbles in lye. She read to them.

When she was courting Jimmy T she didn't have much time to pay to us, but turned all her fault-finding power on him. He *flew* to marry a cheap city girl from a family of ignorant, flashy people. She hardly had time to recompose herself.

When she comes I will meet . . . but there they are!

Maggie attempts to make a dash for the house, in her shuffling way, but I stay her with my hand. "Come back here," I say. And she stops and tries to dig a well in the sand with her toe.

It is hard to see them clearly through the strong sun. But even the first glimpse of leg out of the car tells me it is Dee. Her feet were always neat looking, as if God himself had shaped them with a certain style. From the other side of the car comes a short, stocky man. Hair is all over his head a foot long and hanging from his chin like a kinky mule tail. I hear Maggie suck in her breath. "Uhnnnh," is what it sounds like. Like when you see the wriggling end of a snake just in front of your foot on a road. "Uhnnnh."

Dee, next. A dress down to the ground, in this hot weather. A dress so loud it hurts my eyes. There are yellows and oranges enough to throw back the light of the sun. I feel my whole face warming from the heat waves it throws out. Earrings gold too, and hanging down to her shoulders. Bracelets dangling and making noises when she moves her arm up to shake the folds of the dress out of her armpits. The dress is loose and flows, and as she walks closer, I like it. I hear Maggie go "Uhnnnh" again. It is her sister's hair. It stands straight up like the wool on a sheep. It is black as night and around the edges are two long pigtails that rope about like small lizards disappearing behind her ears.

"Wa-su-zo-Tean-o!" she says, coming on in that gliding way the dress makes her move. The short stocky fellow with the hair to his navel is all grinning and he follows up with, "Asalamalakim, my mother and sister!" He moves to hug Maggie but she falls back, right up against the back of my chair. I feel her trembling there, and when I look up I see the perspiration falling off her skin.

"Don't get up," says Dee. Since I am stout it takes something of a push. You can see me trying to move a second or two before I make it. She turns, showing white heels through her sandals, and goes back to the car. Out she peeks next with a Polaroid. She stoops down quickly and snaps off picture after picture of me sitting there in front of the house with Maggie cowering behind me. She never takes a shot without making sure the house is included. When a cow comes nibbling around the edge of the yard she snaps it and me and Maggie *and* the house. Then she puts the Polaroid on the back seat of the car, and comes up and kisses me on the forehead.

Meanwhile Asalamalakim is going through motions with Maggie's hand. Maggie's hand is as limp as a fish, and probably as cold, despite the sweat, and she keeps trying to pull it back. It looks like Asalamalakim wants to shake hands but wants to do it fancy. Or maybe he don't know how people shake hands. Anyhow, he soon gives up on Maggie.

"Well," I say. "Dee."

"No, Mama," she says. "Not 'Dee,' Wangero Leewanika Kemanjo!"

"What happened to 'Dee'?" I wanted to know.

"She's dead," Wangero said. "I couldn't bear it any longer, being named after the people who oppress me."

"You know well as me you was named after your aunt Dicie," I said. Dicie is my sister. She named Dee. We called her "Big Dee" after Dee was born.

"But who was *she* named after?" asked Wangero.

"I guess after Grandma Dee," I said.

"And who was she named after?" asked Wangero.

"Her mother," I said, and saw Wangero was getting tired. "That's about as far back as I can trace it," I said. Though, in fact, I probably could have carried it back beyond the Civil War through the branches.

"Well," said Asalamalakim, "there you are."

"Uhnnnh, I heard Maggie say.

"There I was not," I said, "before 'Dicie' cropped up in our family, so why should I try to trace it that far back?"

He just stood there grinning, looking down on me like somebody inspecting a Model A car. Every once in a while he and Wangero sent eye signals over my head.

"How do you pronounce this name?" I asked.

"You don't have to call me by it if you don't want to," said Wangero.

"Why shouldn't I?" I asked. "If that's what you want us to call you, we'll call you."

"I know it might sound awkward at first," said Wangero.

"I'll get used to it," I said. "Ream it out again."

Well, soon we got the name out of the way. Asalamalakim had a name twice as long and three times as hard. After I tripped over it two or three times he told me to just call him Hakim-a-barber. I wanted to ask him was he a barber, but I didn't really think he was, so I didn't ask.

"You must belong to those beef-cattle peoples down the road," I said. They said "Asalamalakim" when they met you too, but they didn't shake hands. Always too busy: feeding the cattle, fixing the fences, putting up salt-lick shelters, throwing down hay. When the white folks poisoned some of the herd, the men stayed up all night with rifles in their hands. I walked a mile and a half just to see the sight.

Hakim-a-barber said, "I accept some of their doctrines, but farming and raising cattle is not my style." They didn't tell me, and I didn't ask, whether Wangero (Dee) had really gone and married him.

We sat down to eat and right away he said he didn't eat collards and pork was unclean. Wangero, though, went on through the chitlins and corn bread, the greens and everything else. She talked a blue streak over the sweet potatoes. Everything delighted her. Even the fact that we still used the benches her daddy made for the table when we couldn't afford to buy chairs.

"Oh, Mama!" she cried. Then turned to Hakim-a-barber. "I never knew how lovely these benches are. You can feel the rump prints," she said, running her hands underneath her and along the bench. Then she gave a sigh and her hand closed over Grandma Dee's butter dish. "That's it!" she cried. "I knew there was something I wanted to ask you if I could have." She jumped from the table and went over to the corner where the churn stood, the milk in it clabber by now. She looked at the churn and looked at it.

"This churn top is what I need," she said. "Didn't Uncle Buddy whittle it out of a tree you all used to have?"

"Yes," I said.

"Uh huh," she said happily. "And I want the dasher too."

"Uncle Buddy whittle that too?" asked the barber.

Dee (Wangero) looked up at me.

"Aunt Dee's first husband whittled the dash," said Maggie so low you almost couldn't hear her. "His name was Henry, but they called him Stash."

"Maggie's brain is like an elephant's," Wangero said, laughing. "I can use the churn top as a centerpiece for the alcove table," she said, sliding a plate over the churn, "and I'll think of something artistic to do with the dasher."

When she finished wrapping the dasher the handle stuck out. I took it for a moment in my hands. You didn't even have to look close to see where hands pushing the dasher up and down to make butter had left a kind of sink in the wood. In fact, there were a lot of small sinks; you could see where thumbs and fingers had sunk into the wood. It was beautiful light yellow wood, from a tree that grew in the yard where Big Dee and Stash had lived.

After dinner Dee (Wangero) went to the trunk at the foot of my bed and started rifling through it. Maggie hung back in the kitchen over the dishpan. Out came Wangero with two quilts. They had been pieced by Grandma Dee, and then Big Dee and me had hung them on the quilt frames on the front porch and quilted them. One was in the Lone Star pattern. The other was Walk Around the Mountain. In both of them were scraps of dresses Grandma Dee had worn fifty and more years ago. Bits and pieces of Grandpa Jarrell's paisley shirts. And one teeny faded blue piece, about the size of a penny matchbox, that was from Great Grandpa Ezra's uniform that he wore in the Civil War.

"Mama," Wangero said sweet as a bird. "Can I have these old quilts?"

I heard something fall in the kitchen, and a minute later the kitchen door slammed.

"Why don't you take one or two of the others?" I asked. "These old things was just done by me and Big Dee from some tops your grandma pieced before she died."

"No," said Wangero. "I don't want those. They are stitched around the borders by machine."

"That'll make them last better," I said.

"That's not the point," said Wangero. "These are all pieces of dresses Grandma used to wear. She did all this stitching by hand. Imagine!" She held the quilts securely in her arms, stroking them.

"Some of the pieces, like those lavender ones, come from old clothes her mother handed down to her," I said, moving up to touch the quilts. Dee (Wangero) moved back just enough so that I couldn't reach the quilts. They already belonged to her.

"Imagine!" she breathed again, clutching them closely to her bosom.

"The truth is," I said, "I promised to give them quilts to Maggie, for when she marries John Thomas."

She gasped, like a bee had stung her.

"Maggie can't appreciate these quilts!" she said. "She'd probably be backward enough to put them to everyday use."

"I reckon she would," I said. "God knows I been saving 'em for long enough with nobody using 'em. I hope she will!" I didn't want to bring up how I had offered Dee (Wangero) a quilt when she went away to college. Then she had told me they were old-fashioned, out of style.

"But they're *priceless!*" she was saying now, furiously; for she has a temper. "Maggie would put them on the bed and in five years they'd be in rags. Less than that!"

"She can always make some more," I said. "Maggie knows how to quilt."

Dee (Wangero) looked at me with hatred. "You just will not understand. The point is these quilts, *these* quilts!"

"Well," I said, stumped, "what would *you* do with them?"

"Hang them," she said. As if that was the only thing you *could* do with quilts.

Maggie, by now, was standing in the door. I could almost hear the sound her feet made as they scraped over each other.

"She can have them, Mama," she said, like somebody used to never winning anything, of having anything reserved for her. "I can 'member Grandma Dee without the quilts."

I looked at her hard. She had filled her bottom lip with checkerberry snuff, and it gave her face a kind of dopey, hangdog look. It was Grandma Dee and Big Dee who taught her how to quilt herself. She stood there with her scarred hands hidden in the folds of her skirt. She looked at her sister with something like fear, but she wasn't mad at her. This was Maggie's portion. This was the way she knew God to work.

When I looked at her like that something hit me in the top of my head and ran down to the soles of my feet. Just like when I'm in church and the spirit of God touches me and I get happy and shout. I did something I never had done before: hugged Maggie to me, then dragged her on into the room, snatched the quilts out of Miss Wangero's hands and dumped them into Maggie's lap. Maggie just sat there on my bed with her mouth open.

"Take one or two of the others," I said to Dee.

But she turned without a word and went out to Hakim-a-barber.

"You just don't understand," she said, as Maggie and I came out to the car.

"What don't I understand?" I wanted to know.

"Your heritage," she said. And then she turned to Maggie, kissed her, and said. "You ought to try to make something of yourself too, Maggie. It's really a new day for us. But from the way you and Mama still live you'd never know it."

She put on some sunglasses that hid everything above the tip of her nose and her chin.

Maggie smiled; maybe at the sunglasses. But a real smile, not scared. After we watched the car dust settle I asked Maggie to bring me a dip of snuff. And then the two of us sat there just enjoying, until it was time to go in the house and go to bed.

I STAND HERE IRONING

Tillie Olsen

Born in Omaha, Nebraska, in 1913, Tillie Olsen has lived most of her life in San Francisco, where she married and reared four daughters. She began to write while leading what she calls "the triple life": mother and housewife; full- and part-time worker; and spare-time writer. The title story in her collection *Tell Me a Riddle* won the O. Henry Award for the best American short story of 1961. She has recently been named a Guggenheim fellow and holds honorary academic degrees from several universities.

Other works by Olsen include *Yonnondio: From the Thirties* (1974) and *Mother to Daughter; Daughter to Mother* (1984). However, she is not a prolific writer. "The habits of a lifetime," she says in *Silences*, "when everything else had to come before writing are not easily broken, even when circumstances now often make it possible for writing to be first; habits of years—response to others, distractibility, responsibility for daily matters—stay with you, mark you, become you."

In some sense, it is the "habits of years" which have affected the relationship between mother and daughter in "I Stand Here Ironing." The short story is a mother's inner monologue about her eldest daughter, Emily, whose high school teacher has requested a meeting with her mother. While she irons, the narrator examines her daughter's life and her own conscience, "engulfed with all I did or did not do, with what should have been and what cannot be helped."

I stand here ironing, and what you asked me moves tormented back and forth with the iron.

"I wish you would manage the time to come in and talk with me about your daughter. I'm sure you can help me understand her. She's a youngster who needs help and whom I'm deeply interested in helping."

"Who needs help." . . . Even if I came, what good would it do? You think because I am her mother I have a key, or that in some way you could use me as a key? She has lived for nineteen years. There is all that life that has happened outside of me, beyond me.

And when is there time to remember, to sift, to weigh, to estimate, to total? I will start and there will be an interruption and I will have to gather it all together again. Or I will become engulfed with all I did or did not do, with what should have been and what cannot be helped.

She was a beautiful baby. The first and only one of our five that was beautiful at birth. You do not guess how new and uneasy her tenancy in her now-loveliness. You did not know her all those years she was thought homely, or see her poring over her baby pictures, making me tell her over and over how beautiful she had been—and would be, I would tell her—and was now, to the seeing eye. But the seeing eyes were few or nonexistent. Including mine.

I nursed her. They feel that's important nowadays. I nursed all the children, but with her, with all the fierce rigidity of first motherhood, I did like the books then said. Though her cries battered me to trembling and my breasts ached with swollenness, I waited till the clock decreed.

Why do I put that first? I do not even know if it matters, or if it explains anything.

She was a beautiful baby. She blew shining bubbles of sound. She loved motion, loved light, loved color and music and textures. She would lie on the floor in her blue overalls patting the surface so hard in ecstasy her hands and feet would blur. She was a miracle to me, but when she was eight months old I had to leave her daytimes with the woman downstairs to whom she was no miracle at all, for I worked or looked for work and for Emily's father, who "could no longer endure" (he wrote in his good-bye note) "sharing want with us."

I was nineteen. It was the pre-relief, pre-WPA world of the depression. I would start running as soon as I got off the streetcar, running up the stairs, the place smelling sour, and awake or asleep to startle awake, when she saw me she would break into a clogged weeping that could not be comforted, a weeping I can hear yet.

After a while I found a job hashing at night so I could be with her days, and it was better. But it came to where I had to bring her to his family and leave her.

It took a long time to raise the money for her fare back. Then she got chicken pox and I had to wait longer. When she finally came, I hardly knew her, walking quick and nervous like her father, looking like her father, thin, and dressed in a shoddy red that yellowed her skin and glared at the pockmarks. All the baby loveliness gone.

She was two. Old enough for nursery school they said, and I did not know then what I know now—the fatigue of the long day, and the lacerations of group life in the kinds of nurseries that are only parking places for children.

Except that it would have made no difference if I had known. It was the only place there was. It was the only way we could be together, the only way I could hold a job.

And even without knowing, I knew. I knew the teacher that was evil because all these years it has curdled into my memory, the little boy hunched in the corner, her rasp, "why aren't you outside, because Alvin hits you? that's no reason, go out, scaredy." I knew Emily hated it even if she did not clutch and implore "don't go Mommy" like the other children, mornings.

She always had a reason why we should stay home. Momma, you look sick. Momma, I feel sick. Momma, the teachers aren't there today, they're sick. Momma, we can't go, there was a fire there last night. Momma, it's a holiday today, no school, they told me.

But never a direct protest, never rebellion. I think of our others in their three-, four-year-oldness—the explosions, the tempers, the denunciations, the demands—and I feel suddenly ill. I put the iron down. What in me demanded that goodness in her? And what was the cost, the cost to her of such goodness?

The old man living in the back once said in his gentle way: "You should smile at Emily more when you look at her." What *was* in my face when I looked at her? I loved her. There were all the acts of love.

It was only with the others I remembered what he said, and it was the face of joy, and not of care or tightness or worry I turned to them—too late for Emily. She does not smile easily, let alone almost always as her brothers and sisters do. Her face is closed and sombre, but when she wants, how fluid. You must have seen it in her pantomimes, you spoke of her rare gift for comedy on the stage that rouses a laughter out of the audience so dear they applaud and applaud and do not want to let her go.

Where does it come from, that comedy? There was none of it in her when she came back to me that second time, after I had had to send her away again. She had a new daddy now to learn to love, and I think perhaps it was a better time.

Except when we left her alone nights, telling ourselves she was old enough. "Can't you go some other time, Mommy, like tomorrow?" she would ask. "Will it be just a little while you'll be gone? Do you promise?"

The time we came back, the front door open, the clock on the floor in the hall. She rigid awake. "It wasn't just a little while. I didn't cry. Three times I called you, just three times, and then I ran downstairs to open the door so you could come faster. The clock talked loud. I threw it away, it scared me what it talked."

She said the clock talked loud again that night I went to the hospital to have Susan. She was delirious with the fever that comes before red measles, but she was fully conscious all the week I was gone and the week after we were home when she could not come near the new baby or me.

She did not get well. She stayed skeleton thin, not wanting to eat, and night after night she had nightmares. She would call for me, and I would rouse from exhaustion to sleepily call back: "You're all right, darling, go to sleep, it's just a dream," and if she still called, in a sterner voice, "now go to sleep, Emily, there's nothing to hurt you." Twice, only twice, when I had to get up for Susan anyhow, I went in to sit with her.

Now when it is too late (as if she would let me hold and comfort her like I do the others) I get up and go to her at once at her moan or restless stirring. "Are you awake, Emily? Can I get you something?" And the answer is always the same: "No, I'm all right, go back to sleep, Mother."

They persuaded me at the clinic to send her away to a convalescent home in the country where "she can have the kind of food and care you can't manage for her, and you'll be free to concentrate on the new baby." They still send children to that place. I see pictures on the society page of sleek young women planning affairs to raise money for it, or dancing at the affairs, or decorating Easter eggs or filling Christmas stockings for the children.

They never have a picture of the children so I do not know if the girls still wear those gigantic red bows and the ravaged looks on the every other Sunday when parents can come to visit "unless otherwise notified"—as we were notified the first six weeks.

Oh it is a handsome place, green lawns and tall trees and fluted flower beds. High up on the balconies of each cottage the children stand, the girls in their red bows and white dresses, the boys in white suits and giant red ties. The parents stand below shrieking up to be heard and the children shriek down to be heard, and between them the invisible wall "Not To Be Contaminated by Parental Germs or Physical Affection."

There was a tiny girl who always stood hand in hand with Emily. Her parents never came. One visit she was gone. "They moved her to Rose Cottage" Emily shouted in explanation. "They don't like you to love anybody here."

She wrote once a week, the labored writing of a seven-year-old. "I am fine. How is the baby. If I write my leter nicly I will have a star. Love." There never was a star. We wrote every other day, letters she could never hold or keep but only hear read—once. "We simply do not have room for children to keep any personal possessions," they patiently explained when we pieced one Sunday's shrieking together to plead how much it would mean to Emily, who loved so to keep things, to be allowed to keep her letters and cards.

Each visit she looked frailer. "She isn't eating," they told us.

(They had runny eggs for breakfast or mush with lumps, Emily said later, I'd hold it in my mouth and not swallow. Nothing ever tasted good, just when they had chicken.)

It took us eight months to get her released home, and only the fact that she gained back so little of her seven lost pounds convinced the social worker.

I used to try to hold and love her after she came back, but her body would stay stiff, and after a while she'd push away. She ate little. Food sickened her, and I think much of life too. Oh she had physical lightness and brightness, twinkling by on skates, bouncing like a ball up and down up and down over the jump rope, skimming over the hill; but these were momentary.

She fretted about her appearance, thin and dark and foreign-looking at a time when every little girl was supposed to look or thought she should look a chubby blonde replica of Shirley Temple. The doorbell sometimes rang for her, but no one seemed to come and play in the house or be a best friend. Maybe because we moved so much.

There was a boy she loved painfully through two school semesters. Months later she told me how she had taken pennies from my purse to buy him candy. "Licorice was his favorite and I brought him some every day, but he still liked Jennifer better'n me. Why, Mommy?" The kind of question for which there is no answer.

School was a worry to her. She was not glib or quick in a world where glibness and quickness were easily confused with ability to learn. To her overworked and exasperated teachers she was an overconscientious "slow learner" who kept trying to catch up and was absent entirely too often.

I let her be absent, though sometimes the illness was imaginary. How different from my now-strictness about attendance with the others. I wasn't working. We had a new baby, I was home anyhow. Sometimes, after Susan grew old enough, I would keep her home from school, too, to have them all together.

Mostly Emily had asthma, and her breathing, harsh and labored, would fill the house with a curiously tranquil sound. I would bring the two old dresser mirrors and her boxes of collections to her bed. She would select beads and single earrings, bottle tops and shells, dried flowers and pebbles, old postcards and scraps, all sorts of oddments; then she and Susan would play Kingdom, setting up landscapes and furniture, peopling them with action.

Those were the only times of peaceful companionship between her and Susan. I have edged away from it, that poisonous feeling between them, that terrible balancing of hurts and needs I had to do between the two, and did so badly, those earlier years.

Oh there are conflicts between the others too, each one human, needing, demanding, hurting, taking—but only between Emily and Susan, no, Emily toward Susan that corroding resentment. It seems so obvious on the surface, yet it is not obvious. Susan, the second child, Susan, golden- and curly-haired and chubby, quick and articulate and assured, everything in appearance and manner Emily was not; Susan, not able to resist Emily's precious things, losing or sometimes clumsily breaking them; Susan telling jokes and riddles to company for applause while Emily sat silent (to say to me later: that was *my* riddle, Mother, I told it to Susan); Susan, who for all the five years' difference in age was just a year behind Emily in developing physically.

I am glad for that slow physical development that widened the difference between her and her contemporaries, though she suffered over it. She was too vulnerable for that terrible world of youthful competition, of preening and parading, of constant measuring of yourself against every other, of envy, "If I had that copper hair," "If I had that skin. . . ." She tormented herself enough about not looking like the others, there was enough of the unsureness, the having to be conscious of words before you speak, the constant caring—what are they thinking of me? without having it all magnified by the merciless physical drives.

Ronnie is calling. He is wet and I change him. It is rare there is such a cry now. That time of motherhood is almost behind me when the ear is not one's own but must always be racked and listening for the child cry, the child call. We sit for a while and I hold him, looking out over the city spread in charcoal with its soft aisles of light. "*Shoogily*," he breathes and curls closer. I carry him back to bed, asleep. *Shoogily*. A funny word, a family word, inherited from Emily, invented by her to say: *comfort*.

In this and other ways she leaves her seal, I say aloud. And startle at my saying it. What do I mean? What did I start to gather together, to try and make coherent? I was at the terrible, growing years. War years. I do not remember them well. I was working, there were four smaller ones now, there was not time for her. She had to help be a mother, and housekeeper, and shopper. She had to set her seal. Mornings of crisis and near hysteria trying to get lunches packed, hair combed, coats and shoes found, everyone to school or Child Care on time, the baby ready for transportation. And always the paper scribbled on by a smaller one, the book looked at by Susan then mislaid, the homework not done. Running out to that huge school where she was one, she was lost, she was a drop; suffering over the unpreparedness, stammering and unsure in her classes.

There was so little time left at night after the kids were bedded down. She would struggle over books, always eating (it was in those years she developed her enormous appetite that is legendary in our family) and I would be ironing, or preparing food for the next day, or writing V-mail to Bill, or tending the baby. Sometimes, to make me laugh, or out of her despair, she would imitate happenings or types at school.

I think I said once: "Why don't you do something like this in the school amateur show?" One morning she phoned me at work, hardly understandable through the weeping: "Mother, I did it. I won, I won; they gave me first prize; they clapped and clapped and wouldn't let me go."

Now suddenly she was Somebody, and as imprisoned in her difference as she had been in anonymity.

She began to be asked to perform at other high schools, even in colleges, then at city and statewide affairs. The first one we went to, I only recognized her the first moment when thin, shy, she almost drowned herself into the curtains. Then: Was this Emily? The control, the command, the convulsing and deadly clowning, the spell, then the roaring, stamping audience, unwilling to let this rare and precious laughter out of their lives.

Afterwards: You ought to do something about her with a gift like that—but without money or knowing how, what does one do? We have left it all to her, and the gift has as often eddied inside, clogged and clotted, as been used and growing.

She is coming. She runs up the stairs two at a time with her light graceful step, and I know she is happy tonight. Whatever it was that occasioned your call did not happen today.

"Aren't you ever going to finish the ironing, Mother? Whistler painted his mother in a rocker. I'd have to paint mine standing over an ironing board." This is one of her communicative nights and she tells me everything and nothing as she fixes herself a plate of food out of the icebox.

She is so lovely. Why did you want me to come in at all? Why were you concerned? She will find her way.

She starts up the stairs to bed. "Don't get me up with the rest in the morning." "But I thought you were having midterms." "Oh, those," she comes back in, kisses me, and says quite lightly, "in a couple of years when we'll all be atom-dead they won't matter a bit."

She has said it before. She *believes* it. But because I have been dredging the past, and all that compounds a human being is so heavy and meaningful in me, I cannot endure it tonight.

I will never total it all. I will never come in to say: She was a child seldom smiled at. Her father left me before she was a year old. I had to work her first six years when there was work, or I sent her home and to his relatives. There were years she had care she hated. She was dark and thin and foreign-looking in a world where the prestige went to blondeness and curly hair and dimples, she was slow where glibness was prized. She was a child of anxious, not proud, love. We were poor and could not afford for her the soil of easy growth. I was a young mother, I was a distracted mother. There were the other children pushing up, demanding. Her younger sister seemed all that she was not. There were years she did not want me to touch her. She kept too much in herself, her life was such she had to keep too much in herself. My wisdom came too late. She has much to her and probably little will come of it. She is a child of her age, of depression, of war, of fear.

Let her be. So all that is in her will not bloom—but in how many does it? There is still enough left to live by. Only help her to know—help make it so there is cause for her to know—that she is more than this dress on the ironing board, helpless before the iron.

DIARY

Ellen Birdseye Wheaton

The diary of Ellen Birdseye Wheaton (1816-1858) of Syracuse, NY, provides glimpses into the daily experiences of a woman trying to live up to the white middle class ideal of motherhood in the middle of the nineteenth century. At the time these entries were written, Wheaton was forty years old and the mother of eleven children; the oldest were already adults, and the youngest was still at her breast. She died two years later at the age of forty-two.

Although her merchant husband suffered financial reverses, Wheaton must have had domestic help with the cooking, cleaning, and laundry, since she had time to keep a diary, write letters, and do some of the visiting required of matrons in her class. On the other hand, she indicates that her house was rarely empty, that she took "work" with her when she went calling, that she cared for her sick mother, and that she did not have time for her music, a loss she genuinely regretted.

 TUESDAY, EVE. JAN. 15TH [1856] The family are in bed, and I ought to be there too, but I want to whisper a few words to my journal, ere I go. I am weary, and desponding, & want comfort somewhere. Mother has been more unwell than usual, today, and it makes me very sad and fearful for her. I know not, what is this strange disease she has upon her, but it is something serious, and alarming, and I feel very much the want of some friend and helper to lean upon, some one to advise and to comfort. Now, in the time of trial, I think oftener, than ever, of that dear Father, "who is not lost, but gone before,["] and of those tried and faithful ones, who departed in their prime. Then too, these family troubles, come thicker and faster, and the way looks dark on every side. My Husband is still, far away from home, and my heart grows weary, in longing for him. Oh, it is such a long and weary time, since he left us. Perhaps it may be given me to know in the words of the poet,

> How sublime a thing it is,
> To suffer and be strong—

Tho' I fear, not the latter clause—These trials make me feel how weak I am.

TUESDAY, A.M. [JANUARY 22] Expect my husband to-day, & hope he will not disappoint us.

8 o'c. P.M. Charles has arrived looking very well, and in pretty good spirits—It was an occasion of great rejoicing to us all.

WEDNESDAY, JAN. 30TH I have been trying to do something towards making Edward some shirts, in addition, to my other occupations, for the last few days, and it has confined me to the house very closely—I am troubled somewhat, with the Rheumatism in my right arm, and I don't think sewing helps it

---

DIARY   Excerpts from *The Diary of Ellen Birdseye Wheaton*. Notes by Donald Gordon. Boston: privately printed, 1923. Copyright 1923 by Louise Ayer Gordon. Reprinted by permission of Crawford Gordon, n.p.

much—Yesterday Mr & Mrs Lawrence, came to call [on] us, and kindly brought us a bag of apples—This A.M. they came again, and Julia spent the forenoon with me. We had rather a painful conversation, on matters and things deeply concerning our welfare.—I have about come to the conclusion, that there is neither honor, nor truth, neither gratitude nor friendship in the world—I have been favored for a long period, with prosperity, but now that misfortunes have begun to come, they seem to roll on thicker and faster.— Perhaps we shall be made yet, to drink it to the dregs—May we be sustained under it all, and bear all, as knowing that "he doeth all things well."

Mr. Birdsall took tea with us, and sat a little while afterwards, before leaving for Binghamton. Ellen sang him, his two favorite songs. He seems in Miserable health. Cornelia has been helping her Aunt H. to nurse J. F. to-day, and to-night she & Emma, went to Society to Mr. Leonards. Edward has gone to Mr. Ulvons [?] to a party—But the baby wakes, and I must stop.

FRIDAY FEB.—1ST. We have received an invitation to a party at Mr. Leaven-worths, and Cornelia and Edward think they will go—Of course I cannot think of going—I think it right that they should go, for C. has not been out to a party this winter—tho' it is somewhat inconvenient—for me to prepare her—I have kept her in, very closely, as we seemed to be the subjects of so much censure, and I do not wish to give any occasion—But very likely it will make no difference for our relations are determined to hate and injure us, if possible. Heaven save me, from the tender mercies of blood relations—

We have heard of a situation as teacher, in the South which Cornelia thinks of taking, if she can get it—She has written, applying for it, and is now anxiously awaiting an answer—I think it is best, for her to try and help herself in some way, and this seems to be the most eligible at present—It will be a trial to part with her, and particularly to lose her music, and her help to Ellen, but we must give it all up—There are a great many sad changes, in this wearisome world of ours—

MONDAY, FEB. 11TH. I am quite sick with a cold and sore throat, with severe headache. Went into Mrs MCarthy's, an hour or so with my work, and had a pleasant chat—Mrs Hollister was there, a little while—

TUESDAY [FEBRUARY 12], I was miserable enough all day, and kept my bed part of the day. When Dr Cator came in to see Mother, I got some advice & medicine from him, he says I have an ulcerated sore throat.

SATURDAY [FEBRUARY 16], Frank called on his way to Elbridge with J. B.— —Charlotte and Frank came by the cars, but an accident detained them about two hours. —C. returned to E. in the P.M. and F. to Pompey—There was a little appearance of a thaw this morning, but by three o'c. it is growing cold and snowing fast. We are having a very hard winter. Since Christmas, there has been uninterrupted sleighing, and many very severe snowstorms—I have been in a sleigh twice this winter, and then only for a few minutes. I am really tired of this hard weather, it is so uncomfortable all around the house. All the water pipes are frozen up, the cisterns are nearly empty, and we are in great want of water.

This past week, I have read Grace Lee, a novel by Julia Kavanagh, and have been much interested in it—It is a fascinating but tiresome story. Not quite equal to "North & South" I think. I have also lately read, "King Henry 8th, and his Six Wives"—

Cornelia received a letter this evening from the gentleman, to whom she applied for a situation as teacher. He had written to a lady, at the head of a large school, for a teacher, but had received no answer, and could not tell what he should do, but will write again, in a few days. She feels very much disappointed, and thinks the thing is settled—However I tell her to go on, and get ready for some place all the same.

SATURDAY FEB. 23. Charles went to Binghampton on Thursday,—for two or three days. On Friday Eve. a letter came to Cornelia from Mr Davis, saying, that he had not procured a teacher, & would like her to come on immediately. So that she has her way clear before her.

Charles returned from B. this evening, and says he will go with her next week, as his route to S. C. lies, with hers, to within 36 miles of her destination. But he always has so many hindrances, about getting away, that I fear they will not go so soon,—and yet I dread their going, very much. But as he is circumstanced, I know that he is much more pleasantly situated there than he can be here, and so I am reconciled to his going, and to being left alone. C. takes pleasure in the thought that she shall be enabled to help herself, and relieve her Father somewhat, in this time of trial—

FEB. 27TH WEDNESDAY. Charles told us, this day at noon, that he had recd letters from the South, which make it important for him to be there as soon as possible. He wishes C. to be ready to go on tomorrow—So we have got to be busy—

FRIDAY A.M. [FEBRUARY 29] Ellen finished packing the last trunk, and we had breakfast.—Then Cornelia ran over to Mr. H's and bade goodbye. The man came for the trunks and then for her. At the last moment, I decided to go to the cars with her. When we got there, there was quite a company assembled of friends from all sides. The girls kept up good courage, to the last and went off, apparently in good spirits—I came home feeling almost sick, with fatigue and excitement—I find I have another of those terrible sore throats.

MARCH 1 SATURDAY MORNING, This is the morning Mother had decided upon, to go home, and she and Julia got off, about the same time, that the others did—yesterday. She did not feel quite as well as usual for a day or two, but I think, it was nothing serious—She has been here, about 9 weeks—and is much improved, since she first came. After they left, it seemed very lonely and still—but there was enough to keep us busy putting the house to rights—

MARCH 12TH, WEDNESDAY, This A.M. Edward brought a letter from the P. O. with Charles writing upon it. I was very sure I should have one to-day, and of course was very glad to get it. He had got on safely, as far as Columbia, and was very well. Says the climate there is delightful, streets dry & dusty, and warm enough to do without fires, during the day. A most remarkable contrast to this ice-bound region, we inhabit. The girls parted from him, on Wednesday the 5th, on their route to Warrenton. I do hope to get some news from Cornelia this week. I had a very kind and pleasant letter from Louisa last night, which really was like balm to my wounded spirit—She is a dear, good woman. But I depend most upon Charles' letters. They are so kind, so frequent, and so just the thing, I don't know how I could get along without them. It has snowed very much here, since Sunday [March 9th], and to-day the wind has been high. I have never experienced so severe a winter, since my recollection. There having been now, eleven weeks of constant sleighing, without one really thawy day. I have been very industrious to-day, and am as tired, as a *"man, a mowing"*

Ellen has concluded to sing, at Mr Held's concert next week, and has commenced practising a little for it. Mrs. McE. came in to-night, and I settled with her, and paid her up. I hope I shall be enabled to get along, this Spring, without hiring so much help, as I have formerly done. Sometimes I fear, that I dont realize our position fully, and that I am indolent and forgetful of my duty. I dont mean to be so, and I do not wish to consult my own ease, if I know myself.—But I am willing to sacrifice ease, and leisure, to the welfare of my family, if I may thereby promote these ends—

MARCH 13, THURSDAY This day I am forty years old. Is it possible? I cannot realize it, and yet at times, I feel old and worn. When I look around and see this numerous flock of children, I can realize it, fully, and feel, that the prime of my life is, pretty far gone. But it seems only yesterday, since I was married. And so the years roll by, and if I am permitted to live, shall in a little time find myself, wrinkled, old and gray.

This morning brought me a delightful letter from Cornelia, and two from Charles, that did me good like a medicine. She is pleased with her position and the family of Mr. Davis, tho' she had not begun her duties, as yet. Ellen had not yet got a situation, but there were good prospects for her. I took the letter over to Mrs. Ellis, (who has had no letter yet from Ellen,) and read it to her, & Mrs. Morgan. I sat half an hour or so, and came home to find Sophronia here. She spent the P.M. and Ellen M. W. came about 4 o'c and staid also—Had a pleasant visit with them, and Jarvis called for them about 7. o'clock—

SATURDAY MARCH 22ND brought Sisters Emma and Charlotte, from Pompey, with Mr. Kendall and Frank all to dinner. Then the girls had company in the P.M. and so the day passed in bustle and confusion. It is uncertain whether C. returns to Elbridge, & E. will remain some days, on a visit. Edward having heard some obscure threats about the Sheldon Block being in danger from incendiaries, has kept watch, for the best part of two nights, and I of course am somewhat disturbed, by his coming in about three o'clock in the morning, so that I dont rest very well. My baby is much out of tune lately, owing to teething, I fancy. I am desirous to wean her, next month, but I am much afraid it will be a critical thing for her.

SUNDAY, A.M. [MARCH 23] Went to a meeting at the Market Hall, & heard a sermon read by Mr. Davis. After meeting there was some talk of what had been done towards a settlement between our Church and the Plymouth folks. It looks about as likely to happen as ever, and I don't think they want any settlement, only to get hold of the Church property. I am sick of the whole thing. This P.M. went to the First Pres. Church with Sister E. After waiting a while in the porch, Mr. E. Bradley, invited us to sit with him. The Church was quite full, & [sic] listened to a discourse by Mr. Newell of Salina. Rev. Mr. Hall, was also in the pulpit. The best part of the service, was the music and the organ which was very finely played—

To-night, after tea, to my surprise, had a call from Horace. While he was here, James and Lucy Ellis, came in and sat awhile. Lucy looks sad when she sees my children—poor woman!—10 o'clock, P.M. Edward is sleeping on the lounge, preparatory to going out at midnight, to watch, & the babies are all in bed, so that I am really enjoying a very few minutes of quiet and leisure, the first I have had to-day. To make the most of it, I want to do, at least, half a dozen things, among which are several letters to be written. What shall I do first?

SAT. A.M. [APRIL 5] Very early this morning, the house was astir, to see Emma off, in the cars, and as I did not sleep much thro' the night, in consequence of little Mabel's restlessness, I felt rather poorly today.—

Have had a very trying & exciting day, and have not at last, got matters arranged quite to my satisfaction—It has been quite a new experience for me, and an unpleasant one, but I hope, I am none the worse for it.

SUNDAY P.M. [APRIL 6] This forenoon wrote a letter to Charles, and afternoon went to Sec. Bap. Church. But did not find it specially interesting, and left before the close. E. M. W. was here to lunch and dinner. This evening the girls are gone to meeting. I think of the absent ones, when Sunday night comes, and feel lonely—Cornelia always said she enjoyed the Sunday P.M. dinner the best of any meal, in the week and when that time comes, I always think of her, and then this twilight reminds me of her music and her Fathers. Oh how much we miss the music. I don't hear as often from her as I should like—and yet I know, she has much to occupy her time, in her school, besides all her numerous correspondents, so I will try not to complain—I often picture her to myself surrounded by her pupils, and their attention fixed upon her, as she dispenses the knowledge to them. In all her letters she seems quite cheerful and contented. Oh! for patience to bear all these separations, and mortifications meekly, and rightly, and for wisdom to act rightly in these difficult passes of life—I, who have so long loved to lean upon those stronger than I, must now learn to rely upon myself in trials and emergencies, feeling that all human aid is vain, and help must come alone from above, Ah!

> Life is truly a strife,
> 'Tis a bubble, 'tis a dream

and rudely indeed, are we tossed about upon its billowy surface.—How changed its aspect to me, in the last few years! So lately it seems, that I was so hopeful, so bright, when nothing had power to depress me long, but had always some bright anticipations to cheer me forward. Surrounded by friends, fortune smiled, and life seemed really worth living for. Now, when fortune frowns, friends frown too, or what is worse desert us, entirely. Clouds of care & anxiety, unknown before, settle down upon me, and I walk, from day to day, as in a maze—not seeing my way clearly towards any future object. Many times so weary and heart sick, that life seems utterly worthless—But this is not the right mood, for me to indulge in, and I will be up and doing:

> With a heart for any fate,
> Still achieving, still pursuing,
> Learn to labor and to wait—

WEDNESDAY, APRIL 30TH. I am trying to wean my darling baby, and I find myself rather unstrung by it—I slept very little, last night. Tonight she is to sleep with Betsy, and I fear she will cry a great deal. April 30—It is a trying thing to do. I wrote to Cornelia on Monday A.M. [April 28]—a good long letter, so also did Ellen. Last night, Ellen wrote to her Father, in answer to one from him recd in the morning. I added a few lines and sent a programme of the concert.

IMPRESSIONS OF AN INDIAN CHILDHOOD
Zitkala-Ša

Zitkala-Ša (1875-1938), or Gertrude Simmons Bonnin, was a nationally known writer and lecturer who founded the Council of American Indians in 1926. Born on the Pine Ridge Reservation in South Dakota, Zitkala-Ša (Red Bird) attended Earlham College and taught at the Carlisle Indian School in Pennsylvania. A talented violinist, she studied music at the Boston Conservatory and in Paris. After returning to the reservation in the early 1900s, she married Raymond T. Bonnin, a Sioux who worked for the U.S. Indian Service, and became an activist working for the rights of Native Americans.

The popular images of Native American women include those of the squaw, a large, silent, and inscrutable woman carryng a papoose; and the tender, shy, and submissive maiden. Most of the heroines, such as Pocahontas, the princess; and Kateri Tekakwitha, the saint; served white men. Zitkala-Ša's mother fits into none of these stereotypes. A single parent connected to an extended family, she remembers vividly the past suffering of her people and faces uneasy accommodations with the present for the future benefit of her children.

MY MOTHER.

A WIGWAM of weather-stained canvas stood at the base of some irregularly ascending hills. A footpath wound its way gently down the sloping land till it reached the broad river bottom; creeping through the long swamp grasses that bent over it on either side, it came out on the edge of the Missouri.

Here, morning, noon, and evening, my mother came to draw water from the muddy stream for our household use. Always, when my mother started for the river, I stopped my play to run along with her. She was only of medium height. Often she was sad and silent, at which times her full arched lips were compressed into hard and bitter lines, and shadows fell under her black eyes. Then I clung to her hand and begged to know what made the tears fall.

IMPRESSIONS OF AN INDIAN CHILDHOOD   From *Atlantic Monthly*, January 1900, 37–38, 41, 45–47.

"Hush; my little daughter must never talk about my tears;" and smiling through them, she patted my head and said, "Now let me see how fast you can run to-day." Whereupon I tore away at my highest possible speed, with my long black hair blowing in the breeze.

I was a wild little girl of seven. Loosely clad in a slip of brown buckskin, and light-footed with a pair of soft moccasins on my feet, I was as free as the wind that blew my hair, and no less spirited than a bounding deer. These were my mother's pride,—my wild freedom and overflowing spirits. She taught me no fear save that of intruding myself upon others.

Having gone many paces ahead I stopped, panting for breath, and laughing with glee as my mother watched my every movement. I was not wholly conscious of myself, but was more keenly alive to the fire within. It was as if I were the activity, and my hands and feet were only experiments for my spirit to work upon.

Returning from the river, I tugged beside my mother, with my hand upon the bucket I believed I was carrying. One time, on such a return, I remember a bit of conversation we had. My grown-up cousin, Warca-Ziwin (Sunflower), who was then seventeen, always went to the river alone for water for her mother. Their wigwam was not far from ours; and I saw her daily going to and from the river. I admired my cousin greatly. So I said: "Mother, when I am tall as my cousin Warca-Ziwin, you shall not have to come for water. I will do it for you."

With a strange tremor in her voice which I could not understand, she answered, "If the paleface does not take away from us the river we drink."

"Mother, who is this bad paleface?" I asked.

"My little daughter, he is a sham,—a sickly sham! The bronzed Dakota is the only real man."

I looked up into my mother's face while she spoke; and seeing her bite her lips, I knew she was unhappy. This aroused revenge in my small soul. Stamping my foot on the earth, I cried aloud, "I hate the paleface that makes my mother cry!"

Setting the pail of water on the ground, my mother stooped, and stretching her left hand out on the level with my eyes, she placed her other arm about me; she pointed to the hill where my uncle and my only sister lay buried.

"There is what the paleface has done! Since then your father too has been buried in a hill nearer the rising sun. We were once very happy. But the paleface has stolen our lands and driven us hither. Having defrauded us of our land, the paleface forced us away.

"Well, it happened on the day we moved camp that your sister and uncle were both very sick. Many others were ailing, but there seemed to be no help. We traveled many days and nights; not in the grand happy way that we moved camp when I was a little girl, but we were driven, my child, driven like a herd of buffalo. With every step, your sister, who was not as large as you are now, shrieked with the painful jar until she was hoarse with crying. She grew more and more feverish. Her little hands and cheeks were burning hot. Her little lips were parched and dry, but she would not drink the water I gave her. Then I discovered that her throat was swollen and red. My poor child, how I cried with her because the Great Spirit had forgotten us!

"At last, when we reached this western country, on the first weary night your sister died. And soon your uncle died also, leaving a widow and an orphan daughter, your cousin Warca-Ziwin. Both your sister and uncle might have been happy with us to-day, had it not been for the heartless paleface."

My mother was silent the rest of the way to our wigwam. Though I saw no tears in her eyes, I knew that was because I was with her. She seldom wept before me.

◈◈◈

THE BIG RED APPLES.

The first turning away from the easy, natural flow of my life occurred in an early spring. It was in my eighth year; in the month of March, I afterward learned. At this age I knew but one language, and that was my mother's native tongue.

From some of my playmates I heard that two paleface missionaries were in our village. They were from that class of white men who wore big hats and carried large hearts, they said. Running direct to my mother, I began to question her why these two strangers were among us. She told me, after I had teased much, that they had come to take away Indian boys and girls to the East. My mother did not seem to want me to talk about them. But in a day or two, I gleaned many wonderful stories from my playfellows concerning the strangers.

"Mother, my friend Judéwin is going home with the missionaries. She is going to a more beautiful country than ours; the palefaces told her so!" I said wistfully, wishing in my heart that I too might go.

Mother sat in a chair, and I was hanging on her knee. Within the last two seasons my big brother Dawée had returned from a three years' education in the East, and his coming back influenced my mother to take a farther step from her native way of living. First it was a change from the buffalo skin to the white man's canvas that covered our wigwam. Now she had given up her wigwam of slender poles, to live, a foreigner, in a home of clumsy logs.

"Yes, my child, several others besides Judéwin are going away with the palefaces. Your brother said the missionaries had inquired about his little sister," she said, watching my face very closely.

My heart thumped so hard against my breast, I wondered if she could hear it.

"Did he tell them to take me, mother?" I asked, fearing lest Dawée had forbidden the palefaces to see me, and that my hope of going to the Wonderland would be entirely blighted.

With a sad, slow smile, she answered: "There! I knew you were wishing to go, because Judéwin has filled your ears with the white men's lies. Don't believe a word they say! Their words are sweet, but, my child, their deeds are bitter. You will cry for me, but they will not even soothe you. Stay with me, my little one! Your brother Dawée says that going East, away from your mother, is too hard an experience for his baby sister."

Thus my mother discouraged my curiosity about the lands beyond our eastern horizon; for it was not yet an ambition for Letters that was stirring me. But on the following day the missionaries did come to our very house. I spied them coming up the footpath leading to our cottage. A third man was with them, but he was not my brother Dawée. It was another, a young interpreter, a paleface who had a smattering of the Indian language. I was ready to run out to meet them, but I did not dare to displease my mother. With great glee, I jumped up and down on our ground floor. I begged my mother to open the door, that they would be sure to come to us. Alas! They came, they saw, and they conquered!

Judéwin had told me of the great tree where grew red, red apples; and how we could reach out our hands and pick all the red apples we could eat. I had never seen apple trees. I had never tasted more than a dozen red apples in my life; and when I heard of the orchards of the East, I was eager to roam among them. The missionaries smiled into my eyes, and patted my head. I wondered how mother could say such hard words against them.

"Mother, ask them if little girls may have all the red apples they want, when they go East," I whispered aloud, in my excitement.

The interpreter heard me, and answered: "Yes, little girl, the nice red apples are for those who pick them; and you will have a ride on the iron horse if you go with these good people."

I had never seen a train, and he knew it.

"Mother, I'm going East! I like big red apples, and I want to ride on the iron horse! Mother, say yes!" I pleaded.

My mother said nothing. The missionaries waited in silence; and my eyes began to blur with tears, though I struggled to choke them back. The corners of my mouth twitched, and my mother saw me.

"I am not ready to give you any word," she said to them. "To-morrow I shall send you my answer by my son."

With this they left us. Alone with my mother, I yielded to my tears, and cried aloud, shaking my head so as not to hear what she was saying to me. This was the first time I had ever been so unwilling to give up my own desire that I refused to hearken to my mother's voice.

There was a solemn silence in our home that night. Before I went to bed I begged the Great Spirit to make my mother willing I should go with the missionaries.

The next morning came, and my mother called me to her side. "My daughter, do you still persist in wishing to leave your mother?" she asked.

"Oh, mother, it is not that I wish to leave you, but I want to see the wonderful Eastern land," I answered.

My dear old aunt came to our house that morning, and I heard her say, "Let her try it."

I hoped that, as usual, my aunt was pleading on my side. My brother Dawée came for mother's decision. I dropped my play, and crept close to my aunt.

"Yes, Dawée, my daughter, though she does not understand what it all means, is anxious to go. She will need an education when she is grown, for then there will be fewer real Dakotas, and many more palefaces. This tearing her away, so young, from her mother is necessary, if I would have her an educated woman. The palefaces, who owe us a large debt for stolen lands, have begun to pay a tardy justice in offering some education to our children. But I know my daughter must suffer keenly in this experiment. For her sake, I dread to tell you my reply to the missionaries. Go, tell them that they may take my little daughter, and that the Great Spirit shall not fail to reward them according to their hearts."

Wrapped in my heavy blanket, I walked with my mother to the carriage that was soon to take us to the iron horse. I was happy. I met my playmates, who were also wearing their best thick blankets. We showed one another our new beaded moccasins, and the width of the belts that girdled our new dresses. Soon we were being drawn rapidly away by the white man's horses. When I saw the lonely figure of my mother vanish in the distance, a sense of regret settled heavily upon me. I felt suddenly weak, as if I might fall limp to the ground. I was in the hands of strangers whom my mother did not fully trust. I no longer felt free to be myself, or to voice my own feelings. The tears trickled down my cheeks, and I buried my face in the folds of my blanket. Now the first step, parting me from my mother, was taken, and all my belated tears availed nothing.

Having driven thirty miles to the ferryboat, we crossed the Missouri in the evening. Then riding again a few miles eastward, we stopped before a massive brick building. I looked at it in amazement, and with a vague misgiving, for in our village I had never seen so large a house. Trembling with fear and distrust of the palefaces, my teeth chattering from the chilly ride, I crept noiselessly in my soft moccasins along the narrow hall, keeping very close to the bare wall. I was as frightened and bewildered as the captured young of a wild creature.

IS RACE SUICIDE PROBABLE?
Margaret Sanger

Margaret Sanger (1879-1966) spent most of her life working for the legalization of birth control. In 1916, when the Comstock law prohibited the sale of contraceptives, she opened the first birth control clinic in the United States. By allying herself with health professionals, she gradually gained support for her cause, and in 1936, the courts upheld the right of the medical professions to dispense birth control information. The endorsement of the American Medical Association followed within the year.

Sanger maintained that she was most concerned with freeing working-class women from "involuntary motherhood" by permitting them control over their own bodies. The availability of birth control information would also allow women to express their sexuality more fully, since the fear of pregnancy, according to Sanger, explained in some part the myth of female passivity.

A major objection to the legalization of birth control was that the country would become depopulated. Sanger's response to that objection is based partially on eugenics, the improvement of heredity through genetic control. The fact that this debate was carried on in the pages of *Collier's,* one of the most popular magazines of its day, is indicative of the wide public interest in these issues.

The people of the United States have been warned against the menace of birth control. If they exercise intelligent self-discipline, it is said, Americans may

IS RACE SUICIDE PROBABLE? Margaret Sanger, August 15, 1925, 25. Reprinted by permission of Grant Sanger, M.D.

bring this country to destruction through depopulation. The fear that the present rate of increase in the population of the United States may be decreased and that our population may indeed be brought to a standstill through the practice of birth control is hardly substantiated by the last estimate of the Bureau of the Census. Within the last five years there has been an increase in our native population of approximately 6,000,000, or 1,200,000 a year.

We are a nation of business men and women. We believe in efficiency, accuracy, and sound economic policy. If this is so, it strikes me that it is high time that not only American science but American business as well should begin to analyze the cost to the community of the haphazard, traditional, happy-go-lucky methods in producing the Americans of to-morrow—the *laissez-faire* policy approved by those who forget that the Biblical injunction "be fruitful and multiply" was given to Noah immediately after the Flood, when, according to the Biblical narrative, the entire population of the globe was eight.

It has been conservatively estimated that no less than one quarter of the gross incomes of our states is expended upon the upkeep of asylums for the feeble-minded and insane, the mentally defective, the criminal, the congenitally defective, the delinquent and the dependent. We are spending billions, literally billions, keeping alive thousands who never, in all human compassion, should have been brought into this world. We are spending more in maintaining morons than in developing the inherent talents of gifted children. We are coddling the incurably defective and neglecting potential geniuses.

We have not chosen this Sisyphean task; it has been forced on us because we have left the production of American children to *chance,* instead of bringing this most important of all human functions within the sphere of *choice.*

Until the leaders of American business decide to cooperate in this analysis of our biological and racial problems we shall be at a loss to answer such critics as Luther Burbank, to whom American civilization is deeply indebted. In a recent interview he is quoted as asserting:

"America . . . is like a garden in which the gardener pays no attention to the weeds. Our criminals are our weeds, and weeds breed fast and are intensely hardy. They must be eliminated. Stop permitting criminals and weaklings to reproduce. All over the country to-day we have enormous insane asylums and similar institutions where we nourish the unfit and criminal instead of exterminating them. Nature eliminates the weeds, but we turn them into parasites and allow them to reproduce."

Could any business maintain itself with the burden of such an "overhead"? Could any breeder of live stock conduct his enterprise on such a basis? I do not think so.

It is one of the bad habits of us Americans to estimate everything by magnitude, in terms of millions and billions. But in the matter of increasing population we must hesitate before throwing bouquets at ourselves. I am not a calamity howler, and I think my vision of the future of America is as cheerful as anyone's. But let me conclude with the emphatic statement of my conviction that mere increase in population has nothing to do with progress, nor can a decreasing birth rate by any stretch of the imagination be interpreted as an omen of national calamity.

LESBIAN MOTHERS

Del Martin and Phyllis Lyon

Del Martin and Phyllis Lyon are co-authors of *Lesbian/Woman* and co-founders of a national lesbian organization, the Daughters of Bilitis. Their interest in lesbian mothers grew in part from Martin's experience as a mother and grandmother.

As Martin and Lyon state, "lesbian mother" may appear to be a contradiction in terms, since lesbian relationships are nonprocreative. But children from previous heterosexual relationships are often integrated into lesbian households. In their interviews with women who have established such households, the authors discovered a wide variation in experience. They also considered the reasons why some lesbian mothers are reluctant to enter into such arrangements. The common denominator in both cases is often fear: Some fear the reactions of their children; others fear the loss of custody; many fear both. At the root of these fears, Martin and Lyon point out, is the homophobia of our society.

 Until recently American society has regarded the phrase *lesbian mother* as a contradiction in terms. Because lesbian relationships are between two women and are therefore nonprocreative, it was automatically assumed that there was no such thing as a lesbian mother.

Researchers who have done studies on female homosexuality have directed their attention primarily to sexual behavior. While they have noted that most lesbians have had some heterosexual experience before engaging in lesbian relationships, they have failed to recognize that a significant number of these women do have children.

Lesbians, like other women in our society, have been raised with the expectation of becoming wives and mothers. Those who sought "professional help" were assured that their lesbian feelings would disappear when they met the right man, got married, and had children. But this doesn't happen.

As a result, there are many lesbian mothers trying in various ways to cope with a hostile society which recognizes and seeks to protect only traditional, and often outmoded, concepts of family and parenthood. Lesbian women have in the past been deprived of their children or forced to live a deception. Only now, with a new consciousness and new honesty, are lesbian mothers beginning to emerge as individuals—strong in their concepts of motherhood and determined to fight for their children.

For Sandra and Madeleine, moving their six children, all under the age of eight, into a five-bedroom, three-bathroom house was a joyful experience. "We have a viable and exciting family unit which runs smoothly, each one being taught to love and care for the other. We pooled our financial resources; one of us works and the other takes care of the house and kids. Everything was working out well until our ex-husbands took us to court to try to get the children away from us."

LESBIAN MOTHERS   From *Ms.*, October 1973, pp. 78–80. Reprinted by permission of the authors.

By order of a Seattle court—which rejected the testimony of a psychiatrist and social worker that the children appear adjusted and healthy—the two women have been forced to separate. The judge did not order that the homosexual relationship end, only that it would be in the "best interests" of the children that they not be living under one roof. Considering the high rate of divorce, it is not unusual for homes to have no male models for children, the judge admitted. "But it is unusual to have homes with two mothers as models." He also said he realized separate residences could prove to be a financial burden, but his "prime interest is the welfare of the children."

In a similar decision last year in San Jose, California, the judge awarded custody of three children to their mother Cam, an admitted lesbian. Though it was the first time an admitted or proved lesbian won a child custody contest, the court restricted Cam's relationship with her lover, also a mother. The two women are to see each other only when Cam's children are in school or visiting their father. Joan Bradford ("Found Women," *Ms.*, January, 1973), the attorney for the plaintiff, is appealing the decision on the grounds of the Constitutional right of freedom of association.

Not long ago a Southern California judge awarded two small children, a girl and a boy, to the mother despite inferences about her lesbian tendencies, because "children need their mothers in their earlier years." However, the son is to be turned over to the father at age five. Apparently, there is no similar concern about the daughter.

Lesbian mothers who want to be honest with their children must also be realistic. Children who know the truth often have to be trusted not to tell it to their fathers or friends. Jean, a divorced mother of two—a daughter, eleven, and a son, eight—has instructed her children not to tell their father of her new relationship. She has been criticized for placing too heavy a burden on their young shoulders. Yet an inadvertent remark while visiting with their father, or to a neighbor or relative, could mean permanent separation. In terms of the children themselves, Jean has no qualms. "I have no fear about whether my children will grow up gay or straight. I want to teach them about relationships rather than roles."

Though a 1967 decision of the California appellate court prohibits denying a mother child custody merely because she is a lesbian, Jean, a San Franciscan, is aware that the courts, while ruling in "the best interests of the children," routinely interpret that to be a heterosexual environment. Despite favorable psychiatric testimony regarding the "fitness" of a lesbian as a parent, judges are still inclined to award custody to the father in such cases. These decisions are not based upon the qualifications of the mother, but rather on the assumption that her children will more than likely become homosexuals. Yet, of the thousands of lesbian women we have met over the years, all were products of a heterosexual union, all were raised in a heterosexual environment, all were taught a totally heterosexual value system, and all were assumed to be heterosexual. It happens very rarely, according to Dr. Harvey E. Kaye, a New York psychiatrist who observed numerous homosexual family situations, that such a parent turns her child away from heterosexuality.

Lesbian mothers believe that the problems they face in raising their children would not be much different from those encountered by heterosexual divorcées if it weren't for society's crippling *homophobia*—the fear that gay parents will, wittingly or unwittingly, bring up gay children. Since 10 percent of the population may be homosexual, lesbian mothers estimate that 90 percent of their children will turn out to be heterosexual no matter what the environment—just as they themselves turned out to be lesbian in spite of growing up in heterosexual environments.

Knowing this and being acutely aware of the damage that can be done by pigeonholing children into ill-fitting roles, Jean is simply concerned that her children grow up to be free human beings. "I want them to feel good about themselves, whoever they are and whatever 'other people' may think.

"In the meantime, I'm not trying to hide the pain of our present reality from my children. We all love each other very much. If we want to stay together, we need to protect our family unit together. So far, the kids have been able to deal with it."

Jean's situation is shared by many other women—women who in most cases did not discover, or face up to, their lesbian feelings until after marriage and motherhood; women who then sought divorces without divulging the lesbian identity that would endanger their custody of their children; women who live alone with their children but who may have a personal relationship with another woman outside the home; women who have preferred the constancy of establishing the lesbian lover as an integral part of the family unit, a stepparent, as it were.

Aside from the constant threat of exposure that could result in their losing their children, these women also worry about having male friends with whom their daughters and sons can identify; about when and if they should tell their children of their own lesbian identity; and about the reactions of their children should they bring a lesbian lover into the household. Those who are open about their lesbianism, at least with their friends and children, have joined groups such as San Francisco's Lesbian Mothers Union. Here they can socialize and rap about problems they encounter as lesbian heads-of-household. They also form babysitting co-ops and hold picnics so that their children can mingle and make friends with other youngsters with similar lifestyles.

The question asked most often of lesbian mothers is, "What do you do about the absence of a father image for your sons?" Many lesbians, especially those who are feminists, resent this question because it implies their daughters are not as important. Furthermore, there usually is a biological father who has visiting privileges and whose visits can in some cases disrupt the household, presenting a negative male image rather than a positive one.

For example, when Shirley's exhusband comes to see his two-year-old son on weekends, she must hide any evidence of the woman she lives with. "We scurry around and take things down from the bulletin board and hide the extra toothbrush," she explains indignantly. "Ann even has to get out of the house till he's gone." This gives the child a feeling that his father would be hurt or angered by honesty.

The absence of a father image does not concern many lesbian mothers. In fact, having sons grow up to be like their fathers is frequently considered undesirable. Lesbian mothers are eager to raise sons to relate to women as people, as equals. What really worries these mothers is the influence of their sons' peers, of television, and of the schools which still perpetuate stereotypes.

"We can't control that," Jerry, who has a young son, explains, "but we try.

Some of our gay male friends have become sensitive to the problem and have been helpful with my son, Paul. Also we see to it that we have a wide range of friends coming into our home—both women and men, gay and straight."

"My fourteen-year-old son doesn't have to be *macho* to know that he is a man," a Chicana mother says. "He doesn't have to role-play in order to prove his manhood. He knows he is male and is having no trouble with his identity. What he doesn't understand is what all the fuss is about, why his friends have to pretend to be something they are not."

A lesbian mother, who doesn't relate to men "at all," claims, "My sons don't need a male image. They need a human image. The best thing I can do is make them aware." Other lesbian mothers may not be willing to forgo all relationships with men, yet they agree that nonsexist male models are hard to come by.

Because of their feminist consciousness, many lesbian mothers are confident of giving their daughters a positive self-image. Some, however, are subject to the same societal pressures that affect heterosexual mothers. Laura, for instance, admitted that she had worried about her daughter developing a proper female identification. "A couple of years ago, when Linda was six, she wanted Hot-Wheels for Christmas, and it threw me in to a fit," Laura remembers. "Meg and I sat and discussed it for hours." Linda did not get the toy cars. Laura realizes now, however, that she had given in to those societal pressures that dictate dolls and surrogate household appliances for little girls, and cars and chemistry sets for little boys.

Before the days of Gay Liberation and the Women's Movement, most lesbian mothers were apt to try to conceal their lesbianism from their children. One we know went to the extreme of cutting herself off completely from any contact with the gay community or from any possibility of an adult love relationship. Instead she devoted her energies solely to the job of "mothering." Now, young women prefer to be open and honest with their children, to be free enough to display affection in front of them, as heterosexual couples do. "The important thing," according to Barbara, "is that there is love and security in the home and that my child grows up with the idea of *two people* loving each other."

But it's one thing inside the home, quite another on the outside. Barbara described the time she put her arm around Carole as they were walking down the street, and her nine-year-old son, Jim, stopped her. "Don't do that. I understand, but other people don't."

Sarah and Diane, in their late thirties, merged their families three years ago, which made them responsible for nine children. "Neither of us cares what the girls turn out to be—whatever makes them happy," Sarah says. "If they become lesbians, it's the unfair shake they'd get from society that will bother us. Truthfully, we don't feel they will ever find as beautiful a relationship with a man as they would with a woman. Perhaps we are biased by our own experience. But despite all our efforts to the contrary, we still see the 'typical male' qualities developing in our own sons."

"We didn't have any more problems bringing these kids together than a straight couple would with his, hers, and ours," Diane added. "It's difficult to tell whether they accept or reject our relationship. My eighteen-year-old boy definitely rejects it, and Sarah's nineteen-year-old daughter, who is married, accepts it. The rest would be just guesses. Two sons have been difficult, but we aren't sure if it's because of 'us' or just resentment over the divorce. The sixteen-year-old boy shows definite signs of homosexuality."

Bringing teenage sons into a new family constellation with two women heading the household presents more difficulties than when younger children are involved. Gerri, confused by the responses of her fourteen-year-old son, says, "He genuinely likes Mary and her ten-year-old daughter as people— that's evident. But he is upset to the point of threatening violence and running away (though I don't think he is likely to do either), about living in an all female household where his *machismo* is not honored. I know this is a transition time in his life. Our new family arrangement makes it especially difficult for him. But I don't know how to make him feel good as a human being, a male person, a family member, when he sees male chauvinism as the only example all around him as the way *good* men are. My choice of a woman as the most fulfilling partner must be threatening to him, too, I guess. But he can't articulate any of this very well."

Many lesbian mothers remain captive in unsatisfactory heterosexual marriages because they fear exposure or cannot overcome a traditional need for the male. Others are being blackmailed into giving up their children for the same reasons. As awareness and support grow, more and more lesbian mothers are coming out into the open to declare that their relationships are viable and valid, and that they are just as capable of raising children as are heterosexuals. Many women no longer flinch at taking their cause to the courts. Increasingly. psychologists and sociologists are backing them up, and some courts are acknowledging that mothering abilities exist because of the individual, not because of sex orientation.

After interviewing many of these women, we feel there was only one logical conclusion to make. What is important in deciding custody cases is the relationship between parent and child, not the parent's sexual orientation. If parents stopped worrying about artificial sex roles, and concentrated on teaching their children how to develop healthy human relationships, perhaps we might put an end to the Battle of the Sexes—woman against man, heterosexual against homosexual.

WOMEN, WAR, AND BABIES

Jane Addams

Jane Addams (1860-1935), the most celebrated social feminist of the first third of this century, served as a model for several generations of young women who sought, in her words, a "recognized outlet for their active faculties." The founder of Hull House believed that the domestic role of women as caretakers and as guardians of morality should be expanded into the social and political spheres. Her efforts, described in her autobiography, *Twenty Years at Hull House,* helped to establish social work as a respected profession.

Addams was involved in a variety of social issues, including women's suffrage, education, child labor, and peace. A founder of the Women's International League for Peace and Freedom (WILPF) and president of the Women's International Peace Party, she saw her anti-war position as a natural extension of woman's role. Because such conflicts required women to bear sons to serve in combat, they presented a special threat to the stability of the family. The severe public criticism of her pacifism caused Addams great anguish, but she did not waver, and in 1931 she was awarded the Nobel Prize for Peace.

Many women throughout the world have set their faces unalterably against war. This is our reason for our organization against war. I head a movement planned to unite womanhood, in all parts of the world, in a great protest against Europe's war. It is called the Women's Peace Party and is international in scope. It began its existence at Washington, and is increasing in membership with astonishing rapidity.

As women we are the custodians of the life of the ages and we will not longer consent to its reckless destruction. We are particularly charged with the future of childhood, the care of the helpless and the unfortunate, and we will not longer endure without protest that added burden of maimed and invalid men and poverty-stricken women and orphans which war places on us.

We have builded by the patient drudgery of the past the basic foundations of the home and of peaceful industry; we will not longer endure that hoary evil which in an hour destroys or tolerate that denial of the sovereignty of reason and justice by which war and all that makes for war today render impotent the idealism of the race.

Therefore we demand that our right to be consulted in the settlement of questions concerning not alone the life of individuals but of nations be recognized and respected, that women be given a share in deciding between war and peace.

Some of the objects we are working on to obtain, are limitations of armaments and the nationalization of their manufacture; organized opposition to militarism in our own country and education of youth in the ideals of peace; democratic control of foreign policies; the further humanizing of Governments by the extension of the franchise to women; "concert of nations" to supercede

WOMEN, WAR ...   Reprinted from Harper's Magazine Foundation July 31, 1915. All rights reserved, 101.

"balance of power;" action toward the gradual organization of the world to substitute law for war.

We also believe in the substitution of an international police for rival armies and navies; removal of the economic causes of war; the appointment by our Government of a commission of men and women, with an adequate appropriation, to promote international peace.

At the present moment women in Europe are being told: "Bring children into the world for the benefit of the nation; for the strengthening of future battle lines; forget everything that you have been taught to hold dear; forget your long struggle to establish the responsibilities of fatherhood; forget all but the appetite of war for human flesh. It must be satisfied and you must be the ones to feed it, cost what it may.

This war is destroying the home unit in the most highly civilized countries of the world to an extent which is not less than appalling. Could there be a more definite and dreadful illustration of the tendencies of war to break down and destroy the family unit? All such consequences of war mitigate against the age long efforts of woman to establish the paternity of her child and the father's responsibility for it.

In the interest of this effort the State has made marriage a matter of license and record, and the Church has surrounded it by every possible sanctity. Under the pressure of war, however, both of these institutions have in a large measure withdrawn their protection.

All that women have held dear, all that the Church has worked for and the State has ordered, has been swept away in a breath—the hot breath of war—leaving woman in her primitive, pitiable state of the necessity of self-defence, without the strength with which to compass self-defense. So long as a State, through the exigencies of war, is obliged to place military authority above all civil rights, women can have within it no worthy place, no opportunity for their development, and they cannot hope for authority in its councils.

Thousands of them in Europe, as in the United States had become so thoroughly imbued with the idea that the recognition of the sacredness of human life had at last become established, throughout the world, that the news of this war to them came as an incredible shock. Women are entitled in all justice to some consideration in this matter of war making, if only because they have necessarily been paramount in the nurture of that human life which is now being so lavishly spent.

The advanced nations know very accurately, and we have begun to know in America, how many children are needlessly lost in the first years of infancy. Measures inaugurated for the prevention of infant mortality were slowly spreading from one country to another. All that effort has been scattered to the winds by the war. No one is now pretending to count the babies who are dying throughout the villages and countrysides of the warring nations.

DRAFTING DAUGHTERS

Ellen Goodman

Ellen Goodman (b. 1941) is a journalist whose syndicated column appears in over 250 newspapers. Born in Newton, MA, she graduated *cum laude* from Radcliffe in 1963, married, and had one daughter. Known as "an egghead's Erma Bombeck," she has won many awards, including a Nieman Fellowship in 1973 and the Pulitzer Prize for commentary in 1980.

Goodman wrote the following column before draft registration was reinstituted during President Carter's administration (1977-1981). Because the Equal Rights Amendment was before the states for ratification at the same time, a national debate arose over the question of whether or not young women should also be subject to the draft. Those citizens who opposed the registration of women tended to oppose the ERA as well, but for many women, the issue of registration presented a real dilemma. These women were committed to equality of rights and responsibilities, but they could not support war or the procedures which authorized preparation for war. Although the registration of males only was declared constitutional and females remained exempt, the dilemma remains.

My daughter is eleven, and as we watch the evening news, she turns to me seriously and says, "I don't like the way the world is doing things." Neither do I.

My daughter is eleven years and eight months old, to be precise, and I do not want her to grow up and be drafted. Neither does she.

My daughter is almost twelve, and thinks about unkindness and evil, about endangered species and war. I don't want her to grow up and be brutalized by war—as soldier or civilian.

As I read those sentences over, they seem too mild. What I want to say is that I am horrified by the very idea that she could be sent to fight for fossil fuel or fossilized ideas. What I want to say is that I can imagine no justification for war other than self-defense, and I am scared stiff about who has the power to decide what is "defense."

But now, in the last days before President Carter decides whether we will register young people and whether half of those young people will be female, I wonder about something else. Would I feel differently if my daughter were my son? Would I be more accepting, less anguished, at the notion of a son drafted, a son at war?

Would I beat the drums and pin the bars and stars on his uniform with pride? Would I look forward to him being toughened up, be proud of his heroism, and accept his risk as a simple fact of life?

DRAFTING DAUGHTERS   From *At Large*, New York: Summit Books, 1981, 112–113. © 1980, The Boston Globe Newspaper Company/Washington Post Writers Group. Reprinted with permission.

I cannot believe it.

So, when I am asked now about registering women for the draft along with men, I have to nod yes reluctantly. I don't want anyone registered, anyone drafted, unless it is a genuine crisis. But if there is a draft, this time it can't just touch our sons, like some civilized plague that leaves daughters alone to produce another generation of warriors.

We may have to register women along with men anyway. Women may not have won equal rights yet, but they have "won" equal responsibilities. A male-only draft may be ruled unconstitutional.

But at a deeper level, we have to register women along with men because our society requires it. For generations, war has been part of the rage so many men have held against women.

War is the hard-hat yelling at an equal rights rally, "Where were you at Iwo Jima?" War is in the man infuriated at the notion of a woman challenging veterans' preference. War is in the mind of the man who challenges his wife for having had a soft life.

War has often split couples and sexes apart, into lives built on separate realities. It has been part of the grudge of self-sacrifice, the painful gap of understanding and experience between men's and women's lives. It is the stuff of which alienation and novels are written.

But more awesomely, as a male activity, a rite of passage, a test of manhood, war has been gruesomely acceptable. Old men who were warriors have sent younger men to war as if it were their birthright. The women's role until recently was to wave banners and sing slogans, and be in need of protection from the enemy.

We all pretended that war was civilized. War had rules and battlegrounds. War did not touch the finer and nobler things, like women.

This was, of course, never true. The losers, the enemies, the victims, the widows of war were as brutalized as the soldiers. Under duress and in defense, women always fought.

But, perhaps, stripped of its maleness and mystery, its audience and cheerleaders, war can be finally disillusioned. Without the last trappings of chivalry, it can be seen for what it is: the last deadly resort.

So, if we must have a draft registration, I would include young women as well as young men. I would include them because they can do the job. I would include them because all women must gain the status to stop as well as to start wars. I would include them because it has been too easy to send men alone.

I would include them because I simply cannot believe that I would feel differently if my daughter were my son.

But Mother Teresa reminds us how often we think of the poor of the world as sand. Most of us live according to self-interest. The truly selfless are as rare as Nobel Prize winners.

But it is a question of how wide our definition of self-interest is and how much it rules our lives.

It is hard, at a time when many Americans feel desperate about their heating bills or their ability to buy a home of their own, to think about the emaciated child. It's hard when we haven't eliminated poverty in America to think about Calcutta. I don't fault this. It just is.

SIX

Workers

'Cause I'm a woman. . . .
I can bring home the bacon. . . . Fry it up in the pan. . . .
And never let you forget you're a man.*

SO SINGS THE SULTRY, dressed-for-success siren in the recent television commercial for perfume. Quite simply, this advertisement summarizes the popular image of today's working woman: assertive enough to be an executive, but seductive enough to wear perfume; independent enough to bring home the bacon, but domestic enough to cook it up in the pan. She manages it all—career, home, and family. But the truth of the matter is that the lives of women rarely match the popular images of them perpetuated by the media.

Cooking dinner? Just stir it up in the pan! The image of housework conveyed here belies the extent of the labor involved and the amount of time actually spent by women doing this work. A woman's status in the paid labor force notwithstanding, she does the cooking, along with the rest of the housework, or sees that someone else does. And in spite of all the labor saving devices invented for the home during the present

---

*Lyrics from *Enjoli* perfume commercial used with permission of Charles of the Ritz Group Ltd. © 1978 Charles of the Ritz Group Ltd.

century, women in the United States today spend just about as much time on household tasks as did their colonial sisters. For new duties have evolved to replace the outmoded ones. Whereas most women today no longer carry water from wells to heat for their children's baths, their grandmothers did not feel obligated to bathe their children as frequently as modern standards require. And today, although the laundry is no longer boiled on the stove top, people wash their clothes more than they did a generation ago.

Prior to the 1970s, with the exception of a few women shown in service or "helping" occupations, television commercials rarely portrayed women doing out-of-the-home work. This lack of attention to women's work roles outside the home helped to foster the popular myth that women have only recently entered the paid labor force. However, the facts discredit this image as well. Women were, in fact, among the first wage-earners in this country. Over time what has changed is the proportion of women in paid employment. From 1850 to 1900, for example, women's participation increased from 10 to 20 percent. More recently, the rate grew from 30 percent in 1947, to over 50 percent in 1980. Now more than 50 percent of married women work in paid labor, and the growth in the number of working mothers with preschool children is phenomenal. These figures, however, say nothing about housework and other labor, such as taking in boarders or doing laundry, tasks urban working-class women have done in their homes to stretch the family income.

Like the popular image of the working woman promoted in soap operas, romantic novels, magazine short stories, and countless other advertisements, the perfume commercial leads to the conclusion that women have glamorous, exciting, high-paying careers, and compete with men for top jobs. The sweet smelling superwoman in the perfume commercial is, after all, wearing an expensive suit. But as "Mother" Jones chided over sixty years ago, "women don't have careers, . . . they have jobs." And time has not proved Mother Jones wrong. The employment rates of black, immigrant, and working-class women, groups excluded from high status positions by education and opportunity, always have been higher than those for middle-class white women. Moreover, eight out of ten women in paid employment today work in non-professional, non-technical, non-managerial jobs; more than a third are in clerical jobs. As the documents illustrate, these women face a number of problems generated by the low-status, low-paying, dead-end nature of their work.

Also, women tend to be clustered in a smaller number of occupations than men, and those women in professional or managerial positions find themselves in traditionally "feminine" fields such as nursing and elementary school teaching, not in the more "masculine" ones such as surgery and engineering. This clearly belies the myth that women are contesting with men for jobs. Moreover, women do not hold the high paying jobs. Full-time, year-round women workers earn considerably less than their male counterparts. The discrepancy, amounting to about forty percent, has changed very little in the past thirty-five years, despite passage of the Equal Pay Act in 1963. Thus, the adage, "A woman earns fifty-nine cents for a man's dollar."

Protective legislation, passed early in this century, based on an ideology viewing women as a "national resource" because of their childbearing function, ultimately contributed to the segregation and wage differentials in the labor force. These laws, which restricted the number of hours women could work, limited the shift work they could do, established a separate minimum wage for women, and limited the weight they were allowed to lift, were overturned in 1964 by the provisions of Title VII of the Civil Rights Act. This law also banned sexual discrimination by employers, unions, and employment agencies. Today, much ado is made of the few class action suits rendering large financial compensation to victims of sexual discrimination. But as the article on women coal miners, included here, demonstrates, going through the process of suing can be a harrowing experience. In addition, many claim that in the last few years, the government has not aggressively enforced sexual discrimination laws. Nor, critics charge, has much been done to undo other systematic biases leading to unequal reception of unemployment compensation and social security benefits by women and men. Government inaction upholds the status quo slowing down movements toward equality.

Many analysts speculate that the growing awareness of inequalities, especially among office workers, may put new life in the dying labor movement. Until very recently, neither management nor organized labor saw clerical workers as possible recruits for the unions. They based this assessment on stereotyped assumptions about the women in these jobs: that they identified with management, only worked for "pin money," and were only temporary members of the work force. But groups like Nine-to-Five are organizing office workers to improve their working conditions, increase their wages and upgrade their fringe benefits. Such efforts, along with laws prohibiting sexual discrimination by employers and unions alike, have led management and labor to take a new look at these workers, re-examining their potential for unionization.

Historically women played an active role in the labor movement. They contributed as both leaders and as rank and file members. They were among the first strikers in the early nineteenth century. Many went to jail for their efforts; some lost their lives. And Sarah Bagley and Mary Harris "Mother" Jones rank among the best labor organizers of the past two centuries. Yet, by 1940, in "Union Maid," the most popular song about women in the labor movement, Woody Guthrie's heroine, summing up organized labor's post-Depression perspective toward women, advised, "You girls who want to be free/Just take a tip from me!/Get you a man who's a union man/And join the Ladies' Auxiliary. . . ."

Even if the woman in the perfume commercial does land a job in the executive suite, she will most likely find herself in a position lacking power and opportunity. To add to her ineffectiveness, she will be treated as a token, expected to represent "the woman's point of view," and evaluated as a member of that group, not on the basis of her individual talents. Any inefficaciousness on her part will be blamed on her biological makeup or her "inappropriate upbringing." The saying, "Women just aren't raised to be managers," is part of the ideology justifying women's lack of success in the corporation. The corporation will treat her to seminars and games to teach her how to manage and urge her to improve her self-image and consider her self-interests. The structural arrangements of the corporation itself will seldom, if ever, be listed among the barriers to her advancement. And the organization will expect her to accept the structure if she wants to make her way up the corporate ladder.

But sooner or later, management material or otherwise, she will burn the bacon. For in spite of the superwoman myth, unless she is affluent, she will find her juggling act—job, family, housework—exhausting. The support systems necessary to maintain this triple burden are not in place in our society. But there have been times in our history when these provisions were there. During World War II, companies commonly made child-care facilities available. Unfortunately, employers promptly closed them down at the war's end when they gave many women workers pink slips. Our nation currently lacks an explicit child-care policy, and little hope is in sight that we will develop one providing benefits or services to all working parents. The assumption that child-care and domestic duties are women's work still prevails. And until such imagery disappears, speaking of women's work strictly in terms of their paid employment will be impossible.

A CHAPTER ON HOUSEKEEPING

Fanny Fern

Housework, although necessary to the operations of the economy, continues to be a low power, low status, usually non-remunerative job. And it has not been uncommon for some twentieth-century social commentators to equate housewifery with idleness. Hence, many people were shocked when a contemporary researcher compiled a list of eighty separate tasks involved in doing housework and when other analysts calculated the high cost for a housewife's work were a family forced to pay to have it done commercially.

Although the technology of housework has changed from the nineteenth century, many other characteristics remain the same. In the following amusing portrait of Mrs. Carrot, Fanny Fern takes some potshots at overzealous housekeeping but she captures, as well, much of the unending drudgery of this gender-linked work.

I NEVER could see the reason why your smart housekeepers must, of necessity, be Xantippes. I once had the misfortune to be domesticated during the summer months with one of this genus.

I should like to have seen the adventurous spider that would have dared to ply his cunning trade in Mrs. Carrot's premises! Nobody was allowed to sleep a wink after daylight, beneath her roof. Even her old rooster crowed one hour earlier than any of her neighbors'. "Go ahead," was written on every broom-stick in the establishment.

She gave her husband his breakfast, buttoned up his overcoat, and put him out of the front door, with his face in the direction of the store, in less time than I've taken to tell it. Then she snatched up the six little Carrots; scrubbed their faces, up and down, without regard to feelings or noses, till they shone like a row of milk pans.

"Clear the track" was her motto, washing and ironing days. She never drew a long breath till the wash-tubs were turned bottom upwards again, and every article of wearing apparel sprinkled, folded, ironed, and replaced on the backs of their respective owners. It gave me a stitch in the side to look at her!

As to her "cleaning days," I never had courage to witness one. I used to lie under an apple tree in the orchard, till she was through. A whole platoon of soldiers would n't have frightened me so much as that virago and her mop.

You should have seen her in her glory on "baking days;" her sleeves rolled up to her arm-pits, and a long, check apron swathed around her bolster-like

A CHAPTER ON HOUSEKEEPING   From *Fern Leaves from Fanny's Port-folio, Second Series*, Buffalo, N.Y.: Orton, and Mulligan, 1854, pp. 371–72.

figure. The great oven glowing, blazing, and sparkling, in a manner very suggestive, to a lazy sinner, like myself. The interminable rows of greased pie-plates; the pans of rough and ready gingerbread; the pots of pork and beans, in an edifying state of progression; and the immense embryo loaves of brown and wheaten bread. To my innocent inquiry, whether she thought the latter would "rise," she set her skinny arms akimbo, marched up within kissing distance of my face, cocked her head on one side, and asked if I thought she looked like a woman to be trifled with by a loaf of bread!" The way I settled down into my slippers, without a reply, probably convinced her that I was no longer skeptical on that point.

Saturday evening she employed in winding up everything that was unwound in the house—the old entry clock included. From that time till Monday morning, she devoted to her husband and Sabbatical exercises. All I have to say is, it is to be hoped she carried some of the fervor of her secular employments into those halcyon hours.

AMERICAN WOMAN'S DILEMMA

After World War II the social ideology in the United States shifted its emphasis from woman as worker to woman as homemaker and mother. Changes in social ideologies do not, of course, occur in isolation from other social forces. Many analysts agree that powerful economic inducements lay behind the efforts to convince women that their place was in the home, having and raising children, not in the paid labor force. An inability of the system to provide full employment and an increasing emphasis on the consumption of household durable goods helped create a hothouse for the growth of the "feminine mystique." Although this social ideology focused primarily on white, middle-class women, its repercussions affected the lives of all women in the United States regardless of class or color.

The selection below appeared in *Life*, one of the most popular pictorial magazines of this century. First issued as a weekly at 10 cents a copy in November, 1936, *Life* suspended regular publication in 1972. Ten special issues appeared between 1972 and 1978. In October, 1978 *Life* returned to the newsstands as a monthly, costing $1.50 but still devoted, according to its editors, to the "picture magic" that had made its predecessor so popular. (Note: *Sic* refers to pictures not included.)

 Mrs. John McWeeney of Rye, N.Y. has a big, good-looking husband who works in a nut and bolt company and three children, Shawn, a grave little 4-year-old; John, called "Rusty," almost 2, and baby Mark, 4 months old. She lives in a bright new seven-room house that has a safe backyard for Shawn and Rusty to play in and a number of modern machines to help her with her household chores. She uses a diaper

AMERICAN WOMAN'S DILEMMA *Life*, June 16, 1947, 101. © 1947 Time, Inc. Frances Levison, *Life* Magazine © 1947, Time Inc. Reprinted with permission.

service and she can afford a cleaning woman once a week who does the heavy laundry.

But even under these better than average circumstances Marjorie McWeeney's hours are long and her work demanding. She must keep an eye on her children during their 70 waking hours a week and also watch over them when they are supposed to be in bed but may actually be popping down the stairs to ask for water or an extra goodnight kiss.

The picture at the left [sic] shows the household tasks that Marjorie must accomplish every week. She has a crib and four beds to make up each day, totaling 35 complete bed-makings a week. She has hundreds of knives, forks and utensils to wash, food to buy and prepare for a healthy family of five and a whole house to dust and sweep. Every day of the week Marjorie must stick to the minimum schedule of chores listed in the time column.

Actually Marjorie's chores are much lighter than they would have been a few generations ago. She cleans with machinery propelled by electricity, she uses food prepared in canneries, she buys clothes factory-made to fit every member of the family. But her jobs, though relieved of old-time drudgery, have none of the creative satisfactions of home baking, home preserving, home dressmaking. And, because her family unit is small with no aunts or cousins in the household, all the time she saves from housework must go into supervision of her children. Unless she makes special arrangements with a baby-sitter, she has no relief from child care.

Many women in Marjorie's position feel that this is a life of drudgery, that it is not good for Marjorie, a graduate of a junior college, to stay with small children long, continuous hours. Marjorie herself has no desire to work outside. Because as an individual she likes the job that she does, she has no problem right now. Like most busy young housewives, however, she gives little thought to the future—to satisfactory ways of spending the important years after her children have grown up and left home.

HER WORK

    6:30 NURSE BABY
    7:15 DRESS SHAWN, RUSTY
    7:30 FIX BREAKFAST
    7:45 BREAKFAST FOR ALL
    8:00 HUSBAND JOHN TO WORK
          WASH DISHES
          CLEAN DOWNSTAIRS
          CALL GROCER'S
    9:00 SHAWN, RUSTY IN YARD
          BATHE BABY
          MAKE BEDS
          CLEAN UPSTAIRS
   10:30 NURSE BABY
   11:00 FIX LUNCH
   11:30 LUNCH FOR SHAWN, RUSTY
   12:00 JOHN HOME
          LUNCH WITH JOHN

```
1:00  JOHN TO WORK
      NAPS FOR SHAWN, RUSTY
      WASH DISHES
      NAP FOR MARJORIE
2:30  NURSE BABY
2:45  ROUSE SHAWN, RUSTY
3:00  SHAWN, RUSTY PLAY
      GARDENING OUTDOORS
              OR
      MENDING INDOORS
5:00  FRUIT JUICE FOR BABY
      FIX SUPPER
5:30  SUPPER FOR SHAWN, RUSTY
6:00  JOHN HOME
      BATHS FOR SHAWN, RUSTY
6:30  SHAWN, RUSTY IN BED
      NURSE BABY
7:00  DRESS FOR DINNER
7:15  COCKTAIL WITH JOHN
7:30  FIX DINNER
8:00  DINNER WITH JOHN
9:00  WASH DISHES
10:30 NURSE BABY
10:45 TAKE SHAWN, RUSTY
      TO BATHROOM
11:00 BED
```

FULL-TIME CAREER

Many young girls go right on working at fulltime jobs after they get married because they find offices and factories more satisfying than housework and child care. This is a good plan but only if they are very successful and earn enough money to provide their children with secure and well-run homes.

The two women pictured [sic] at left have exceptional careers. One runs her own public relations firm, the other is a top-ranking lawyer. Together with their husbands they have family incomes which run well into five figures. Their households are staffed with expertly trained help, so that they can enjoy their non-working hours in leisurely comfort with their children.

But for Mrs. Joseph Gloss, a factory employee, things are not so simple. She and her husband do not make enough money to hire a servant and have had to board out their 4-year-old son during the week. Recently a sister came to stay and look after the child, but if she leaves, the mother will again have to resign herself to seeing her boy only on weekends.

IDLENESS

MILLIONS OF WOMEN FIND TOO MUCH LEISURE CAN BE HEAVY BURDEN

The Bureau of Labor Statistics lists 20 million women, nearly half of all adult female Americans, as essentially idle. They do not have children under 18, they are not members of the labor force, they do not work on farms, nor are they aged or infirm. With not nearly enough to do, many of them are bored stiff.

The fact that time hangs heavily on their hands is not entirely their fault. Many are over 40 and belong to a generation which frowned on work for any but poverty-stricken women. Their husbands have worked hard to give them an easeful life. Now that they have it, it is a burden. This is because an untrained woman has difficulty finding satisfying tasks to fill her days. Social work, which once busied many women, is now largely handled by professionals. As a result, many of these "idle" women fall back on numbing rounds of club meetings and card-playing. They read too much low-grade fiction and escape too readily into dream realms of movies and soap operas.

It is this group that has become the butt of the cartoonists and of critical social commentators. Marynia Farnham and Ferdinand Lundberg, in their best-seller, *Modern Woman: The Lost Sex*, complain, "Some unknown percentage of the women classified as housewives are functionally little more than wastrels seething into afternoon movies, tea shops, cocktail lounges, expensive shopping centers."

In this desert of wasted time, a few women, particularly young ones, nevertheless, are discovering that there are more satisfying and useful ways of spending their days.

PART-TIME CAREER

One solution for a bored housewife or an idle woman is the part-time career. It is usually possible for a housewife, once her children are off to school, to find a few hours a week to begin a program of absorbing work. As her children grow independent, she can give more and more time to her outside interests.

Young women who can afford to work without pay can make useful, satisfying careers out of civic and charitable work if they take time to develop professional skills like Mrs. Johnson. Part-time jobs are harder to find and not all are as glamorous as that of the television announcer on the opposite page [sic]. But the other women shown here have all found jobs they like.

In some communities play clubs for children and group sitter plans are giving housewives time to spend away from home. Multiple laundries, "washeterias," where women can do their washing pleasantly and quickly by machine, are helping too. Once she has arranged for free hours, it is up to each woman to fill this time with really satisfying efforts. She will find it much easier to make a beginning at this while still in her 20s and 30s.

If she finds none of the jobs in these pictures suited to her individual needs, she might read books for a publisher, do research projects for an author, write scripts for local radio broadcasts. She might prefer to bake cakes at home for community sale. She might open a bookshop, run a circulating library of art prints for the town museum, design Christmas cards, sell real estate, open a school for women's handwork, become a laboratory assistant in a hospital or work on a town slum-clearance project with other women. She might discover that certain businesses in her locale such as department stores are giving their regular staff two-day weekends and need part-time help to fill in the extra days.

When she finds really satisfying work to do she will discover that she is more interesting to her friends, to her husband and to herself. . . .

I'M NOT YOUR GIRL

Jill Nelson

While the popular television image of the domestic service worker, be it Hazel or Florida, portrays her as ruling the roost, the opposite is true for most women in these jobs. In many instances, the employer's evaluation of "good help" tends to be based as much on a domestic's willingness to appear docile as on her ability to cook and clean. To add to their powerlessness, domestic service workers, many of whom come from minority or immigrant backgrounds, are locked into the subterranean economy. And, they work in isolation making it difficult for them to share problems or vent frustrations with peers. Some observers see it as ironic that the liberation of middle-class women comes, in part, at the expense of their lower-class sisters. As the one group moves into the paid labor force in ever increasing numbers, it seeks to employ domestic help from the other.

In the article below, *Essence* contributor Jill Nelson notes some of the attempts underway to organize domestic service workers, enhance their wage-earning and bargaining power, and increase their control over hiring and other labor-relations practices.

"She just called me up and told me it wasn't going to work out—after eight years," says Geraldine Miller, shaking her gray head. "There was no unemployment, no two weeks notice, no nothing," she finishes in disgust. The call firing Geraldine from her job with a Larchmont, N.Y., family came in 1975. Miller was hurt and angry at being fired by the woman whose children she had taken care of for eight years, but she was not surprised. Geraldine has been a household worker for nearly 30 years, ten of them as an organizer with the Bronx Household Technicians union (BHT). These years have taught Geraldine that there are few legal protections in her profession, fewer courtesies and no adequate safeguards against employers' abuses.

Geraldine grew up in Sabetha, Kan., and planned to go to college on money her aunt had put aside for that. She left school at 16, however, to work as a professional dancer, having studied dance since she was five. She danced all over the United States, "from Omaha to Ocean City, N.J.," she says with a laugh, but quit at 35 because she "was never going to be a big wiz" and "was tired of living out of a bag." Geraldine found herself in New York City without a job. She worked briefly as a wrapper at Saks Fifth Avenue, waitressed at Bickford's (a local cafeteria chain) and tried various other jobs.

But after nearly 20 years of being her own boss, her self-respect, coupled with a stubborn sense of her own worth, led to personality clashes with employers and co-workers, which usually ended with her looking for other work. "I got into household work for two reasons," says Geraldine. "It's something that's constant, the kind of work you can always get if you're good at it. It's also a good line of work for independent people like me. I found that,

---

in other jobs, the workers or the bosses resented excellence. With household work the better you are at it, the less trouble you have."

Geraldine Miller likes household work because it suits her personality. To Carolyn Reed household work is her creative art. "I get the same satisfaction out of it that I assume you do from being a journalist," she says. "When I can organize and manage a house, plan a dinner party—especially when it's someone else's money—I enjoy doing that."

Carolyn, director of the National Committee on Household Employment (NCHE) since 1978, lived in Orangeburg, S.C., as a child and returned to her native New York at 16. Now 40, she's a plump woman with large round eyes and cheeks that rise when she smiles. NCHE was founded in 1964 by the U.S. Department of Labor to upgrade the status of private household workers; it came under the National Urban League umbrella in 1971.

"I don't think people expected us to become the activist organization that we are," Carolyn says. "But if we're ever to professionalize the job and not be excluded from the labor laws, we have to organize."

Of course that's easier said than done. It's even hard to know how many women need to be organized. Geraldine Miller's Bronx Household Technicians is one of 45 NCHE affiliates. NCHE represents 10,000 of the estimated 1.2 million household workers. Both Carolyn and Geraldine, however, insist that this U.S. Department of Labor figure is inaccurate. "To any figures the government puts out about household workers, I add 500,000," says Carolyn with a laugh, "and even that figure is probably low." The nature of household work makes an accurate count difficult. Most jobs are found by word of mouth, and women either work for three or four households simultaneously or move rapidly from family to family.

Household workers have been covered by the Federal Social Security Act since 1951 and by the Fair Labor Law requiring minimum wage and overtime coverage since 1974. These laws, hard to enforce, are often ignored. For instance most states' laws clearly deny household workers minimum wage and collective bargaining protections. Those states, such as New York, that include household workers in labor laws do so by provisions that are vague and are essentially unenforceable.

The real stumbling block to dignity and decent wages for household workers is the stigma of the work itself. Both workers and employers think there's something somehow wrong with cleaning house for a living. "There are domestic workers who feel they're not as good as other people because of the work they do. They hide the fact that they do housework," says Geraldine Miller. "You see them with their little attaché cases, dressed to a tee like they're secretaries, but the truth is they're household workers." Geraldine laughs when she says this, a bitter laugh. How can you organize workers who won't admit that they do the work?

"Household work has always been demeaning in the eyes of both the worker and the employer," states Geraldine. "Pay is low and there are no benefits. You're given certain things instead of being paid enough to buy them."

She talks about the centuries-old division of Black labor: "Many slave women worked in the homes. There was a division between the house slaves and the field slaves. I don't see any wrong in doing either job," she says, shrugging. "The fact is, they were alive. Both types were slaves as far as I'm concerned, but most people don't look at it that way. What's happened is, these two types of slaves have been put against each other, and I think it has come down through the ages since slavery." Thoughtfully she adds, "After a certain length of time, other work became 'something' and household work stayed the same. It's as if it hasn't changed since slavery."

Though slavery was abolished over 100 years ago and numerous laws have since been written to protect workers from such servitude, the stigma of slavery still haunts household work. Those of us who aren't household workers often think less of those who are—in a way, we accuse them of volunteer slavery. For many household workers the work they do is an embarrassing secret, referred to—if at all—by euphemisms.

One New York household worker is a 61-year-old woman who receives no social security, health care or unemployment benefits. Soon she will be too old to work and without any means of support. Asked what kind of work she does, she avoids the question, then finally answers, "I'm a domestic," in a hushed, shamed voice. "I'm just doing this temporarily" or "My family is very nice to me" or "What do we need a union for?"—these are the responses of the women pushing white children in prams along the sidewalks of the more expensive neighborhoods in this country. The realities of life for household workers are harsher than these women even admit, especially to themselves.

The average domestic worker in the United States is a Black woman in her fifties. She heads her household alone and has an eighth grade education. "Most household workers haven't had the education or the experience to go into other types of work. If you're a woman, it's a given that you know how to do housework," Carolyn Reed says. Recently, a New York Bar Association report on household workers advocated their unionizing. Their average yearly wage was cited as $2,609. While Carolyn estimates a slightly higher $3,167 per year, both figures are well below $5,500, the Social Security Administration's assessment of the annual value of work done by a homemaker. In addition both figures fall below the maximum welfare grant allowable in New York State for a single woman with one child: $3,996 annually.

In the ignored, often illegal, world of the household worker, Lily Harrison is one of the lucky ones. She works in five different homes five days a week. Her annual salary is $4,000. On that she supports herself and her 14-year-old son. Her older daughter (a student in Washington, D.C., who works at IBM) is self-supporting. Lily spends a good portion of her wages calling or going to see her daughter. Like any mother, she buys her children an occasional gift or sends her daughter a package from home.

Lily is youthful and active at 43. The color of polished mahogany, she wears her hair in a French twist and dresses like the Southern school girls of the 1950s—a neat skirt, blouse with Peter Pan collar and a cardigan. Although she has lived in New York City since 1956, she still speaks with a Southern accent. In Wadley, Ga., she was the daughter of a sharecropper and a household worker. Lily naturally "helped out" around the farm after school, being paid only at the owner's discretion.

"I was makin' ten dollars a week at a restaurant at home when I was offered $20 a week to work in New York. At the time $20 a week sounded like a lot," Lily says, laughing. "I was sleeping in with a family. I prepared the meals, did the laundry, took care of the kids—everything. The people I worked for were always out; so I took care of the kids 24 hours a day except Thursday and every other Sunday, my days off."

When she was let go after five years, Lily ran a department store elevator in White Plains, N.Y., but returned to household work because the store's air conditioning bothered her. She made the same money—$42 a week *gross* in the 1960s.

"I really like the work I do," Lily says softly, sitting in her cheerful, worn but spotless kitchen. "I like to do things around the house. I've learned the value of things, how to take care of this, how to clean that. I am also somewhere that I'm not just a number. At work people really appreciate what I do. I get honor from what I do."

It wasn't always that way. The physical demands of household work and the slave hours combine with the stigma to wear on the worker and other people who are close to her. "I had a friend. He was a teacher. I think he really did like me," says Lily, who is divorced. "It was just that I figured, 'What would he want with a household worker?' So I didn't pursue the relationship. I guess I must have thought less of myself at that time. I just let that one go by."

Lily Harrison met Geraldine Miller on the train nearly ten years ago. Lily was going to work in Larchmont when Geraldine—working in Crestwood at the time—walked from car to car handing out literature on household workers' rights and talking with women on their way to work. "She bugged me every day," Lily says, shaking her head at the memory. "She used to talk about getting us together, how we needed more benefits. In those days no one was getting any benefits at all."

In 1975, following seven years of Geraldine's bugging, Lily joined BHT. "I feel I'm just as good as anyone else now. I really do," Lily says proudly, the shyness that usually covers her momentarily gone. "When I walk the street I can hold my head up against anyone who's walking that street, because I'm proud of what I do." Her first action as an activist was to give literature from BHT and NCHE to her five employers and demand the workers' benefits to which she was legally entitled. "I just told them," she says with pride, modestly smoothing her hair. "They read the laws and agreed to pay the benefits—social security, unemployment, minimum wage."

Lily's experience is unique. Geraldine has been fired for asking her employer to pay her workers' benefits, and both she and Carolyn Reed say that's not uncommon. A strong organization of household workers, both women agree, would make it nearly impossible for someone to hire household help without paying these benefits. "Sometimes women will work months and months with no time off and very low pay, especially foreigners who are not in this country legally," Lily says. "If more people took the risk and spoke up for their rights, we'd *all* be a lot further along," she insists.

Carolyn Reed dismisses the suggestion that an influx of women from the Caribbean and Latin America has "stolen" household jobs that would have gone to American women. "We don't have enough women to fill all the places," she says. "That's a split that people are trying to create. If you keep people at the bottom fighting among themselves, they won't fight the person who is really ripping them off," she says angrily. Carolyn thinks that many employers deliberately hire illegal aliens from the Caribbean, Latin America or Mexico. Women in the United States illegally are unlikely to report employers' abuses. "When I pick up *The New York Times* and see 'Jamaican preferred,' I say, 'Aha, that's somebody who wants to rip off a household worker,'" Carolyn says. "Our fight is for these women, not against them." "What difference is there," asks Geraldine Miller, "if a household worker from Jamaica, West Indies, is paid less than minimum wage and so is a household worker from Jamaica, N.Y.?"

Carolyn Reed's organizing efforts for NCHE have found support in unlikely places. To her surprise it has been easier to organize in the South than anywhere else in the country. She remembers an early NCHE effort in Auburn, Ala., where, in 1971, household workers organized and won pay levels well above the minimum wage. It was a success that's been hard for NCHE to duplicate.

"There aren't nearly as many cultural differences in the South," Carolyn notes. "Most of the women are Black and from similar backgrounds." She's found the most resistance to a household workers' union in Northern areas, where the workers' market is shared by white ethnic and Caribbean women. "Many of these women have a deep distrust of each other," Carolyn says. "It's gotten to the point that people think this is a Black women's organization. Of course it isn't but it is hard recruiting a variety of women for NCHE."

A basic element in organizing household workers is building a support base among organizations already existing in the community. NCHE has worked with organizations as diverse as the United Auto Workers and the National Congress of Neighborhood Women. "We go and contact civil rights groups, women's groups, church organizations," Carolyn explains. "We give them our code of standards and propaganda and talk with them about what we are trying to do.

"We also go into neighborhoods where household workers are and try to get stories from them regarding the conditions under which they work. We plan a social event at every meeting, too, because a lot of people, after working hard, don't want to get together and work hard again. We hold educational events to tell women how to find out if their employer is paying social security, or we have someone from a union come in and speak."

Geraldine's work with Bronx Household Technicians is much the same. "It's very difficult," she says with a sigh and shake of her head. "I make up leaflets and give them out in neighborhoods where household workers live. We hand them out on corners where people get buses to go to work." BHT has monthly meetings to discuss workers' and community issues, job-related problems and possible solutions.

Carolyn Reed and Geraldine Miller emphasize that many of the women who do household work are regular church members. They feel sure that if they could take their organizing efforts into the churches, it would be a giant step forward. This step, too, has been difficult. "Even in the church I attend," says Geraldine, "they don't want to hear about organizing household workers. I have found that it's not so much the pastor as the women themselves. They do not want to relate to household workers, even though a lot of them are doing household work themselves."

In the last few years feminist organizations have begun to work with NCHE and some of its affiliates. This help is viewed with some skepticism and a big dose of pragmatism. "It's out of their guilt that they're helping," declares

Carolyn Reed. "I will take that help out of guilt, out of anything, as long as they're helping and they come across with the money." Recently Carolyn has been interviewing the household workers of prominent feminists to see if feminist theories about the dignity of women are being put into practice. Her findings so far here have been unsettling. "The majority of them are exploiting their housekeepers," she says indignantly. "The workers tell stories you would not believe. The only one who has been consistent is Gloria Steinem, and I swear that's because she knows I live across the street and can see what she is doing," Carolyn says with a laugh.

According to Carolyn, many feminist employers do not pay social security or other benefits. They argue that their household workers ask them not to make deductions and prefer to receive all the money in cash at the end of the week. "I tell them, 'Listen,'" Carolyn says, leaning forward in her chair and pointing with her index finger, "'if this person was working in your office and said, "Don't take social security out," you wouldn't have that person working for you. So what's the difference?'"

Interestingly Black women—in some sense a natural constituency—have ignored the issue of organizing household workers until recently. Their reluctance to discuss it discourages the organizers. "Black women who have made it a little higher than we have, who have a little more education, feel as if we're not worthy of their help," says Carolyn. "Possibly they feel that it's beneath them, it's something they'd like to forget, as if nobody in their family ever did housework. It's ridiculous. Every last one of us has had somebody in our lives who did housework.

"Most of our support in the last ten years has come from the white women's movement," Carolyn concedes, "more than from organizations like the Urban League or the other civil rights groups. The problem seems to be that those who are in other professions aren't dealing with the fact that their mothers and grandmothers have scrubbed floors so that they could get that education."

Carolyn and Geraldine frequently address this lack of awareness in their organizing work. Carolyn travels around the country making speeches and attending conferences as NCHE's representative. She publishes a monthly newsletter with information about NCHE affiliate activities and a calendar of events and collects data on household workers nationally through brief questionnaires. Geraldine Miller has directed a program funded by the Comprehensive Employment and Training Act (CETA) under the auspices of the National Congress of Neighborhood Women. The program offered workshops and training sessions for workers, employers and the public on such topics as professionalism, consumerism and health issues.

Besides feeling embarrassed about their work, being isolated by its stigma, being intimidated by their employers and being ignorant of their employee rights, many household workers also resist the idea of unionizing. Even among women who are members of NCHE affiliates, the resistance is present. "Unions frighten me off," says Lily Harrison shyly. "Mention 'union' and that really frightens off a lot of folks. When the leader of the union says, 'Do this or do that,' everybody has to fall right in," she explains. "If he says you don't work, you don't. And you sure don't get paid."

"There's a great deal of education that has to take place before we can even approach the prospect of forming a union," Geraldine Miller admits. Carolyn

Reed, however, adamantly supports unionizing, though she insists that household technicians must form their own union and not be absorbed as another category covered by an existing union. "In 1990 I would like there to be a household workers' union controlled by the workers themselves," Carolyn says.

"NCHE can't do it all," Geraldine insists. "We need the help of Black groups, white groups, any other kind of groups—groups that can help pass the word about household workers. That's the only way we're ever going to make gains—if groups of people come together and say, 'This is what we are for.'"

Carolyn Reed sits in her cubicle at the Urban League's New York City headquarters. Neat files and shelves line one wall; everything is in place and accessible. While Carolyn firmly insists she feels "uncomfortable" in her work as an administrator, she acknowledges that the benefits of working in a bureaucracy include file cabinets, Xerox machines and not having to dig for papers now at her fingertips. Asked what she hopes to accomplish in the next decade, she says, "I would like to work myself out of this job. I would like to return to household work, the work I really enjoy."

Every weekday morning Lily Harrison and dozens of other household workers gather at a bus stop in the Bronx to go to their jobs in Larchmont, Crestwood and other New York suburbs. During her 40-minute ride Lily Harrison talks to other workers about organizing for their rights. Sometimes it seems that the last thing the women want to talk about is the work they do; they prefer to forget it until they step off the bus at their destinations and go into the houses they maintain. But Lily Harrison is persistent, as Geraldine Miller was persistent with her. She takes the bus every day. It is not a burden talking about the organization because, for her, the issue is simple and clear. "I just want decent wages and the benefits that are due us," she says firmly. Maybe these are small goals, but for Lily, Carolyn and Geraldine, they seem large and elusive, as elusive as the women they are organizing.

HOW I FOUND AMERICA

Anzia Yezierska

In 1920, Yezierska's story, "The Fat of the Land" was named the best short story of 1919 and *Hungry Hearts,* containing "How I Found America," was published. Yezierska's writing career, spanning over fifty years, included short stories, novels, essays, and critical reviews. Whereas her earlier writings focused on the immigrant Jewish girl, she turned, in her seventies, to the theme of the mistreatment of the elderly. As her biographer, Carol Schoen says of her, "To both she brought a prophet's zeal for pointing out injustice at a time when the difficulties were only dimly appreciated." Born in Russia in 1880, Anzia Yezierska died in California in 1970.

Like other Jewish immigrant women from Eastern Europe, the narrator has come to America with her family in search of freedom from religious oppression as well as for economic security and political openness. Yezierska's story tells of the New York sweatshops of the early twentieth century to which the East Europeans were forced to look for work as the "No Irish Need Apply" signs of the 1850s and 1860s had been replaced by "No Jews . . ." for most other types of employment. The myth of America was sharply displaced by the misery of working and living conditions awaiting the unsuspecting immigrants.

. . . My eyes were shutting themselves with sleep. Blindly, I felt for the buttons on my dress, and buttoning I sank back in sleep again—the deadweight sleep of utter exhaustion.

"Heart of mine!" my mother's voice moaned above me. "Father is already gone an hour. You know how they'll squeeze from you a nickel for every minute you're late. Quick only!"

I seized my bread and herring and tumbled down the stairs and out into the street. I ate running, blindly pressing through the hurrying throngs of workers—my haste and fear choking each mouthful.

I felt a strangling in my throat as I neared the sweatshop prison; all my nerves screwed together into iron hardness to endure the day's torture.

For an instant I hesitated as I faced the grated window of the old dilapidated building—dirt and decay cried out from every crumbling brick.

In the maw of the shop, raging around me the roar and the clatter, the clatter and the roar, the merciless grind of the pounding machines. Half maddened, half deadened, I struggled to think, to feel, to remember—what am I—who am I—why was I here?

I struggled in vain—bewildered and lost in a whirlpool of noise.

"America—America—where was America?" it cried in my heart.

The factory whistle—the slowing-down of the machines—the shout of release hailing the noon hour.

I woke as from a tense nightmare—a weary waking to pain.

In the dark chaos of my brain reason began to dawn. In my stifled heart feelings began to pulse. The wound of my wasted life began to throb and ache. My childhood choked with drudgery—must my youth too die—unlived?

HOW I FOUND AMERICA   Anzia Yezierska, *Hungry Hearts,* Cambridge, MA: Houghton Mifflin Company, 1920, 265–73. Reprinted by permission.

The odor of herring and garlic—the ravenous munching of food—laughter and loud, vulgar jokes. Was it only I who was so wretched? I looked at those around me. Were they happy or only insensible to their slavery? How could they laugh and joke? Why were they not torn with rebellion against this galling grind—the crushing, deadening movements of the body, where only hands live and hearts and brains must die?

A touch on my shoulder. I looked up. It was Yetta Solomon from the machine next to mine.

"Here's your tea."

I stared at her, half hearing.

"Ain't you going to eat nothing?"

"Oi weh! Yetta! I can't stand it!" The cry broke from me. "I did n't come to America to turn into a machine. I came to America to make from myself a person. Does America want only my hands—only the strength of my body—not my heart—not my feelings—my thoughts?"

"Our heads ain't smart enough," said Yetta, practically. "We ain't been to school like the American-born."

"What for did I come to America but to go to school—to learn—to think—to make something beautiful from my life . . ."

"Sh-sh! Sh-sh! The boss—the boss!" came the warning whisper.

A sudden hush fell over the shop as the boss entered. He raised his hand.

Breathless silence.

The hard, red face with pig's eyes held us under its sickening spell. Again I saw the Cossack and heard him thunder the ukaz.

Prepared for disaster, the girls paled as they cast at each other sidelong, frightened glances.

"Hands," he addressed us, fingering the gold watch-chain that spread across his fat belly, "it's slack in the other trades and I can get plenty girls begging themselves to work for half what you're getting—only I ain't a skinner. I always give my hands a show to earn their bread. From now on, I'll give you fifty cents a dozen shirts instead of seventy-five, but I'll give you night-work, so you need n't lose nothing." And he was gone.

The stillness of death filled the shop. Each one felt the heart of the other bleed with her own helplessness.

A sudden sound broke the silence. A woman sobbed chokingly. It was Balah Rifkin, a widow with three children.

"Oi weh!" She tore at her scrawny neck. "The blood-sucker—the thief! How will I give them to eat—my babies—my babies—my hungry little lambs!"

"Why do we let him choke us?"

"Twenty-five cents less on a dozen—how will we be able to live?"

"He tears the last skin from our bones!"

"Why did n't nobody speak up to him?"

"Tell him he could n't crush us down to worse than we had in Russia?"

"Can we help ourselves? Our life lies in his hands."

Something in me forced me forward. Rage at the bitter greed tore me. Our desperate helplessness drove me to strength.

"I'll go to the boss!" I cried, my nerves quivering with fierce excitement. "I'll tell him Balah Rifkin has three hungry mouths to feed."

Pale, hungry faces thrust themselves toward me, thin, knotted hands reached out, starved bodies pressed close about me.

"Long years on you!" cried Balah Rifkin, drying her eyes with a corner of her shawl.

"Tell him about my old father and me, his only bread-giver," came from Bessie Sopolsky, a gaunt-faced girl with a hacking cough.

"And I got no father or mother and four of them younger than me hanging on my neck." Jennie Feist's beautiful young face was already scarred with the gray worries of age.

America, as the oppressed of all lands have dreamed America to be, and America *as it is*, flashed before me—a banner of fire! Behind me I felt masses pressing—thousands of immigrants—thousands upon thousands crushed by injustice, lifted me as on wings.

I entered the boss's office without a shadow of fear. I was not I—the wrongs of my people burned through me till I felt the very flesh of my body a living flame of rebellion.

I faced the boss.

"We can't stand it!" I cried. "Even as it is we're hungry. Fifty cents a dozen would starve us. Can you, a Jew, tear the bread from another Jew's mouth?"

"You, fresh mouth, you! Who are you to learn me my business?"

"Were n't you yourself once a machine slave—your life in the hands of your boss?"

"You—loaferin—money for nothing you want! The minute they begin to talk English they get flies in their nose. . . . A black year on you—trouble-maker! I'll have no smart heads in my shop! Such freshness! Out you get . . . out from my shop!"

Stunned and hopeless, the wings of my courage broken, I groped my way back to them—back to the eager, waiting faces—back to the crushed hearts aching with mine.

As I opened the door they read our defeat in my face.

"Girls!" I held out my hands. "He's fired me."

My voice died in the silence. Not a girl stirred. Their heads only bent closer over their machines.

"Here, you! Get yourself out of here!" The boss thundered at me. "Bessie Sopolsky and you, Balah Rifkin, take out her machine into the hall. . . . I want no big-mouthed Americanerins in my shop."

Bessie Sopolsky and Balah Rifkin, their eyes black with tragedy, carried out my machine.

Not a hand was held out to me, not a face met mine. I felt them shrink from me as I passed them on my way out.

In the street I found I was crying. The new hope that had flowed in me so strong bled out of my veins. A moment before, our togetherness had made me believe us so strong—and now I saw each alone—crushed—broken. What were they all but crawling worms, servile grubbers for bread?

I wept not so much because the girls had deserted me, but because I saw for the first time how mean, how vile, were the creatures with whom I had to work. How the fear for bread had dehumanized their last shred of humanity! I felt I had not been working among human beings, but in a jungle of savages who had to eat one another alive in order to survive.

And then, in the very bitterness of my resentment, the hardness broke in me. I saw the girls through their own eyes as if I were inside of them. What else could they have done! Was not an immediate crust of bread for Balah Rifkin's children more urgent than truth—more vital than honor?

Could it be that they ever had dreamed of America as I had dreamed? Had their faith in America wholly died in them? Could my faith be killed as theirs had been?

Gasping from running, Yetta Solomon flung her arms around me.

"You golden heart! I sneaked myself out from the shop—only to tell you I'll come to see you to-night. I'd give the blood from under my nails for you—only I got to run back—I got to hold my job—my mother—"

I hardly saw or heard her—my senses stunned with my defeat. I walked on in a blind daze—feeling that any moment I would drop in the middle of the street from sheer exhaustion.

Every hope I had clung to—every human stay—every reality was torn from under me. I sank in bottomless blackness. I had only one wish left—to die.

Was it then only a dream—a mirage of the hungry-hearted people in the desert lands of oppression—this age-old faith in America—the beloved, the prayed-for "golden country"?

Had the starved villagers of Sukovoly lifted above their sorrows a mere rainbow vision that led them—where—where? To the stifling submission of the sweatshop or the desperation of the streets!

"O God! What is there beyond this hell?" my soul cried to me. "Why can't I make a quick end to myself?"

A thousand voices within me and about me answered:

"My faith is dead, but in my blood their faith still clamors and aches for fulfillment—*dead generations whose faith though beaten back still presses on—a resistless, deathless force!*

"In this America that crushes and kills me, their spirit drives me on—to struggle—to suffer—but never to submit."

In my desperate darkness their lost lives loomed—a living flame of light. Again I saw the mob of dusty villagers crowding around my father as he read the letter from America—their eager faces thrust out—their eyes blazing with the same hope, the same age-old faith that drove me on—

A sudden crash against my back. Dizzy with pain I fell—then all was darkness and quiet. . . .

FEMININE WAITERS AT HOTELS
Fanny Fern

Although women dominate the waiting world numerically, male waiters tend to receive higher wages as they are more likely to be employed in exclusive restaurants. Whatever their title, most waitress jobs share the characteristics of other occupations in the secondary labor force: part-time work, unstable employment, low wages and little or no fringe benefits. In addition, waitresses must mediate between customers and cooks or bartenders. If the meal or drink is not satisfactory to the customer, she faces the threat of lost wages (tips). When praises are to be given, she is asked to relay compliments to the chef, manager or bartender. She bears the brunt of bad tempers on both ends of her tray, but she must always obey the dictum, "service with a smile."

Having worked as a seamstress herself, Fanny Fern nonetheless probably had good reason in 1854 to advise "poor pale-faced sempstresses" to "Throw your thimbles at the heads of your penurious employers". . . and apply for work as female waiters.

"Some of our leading hotel-keepers are considering the policy of employing female waiters."

Good news for you, poor pale-faced sempstresses! Throw your thimbles at the heads of your penurious employers; put on your neatest and *plainest* dress; see that your feet and fingers are immaculate, and then rush *en masse* for the situation, ousting every white jacket in Yankeedom. Stipulate with your employers, for leave to carry in the pocket of your French apron, a pistol loaded with cranberry sauce, to plaster up the mouth of the first coxcomb who considers it necessary to preface his request for an omelette, with *"My dear."* It is my opinion that one such hint will be sufficient; if not, you can vary the order of exercises, by anointing him with a "HASTY plate of soup" at dinner.

Always make a moustache wait twice as long as you do a man who wears a clean, presentable lip. Should he undertake to expedite your slippers by "a fee," tell him that hotel bills are *generally* settled at the clerk's office, except by *very* verdant travelers.

Should you see a woman at the table, digging down to the bottom of the salt cellar, as if the top stratum were too plebeian; or ordering ninety-nine messes (turning aside from each with affected airs of disgust,) or rolling up the whites of her eyes, declaring that she never sat down to a dinner-table before minus "finger glasses," you may be sure that her aristocratic blood is nourished, *at home,* on herrings and brown bread. When a masculine comes in with a white vest, flashy neck-tie, extraordinary looking plaid trousers, several yards of gold chain festooned over his vest, and a mammoth seal ring on his little finger, you may be sure that his tailor and his laundress are both on the anxious seat; and whenever you see travelers of *either* sex peregrinating the country in their "best

FEMININE WAITERS AT HOTELS   From *Fern Leaves from Fanny's Port-folio, Second Series,* Buffalo, NY: Miller, Orton and Mulligan, 1854, pp. 332–33.

bib and tucker," you can set them down for unmitigated "snobs," for high-bred people can't afford to be so extravagant!

I dare say you'll get sick of so much pretension and humbug. Never mind; it is better than to be stitching yourselves into a consumption over six-penny shirts; you'll have your fun out of it. This would be a horridly stupid world, if every body were sensible. I thank my stars every day, for the share of fools a kind Providence sends in my way.

STENOGRAPHY IN NEW YORK CITY
G.E.D.

We know little about the author of this letter except that she, like hundreds of other women, responded to a call from *Harper's Bazar* in January 1908 to write about their working experiences for a series called "The Girl Who Comes to the City: A Symposium." Letters submitted were to be "written by those girl readers who have gone through the experience of coming to the city and either succeeding or failing there, during the last ten years." Quite predictably, in September of that year, the editor announced, "Owing to the great amount of accepted material now awaiting publication in this department, no more contributions are desired."

Although the media has publicized the problem of sexual harassment of working women over the past decade or so, the following selection suggests that sexual harassment appears to be a perennial problem for women.

Five years ago my father and mother died within one month of each other, leaving me, at nineteen years of age, wholly dependent upon my own exertions. I had graduated from the high school at seventeen, taken a post-graduate course the year after, won a scholarship for college, where I had spent one year, when I was called home, not to return again.

After paying the expenses of my parents' illness and the funeral expenses, I counted as my sole worldly possession one hundred dollars. With this I determined to make my worldly career. A friend of mine advised me to become a stenographer as the surest and swiftest way of making a living. I took fifty dollars and learned stenography, and during the three months I spent in mastering it, I worked every spare moment I had, doing embroidery and other odd "jobs" which my friends or acquaintances happened to have and, knowing my circumstances, kindly let me do for them. This gave me sufficient spare money to pay my board and lodging, while I did my laundry work myself, thus leaving intact my remaining fifty dollars, which I wished to guard jealously to assist me until I could secure a much-needed position in some city.

After my three months of study and hard work I completed my course.

I left my native town in the Mohawk Valley one cold, blistering day in March for New York. The fear and trembling which filled my heart on that

---

STENOGRAPHY IN NEW YORK CITY   From *The Girl Who Comes to the City: A Symposium, Harper's Bazar*, March 3, 1908, pp. 277–78.

eventful day would be impossible to describe. When I arrived at the Grand Central Station I was met by some school acquaintances, who assured me that I would have no trouble in getting a position in a week or two at the longest. Their buoyant hopes helped to revive my spirits, and I felt quite like a new being as they took me to their boarding-place on West Twenty-fourth Street.

After a night's rest, I felt more like doing something. There is something about the noises, the teeming life, of New York which always puts new life into me, something of the fighting spirit; a feeling, as it were, that the fittest will survive.

I purchased several papers, and plodded faithfully through their multitude of "ads." I took the addresses of some I intended to call upon, and wrote several letters to those who gave no address. The first office I visited was a lawyer's. He wanted a stenographer, and would pay six dollars a week. I asked him if he thought a young lady could live in New York on that, and clothe herself. He said he expected young women had friends who helped them out. I was too indignant to speak for a moment, but when I got my breath I politely informed him that I was not that kind of a young woman, and bade him good afternoon. I went no farther that day; to be quite frank, I went back to my boarding-place and had a good cry, wondering if all men were like that. The next day I started out again, though in rather a dejected mood. The first "ad" I answered the second day was that of a doctor who desired a stenographer at once, good wages paid. It sounded rather well, I thought, and I felt that this time I would meet a gentleman. The doctor was very kind and seemed to like my appearance and references; as to salary, he offered me fifteen dollars a week, with a speedy prospect of more. As I was leaving his office, feeling that at last I was launched safely upon the road to a good living, he said, casually, "I have an auto, and as my wife doesn't care for that sort of thing, I shall expect you to accompany me frequently on pleasure trips." That settled the doctor; I never appeared. After that experience I was ill for two weeks, a result of my hard work, suffering, and discouragement.

One day as I sat rather hopelessly gazing out of my window, I received a gentleman's card, with a request that I call at once at a large wholesale dry-goods house in the lower part of the city in reference to my application sent in two weeks before. I hastened to call, and was greeted by a kindly, grayhaired old gentleman of the old school, the kind who respects all woman-kind because his mother was a woman. He looked my letters of reference over carefully, and hired me at once. The wages were not high—only nine dollars to start; but it seemed to me that nine dollars from such a man was worth twenty or a hundred from some others. I worked at this place for two years, and I endeavored faithfully to give two dollars' worth of work for every dollar I received, and I think I succeeded. That my desire to please was not unnoticed by the firm was proved by the fact that my salary was steadily increased until, when I left, a year ago, I was getting twenty-two dollars a week.   G. E. D.

A PINK-COLLAR WORKER'S BLUES

Karen Kenyon

As the selection from Whitcomb and Lang's *Charm* demonstrated, secretaries are often chosen for their youthfulness, sexual attractiveness, and compliance as much as for their stenographic skills. Regardless of their age or professionalism, it is still common to hear secretaries referred to as "girls." They are called by their first names while being expected to address male bosses by their formal titles. Many secretaries are expected to be office wives—listening sympathetically to others, cheering them up, making coffee, cleaning off desks, and running personal errands for them.

This short essay, written for *Newsweek*'s "My Turn," a column open for editorials on issues of current interest, addresses some of the dilemmas faced by women, particularly secretaries, working in the pink-collar ghetto.

More and more women every day are going out to work. A myth has grown around them: the myth of the "new woman." It celebrates the woman executive. It defines her look (a suit), and her drink (Dewar's or perhaps a fine white wine). It puts her "in charge." But it neglects to say whom she is in charge of—probably some other women.

The world still needs helpers, secretaries and waitresses, and the sad truth is that mostly woman fill these serving roles. Today more women hold clerical jobs than ever before (4 million in 1950 and 20 million in 1981). Wherever we look, we see the image of the successful woman executive but, in fact, most women are going out to become secretaries. The current totals: 3 million women in management and 20 million clerical employees. So for the majority of working women—the so-called "pink-collar workers"—liberation from home is no liberation at all.

Recently I took a job as a part-time secretary in a department office of a university. I thought the financial security would be nice (writers never have this) and I needed the sense of community a job can bring. I found there is indeed a sense of community among secretaries. It is, in fact, essential to their emotional survival.

HUMAN BEINGS: I felt a bit like the author of "Black Like Me," a Caucasian who had his skin darkened by dye and went into the South, where he experienced what it was like to be black. Here I was, "a person," disguised as "a secretary." This move from being a newly published author to being a secretary made it very clear to me that the same people who are regarded as creative human beings in one role will be demeaned and ignored in another.

I was asked one day to make some Xerox invitations to a party, then told I could keep one (not exactly a cordial invitation, I thought). The next day I was asked, "Are you coming to the party?" I brightened and said, "Well, maybe I will." I was then told, "Well, then, would you pick up the pizza and we'll reimburse you."

A friend of mine who is an "administrative assistant" told me about a campus party she attended. She was engaged in a lively, interesting conversation with a faculty wife. The wife then asked my friend, "Are you teaching here?" When my friend replied, "Well, no, actually I'm a secretary," the other woman's jaw dropped. She then said, "Don't worry. Nobody will ever guess."

I heard secretaries making "grateful" remarks like, "They really treat us like human beings here." To be grateful for bottom-line treatment was, I felt, a sorry comment.

We think we have freed our slaves, but we have not. We just call them by a different name. Every time people reach a certain status in life they seem to take pride in the fact that they now have a secretary.

It is a fact that it has to be written very carefully into a job description just what a secretary's duties are, or she will be told to clean off the desk, pick up cleaning and the like. Women in these jobs are often seen as surrogate wives, mothers and servants—even to other women.

Many times, when a secretary makes creative contributions she is not given her due. The work is changed slightly by the person in charge, who takes the credit. Most secretaries live in an area between being too assertive and being too passive. Often a secretary feels she has to think twice before stepping in and correcting the grammar, even when she knows her "superior" can't frame a good sentence.

ENVY: When after three months I announced to my co-workers that I was quitting, I was met with kind goodbyes. In some I caught a glimpse of perhaps a gentle envy, not filled with vindictiveness at all, but tinged with some remorse. "I'm just a little jealous that someone is getting out of prison," admitted one woman. "I wish I'd done that years ago," said another.

Their faces remain in my heart. They stand for all the people locked into jobs because they need the money, because they don't know where else to go, afraid there's no place else, because they don't have the confidence or feel they have the chance to do anything else.

I was lucky. I escaped before lethargy or repressed anger or extreme eagerness to please took over. Before I was drawn over the line, seduced by the daily rewards of talk over coffee, exchanged recipes, the photos of family members thumbtacked to the wall near the desk, the occasional lunches to mark birthdays and departures.

I am free now, but so many others are trapped in their carpeted, respectable prisons. The new-woman myth notwithstanding, the true tale of the woman on her own most often ends that way.

As I see it, the slave mentality is alive and well. It manicures its nails. It walks in little pumps on tiny cat feet. It's there every time a secretary says, "Yes, I'll do that. I don't mind" or finds ashtrays for the people who come to talk to someone else. The secretary has often forgotten her own dream. She is too busy helping others to realize theirs.

THE WOMEN OF THE BOYCOTT

Barbara Baer and Glenna Matthew

Women face a triple work burden as productive childbearers, household workers, and wage earners, with all the contradicting expectations these roles entail. But Hispanic women confront some additional culture-specific problems as well. They live in a culture stressing a "machismo" norm, emphasizing men's virility and power and women's domesticity and submissiveness. Often, they face language barriers since many are immigrants or first-or-second-generation citizens; and some are illegal aliens. Many toil in sweatshops as piece workers or in the fields as migrant workers, settings rife with exploitative conditions—long hours for little pay, no fringe benefits, hazardous environments, and menacing sexual harassment. Illegal aliens suffer the constant threats of exposure and deportation.

The excerpt below concerns the women of the United Farm Workers movement of the 1970s. They represent the potential for Hispanic women in such labor movements and their tribulations aptly illustrate the sacrifices made by women who commit themselves to a cause conflicting with their wife-mother role. The women of the boycott, however, see themselves as stronger for having faced these obstacles.

Los Altos, Calif.

Dolores Huerta, vice president of the United Farm Workers, was standing on a flat-bed truck beside Cesar Chavez. She didn't show her eight-and-a-half months' pregnancy, but she looked very tired from the days and nights of organizing cross-country travel plans for the hundreds of people who were now waiting in the parking lot alongside the union headquarters at Delano, Calif. She leaned down and talked with children, her own and others. Small children held smaller ones, fathers carried babies on their shoulders.

The parking lot was filled with cars, trucks and busses, decorated with banners and signs. People sang strike songs and Chavez spoke to them about the boycott. Dolores listened intently, nodding, brushing her straight black hair away from her face from time to time and smiling softly at the children. A priest blessed the cars and busses whose destinations read like a history of the great American migrations—in reverse: *"Hasta la Victoria*—Miami!"; *"Viva la Huelga*—Cleveland!"; *Hasta La Boycott*—Pittsburgh!"

Five years ago there would have been nothing unusual about hundreds of families assembling to move out with the crops, but this time the decision to pull up roots was different. The people on the dusty blacktop were UFW members and until a week earlier they had had a commitment to stay in the area. The union had made it possible for most to have a house or rent one, send their children to a school all year, get medical care. Most of these people had spent the summer on strike lines or in jails. Then, within one week of Cesar Chavez's announcement of a second national boycott of grapes, they had sold their houses and everything they could not carry with them to buy the cars,

THE WOMEN OF THE BOYCOTT From *The Nation*, February 23, 1974, 232–38. Copyright 1974, *Nation* Magazine, The Nation Associates, Inc.

winter clothing, whatever else they might need for years outside the San Joaquin Valley. They were ready to leave by the last day in August.

We had come to Delano specifically to meet Dolores Huerta. As we waited for the caravan to leave, she told us to look well at the other women. These women were "nonmaterialistic." They packed up their families and pledged them to stay out on the boycott until the union got its grape and lettuce contracts back. If the woman of a family refuses, Dolores said, the family either breaks up or is lost to the union. Families are the most important part of the UFW because a family can stick it out in a strange place, on $5 a week per person, the wage everyone in the union is paid (plus expenses). Often the leaders would be women because women were strong in the home and becoming stronger in the union. The women decided the fate of the union, Dolores told us.

Chavez and Dolores Huerta knew the people they were talking about—and what they were asking of UFW members they asked of themselves first. All summer the union had fought to win second contracts from the grape growers in southern and central California valleys who had signed with them first in 1970. But as each contract expired, the Teamsters signed up the growers immediately—thirty at once around Delano. Chavez called the contracts illegal, "sweetheart agreements," because the workers had not voted on their representatives. Chavez called for pickets on the Teamsters-contracted fields. County courts, sympathetic to the growers, enjoined the UFW strikers from effective picketing. Thousands of clergy and students came to support the farm workers and some were jailed. Jailings and trials went on all summer.

Farm workers have never won a major strike in the fields because they are not protected by the National Labor Relations Act, whose provisions guarantee the right to picket; because growers and their allies have used violence and, most important, because there is an unlimited scab labor force across the Mexican border. There is no way to win a strike when men will scab at any price.

Toward the end of the summer the picket lines became violent. In separate incidents in the town of Arvin, two union men were killed. A sheriff struck Nagi Daifullah, a Yemenite, on the head with a flashlight. Juan de la Cruz was shot as he came off the picket line.

The United Farm Workers would not fight violence with violence. When the funerals were over, Chavez called for all strikers to get ready to leave on a second national boycott. The first had lasted five years. This one, though better organized, was more complicated: there were now grapes, wines, lettuce and Teamsters as well as the growers.

By noon the dust had settled in a low haze on this crossroads between vineyards—the stucco buildings the UFW calls "Forty Acres." The union offices were nearly empty, though telephones kept ringing. We went into a bare room with a long table to talk to Dolores Huerta.

Dolores was the first person Chavez called upon to work with him organizing farm workers into a union. That was more than a dozen years ago. She became the UFW's first vice president, its chief negotiator, lobbyist, boycott strategist and public spokeswoman. And in partnership, Dolores and Chavez formulated the UFW's nonviolent and democratic philosophy.

In 1955, Fred Ross brought Dolores Huerta to a meeting of the Community

Service Organization in Stockton, and she has been in political action ever since. Ross, working in San Jose with Saul Alinsky, had taken Cesar Chavez to his first CSO meeting there. Both Dolores and Cesar say they owe their present lives to Fred Ross, and they keep drawing the thin, spare man, now 60, away from his book about the union and back into UFW struggles.

When Dolores began organizing, she already had six children and was pregnant with a seventh. Nearly twenty years later, there are ten children, and Dolores is still so slim and graceful that we find it hard to imagine her in her youth, the age of her daughter. She has not saved herself for anything, has let life draw and strain her to a fine intensity. It hasn't made her tense, harsh or dry. She shouts a lot and laughs with people. She tells us she has a sharp tongue but it seems to us she has an elusiveness of keeping her own counsel, mixed with complete directness and willingness to spend hours talking. Her long black hair is drawn back from high cheek bones, her skin is tanned reddish from the sun on the picket line, and in her deep brown eyes is a constant humor that relieves her serious manner.

Contradictions in her life must have taken, and continue to take, a toll: her many children, Catholic faith and a divorce, her high-strung nerves and the delicate health we know she disregards. It must be that her work, the amount she has accomplished and the spirit she instills in others, have healed the breaks. We talked to Dolores Huerta for several hours in the union offices when the last cars had left Delano.

"I had a lot of doubts to begin with, but I had to act in spite of my conflict between my family and my commitment. My biggest problem was not to feel guilty about it. I don't any more, but then, everybody used to lay these guilt trips on me, about what a bad mother I was, neglecting my children. My own relatives were the hardest, especially when my kids were small; you know, they were stair steps—I had six and one on the way when I started—and I was driving around Stockton with all these little babies in the car, the different diaper changes for each one. It's always hard, not just because you're a woman but because it's hard to really make that commitment. It's in your own head. I'm sure my own life was better because of my involvement. I was able to go through a lot of very serious personal problems and survive them because I had something else to think about. Otherwise, I might have gotten engulfed in my personal difficulties and, I think, I probably would have gone under.

"If I hadn't met Fred Ross then, I don't know if I ever would have been organizing. People don't realize their own worth and I wouldn't have realized what I could do unless someone had shown faith in me. At that time we were organizing against racial discrimination—the way Chicanos were treated by police, courts, politicians. I had taken the *status quo* for granted, but Fred said it could change. So I started working.

"The way I first got away from feeling guilty about neglecting my family was a religious cop-out, I guess. I had serious doubts whether I was doing the right thing, giving kids a lousy supper to go to a council meeting. So I would pray and say, if what I was doing wasn't bearing fruit, then it would be a sign I shouldn't be doing it. When good things came out of my work, when it bore fruit, I took that as a sign I should continue and that the sacrifices my family and I were making were justified.

"Of course, I had no way of knowing what the effects on my kids would be. Now, ten years later, I can look back and say it's O.K. because my kids turned out fine, even though at times they had to fend for themselves, other people took care of them, and so on. I have a kind of proof: my ex-husband took one of my kids, Fidel, during the first strike. We didn't have any food or money, there was no way I could support him. He was eating all right, like all the strikers' kids, but on donations. So my ex-husband took the boy until he was 11. I got him back just last year. He had a lot of nice clothes and short hair, but he was on the verge of a nervous breakdown. When my ex-husband tried to take another boy, the judge ruled against him. You could see the difference when you compared the two kids—one was skinny and in raggedy clothes and with long hair, but real well, happy. Fidel is coming back now to the way he used to be, and he's got long hair too.

"We haven't had a stable place to live—I haven't been anywhere for more than two months, except in New York on the boycott—since 1970. But taking my kids all over the states made them lose their fear of people, of new situations. Most of us have to be mobile. But the kids are in school, they go to school and work on the boycott. Even the 10-year-olds are out on the boycott in the cities.

"My kids are totally politicized mentally and the whole idea of working without materialistic gain has made a great difference in the way they think. When one of our supporters came to take my daughter to buy new clothes in New York, she was really embarrassed. We never buy new clothes, you know, we get everything out of the donations. She said, 'Mama, the lady wanted to buy me a lot of new things, but I told her they didn't fit me.' You know, she came home with a couple of little things to please the lady, but she didn't want to be avaricious. Her values are people and not things. It has to be that way—that's why everyone who works full-time for the union gets $5 a week, plus gas money and whatever food and housing they need to live on, live on at the minimum they can."

How has it happened, we asked, that in the very culture from which the word *"machismo"* derives, the women have more visible, vocal and real power of decision than women elsewhere? Delores told us that the union had made a conscious effort to involve women, given them every chance for leadership, but that the men did not always want it.

"I really believe what the feminists stand for. There is an undercurrent of discrimination against women in our own organization, even though Cesar goes out of his way to see that women have leadership positions. Cesar always felt strongly about women in the movement. This time, no married man went out on the boycott unless he took his wife. We find day care in the cities so the women can be on the picket line with the men. It's a great chance for participation. Of course we take it for granted now that women will *want* to be as involved as men. But in the beginning, at the first meetings, there were only men. And a certain discrimination still exists. Cesar—and other men—treat us differently. Cesar's stricter with the women, he demands more of us. But the more I think of it, the more I'm convinced that the women have gotten stronger because he expects so much of us. You could even say it's gotten lopsided . . . women are stronger than the men.

"Women in the union are great on the picket line. More staying power, and we're nonviolent. One of the reasons our union *is* nonviolent is that we want our women and children involved, and we stay nonviolent because of the women and children.

"One time the Teamsters were trying to provoke a fight to get our pickets arrested. Forty, fifty police were waiting with paddy wagons. We had about 300 people. The Teamsters attacked the line with 2 X 4 boards. I was in charge of the line. We made the men go to the back and placed the women out in front. The Teamsters beat our arms but they couldn't provoke the riot they wanted, and we didn't give in. The police stood there, watched us get beaten; the D.A. wouldn't even let us sign a *complaint*. But we had gained a lot of respect from our men. Excluding women, protecting them, keeping women at home, that's the middle-class way. Poor people's movements have always had whole families on the line, ready to move at a moment's notice, with more courage because that's all we had. It's a class not an ethnic thing."

We knew that the women of the UFW found themselves in a unique situation. Unlike the sex-determined employment of the urban poor, the jobs of farm worker women and men had always been the same. They *had* to work, but it wasn't housework or even factory work, separating them from men. Women had picked, pruned and packed in fields, cannery and shed side by side with men. But would the women decide to let the men organize the union? Dolores Huerta had spoken for herself alone; the resolution of conflicts between family and political, union action, would come to each UFW woman in her own terms.

Lupe Ortiz has been an organizer in a union field office since she left school. She is about 25, a natural leader, with a quality of making people laugh to get work done. Yet for all her big voice and humor, she didn't know how women could assert themselves at home as they did at work. What she told us seemed the reverse of our more familiar, middle-class feminism; here, by contrast, a woman insisted on work equality, and in large part received it, but she wouldn't challenge the traditional order of the family.

As Lupe directed her male co-workers in Spanish, she expounded to us in English the differences between "Anglo" and Chicano women. "You Anglo women, you do it your way, but I don't ever want to be equal to my husband."

"You get the same salary; don't you want the same voice at home?"

"In work, but not at home. No, at home you have to know when to open your mouth and when not to. You have to learn you can't go places men go, like bars."

"Don't you want it to change? For men to act as though you're equal?"

"It's not exactly equality. It's our culture. I don't want our Chicano culture to change. Let men have the say-so." Lupe laughed, this time openly, as she looked at the men in the office. "I bet *you* split up with your husbands more often than we do because you make head-on conflicts."

Ester Yurande, a generation older than Lupe, showed a generation difference in her appearance: she was as carefully, femininely dressed, with lovely long hair and glittering earrings, as Lupe had been rugged in jeans, sweatshirt and close-cropped curls. Ester had worked in the fields until she became the bookkeeper for the Medical Clinic at Forty Acres. She had been a UFW member from the start, been jailed in the early 1960s. How, we asked her, had the union changed the lives of the women who came to the clinic?

"A doctor treats us with dignity now. We don't get charity when we're having a baby, we get care. It's to do with pride. Mexican women around here used to do what the men said, but Dolores Huerta was our example of something different. We could see one of our leaders was a woman, and she was always out in front, and she would talk back. She wasn't scared of anything."

Dolores herself had told us that she didn't hesitate to argue. "You know, Cesar has fired me fifteen times, and I must have quit about ten. Then, we'll call each other up and get back to work. There have been times when I should have fought harder. When he tells me now, 'you're getting really impossible, arguing all the time,' I say, 'you haven't seen anything yet. I'm going to get worse.' Because from now on I'm going to fight really, really hard when I believe something. There have been times I haven't. I can be wrong, too, but at least it will be on the record how I felt."

When we asked Ester how she felt about fighting back herself, she didn't want to answer. We had become outsiders once more, women who didn't comprehend her way. Men have accepted strong women in the union, but there remains deeply engrained in these women a respect for their men's *machismo*.

There is a religious fervor about the union, which has made its members call it La Causa. Perhaps the closeness of the Catholic Church to the movement is one more reason women have been able to identify with its goals. The UFW women have brought their personal strength and their faith to the union; the union in turn has reinforced and completed their lives by giving them a direct form of action and an ideal.

Dolores, very religious herself, told us that women were most important to the union because a woman determined the fate of a whole family. If a *wife* was for the union, Dolores said, then the husband would be, too. If she was not, if she was afraid or too attached to her home and possessions, then the family usually stayed out of the union, or it broke up. There had been a number of broken marriages that had cost the union the strength of a united family.

Maria-Luisa Rangel did not want to go out on the first boycott. At that time—in 1968—many women were staying in California while the men lived together in boycott houses in Eastern cities. The Rangels, parents of eight children, had saved enough money to own part of a family store, and they owned their home in the small town of Dinuba, near Fresno. They would have to part with both if they went to Detroit for two years. Hijino Rangel was determined to go. So Maria-Luisa went. Looking at her unsoftened features, her inaccessible but not unfriendly black eyes, we sensed the strength that had enabled her then to wrench herself away from everything she owned and keep her family together. She had a hard time in Detroit; she didn't know much English, the climate was completely strange and she had two operations in the city. But when they returned to the valley in 1970, the Rangels knew that they had helped win the boycott that secured the 180 union contracts with grape growers of the Coachella and San Joaquin Valleys. And the experience had worked on Maria-Luisa. She spoke out as a representative of the union about the present boycott. "It's just like it was then. The struggle is for the people to win, not the growers but the people. I know it, and *they*—the growers—know it."

Women have paid different prices for making the union part of their lives. The 100 women who spent many weeks in Fresno jails last summer (for violating anti-picket injunctions) ranged from minors to great-grandmothers. There were field workers and nuns, lay religious women and union officials. For some of the Chicano women, it was a reminder of previous jailings when no nuns had been present and the guards had beaten "the Mexicans." For others, it was the first time, and almost a vacation from their daily lives. Workhardened baked hands became almost soft. All the women shared their experiences—the farm workers told city women like Dorothy Day, editor of the *Catholic Worker*, about their struggle, and learned from her about women's movements in the cities and in the Church.

Maximina de la Cruz and her husband, Juan, were born around 1910 in Mexico. Juan entered America on the bracero program, picked crops in Texas, and then in New Mexico, where Maximina worked in a clothing factory. They married, moved with their son to the San Joaquin Valley in 1960, and joined the union during the first strikes in 1965. Juan de la Cruz was killed last summer by a man who fired his .22-caliber rifle into the picket line from a truck. Maximina told us she remembers that many times the growers or the Teamsters put on deputy badges, joined in beating the farm workers, and then arrested them on grounds of self-defense. The man who shot de la Cruz has entered a plea in the valley courts that he shot defending himself from the picket line.

Maximina was observing the thirty-day mourning period when we came to her home in Arvin. Hearing us arrive, she and her mother, Porfiria Coronado, met us at their gate, and without a word, in the dark, she took us, with hands that felt like warm, worked clay, into her living room. Candles beneath pictures of saints and near a wedding photograph were the only light. As the night went on, she told us of her early life of hardship, the many moves, purchase of their small house, and the changes the UFW had made in their lives.

"We *know* the growers. They want to go back to the old days, the way it was before we had a union, when we got a dollar an hour, no toilets or water in the fields, no rest periods, and they could kick you out without any pay for not picking fast enough. A whole family earned less than one union man today. They fought us hard and dirty each time, but we didn't give in. We won't. This time we're out in the cities again to tell the good people what it is like to work here. I'm staying on here, and I'll be back at work in the fields, but not until the union gets its contracts back. I might have to wait a while but I know people will undertand and help us win back our union. I'm proud to be a woman here. Juan was proud of the union. You know, on the picket lines, we were so gay, peaceful and *attrativas*, even the grandmothers. Until *they* shot their gun."

Except for the Catholic Church, the powerful and wealthy institutions of California have opposed the UFW at one time or another. Grower-biased central valley law enforcement and the courts have made a mockery of legal institutions; agri-business has never given up trying to break the union through legislation; Gov. Ronald Reagan has been photographed eating scab grapes; even the U.S. Government helped the growers by buying non-union lettuce in great quantity to ship to troops in Vietnam. Yet the greater the odds, the more the union has come to represent poor people against the rich and mighty. Dolores Huerta fights best when the situation looks bleakest. She attributes her refusal to give up to her mother's influence.

"My mother was one of those women who do a lot. She was divorced, so I never really understood what it meant for a woman to take a back seat to a man. My brothers would say, 'Mama spoiled you,' because she pushed me to the front. When I was first involved in organizing, my mom would watch the kids for me, but then she got involved herself and she couldn't baby-sit any more. She won the first prize in Stockton for registering voters and increasing membership.

"To tell the truth, I was prejudiced against women for a long time and I didn't realize it. I always liked to be with men because I thought they were more interesting and the women only talked of kids. But I was afraid of women, too. It was in the union that I lost my fear of being around women. Or put it this way, I learned to respect women. Cesar's wife, Helen Chavez, helped me more than anyone else. She was really committed to home. Actually, Cesar's toughest organizing jobs were on Helen, his wife, and Richard, his brother. They wanted to lead their own lives. Helen kept saying she wouldn't do anything, and she's so strong and stubborn you couldn't convince her to change her mind. She took care of the food and the kids, and while Cesar was organizing she was supporting them, too, working in the fields. Cesar, keeping his *machismo* intact in those days, would make her come home and cook dinner.

"We wanted her to learn the credit union bookkeeping. We yelled at her one night into the kitchen, 'You're going to be the assistant bookkeeper.' She yelled back, 'No, I won't either,' but we voted her the job. Boy was she mad! But you should see her books. We've been investigated a hundred times and they never find a mistake."

The union had to teach its members—farm workers with almost no education or training—the professional skills it required. Marie Sabadado, who directs the R. F. Kennedy Medical Plan, Helen Chavez, head of the credit union, and Dolores, chief negotiator and writer of labor contracts, taught themselves. Dolores made it sound almost easy to learn very specialized skills in a week's time.

"When Cesar put me in charge of negotiations in our first contract, I had never seen a contract before. I talked to labor people, I got copies of contracts and studied them for a week and a half, so I knew something when I came to the workers. Cesar almost fell over because I had my first contract all written and all the workers had voted on the proposals. He thought we ought to have an attorney, but really it was better to put the contracts in a simple language. I did all the negotiations myself for about five years. Women should remember this: be resourceful, you can do anything, whether you have experience or not. Cesar always says that the first education of people is how to be people and then the other things fall into place.

"I think women are particularly good negotiators because we have a lot of patience, and no big ego trips to overcome. Women are more tenacious and that helps a great deal. It unnerves the growers to negotiate with us. Cesar always wanted to have an *all-woman* negotiating team. Growers can't swear back at us or at each other. And then we bring in the ethical questions, like how our kids live. How can the growers really argue against what should be done for human beings just to save money?"

We knew everyone was immensely proud of the union services. We also knew that the legal staff (as well as the doctors and nurses at the clinic) were volunteer lawyers from the outside. In the past, the growers got rid of nascent farm-worker organizations by breaking them in the courts. The UFW has an excellent, tough legal staff. But to stay permanently with the union doctors and lawyers need to come from the farm workers themselves. The union will have to send its men and women out of the community for training. There has never been the luxury of a few years in which to do so, and there is a certain fear of becoming "corrupted" by the universities.

The United Farm Workers headquarters are located in Delano, between Bakersfield and Fresno, and also at La Paz, a town no larger than a half-block of post office, store and gas station, east of Bakersfield in the Tehachapi range. Union field offices lie in small towns in the central valleys. From anywhere in these valleys it is about three hours, north to San Francisco, or south to Los Angeles on any of the state's three parallel freeways. Meeting only union people, in their austere but clean and bright offices, we hadn't seen what local fieldworker conditions were like. We took a look at some company towns by leaving the freeways and taking side roads at random into the fields.

Company towns are wholly dependent for their income on the prosperity and good will of the growers. Since the big growers are the last employers in America to escape collective bargaining, one can judge their civic responsibility by the looks of the town: boarded-up or gutted buildings, cracked sidewalks, decaying stores—they all show that the growers spend their profits on themselves. Only the bars, preserves of the men, where the wine is sold, do business.

Livingston is a company town of Gallo wines near Merced on Highway 99. Outside the town, the Gallo brothers haven't hidden their wealth. They have splendid houses, isolated even from one another, surrounded by velvety slopes leading to pools, tennis courts and greenhouses. Not far away, but well hidden, the Gallo workers live in company camps lost at dusty terminals of country roads in the shadow of enormous vats guarded by armed men. When we were there, a determined nucleus of UFW strikers who had refused to work under Gallo's new Teamster contract, had also refused to obey the grower's eviction notices. For that, they had been deprived of garbage collection and water.

Downtown Livingston seemed only slightly less bleak than the camps. Fifty people had gathered in front of the local courthouse for a silent protest against the imprisonment of fellow strikers. Aggie Rose, a former elementary school-teacher of Portuguese ancestry, was head of the union office. As she spoke to the men and women forming the procession, encouraging and exhorting them in Spanish and Portuguese to keep their spirits up, the intensity of her light eyes, her constantly moving thin figure, momentarily brought life back into the town. The line of marchers circled the courthouse for a while. Police in squad cars hovered along dark streets. There was nothing to do but disperse.

Dolores would soon be back in New York directing the East Coast boycott. She was determined that we understand, before we left, why the union would not be defeated, not even in Livingston.

"One of the reasons the growers are fighting us so hard is that they realize we're changing people, not just getting a paycheck for them. Without our militancy we wouldn't have a union. So we keep pushing our people, getting them out on other issues, like the tuition rise in California colleges, or the Presidential campaign. We had farm workers out door to door for McGovern. And when our people come back from the boycott, they will be stronger than ever."

We asked Dolores whether she had ever been scared, or lacked confidence in her ability to organize people.

"Of course. I've been afraid about everything until I did it. I started out every time not knowing what I was to do and scared to death. When Cesar first sent me to New York on the boycott it was the first time we'd done anything like that. There were no ground rules. I thought, 11 million people in New York, and I have to persuade them to stop buying grapes. Well, I didn't do it alone. When you need people, they come to you. You find a way . . . it gets easier all the time."

WOMEN COAL MINERS FEAR LOSS OF NEWLY WON EQUALITY

Leon Daniels

While not a new problem, sexual harassment is a growing occupational hazard for women as their number in the paid labor force increases. For this reason, and because sexual harassment has been classified as sexual discrimination, an unlawful practice, more women are choosing collective action against offenders. At the present time, employers must take responsibility for the occurrence of sexual harassment on their property. Some have hailed this charge as a victory for women as it would seem to be in the employer's interests to control the incidence of sexual abuse on the job. Others, however, point out that pressure on offended women by company officials and co-workers alike not to take action becomes more likely given the employer's desire to project a good public image as well as power to threaten closure in the face of an expensive suit. And as this article illustrates, sexual harassment is just one of many problems women in male-dominated, blue-collar occupations face.

From the wires of UPI, Charleston, West Virginia, the selection below appeared in the *New Hampshire Sunday News*, the Sunday edition of the *Union Leader*.

BECKLEY, W. VA. (UPI)—   The collapse of America's coal industry, like a dreaded mine cave-in, threatens to bury a decade of slow progress won by women miners against discrimination and sexual harassment.

The 1930s-style depression afflicting the coalfields of West Virginia, Virginia and Kentucky has been particularly devastating to women who dig coal.

Last hired, first fired, many of them believe they will never be called back down into the shafts where they were earning $90-$100 a day.

WOMEN COAL MINERS... From *New Hampshire Sunday News*, July 31, 1983, 7D. Reprinted by permission of United Press International.

The sagging of coal markets a year ago has idled one in three members of the United Mine Workers of America. The plight of women miners is worse. Of the 3,730 women who have gone into the mines since 1973, only about half are still working.

"I went into the mines for the money," said Patricia Runion, 35, a divorced mother of two teenage sons who has been laid off since last Nov. 15.

The matronly miner is a plaintiff in an $8.8 million suit she and six other women filed last February against Pittston Coal Co., charging their privacy was invaded by foremen who regularly peeped at them through a hole in the wall of a mine bathhouse.

"When I found out what they had been doing I felt totally stripped, like I'd been raped," Mrs. Runion said in an interview in the modest house she built atop a mountain outside this coal town with money she earned deep underground.

With such lawsuits, women miners have fought hard against sexual abuse on the job. Their union has pledged to help them fight discrimination in the mines.

Coal-mining women have no real strategy, however, to bring back the jobs they have lost, perhaps irrevocably, to modern equipment installed during this period of slow production.

Married at 15 to a miner, Mrs. Runion went on to finish high school and hold minimum-wage jobs in a grocery and as a hospital ward clerk.

She remembered once mentioning to her husband that she would like to be a miner.

"He just laughed," she recalled. "He didn't like the idea at all."

After divorce from the well-paid miner, she said, "I didn't want to give up things. I told my sons it wouldn't be easy but we'd be okay. I was bound and determined not go on welfare."

Mrs. Runion, after 80 hours of underground training, became a fullfledged "black hat" miner within six months.

"At first, I was scared," she said. "It was a totally different world. We were working 600 feet underground. I was afraid of roof falls. Any smart miner will respect the top."

Mrs. Runion remembers that she "felt sorry" for a fellow trainee, a male, who quit in fear the first time he was sent underground.

As for herself, she said, "I was determined to make it. I was going to do it or die."

In time, she came to love her work in the underground darkness.

"I was seeing a place nobody had ever seen before and I just loved it," she said. "It was like a new city down there."

Mrs. Runion took "a lot of teasing and joking from the men," much of it sexually based, but eventually they respected her enough to elect her to a union safety committee.

She said the new life for which she had worked so hard collapsed when she learned foremen who had discriminated against her on the job also had peeped at her in the bathhouse.

"Now I don't want to go back into the mines," she said. "It's been a humiliation, an embarrassment to my children."

"I went into the mines to keep him out of the mines," Mrs. Runion said, pointing at her older son, Bob, 17. "This one is going to be a lawyer."

Mrs. Runion still has difficulty understanding male miners.

"When they're underground they talk about hunting, drinking and sex," she said. "When they go home they talk about coal mining."

Betty Jean Hall, an attorney for the Coal Employment Project which aids women miners, urges political action but acknowledges that alone cannot solve the job crisis.

Mrs. Hall's organization contends women miners get less rewarding jobs than men. It investigates cases of sexual harassment.

"The Reagan administration leaves no hope for women and minorities," she charged.

Robin Keener said she went into the mines with the goal of becoming "a boss."

"I loved my job," said the woman who became a miner after divorcing one. "I felt a great sense of accomplishment. This was something I could do well."

Mrs. Keener, who earns money as a sketch artist and has taken business courses at a local community college, went into the mines to support three children. She worked only a year before she was laid off. As a roof bolter, she used a machine to drive 6-foot metal pins into the top of the shaft to prevent cave-ins.

Mrs. Keener said that since filing their lawsuit she and the other plaintiffs often have received anonymous telephone threats and have been snubbed by male miners who fear the company will shut down the mine.

THE NEW CORPORATE FEMINISM
Suzanne Gordon

While creators of seminars on teaching women to be managers search for ways to help integrate women into the higher managerial circles, some analysts question the desirability of such action altogether. They remind us that originally the objectives of the modern woman's movement focused on a more radical platform. They sought collective actions rather than individual solutions to the problems women in the workplace confront; developed the strategy of networking to support women at all levels of the organization, not just the elites; and aspired to change the hierarchical arrangements of male dominated organizations, not simply embrace them.

Suzanne Gordon best known for her book, *Off Balance: The Real World of Ballet* (1983) an account of the unglamorous side of that life, especially for women, turns, in the following article from *The Nation*, to a critique of the corporate world and the place of women in it. The observations Gordon makes have led some critics to proclaim that we have reached a post-feminist era.

About four weeks ago a friend of mine, who is an editor at a major New York City publishing house, went to one of her company's biannual sales conferences. She departed full of ideas about books on feminism—books about feminist psychology, about socialist feminism, about women and culture. After

THE NEW CORPORATE FEMINISM From *The Nation*, February 5, 1983, 129. Copyright 1983, *Nation* Magazine, The Nation Associates, Inc.

a week in Puerto Rico, she returned well tanned and well deflated. She told me that when she explained her ideas to the company's salespeople, they did not respond enthusiastically. They insisted that women's books were still high on their list and so was feminism. But the kinds of books they felt would sell and the feminism they described had little to do with my friend's political ideals.

What publishers are looking for these days isn't radical feminism. It's corporate feminism—a brand of feminism designed to sell books and magazines, three-piece suits, airline tickets, Scotch, cigarettes, and, most important, corporate America's message, which runs: Yes, women were discriminated against in the past, but that unfortunate mistake has been remedied; now every woman can attain wealth, prestige and power by dint of individual rather than collective effort.

At a time when hundreds of thousands of women are still trying to realize the ideals of radical feminism, business has set about redefining and depoliticizing one of the most compelling social movements of the late twentieth century. Indeed, what has happened to reformist feminism in the past decade is perhaps the most dramatic example of American capitalism's genius at defusing protest by winning the protesters over to the very values and institutions they once attacked.

Evidence of the success of this effort is not hard to find. Ten years ago, you could walk into any large bookstore and browse among shelves of books and magazines carrying the kind of message my editor friend longs to publish. Today, things are different. Walk into any large bookstore and you'll find racks of primers on appropriate managerial and entrepreneurial conduct. Covers with clenched fists and feminist symbols are no longer in vogue. Now we have photographs of smartly dressed women standing in front of imposing desks in elegant but efficiently furnished offices. This role model of success—a tailored Charlie's Angel who carries an attaché case instead of a .38—will teach her sisters about the virtues of action, as well as how to "network," cut deals, make killings, be the boss and get to the top of the corporate heap.

The helpful tips our sisters in business provide are necessary, they say, because women face serious obstacles as they travel the road to success. First, they must overcome their feminine socialization. Their upbringing has, sadly, made them nurturers rather than predators and thus ill suited for the marketplace. More important, women must also overcome the scruples instilled by their feminist education, for feminism and the radical movements from which it sprang had little positive to say about corporate America and the power relations and values that prevail therein. In the late 1960s and early 1970s, women who came to feminism from the antiwar and civil rights movements shared certain ideals and goals: they shared the desire, as Eugene Debs so aptly put it, "to rise with the ranks, rather than from the ranks." Wealth, ambition, jockeying for power, the subordination of one's personal life to one's professional life and the delight in wielding authority—in short, precisely what many women are now choosing to pursue—were not highly regarded. Now many of the same women who once hoped to revolutionize the system are being trained as its administrators, and they need a corporate education as well as an ideology that will allow them to reconcile the hopes of the past with the realities of the present.

That is exactly what book after book and article after article, not to mention the myriad seminars on entrepreneurial feminism, are offering them. To draw the fainthearted or skeptical woman into the fray, these voices of corporate America start by calming her fear that she must become a "company woman." The first lesson the would-be managerial woman receives is that she can be totally committed to both her sisters and herself. For the managerial woman will be less competitive and callous, more humane and supportive, than the managerial man.

"Today women managers are bringing a new dimension to the administrative process," writes Margaret Fenn in *In the Spotlight: Women Executives in a Changing Environment*. "Women managers are helping to move business toward the adoption of an administrative philosophy that provides the opportunity for all members to participate and contribute their skills and knowledge to the processes affecting them." "Women," writes Nancy Lee in *Targeting the Top*, "have generally trained themselves to pay close attention to others in order to understand their motivations and predict what is apt to happen. Intuition or accurately reading verbal and non-verbal signals, coupled with genuine concern for other people, are the great strengths that women are bringing with them into the organization."

Lest women worry that wielding power will corrupt them as it has corrupted so many men, *Ms.* magazine's recent issue on power reassures them that "the solidarity fostered by the women's movement" is "setting precedents for the next generation and they [powerful women] are creating a reality, a way to think about and perceive powerful women, where before we only had myths and caricatures."

The question, of course, is what kind of reality are those women creating? Are women in business any different from their male counterparts?

The women's movement grew out of a critique of male power and out of a close accounting of the price men pay for their dominant position. Feminists argued that men have forfeited the ability to lead a life that can bring both personal and professional fulfillment; feminism's promise was a life that balanced love, friendship and work. Yet the same corporate feminists who spout volumes about the need to combine personal and professional fulfillment also write that the woman manager must, like so many men before her, subordinate the personal to the professional. Margaret V. Higginson and Thomas L. Quick in *The Ambitious Woman's Guide to a Successful Career* make it quite clear that if a woman is to succeed in business she must play by the rules: "The separation of personal, private self from public self may be distasteful but most managers find it necessary. Managerial performance requires that the manager be where the action is. This requirement may entail long hours, travel movement outside work hours and public review of one's action."

"Managerial performance" also involves making one's personal life serve one's professional goals. "Your relationships with former associates," say Higginson and Quick, "must reflect position not emotion." "Women," they complain, "seem to have a special problem in this area. In the company cafeteria, for example, they will sit down with other women—even if these women are on a lower job level, rather than joining the men who are now their peers."

Margaret Fenn put it even more bluntly: "Associations and friendships reflect managerial values. These imply a degree of social distancing from subordinates." And according to Gay Norton Edelman, in an article on office politics, "The fact is, you were hired to get the job done, not to win friends, fulfill needs left from your childhood or work out unresolved conflicts from your past. You don't have to be a cold fish or a cutthroat . . . but it's good politics to avoid becoming too people-oriented. You don't want personal relationships in the office to harm your work and career." In other words, the recognition that we all need intimacy is not a strength but a weakness, a holdover from childhood that must be shed by women seeking to take their places in the adult world.

Thus friendships are inappropriate and sticking together must give way to looking out for number one, say the corporate Machiavellis. When one troubled executive wrote to *Savvy* magazine's column "Ideas and Strategies for Doing Better Business," she learned that better business is simply business as usual. New to her company, she had been beset by a gang of employees who challenged her authority. What was *Savvy's* solution? "Divide and conquer. The way your gang is acting, the time for group talk is over. Now you must deal with each one privately. You must make each see that her future self-interest is linked to pleasing you and not to pleasing others in the group."

In the same issue, a disgruntled employee who had joined her co-workers to fight an authoritarian boss was given similar counsel: "You have probably already hurt yourself by joining the grumblers, but it's still not too late to do what you should have done in the beginning. Request a private meeting and tell her that you are committed to working with her. As for your colleagues— remember, old alliances often go through radical swings during the first months under a new leadership. . . . One thing you can depend on: Change at the top provides opportunities for new alliances."

These new alliances, of course, should be alliances with the powerful, and the effect of them is to maintain that power, not redistribute it. And so it is no surprise that these books and articles place great emphasis on the virtues of networking and role-modeling. Indeed, the adoption of networking by women in business has been lauded as one of modern feminism's foremost achievements. Women realized that affirmative action suits would take them only so far. What they needed was contact with the rich and powerful, so they began to form replicas of the "old boy networks" through which powerful men have traditionally passed on their power to a select few. As a result of these networks, more women are now in, or near, positions of power and can thus serve as role models who, according to *Ms.*, pave the road that millions of other women will travel.

In reality, however, the relationships cemented in the old girl networks are no different from those the old boy networks foster. For no matter which sex uses it, the network is a vehicle for the advancement of an elite. Moreover, the role-model concept turns feminist politics into fantasy: women cease to be the architects of a radical vision of the world and become spectators, watching the drama of other women's success.

The power of collective action, these books and articles say, is no longer the goal; corporate feminism seeks the legitimation of the individual manager's power over others. And so Fenn informs us:

> An effective manager recognizes that power and influence are parts of everyday life. It's true that all organizational members are positioned in a hierarchy which implies unequal power distribution. But such distribution emerges naturally from ideas about social organization and behavior. As a

condition of employment employees accept as legitimate the exercise of authority over areas related to performance and are indifferent to the fact that they have the ability to choose other alternatives.

If they're not worried about your authority, why should you be?

The message of these self-help books is expounded with great enthusiasm when businesswomen gather to march off into the corporate sunset. At the third Women in Business Conference in New York City, attended by 3,000 executives, entrepreneurs and owners of small and large businesses, the participants were treated to seminars on business skills that emphasized the virtues of wealth and status. Women were not told how to nurture their subordinates, how to fight for the underprivileged or how to imbue the corporation with radical feminist values. They were schooled in the arts of adaptation.

In a seminar entitled "Dressing for Success," women were taught that the way they present themselves is no less important than the business equipment they purchase. Four panelists—Beverly Stephen, a syndicated columnist for the New York *Daily News;* Maria Rios, a psychotherapist; Ruth McCarthy Manton, president of a design management company; and Barbara Munder, a hgh-level executive at McGraw-Hill—explained that finding a "self and self-style" appropriate to the corporate world involves change and risk. They also pointed out that one's clothes, like one's friendships, must reflect managerial values. "In corporate or financial institutions you can show some individuality, but not too much," Munder said candidly. "You can't show too much individuality, not even at the top. I would never go into a presentation without a suit."

While most of the conference participants were trying to make contacts, I talked with Marie Robinson, who owns a business and is an avid proponent of the corporate feminist success gospel. I asked her if she thinks women function differently from men in the business world. She answered unequivocally in the affirmative: "Women's leadership style is to reach a consensus rather than be authoritarian. My style is generally to reach a consensus, to build a team.

"I think women generally have tremendous empathy for the women working under them. They're part of the family women create." This means, she elaborated, that if you "make them feel they belong," they'll be willing to work longer hours without demanding overtime.

Grace Fippinger, a vice president at New York Telephone and honorary chair of the conference, amiably informed me that she wants all women in business to consider themselves part of her team. But she feels she has a responsibility only to women at her own level. When I asked if she thought she should help her female subordinates advance, she was aghast: "I wouldn't treat a woman who reports to me any different than a man. That wouldn't be fair."

A reading of the literature on corporate feminism and an examination of corporate feminist values lead to one inescapable conclusion: women exercising their entrepreneurial skills, wielding power and flexing their financial muscles are joining the system, not changing it. Some women have noted this with dismay and exhorted feminists to return to their roots. In an article in *The New York Times Magazine,* for example, Anne Taylor Flemming ruefully reported the sad fact that women have not responded to success as feminists had hoped they would. On their "way to the top," women are not being "as gentle with one another as we once hoped we'd be," she wrote, and recalled the promise of feminism—that women would "be tender with one another because our wombs had somehow bequeathed us an extra empathy, a kind of biologic tenderness." She doesn't question the pursuit of careerist goals; she merely seeks a "gentler jungle."

This Victorian vision of femininity is precisely the vision that fuels corporate feminism. Femininity, the corporate feminists argue, is a kind of armor that magically protects women from the compromises the business world forces men to make every day of their professional lives. Because of femininity—and corporate feminism—women can enter that world and remain pure; they can manage and administer without power corrupting them because it is the sex, not the system, that determines what people believe and how they act.

The reality, of course, is quite the opposite. As these books and articles and seminars show, it is the system, not the sex, that determines values and behavior. For centuries men have been in charge, and so feminism has associated capitalism's ills with masculinity. But putting a corporate feminist in charge won't cure those ills; she'll simply perpetuate them—though her rhetoric will be more gentle.

Women cannot do it differently because they're not allowed to. They cannot live by the values of radical feminism (or any other ism—except, of course, capitalism) in the business world because no one in corporate America has the freedom to live by values other than those of corporate America. As Barbara Munder said in her disquisition on dress: women in business can't even escape the uniform when they're on top. Ostensibly, she was referring only to appearances. In fact, standardization in fashion is indicative of a more extensive standardization. When women—or men for that matter—enter the business world, they must shed their politics, their emotions and their ideals, and they must standardize their attire, their attitudes, their behavior and even their skills.

Given the current state of the women's movement and the fragmentation of progressive politics, this is hardly surprising. If reform feminism had chosen to be an aggressive partner in a strong progressive movement for broad social change, the outlook would not be so grim. One could safely counsel women to take their places at all levels of economic and political life, knowing that a political community would reinforce their ideals, help them withstand the institutional pressures to adapt to the status quo and encourage action that might lead to changes within America's major institutions.

Without such a movement, and in the face of reformist feminism's affair with careerism, it is hard to imagine a scenario other than the one thousands of women are enacting today. For once collective ideals are abandoned, everything else—the fine feelings and fond wishes—goes with it. Women must become company women because there is nothing left to be.

LETTERS OF A WOMAN HOMESTEADER

Elinore Rupert Stewart

The letter reprinted below comes from a series of letters published in *The Atlantic Monthly* in 1913 and 1914. According to the editors, they were "genuine letters, written without thought of publication, simply to tell a friendly story." The writer of the letters, they noted, was a young widow whose husband was killed in a railroad accident, moved to Denver where she supported herself and her two-year old daughter, Jerrine, by working as a "house-cleaner and laundress." "Later, seeking to better herself, she accepted employment as a housekeeper for a well-to-do Scotch cattleman, Mr. Stewart. . . " Her letters, written to a former employer, began in April, 1909, shortly after her arrival at the Stewart ranch in Wyoming, and ended in 1913, by which time she and Stewart had wed.

Elinore Rupert was indeed a homesteader, for in the letter preceding this one she described her sixty-mile journey with neighbors to Green River, the county seat, to file on her land. Like many others in the late nineteenth and early twentieth centuries, she filed for ownership of land under the provisions set up by the Homestead Act of 1862. The law provided one quarter section (160 acres) of land on the public domain to any adult willing to occupy and farm the land for five years.

Life was not easy for women on the homesteads. In her letter Elinore Rupert described a summer's work that would put Mrs. Carrot to shame.

Burnt Fork, Wyo., Sept. 11.

DEAR MRS. CONEY,—

 This has been for me the busiest, happiest summer I can remember. I have worked very hard but it has been work that I really enjoy. Help of any kind is very hard to get here, and Mr. Stewart had been too confident of getting men, so that haying caught him with too few men to put up the hay. He had no man to run the mower and he could n't run both the mower and the stacker, so you can fancy what a place he was in.

I don't know that I ever told you, but my parents died within a year of each other and left six of us to shift for ourselves. Our people offered to take one here and there among them until we should all have a place, but we refused to be raised on the halves and so arranged to stay at Grandmother's and keep together. Well, we had no money to hire men to do our work so had to learn to do it ourselves. Consequently I learned to do many things which girls more fortunately situated don't even know have to be done. Among the things I learned to do was the way to run a mowing machine. It cost me many bitter tears because I got sunburned, and my hands were hard, rough, and stained with machine oil, and I used to wonder how any Prince Charming could overlook all that in any girl he came to. For all I had ever read of the Prince had to do with his 'reverently kissing her lily-white hand,' or doing some other fool trick with a hand as white as a snowflake. Well, when my Prince showed up he did n't lose much time in letting me know that 'Barkis was willing,' and I wrapped my hands in my old checked apron and took him up before he could catch his breath. Then there was no more mowing, and I almost forgot that I knew how until Mr. Stewart got into such a panic. If he put a man to mow, it kept them all idle at the stacker, and he just could n't get enough men. I was afraid to tell him I could mow for fear he would forbid me to do so. But one morning, when he was chasing a last hope of help, I went down to the barn, took out the horses and went to mowing. I had enough cut before he got back to show him I knew how, and as he came back man-less he was delighted as well as surprised. I was glad because I really like to mow, and besides that, I am adding feathers to my cap in a surprising way. When you see me again you will think I am wearing a feather duster, but it is only that I have been said to have almost as much sense as a 'mon,' and that is an honor I never aspired to, even in my wildest dreams.

I have done most of my cooking at night, have milked seven cows every day, and have done all the hay-cutting, so you see I have been working. But I have found time to put up thirty pints of jelly and the same amount of jam for myself. I used wild fruits, gooseberries, currants, raspberries and cherries. I have almost two gallons of the cherry butter, and I think it is delicious. I wish I could get some of it to you, I am sure you would like it.

We began haying July 5 and finished September 8. After working so hard and so steadily I decided on a day off, so yesterday I saddled the pony, took a few things I needed, and Jerrine and I fared forth. Baby can ride behind quite well. We got away by sun-up and a glorious day we had. We followed a stream higher up into the mountains and the air was so keen and clear at first, we had on our coats. There was a tang of sage and of pine in the air, and our horse was midside deep in rabbit-brush, a shrub just covered with flowers that look and smell like goldenrod. The blue distance promised many alluring adventures, so we went along singing and simply gulping in Summer. Occasionally a bunch of sage chickens would fly up out of the sage-brush, or a jack-rabbit would leap out. Once we saw a bunch of antelope gallop over a hill, but we were out just to be out, and game did n't tempt us. I started, though, to have just as good a time as possible, so I had a fish-hook in my knapsack.

Presently, about noon, we came to a little dell where the grass was as soft and as green as a lawn. The creek kept right up against the hills on one side and there were groves of quaking asp and cotton-woods that made shade, and service-bushes and birches that shut off the ugly hills on the other side. We dismounted and prepared to noon. We caught a few grasshoppers and I cut a birch pole for a rod. The trout are so beautiful now, their sides are so silvery, with dashes of old rose and orange, their speckles are so black, while their backs look as if they had been sprinkled with gold-dust. They bite so well that it does n't require any especial skill or tackle to catch plenty for a meal in a few minutes.

In a little while I went back to where I had left my pony browsing, with eight beauties. We made a fire first, then I dressed my trout while it was burning down to a nice bed of coals. I had brought a frying pan and a bottle of lard, salt, and buttered bread. We gathered a few service-berries, our trout were soon browned, and with water, clear, and as cold as ice, we had a feast. The quaking aspens are beginning to turn yellow, but no leaves have fallen. Their shadows dimpled and twinkled over the grass like happy children. The sound of the dashing, roaring water kept inviting me to cast for trout, but I did n't want to carry them so far, so we rested until the sun was getting low and then started for home, with the song of the locusts in our ears warning us that the melancholy days are almost here. We would come up over the top of a hill into the glory of a beautiful sunset with its gorgeous colors, then down into the little valley already purpling with mysterious twilight. So on, until, just at dark, we rode into our corral and a mighty tired, sleepy little girl was powerfully glad to get home.

After I had mailed my other letter I was afraid that you would think me plumb bold about the little Bo-Peep, and was a heap sorrier than you can think. If you only knew the hardships these poor men endure. They go two together and sometimes it is months before they see another soul, and rarely ever a woman. I would n't act so free in town, but these men see people so seldom that they are awkward and embarrassed. I like to put them at ease, and it is to be done only by being kind of hail-fellow-well-met with them. So far not one has ever misunderstood me and I have been treated with every courtesy and kindness, so I am powerfully glad you understand. They really enjoy doing these little things like fixing our dinner, and if my poor company can add to any one's pleasure I am too glad.

Sincerely yours,
Elinore Rupert.

Mr. Stewart is going to put up my house for me in pay for my extra work.

I am ashamed of my long letters to you, but I am such a murderer of language that I have to use it all to tell anything.

Please don't entirely forget me. Your letters mean so much to me and I will try to answer more promptly.

TONI MORRISON'S BLACK MAGIC

Jean Strouse

In her essay, "Silences," Tillie Olsen speaks of the silences of women writers that result from their commitments to families and the necessity to work at other jobs for a living, thus allowing only snatches of time, if any, for writing. For Olsen, it was, "Time on the bus, even when I had to stand, . . . the stolen moments at work . . . the deep night hours for as long as I could stay awake after the kids were in bed, after the household tasks were done, sometimes during." She then tells of the many great women writers who remained unmarried, were childless, who had household help, allowing them to pursue with luxurious single-mindedness their art, and later she writes of "the silences where the lives never come to writing." She continues

> Among these, the mute inglorious Miltons: those whose waking hours are all struggle for existence; the barely educated; the illiterate; women. Their silence the silence of centuries as to how life was, is for most of humanity. Traces of their making, of course, in folk song, lullaby, tales, language itself, jokes, maxims, superstitions—but we know nothing of the creators or how it was with them.

After reading Strouse's interview below, one gets the feeling that Morrison speaks for much of this silenced segment of humanity. And her commitments to her family, like those to her writing, come from a deep-seated reverence for her ancestors who demonstrated that in a hostile world, a race's survival may depend on the strength of familial bonds.

"Are you really going to put a middle-aged, gray-haired colored lady on the cover of this magazine?" laughed Toni Morrison on a recent visit to NEWSWEEK. Well, yes—but her autobiographical one-liner leaves out just about everything.

She *is* middle-aged (50), graying, female and black. She has been a dancer, an actress and a college beauty queen. She is now, among other things, an editor at Random House, a teacher (formerly at Yale, currently at Bard College), a member of the American Academy and Institute of Arts and Letters, a public lecturer, a wicked mimic (strictly off the record), an active member of the National Council of Arts, the mother and single parent of two sons, Harold and Slade, and a prize-winning novelist. Her third book, "Song of Solomon," won the National Book Critics Circle Award in 1977; her fourth, "Tar Baby" *(306 pages. Knopf. $11.95)*, has just been published.

She moves through this complicated life with regal grace and extraordinary self-possession. Yet she wears her dignity lightly, always ready to laugh, or to tell somebody where to get off, or to listen seriously. In Washington, she delivers a ringing defense of the artist in American society—to a standing ovation—as the National Council on the Arts discusses the Reagan Administration's budget cuts, and two hours later is chatting and joking with students at her alma mater, Howard University. One rainy Saturday afternoon, she chauffeurs 16-year-old Slade around Manhattan from a jazz lesson to a haircut

---

while being interviewed, without slighting either the interview or Slade. Toward the end of taping a Dick Cavett show, Cavett asks whether it wouldn't have been nice to do the whole hour without mentioning the word *black*. "I guess so," Morrison smiles, "but you started it."

She speaks and writes in a voice that ranges from Biblical and incantatory to down home and streetwise. "She paints pictures with words," says her look-alike friend, opera star Leontyne Price, "and reading or hearing those words is like listening to music." "That voice of hers is so *sure*," observes writer Toni Cade Bambara. "She lures you in, locks the doors and encloses you in a special, very particular universe—all in the first three pages."

WRY WISDOM: In the new novel, "Tar Baby," Morrison takes on a much larger world than she has before, drawing a composite portrait of America in black and white. She has produced that rare commodity, a truly public novel about the condition of society, examining the relations between blacks and whites, men and women, civilization and nature circa 1981. That may sound like it's good for you but no fun, but "Tar Baby" keeps you turning pages as if to find out who killed J. R.: a melodrama full of sex, violence, myth, wit, wry wisdom and the extraordinary sense of place that distinguishes all Morrison's writing, it wraps its urgent messages in a highly potent love story.

"Tar Baby" moves from a lush, Caribbean island to jazzy, modern New York to a tiny town in Florida, and it features four couples, one white and three black. There is wealthy, patrician Valerian Street, a retired Philadelphia candy manufacturer, and his wife, Margaret, the former "Principal Beauty of Maine." Serving the Streets are a black butler and cook, Sydney and Ondine Childs. Two island people, Gideon and Thérèse, do Valerian's yardwork and laundry. And at the center of it all is the Childses' niece, Jadine, a gorgeous young Sorbonne-educated model, who falls in love with a black American renegade called Son—a character in the tradition of Huck Finn, Nigger Jim, Stagger Lee and John Henry. Some readers may find "Tar Baby's" plot contrived and too consciously wrought, but if there are flaws in the novel's construction they don't matter: Morrison's voice, with its precision and musical cadence, is so original, she has so much to say about modern life and she creates such indelible characters that she leaves you affected, astonished and appalled.

The black writing of the 1960s had very specific things to say about America's most visible underclass. The revolutionary fervor of those years quieted down, but the pain did not. America still consists, for the most part, of two nations, separate and unequal. The black writing of the last ten years makes that point but has moved far away from political rhetoric; instead, like the best fictional portraits of an age, it holds up mirrors to show what most white people do not take the trouble to see.

BLEAKEST IMAGE: Toni Morrison's four books, written between 1967 and 1980, reflect an ugly America, and "Tar Baby" shows the bleakest image so far. Jadine is everything integration aims to produce. Fully assimilated into white American culture, she should be wonderful; instead, she is tragic, because "she has lost the original and ancient characteristics of her tribe."

Morrison hates it when people say she is not a "black writer." "Of course

I'm a black writer. That's like saying Dostoevski's not a Russian writer. They mean I'm not *just* a black writer, but categories like black writer, woman writer and Latin American writer aren't marginal anymore. We have to acknowledge that the thing we call 'literature' is pluralistic now, just as society ought to be. The melting pot never worked. We ought to be able to accept on equal terms everybody from the Hasidim to Walter Lippmann, from the Rastafarians to Ralph Bunche."

Morrison, like many of the powerful women in her fiction, has capacities that strike her friends as otherworldly. "I have a sense of Toni as a mythic character—as somehow larger than life," says novelist Mary Gordon. "I once dreamed that she bought a huge old Victorian mansion. It would one day be beautiful, but now it was a wreck, with cobwebs, broken windows, mice, rats and vermin everywhere. I asked her how she was going to deal with all that mess. She simply said, 'No problem,' and waved her arms in the air. Immediately the rats and roaches disappeared and the house was beautiful."

To Toni Morrison, however, there is no magic in writing, editing, teaching and raising two boys alone. Interviewed at home—a lovely, four-story former boathouse on the Hudson River north of Manhattan—she finishes fixing breakfast for 19-year-old Harold, then looks out of her bright kitchen window over the frozen expanse of river and muses: "Sure it's hard, but you do what you have to do. You *make* time; I don't go to theater or operas or dinners. But I think women dwell quite a bit on the duress under which they work, on how hard it is just to do it at all. We are traditionally rather proud of ourselves for having slipped creative work in there between the domestic chores and obligations. I'm not sure we deserve such big A-pluses for all that." She comes from a long line of people who did what they had to do to survive. It is their stories she tells in her novels—tales of the suffering and richness, the eloquence and tragedies of the black American experience. She saw a great deal of that pain and that strength in her own family's past.

Born in Lorain, Ohio, in 1931, she was christened Chloe Anthony Wofford. Her mother's family had migrated north from Greenville, Ala., around 1910. "They had lost their land, like a lot of black people at the turn of the century, and they were sharecroppers, which meant they were never able to get out of debt. My grandfather had left Greenville for Birmingham to earn money playing the violin. He sent money back, but my grandmother began to get nervous, all alone in Greenville, because her daughters were reaching puberty and that was a dangerous business in the South, in the country, because white boys began to circle. So my grandmother decided to leave. She sent her husband an oral message: 'We're heading north on the midnight train. If you ever want to see us again, you'll be on that train.'

"She didn't know if he got the message, but with $18 to her name she packed up her six or seven children and got them all to the train in Birmingham. It was the first city my mother had ever seen—she still remembers, 'We had *white* bread!' My grandfather was nowhere in sight. As the train left the station the children began to cry—then about an hour later, he showed up. He'd been there all along, hiding, for fear somedy would recognize him and stop them for owing money."

They traveled to Kentucky, where her grandfather worked in a coal mine. "My grandmother did washing, and my mother and her sister went to a little one-room school. One day the teacher, who was about 16 and white, was doing long division and having trouble explaining it. Since my mother and her sister already knew long division, they explained it to the teacher and the class. They came home all excited and proud of themselves, crowing, 'Mama, guess what we did? We taught the teacher long division!' My grandmother just said to her husband, 'Come on, Johnny, we have to move'."

They continued north, settling in the steel-mill town of Lorain on Lake Erie. The story of Morrison's father is "different but the same." "My father was a racist," she declares with a smile that does nothing to detract from the seriousness of what she is saying. "As a child in Georgia, he received shocking impressions of adult white people, and for the rest of his life felt he was justified in despising all whites, and that they were not justified in despising him." Did his racial attitudes cause his children to distrust whites? "Not when we were little," says Morrison. "I knew he was wrong. I went to school with white children—they were my friends. There was no awe, no fear. Only later, when things got . . . sexual . . . did I see how clear the lines really were. But when I was in first grade nobody thought I was inferior. I was the only black in the class and the only child who could read!"

Her father did provide her with a strong sense of her own value on her own terms. At 13, she cleaned house for a white family after school. One day she complained to her father because the work was hard and the woman was mean. He said: "Girl, you don't live there. You live *here*. So you go do your work, get your money and come on home."

GHOST STORIES: All her early life she absorbed the black lore, music, language, myths and rituals that give her prose its special flavor and tone. "We were intimate with the supernatural," she recalls. Her parents told thrillingly terrifying ghost stories. Her mother sang constantly. Her grandmother kept a dream book and played the numbers off it, decoding dream symbols to determine what number to bet on. Morrison's world, like the world of her novels, was filled with signs, visitations, ways of knowing that reached beyond the five senses.

As a studious adolescent, she read the great Russian novels, "Madame Bovary," Jane Austen. "Those books were not written for a little black girl in Lorain, Ohio, but they were so magnificently done that I got them anyway— they spoke directly to me out of their own specificity. I wasn't thinking of writing then—I wanted to be a dancer like Maria Tallchief—but when I wrote my first novel years later, I wanted to capture that same specificity about the nature and feeling of the culture *I* grew up in."

She does. In that astonishing first novel, "The Bluest Eye," she wrote about "the people who in all literature were always peripheral—little black girls who were props, background; those people were never center stage, and those people were me." Pecola Breedlove, the little black girl in "The Bluest Eye," thinks everything would be all right if only she had beautiful blue eyes. Here, a black woman who explains to her son the difference between colored people and niggers ("colored people were neat and quiet, niggers were dirty and loud") looks at Pecola:

She had seen this little girl all of her life. Hanging out of windows over saloons in Mobile, crawling over the porches of shotgun houses on the edge of town, sitting in bus stations holding paper bags and crying to mothers who kept saying "Shet up!" Hair uncombed, dresses falling apart, shoes untied and caked with dirt. They had stared at her with great uncomprehending eyes. Eyes that questioned nothing and asked everything. Unblinking and unabashed, they stared up at her. The end of the world lay in their eyes, and the beginning, and all the waste in between.

In "The Souls of Black Folk," published in 1903, W. E. B. Du Bois described the peculiar "double consciousness" constantly experienced by the American black—"this sense of always looking at one's self through the eyes of others, of measuring one's soul by the tape of a world that looks on in amused contempt and pity. One ever feels his twoness—an American, a Negro; two souls, two thoughts, two unreconciled strivings; two warring ideas in one dark body, whose dogged strength alone keeps it from being torn asunder."

That consciousness, in Toni Morrison's case, is triple: American, black and female. Until recently, the principal black voices heard by white America were male. So were the famous titles: Richard Wright's "Native Son," Ralph Ellison's "Invisible Man," Claude Brown's "Manchild in the Promised Land," James Baldwin's "Notes of a Native Son." There was also Du Bois himself, and Jean Toomer, whose haunting montage novel, "Cane," came out in 1923 at the beginning of the Harlem renaissance. The collected works of these writers amounted to an eloquent cry of protest and rage: America had freed its slaves only to take away their manhood. "I am invisible," wrote Ellison, "simply because people refuse to see me." "Dear James," wrote Baldwin to a nephew in "The Fire Next Time": "Your grandfather . . . was defeated long before he died because, at the bottom of his heart, he really believed what white people said about him. . . . You can only be destroyed by believing that you really are what the white world calls a *nigger*. I tell you this because I love you, and please don't you ever forget it."

The words of these writers echoed throughout the country in the civil-rights movement of the 1960s. Toward the end of that decade, as the cry "Black power!" rose from the streets of Newark and Detroit, other writers and speakers emerged: Stokely Carmichael, LeRoi Jones, Eldridge Cleaver, H. Rap Brown. "Those books and political slogans about power were addressed to white men," observed Toni Morrison, "trying to explain or prove something to them. The fight was between men, for king of the hill." There had always been black women bards telling slave narratives, and "moral uplift" writers such as Margaret Walker, Lorraine Hansberry, Alice Childress and Gwendolyn Brooks, but their voices were rarely heard outside the black community. Baldwin referred, in "Nobody Knows My Name," to the "as yet unwritten history of the Negro woman."

SPECIAL VANTAGE POINT: That history has now begun to be written. In the embattled '60s, poets Nikki Giovanni, Mari Evans, June Jordan and Sonia Sanchez made art out of their anger at the white world. By the early '70s the political ground had shifted; there was less talk of black power, more talk of women's liberation, and writers such as Morrison, Bambara, Alice Walker and Gayl Jones wrote fiction from a very special vantage point. To be young, gifted, female and black was to be able to speak in a voice the reading public had not heard before.

*A Portuguese seaman turned plantation owner, he took her out of the field
when she was still a child and put her to work in his whorehouse while she was
a child. . . . She was the pretty little one with the almond eyes and coffee-bean
skin, his favorite. "A good little piece. My Best. Dorita. Little good piece."*

—Gayl Jones, "Corregidora"

*Gretchen smiles, but it's not a smile and I'm thinking that girls never really
smile at each other because they don't know how and don't want to know how
and there's probably no one to teach us how, cause grown-up girls don't know
either.*

—Toni Cade Bambara, "Raymond's Run" in "Gorilla My Love"

As an editor at Random House, Toni Morrison has presided over this
cultural awakening, publishing Bambara and Jones, as well as Angela Davis
and some of the best recent works in black history—notably, "The Black
Book," a scrapbook of 300 years of black American life, and Ivan Van
Sertima's "They Came Before Columbus." "Toni has done more to encourage
and publish other black writers than anyone I know," says another of her
authors, Andrew Young. Bambara calls her "a superb editor, a real wizard. She
floats little suggestions past my eyeballs and smiles her magical smile—I trust
her judgment absolutely."

Of Morrison as a writer, Bambara says: "The fact that she is there, with her
canny, spooky voice, gives other people inspiration to develop, to fly." And her
friend James Baldwin says, "We still overlook the incredible stamina—Toni
would say 'sheer intelligence'—of black women in their ability to be all those
things which somehow hold a man together. Toni shows this, with a sense of
humor that is the key to a sense of life."

PAIN OF OPPRESSION: There are virtually no white people in Morrison's first
three novels. She concentrates instead on the "village" culture of blacks in
small, Midwestern cities like Lorain, where people have names like Chicken
Little, First Corinthians and Milkman Dead—and where the owner of Reba's
Grill "cooked in her hat because she couldn't remember the ingredients without it." The pain of oppression makes itself constantly felt.

Pecola Breedlove in "The Bluest Eye" gets ignored by her mother, taunted by
her schoolmates, raped by her father and driven eventually to madness. In one
heartbreaking scene she takes two friends to see her mother, Pauline, a domestic in a white man's house. When Pecola inadvertently knocks a blueberry pie
all over the clean kitchen floor, Pauline flies into a rage and shoos her out—
then turns to comfort the terrified, flaxen-haired little girl of the house who
keeps asking, "Who were they, Polly?"

As a christening present in February, Toni Morrison gave Mary Gordon's
infant daughter a copy of "The Arabian Nights," with the inscription: "Here
are some stories a woman made up and told in order to save her life. They
contain all the wisdom there is and all you will ever need." Morrison wrote
"The Bluest Eye" in her 30s—in a sense, in order to save her life. She was
working as a textbook editor in Syracuse, N.Y., and caring for her two small
boys. She had by this time gone to Howard, to Cornell for an M.A. in English
and then eventually back to Howard to teach. There she had met a number of
people who came to prominence in the '60s, including Amiri Baraka, then
named LeRoi Jones ("He really turned that campus around"), and Andrew

Young. She taught Stokely Carmichael, "the kind of student you always want in a class—smart, perceptive, funny and a bit of a rogue. He *never* worked, and he stimulated all the others to think." The day Carmichael graduated in 1964 he told her he'd been accepted at New York's Union Theological Seminary—but first he was going to Mississippi to spend a summer in the field. Another student, Claude Brown, asked her to read his 800-page manuscript. "I said, what? Eight hundred pages? Claude, *come on!* A nickel a word I'll read it for you." The book turned out, of course, to be "Manchild in the Promised Land."

At Howard she also met the man she married, an architecture student from Jamaica named Harold Morrison. The marriage lasted six years, and when it "dissolved in smoke" in 1964, she found herself alone with a 3-year-old and another child on the way. For all her forthrightness, Morrison remains a very private person and refuses to discuss her husband (he lives in Jamaica, and she and the boys see him occasionally) or her current relationships in print.

She went home to Lorain, had her baby, took the job in Syracuse and started "The Bluest Eye." She says: "That was 1967 and the slogan 'Black is beautiful' was in the air. I loved it, but something was missing. Everybody kept saying how beautiful the Vietnamese people were—'and such beautiful people, too,' they said. And I thought, well, if they were ugly would it have been better? So I wrote about a child who was ugly—Pecola is a perfect, defeated victim—only she was also beautiful."

One of Morrison's greatest gifts as a storyteller is her wide-spirited sympathy for the villains as well as the victims. Even Pecola's father, who would be a monster in less skillful hands, becomes truly tragic, trapped by social circumstances, able to express love only in the horrifying rape of his daughter. The huge sorrow that inhabits all of Morrison's work has more in common with Greek tragedy than any other form. Like classical heroes at the hands of their gods and fates, her people are moved by forces beyond their control—and their pain is deeply personal.

"The Bluest Eye" came out in 1970 and sold modestly. Six months later, Morrison began work on her second novel, "Sula." By this time she had moved to New York to edit books for Random House; she made up a lot of "Sula" in her head on the subway commuting between her home in Queens and work in Manhattan.

TOWN PARIAH: Like the first novel, the second deals with a subject nobody had written much about—female friendships. It takes place in a town called Medallion, Ohio, between 1919 and 1965. Because Sula Peace and her friend Nel Wright had discoverd that they were "neither white nor male, and that all freedom and triumph was forbidden to them, they had set about creating something else to be." Nel eventually marries and settles into conventional life. The experimental Sula takes off for a larger world. She returns after ten years to seduce Nel's husband and become the town pariah, capable of inflicting pain in all directions because she doesn't feel a thing—not for Nel, or Nel's husband or her own mother burning to death. Then she falls in love with Ajax, who says that "all [women] want, man, is they own misery. Ax em to die for you and they yours for life." But he doesn't want Sula for life, and leaves her.

Relations between the sexes never have happy endings in Morrison's novels. "Racism will destroy love," she tells the students at Howard. "It will. It's not some abstract something floating around in The New York Times, it's a real thing. It hurts." Ajax knows who he is and flees Sula's possessive desire. Sula's attempt to escape who *she* is—"neither white nor male"—and to achieve an absolute freedom from the past costs not only love but her life.

In all of Morrison's stories, seeking or denying one's cultural roots is more important than happy endings. In the stunningly powerful "Song of Solomon," Milkman Dead leaves his native Michigan for the South to find a cache of gold. Instead, he finds the much more valuable treasure of the Dead family past and the heritage of slavery with its anguish and truth. Milkman learns about himself on that journey—learns everything from the grim nature of his parents' marriage ("Ruth began her days stunned into silence by her husband's contempt and ended them wholly animated by it") through the weird wisdom of his aunt, Pilate, to the real meaning of the ancient myth that blacks can fly. Morrison establishes intimacy with the supernatural by giving Pilate no navel (the selfless, all-seeing Pilate may be the best character she has yet created) and so deftly weaves her fictional spell that you willingly believe in Milkman's final discovery: "If you surrendered to the air, you could *ride* it." If she has a certain literary kinship with the Greeks, she has another with the supernaturalism of such contemporary Latin American novelists as Gabriel García Márquez, whose sense of cultural diversity and social commitment she greatly admires: "Art can be both uncompromisingly beautiful and socially responsible."

"Song of Solomon" was a resounding success, winning Morrison prizes and thousands of new fans and establishing her as a major American writer. Unlike many successful authors who keep writing the same novel, Morrison has kept moving, taking risks, trying something larger with each new book. She wrote about little girls in "The Bluest Eye," older girls and young women in "Sula" and a man in "Song of Solomon."

AMBITIOUS STEP: She has often been said to be one of the few women writing today able fully to imagine her way inside male characters. How does she do it? "I didn't think I could at first, but I had to try. I learned a lot from my sons, seeing how excited they got by going near danger, for instance—they'd come away *charged,* lifted, as if somebody'd turned the volume up. And my father taught me, too. He died before I started 'Song of Solomon,' but I had long conversations with him in my head anyway, to learn what he knew about men. So you see, I have my own version of the supernatural."

In "Tar Baby" she takes her most ambitious step yet. She moves from the midwest to an island in the Caribbean; she uses less narrative exposition, giving her characters dramatic life through their own actions and dialogue; and she moves nature and myth, always strong and subtle forces in her work, to the foreground—emperor butterflies think, ghosts of blind slaves ride horses in the hills and the trees are marshaling for war.

"Tar Baby" takes as its point of departure the old folk tale (antedating Uncle Remus) that Morrison heard as a child: a farmer sets out a tar baby dressed in bonnet and skirt to trap the troublesome rabbit. The rabbit hits the tar baby when it doesn't answer his "Good morning," gets stuck and is caught. He begs the farmer, "Boil me in oil, skin me alive, but *please* don't throw me in that briar patch." The farmer falls for the trick and throws him in the briar patch; as the clever rabbit lickety-splits away, he sings, "This is where I was born and bred at."

As Morrison's novel opens, Jadine has left Paris to visit the Streets in the Caribbean. Valerian has paid for her education, and she is living as a guest in his house, sleeping upstairs and eating in the dining room, waited on by her doting uncle and aunt. When the proud outlaw Son jumps ship and intrudes on their lives, his presence shakes out all of the household's worst secrets, violent hostilities, pent-up racial, sexual and familial furies. As the house of Atreus crashes around them, Son and Jadine fall in love—and here the strong Morrison themes come into play. High-yellow Jadine, cut off from all the funk and blackness of her past, essentially bought and raised by a white man, cannot be the woman Son needs her to be—she can't live with him in the briar patch; and he cannot live without her. The tar baby and the rabbit lock in a fatal embrace.

Morrison's genius lies in her uncanny ability to immerse you totally in the world she creates. Listen to her lure you in, sense by sense: "Fog came to that place in wisps sometimes, like the hair of maiden aunts. . . . Salt crystals clung to each other. Oysters uncurled their fringes and sank to the bottom of the tureen. Patience was difficult to come by in that fuzzy caul and breathing harder still. It was then that the word 'island' had meaning." And watch her sketch a complex character in a few swift strokes: the blind old island visionary, Thérèse, refuses "to speak to the American Negroes, and . . . even to acknowledge the presence of the white Americans in her world. To effect this she believed all she had to do was not look at them . . . So her face was always turned away when they addressed her and her glance . . . went to a distant point on the horizon which she could not have seen if her life depended on it. What they took for inattentiveness was a miracle of concentration."

MORAL VISION: Morrison never preaches, and her books score no narrow political points. Still, like all the best stories, hers are driven by an abiding moral vision. Implicit in all her characters' grapplings with who they are is a large sense of human nature and love—and a reach for understanding of something larger than the moment or the self. By showing the inside of Pecola's destruction, Sula's narcissism, Milkman's quest and Jadine's loss, Toni Morrison explores not only the ways in which social forces batter the human spirit, but also the ways in which that spirit lives. "I wish I'd a knowed more people," says the dying Pilate in "Song of Solomon." "I would of loved 'em all. If I'd a knowed more, I would a loved more."

That rainy Saturday as Morrison drove Slade around Manhattan, she talked at some length about her father and the specific, appalling incidents in his family past that led him to despise whites. When I got home later, I found that my tape recorder had failed to record the conversation. I told Toni the next day. She was silent a moment, then said, "I know why. I told you something I wasn't supposed to tell you. So my father took care of it. I'm not surprised. He's done that before."

For all her ease and success in the white world, Morrison's strongest attachments are to her sons, her family in Lorain and a few intimate black friends.

She bought her boathouse on the Hudson two years ago, after the success of "Song of Solomon." The day she first saw it, she walked out along the dock for a view of the river and felt her father's voice expressing his extreme delight in this particular place. Seeing her there now, ensconced with her work, her kids and her wonder-woman life, you can hear her father approving: "Girl, you don't live there. You live *here*."

SEVEN

Sisters

ALTHOUGH SOME WOMEN MAY have broken from convention, custom prescribes that women's associations with one another must necessarily take a backseat to their relationships with men. So commonly understood is this norm that a current telephone commercial plays upon it with predictable results. Two women friends are together; one gets a call from a man. "He's back, . . . " she excitedly tells the other, cupping her hand over the receiver. "I'm not very good at writing either," she helps him apologize for not keeping in touch. "Saturday night?" She repeats his inquiry, looking questioningly at her friend who then raises her hands in mock surrender. And so the message is clear: Women's plans with each other can be preempted by a man without as much as a whimper of protest from the rejected friend. Enter lover or husband and exit (female) friend remains the unwritten rule governing women's friendships. The maxim teaches women not to feel guilty about breaking an engagement with a woman friend to go out with a man (any man).

341

The jilted friend must act delighted about the disrupted plans, too. To do otherwise, to show anger, hurt, or disappointment, breaches the tacit understanding.

The order of the day tells women that because of their competition for men, they cannot and should not ally with each other. Self-appointed advice givers warn against trusting another woman for she will stab you in the back, connive against you, lie to you, gossip about you, and surely steal your man. A legion of characters from novels, stories, films and soap operas act out these stereotypes, and, to complicate matters, some women do fulfill these prophesies.

But in spite of the popular image depicting women as incapable of maintaining lasting relationships and associations, female friendships have played a crucial role in the lives of women in all eras and social classes. Carroll Smith-Rosenberg, in her highly acclaimed essay on the female world of love and ritual in the nineteenth century, found evidence for the existence of large, intergenerational networks of supportive female friends and relatives among middle- and upper-class women. Working-class and poor women have long maintained informal networks, too, taking turns baby sitting, swapping children's clothing, lending a knowing ear, and sometimes sharing food. Other informal female networks come to mind as well. Suburban coffee klatches arose from the loneliness created by post World War II geographic and social mobility as young families moved in unprecedented numbers to the suburbs. Life on the prairie represents an earlier form of isolation women suffered. But there, too, women came together to help one another, as Susan Glaspell's popular play *Trifles*, reprinted below, illustrates.

But all of the networks described above require women to schedule their meetings around the daily needs of men. Should a woman not want her female friendships to be second place to her relationships with men, or should she entertain the possibility of going through life without a man, she is again presented with a number of negative pictures, giving her pause for thought. Many people regard women without men as incomplete, lonely, frustrated, sick, or monstrous. A woman who chooses the convent, people whisper, must have done so because she couldn't get a man, was jilted by a man, or is suffering from the unrequited love of a man. Widows, especially those who lose husbands early in life, are almost always described as lonely and are expected to remarry after a certain period of time. Friends and neighbors pitied nineteenth-century spinsters for not having husbands and children, and in the middle of the twentieth century experts like Farnham and Lundberg described single career women as sexually perverse. And regardless of the growing literature presenting lesbian themes, perspectives, and experiences, "coming out" continues to be a decision fraught with fear and trepidation for many gay women. So the popular picture of women without men is not a pretty one, and the portrayal of women who opt to live with women rather than men is even less kind.

Yet, whether sexual in nature or not, many women have chosen to go against the grain, living most of their private lives in a female-defined and female-dominated world. Women's friendship groups have acted as buffers between women and the male-dominated public world. "Thine in the bonds of womanhood," feminist and abolitionist Sarah Grimke signed her *Letters on the Equality of the Sexes and the Conditions of Women* in 1838, recognizing one may be sure, the double meaning of her words. The correspondence between many nineteenth-century feminists, for example, illustrates the succor these women gave one another in the face of skeptical, if not hostile, responses from family, acquaintances, and the public at large. Similarly, "consciousness-raising" and other female-centered support groups developed during the modern women's movement, acting as asylums from an unaccepting world.

As a result of their banding together, then, women have enacted changes unimaginable if women were indeed incapable of working together. The late nineteenth century and early twentieth century stands out as a time when large numbers of women came together in religious, social, and civic voluntary associations for purposes of social reform. Some of these organizations, like the Women's Christian Temperance Union, began in the nineteenth century but many others evolved in response to the times. Formed in 1890, the Consumers League worked hard for improvement in working conditions for women and for passage of child labor laws. And the Settlement House movement was in full swing. Although most of the women participating in these activities were white, middle- and upper-class Protestants, other social classes and ethnic groups organized for change, too. Working-class women helped to found the Women's Trade Union League in 1903, and in 1912, Jewish women established Hadassah, the women's Zionist organization.

The formation of black women's clubs represents a notable historical movement of this time. Along with fighting for equality for blacks and providing companionship, the black reform societies helped black women find employment, set up day nurseries and kindergartens, and established homes to protect young black women from sexual abuse. Like many middle-class white women of the day, the women drawn to the black club movement were middle-class and educated, but unlike many of their white counterparts the vast majority worked outside the home, knowing firsthand the problems their black sisters faced in a racially and sexually hostile labor market.

There is, then, an abundant history of female friendships and associations that conventional wisdom fails to acknowledge. Moreover, serious clubwomen have been misrepresented often as frivolous social butterflies and snobbish matrons. And although these images have some basis in fact, women in voluntary associations have accomplished important social changes in this country, calling into question the appropriateness of the stereotype.

Negative stereotypes of sorority die hard, but recently scholars have rescued from oblivion many documents demonstrating the richness of the history of women's friendships and associations. Coupled with a growing collection of contemporary works, this literature provides a source for a continuing elaboration of models of female friendship and networking experiences. Perhaps the current emphasis on sisterhood, along with the rediscovery of women's history, will help lay to rest the myth that women are incapable of loving one another.

PASTORALE
Paule Marshall

Paule Marshall, like Selina Boyce, the heroine of her novel, *Brown Girl, Brownstones* (1959), grew up in the Barbadian community in Brooklyn during the Depression and World War II. Marshall graduated Phi Beta Kappa from Brooklyn College in 1953 and later worked as a magazine writer and researcher. In addition to *Brown Girl,* Marshall has published a collection of short stories, *Soul Clap Hands and Sing* (1961), and two other novels, *The Chosen Place, the Timeless People* (1969) and *Praisesong for the Widow* (1983).

Although "Pastorale" focuses on the early asdolescent friendship of Selina and her childhood companion, Beryl Challenor, in *Brown Girl* Marshall has captured a rich diversity of female-female relationships, supportive and antagonistic, throughout the life cycle. Much of *Brown Girl* centers on the world of the Bajan (Barbadian) immigrant women. We learn about the social network of the community, especially its women, through Silla Boyce, "the mother," and her intimates, Florrie Trotman and Iris Hurley. We witness the power of the mother-daughter bond in the stormy relationship between Silla and Selina. Through the character of Miss Thompson, the Afro-American hairdresser, we hear, with Selina, the gruesome tales of growing up black and female in the South.

. . . It was summer again now and Sunday, and Selina had been wandering the house since dawn. When Maritze was at mass she sat with Miss Mary in the dust-yellow room while she wheezed and gasped her dirge of memories. Afterward she stopped at Suggie's and found her sprawled amid her rumpled sheets, sluggish from the rough pleasures of her night. She laughed a good deal, a lovely sensual sound, and Selina gazing shyly at her from the foot of the bed said, "You're a summer woman, Miss Suggie."

The laugh became more wanton; Suggie struggled up, wrapped her naked body in the sheet and trailing it behind her, sauntered into the kitchen. She returned with a small glass of rum. "Come," she beckoned, "I gon make you a summer woman too, just for your womanishness."

Despite Selina's struggles she forced open her lips and the rum bit into her tongue and spurted hot down her throat. They stood quietly afterward, Selina rubbing her chest and frowning.

"Y'know, it feels kinda good," she said after a time.

"'Deed it does, faith!"

On her way downstairs, the rum coiling hot in her stomach, she felt that she, like Suggie, carried the sun inside her. Passing the parlor she glimpsed her sister at the piano and gave her a shout, receiving only an exasperated sigh in answer. Ina's body was bent in the same exasperated pose, her head bowed as if pressed down by the heat. Selina peered at her through the parlor's embalmed gloom, wondering at her strangeness, wincing at the wrong notes that punctuated her playing.

"Hey, cut out that noise," she called, passing on. "Daddy's in by now and trying to sleep."

He had come while she was upstairs and was asleep in the sun parlor with his clothes on. One arm shielded his eyes from the sun; his body seemed sapped like Suggie's from his night with the woman. For a long time Selina sat on the bed, gazing down at his face, innocent in sleep, at his chest moving lightly under the shirt. He was a dark god, she dreamed, tiptoeing away, who had fallen from his heaven and lay stunned on earth . . .

The mother was the only one who had not succumbed to the day's torpor, and as Selina entered the kitchen she helplessly admired her. She sat cool, alert, caged in sunlight from the barred window, holding the newspaper a little away from her as though the news of the war in Europe might contaminate her.

Selina said, "Let's have some lemonade."

The mother gave her a look that was shifting and complex. On one hand it dismissed her and the offer of the lemonade; on the other, it beckoned her close as though to embrace her. She said, "The best thing in heat like this is a hot-hot cup of tea."

"I'll make tea then."

"What kind of tea you could make?"

"I can make it."

The mother was silent and Selina made the tea and brought it to the table. Silla put down the newspaper and, without looking at her but frowning scornfully, took a quick sip. "Lord-God, tea strong enough to choke a horse," she complained but drank it, and they sat within the cage of sunlight, drinking the hot tea, reading and sweating, an ease and intimacy between them. Selina grew bold as the rum and hot tea fired her blood and asked after a time, "Can I go to Prospect Park with Beryl?"

"Pestilence," Silla said without annoyance, "here it tis the world is almost in war and all you thinking 'bout is patrolling the streets."

"Can I go?"

"You must gon hoof it there 'cause I'm not giving you penny one."

"But can I go without Ina? Just this once, please."

"What you need Ina for any more? You's more woman now than she'll ever be, soul. G'long."

Selina folded the funnies and placed them on the table. She did not hurry, afraid that if she did the mother might renege. But once outside the kitchen she ran, fleeing the house and its tumid silence, racing down Chauncey Street, which dozed in the Sunday torpor. The brownstones leaned against the soft sky, the ones owned or leased by the West Indians looking almost new with their neat yards, new shades and fresh painted black iron fences, while the others where the whites still lived looked more faded in the hard sunlight.

Selina thought of the white people behind those drawn green shades as having wasted faces and worn hands, as sitting all day in bare rooms. She was annoyed, for they seemed to disdain her by never showing themselves. She picked up a stick and ran, rasping it on their fences, hoping to startle them out of their dusty silence and bring them to the window . . .

There were new cream-colored shades with fringes at every window of the Challenor house and behind them filmy curtains waving in the warm wind. The Challenors had started buying the house two years ago. The wife, Gert Challenor, despised by the Bajan women because of her docility, did day's work. The husband, Percy, worked in the same mattress factory with Selina's father and sold stockings at night to meet the two mortgages. Silla always said with grudging respect, "But look at Percy. He's nothing but a work horse."

Selina stood in the dining room now, looking at him where he sat at the head of his table with his six children arrayed around him and his plump anxious wife facing him. To Selina he was a pagan deity of wrath, his children the subjects cowering before the fire flaring from his nostrils, his wife the priestess ministering to his needs. A thought cringed in the corner of her mind as she greeted him: he was too big to live among ordinary people . . .

"Selina getting big," he said, and it was like the pronouncement of an oracle.

"In truth," Gert Challenor agreed hurriedly, "these New York children does shoot up fast enough. How old you is, girl?"

"Eleven."

"How things at the house?" he commanded.

"All right."

"Silla and yuh fatha?"

"Fine."

"And Ina there? I guess she's a half a woman by now."

"She's okay."

"Yuh fatha still studying figures?"

"It's accounting. Yes"

"These white people ain gon hire him."

"Selina mussa get she smartness from Deighton," Gert Challenor added quickly.

He excluded this with a blunt gesture. "How his piece of ground home?"

"All right, I guess," she murmured and her stomach tightened.

"He done anything about it?"

"Like what?"

"Sell it?"

"No."

"Percy . . ."

He silenced his wife with a hard look. "He ain renting it either?"

"I dunno."

"But c'dear, how the child could know that?" his wife said.

"How yuh mean? Selina know full-well everybody in Brooklyn talking 'bout she fatha and his piece of ground. I tell you those men from Bridgetown home is all the same. They don know a thing 'bout handling money and property and thing so. They's spree boys. Every last one them . . . There ain nothing wrong with wanting piece of ground home but only when you got a sufficient back-prop here. I tell you, he's a disgrace!"

And for Selina, listening with lowered eyes, Percy Challenor had established irrevocably that her father was a disgrace. She felt the hate uncoil and tears prick her eyes. She waited eagerly for his next question, ready to meet his eyes with venom.

But Beryl rose between them, asking, "Can I go to Prospect Park with Selina, Daddy?" and his eyes swept across to her.

"Where wunna getting the money?"

"We've been saving what people gave us . . ."

Even the smaller children stopped eating while he deliberated. Finally he declared, "All right then. But make haste back here."

Outside, under the poised sun, they stood apart, suddenly shy. Then glancing up, they smiled secretly, and Selina hooted loud and began to spin. Beryl, laughing, rushed around her, snatching at her dress to stop her. Their hands met and Selina separated Beryl's fingers and meshed them with hers. Together, their hands closed into one fist, their bodies joined in a single rhythm, they skipped the three blocks to the Tompkins Avenue trolley.

They took separate window seats on the trolley so that they could watch the panorama of Sunday in Brooklyn strung out under the sun. To Selina the colors, the people seemed to run together. Dark, lovely little girls in straw bonnets flowed into little boys with their rough hair parted neatly on the side; into women in sheer dresses which whipped around their brown legs; into a bevy of church sisters swathed in black as though mourning their own imminent deaths; into the vacant, sun-grazed windows of the closed stores; into endless colonnades of trees down the side streets; into a blue sweep of sky; into dark little girls in straw bonnets . . . Life suddenly was nothing but this change and return . . .

Those colors, those changing forms were the shape of her freedom, Selina knew. She had finally passed the narrow boundary of herself and her world. She could no longer be measured by Chauncey Street or the park or the nearby school. "Lord," she whispered behind her hand, "I'm free."

In Prospect Park, with her hand in Beryl's and the sun shimmering before her eyes, she was drunk with freedom. She swaggered, Beryl in tow, into the zoo; she breathed deep the rank animal smells even as Beryl held her nose; she stopped at every vendor stand and bought ices, popcorn and peanuts and scattered the wrappers and shells behind her. At the seals' pond she leaped as they leaped into the sun and cried loud with them as they crashed sobbing into the water. Holding Beryl's waist she watched a lioness with her cubs sucking savagely at her teats.

"It looks just like Virgie Farnum," she said.

Beryl nodded. "It does a little. I'm only having two children when I get married. A boy and a girl. The boy first."

"I'm not having any. I'd never let them chop loose my stomach."

"Whaddya talking about—chop loose your stomach?"

"Don't you know yet that's what they do when you have a baby?"

"That's not so. They don't chop anything. It just pops out."

"Pops out?" she laughed. "Pops outta where?"

"Underneath," Beryl cried, angering.

"Underneath, where? Who told you that lie?"

"A girl in school. And it's not a lie." Beryl pushed Selina's arm from around her waist.

"Ya see. Somebody in school. A kid. When I heard Virgie Farnum telling my mother how they chopped loose her stomach and took out the baby. Grown-up people now who have children and should know."

Beryl glowered across at her, "I'm a year older than you, Selina Boyce, and I know too. You might be smart in school but you don't know anything else. You're a kid, a silly little kid still. Besides, I saw my mother naked once and she didn't have any scars on her stomach."

"They had healed."

Beryl turned away in disgust. "You think you know everything."

Silent, not touching, they walked out of the zoo into the picnic grounds, where families ate a Sunday dinner of potato salad and fried chicken out of paper plates and small children screamed and raced across the scarred grass. On the slopes, amid the rocks and trees there, lovers lay in each other's arms, their faces close and murmuring. Selina gazed at them and slowly her lips parted, blindly her hand groped for Beryl as she was shaken by something she sensed in them. It seemed that they—those laughing girls with grass in their hair, those bold boys with daring hands—had attained the fullest freedom. Back on the trolley she had had the merest glimpse of it; it had charged her blood like a stimulant when she was walking in the zoo. But their freedom was richer, fuller and denied her.

"Look, two of them are kissing," Beryl said, clinging to her arm.

It was more than just kissing, Selina wanted to say, watching their mouths open into each other and their bodies slowly sink into the grass. They were pouring themselves into each other. Suddenly she could not look any more. Tears stung her eyes. Pushing Beryl away she raced into a small wood near by and bounded up a low ridge there. Yelping, she plunged up and down the rise, the shrubbery cracking loud and the twigs whipping her legs, while Beryl stared open-mouthed below. Finally she paused on the crest, her wild shouts died and she stared, rapt, down onto a field where boys were playing baseball. From this height, she felt a profound detachment from them, from everyone, even Beryl. She was no longer human, she told herself, but a bit of pollen floating over the field and circling the world on a wind.

"Wait till your mother sees your dress," Beryl said when she climbed down.

"I don't give one damn."

"You're mad again," Beryl said helplessly. "Well come on let's get outta this sun. My mother says I'm getting black running around with you in the sun."

They searched until they found a shaded place within the shadow of a high rock. Beryl sat on her handkerchief and modestly tucked her dress under her knees while Selina sprawled flat on the ground, her face pressed to the earth, which was fecund with the oncoming summer; her lips brushed the grass, which was still cool and a little damp from the dew.

"I'm sorry I cursed," she said gently, touching Beryl's silver bangles. "You got new bangles?"

"Uh-huh. My grandmother sent them from home."

"I've still got the ones I wore as a baby."

"Me too. In a drawer someplace."

"Mine turn black when I'm sick."

"So do mine. My father says they know what goes on inside your body."

"It's funny," she began musingly, thinking of Percy Challenor presiding at the table. "I can't imagine your father ever being small. Or my mother either . . ."

"Well they were and my father was smart in school too. Maybe that's why he beats us so when we get bad marks."

"My father only beat me once. Long ago. I can't even remember why now." What she could remember was that after the first blow she had been strangely numb to the others. Instead she had been aware only of his body against hers, his muscles moving smoothly under his skin as he flailed her, and his heaving chest crushed against hers. She had been fused with him; not only had he breathed for her but his heart had beaten for them both.

She slapped at a fly on her leg and killed it.

"My mother never beats me," Beryl was saying.

"See, I killed it." Selina showed her the squashed fly and then wiped her hand on the grass. "Ugh, they've got blood like people." Then in the ample silence of rock and sky she said, "I imagine sometimes that I don't belong to them."

"Them who?"

"My family."

"What makes you imagine that?"

"I dunno. I saw a dead girl once. Ina took me." She ran her hand hard over the grass, still cleaning it.

"What'd she die from?"

"I dunno, but she was pretty. I think of her a lot and think of me instead of her in the box and everybody crying."

"Those aren't good thoughts, Selina."

"I know. And then maybe being dead is like before you was born, not knowing what's going on and not being able to see. Then I wouldn't know who was crying and who wasn't."

"My father wants me to be a lawyer since I'm the oldest. He told me the other day," Beryl said brightly after a long silence. "My father says you can always make money at that among your own people. What does your father want you to be?"

Selina still wiped her hand on the grass.

"Selina!"

"What?"

"What does your father want you to be?"

"He never said I had to be anything."

"Doesn't he care?"

"Of course he cares," she shouted.

"Maybe he'll let you be a poet."

"A poetess."

"If I get good marks this term I'm getting ice skates."

"Doris has some."

"Doris, I can't stand her!" Beryl said venomously. "She thinks she's cute because she's light and has good hair and all the boys like her. D'ya know she's got boys coming to see her already?"

"I hate boys," Selina cried.

After a hesitant silence, Beryl said, "So do I."

They lay in the ample silence of rock and trees, staring into the enormous blue expanse of sky and at the rock shutting out the sun. They heard a sharp crack and shouts from the baseball field and Beryl said, her eyes averted,

"Remember what we were talking about in the zoo when you got so mad?"

"You got mad, not me."

"Okay. Well anyway what I was saying is true. I can prove it. I bleed sometimes," she said quietly.

"What?"

"I bleed sometimes."

"So what. Everybody does."

"Not from a cut or anything but from below. Where the baby pops out. Ina does too. That's why she gets pains every once in a while. I'll tell you, if you want to hear . . ."

"Tell me." And beneath her eagerness there was dread.

Beryl raised up, gathering her dress neatly under her. Her eyes flitted nervously across Selina's intense face. Then, with her head bowed and a squeamish look she explained it all. "That's why I'm getting these things," she concluded, jabbing her small breasts. "It happens to all girls."

Selina stared very quietly at her and, for that moment, she was quiet inside, her whole self suspended in disbelief. Then an inexplicable revulsion gripped her and her face screwed with disgust. "It's never gonna happen to me," she said proudly.

"If it doesn't happen by the time you're twenty you die."

"Well then I'll just die."

"It'll happen. It hurts sometimes and it makes you miserable in the summer and you can't jump rope when you have it but it gives you a nice figure after a time."

Her eyes searched Beryl's face. "How come?"

"I dunno. It just does. Look what's happening to Ina."

"Well if it ever happens to me nobody'll ever know. They'll see me change and think it's magic."

"Besides, it makes you feel important."

"How could anyone walking around dripping blood feel important?"

"It's funny but you do. Almost as if you were grown-up. It's like . . . oh, it's hard to explain to a kid . . ."

"Who's a kid?"

"You, because you haven't started yet."

"I'll never start!" And beneath her violent denial there was despair.

"Oh yes, you'll start." Beryl nodded wisely. "Wait, lemme try to explain how it makes you feel. The first time I was scared. Then I began to feel different. That's it. Even though nothing's changed and I still play kid games and go around with kids, even though my best friend's a kid"—she bowed to Selina—"I feel different. Like I'm carrying something secret and special inside . . . Oh, you can't really explain it to a kid . . ."

"Who's a kid? I was drinking rum today with Miss Suggie and I didn't bat an eye."

"Oh, Selina, nothing will help till you start."

Selina drew aside in a sullen despairing anger. A bit of the sun edged around the rock as though it had been hiding there listening and was coming now to upbraid them. As she squinted through her tears at the sun's bright fringe, the promise of the day was lost. The mother had deceived her, saying that she was more of a woman than Ina yet never telling her the one important condition.

She had deceived herself on the trolley and on the rise in the park. She was not free but still trapped within a hard flat body. She closed her eyes to hide the tears and was safe momentarily from Beryl and Ina and all the others joined against her in their cult of blood and breasts.

After a time Beryl came and lay close to her. She placed her arm comfortingly around her. "What was that poem you wrote about the sky?" she asked. And always her voice calmed Selina. Her disappointment, her anguish tapered slowly until finally her tears were gone and she turned to Beryl and held her so that they were like the lovers on the slope. "It wasn't about this kind of sky," she said and began to recite, her thin voice striking the rock and veering off into the sky, her eyes closed. When she finished and opened her eyes Beryl's were closed, her face serene in sleep. Whispering, Selina recited then to the rock, to the dome of sky, to the light wind, all the poems she had scribbled in class, that came bright and vivid at night.

Beryl stirred in her sleep and pressed Selina closer. Just then the sun rose above the rock. The strong light seemed to smooth the grass, to set the earth steaming richly. They were all joined it seemed: Beryl with the blood bursting each month insider her, the sun, the seared grass and earth—even she, though barren of breasts, was part of the mosaic. With a cry she buried her face between Beryl's small breasts, and suddenly her happiness was like pain and a long leap into space.

On their way home a summer rain fell even as the sun shone. Holding each other close, they laughed and, pointing to the sunlit rain, chanted softly, "The devil's beating his wife. The devil's beating his wife . . ."

THE LETTERS OF EMILY DICKINSON

Known to her contemporary and friend, Thomas Wentworth Higginson, editor of the *Atlantic*, as my "half cracked poetess," known to us as one of the greatest American poets, Emily Dickinson's letters possess literary value of their own. The letters below, but a tiny sample of the hundreds she wrote throughout her life, were penned between the ages of fifteen and twenty-four years and addressed to her friend, Abiah Root. Emily and Abiah met while attending Amherst Academy in 1843-44. Abiah then transferred to another academy, closer to her home in West Springfield and Emily later left the academy to attend Mt. Holyoke Female Seminary in South Hadley, Massachusetts. Although Emily Dickinson is hardly a typical young woman of her day or any other, we can garner from her letters to Abiah Root much that is representative of the experiences of a young woman of her social class during that era.

Although Emily's network of intimates decreased as she became more reclusive, over time she became very close to her mother, sister, and sister-in-law. Emily Dickinson wrote well over seventeen hundred poems which she arranged in tidy bundles in her bedroom dresser drawer. Of these, only seven were published in her lifetime. After suffering a two and a half year illness, Emily Dickinson died in 1885. She was fifty-five years old.

THE LETTERS OF EMILY DICKINSON   Thomas Johnson, ed., Cambridge, MA: The Belknap Press of Harvard University Press, 1958, I, 12–15, 19–21, 65–67, 297–99.

7 May 1845

To Abiah Root

Dear Abiah,

It seems almost an age since I have seen you, and it is indeed an age for friends to be separated. I was delighted to receive a paper from you, and I also was much pleased with the news it contained, especially that you are taking lessons on the "piny," as you always call it. But remember not to get on ahead of me. Father intends to have a piano very soon. How happy I shall be when I have one of my own! Old Father Time has wrought many changes here since your last short visit. Miss S. T. and Miss N. M. have both taken the marriage vows upon themselves. Dr. Hitchcock has moved into his new house, and Mr. Tyler across the way from our house has moved into President Hitchcock's old house. Mr. C. is gong to move into Mr. T.'s former house, but the worst thing old Time has done here is he has walked so fast as to overtake Harriet Merrill and carry her to Hartford on last week Saturday. I was so vexed with him for it that I ran after him and made out to get near enough to him to put some salt on his tail, when he fled and left me to run home alone. . . . Viny went to Boston this morning with father, to be gone a fortnight, and I am left alone in all my glory. I suppose she has got there before this time, and is probably staring with mouth and eyes wide open at the wonders of the city. I have been to walk to-night, and got some very choice wild flowers. I wish you had some of them. Viny and I both go to school this term. We have a very fine school. There are 63 scholars. I have four studies. They are Mental Philosophy, Geology, Latin, and Botany. How large they sound, don't they? I don't believe you have such big studies. . . . My plants look finely now. I am going to send you a little geranium leaf in this letter, which you must press for me. Have you made you an herbarium yet? I hope you will if you have not, it would be such a treasure to you; 'most all the girls are making one. If you do, perhaps I can make some additions to it from flowers growing around here. How do you enjoy your school this term? Are the teachers as pleasant as our old schoolteachers? I expect you have a great many prim, starched up young ladies there, who, I doubt not, are perfect models of propriety and good behavior. If they are, don't let your free spirit be chained by them. I don't know as there [are] any in school of this stamp. But there 'most always are a few, whom the teachers look up to and regard as their satellites. I am growing handsome very fast indeed! I expect I shall be the belle of Amherst when I reach my 17th year. I don't doubt that I shall have perfect crowds of admirers at that age. Then how I shall delight to make them await my bidding, and with what delight shall I witness their suspense while I make my final decision. But away with my nonsense. I have written one composition this term, and I need not assure you it was exceedingly edifying to myself as well as everybody else. Don't you want to see it? I really wish you could have a chance. We are obliged to write compositions once in a fortnight, and select a piece to read from some interesting book the week that we don't write compositions.

We really have some most charming young women in school this term. I sha'n't call them anything but women, for women they are in every sense of the word. I must, however, describe one, and while I describe her I wish Imagination, who is ever present with you, to make a little picture of this self-same young lady in your mind, and by her aid see if you cannot conceive how she looks. Well, to begin. . . . Then just imagine her as she is, and a huge string of gold beads encircling her neck, and don't she present a lively picture; and then she is so bustling, she is always whizzing about, and whenever I come in contact with her I really think I am in a hornet's nest. I can't help thinking every time I see this singular piece of humanity of Shakespeare's description of a tempest in a teapot. But I must not laugh at her, for I verily believe she has a good heart, and that is the principal thing now-a-days. Don't you hope I shall become wiser in the company of such virtuosos? It would certainly be desirable. Have you noticed how beautifully the trees look now? They seem to be completely covered with fragrant blossoms. . . . I had so many things to do for Viny, as she was going away, that very much against my wishes I deferred writing you until now, but forgive and forget, dear A., and I will promise to do better in future. Do write me soon, and let it be a long, long letter; and when you can't get time to write, send a paper, so as to let me know you think of me still, though we are separated by hill and stream. All the girls send much love to you. Don't forget to let me receive a letter from you soon. I can say no more now as my paper is all filled up.

Your affectionate friend,
Emily E. Dickinson.

25 September 1845

To Abiah Root

Dearest Abiah,

As I just glanced at the clock and saw how smoothly the little hands glide over the surface, I could scarcely believe that those self-same little hands had eloped with so many precious moments since I received your affectionate letter, and it was still harder for me to believe that I, who am always boasting of being so faithful a correspondent, should have been guilty of negligence in so long delaying to answer it. . . . I am very glad to hear that you are better than you have been, and I hope in future disease will not be as neighborly as he has been heretofore to either of us. I long to see you, dear Abiah, and speak with you face to face; but so long as a bodily interview is denied us, we must make letters answer, though it is hard for friends to be separated. I really believe you would have been frightened to have heard me scold when Sabra informed me that you had decided not to visit Amherst this fall. But as I could find no one upon whom to vent my spleen for your decision, I thought it best to be calm, and therefore I have at length resigned myself to my cruel fate, though with not a very good grace. I think you do well to inquire whether anything has been heard from H. I really don't know what has become of her, unless procrastination has carried her off. I think that must be the case. I think you have given quite a novel description of the wedding. Are you quite sure Mr. F., the minister, told them to stand up and he would tie them in a great bow-knot? But I beg pardon for speaking so lightly of so solemn a ceremony. You asked me in your letter if I did not think you partial in your admiration of Miss Helen H[umphrey], ditto Mrs. P[almer]. I answer, Not in the least. She was universally beloved in Amherst. She made us quite a visit in June, and we regretted more than ever that she was going where we could not see her as often as we had been accustomed. She seemed very happy in her prospects, and seemed to think distance nothing in comparison to a home with the one of her choice. I hope she will be happy, and of course she will. I wished much to see her once more, but was denied the privilege. Abby Wood, our particular friend, and the only particular friend among the girls, is well and sends much love to you. . . . You asked me if I was attending school now. I am not. Mother thinks me not able to confine myself to school this term. She had rather I would exercise, and I can assure you I get plenty of that article by staying at home. I am going to learn to make bread to-morrow. So you may imagine me with my sleeves rolled up, mixing flour, milk, salaratus, etc., with a deal of grace. I advise you if you don't know how to make the staff of life to learn with dispatch. I think I could keep house very comfortably if I knew how to cook. But as long as I don't, my knowledge of housekeeping is about of as much use as faith without works, which you know we are told is dead. Excuse my quoting from the Scripture, dear Abiah, for it was so handy in this case I couldn't get along very well without it. Since I wrote you last, the summer is past and gone, and autumn with the sere and yellow leaf is already upon us. I never knew the time to pass so swiftly, it seems to me, as the past summer. I really think some one must have oiled his chariot wheels, for I don't recollect of hearing him pass, and I am sure I should if something had not prevented his chariot wheels from creaking as usual. But I will not expatiate upon him any longer, for I know it is wicked to trifle with so reverend a personage, and I fear he will make me a call in person to inquire as to the remarks which I have made concerning him. Therefore I will let him alone for the present. . . . How are you getting on with your music? Well, I hope and trust. I am taking lessons and am getting along very well, and now I have a piano, I am very happy. I feel much honored at having even a doll named for me. I believe I shall have to give it a silver cup, as that is the custom among old ladies when a child is named for them. . . . Have you any flowers now? I have had a beautiful flower-garden this summer; but they are nearly gone now. It is very cold to-night, and I mean to pick the prettiest ones before I go to bed, and cheat Jack Frost of so many of *the treasures* he calculates to rob to-night. Won't it be a capital idea to put him at defiance, for once at least, if no more? I would love to send you a bouquet if I had an opportunity, and you could press it and write under it, The last flowers of summer. Wouldn't it be poetical, and you know that is what young ladies aim to be now-a-days. . . . I expect I have altered a good deal since I have seen you, dear Abiah. I have grown tall a good deal, and wear my golden tresses done up in a net-cap. Modesty, you know, forbids me to mention whether my personal appearance has altered. I leave that for others to judge. But my [*word omitted*] has not changed, nor will it in time to come. I shall always remain the same old sixpence. . . . I can say no more now, as it is after ten, and everybody has gone to bed but me. Don't forget your affectionate friend,

Emily E.D.

South Hadley, 16 May 1848

To Abiah Root

My dear Abiah,

You must forgive me, indeed you must, that I have so long delayed to write you, and I doubt not you will when I give you all my reasons for so doing. You know it is customary for the first page to be occupied with apologies, and I must not depart from the beaten track for one of my own imagining. . . . I had not been very well all winter, but had not written home about it, lest the folks should take me home. During the week following examinations, a friend from Amherst came over and spent a week with me, and when that friend returned home, father and mother were duly notified of the state of my health. Have you so treacherous a friend?

Now knowing that I was to be reported at home, you can imagine my amazement and consternation when Saturday of the same week Austin arrived in full sail, with orders from head-quarters to bring me home at all events. At first I had recourse to words, and a desperate battle with those weapons was waged for a few moments, between my *Sophomore* brother and myself. Finding words of no avail, I next resorted to tears. But woman's tears are of little avail, and I am sure mine flowed in vain. As you can imagine, Austin was victorious, and poor, defeated I was led off in triumph. You must not imbibe the idea from what I have said that I do not love home—far from it. But I could not bear to leave teachers and companions before the close of the term and go home to be dosed and receive the physician daily, and take warm drinks and be condoled with on the state of health in general by all the old ladies in town.

Haven't I given a ludicrous account of going home sick from a boarding-school? Father is quite a hand to give medicine, especially if it is not desirable to the patient, and I was dosed for about a month after my return home, without any mercy, till at last out of mere pity my cough went away, and I had quite a season of peace. Thus I remained at home until the close of the term, comforting my parents by my presence, and instilling many a lesson of wisdom into the budding intellect of my only sister. I had almost forgotten to tell you that I went on with my studies at home, and kept up with my class. Last Thursday our vacation closed, and on Friday morn, midst the weeping of friends, crowing of roosters, and singing of birds, I again took my departure from home. Five days have now passed since we returned to Holyoke, and they have passed very slowly. Thoughts of home and friends "come crowding thick and fast, like lightnings from the mountain cloud," and it seems very desolate.

Father has decided not to send me to Holyoke another year, so this is my *last term.* Can it be possible that I have been here almost a year? It startles me when I really think of the advantages I have had, and I fear I have not improved them as I ought. But many an hour has fled with its report to heaven, and what has been the tale of me? . . . How glad I am that spring has come, and how it calms my mind when wearied with study to walk out in the green fields and beside the pleasant streams in which South Hadley is rich! There are not many wild flowers near, for the girls have driven them to a distance, and we are obliged to walk quite a distance to find them, but they repay us by their sweet smiles and fragrance.

The older I grow, the more do I love spring and spring flowers. Is it so with you? While at home there were several pleasure parties of which I was a member, and in our rambles we found many and beautiful children of spring, which I will mention and see if you have found them,—the trailing arbutus, adder's tongue, yellow violets, liver-leaf, blood-root, and many other smaller flowers.

What are you reading now? I have little time to read when I am here, but while at home I had a feast in the reading line, I can assure you. Two or three of them I will mention: *Evangeline, The Princess, The Maiden Aunt, The Epicurean,* and *The Twins and Heart* by Tupper, complete the list. Am I not a pedant for telling you what I have been reading? Have you forgotten your visit at Amherst last summer, and what delightful times we had? I have not, and I hope you will come and make another and a longer, when I get home from Holyoke. Father wishes to have me at home a year, and then he will probably send me away again, where I know not. . . .

Ever your own affectionate
Emilie E. Dickinson.

P. S. My studies for this series are Astronomy and Rhetoric, which take me through to the Senior studies. What are you studying now, if you are in school, and do you attend to music? I practise only one hour a day this term.

about May 1852

To Abiah Root

I love to link you, A. and E., I love to put you together and look at you side by side—the picture pleases me, and I should love to watch it until the sun goes down, did I not call to mind a very precious letter for which I have not as yet rendered a single farthing, so let me thank you that midst your many friends and cares and influenzas, you yet found time for me, and loved me. You remarked that I had written you more affectionately than wont—I have thought that word over and over, and it puzzles me now; whether our few last years have been cooler than our first ones, or whether I write indifferently when I truly know it not, the query troubles me. I do believe sincerely, that the friendship formed at school was no warmer than now, nay more, that *this* is warmest—they differ indeed to me as morning differs from noon—one may be fresher, cheerier, but the other fails not.

You and I have grown older since school-days, and our years have made us soberer—I mean have made *me* so, for you were always dignified, e'en when a little girl, and *I* used, now and then, to cut a timid caper. That makes me think of you the very first time I saw you, and I can't repress a smile, not to say a hearty laugh, at your little girl expense. I have roused your curiosity, so I will e'en tell you that one Wednesday afternoon, in the days of that dear old Academy, I went in to be entertained by the rhetoric of the gentlemen and the milder form of the girls—I had hardly recovered myself from the dismay attendant upon entering august assemblies, when with the utmost equanimity you ascended the stairs, bedecked with dandelions, arranged, it seemed, for curls. I shall never forget that scene, if I live to have gray hairs, nor the very remarkable fancies it gave me then of you, and it comes over me now with the strangest bygone funniness, and I laugh merrily. Oh, Abiah, you and the early flower are forever linked to me; as soon as the first green grass comes, up from a chink in the stones peeps the little flower, precious "leontodon," and my heart fills toward you with a warm and childlike fullness! Nor do I laugh now; far from it, I rather bless the flower which sweetly, slyly too, makes me come nearer you.

But, my dear, I can't give the dandelion the privilege due to you, so good-by, little one!

I would love to see you, Abiah, I would rather than write to you, might I with equal ease, for the weather is very warm, and my head aches a little, and my heart a little more, so taking me *collectively,* I seem quite miserable, but I'll give you the sunny corners, and you must'nt look at the shade. You were happy when you wrote me; I hope so now, though I would you were in the country, and could reach the hills and fields. I can reach them, carry them home, which I do in my arms daily, and when they drop and fade, I have only to gather fresh ones. Your joy would indeed be full, could you sit as I, at my window, and hear the boundless birds, and every little while feel the breath of some new flower! Oh, do you love the spring, and isn't it brothers and sisters, and blessed, ministering spirits unto you and me, and us all?

I often see Abby—oftener than at sometimes when friendship drooped a little. Did you ever know that a flower, once withered and freshened again, became an immortal flower,—that is, that it rises again? I think resurrections here are sweeter, it may be, than the longer and lasting one—for you expect the one, and only hope for the other. . . . I will show you the *sunset* if you will sit by me, but I cannot bring it there, for so much gold is heavy. Can you see it in Philadelphia?

Abby's health does not change—I fear the wide world holds but little strength for her—I would it were otherwise. Abby is sweet and patient, does n't it ever seem as if her lovely patience was shriving her for God? We cannot tell, but I trust that her sweet face may not be hidden yet. Dear Abiah, do write me whenever you love to do, yet *oftener* I am not confident I ever would hear at all, should I conclude the bargain.

Emilie.

about 25 July 1854

To Abiah Root

My dear Child.

Thank you for that sweet note, which came so long ago, and thank you for asking me to come and visit you, and thank you for loving me, long ago, and today, and too for all the sweetness, and all the gentleness, and all the tenderness with which you remember me—your quaint, old fashioned friend.

I wanted very much to write you sooner, and I tried frequently, but till now in vain, and as I write tonight, it is with haste, and fear lest something still detain me. You know my dear Abiah, that the summer has been warm, that we have not a girl, that at this pleasant season, we have much company—that this irresolute body refuses to serve sometimes, and the indignant tenant can only hold it's peace—all this you know, for I have often told you, and yet I say it again, if mayhap it persuade you that I do love you indeed, and have not done neglectfully. Then Susie, our dear friend, has been very ill for several weeks, and every hour possible I have taken away to her, which has made even smaller my "inch or two, of time." Susie is better now, but has been suffering much within the last few weeks, from a Nervous Fever, which has taken her strength very fast. She has had an excellent Nurse, a faithful Physician, and her sister has been unwearied in her watchfulness, and last of all, *God* has been loving and kind, so to reward them all, poor Susie just begins to trudge around a little—went as far as her garden, Saturday, and picked a few flowers, so when I called to see her, Lo a bright bouquet, sitting upon the mantel, and Susie in the easy-chair, quite faint from the effort of arranging them—I make my story long, but I knew you loved Susie—Abiah, and I thought her mishaps, quite as well as her brighter fortunes, would interest you.

I think it was in June, that your note reached here, and I did snatch a moment to call upon your friend. Yet I went in the dusk, and it was Saturday evening, so even then, Abiah, you see how cares pursued me—I found her very lovely in what she said to me, and I fancied in her face so, although the gentle dusk would draw her curtain close, and I did'nt see her clearly. We talked the most of you—a theme we surely loved, or we had not discussed it in preference to all. I would love to meet her again—and love to see her longer.

Please give my love to her, for your sake. You asked me to come and see you—I must speak of that. I thank you Abiah, but I don't go from home, unless emergency leads me by the hand, and then I do it obstinately, and draw back if I can. Should I ever leave home, which is improbable, I will with much delight, accept your invitation; till then, my dear Abiah, my warmest thanks are your's, but don't expect me. I'm so old fashioned, Darling, that all your friends would stare. I should have to bring my work bag, and my big spectacles, and I half forgot my grandchildren, my pin-cushion, and Puss—Why think of it seriously, Abiah—*do* you think it my *duty* to leave? Will you write me again? Mother and Vinnie send their love, and here's a kiss from me—

Good Night, from Emily—

FRIENDSHIP, FEMINISM AND BETRAYAL

Susan Lee

What happens to an intimate friendship between two women after one of them marries? Conventional wisdom predicts the demise of the friendship for, as the saying goes, three's a crowd. But Susan Lee's essay reflects the rethinking many contemporary women have been doing about the nature of their friendships and the observations she makes belie the simplicity implied by the old saw. Ultimately, she ponders the complications women face as they struggle to develop models of female friendships which defy conventional expectations.

Susan Lee has written a novel *Dear John* (1980) with Sandra Till Robinson, and she has another one in progress.

FRIENDSHIP, FEMINISM AND BETRAYAL   From *The Village Voice*, June 9, 1975, 11–12. Reprinted by permission of the author and *The Village Voice*.

Home for Christmas my first year in college, I spoke to my best friend from high school. Elizabeth and I stayed on the phone for 45 minutes, but we had nothing very much to say to each other. After the conversation, I was upset. I remember wanting to tell my mother, who asked what the matter was, about the weirdness of discovering that this woman and I, who had talked every school day for five years no longer had anything in common. All I could do was cry.

Except for a brief, awkward visit to my house a month later when my father died, a church wedding where Elizabeth married a man I'd gone out with in seventh grade, and two short stopovers in southern New Jersey, I don't remember ever seeing or speaking to her again.

We used to spend hours talking about our relationships with boys. We never discussed our relationship with each other. Except for the few minutes with my mother who told me she thought Elizabeth and I never had anything in common, and my once making a distinction between acquaintances and friends, I'd never spoken about what I considered a real friendship.

Many people have expressed agreement with Cicero that "friendship can only exist between good men." I'm not one of them. As a 30-year-old woman who has had friends since grade school, I have been very concerned with those friendships. Yet only in the last few years have such relationships been acknowledged as being as important as they've always been.

It was always commonplace for girls in my high school to spend a great deal of time together. It was also commonplace for a girl to spend Saturdays with another girl listening to Johnny Mathis albums, trying on clothes to find something that fit right, or babysitting and then having the evening that was planned together usurped by some boy calling up for a date. When this happened to me, I felt betrayed. I never said anything. It didn't occur to me that this wasn't the natural order of things. I didn't know anyone who complained, nor do I remember anyone who ever turned down a boy because she'd already made plans with a girl.

One woman I know said that if as a teenager she had told her parents she'd prefer being with a girl than a boy, they would have sent her to a doctor.

Even now, this past summer, when I was home for a few weeks because my mother was sick, my mother only asked questions about the men who called. One night when I was coming into the city, she discovered I was going to see a woman instead of the man who had just called.

All she said was, "Oh?" Within that one word was more archness than I'd ever heard placed in such a small space.

A male friend of mine suggested that, as kids, if a girl could turn down another girl, for a boy, maybe the girls weren't friends. What he didn't understand is how power works, how it matters who gets to set the dates, how important one telephone call can be, and how helpless someone can feel waiting for it.

But girls didn't deny each other because we weren't friends. We could only do it because we were and because boys weren't, and because they got to make the call and we didn't.

Still, a friend of mine recently remembered that she once was leaving a girl to go out on a date. Her girlfriend's mother, who was very hurt for her daughter, stopped her and said that when she was young, girls knew the value of friendship.

Now, each of us knows what this woman meant. We might express it in terms of a heightened woman's consciousness. We might talk of it in terms of respect for each of our relationships. My friend didn't. She went out on her date. She knew what was flexible in her life and what wasn't. The given of having friends then was that we understood the same rules. The same given remains except that some of the rules are changing.

◈◈◈

The Greeks and Romans featured "friendship" in their society. From what I can tell, such friendship was a code word for male homosexual relationships.

The Old Testament emphasizes loyalty to family. Friendship, as we understand it, was hardly known. The New Testament uses the word "friend" slightly more but is as little interested in the relationships outside the family or group of coreligionists as the Old Testament.

While members of African tribes have exchanged names and had friendship ceremonies for generations, friendships have not been considered very important in Western cultures until fairly recently.

It would be difficult to date the advent of magnanimity, trust, and accord first manifesting itself as friendship among westerners. Studying friendship in the Plymouth Bay Colony, one historian decided that friendship, as we know it, did not exist. Far more central was devotion to a religious ideal. If you were in concord with that, you remained in relationship with your neighbors. If not, the relationship would be severed. Very possibly, regardless of your history, you were expelled.

American literature is full of male buddies who are supposedly friends; although they may hardly speak to each other, they would only be too glad to die for each other. I'm not sure if this palship is friendship.

Hardly any fiction deals with friendship between women. Doris Lessing's "The Golden Notebook" uses a relationship between two women as the backdrop for examining one of their lives in depth. Fay Weldon's recent "Female Friends" deals more directly with the subject. The women, unfortunately, are victims who continually slash at each other and whose friendship somehow remains as eternal as the sea.

Many studies have been done about interpersonal relationships. These however, usually deal with dating heterosexual couples. Most, like Erich Fromm in his book about different kinds of love, ignore friendship. The closest Fromm could come was brotherly love. The few that mention friendship concentrate on the architecture of friendship and on the network of who is friendly with whom. The conclusions usually have to do with the proximity of a physical, mental, or emotional sort. One study, for example, reveals that boys of the same height tend to be friends.

Friendship has become so institutionalized in our culture that a recent book combined the notion that everyone should have a good friend with the alienated sense that each person should be her or his own best friend.

My guess is that as the family breaks down, friendships will grow in importance. In my own life, as I have relied less and less on the idea of marriage for myself, the more I've come to see the friendships that I've had for years and years as the on-going relationships in my life.

College was a relatively easy place to find people I liked. Condescending as it might have sounded to me then, we each had our futures ahead of us. It seemed possible to get on with a large number of people. Still, most of my college friends and acquaintances disappeared from my life almost as soon as I left the campus. Like Elizabeth and I, we had little more in common than living near each other.

I used to think affection was enough for friendship, but I no longer believe that. Affection can be sufficient for lovers in a way it isn't for friends. But then, people "fall in" love. Someone is a lover after a few days. A friendship, where love develops, often takes years.

A friend is someone I can be myself with; with a lover, I'm all too often someone else, someone I'd rather be. With a friend, I'm a person; with a lover, I'm a person [sic].

I can only be myself when there is a shared community of interests between the other person and me. I began to realize how important this was when I got to graduate school in San Francisco and met other people who cared intimately about the same work I did. No longer was someone's impending wedding date the ongoing center of a conversation.

I found people who perceived what went on outside of them and how they acted in the world in many of the same ways I did. I was not as aware of the need for loyalty to friends as I am now. If I fall under the illusion that I was particularly unusual in the way that I treated other women, I remind myself of the green rocking chair in my San Francisco living room. I gave this chair up to any man who came into my house and kept it for myself if another woman was there.

One relationship developed into something more than shared after class-room time. Both Linda and I were dedicated to writing fiction and to working out our lives so that we'd be able to write. And, however different Linda and I were, I was conscious that our friendship had a loyalty and a respect for each other that other friendly relationships did not have.

We spent hours discussing our lives, our work, our dailyness. Where a lover and I take endless time concerning ourselves with ourselves and our specific relationship, Linda and I were spectators at the landscapes of each other's lives. We were more like adjacent lands sharing common borders than the same property itself. It seemed to me that not only did I have my life, but I had hers as well, to see the working out of our goal to become the best writers we possibly could.

A friend like Linda is a reflection of what I value, in a way a lover is not necessarily. I like to be friends with what is best in me and with what I'm interested in. While I, and several of my friends, too often excuse our choice of lovers as irrational or necessary acts, we take the responsibility for whom we've chosen as friends.

Still, I'm far more conscious of lovers than I am of friends. Though this is changing, I usually think about friends when something is wrong between us. When I'm in love, I'm almost always aware of my lover.

When I was in California and Linda didn't call or was late for an appointment, I assumed there was a good reason. When a lover messes up, I'm quick to think it's our relationship. Friends don't take things as personally as lovers do. There's less expectation and more politeness with friends, who are taken far more for granted than lovers. Yet the reality in my life is that friends are more constant. Lovers come and go except for those who become my friends and stay near me.

Even understanding this, it didn't occur to me to stay in California because of my friends. Linda, abiding by the same implicit rules I did, never mentioned my remaining to me; I don't know if she thought of it. Another friend confronted me; he asked how I could leave the people I freely acknowledged loving more than anyone else. It was enough for me that I was bored and dissatisfied in San Francisco and wanted to come back to New York.

The following year, I returned to the West Coast for Linda's wedding to another writer. Our relationship had deepened into the assumption that we were each other's friend. Although I had fears about the marriage which Linda was all too aware of, I didn't think of not going to give support. I hoped that if any woman could manage writing and a marriage, Linda would.

I tried seeing her for several weeks yearly in Italy or France where she lived. What I didn't admit to myself after one visit to Praiano was how the three of us were developing. I was writing; Thomas, Linda's husband, was writing; only Linda wasn't.

A year and a half later in Paris, I couldn't help seeing what I hadn't wanted to see in Italy. Thomas wrote constantly, and Linda talked about writing. When he worked, we had to whisper. One night when Linda went into her study to work, Thomas interrupted her. I expected her to tell him to leave her alone as she so assiduously left him. Instead, he talked her out of doing anything but spending time with him and me. She acceded to him as she did in much else of what he wanted. She had become a wife.

My visit to Paris was disastrous. Whenever I tried talking about what I found appalling, Linda turned the discussion to my love relationships of the previous year which had not been ones she would have liked to have had. My anger at what I construed as her growing passivity remained unarticulated and high.

I came home and didn't answer a cheery letter ignoring the realities of my stay. A few months later, I wrote a very disturbed explanatory response and did not hear from Linda again.

I knew she'd stopped speaking to her childhood best friend because the woman had once flirted with Thomas. I was aware she'd given me up because of what she thought was an opposite reaction to the man she chose to live with and to the way she led her life.

Six months later, I was speaking to an editor in the publishing house which had signed Thomas's novel and found out Linda and Thomas were in New York for a few weeks.

Sorting out my resentment at having lost my closest friendship, I called them. Linda answering, we talked awkwardly and arranged dinner for that night. I thought the two of us might be able to resolve our difficulties. Perhaps I had been wrong. Deep friendship is hard to come by, and I was prepared to do what I could to salvage this one.

When Linda arrived at the restaurant, she said Thomas would be there with some of his friends within half an hour. I was dumbfounded. She and I were to have had dinner alone.

By the next day, I was furious. Living outside English-speaking countries,

Linda might have missed the American women's movement. Still, she taught a college course on women in Paris. She couldn't be as unaware of turning into a passive, dependent person as she seemed to be. If she and I weren't going to be friends, I at least wanted to make clear what bothered me.

But she didn't want to hear it. As far as she was concerned, I was hostile. Finally, she agreed to meet.

There we were at the Buffalo Road House: I, with a tennis racket, T-shirt, and dungarees; she, with the latest long Parisian swirl skirt. We were surrounded by four booths of male couples who all stopped talking as we began.

I gathered they all thought we were the lovers Thomas had believed we were years before. I wanted to turn around and say, "No, no. This is worse. We were friends, and now we're not going to be."

We drank wine and were each very upset. Surprising me, she told me that I had betrayed her. She, who long before defined a friend as someone who knew you and loved you anyway, said I didn't trust her. On my side, I was sure she was the one who betrayed our original friendship. She was the one who'd given up her life for someone else's needs.

I argued, somewhat disingenuously, that I was never hostile to her but to her role as wife. I remember thinking that we were never as close as I had thought.

Linda said, "If Thomas ever was as nasty about you as you've been about him, I would have divorced him a long time ago."

I thought this was not only untrue but gratuitous. Thomas, whose novel includes such lines as, "He stuck his throbbing cock into her Hawaiian cunt," could afford to be magnanimous. There was little reason for him to complain. I could talk all I wanted of the need for women to struggle. While he and his friends discussed how liberated they were, he knew Linda's allegiance and investment were more and more in him and his future and less so in her own.

Then she said that since she and I had stopped corresponding, she's started a novel about the friendship between two women and had gotten more than 100 pages into it.

She and I haven't spoken since. I've hoped she would finish that novel. Not only do I want her to write, I want to read about a friendship through her eyes, and I want something to come out of our relationship.

But I'm being disingenuous again. While acting as an external conscience to a friend might sound touching and be theoretically correct, the reshaping of people, luckily for friendship, is traditionally—and usually without success— left to lovers. Linda knew what I was upset about. At one point when I was in Paris talking to Thomas about each of our projects, Linda burst out, "Don't you both see? *I'm* the one in trouble." Thomas denied what I perceived was true. Linda didn't need me to be tiresome or beligerent about it. Even more, she didn't need someone who she sensed didn't trust her enough to overcome it.

While I now know I can no longer be friendly with someone who acts like a "wife," I think Linda was right about my betraying her. I acted like one of the Plymouth Bay colonists. In effect, I said that specific beliefs and actions meant more than our history together.

Still, I'm angry. I know very well that other people's supposedly durable friendships turn out unexpectedly fragile and break fairly easily. Yet, however necessary my betrayal was, this woman and I had made a commitment to each other, the alternative was not to have gone on being friends. We were too on edge with each other to do that. All we could have done was to fade away from each other without having had the courage to talk about our differences at all.

When I was young, I thought my friends *had* to act as they did. As a result, I overlooked many decisions that I fundamentally disagreed with. Now, due to the women's movement, I assume each of my friends takes responsibility for her life. Because I no longer consider us powerless, I no longer can forgive acting as if we were.

While a heightened women's consciousness has resulted in our openly valuing friendships more highly than we did before, this same consciousness has caused me, and other women, to demand more of these relationships. The validity of each of our lives has become an issue that might have been passed by before and now can no longer be.

Often, these new pressures are too great for many of these friendships to bear. I know there are no models to go by to put them back together. I know we have to develop new models of not only keeping friendships but having them at all.

Yet to venture that friendships often break apart because of social and political dislocations doesn't alleviate my wanting friendships that last or my being hurt that this relationship with Linda, which I had assumed would be one of these, no longer exists.

Looking back on what happened between us, I can understand the pressures on her to choose as she did. I can wish her well. I can understand my own development which made me make demands that others might find unreasonable. I can do a lot of things, but what I feel—not by Linda so much as by historical circumstance—is cheated.

THE CLOISTERED LIFE

Julia Lieblich

Prior to the 1960s, a veil of secrecy shrouded life within convent walls. Novels like Kathryn Hume's *The Nun's Story* helped perpetuate the public's image of the cloister as an enigmatic, if not medieval, world. But during the sixties, most dramatically after the decree issued by the Second Vatican Council encouraging religious orders to adjust to the changed conditions of the times, and Pope Paul VI's *Motu Proprio*, a letter to the superiors general of all religious orders mandating changes, the convent shed most of its mysterious aura. Nuns now participate more actively in public life, and outsiders have been given greater access to what goes on in the cloister. But the winds of change began blowing around convent walls at least a decade before Vatican II. A movement among women religious themselves evolved into the Sister Formation Conference directed toward improving the spiritual and professional education of nuns. These efforts led to a marked increase in the educational level of many women in religious orders and a more open exchange between convent and outside world.

Lieblich's view of the cloister contradicts many of the popular images of the types of women who join these religious orders and of the reasons for doing so. Although their definition of community may not be a common one, their choice of the cloistered life adds to the growing list of instances demonstrating women's capacities to live complete lives without men and their ability to exist quite peaceably with other women as well.

Julia Lieblich writes for Time Inc.'s Teletext information service.

When Carolyn O'Hara received her master's degree in philosophy at age 24, she did something she had secretly been planning ever since her freshman year at Boston College. She entered a Carmelite cloister and became a member of a community of nuns who spend their days in silent prayer. "My mother thought she'd failed in some terrible way," the now 41-year-old Sister Carolyn recently recalled at the order's cloister in Beacon, N.Y. "She was sure there was something deeply wrong with me. My friends also thought I was crazy. A few could understand a religious vocation, but not a call to the cloister."

Sister Rachel Lauzé, who at 33 looks more like a college student than a nun, spent five years working as a Maryknoll nurse in Indonesia before deciding to enter her order's Maryknoll, N.Y., cloister. Her family, she says, "thought I was going through a masochistic phase."

Sisters Carolyn and Rachel are among the more than 3,800 Roman Catholic nuns in the United States who have removed themselves from the distractions of a worldly life to the cloister, devoting their lives to the search for God through prayer. It is not a self-centered meditation. They believe that their union with God contributes to the salvation of all people, and that their prayers for humanity touch the lives of the suffering everywhere. In an earlier century, they might have been respected by families and friends as women with an exceptional calling. Today, they are often viewed as rebels by a secular

---

THE CLOISTERED LIFE   From *The New York Times*, July 10, 1983, 12. Copyright © 1983 by The New York Times Company.

society that values action over contemplation. Their special way of life sets them apart in a world where even many Catholics dismiss the cloister as an archaic institution and the nuns inside as people with an unhealthy attraction to solitude—weak women who are not carrying their weight in the world.

Sister Marjorie Robinson, 35, a former teacher from Philadelphia and now a Carmelite at the Beacon cloister, recognizes that "to our society, it's almost like we're marginal people, a countersign to a lot of what our society goes after—the practical and the material." What she and her sisters are saying, however, she points out, is that "there are deeper realities—something beyond the everyday illusions and distractions." As a symbol of her permanent commitment to God, she, like many sisters, wears a plain gold ring inscribed with the word "Jesus," which she received at her final vows ceremony.

The timeworn image of cloistered nuns as escapists, spurned lovers or naïve waifs has little basis in reality today. It takes more than a botched-up love affair to lure educated women in their 20's and 30's to the cloister in the 1980's. For many, choosing to leave behind family and friends, the possibility of marriage and children and worldly careers that offer tangible rewards is a long, difficult and frequently painful decision. And opting to stay in the cloister after all romantic notions about the life have been stripped away is tougher still.

Yet at a time when almost three times as many nuns are leaving than entering active teaching, nursing and missionary orders each year, the number of cloistered nuns in the United States is slowly increasing. Some still elect to enter highly traditional orders as "brides of Christ," to live behind grilles, to walk barefoot and to practice penances, such as self-flagellation, that date back to the Middle Ages. A few seek even greater solitude in hermitages. But most of those who choose the contemplative life today gravitate toward orders whose broad interpretation of the guidelines set out by the Second Vatican Council have freed their members from the hairshirt habits and the almost total silence of the past.

The wrong reason to enter any kind of cloister, says Sister Carolyn, "is to escape. It takes a certain amount of psychic strength to face yourself and your reactions to the same people in a cloister 365 days a year. You go to the convent to find solitude, and you find God, and you find yourself."

The majority of the more than 200 Catholic cloisters in the United States today are offshoots of convents founded in Europe during the Middle Ages. The largest order—about 850 sisters in 65 convents—is the Discalced (shoeless) Carmelites, founded by St. Teresa of Avila in Spain in 1562 and brought to the United States in 1790. There are at least a dozen other major American cloistered orders, including the Poor Clares, the Sister Adorers of the Precious Blood, the Sacramentines, the Passionists, the Cistercians, the Redemptoristines and the branches of the Dominicans, the Visitation Nuns and the Benedictines. While other Christian religions also have cloistered communities, their numbers are far fewer.

In all but two of the six American Catholic cloisters and the community of hermit nuns visited over a recent period of four months, it was possible to speak to the sisters without any physical barrier separating us. At one, conversations had to be conducted through a grille; at another, from behind the wooden turn used to pass items in and out of the convent. It was also possible to talk to some sisters on the telephone, although at times only after a call back from a message left on an answering machine, which in one order notifies callers that "The sisters are at prayer . . . remembering your intentions." More open discussions took place at a two-day meeting last September of the Metropolitan Association of Contemplative Nuns in Yonkers, N.Y. And during a visit this spring to Israel and France, several cloistered nuns on Mount Carmel and in Paris spoke of their concerns, the former, through a grille, the latter, face-to-face.

That the special role of the contemplatives has continuing relevance was emphasized by Pope John Paul II last November when he praised cloistered nuns in Spain for their devotion to absolute principle in a world that, he said, "exalts relative values."

Between A.D. 500 and 1200, all nuns were cloistered. Because a large dowry was generally required for entry, most of the sisters were daughters of the aristocracy. For centuries, a religious life was considered the respectable alternative to marriage. In many cases, it also offered women a more independent and intellectually stimulating life—in northern France and Germany, several orders were renowned for the academic level of the all-girl schools they operated.

During the late Middle Ages, the public began to view the cloister less as a holy institution and more as a dumping ground for the nobility's rebellious daughters, discarded mistresses and the widows of enemies. Some of these unwilling recruits were notorious for their neglect of religious duties and their general disregard for the vows of poverty, obedience and chastity. Although several Catholic reformers, notably St. Teresa of Avila, restored strict monastic order to dissolute convents, nuns never quite regained their exalted stature.

In the last century, a few former sisters have reinforced the negative image of nuns through highly publicized, sometimes factually suspect, accounts of cruel penitential practices in some North American convents. While some overly zealous convent heads may have stretched the concept of penance to extremes in the belief that intense physical pain and humiliation led to holiness, they were certainly exceptions. Film makers further colored the public's perception by sometimes portraying nuns as inane schoolgirls, ethereal creatures or despotic spinsters. Rarely have contemplatives been presented as mature women with a vocation as challenging as any other "career."

Before turning to cloistered life, Baltimore Carmelite Sister Barbara Jean LaRochester had spent 17 years as an active nun in Philadelphia. During the week, she worked as an X-ray technologist in a Catholic hospital and on weekends as a volunteer teacher's aide in an inner-city school. As a board member of the National Black Sisters Conference in 1968, she was active in the civil rights movement during the height of the race riots. But in 1972, she decided her real call was to contemplation.

"As a physical presence out in the world I could only be one person with two hands and two feet," says the now 50-year-old nun. "But through prayer, I felt I could reach more of my brothers and sisters. The spiritual dimension is limitless."

For Carmelite Sister Annamae Dannes, the decision came 15 years ago, when she was 26 years old and well-launched on a career as a teacher in a northern Ohio public school. "When I was in school, I felt that if I dated the right person I'd be happy," she says. "After college, I thought that if I traveled in

Europe I'd be satisfied. Then I got the idea that moving to New York City and going to Columbia Teachers College would be grand. Later, it was getting the right job. But, somehow, it was never enough."

"I delighted in teaching, but I was beginning to question the meaning of my life. I have a friend who used to pray with the nuns at the Cleveland Carmelite and one day I joined her. I felt right at home here from the start. I just knew that was where I belonged."

Cloistered nuns believe that their vocation is to witness the primacy of prayer in the Church, to serve as a reminder of the contemplative dimension in all lives, and to intervene for others before God. "If people are aware that I'm praying for them," says Sister Michaelene Devine, prioress at the Beacon Carmelite, "it's a real source of comfort. Even if they're not aware, I feel that our intercessory prayers help them to be more open to the influence of God." Desert Mother Mary of Jesus, who heads the Carmel of the Immaculate Heart of Mary, a hermitage in Chester, N.J., expresses the effect in terms of secular linkages. "People are conscious of radio, TV and the telephone," she says, "but they're not always conscious of this spiritual network of communication through prayer." Contemplatives, do not, however, says Sister Annamae Dannes, feel that their prayers have more weight than those of anyone else.

If the sisters come to the cloister to pray for the world they stay because of the relationship they develop with God. Contemplation may be deep and mysterious but it is not abstract.

"It's not a psychological mind-game we're playing," says Sister Rachel. "When we pray, we meet a real person—God. It's like a regular relationship with anyone. On some days, it's ecstatic. On others, I wonder how I ended up here."

"For prayer, you need silence and you need solitude," declares Sister Michaelene. "In community, we provide this for one another."

But just how cloistered a convent must be to facilitate prayer is a matter of debate among contemplatives. In affirming the role of the cloister in 1965, Vatican II stated that "it should be modified according to conditions of time and place, and outdated customs done away with." It did not, however, decree specific changes. Individual orders consequently reached different conclusions.

Until the 1960's, the inner-sanctums of almost all cloistered convents were cut off from the world by heavy iron or wooden grilles, some with sharp spikes pointing outward to discourage persistent lovers or distraught fathers. Nuns rarely left the convent grounds. Extern sisters, who were not part of the cloister, greeted visitors, answered the telephone, shopped for food and supplies and conducted other worldly business.

All contemplatives then wore heavy wool habits, whatever the weather. Some went barefoot, even in winter. Rules of silence were rarely broken, and then only after saying a prayer and kissing the floor. In some convents, nuns communicated much of the time in writing or through sign language.

The Mother Superior was the unquestioned leader of the community. The sisters had to ask her for permission for everything from getting supplies to staying up an extra hour. Mortification was considered an essential part of most cloistered life, and common penances included frequent fasting, kneeling during meals and praying for extended periods of time with arms outstretched.

After Vatican II, many communities decided it was time for a change. Some began with the convent building itself. One morning in 1969, the Yonkers Sacramentines voted to remove the grille in their front parlor, and by noon it was down, thanks to a sister who knew how to use an electric saw. "I was so happy," recalls Sacramentine Sister Mary of the Eucharist. "When my mother visited, I could hug her for the first time in years."

In all but the most traditional cloisters, the rules have been relaxed considerably. A sister may now leave the grounds alone to go to a doctor, to visit a sick parent, to shop or to vote. The emphasis is less on conformity and more on the intellectual, emotional and artistic development of each sister. A few nuns have even attended college classes.

Many traditional vows are differently interpreted today. Poverty does not mean going without nutritious meals or forgoing an occasional treat. According to Sister Michaelene, "It means respect and enjoyment of material things without being attached to them." Obedience no longer means asking the Mother Superior for "permissions." Rather, says Sister Helen Werner, the 63-year-old coordinator of the Maryknoll cloister, "it means being accountable to God and the rest of the community." And the rule of silence is no longer "enforced." Instead, Sister Helen says, it is "looked upon as a value, but so is sharing in relationships."

For many nuns, sharing means communicating with other orders. In the past, one community had virtually no contact with another, even when their convents were within walking distance of each other. In 1969, 130 sisters from all over the United States gathered in Woodstock, Md., to form the Association of Contemplative Sisters. Today, the A.C.S., which meets every two years, has 400 members who pool their financial resources to sponsor workshops and lectures on theology, psychology and the role of the contemplative in the modern world.

"Getting together as a group of women with common needs," says Sister Annamae Dannes, president of the A.C.S., gave the nuns "the strength to stand up for themselves," in a male-dominated church.

Sisters are also communicating more with their lay neighbors. Some of them, says Sister Annamae, "hold prayer groups and act as spiritual counselors for people who want to talk about prayer or their lives in general." And in many cloisters, the chapel is open to the public during daylight hours and invited visitors may attend mass.

But the nuns say they try not to let these involvements disrupt their lives of prayer. "We want to stay in touch with the world and be available to people, but we can't get overly active," says Sister Mary Devereux, of the Blessed Sacrament cloister in Yonkers, N.Y., an order of perpetual adoration whose nuns keep a constant vigil of prayer in their chapel. "It's a constant struggle. We're living in the world, but we're not of it."

Perhaps no contemplative community is more aware of the world outside its walls than the Maryknoll cloister. The 12 nuns in the tan brick convent on the grounds of the Maryknoll Sisters' headquarters are all former missionaries who have spent at least two years in active service, a prerequisite for entering the order's cloisters. Their special calling is to focus their prayers on the more than 1,900 Maryknoll priests, brothers, sisters and layworkers in their "loneliness and struggles on the mission." In December 1982, two Maryknoll sisters were murdered in El Salvador.

In the mid-1960's, the role of the cloister was questioned by many within the Maryknoll community, as it was throughout the Catholic Church. Now, many Maryknoll missionary nuns on home leave go to the cloister to make a retreat. "When you're out on the mission," says Sister Muriel Vollmer, "you see your own helplessness. Very often the missionaries can't even work because they're so curtailed by governments. Many come home because they're on hit lists. You can't survive in these times without prayer." . . .

◈◈◈

The always rigid cloister entry requirements have never been more difficult. Contemplative orders are looking for evidence of a genuine calling from God—not an easy thing to discern. Most orders today require psychological testing and interviews with several members of the clergy before a candidate is accepted. Two years of college, or work experience, is preferred.

"We want women, not girls," says Sister Michaelene. "You can't make choices about your life until you know what your options are."

A nun must live in the cloister for five to seven years before she makes her final vows. The sisters say that's how long it takes to determine if a vocation is real and if a woman has what it takes to live an often stark life devoid of everyday distractions.

Between 1977 and 1979, the most recent years for which comparable statistics have been compiled, 288 women entered, and 267 women left, American cloisters. By contrast, 1,887 women entered active orders and 5,694 left during that same period. For those who stay in the cloister, it is a life of extreme faith. If an active nun occasionally sees the sick healed or the poor fed, the cloistered nun has no such visible satisfaction. "It's not easy," says Sister Michaelene. "We don't see the hostilities in Lebanon ceasing because of our prayers."

The lack of concrete evidence inevitably leads to periods of near devastating doubt. "One day you come to your hour of prayer and you feel nothing," says Sister Annamae. "You begin to think, 'Am I making this all up?' Sometimes a spiritual counselor or a friend who's been through it can comfort you," she says. "But essentially you go through it alone. Once you get beyond the doubt, you're purified. You can give yourself completely to God—not in a servile sense, but as a free person."

Dealing with loneliness and the pull toward an active life is an ongoing challenge. Most communities are now quite open about discussing sexuality and the psychological implications of a celibate life, and Mother Superiors, priests and Catholic psychologists, who no longer view psychology and theology as contradictory sciences, provide sympathetic counseling.

For Sister Annamae, "The hardest thing is not to be loved exclusively by one person. We go through the gamut of emotions as much as anyone," she says, "maybe more, because we lead such a reflective life."

"I'm a red-blooded American woman," says Maryknoll Sister Rachel. "I love kids. I love men, too. I think it would be nice to have a husband. I face it. I admit it has an appeal, but I feel the pull toward religious life is stronger."

Sister Helen Werner points out that living in a cloister today does not rule out the possibility of deep platonic relationships with the men and women who visit, and with the sisters in the convent. In the past, close or "particular friendships," from the French, amitiés particulières, were forbidden. In some convents, two nuns were not allowed to be together without the presence of a third. Some sisters said the intent was to discourage exclusiveness or platonic friendships that would interfere with the primary relationship with God. Others say the unspoken reason was to prevent lesbian relationships from developing. Today, many nuns discuss the once-taboo subject quite matter-of-factly.

"We've talked about lesbianism," says Sister Michaelene. "I'm sure it happens, but it's not something we've experienced. If we did have a problem, we'd deal with it openly and sensitively. Anything that involves people living together in a small community you have to treat gently."

As to what the future holds for cloisters, Sister Michaelene thinks the contemplative life "may not be lived exactly the same way, but I think the life of prayer will continue. It's so much a part of human nature."

Despite the loneliness and doubts, most of the sisters interviewed say they are at peace in the cloister. "Like any life, if it's not for you, it can be a living hell," says Sister Marjorie. "But if the cloister is where you truly belong, it can be a beautiful life, a life of pain and sorrow balanced with peace and joy."

Many veteran nuns say their families and friends still have a hard time understanding a contemplative vocation. Sister Mary Devereux, who has been in a cloister for a quarter of a century, says her mother recently asked her, "Why do you have to get up so early when you have nothing to do all day?"

Occasionally, there are surprises. "My opinion of a cloistered vocation has changed drastically," says Helen O'Hara, who first thought "What a waste," when her daughter, now Sister Carolyn, told her she was entering a Carmelite cloister. But after reading everything she could get her hands on about the order and its founder, Mrs. O'Hara says she began to understand the contemplative life "as much as a lay person can. My husband and I began to respect Carolyn's choice. She was always quiet and strong. Now I notice an inner peace in her. It's been a gift. I feel we have a powerhouse of prayer in Beacon."

TRIFLES: A PLAY IN ONE ACT

Susan Glaspell

Susan Glaspell, born in Davenport, Iowa in 1876 or 1882—the correct date being in dispute, attended Drake University in Des Moines and later pursued graduate studies at the University of Chicago as well. She worked as a reporter in her hometown, eventually having her own column, "The News Girl." She gave up journalism in 1901, beginning a career as a full-time writer. She published at least two short stories a year from 1903 to 1922, mostly romances, appearing in popular magazines such as *Harper's Bazar* and the *Ladies' Home Journal*. In addition, three of her ten novels came out during those years. In 1913, Glaspell married George Cram Cook, moved to Cape Cod, and began writing plays, many of which were first performed by the experimental theater group, the Provincetown Players, remembered today for launching the career of Eugene O'Neill. Glaspell appeared in the role of Mrs. Hale in the first performance of *Trifles* at the Wharf Theater in 1916. Her last play, *Alison's House* (1930), based on the life of Emily Dickinson, won the 1931 Pulitzer Prize for drama.

Glaspell married Norman Mateson in 1925, a year after Cook's death. This second marriage ended in 1931.

Trifles is one of the most frequently performed one-act plays ever written in the United States. And Glaspell's short-story version, "A Jury of Her Peers," has also proved to be very popular. In it, while skillfully capturing the extreme isolation and loneliness of women living on the bleak Iowan prairie, Susan Glaspell portrays one of the many types of commitments women have to one another.

SCENE:

The kitchen in the now abandoned farmhouse of JOHN WRIGHT, *a gloomy kitchen, and left without having been put in order—unwashed pans under the sink, a loaf of bread outside the bread-box, a dish-towel on the table—other signs of incompleted work. At the rear the outer door opens and the* SHERIFF *comes in followed by the* COUNTY ATTORNEY *and* HALE. *The* SHERIFF *and* HALE *are men in middle life, the* COUNTY ATTORNEY *is a young man; all are much bundled up and go at once to the stove. They are followed by the two women—the* SHERIFF'S *wife first; she is a slight wiry woman, a thin nervous face.* MRS. HALE *is larger and would ordinarily be called more comfortable looking, but she is disturbed now and looks fearfully about as she enters. The women have come in slowly, and stand close together near the door.*

COUNTY ATTORNEY

[*Rubbing his hands.*]   This feels good. Come up to the fire, ladies.

MRS. PETERS

[*After taking a step forward.*]   I'm not—cold.

SHERIFF

[*Unbuttoning his overcoat and stepping away from the stove as if to mark the beginning of official business.*]   Now, Mr. Hale, before we move things about, you explain to Mr. Henderson just what you saw when you came here yesterday morning.

COUNTY ATTORNEY

By the way, has anything been moved? Are things just as you left them yesterday?

SHERIFF

[*Looking about.*]   It's just the same. When it dropped below zero last night I thought I'd better send Frank out this morning to make a fire for us—no use getting pneumonia with a big case on, but I told him not to touch anything except the stove—and you know Frank.

COUNTY ATTORNEY

Somebody should have been left here yesterday.

SHERIFF

Oh—yesterday. When I had to send Frank to Morris Center for that man who went crazy—I want you to know I had my hands full yesterday. I knew you could get back from Omaha by today and as long as I went over everything here myself—

COUNTY ATTORNEY

Well, Mr. Hale, tell just what happened when you came here yesterday morning.

HALE

Harry and I had started to town with a load of potatoes. We came along the road from my place and as I got here I said, "I'm going to see if I can't get John Wright to go in with me on a party telephone." I spoke to Wright about it once before and he put me off, saying folks talked too much anyway, and all he asked was peace and quiet—I guess you know about how much he talked himself; but I thought maybe if I went to the house and talked about it before his wife, though I said to Harry that I didn't know as what his wife wanted made much difference to John—

COUNTY ATTORNEY

Let's talk about that later, Mr. Hale. I do want to talk about that, but tell now just what happened when you got to the house.

HALE

I didn't hear or see anything; I knocked at the door, and still it was all quiet inside. I knew they must be up, it was past eight o'clock. So I knocked again, and I thought I heard somebody say, "Come in." I wasn't sure, I'm not sure yet, but I opened the door—this door [*indicating the door by which the two women are still standing*] and there in that rocker—[*pointing to it*] sat Mrs. Wright.
[*They all look at the rocker.*

COUNTY ATTORNEY

What—was she doing?

HALE

She was rockin' back and forth. She had her apron in her hand and was kind of—pleating it.

COUNTY ATTORNEY

And how did she—look?

HALE

Well, she looked queer.

COUNTY ATTORNEY

How do you mean—queer?

HALE

Well, as if she didn't know what she was going to do next. And kind of done up.

COUNTY ATTORNEY

How did she seem to feel about your coming?

HALE

Why, I don't think she minded—one way or other. She didn't pay much attention. I said, "How do, Mrs. Wright, it's cold, ain't it?" And she said, "Is it?"—and went on kind of pleating at her apron. Well, I was surprised; she didn't ask me to come up to the stove, or to set down, but just sat there, not even looking at me, so I said, "I want to see John." And then she—laughed. I guess you would call it a laugh. I thought of Harry and the team outside, so I said a little sharp: "Can't I see John?" "No," she says, kind o' dull like. "Ain't he home?" says I. "Yes," says she, "he's home." "Then why can't I see him?" I asked her, out of patience. " 'Cause he's dead," says she. *"Dead?"* says I. She just nodded her head, not getting a bit excited, but rockin' back and forth. "Why—where is he?" says I, not knowing what to say. She just pointed upstairs—like that [*himself pointing to the room above*]. I got up, with the idea of going up there. I walked from there to here—then I says, "Why, what did he die of?" "He died of a rope around his neck," says she, and just went on pleatin' at her apron. Well, I went out and called Harry. I thought I might—need help. We went upstairs and there he was lyin'—

COUNTY ATTORNEY

I think I'd rather have you go into that upstairs, where you can point it all out. Just go on now with the rest of the story.

HALE

Well, my first thought was to get that rope off. It looked . . . [*Stops, his face twitches*] . . . but Harry, he went up to him, and he said, "No, he's dead all right, and we'd better not touch anything." So we went back down stairs. She was still sitting that same way. "Has anybody been notified?" I asked. "No," says she, unconcerned. "Who did this, Mrs. Wright?" said Harry. He said it business-like—and she stopped pleatin' of her apron. "I don't know," she says. "You don't *know*?" says Harry. "No," says she. "Weren't you sleepin' in the bed with him?" says Harry. "Yes," says she, "but I was on the inside." "Somebody slipped a rope round his neck and strangled him and you didn't wake up?" says Harry. "I didn't wake up," she said after him. We must 'a looked as if we didn't see how that could be, for after a minute she said, "I sleep sound." Harry was going to ask her more questions but I said maybe we ought to let her tell her story first to the coroner, or the sheriff, so Harry went fast as he could to Rivers' place, where there's a telephone.

COUNTY ATTORNEY

And what did Mrs. Wright do when she knew that you had gone for the coroner?

HALE

She moved from that chair to this one over here [*Pointing to a small chair in the corner*] and just sat there with her hands held together and looking down. I got a feeling that I ought to make some conversation, so I said I had come in to see if John wanted to put in a telephone, and at that she started to laugh, and then she stopped and looked at me—scared. [*The* COUNTY ATTORNEY, *who has had his notebook out, makes a note.*] I dunno, maybe it wasn't scared. I wouldn't like to say it was. Soon Harry got back, and then Dr. Lloyd came, and you, Mr. Peters, and so I guess that's all I know that you don't.

COUNTY ATTORNEY

[*Looking around.*] I guess we'll go upstairs first—and then out to the barn and around there. [*To the* SHERIFF.] You're convinced that there was nothing important here—nothing that would point to any motive.

SHERIFF

Nothing here but kitchen things.
[*The* COUNTY ATTORNEY, *after again looking around the kitchen, opens the door of a cupboard closet. He gets up on a chair and looks on a shelf. Pulls his hand away, sticky.*

COUNTY ATTORNEY

Here's a nice mess.
[*The women draw nearer.*

MRS. PETERS

[*To the other woman.*]   Oh, her fruit; it did freeze. [*To the* LAWYER.] She worried about that when it turned so cold. She said the fire'd go out and her jars would break.

SHERIFF

Well, can you beat the women! Held for murder and worryin' about her preserves.

COUNTY ATTORNEY

I guess before we're through she may have something more serious than preserves to worry about.

HALE

Well, women are used to worrying over trifles.
[*The two women move a little closer together.*

COUNTY ATTORNEY

[*With the gallantry of a young politician.*] And yet, for all their worries, what would we do without the ladies? [*The women do not unbend. He goes to the sink, takes a dipperful of water from the pail and pouring it into a basin, washes his hands. Starts to wipe them on the roller-towel, turns it for a cleaner place.*] Dirty towels! [*Kicks his foot against the pans under the sink.*] Not much of a housekeeper, would you say, ladies?

MRS. HALE

[*Stiffly.*]   There's a great deal of work to be done on a farm.

COUNTY ATTORNEY

To be sure. And yet [*With a little bow to her*] I know there are some Dickson county farmhouses which do not have such roller towels.
[*He gives it a pull to expose its full length again.*

MRS. HALE

Those towels get dirty awful quick. Men's hands aren't always as clean as they might be.

COUNTY ATTORNEY

Ah, loyal to your sex, I see. But you and Mrs. Wright were neighbors. I suppose you were friends, too.

MRS. HALE

[*Shaking her head.*]   I've not seen much of her of late years. I've not been in this house—it's more than a year.

COUNTY ATTORNEY

And why was that? You didn't like her?

MRS. HALE

I liked her all well enough. Farmers' wives have their hands full, Mr. Henderson. And then—

COUNTY ATTORNEY

Yes—?

MRS. HALE

[*Looking about.*]   It never seemed a very cheerful place.

COUNTY ATTORNEY

No—it's not cheerful. I shouldn't say she had the homemaking instinct.

MRS. HALE

Well, I don't know as Wright had, either.

COUNTY ATTORNEY

You mean that they didn't get on very well?

MRS. HALE

No, I don't mean anything. But I don't think a place'd be any cheerfuller for John Wright's being in it.

COUNTY ATTORNEY

I'd like to talk more of that a little later. I want to get the lay of things upstairs now.
[*He goes to the left, where three steps lead to a stair door.*]

SHERIFF

I suppose anything Mrs. Peters does'll be all right. She was to take in some clothes for her, you know, and a few little things. We left in such a hurry yesterday.

COUNTY ATTORNEY

Yes, but I would like to see what you take, Mrs. Peters, and keep an eye out for anything that might be of use to us.

MRS. PETERS

Yes, Mr. Henderson.
[The women listen to the men's steps on the stairs, then look about the kitchen.

MRS. HALE

I'd hate to have men coming into my kitchen, snooping around and criticising.
[She arranges the pans under sink which the LAWYER had shoved out of place.

MRS. PETERS

Of course it's no more than their duty.

MRS. HALE

Duty's all right, but I guess that deputy sheriff that came out to make the fire might have got a little of this on. [Gives the roller towel a pull.] Wish I'd thought of that sooner. Seems mean to talk about her for not having things slicked up when she had to come away in such a hurry.

MRS. PETERS

[Who has gone to a small table in the left rear corner of the room, and lifted one end of a towel that covers a pan.]   She had bread set.
[Stands still.

MRS. HALE

[Eyes fixed on a loaf of bread beside the breadbox, which is on a low shelf at the other side of the room. Moves slowly toward it.]   She was going to put this in there. [Picks up loaf, then abruptly drops it. In a manner of returning to familiar things.] It's a shame about her fruit. I wonder if it's all gone. [Gets up on the chair and looks.] I think there's some here that's all right, Mrs. Peters. Yes—here; [Holding it toward the window] this is cherries, too. [Looking again.] I declare I believe that's the only one. [Gets down, bottle in her hand. Goes to the sink and wipes it off on the outside.] She'll feel awful bad after all her hard work in the hot weather. I remember the afternoon I put up my cherries last summer.

[*She puts the bottle on the big kitchen table, center of the room. With a sigh, is about to sit down in the rocking-chair. Before she is seated realizes what chair it is; with a slow look at it, steps back. The chair which she has touched rocks back and forth.*]

MRS. PETERS

Well, I must get those things from the front room closet. [*She goes to the door at the right, but after looking into the other room, steps back.*] You coming with me, Mrs. Hale? You could help me carry them.

[*They go in the other room; reappear,* MRS. PETERS *carrying a dress and skirt,* MRS. HALE *following with a pair of shoes.*]

MRS. PETERS

My, it's cold in there.
[*She puts the clothes on the big table, and hurries to the stove.*]

MRS. HALE

[*Examining the skirt.*]   Wright was close. I think maybe that's why she kept so much to herself. She didn't even belong to the Ladies Aid. I suppose she felt she couldn't do her part, and then you don't enjoy things when you feel shabby. She used to wear pretty clothes and be lively, when she was Minnie Foster, one of the town girls singing in the choir. But that—oh, that was thirty years ago. This all you was to take in?

MRS. PETERS

She said she wanted an apron. Funny thing to want, for there isn't much to get you dirty in jail, goodness knows. But I suppose just to make her feel more natural. She said they was in the top drawer in this cupboard. Yes here. And then her little shawl that always hung behind the door.   [*Opens stair door and looks.*]   Yes, here it is.
[*Quickly shuts door leading upstairs.*]

MRS. HALE

[*Abruptly moving toward her.*]   Mrs. Peters?

MRS. PETERS

Yes, Mrs. Hale?

MRS. HALE

Do you think she did it?

MRS. PETERS

[*In a frightened voice.*]   Oh, I don't know.

MRS. HALE

Well, I don't think she did. Asking for an apron and her little shawl. Worrying about her fruit.

MRS. PETERS

[*Starts to speak, glances up, where footsteps are heard in the room above. In a low voice.*] Mr. Peters says it looks bad for her. Mr. Henderson is awful sarcastic in a speech and he'll make fun of her sayin' she didn't wake up.

MRS. HALE

Well, I guess John Wright didn't wake when they was slipping that rope under his neck.

MRS. PETERS

No, it's strange. It must have been done awful crafty and still. They say it was such a—funny way to kill a man, rigging it all up like that.

MRS. HALE

That's just what Mr. Hale said. There was a gun in the house. He says that's what he can't understand.

MRS. PETERS

Mr. Henderson said coming out that what was needed for the case was a motive; something to show anger, or—sudden feeling.

MRS. HALE

[*Who is standing by the table.*] Well, I don't see any signs of anger around here. [*She puts her hand on the dish towel which lies on the table, stands looking down at table, one half of which is clean, the other half messy.*] It's wiped to here. [*Makes a move as if to finish work, then turns and looks at loaf of bread outside the breadbox. Drops towel. In that voice of coming back to familiar things.*] Wonder how they are finding things upstairs. I hope she had it a little more red-up up there. You know, it seems kind of *sneaking*. Locking her up in town and then coming out here and trying to get her own house to turn against her!

MRS. PETERS

But Mrs. Hale, the law is the law.

MRS. HALE

I s'pose 'tis. [*Unbuttoning her coat.*] Better loosen up your things, Mrs. Peters. You won't feel them when you go out.
[MRS. PETERS *takes off her fur tippet, goes to hang it on hook at back of room, stands looking at the under part of the small corner table.*

MRS. PETERS

She was piecing a quilt.
[*She brings the large sewing basket and they look at the bright pieces.*]

MRS. HALE

It's log cabin pattern. Pretty, isn't it? I wonder if she was goin' to quilt it or just knot it?
[*Footsteps have been heard coming down the stairs. The* SHERIFF *enters followed by* HALE *and the* COUNTY ATTORNEY.]

SHERIFF

They wonder if she was going to quilt it or just knot it!
[*The men laugh, the women look abashed.*

COUNTY ATTORNEY

[*Rubbing his hands over the stove.*]   Frank's fire didn't do much up there, did it? Well, let's go out to the barn and get that cleared up.
[*The men go outside.*]

MRS. HALE

[*Resentfully.*]   I don't know as there's anything so strange, our takin' up our time with little things while we're waiting for them to get the evidence. [*She sits down at the big table smoothing out a block with decision.*] I don't see as it's anything to laugh about.

MRS. PETERS

[*Apologetically.*]   Of course they've got awful important things on their minds.
[*Pulls up a chair and joins* MRS. HALE *at the table.*]

MRS. HALE

[*Examining another block.*]   Mrs. Peters, look at this one. Here, this is the one she was working on, and look at the sewing! All the rest of it has been so nice and even. And look at this! It's all over the place! Why, it looks as if she didn't know what she was about!
[*After she has said this they look at each other, then start to glance back at the door. After an instant* MRS. HALE *has pulled at a knot and ripped the sewing.*

MRS. PETERS

Oh, what are you doing, Mrs. Hale?

MRS. HALE

[*Mildly.*]   Just pulling out a stitch or two that's not sewed very good. [*Threading a needle.*] Bad sewing always made me fidgety.

MRS. PETERS

[*Nervously.*]   I don't think we ought to touch things.

MRS. HALE

I'll just finish up this end.   [*Suddenly stopping and leaning forward.*]   Mrs. Peters?

MRS. PETERS

Yes, Mrs. Hale?

MRS. HALE

What do you suppose she was so nervous about?

MRS. PETERS

Oh—I don't know. I don't know as she was nervous. I sometimes sew awful queer when I'm just tired. [MRS. HALE *starts to say something, looks at* MRS. PETERS, *then goes on sewing.*] Well I must get these things wrapped up. They may be through sooner than we think. [*Putting apron and other things together.*] I wonder where I can find a piece of paper, and string.

MRS. HALE

In that cupboard, maybe.

MRS. PETERS

[*Looking in cupbord.*]   Why, here's a bird-cage. [*Holds it up.*] Did she have a bird, Mrs. Hale?

MRS. HALE

Why, I don't know whether she did or not—I've not been here for so long. There was a man around last year selling canaries cheap, but I don't know as she took one; maybe she did. She used to sing real pretty herself.

MRS. PETERS

[*Glancing around.*]   Seems funny to think of a bird here. But she must have had one, or why would she have a cage? I wonder what happened to it.

MRS. HALE

I s'pose maybe the cat got it.

MRS. PETERS

No, she didn't have a cat. She's got that feeling some people have about cats—being afraid of them. My cat got in her room and she was real upset and asked me to take it out.

MRS. HALE

My sister Bessie was like that. Queer, ain't it?

MRS. PETERS

[*Examining the cage.*] Why, look at this door. It's broke. One hinge is pulled apart.

MRS. HALE

[*Looking too.*] Looks as if someone must have been rough with it.

MRS. PETERS

Why, yes.
[*She brings the cage forward and puts it on the table.*

MRS. HALE

I wish if they're going to find any evidence they'd be about it. I don't like this place.

MRS. PETERS

But I'm awful glad you came with me, Mrs. Hale. It would be lonesome for me sitting here alone.

MRS. HALE

It would, wouldn't it? [*Dropping her sewing.*] But I tell you what I do wish, Mrs. Peters. I wish I had come over sometimes when *she* was here. I—[*Looking around the room*]—wish I had.

MRS. PETERS

But of course you were awful busy, Mrs. Hale—your house and your children.

MRS. HALE

I could've come. I stayed away because it weren't cheerful—and that's why I ought to have come. I—I've never liked this place. Maybe because it's down in a hollow and you don't see the road. I dunno what it is, but it's a lonesome place and always was. I wish I had come over to see Minnie Foster sometimes. I can see now—
[*Shakes her head.*

MRS. PETERS

Well, you mustn't reproach yourself, Mrs. Hale. Somehow we just don't see how it is with other folks until—something comes up.

MRS. HALE

Not having children makes less work—but it makes a quiet house, and Wright out to work all day, and no company when he did come in. Did you know John Wright, Mrs. Peters?

MRS. PETERS

Not to know him; I've seen him in town. They say he was a good man.

MRS. HALE

Yes—good; he didn't drink, and kept his word as well as most, I guess, and paid his debts. But he was a hard man, Mrs. Peters. Just to pass the time of day with him—[Shivers.] Like a raw wind that gets to the bone. [Pauses, her eye falling on the cage.] I should think she would 'a wanted a bird. But what do you suppose went with it?

MRS. PETERS

I don't know, unless it got sick and died.
[She reaches over and swings the broken door, swings it again, both women watch it.

MRS. HALE

You weren't raised round here, were you? [MRS. PETERS shakes her head.] You didn't know—her?

MRS. PETERS

Not till they brought her yesterday.

MRS. HALE

She—come to think of it, she was kind of like a bird herself—real sweet and pretty, but kind of timid and—fluttery. How—she—did—change. [Silence; then as if struck by a happy thought and relieved to get back to every day things.] Tell you what, Mrs. Peters, why don't you take the quilt in with you? It might take up her mind.

MRS. PETERS

Why, I think that's a real nice idea, Mrs. Hale. There couldn't possibly be any objection to it, could there? Now, just what would I take? I wonder if her patches are in here—and her things.
[They look in the sewing basket.

MRS. HALE

Here's some red. I expect this has got sewing things in it. [Brings out a fancy box.] What a pretty box. Looks like something somebody would give you. Maybe her scissors are in here. [Opens box. Suddenly puts her hand to her *nose.*] Why—[MRS. PETERS *bends nearer, then turns her face away.*] There's something wrapped up in this piece of silk.

MRS. PETERS

Why, this isn't her scissors.

MRS. HALE

[*Lifting the silk.*]   Oh, Mrs. Peters—its—
[MRS. PETERS *bends closer.*

MRS. PETERS

It's the bird.

MRS. HALE

[*Jumping up.*]   But, Mrs. Peters—look at it! It's neck! Look at its neck! It's all—other side *to.*

MRS. PETERS

Somebody—wrung—its—neck.
[*Their eyes meet. A look of growing comprehension, of horror. Steps are heard outside.* MRS. HALE *slips box under quilt pieces, and sinks into her chair. Enter* SHERIFF *and* COUNTY ATTORNEY. MRS. PETERS *rises.*

COUNTY ATTORNEY

[*As one turning from serious things to little pleasantries.*]   Well, ladies have you decided whether she was going to quilt it or knot it?

MRS. PETERS

We think she was going to—knot it.

COUNTY ATTORNEY

Well, that's interesting, I'm sure.   [*Seeing the birdcage.*] Has the bird flown?

MRS. HALE

[*Putting more quilt pieces over the box.*]   We think the—cat got it.

COUNTY ATTORNEY

[*Preoccupied.*]   Is there a cat?
[MRS. HALE *glances in a quick covert way at* MRS. PETERS.

MRS. PETERS

Well, not *now.* They're superstitious, you know. They leave.

COUNTY ATTORNEY

[*To* SHERIFF PETERS, *continuing an interrupted conversation.*] No sign at all of anyone having come from the outside. Their own rope. Now let's go up again and go over it piece by piece.   [*They start upstairs.*]   It would have to have been someone who knew just the—

[MRS. PETERS *sits down. The two women sit there not looking at one another, but as if peering into something and at the same time holding back. When they talk now it is in the manner of feeling their way over strange ground, as if afraid of what they are saying, but as if they can not help saying it.*]

MRS. HALE

She liked the bird. She was going to bury it in that pretty box.

MRS. PETERS

[*In a whisper.*]   When I was a girl—my kitten—there was a boy took a hatchet, and before my eyes—and before I could get there—[*Covers her face an instant.*] If they hadn't held me back I would have—[*Catches herself, looks upstairs where steps are heard, falters weakly*]—hurt him.

MRS. HALE

[*With a slow look around her.*]   I wonder how it would seem never to have had any children around. [*Pause.*]   No, Wright wouldn't like the bird—a thing that sang. She used to sing. He killed that, too.

MRS. PETERS

[*Moving uneasily.*]   We don't know who killed the bird.

MRS. HALE

I knew John Wright.

MRS. PETERS

It was an awful thing was done in this house that night, Mrs. Hale. Killing a man while he slept, slipping a rope around his neck that choked the life out of him.

MRS. HALE

His neck. Choked the life out of him.
[*Her hand goes out and rests on the bird-cage.*]

MRS. PETERS

[*With rising voice.*]   We don't know who killed him. We dont *know.*

MRS. HALE

[*Her own feeling not interrupted.*] If there'd been years and years of nothing, then a bird to sing to you, it would be awful—still, after the bird was still.

MRS. PETERS

[*Something within her speaking.*] I know what stillness is. When we homesteaded in Dakota, and my first baby died—after he was two years old, and me with no other then—

MRS. HALE

[*Moving.*] How soon do you suppose they'll be through, looking for the evidence?

MRS. PETERS

I know what stillness is. [*Pulling herself back.*] The law has got to punish crime, Mrs. Hale.

MRS. HALE

[*Not as if answering that.*] I wish you'd seen Minnie Foster when she wore a white dress with blue ribbons and stood up there in the choir and sang. [*A look around the room.*] Oh, I *wish* I'd come over here once in a while! That was a crime! That was a crime! Who's going to punish that?

MRS. PETERS

[*Looking upstairs.*] We mustn't—take on.

MRS. HALE

I might have known she needed help! I know how things can be—for women. I tell you, it's queer, Mrs. Peters. We live close together and we live far apart. We all go through the same things—it's all just a different kind of the same thing. [*Brushes her eyes, noticing the bottle of fruit, reaches out for it.*] If I was you I wouldn't tell her her fruit was gone. Tell her it *ain't*. Tell her it's all right. Take this in to prove it to her. She—she may never know whether it was broke or not.

MRS. PETERS

[*Takes the bottle, looks about for something to wrap it in; takes petticoat from the clothes brought from the other room, very nervously begins winding this around the bottle. In a false voice.*] My, it's a good thing the men couldn't hear us. Wouldn't they just laugh! Getting all stirred up over a little thing like a—dead canary. As if that could have anything to do with—with— wouldn't they *laugh*!
[*The men are heard coming down stairs.*

MRS. HALE

[*Under her breath*.]   Maybe they would—maybe they wouldn't.

COUNTY ATTORNEY

No, Peters, it's all perfectly clear except a reason for doing it. But you know juries when it comes to women. If there was some definite thing. Something to show—something to make a story about—a thing that would connect up with this strange way of doing it—
[*The women's eyes meet for an instant. Enter* HALE *from outer door.*

HALE

Well, I've got the team around. Pretty cold out there.

COUNTY ATTORNEY

I'm going to stay here a while by myself.   [*To the* SHERIFF.]   You can send Frank out for me, can't you? I want to go over everything. I'm not satisfied that we can't do better.

SHERIFF

Do you want to see what Mrs. Peters is going to take in?
[*The* LAWYER *goes to the table, picks up the apron, laughs.*

COUNTY ATTORNEY

Oh, I guess they're not very dangerous things the ladies have picked out. [*Moves a few things about, disturbing the quilt pieces which cover the box. Steps back.*] No, Mrs. Peters doesn't need supervising. For that matter, a sheriff's wife is married to the law. Ever think of it that way, Mrs. Peters?

MRS. PETERS

Not—just that way.

SHERIFF

[*Chuckling.*]   Married to the law. [*Moves toward the other room.*] I just want you to come in here a minute, George. We ought to take a look at these windows.

COUNTY ATTORNEY

[*Scoffingly.*]   Oh, windows!

SHERIFF

We'll be right out, Mr. Hale.   [HALE *goes outside. The* SHERIFF *follows the* COUNTY ATTORNEY *into the other room. Then* MRS. HALE *rises, hands tight together, looking intensely at* MRS. PETERS, *whose eyes make a slow turn, finally meeting* MRS. HALE'S. *A moment* MRS. HALE *holds her, then her own eyes point the way to where the box is concealed. Suddenly* MRS. PETERS *throws back quilt pieces and tries to put the box in the bag she is wearing. It is too big. She opens box, starts to take bird out, cannot touch it, goes to pieces, stands there helpless. Sound of knob turning in the other room.* MRS. HALE *snatches the box and puts it in the pocket of her big coat. Enter* COUNTY ATTORNEY *and* SHERIFF.

COUNTY ATTORNEY

[*Facetiously.*]   Well, Henry, at least we found out that she was not going to quilt it. She was going to—what is it you call it, ladies?

MRS. HALE

[*Her hand against her pocket.*]   We call it—knot it, Mr. Henderson.

(CURTAIN)

IN AMERIKA THEY CALL US DYKES

The Boston Gay Collective

The selection below is reprinted from the first commercial edition of *Our Bodies, Ourselves,* a compendium of medical, sexual, and political information originally developed for a course about women and their bodies by the Boston Women's Health Collective. The chapters included in the book went through several locally-published revisions until a growing demand warranted its commercial publication. The book has undergone two major revisions, in 1976 and in 1983 (*The New Our Bodies, Ourselves*). Royalties earned from the book support the nonprofit organization's distribution of other health-related material. In addition to selling over two million copies in the United States, the book has been published in twelve foreign-language editions.

Not without controversy, *Our Bodies, Ourselves,* once hailed as a "best book for young adults" by the American Library Association, later came under attack by the Moral Majority's the Reverend Jerry Falwell who denounced it as "out and out humanistic garbage" that would "distort and warp our children's minds and moral values."

 ...**SARAH.**   I'm twenty-five, and I "came out" when I slept with a friend a year ago. We have been lovers ever since. But it took me about six months to actively assert my gay identity and feel bound to figuring out what gay politics was or could be. I understood my reluctance to being labeled "lesbian" after listening to a couple of gay women at a gay bar react violently to the word. They saw themselves as human beings, not as labels. But, I thought, that's just not the way people deal with each other in this society. They give you labels whether you take them or

IN AMERIKA THEY CALL US DYKES   From The Boston Women's Health Collective, *Our Bodies, Ourselves,* New York: Simon and Schuster, 1971, 57–59. Copyright 1971, 1973, 1976 by the Boston Women's Health Collective, Inc. Reprinted by permission of Simon & Schuster, Inc.

not. They reminded me too much of myself ten or fifteen years ago when I responded similarly to being called a Jew.

From the sixth grade on, I was the only Jew in my school. Everyone informed me of that; and it was no compliment coming from their mouths. I thought of myself as smart, capable, good at science and math. I was going to be another Marie Curie. But I was also intimidated by other peoples' judgments; I had to figure out how to fit in. "No, we don't bury our dead standing up," I would say. I really wanted to have friends, and I did get close to girls and boys. But I was always on the fence; they might always turn around and say "You're a Jew." This explains a lot of my reluctance to identify myself as gay and say "I'm a lesbian."

I thought I could have what people would call a gay relationship with my friend and not have to get into gay women's liberation or see myself as a lesbian. I had the choice not to do that. I knew by calling myself a lesbian I was asking for disapproval, distance, and pehaps violence, from most people. And since I had gone through it once, why ask for it again? So for a long time I did not identify. Then I realized that while ideally no one wants to be labeled, I do live in a society where people react to each other that way, and I don't have any control over that. I can't deny how people relate to me. Yes, I'm Jewish and I'm a lesbian.

I'm one of those women who "came out" with the women's movement. Women's Liberation made me think about my past, about when I was a kid and liked to play football and baseball. To me the accusation "You throw like a girl" was a terrible put-down—I didn't want to be lumped in with the "girl" category. I realized when thinking about my family that my parents had similar expectations for me and my brother—except that it was impressed on me to be nice, considerate, concerned for others in ways my brother was rarely pressed to show.

I thought about how, in junior high, the boys looked at the girls as developing bodies. They would yell, "Pearl Harbor, surprise attack!" as they grabbed our breasts and forced us down on the ground to get the "big feel." I know it scared me then, but how could I deal with my anger and fear when what was so important among girls was to be accepted by the boys? And having a boyfriend was often a protection from those other boys.

In ninth grade, a group of girls got close. We used to hug and kiss each other a lot and have slumber parties. Most of us had boyfriends, but we seemed very important to each other. Once in a while someone would say, "What are you, a homo?" and we'd laugh. It didn't mean anything and it didn't change our behavior in any way.

That's the only reference to homosexuality before college that I can remember. In college I got hit with Freud and latent homosexual tendencies. What did this mean for me, who had always been more emotionally attached to women than to men? In freshman year my roommate and I became very close and dependent on each other, but neither of us could handle the intensity; that happened to me a lot with female friends. In psychotherapy I asked (indirectly of course) if I had "those tendencies." After about fifteen minutes the therapist figured out the question and asked, "Are you wondering if you're a lesbian?" Me: "Not really—ahh, I'm just wondering what you think about those tendencies." "You've given no indications of that," he said. Phew! was my reaction, not knowing what those "indications" were! (That's a story of how expertise has power over people's lives.) So I didn't worry about being a lesbian, but continued to build close friendships with women; and the problems those emotional attachments brought weren't lessened.

After college I felt the sadness of women friends going in different directions without the question of sharing our lives, like there would be with boyfriends. I went with a guy for three years, but he was never more important to me than two of my female friends. That was to my liking, not his. He wanted to get married, but since marriage wasn't part of any world I could imagine for myself, he married another woman two months after we split up. Sometimes my friendships with women were threatened by their jealous boyfriends. With these feelings, I could no longer ignore the women's movement. I read something another woman had written about her—and my—experiences. Fantastic! I wasn't alone. I began thinking that men didn't understand friendship, that they were sexual prowlers wanting all the attention focused on them; whereas my relationships with women seemed natural, exciting, and intense.

Working with Women's Liberation in Boston meant being with women all the time. A group of us who weren't really close but were friends would hang out together, circle-danced at a bar, played basketball. Diana was one of them. She and I found we could tune into each other's survival tactics: her piercing, allusive quips weren't offensive to me. What a relief. We could accept each other without many hurt feelings, we shared a lot of interests and criticisms of the women's movement. Eventually we slept together. That was over a year ago.

DIANA.   When I was a kid, I was always a tomboy. In seventh grade the situation changed—I went to a private school where I didn't know anyone and all my friends were girls. I never got to know any of the boys and couldn't see why anyone would want to—they were picking on younger kids, harassing women teachers, and so on. It seemed as though you couldn't get to know them as friends, but only flirt with them. I didn't want to flirt, so I didn't go to parties everyone else was going to. I knew of course that when boys and girls grew up they were supposed to mysteriously start being attracted to each other. I thought that would happen to me, too, later. But the kids in my class just seemed to be playing at being grown up.

In junior high I started identifying more strongly as a girl. Boys were becoming more and more of an alien group. I still hated stockings and frills, but I certainly didn't want to be a boy anymore.

We had dancing classes in junior high. One night between dances a cold breeze started blowing through the open window. I reached over and touched Margaret's knee and asked her if she was getting cold too. She shrank back in mock horror and said, "What's the matter, Diana, are you a lesbian?" Everyone nearby started snickering. I didn't know what a lesbian was, but I knew I didn't want to be one. Later I found out; there was a lot of joking and taunting among girls in my class about lesbianism, which they viewed as sick and disgusting.

I went to an all-girls boarding school for high school. I was happy to be in an all-girls school, because I thought of boys as people you couldn't act naturally with, people who would make the classroom atmosphere tense and uptight. I began to worry consciously about being a lesbian. I knew that wherever I went, women attracted my attention, never men. If I rode on a bus or subway I would watch the faces of all the women. My emotional attachments were all to women and I had crushes on women friends. But I thought that if my attachments weren't sexual I was okay. I tried imagining sex with one of the seniors and was repelled by the thought. That was a relief. I said to myself that I was attracted to girls' *faces*, not their bodies. I told myself, "I just think Kitty's body is beautiful from an *esthetic* point of view, not a sexual one."

I was a tactophobe—a word we invented to mean someone who was afraid of touching people. I was afraid that if I touched other girls I would like it and keep on touching them. So I became repulsed at the idea, to save myself from perversion.

I went to college, and as I began sleeping with boys I began to lose some of my fear of being a lesbian. I enjoyed sex with boys at first, though I didn't much enjoy being with them otherwise, and was always trying to think up reasons not to see my boyfriend. I thought men were boring, and I still felt I had to act very artificially with them.

I began to go on a campaign to become more boy-oriented. I tried consciously to watch more men and fewer women in the subway. I wanted to feel turned on to men, not because it would be enjoyable, but because I was afraid I would not be a complete woman otherwise.

One sumnmer I went to Latin America. There the women are much more physical with each other, walking arm in arm, dancing close together, and touching each other more. I liked this freedom and thought that it showed how culture-bound our definitions of homosexuality are. I got close to one woman, a nurse named Edna. Before I left I spent a day at her house. We were sitting on her bed and she started sucking my finger. I was totally turned on. As I left I thought, Oh no, there's no denying it anymore. I'm a lesbian. Bisexuality did not occur to me as a possibility, although I knew the term. I thought if I was turned on to women, I must accept the fact of being a total queer.

I got into the women's movement, and felt an enormous relief that I would no longer have to play roles with men and act feminine and sweet, dress in skirts and heels, and do all the things I'd done on dates. Then I began to feel hatred for men for having forced me into these roles. During this time I would buy women's papers as soon as they came out and look immediately for articles by gay women. I began to hang out with gay women, who turned out to be regular people, not the stereotypes I had imagined. On a gut level I was beginning to realize that gayness was not a sickness. One night I went out for a long walk, and when I got home I had decided I was a lesbian. For me it was not a decision to become a lesbian. It was a question of accepting and becoming comfortable with feelings that I had always had.

I don't know if I would ever have "come out" if it hadn't been for the women's movement. The women's movement first led me to question the "naturalness" of the male-female roles that I had always largely accepted. Because I thought that role-playing heterosexuality was "the way it's supposed to be," whenever I rebelled against these roles I was afraid that this meant I was not a complete woman, that there was something wrong with me—not enough sex hormones, no doubt. The women's movement helped me to reject these roles, and with them every reason for struggling to be heterosexual. I realized femaleness was something I was born with, it was not something others could reward me with when I acted "feminine," or take away from me as a punishment. . . .

LETTER TO FANNY QUINCY HOWE
Maimie Pinzer

The Maimie Papers, a set of letters ex-prostitute Maimie Pinzer wrote to Fanny Quincy Howe, her benefactor and dear friend, from 1910 to 1922, provide a rare glimpse into the life of a working-class woman in the early twentieth century.

Born in 1885 to Polish-Russian immigrant parents, Maimie lived comfortably in Philadelphia until she was thirteen when the murder of her father plunged the family into poverty. Forced to quit school and keep house by her mother, an embittered Maimie then took a job as a salesgirl in a downtown department store to earn spending money. After staying away from home for several days and nights with a man, her mother, declaring her a prostitute, had her arrested, thrown into jail and sent to the Magdalen Home for wayward girls.

In 1910, Maimie met social worker Herbert Welsh, who came to her aid while she was hospitalized, encouraged her reform, and recommended the correspondence with the Bostonian philanthropist to help Maimie keep on the straight and narrow. After searching for respectable employment that would support her adequately, but finding herself locked out of the better paying jobs because of lack of training, she considered returning to her former life. With financial aid from Welsh, however, Maimie completed stenography school, eventually moving to Montreal where, in 1914, she and a friend started a letter writing and duplicating firm. Following Canada's entry into the war, the business faltered. It was at that time that Maimie began giving aid to young prostitutes. In 1915, she opened the Montreal Mission, a halfway house, but financial problems and police harassment forced its closing in 1917. She married Ira Benjamin that year and in 1918 they returned to the United States. The last existing letter from Maimie to Fanny was written in 1922.

Throughout her life, in spite of various attempts at reconciliation, Maimie remained estranged from her family, especially her mother. They could never forgive her for her transgressions, it seems.

At the time of the letter below, Maimie had recently returned to Montreal from Philadelphia with Stella, one of the young prostitutes she was trying to help, who had received treatment for venereal disease.

May, 1915

Will you just forget that I wrote the last two or three pages of the letter you received the other day?

I feel they were written under conditions that made me overdraw the conditions. I've no doubt they made me appear a martyr—and occasionally I am not above playing that role, even though there is only a tiny excuse for it.

It is true my mother was most exasperating on that day, but I think my description of the annoyance was a bit overdrawn. You know the old adage about it taking "two to make a quarrel"—it still holds good. Unconsciously, I did make this quarrel. And had my mother, during a great stress of mind, written to a sympathetic friend, her views of the situation—I've no doubt, I should appear to be the terrible one.

I don't really know what "riled" her—only that I am sure I am as much to blame as she. She left that night. I was not able to go to the depot to see her off, as my head and eye ached. I cried myself into this condition. She was seen off by Mr. B. and five girls—Gabrielle, Stella, Alice, Lou and Margaret.

She told Mr. Benjamin (who knew of the "rift in the lute," but not of the conditions) that I lost sight of the fact that her "boys" were very dear to her—hence, our quarrel. But to save my life, I don't know how this applies. For I've no recollection of their names being mentioned in anything unusual, until my brother wrote a very trying letter—insulting, inasmuch as he knew that I, or some friend of mine, must read it to her. Even when the letter came, I said nothing. But I confess I cried a great deal, for I was hurt—because I always counted on this brother's love, and hoped sometime to go to see him. That he lived in comparative ease and luxury, I never commented upon, nor asked him for any assistance. I always thought that he must know my condition. And he knows, too, that I have been trying to live clean; and as he did not send me at any time a penny or a gift, no matter how slight, I thought probably he did not credit the fact that I had been living the life where one receives nothing except that which they earn—and gave it no more thought.

Enough of this. I hope they all have plenty—and I will hope some day to have them all feel downright sorry for their neglect. For I am a sister—and they throw away daily what I suffer for lack of.

My mother left, having made peace with me, for which I was duly grateful—for it would have been a pity to have her go in anger, when she stopped here through two months of continual harmony.

I wish to write you a little about Stella—for I recall I left off directly in the part where I expected to tell you of her.

This girl is no different than thousands of girls, except in appearance—she is "different" in that she is far more beautiful than most girls.

She is a type, and I know the type well.

When I act in anything for her, I see a composite picture of Stellas, Maimies, etc.—their number is legion. I know so well her every thought and action. And even better than she does, I know her hopes. You will hardly be able to grasp this, not ever having lived thru it, but my recollections of the same thing when I was seventeen are very fresh, and very readily brought to mind.

Stella and her type are innately refined. Perhaps not in the sense that some might call refined, but that word suffices to explain that she is the opposite of "bourgeois." That her parents and environments are sordid is an accepted fact; and that [they] have refused to drop into the same rut and have had an idea to outgrow the conditions they were born into, makes them "different." And this difference is frowned upon, and only bad can be seen in it.

If she and the rest of her type were ugly in face or form, they would have no trouble, no matter how different their views. But there's the rub. Stella, being pretty, is the subject of petty jealousies. When the mother is a natural one and has the love of God in her heart, she takes pride in her daughter's pretty face and pretty ways. But Stella's mother and my mother, and many mothers of this type, prefer their children to run along in the same groove that they've made, and any indication of anything else is sensed as immoral, and done to lure men.

I can recall one incident in my life that will furnish proof that this is so.

When I was sixteen, I was home for a week or two—and a man who delivered crackers to our store spoke to me at the door, then went in; and I heard him say to my mother, "Who is that girl?" and, my mother telling him, he went off on a long string of compliments. I could hear them, and see their faces in a reflection from the showcase mirror. Among other things, I heard him say, "Are they her own teeth?" And my mother answered she *thought* so. All the time, the expression on my mother's face never changed; and the expression was plainly that she experienced great agony of mind when I was discussed. I was young, and though I had always been conscious that I had wonderfully regular teeth and that they were generally thought false because their formation was so perfectly even—still, this man's compliments seemed to stay with me.

I had a little money—for I was posing then, in the nude, for the art classes—and that evening I asked a drug clerk, showing him my teeth, what I should buy to preserve them. For everyone, directly after admiring them, would say, "You should take every precaution to preserve them"—and yet I did nothing except rub them with a rough towel to make them shine.

He advised Listerine and toothbrush and prepared chalk. I bought the outfit and, taking it home, placed it on my table, after having used it. The next day when I returned, I knew something had happened by Mother's threatening face and by the scared attitude of my brother and sis.

Nothing daunted, I went upstairs to clean up—for at that time Mr. Benjamin was my "beau," and I was home so as to see him. He lived directly across the road. I found my Listerine, chalk and powder gone! I called downstairs and learned that Mom had them. I came downstairs, and when I asked her for them, she turned on me and before my brother and sister. She attacked me after this fashion: "You have no shame to bring those kind of things in to a decent home! Your poor sister—everyone will damn her along with you. You disgraceful hussy—to put such things on a table!" etc. All this in Yiddish.

I wasn't surprised, because this wasn't anything unusual. Anything I introduced was frowned upon. But I couldn't understand the "disgraceful" part of it until when I met Mr. Benjamin . . . and he knew of it too; for my mother always liked to parade her troubles in order to win sympathy, and she had confided the whole affair to Mr. Benjamin's father.

It developed that she went to a drugstore conducted by a Hebrew and asked what these things were for—the Listerine and the white lumps. The man no doubt told her it was used to keep the mouth in condition, the Listerine being a wash prepared to keep the mouth free from disease. That was enough. Of course, I only surmised this explanation—for how could a druggist say otherwise? She had it (and told Bernard Benjamin) that I was doing unnatural things with my mouth and that the druggist told her the solution was used only to prevent disease from such practices—and that explained why I didn't become pregnant. And I had to live in that neighborhood and know for certain everyone who would listen had been told this.

Now then: this one circumstance is repeated daily by thousands of mothers whose daughters, naturally, living in a new age and learning the newer things, want them, and are continually hounded because they want to live different. I could write everlastingly of experiences such as I wrote in the above, one surprising you more than the other. But they wouldn't surprise Stella—or her type, whatever her name—for they are living thru the same thing with variations.

And somehow—Stella is Maimie. Do you get the idea?

I am afraid I am not able enough to describe how I mean this. But I know every heartache and longing "Maimie" had. And instead of running true to form—which is, that being older and not desiring the same pleasures, one must condemn them in a younger person—I foresee what will make this girl's lot easier and relieve that terrible pressure that everyone condemns her—and love her instead.

Do you know, it is a bit selfish? For I never think of her as Stella, but as Maimie at seventeen—and any kindness shown her is really shown to the Maimie of about ten years ago.

Last night, we were returning home at a little before tea time. Stella said, looking in the window of a very fine shop, "Gee! I could eat one of those cucumbers." I said, "I like them too, but they are too expensive yet," and we walked on. As we passed other grocer shops, I could see her eyes hunting down the cucumbers, but she said no more. As we neared St. Lawrence Main (where there are tiny shops and things are cheaper), I said, "Stella, you run along the Main and buy a cucumber, while I go in and get tea ready." I figured in my mind how to make up for this extravagence. (The cucumber was 15 cents—and we could get a half-dozen eggs for that.) I got tea ready, and though Stella should have been back in five minutes, there was no Stella. I was very hungry. I walked to the door several times, but no Stella in sight. Then I telephoned to nearby grocers, asking if the "red-haired girl" [was there] (or, rather, as I really said, *Est La tete rouge elle la?"*) [sic], but no one had seen Stella. Finally, when three-fourths of an hour had elapsed, I decided to eat alone, for I was certain she had run into her mother or drunken father and was obliged to go home with them. I ate with a heavy heart—for Stella had on a new suit that Mr. Welsh sent her and a hat newly retrimmed (it was my last summer's one), and I knew her mother would tear it off her back. She has had the suit a month or more, but does not wear it home, as her mother would say she had only gotten it one way, and perhaps destroy it. Imagine my surprise, then, when the bell rang and in walked Stella . . . frisky, and she danced around for several seconds before she saw the displeasure on my face. She immediately become serious, and got her broth off the stove and brought it out and began eating it. But it seemed every mouthful was choking her. Still, I said nothing—only about our food and the necessity that she eat bread with her broth (she has broth twice a day but I live on vegetables, cereals, eggs, etc.)

Had I soundly berated her and demanded to know where she had been, I would have done as her mother and Maimie's mother would do—and I wanted to do as Helen Howe's mother would do. For I know girls of seventeen years can't have perfect understanding of things. When she finished her tea, the tears were falling, though she made no sound. I cleared the table while she washed and dried the few dishes. After that, I got a book that we are reading. It is a little girl's book, but I read it for Stella's sake, and I like it myself. It is called *Little Women*—you surely know it. As I settled down to read it, she walked over and put her head in my lap while she sat on the floor. And she cried steadily while I patted her head. (Such wonderful hair as she has—I believe I will enclose a lock to show you the colour and texture, which is like wire.) As she got quieter, I began reading, and she stayed on the floor. Still I didn't ask her where she had been.

We undressed and retired. And after I put the light out, she asked me if she might tell me. It was that she had met a chap, and he was going to meet a girl whom Stella knew from her church. And she wanted the girl to see her suit, and she didn't think it would take so long—etc., etc. Now, what an unusual thing! Doesn't this happen almost every day with young girls—and what of it? But Stella's mother (or mine, for that matter) would beat her and tirade for hours.

I will guarantee that this girl will never do that particular thing again— though tomorrow she may do something equally exasperating.

I hope I have been able to make you understand about Stella. I never permit myself to feel anything toward her but the love "Maimie" never got any in her youth, except from men, for short periods—and she was always hungry for a woman's love. And when, as I wrote you, Mr. Welsh shows her more attention than he does to me—I confess, I feel hurt; but she never knows it (nor does he). And I never permit jealousy to hurt Stella thru the other girls—for this was the bane of "Maimie's" existence in her youth.

I don't recall whether I wrote you before of her parents, home, etc. . . . . .Her mother is a sober, industrious woman, but a horrible shrew. This she isn't altogether to blame for, as her husband (Stella's father) is a common drunk, having helped to support their six children only in fits and starts. The mother was before her marriage a domestic, and since then has done "day work." The father is a street laborer. Their home is typical; but poverty has made it even more squalid than the usual home of this sort of people.

From such a place this Stella came—and it is hardly to be believed. She is absolutely beautiful. Just now, due to the ravages of the disease, of which (I believe) I wrote you, she is painfully thin. Last night, I bathed and massaged her, and the thought came to me . . . that to describe the physical condition of this girl, I couldn't say anything better than that she looks when naked as do the pictures of people depicting famine in India, or some such place. This isn't a bit overdrawn. But this will be changed, now that we have the disease in check.

When Stella was eight years old, she was already with men. Now, the phenomenal part of it all is, that she could meet people who have had experience with girls of her sort, and they would never detect that she was anything but a nice girl out of a home where there is harmony and contentment.

I can recall distinctly that I was ever on the alert as a girl to learn the things that distinguished "nice" people from the other kind. I don't know just why I thought this desirable, inasmuch as I didn't show any desire to live as "nice" people did. But I can recall hundreds of times when I would meet a man, son of "nice" people; and he, thinking to come down to the level of a girl of my sort, would either express himself coarsely or in language that would not be considered good English by "nice" people; and I would take great pleasure in correcting him, thinking to show that it wasn't necessary to come down—I would come up. In this way, I learned much. Often it wasn't their speech, sometimes their mannerisms at or away from table. But I knew all this because I wanted to know, and nothing ever escaped me. If I was with a man in a restaurant and I knew he was of plebeian people, I never troubled to study him, but kept my eyes glued on someone at a nearby table whose appearance stamped them as of "nice" people; and if I saw once that people of this sort did not bite bread but broke it, I never bit bread again in my life—etc. I had no trouble to learn, because I wanted to so much. But with Stella it is all different. She isn't as keen witted as I was; and she never has a "purpose" for anything— and I was full of them. She isn't observing. Apparently when she did associate promiscuously with men, they were of various sorts. And while she knew some . . . sons of nice people—I refused to know any other kind. Yet in spite of all this, she has the earmarks of a lady bred and born. When it is necessary for her to act on her initiative, she will instinctively do what a lady would do. Isn't this surprising, for a girl from a home of that sort, who has had no experience in any other home until she came here?

As for cleanliness—though perhaps I had to teach her a few things, she is wonderfully cleanly in her habits. All this appeals to me. I am anxious to see what she will be, if I am permitted to do for her as I should have been done by as a child.

Last month I advertised for work, offering my services as a worker in a home for my keep. The night the ad appeared, Stella perused the paper indifferently, but noticed this ad. She asked if I meant the place for myself. And when I said I did, I noticed she was very white, and her eyes a bit staring. All of a sudden she keeled over into a dead faint, without another word. I was alone. (Mother had gone to see Alice, who didn't stay here then and who was ill.) I tried simple means to revive her. But as I became frightened, I started to shriek, and my front neighbor came in and then brought a doctor from two doors above. The doctor said, after reviving her, she had a shock, and her heart isn't very strong.

When Mother came, I had Stella in bed and resting, though she wasn't asleep and her eyes still staring. . . . I got into bed and soothed her. She put her mouth to my ear and repeated, over and over, "Maimie don't go away"—but softly, so that Mother couldn't hear. I assured her I wouldn't. And I won't—now that you and Miss Huntington have made it possible for me to stay.

Will you let me know whether you think I am right—or rather, whether it is foolish of me to live over Maimie's youth in Stella?

ADDRESS TO THE FIRST NATIONAL CONFERENCE OF COLORED WOMEN

Josephine St. Pierre Ruffin

Josephine St. Pierre Ruffin grew up in Boston where she attended public schools after they were desegregated in 1855. At sixteen she married George Lewis Ruffin of a prominent black family and the couple moved to England. Returning after the outbreak of the Civil War, she worked actively in the war relief effort and for other civic causes. Her husband attended Harvard Law School and eventually became the first black municipal judge in Massachusetts. The Ruffins raised five children.

Described as a self-assured, talented woman, her abilities for organizing led her into the reform society movement. She established the Woman's Era Club in 1894, served as its president for a decade, and edited its newspaper, *The Woman's Era* for many years. Recognizing the need to consolidate their efforts, Ruffin called for the federation of black women's clubs and arranged the first national conference of black women to whom she delivered the speech below in 1895. In it Ruffin not only appeals for cooperation among black clubwomen but challenges white women to join with blacks to achieve their common goals. Ruffin also refuted charges of the immorality of black women, for at the time of her address a southern journalist who called all black women prostitutes, liars and thieves had further perpetuated this widely held defamatory image.

In 1900 Ruffin, acting as a delegate from the Woman's Era Club and the Massachusetts State Federation of Women's Clubs, attended the convention of the General Federation of Women's Clubs held in Milwaukee where she became embroiled in a widely publicized "incident." For when it was learned that she represented a "colored club," someone tried to seize from her the badge she had been handed upon entering the convention. In spite of her staunch resistance, the credential committee opposed seating her as a delegate from a black club, saying, however, that she could be admitted as a representative of the Massachusetts State Federation of Women's Clubs since it was a "white club"; but Ruffin stood her ground and refused to participate under these conditions. The segregationist policies of the GFWC persisted long into the twentieth century.

Ruffin remained a tireless community leader all her life; she founded and served a number of social welfare associations in Boston. She died in 1924 at the age of eighty-one.

It is with especial joy and pride that I welcome you all to this, our first conference. It is only recently that women have waked up to the importance of meeting in council, and great as has been the advantage to women *generally*, and important as it is and has been that they should confer, the necessity has not been nearly so great, matters at stake not nearly so vital, as that *we*, bearing peculiar blunders, suffering under especial hardships, enduring peculiar privations, should meet for a "good talk" among ourselves. Although rather hastily called, you as well as I can testify how long and how earnestly a conference has been thought of and hoped for and even prepared for. These women's clubs, which have sprung up all over the country, built and run upon broad and strong lines, have all been a preparation, small conferences in

ADDRESS... From *The Woman's Era*, September 1895, 12–15. Smith College Library, Smith College.

themselves, and their spontaneous birth and enthusiastic support have been little less than inspirational on the part of our women and a general preparation for a large union such as it is hoped this conference will lead to. Five years ago we had no colored women's clubs outside of those formed for special work; to-day, with little over a month's notice, we are able to call representatives from more than twenty clubs. It is a good showing, it stands for much, it shows that we are truly American women, with all the adaptability, readiness to seize and possess our opportunities, willingness to do our part for good as other American women.

The reasons why we should confer are so apparent that it would seem hardly necessary to enumerate them, and yet there is none of them but demand our serious consideration. In the first place we need to feel the cheer and inspiration of meeting each other, we need to gain the courage and fresh life that comes from the mingling of congenial souls, of those working for the same ends. Next, we need to talk over not only those things which are of vital importance to us as women, but also the things that are of especial interest to us as *colored* women, the training of our children, openings for our boys and girls, how they can be prepared for occupations and occupations may be found or opened for them, what *we* especially can do in the moral education of the race with which we are identified, our mental elevation and physical development, the home training it is necessary to give our children in order to prepare them to meet the peculiar conditions in which they shall find themselves, how to make the most of our own, to some extent, limited opportunities, these are some of our own peculiar questions to be discussed. Besides these are the general questions of the day, which we cannot afford to be indifferent to:

temperance, morality, the higher education, hygienic and domestic questions. If these things need the serious consideration of women more advantageously placed by reason of all the aid to right thinking and living with which they are surrounded, surely we, with everything to pull us back, to hinder us in developing, need to take every opportunity and means for the thoughtful consideration which shall lead to wise action.

I have left the strongest reason for our conferring together until the last. All over America there is to be found a large and growing class of earnest, intelligent, progressive colored women, women who, if not leading full useful lives, are only waiting for the opportunity to do so, many of them warped and cramped for lack of opportunity, not only to do more but to *be* more; and yet, if an estimate of the colored women of America is called for, the inevitable reply, glibly given, is, "For the most part ignorant and immoral, some exceptions, of course, but these don't count."

Now for the sake of the thousands of self-sacrificing young women teaching and preaching in lonely southern backwoods for the noble army of mothers who have given birth to these girls, mothers whose intelligence is only limited by their opportunity to get at books, for the sake of the fine cultured women who have carried off the honors in school here and often abroad, for the sake of our own dignity, the dignity of our race and the future good name of our children, it is "mete, right and our bounden duty" to stand forth and declare ourselves and principles, to teach an ignorant and suspicious world that our aims and interests are identical with those of all good aspiring women. Too long have we been silent under unjust and unholy charges; we cannot expect to have them removed until we disprove them through *ourselves*. It is not enough to try to disprove unjust charges through individual effort, that never goes any further. Year after year southern women have protested against the admission of colored women into any national organization on the ground of the immorality of these women, and because all refutation has only been tried by individual work the charge has never been crushed, as it could and should have been at the first. Now with an army of organized women standing for purity and mental worth, we in ourselves deny the charge and open the eyes of the world to a state of affairs to which they have been blind, often willfully so, and the very fact that the charges, audaciously and flippantly made, as they often are, are of so humiliating and delicate a nature, serves to protect the accuser by driving the helpless accused into mortified silence. It is to break this silence, not by noisy protestations of what we are not, but by a dignified showing of what we are and hope to become that we are impelled to take this step, to make of this gathering an object lesson to the world. For many and apparent reasons it is especially fitting that the *women* of the race take the lead in this movement, but for all this we recognize the necessity of the sympathy for our husbands, brothers and fathers.

Our woman's movement is woman's movement in that it is led and directed by women for the good of women and men, for the benefit of *all* humanity, which is more than any one branch or section of it. We want, we ask the active interest of our men, and, too, we are not drawing the color line; we are women, American women, as intensely interested in all that pertains to us as such as all other American women; we are not alienating or withdrawing, we are only coming to the front, willing to join any others in the same work and cordially inviting and welcoming any others to join us.

If there is any one thing I would especially enjoin upon this conference it is union and earnestness. The questions that are to come before us are of too much import to be weakened by any trivialities or personalities. If any differences arise let them be quickly settled, with the feeling that we are all workers to the same end, to elevate and dignify colored American womanhood. This conference will not be what I expect if it does not show the wisdom, indeed the absolute necessity of a national organization of our women. Every year new questions coming up will prove it to us. This hurried, almost informal convention does not begin to meet our needs, it is only a beginning, made here in dear old Boston, where the scales of justice and generosity hang evenly balanced, and where the people "dare be true" to their best instincts and stand ready to lend aid and sympathy to worthy strugglers. It is hoped and believed that from this will spring an organization that will in truth bring in a new era to the colored women of America.

EIGHT

Struggles and Visions

A woman is nobody. A wife is everything. A pretty girl is equal to ten thousand men, and a mother is, next to God, all powerful. . . . The ladies of Philadelphia, therefore, under the influence of the most serious "sober second thoughts," are resolved to maintain their rights as Wives, Belles, Virgins, and Mothers, and not as Women.

[Philadelphia] *Public Ledger and Daily Transcript* (c. 1848)

THE *LEDGER'S* EDITORIAL WAS a response to the Seneca Falls "Declaration of Sentiments," reprinted below. Millions of words would follow as American women struggled to gain a more equal place. But, nowhere would the basic opposition to woman's rights be stated as baldly or as clearly. "A woman is nobody." Her life, according to the *Ledger*, had meaning only in relation to men. She could, that is, be somebody only as belle or virgin, wife or mother.

This is precisely the set of ideas which feminists, from the very outset of the woman's movement, have rejected. They have discovered, to their chagrin, that establishing a woman's right to be someone in her own right rather than merely an appendage of her father or husband is an unending task. And the *Ledger's* editorial provides an important clue as to why this has been so. This is the power of cultural images to reduce women to the sum of the roles they play

According to the dominant cultural view, echoed so faithfully in this editorial, a woman is a cipher, a *tabula rasa*. On this blank surface men write whatever they want women to be. Sometimes they write "belle." And women find themselves staring into mirrors trying to decide if they are really pretty. Sometimes men write "wife." And women find themselves putting their husbands' wealth on display. Sometimes men write "mother." And women find themselves living not for themselves but for their offspring.

Here indeed is the heart of the matter. Shall women be able to live their own lives for themselves? Or shall they continue to live for others? Since the whole of life is at stake in these questions, political struggles—be they for the vote or for the equal rights amendment—are only the beginning of women's crusade to gain control of their lives.

This is not, however, to denigrate the importance of politics. Beginnings are of vital import. As a a consequence, the first documents in this chapter offer an overview of the suffrage and equal rights campaigns. They reflect some of the different arguments women have advanced on their behalf, and some of the criticism they have encountered. It is important to recognize the diverse reasons women have had, at different times, for demanding the vote or the ERA. It is important too to appreciate the fact that some of the opposition to both measures came—and continues to come—from other women.

One of the lessons of the suffrage movement surely is that access to the formal means of exercising power, in this case the right to vote, is no guarantee that women will actually exercise that power. One need only look at the male monopoly, only recently challenged, of high political office to see that suffrage advocates underestimated the intransigence of the male establishment. A key tactic used to keep women in their traditional "place" and out of the corridors of political power was the cultural message that women could only find fulfillment as belles, wives, and mothers. Men find they need not choose between fatherhood, say, and a public career. But, women were told—in sermons, magazine articles, movie scripts, advertising copy, popular song lyrics, and newspaper editorials—that they did have to choose between family and career.

So long as that message is heard on all sides, only the exceptionally brave or gifted woman will resist. Changing the message, on the other hand, is more than a matter of gaining formal political rights. It is also a matter of gaining a measure of control over those command posts of culture which tell us what life is all about. One of the most important of these is the pulpit. Another is the university lecture hall. Here, as well as in the editorial offices of magazines and the programming offices of studios, are the people who tell us what a good mother (or belle or wife or whatever) is like. They are the ones, that is, who propagate our culture's norms. That is why several of the documents reprinted here deal with the efforts of women to gain access to these command posts.

Throughout the century and a half this chapter surveys, the constant, underlying issue has been: What else must change if women are to have lives of their own? Opponents of suffrage were given to answering this question with dire prophesy concerning the decline of marriage and the family should women gain the vote. Opponents of the equal rights amendment sometimes offer the same gloomy forecast. Feminists, for their part, have sometimes argued that just the opposite would prove true. The vote, National American Suffrage

Association president Carrie Chapman Catt repeatedly claimed, would not change the family or marriage at all. Other feminists, however, such as Charlotte Perkins Gilman or Elizabeth Cady Stanton, have argued that these bedrock institutions were precisely what most needed changing.

How one answers this question of how liberation would change the rest of the social order largely determines where one stands on woman's issues. So the concluding part of this chapter consists of three contrasting visions of what a society in which men and women are equal might be like. These three do not, needless to say, exhaust the possibilities. We hope, on the other hand, that they are sufficiently diverse and thought-provoking to challenge you to formulate your own vision of a non-sexist future. We cannot, as history teaches, directly translate our visions into reality. Yet, as the prophet Isaiah (no feminist he) taught, "Where there is no vision, the people perish."

THE PASTORAL LETTER OF THE GENERAL ASSOCIATION OF CONGREGATIONAL MINISTERS OF MASSACHUSETTS

Sarah Moore Grimke

Sarah Grimke's *Letters on the Equality of the Sexes,* from which the following document is taken, is perhaps the earliest full statement of the feminist critique of woman's "sphere" by an American. It predates the famous Seneca Falls Declaration of Sentiments (1848), for example, by a full decade.

Grimke (1792-1873), along with her equally celebrated sister Angelina, first achieved renown as an advocate of the abolition of slavery. Their fame in this regard came, in the first instance, because they had been raised as part of the slaveholding class on a South Carolina plantation. They could thus claim to be speaking from personal knowledge when detailing the evils of the South's "peculiar institution." Their prominence in the anti-slavery crusades of the 1830s soon catapulted the sisters into a second, equally stormy, controversy. This was over the propriety of women taking an active role in public affairs of any kind.

It is, as a result, no coincidence that Sarah Grimke wrote her letters on the equality of the sexes to Mary S. Parker, president of the Boston Female Anti-Slavery Society. The Pastoral Letter of the General Association of Congregational Ministers which Grimke subjected to such withering analysis follows here in excerpted form.

We invite your attention to the dangers which at present seem to threaten the female character with wide spread and permanent injury.

The appropriate duties and influence of women, are clearly stated in the New Testament. Those duties and that influence are unobtrusive and private, but the sources of mighty power. When the mild, dependant, softening influence of woman upon the sternness of man's opinions is fully exercised, society feels the effects of it in a thousand forms. The power of woman is in her dependence, flowing from the consciousness of that weakness which God has given her for her protection and which keeps her in those departments of life that form the character of individuals and of the nation. There are social influences which females use in promoting piety and the great objects of christian benevolence, which we cannot too highly commend. We appreciate the unostentatious prayers and efforts of woman, in advancing the cause of religion at home and abroad:—in Sabbath schools, in leading religious inquirers to their pastor for instruction, and in all such

THE PASTORAL LETTER ... From *Letters on the Equality of the Sexes and the Condition of Woman,* Boston: Isaac Knapp, 1838, pp. 14–21.

associated effort as becomes the modesty of her sex; and earnestly hope that she may abound more and more in these labours of piety and love. But when she assumes the place and tone of a man as a public reformer, our care and protection of her seem unnecessary, we put ourselves in self defence against her, she yields the power which God has given her for protection, and her character becomes unnatural. If the vine, whose strength and beauty is to lean upon the trellis work and half conceal its clusters, thinks to assume the independence and the overshadowing nature of the elm, it will not only cease to bear fruit, but fall in shame and dishonour into the dust.

We cannot, therefore, but regret the mistaken conduct of those who encourage females to bear an obtrusive and ostentatious part in measures of reform, and countenance any of that sex who so far forget themselves as to itinerate in the character of public lecturers and teachers.

We especially deplore the intimate acquaintance and promiscuous conversation of females with regard to things "which ought not to be named;" by which that modesty and delicacy which is the charm of domestic life, and which constitute the true influence of women in society are consumed, and the way opened, as we apprehend, for degeneracy and ruin. We say these things, not to discourage proper influences against sin, but to secure such reformation as we believe is scriptural and will be permanent.

❖❖❖

Haverhill, 7th Mo. 1837

DEAR FRIEND,—When I last addressed thee, I had not seen the Pastoral Letter of the General Association. It has since fallen into my hands, and I must digress from my intention of exhibiting the condition of women in different parts of the world, in order to make some remarks on this extraordinary document. I am persuaded that when the minds of men and women become emancipated from the thraldom of superstition and 'traditions of men,' the sentiments contained in the Pastoral Letter will be recurred to with as much astonishment as the opinions of Cotton Mather and other distinguished men of his day, on the subject of witchcraft; nor will it be deemed less wonderful, that a body of divines should gravely assemble and endeavor to prove that woman has no right to 'open her mouth for the dumb,' than it now is that judges should have sat on the trials of witches, and solemnly condemned nineteen persons and one dog to death for witchcraft.

But to the letter. It says, 'We invite your attention to the dangers which at present seem to threaten the FEMALE CHARACTER with wide-spread and permanent injury.' I rejoice that they have called the attention of my sex to this subject, because I believe if woman investigates it, she will soon discover that danger is impending, though from a totally different source from that which the Association apprehends,—danger from those who, having long held the reins of *usurped* authority, are unwilling to permit us to fill that sphere which God created us to move in, and who have entered into league to crush the immortal mind of woman. I rejoice, because I am persuaded that the rights of woman, like the rights of slaves, need only be examined to be understood and asserted, even by some of those, who are now endeavoring to smother the irrepressible desire for mental and spiritual freedom which glows in the breast of many, who hardly dare to speak their sentiments.

'The appropriate duties and influence of women are clearly stated in the New Testament. Those duties are unobtrusive and private, but the sources of *mighty power.* When the mild, *dependent,* softening influence of woman upon the sternness of man's opinions is fully exercised, society feels the effects of it in a thousand ways.' No one can desire more earnestly than I do, that women may move exactly in the sphere which her Creator has assigned her; and I believe her having been displaced from that sphere has introduced confusion into the world. It is, therefore, of vast importance to herself and to all the rational creation, that she should ascertain what are her duties and her privileges as a responsible and immortal being. The New Testament has been referred to, and I am willing to abide by its decisions, but must enter my protest against the false translation of some passages by the MEN who did that work, and against the perverted interpretation by the MEN who undertook to write commentaries thereon. I am inclined to think, when we are admitted to the honor of studying Greek and Hebrew, we shall produce some various readings of the Bible a little different from those we now have.

The Lord Jesus defines the duties of his followers in his Sermon on the Mount. He lays down grand principles by which they should be governed, without any reference to sex or condition:—'Ye are the light of the world. A city that is set on a hill cannot be hid. Neither do men light a candle and put it under a bushel, but on a candlestick, and it giveth light unto all that are in the house. Let your light so shine before men, that they may see your good works, and glorify your Father which is in Heaven.' I follow him through all his precepts, and find him giving the same directions to women as to men, never even referring to the distinction now so strenuously insisted upon between masculine and feminine virtues: this is one of the anti-christian 'traditions of men' which are taught instead of the 'commandments of God.' Men and women were CREATED EQUAL; they are both moral and accountable beings, and whatever is *right* for man to do, is *right* for woman.

But the influence of woman, says the Association, is to be private and unobtrusive; her light is not to shine before man like that of her brethren; but she is passively to let the lords of the creation, as they call themselves, put the bushel over it, lest peradventure it might appear that the world has been benefitted by the rays of *her* candle. So that her quenched light, according to their judgment, will be of more use than if it were set on the candlestick. 'Her influence is the source of mighty power.' This has ever been the flattering language of man since he laid aside the whip as a means to keep woman in subjection. He spares her body; but the war he has waged against her mind, her heart, and her soul, has been no less destructive to her as a moral being. How monstrous, how anti-christian, is the doctrine that woman is to be dependent on man! Where, in all the sacred Scriptures, is this taught? Alas! she has too well learned the lesson which MAN has labored to teach her. She has surrendered her dearest RIGHTS, and been satisfied with the privileges which man has assumed to grant her; she has been amused with the show of power, whilst man has absorbed all the reality into himself. He has adorned the creature whom God gave him as a companion, with baubles and gewgaws, turned her attention to personal attractions, offered incense to her vanity, and made her the instrument of his selfish gratification, a plaything to please his eye and amuse his hours of leisure. 'Rule by obedience and by submission sway,' or in other words, study to be a hypocrite, pretend to submit, but gain your point, has been the code of household morality which woman has been taught. The poet has sung, in sickly strains, the loveliness of woman's dependence upon man, and now we find it re-echoed by those who profess to teach the religion of the Bible. God says, 'Cease ye from man whose breath is in his nostrils, for wherein is he to be accounted of?' Man says, depend upon me. God says, 'HE will teach us of his ways.' Man says, believe it not, I am to be your teacher. This doctrine of dependence upon man is utterly at variance with the doctrine of the Bible. In that book I find nothing like the softness of woman, nor the sternness of man: both are equally commanded to bring forth the fruits of the Spirit, love, meekness, gentleness, &c.

But we are told, 'the power of woman is in her dependence, flowing from a consciousness of that weakness which God has given her for her protection.' If physical weakness is alluded to, I cheerfully concede the superiority; if brute force is what my brethren are claiming, I am willing to let them have all the honor they desire; but if they mean to intimate, that mental or moral weakness belongs to woman, more than to man, I utterly disclaim the charge. Our powers of mind have been crushed, as far as man could do it, our sense of morality has been impaired by his interpretation of our duties; but no where does God say that he made any distinction between us, as moral and intelligent beings.

'We appreciate,' says the Association, 'the *unostentatious* prayers and efforts of woman in advancing the cause of religion at home and abroad, in leading religious inquirers TO THE PASTOR for instruction.' Several points here demand attention. If public prayers and public efforts are necessarily ostentatious, then 'Anna the prophetess, (or preacher,) who departed not from the temple, but served God with fastings and prayers night and day,' 'and spake of Christ to all them that looked for redemption in Israel,' was ostentatious in her efforts. Then, the apostle Paul encourages women to be ostentatious in their efforts to spread the gospel, when he gives them directions how they should appear, when engaged in praying, or preaching in the public assemblies. Then, the whole association of Congregational ministers are ostentatious, in the efforts they are making in preaching and praying to convert souls.

But woman may be permitted to lead religious inquirers to the PASTORS for instruction. Now this is assuming that all pastors are better qualified to give instruction than woman. This I utterly deny. I have suffered too keenly from the teaching of man, to lead any one to him for instruction. The Lord Jesus says,—'Come unto me and learn of me.' He points his followers to no man; and when woman is made the favored instrument of rousing a sinner to his lost and helpless condition, she has no right to substitute any teacher for Christ; all she has to do is, to turn the contrite inquirer to the 'Lamb of God which taketh away the sins of the world.' More souls have probably been lost by going down to Egypt for help, and by trusting in man in the early stages of religious experience, than by any other error. Instead of the petition being offered to God,—'Lead me in thy truth, and TEACH me, for thou art the God of my salvation,'—instead of relying on the precious promises—'What man is he that feareth the Lord? him shall HE TEACH in the way that he shall choose'—'I will instruct thee and TEACH thee in the way which thou shalt go—I will guide thee with mine eye'—the young convert is directed to go to man, as if he were in the place of God, and his instructions essential to an advancement in the path of righteousness. That woman can have but a poor conception of the privilege of being taught of God, what he alone can teach, who would turn the 'religious inquirer aside' from the fountain of living waters, where he might slake his thirst for spiritual instructions, to those broken cisterns which can hold no water, and therefore cannot satisfy the panting spirit. The business of men and women, who are ORDAINED OF GOD to preach the unsearchable riches of Christ' to a lost and perishing world, is to lead souls to Christ, and not to Pastors for instruction.

The General Association say, that 'when woman assumes the place and tone of man as a public reformer, our care and protection of her seem unnecessary; we put ourseles in self-defence against her, and her character becomes unnatural.' Here again the unscriptural notion is held up, that there is a distinction between the duties of men and women as moral beings; that what is virtue in man, is vice in woman; and women who dare to obey the command of Jehovah, 'Cry aloud, spare not, lift up thy voice like a trumpet, and show my people their transgression,' are threatened with having the protection of the brethren withdrawn. If this is all they do, we shall not even know the time when our chastisement is inflicted; our trust is in the Lord Jehovah, and in him is everlasting strength. The motto of woman, when she is engaged in the great work of public reformation should be,—'The Lord is my light and my salvation; whom shall I fear? The Lord is the strength of my life; of whom shall I be afraid?' She must feel, if she feels rightly, that she is fulfilling one of the important duties laid upon her as an accountable being, and that her character, instead of being 'unnatural,' is in exact accordance with the will of Him to whom, and to no other, she is responsible for the talents and the gifts confided to her. As to the pretty simile, introduced into the 'Pastoral letter,' 'If the vine whose strength and beauty is to lean upon the trellis work, and half conceal its clusters, thinks to assume the independence and the overshadowing nature of the elm,' &c. I shall only remark that it might well suit the poet's fancy, who sings of sparkling eyes and coral lips, and knights in armor clad; but it seems to me utterly inconsistent with the dignity of a Christian body, to endeavor to draw such an anti-scriptural distinction between men and women. Ah! how many of my sex feel in the dominion, thus unrighteously exercised over them, under the gentle appellation of *protection*, that what they have leaned upon has proved a broken reed at best, and oft a spear.

Thine in the bonds of womanhood,
SARAH M. GRIMKE.

SENECA FALLS CONVENTION DECLARATION OF SENTIMENTS

The 1848 Seneca Falls "Declaration" is without doubt, and quite properly, the most famous document produced by the woman's movement in the United States. Elizabeth Cady Stanton, Lucretia Mott, Martha C. Wright, and Mary Ann McClintock wrote it in "Mrs. McClintock's parlor." The Declaration of Independence served as their model.

The secrets of its power are several. One is, as Stanton and her co-editors of the *History of Woman Suffrage* put it almost forty years later, "the Declaration and resolutions . . . demanded all [that] the most radical friends of the movement have since claimed. . . ." A second source of its continuing hold over the imagination is its faithful echoing of Jefferson's Declaration. This simple literary device enabled Stanton and her co-authors to claim, as their birthright, the same republican political creed male Americans professed to live by. It allowed them to claim too the revolutionary tradition which the, by the mid-nineteenth century, almost god-like Founding Fathers had invoked to justify the overthrow of established but unjust conditions.

Finally, the Seneca Falls "Declaration" marked the birth, not of feminist thinking, but of the feminist movement in the United States. So it stood as the model for the countless subsequent declarations women's rights conventions would adopt.

When, in the course of human events, it becomes necessary for one portion of the family of man to assume among the people of the earth a position different from that which they have hitherto occupied, but one to which the laws of nature and of nature's God entitle them, a decent respect to the opinions of mankind requires that they should declare the causes that impel them to such a course.

We hold these truths to be self-evident: that all men and women are created equal; that they are endowed by their Creator with certain inalienable rights; that among these are life, liberty, and the pursuit of happiness; that to secure these rights governments are instituted, deriving their just powers from the consent of the governed. Whenever any form of government becomes destructive of these ends, it is the right of those who suffer from it to refuse allegiance to it, and to insist upon the institution of a new government, laying its foundation on such principles, and organizing its powers in such form, as to them shall seem most likely to effect their safety and happiness. Prudence, indeed, will dictate that governments long established should not be changed for light and transient causes; and accordingly all experience hath shown that mankind are more disposed to suffer, while evils are sufferable, than to right themselves by abolishing the forms to which they were accustomed. But when a long train of abuses and usurpations, pursuing invariably the same object evinces a design to reduce them under absolute despotism, it is their duty to throw off such government, and to provide new guards for their future security. Such has been the patient sufferance of the women under this government, and such is now the necessity which constrains them to demand the equal station to which they are entitled.

SENECA FALLS DECLARATION . . .   From: Elizabeth Cady Stanton et al., eds., *History of Woman Suffrage*, Rochester, N.Y.: Charles Mann, 1889, Second edition, I, pp. 70–73.

The history of mankind is a history of repeated injuries and usurpations on the part of man toward woman, having in direct object the establishment of an absolute tyranny over her. To prove this, let facts be submitted to a candid world.

He has never permitted her to exercise her inalienable right to the elective franchise.

He has compelled her to submit to laws, in the formation of which she had no voice.

He has withheld from her rights which are given to the most ignorant and degraded men—both natives and foreigners.

Having deprived her of this first right of a citizen, the elective franchise, thereby leaving her without representation in the halls of legislation, he has oppressed her on all sides.

He has made her, if married, in the eye of the law, civilly dead.

He has taken from her all right in property, even to the wages she earns.

He has made her morally, an irresponsible being, as she can commit many crimes with impunity, provided they be done in the presence of her husband. In the covenant of marriage, she is compelled to promise obedience to her husband, he becoming, to all intents and purposes, her master—the law giving him power to deprive her of her liberty, and to administer chastisement.

He has so framed the laws of divorce, as to what shall be the proper causes, and in case of separation, to whom the guardianship of the children shall be given, as to be wholly regardless of the happiness of women—the law, in all cases, going upon a false supposition of the supremacy of man, and giving all power into his hands.

After depriving her of all rights as a married woman, if single, and the owner of property, he has taxed her to support a government which recognizes her only when her property can be made profitable to it.

He has monopolized nearly all the profitable employments, and from those she is permitted to follow, she receives but a scanty remuneration. He closes against her all the avenues to wealth and distinction which he considers most honorable to himself. As a teacher of theology, medicine, or law, she is not known.

He has denied her the facilities for obtaining a thorough education, all colleges being closed against her.

He allows her in Church, as well as State, but a subordinate position, claiming Apostolic authority for her exclusion from the ministry, and, with some exceptions, from any public participation in the affairs of the Church.

He has created a false public sentiment by giving to the world a different code of morals for men and women, by which moral delinquencies which exclude women from society, are not only tolerated, but deemed of little account in man.

He has usurped the prerogative of Jehovah himself, claiming it as his right to assign for her a sphere of action, when that belongs to her conscience and to her God.

He has endeavored, in every way that he could, to destroy her confidence in her own powers, to lessen her self-respect, and to make her willing to lead a dependent and abject life.

Now, in view of this entire disfranchisement of one-half the people of this country, their social and religious degradation—in view of the unjust laws above mentioned, and because women do feel themselves aggrieved, oppressed, and fraudulently deprived of their most sacred rights, we insist that they have immediate admission to all the rights and privileges which belong to them as citizens of the United States.

In entering upon the great work before us, we anticipate no small amount of misconception, misrepresentation, and ridicule; but we shall use every instrumentality within our power to effect our object. We shall employ agents, circulate tracts, petition the State and National legislatures, and endeavor to enlist the pulpit and the press in our behalf. We hope this Convention will be followed by a series of Conventions embracing every part of the country.

The following resolutions were discussed by Lucretia Mott, Thomas and Mary Ann McClintock, Amy Post, Catharine A. F. Stebbins, and others, and were adopted:

WHEREAS, The great precept of nature is conceded to be, that "man shall pursue his own true and substantial happiness." Blackstone in his Commentaries remarks, that this law of Nature being coeval with mankind, and dictated by God himself, is of course superior in obligation to any other. It is binding over all the globe, in all countries and at all times; no human laws are of any validity if contrary to this, and such of them as are valid, derive all their force, and all their validity, and all their authority, mediately and immediately, from this original; therefore,

Resolved, That such laws as conflict, in any way, with the true and substantial happiness of woman, are contrary to the great precept of nature and of no validity, for this is "superior in obligation to any other."

Resolved, That all laws which prevent woman from occupying such a station in society as her conscience shall dictate, or which place her in a position inferior to that of man, are contrary to the great precept of nature, and therefore of no force or authority.

Resolved, That woman is man's equal—was intended to be so by the Creator, and the highest good of the race demands that she should be recognized as such.

Resolved, That the women of this country ought to be enlightened in regard to the laws under which they live, that they may no longer publish their degradation by declaring themselves satisfied with their present position, nor their ignorance, by asserting that they have all the rights they want.

Resolved, That inasmuch as man, while claiming for himself intellectual superiority, does accord to woman moral superiority, it is pre-eminently his duty to encourage her to speak and teach, as she has an opportunity, in all religious assemblies.

Resolved, The the same amount of virtue, delicacy, and refinement of behavior that is required of woman in the social state, should also be required of man, and the same transgressions should be visited with equal severity on both man and woman.

Resolved, That the objection of indelicacy and impropriety, which is so often brought against woman when she addresses a public audience, comes with a very ill-grace from those who encourage, by their attendance, her appearance on the stage, in the concert, or in feats of the circus.

Resolved, That woman has too long rested satisfied in the circumscribed limits which corrupt customs and a perverted application of the Scriptures have marked out for her, and that it is time she should move in the enlarged sphere which her great Creator has assigned her.

Resolved, That it is the duty of the women of this country to secure to themselves their sacred right to the elective franchise.

Resolved, That the equality of human rights results necessarily from the fact of the identity of the race in capabilities and responsibilities.

Resolved, therefore, That, being invested by the Creator with the same capabilities, and the same consciousness of responsibility for their exercise, it is demonstrably the right and duty of woman, equally with man, to promote every righteous cause by every righteous means; and especially in regard to the great subjects of morals and religion, it is self-evidently her right to participate with her brother in teaching them, both in private and in public, by writing and by speaking, by any instrumentalities proper to be used, and in any assemblies proper to be held; and this being a self-evident truth growing out of the divinely implanted principles of human nature, any custom or authority adverse to it, whether modern or wearing the hoary sanction of antiquity, is to be regarded as a self-evident falsehood, and at war with mankind.

At the last session Lucretia Mott offered and spoke to the following resolution:

Resolved, That the speedy success of our cause depends upon the zealous and untiring efforts of both men and women, for the overthrow of the monopoly of the pulpit, and for the securing to woman an equal participation with men in the various trades, professions, and commerce.

The only resolution that was not unanimously adopted was the ninth, urging the women of the country to secure to themselves the elective franchise. Those who took part in the debate feared a demand for the right to vote would defeat others they deemed more rational, and make the whole movement ridiculous.

But Mrs. Stanton and Frederick Douglass seeing that the power to choose rulers and make laws, was the right by which all others could be secured, persistently advocated the resolution, and at last carried it by a small majority.

Thus it will be seen that the Declaration and resolutions in the very first Convention, demanded all the most radical friends of the movement have since claimed—such as equal rights in the universities, in the trades and professions; the right to vote; to share in all political offices, honors, and emoluments; to complete equality in marriage, to personal freedom, property, wages, children; to make contracts; to sue, and be sued; and to testify in courts of justice. At this time the condition of married women under the Common Law, was nearly as degraded as that of the slave on the Southern plantation. The Convention continued through two entire days, and late into the evenings. The deepest interest was manifested to its close.

WOMAN'S RIGHTS CONVENTION

James Gordon Bennett

The Seneca Falls "Declaration" was widely publicized, and—as Stanton and her co-editors of *History of Woman Suffrage* later said—"unsparingly ridiculed by the press, and denounced by the pulpit, much to the surprise and chagrin of the leaders." Whether or not they were "wholly unprepared to find themselves the target for the jibes and jeers of the nation," as they claimed forty years afterwards, become such a target they did.

One leading critic was James Gordon Bennett, probably the most famous newspaper publisher of the day. In the editorial reprinted here he struck a note of amused condescension much favored by early opponents of feminism.

This is the age of revolutions. To whatever part of the world the attention is directed, the political and social fabric is crumbling to pieces; and changes which far exceed the wildest dreams of the enthusiastic Utopians of the last generation, are now pursued with ardor and perseverance. The principal agent, however, that has hitherto taken part in these movements has been the rougher sex. It was by man the flame of liberty, now burning with such fury on the continent of Europe, was first kindled; and though it is asserted that no inconsiderable assistance was contributed by the gentler sex to the late sanguinary carnage at Paris, we are disposed to believe that such a revolting imputation proceeds from base calumniators, and is a libel upon woman.

By the intelligence, however, which we have lately received, the work of revolution is no longer confined to the Old World, nor to the masculine gender. The flag of independence has been hoisted, for the second time, on this side of the Atlantic; and a solemn league and covenant has just been entered into by a Convention of women at Seneca Falls, to "throw off the depotism under which they are groaning, and provide new guards for their future security." Little did we expect this new element to be thrown into the cauldron of agitation which is now bubbling around us with such fury. We have had one Baltimore Convention, one Philadelphia Convention, one Utica convention, and we shall also have, in a few days, the Buffalo Convention. But we never dreamed that Lucretia Mott had convened a fifth Convention, which, if it be ratified by those whom it purposes to represent, will exercise an influence that will not only control our own Presidential elections, but the whole governmental system throughout the world. . . . The declaration is a most interesting document. We published it in *extenso* the other day. The amusing part is the preamble, where they assert their equality, and that they have certain inalienable rights, to secure which governments, deriving their just powers from the consent of the governed, are instituted; and that after the long train of abuses and usurpations to which they have been subjected, evincing a design to reduce them under absolute depotism, it is their right, it is their duty, to throw off such government.

WOMEN'S RIGHTS ...   From: Elizabeth Cady Stanton et al., eds., *History of Woman Suffrage*, I, p. 805.

The declaration is, in some respects, defective. It complains of the want of the elective franchise, and that ladies are not recognized as teachers of theology, medicine, and law. . . . . These departments, however, do not comprise the whole of the many avenues to wealth, distinction, and honor. We do not see by what principle of right the angelic creatures should claim to compete with the preacher, and refuse to enter the lists with the merchant. A lawyer's brief would not, we admit, sully the hands so much as the tarry ropes of a man-of-war; and a box of Brandreth's pills are more safely and easily prepared than the sheets of a boiler, or the flukes of an anchor; but if they must have competition in one branch, why not in another? There must be no monopoly or exclusiveness. If they will put on the inexpressibles, it will not do to select those employments only which require the least exertion and are exempt from danger. The laborious employments, however, are not the only ones which the ladies, in right of their admission to all rights and privileges, would have to undertake. It might happen that the citizen would have to doff the apron and buckle on the sword. Now, though we have the most perfect confidence in the courage and daring of Miss Lucretia Mott and several others of our lady acquaintances, we confess it would go to our hearts to see them putting on the panoply of war, and mixing in scenes like those at which, it is said, the fair sex in Paris lately took prominent part.

It is not the business, however, of the despot to decide upon the rights of his victims; nor do we undertake to define the duties of women. Their standard is now unfurled by their own hands. The Convention of Seneca Falls has appealed to the country. Miss Lucretia Mott has propounded the principles of the party. Ratification meetings will no doubt shortly be held, and if it be the general impression that this lady is a more eligible candidate for the Presidential chair than McLean or Cass, Van Buren or old "Rough and Ready," then let the Salic laws be abolished forthwith from this great Republic. We are much mistaken if Lucretia would not make a better President than some of those who have lately tenanted the White House.—*New York Herald*, James Gordon Bennett, Proprietor.

ADDRESS ON WOMAN'S RIGHTS

Sojourner Truth

This speech was delivered at the 1853 Woman's Rights Convention which was held in New York City. Feminism had, even within the five years since the Seneca Falls meeting, attracted a host of enemies; large numbers of hostile men attended the 1853 convention to jeer and harass the speakers. It was the antics of these hecklers that brought Sojourner Truth, a noted advocate of abolition, to the podium. A former slave, Truth could draw parallels between the positions of women and black people from her own experience. And she did so with a deeply held religious fervor.

ADDRESS . . .   From: Elizabeth Cady Stanton et al., eds., *History of Woman Suffrage*, I, pp. 193–4.

 Sojourner Truth, a tall colored woman, well known in antislavery circles, and called the Lybian Sybil, made her appearance on the platform. This was the signal for a fresh outburst from the mob; for at every session every man of them was promptly in his place, at twenty-five cents a head. And this was the one redeeming feature of this mob—it paid all expenses, and left a surplus in the treasury. Sojourner combined in herself, as an individual, the two most hated elements of humanity. She was black, and she was a woman, and all the insults that could be cast upon color and sex were together hurled at her; but there she stood, calm and dignified, a grand, wise woman, who could neither read nor write, and yet with deep insight could penetrate the very soul of the universe about her. As soon as the terrible turmoil was in a measure quelled

SHE SAID: Is it not good for me to come and draw forth a spirit, to see what kind of spirit people are of? I see that some of you have got the spirit of a goose, and some have got the spirit of a snake. I feel at home here. I come to you, citizens of New York, as I suppose you ought to be. I am a citizen of the State of New York; I was born in it, and I was a slave in the State of New York; and now I am a good citizen of this State. I was born here, and I can tell you I feel at home here. I've been lookin' round and watchin' things, and I know a little mite 'bout Woman's Rights, too. I come forth to speak 'bout Woman's Rights, and want to throw in my little mite, to keep the scales a-movin'. I know that it feels a kind o' hissin' and ticklin' like to see a colored woman get up and tell you about things, and Woman's Rights. We have all been thrown down so low that nobody thought we'd ever get up again; but we have been long enough trodden now; we will come up again, and now I am here.

I was a-thinkin', when I see women contendin' for their rights, I was a-thinkin' what a difference there is now, and what there was in old times. I have only a few minutes to speak; but in the old times the kings of the earth would hear a woman. There was a king in the Scriptures; and then it was the kings of the earth would kill a woman if she come into their presence; but Queen Esther come forth, for she was oppressed, and felt there was a great wrong, and she said I will die or I will bring my complaint before the king. Should the king of the United States be greater, or more crueler, or more harder? But the king, he raised up his sceptre and said: "Thy request shall be granted unto thee—to the half of my kingdom will I grant it to thee!" Then he said he would hang Haman on the gallows he had made up high. But that is not what women come forward to contend. The women want their rights as Esther. She only wanted to explain her rights. And he was so liberal that he said, "the half of my kingdom shall be granted to thee," and he did not wait for her to ask, he was so liberal with her.

Now, women do not ask half of a kingdom, but their rights, and they don't get 'em. When she comes to demand 'em don't you hear how sons hiss their mothers like snakes, because they ask for their rights; and can they ask for anything less? The king ordered Haman to be hung on the gallows which he prepared to hang others; but I do not want any man to be killed, but I am sorry to see them so short-minded. But we'll have our rights; see if we don't; and you can't stop us from them; see if you can. You may hiss as much as you like, but it is comin'. Women don't get half as much rights as they ought to; we want more, and we will have it. Jesus says: "What I say to one, I say to all—watch!" I'm a-watchin'. God says: "Honor your father and your mother." Sons and daughters ought to behave themselves before their mothers, but they do not. I can see them a-laughin', and pointin' at their mothers up here on the stage. They hiss when an aged woman comes forth. If they'd been brought up proper they'd have known better than hissing like snakes and geese. I'm 'round watchin' these things, and I wanted to come up and say these few things to you, and I'm glad of the hearin' you gave me. I wanted to tell you a mite about Woman's Rights, and so I came out and said so. I am sittin' among you to watch; and every once and awhile I will come out and tell you what time of night it is.

EDITOR'S TABLE

While Truth and other crusaders for woman's rights met and petitioned and struggled, they were by no means alone in claiming to speak for American women. One prominent competitor was *Godey's Lady's Book* which, from the 1830s on, had advised women about virtually every aspect of their lives. The first issue of 1868 marked *Godey's* thirty-fifth anniversary, and the editor (Sarah Josepha Hale) took the occasion to review some of the magazine's major accomplishments.

Godey's quite properly prided itself on being the very soul of propriety, and had always proclaimed its commitment to conventional ideas about women and their roles in society. This did not prevent it, however, from supporting some changes. This moderate reformism separates *Godey's* from the more doctrinaire supporters of the *status quo*.

EIGHTEEN HUNDRED AND SIXTY-EIGHT

A HAPPY New Year to all our friends!

As we thus welcome the day with cheer and hope for the future, it naturally occurs to compare these expectations with what we have done during the last thirty-five years.

The purpose of GODEY'S LADY'S BOOK has been to help womankind, and to carry the sunshine of peace, intelligence, and happiness into the homes of the people. The tendencies of thought and the conditions of life in our Republic, as we gladly acknowledge, have been propitious to our work. Still, the good results of the plans suggested and advocated by us are important, and we think it will be interesting to our readers to know the LADY'S BOOK has had its share in bringing them to pass.

Woman as the Teacher.—This privilege or duty we have claimed for the sex, and steadily advocated a higher culture for girls, showing that mothers in their homes and young women in the school-room were, if properly fitted, the best teachers for the children of the Republic. When we began this plea the profession was almost monopolized by men; only in summer, when the

EDITOR'S TABLE   From *Godey's Lady's Book And Magazine*, January, 1868, p. 93.

scholars were small children, was the school-mistress abroad. Now mark the change. According to the report of the Census Bureau there are in the United States 115,224 public schools, colleges, and academies; these are taught by 150,241 persons, the number of women employed being over *one hundred thousand.* Thus we see that two thirds of the educational duties and influences in our public seminaries are now committed to the young single women of the United States.

Fashions of Dress and their Influence.—This subject of good clothing, in its effect on character and civilization, is one which we have studied and kept constantly before our readers. By the illustrations and patterns, their taste and skill have been awakened, household industry has been developed, and this important art of economy, that of fitting and making the family clothing at home, has become fashionable. We consider this one of the great movements of American ingenuity, that will add much to the comfort and refinement of society.

Medical Education for Women.—As we believe that woman is the conservator of health and morals, it seems but justice to society that she should be fitted for her duties. They have now opportunities. In our country three medical colleges are incorporated for them; and more than two hundred women have graduated with the full diploma. We have encouraged this progress, and are happy to say that the experiment has been successful.

The Bible Name of Woman for feminine humanity had been for many years degraded in our language by using the animal term of sex, *female,* as the synonym for *woman,* and the feminine terminations had been allowed to fall into disuse. These errors we have been endeavoring to rectify, with what we consider great success. The reform, in speaking or writing of woman, is observable in every book we read, in every speech or sermon we hear; and in the terminations there is a return to that early English text which always had the appropriate feminine endings.

The American National Thanksgiving Day may now be regarded as an institution. We congratulate our readers that in future they will celebrate a united festival.

Thus our plans set forth in the Editors' Table have prospered, while the general interest of the work has been increasing—as the present enlarged volume proves. Mr. Godey deserves the patronage of American ladies, for he encourages and liberally rewards their genius.

The LADY'S BOOK has never advocated the education of woman for man's work. Her own duties are large enough to satisfy the widest claims. The hard work and the government of the world belong alike to men; and we have no desire to trench upon either. But education for her own work of household economy she requires, and should have.

CONTROVERSY OVER THE EQUAL RIGHTS AMENDMENT

More than half a century after it was originally proposed by the Woman's Party, and more than forty years after the Republican Party endorsed it in its 1940 platform, the controversy over the Equal Rights Amendment rages on. Originally it was a battle between feminists. This of course is no longer the case. Those who fear that the amendment will strip women of important legal protections no longer point to widow's pensions or maximum hours legislation but to exemption from the draft and child custody. Nonetheless, there is an underlying continuity to the arguments of opponents. It consists of the presumption that women have much to gain from special legal protections (and much to lose should they be taken away) because in crucial ways they really are different from men.

The arguments in favor of the amendment display an equally strong similarity over time. They of course rest upon the opposite presumption, that women need no special protections because they do not differ from men in fundamental ways. Further, present-day advocates of the E.R.A. contend that "special protection" under the law for women has done them more harm than good.

The following statements are reprinted from *The Congressional Digest*, a non-partisan public affairs journal. The first is by Melissa A. Thompson, a legislative coordinator for the National Organization for Women. As such she was a chief lobbyist for the amendment. The second is by Phyllis Schlafly, national chairman (an interesting choice of title) of STOP E.R.A. Schlafly has been the most visible opponent of the amendment over the past dozen years.

NATIONAL ORGANIZATION FOR WOMEN

MELISSA A. THOMPSON, LEGISLATIVE COORDINATOR

The Equal Rights Amendment was first introduced in 1923 at the urging of Alice Paul, its author, and the National Woman's Party. She and her organization have been urging the ERA's adoption since 1920 because they knew that the right to vote for women was only the first step. The ERA was introduced in every Congress after that and in 1943 the language was revised to its present wording. It took until the 1940's to get the ERA out of committee and in 1946 the full Senate voted down the ERA. Then in the late 60's the push was on again—inspired partly by the formation of the National Organization for Women and the new feminist wave. The Women's Bureau and the Department of Labor joined the list of supporters in 1969 with the appointment of Elizabeth Koontz as Director of the Women's Bureau. In 1970 the Citizen's Advisory Council on the Status of Women endorsed the ERA for the first time and also, the United Auto Workers, the first major union to support ratification.

In 1970 the House finally voted to approve the ERA, 350-15 over the resistance of House Judiciary Chairman Emanual Celler. Senator Sam Ervin was able to kill it on the Senate side. Representative Martha Griffiths again got the House to pass the ERA after six days of hearings and a strong fight on amendments aimed at nullifying the intent of the ERA. On the Senate side. Senator Birch Bayh led the fight again, and again the Senate held extensive

CONTROVERSY... From The Congressional Digest, June-July, 1977, 182, 184, 186, 188; 189, 191. Reprinted by permission.

hearings. Senator Ervin fought hard to kill or amend the bill but on March 22, 1972, the ERA passed the Senate 84-8.

Within an hour, Hawaii ratified, then Nebraska. By the end of 1973 30 states had ratified. In 1974, three more states ratified and then North Dakota in 1975 and Indiana in 1977. If nothing else, we always seem to set records— such as the longest to ratify. We have until March 22, 1979, to ratify or else we must start the process all over again.

What happened? Why did the momentum slow down? We got caught in our own naivete—we thought that because it was right and just and polls showed that the majority of Americans were in support we would ratify quickly. We misjudged the conservative right wing's ability to organize against the ERA. It was no longer proper to fight for racial segregation and discrimination. They had lost the bulk of their constituency on the race issue. They quickly spotted the ERA as an easy vehicle for building up their waning forces by use of sophisticated propaganda and scare tactics. It was a way of keeping their old boy power network intact.

We have until March 22, 1979 to ratify in three more states and we have our work cut out for us.

What does the Equal Rights Amendment really mean? Money! Money in the pockets of women. The heart of all discrimination against women is money, whether it is state marriage property laws giving ownership and control to the male spouse or Federal laws limiting a woman's access to the military and its training and jobs. The world of big business knows this as does the old boy network because with money comes power.

And for those of you who might argue that ratification of the ERA is just symbolic, I would like to remind you that the only right *constitutionally* guaranteed women is the right to vote! Other constitutional rights have been allowed to cover women but it has been limited to a case by case judicial ruling. Those who argue that the Fourteenth Amendment is adequate should re-read it. The Fourteenth Amendment specifically uses the word male in the second section—it was not meant to cover women and subsequent court rulings have confirmed this. Neither the founding fathers nor the Reconstruction Congress had women's emancipation in mind. This is not to say that the Supreme Court has not recognized women as "persons"; they did as early as 1874 in *Minor v. Happersett*. To quote from attorney Ruth Bader Ginsburg: "They said, 'Beyond doubt women are "persons" and may be "citizens" within the meaning of the Fourteenth Amendment . . . So are children,' it (the Court) went on to explain, and no one would suggest children have a constitutional right to franchise."

The ratification of the Equal Rights Amendment would clearly establish that adult women are to have the same rights and responsibilities guaranteed adult men by the Constitution. It would also act to reinforce all the anti-discrimination statutes that feminists have gotten enacted in the last 15 years— statutes that can easily be legislated away by the whim of Congress or state legislatures otherwise.

What about women's special privileged status? What special status, may I ask you? How can women be told in glowing terms of their "special" status when the poorest of the poor are women? Is that a special status that anyone wants? I really think it is a status that we should share equally with men.

In South Carolina recently, I was discussing the ERA with a State Senator who was arguing that the South Carolina dower law was a benefit he did not wish to take from the "ladies." This law gives a widow a one-third interest in the real property of the marriage. The wife has no right to the property during the marriage. I suggested to him that it would be more equitable for the wife to be entitled to one-half the marital property, whether or not the husband was dead—such as is the case in community property law states. The Senator gasped that this was too much! Outrageous! Now I ask you, do you really think that this State Senator was truly interested in protecting the women of his state?

If there is any benefit that women presently have, it should be extended to men, or I question that it is a benefit.

I have no intention of reviewing all the arguments of those opposed to the Equal Rights Amendment, mainly since they are not based on fact and therefore are not worth the time. Actually, the basic arguments used against the ERA are the same ones used against giving women the right to vote. For example, that it will break up the family or cause women to be men. Well, giving women the right to vote did not lead to the break-up of families or women to be men and neither will the ERA. The ERA means that both spouses will be treated the same by the law, but no legislation can go beyond the bedroom door, no legislation can control which spouse really rules the home, who really makes the major family decisions. No law can make people treat each other with love and respect. All this argument does is confuse law with custom—it makes for good propaganda but bad law.

The ERA will mean that both spouses will have the same legal rights and responsibilities. This does not mean that both spouses will or can be required to pay 50 per cent of the marital expenses. It does mean that either spouse could be held liable for the support of the other based on individual ability.

Some of you may argue that the ERA is a state's rights issue. The right of a state to discriminate on the basis of sex is what you really mean.

The ERA is an amendment to the United States Constitution, affecting both Federal and state action, not private or religious. It is clearly a Federal issue affecting every U.S. citizen. State ERA's are inadequate because they do not cover Federal action. Statute by statute is inadequate—it does not have constitutional weight. The ERA would allow states to make individual laws, but not sexually discriminatory. For example, one state could set the age of marital consent at 18, another at 16, just as they do now, except the ERA would not allow a different age for men and women. Whatever age, it would have to be the same.

Don't ever let anyone tell you that the ERA is a Federal power grab, because it gives the Federal Government no additional power. A state or the Federal Government should no more have the right to discriminate on the basis of sex than they have the right to discriminate on the basis of race, and the Constitution should say so.

President Carter has well recognized this and the importance of the Equal Rights Amendment as a human rights issue. He has included it in his program in his world-wide campaign for human rights. A few people are saying his involvement is inappropriate or even illegal. Inappropriate for a President to provide moral leadership on a Federal issue? Bunk! President Wilson thought otherwise on the 19th Amendment and even used his influence to get several states to convene special sessions of their Legislature in order to ratify the amendment to give women the vote. It would be immoral for the President to allow the ERA to go down to defeat.

Who supports the ERA? The list of National groups is now well over 200. Also, every U.S. President from Eisenhower to Carter, and each year the number of groups in support of the ERA grows. These groups and individuals have studied the ERA and are very secure in their support for the Amendment. I am aware of no group that has changed its position of support, once taken, to one of opposition.

Who is opposed to the ERA? Here the number of National groups is very small. I have seen no list over twenty-five. This small group of people should not be allowed to stop the majority in our quest for equal legal rights. The latest Harris poll (taken November, 1976) showed that well over 62% of the people in this country are in support of the Amendment.

Where do we go from here? We have just under two years to ratify and we intend to do it. We have learned that it is not enough to defeat anti-legislators if we do not break up the old guard power block. The opposition has taught us some hard lessons and in many ways done us a favor by forcing ERA proponents to learn hard-nosed politics and legislative skills. We've had some major setbacks this year but not without repercussions to the old guard.

Who's playing who for the fool, who's playing underhanded and deceitful politics and lying to the voters? We plan to show them that they cannot get away with it—we know we are not losing the votes based on the ERA and its merits. We intend to fight hard on the elective and legislative battlefield these next two years—and we plan to win!

PHYLLIS SCHLAFLY

NATIONAL CHAIRMAN, STOP ERA

The Equal Rights Amendment pretends to be an advance for women, but actually it will do nothing at all for women. It will not give women equal pay for equal work or any new employment advantages, rights or benefits. There is no way it can extend the rights already guaranteed by the Equal Employment Opportunity Act of 1972. Under this act and the commission it created women have already won multi-million-dollar back-pay settlements against the largest companies in our land.

The Education Amendments of 1972 have already given women full equal rights in education at every level, from kindergarten through graduate schools. The Equal Credit Opportunity Act of 1974 has already given women equal rights and ended all discrimination in credit. There is no law that discriminates against women.

What ERA will do is to require us to "neuterize" all Federal and state laws, removing the "sexist" words such as male, female, man, woman, husband and wife, and replacing them with the sex-neutral words such as person and spouse. Every change this requires will deprive women of a right, benefit or exemption that they now enjoy.

At the federal level the most obvious result would be on the draft and military combat. ERA will take away a young girl's exemption from the draft in all future wars and force her to register for the draft just like men. The

Selective Service Act would have to read "all persons" instead of "all male citizens."

Likewise, ERA will require the military to assign women to all jobs in the armed services, including combat duty. Present federal laws that exempt women from combat duty will become unconstitutional under ERA because the U.S. Constitution is "the supreme law of the land."

Last month's newspapers featured headlines such as "Draft is Inevitable, Arms Chairman Says" and "Pentagon Urges Standby Draft." You have to be kidding to call it an advance for women to make our girls subject to military induction and combat duty in all our country's future wars!

When the laws pertaining to family support are neuterized, this will void the husband's obligation to support his wife, to provide her with a home, and to support their minor children. Those present obligations are not sex equal, and they could not survive under ERA.

When I debated the leading pro-ERA legal authority, Professor Thomas I. Emerson, he stated that ERA will change the family support law so that the financial obligation will be "reciprocal" or "mutual," and husband and wife will be obliged to support each other only if he or she is incapacitated. That would be a tremendous ripoff of the legal rights of homemakers.

The neuterization of our laws under ERA would have a great effect on the legal definition of marriage. Most people do not think a union of a person and a person is the same thing as a union of a man and a woman. No wonder Senator Sam J. Ervin, Jr., stated on Feb. 22, 1977: "I don't know but one group of people in the United States the ERA would do any good for. That's homosexuals."

Since it is the law of our land that "separate but equal is not equal" and the elimination of discrimination requires full integration, every aspect of our school system would have to be fully coed, whether our citizens want it or not. Private schools and colleges that admit only girls or only boys would be constitutionally required to go fully coed; otherwise they would be in violation of the constitutional mandate against sex discrimination.

In other words, ERA will deprive you of your freedom of choice to attend an all-girls' or all-boys' school or college. All sports, including contact sports, would have to be coed for practice and competition. If you thought the department of Health, Education and Welfare was behaving foolishly and arrogantly when it tried to outlaw mother-daughter and father-son events, that's nothing to the mischief it will do under ERA!

Probably the greatest danger in ERA is Section Two, the provision that Congress will have the power of enforcement. This means that the executive branch will administer ERA and the federal courts will adjudicate it. Section Two will transfer into the hands of the federal government the last remaining aspects of our life that the feds haven't yet got their meddling fingers into, including marriage, divorce, child custody, prison regulations, protective labor legislation, and insurance rates.

Why anyone would want to give the federal politicians, bureaucrats, and judges more power, when they can't solve the problems they have now, is difficult to understand. Yet, ERA will, in the words of former Sen. Sam J. Ervin, Jr., "virtually reduce the states of the union to meaningless zeroes on the nation's map."

While we all want equality of treatment in many aspects of life, such as freedom of speech, press, and religion, trial by jury, and due process, in other aspects, equal treatment of all our citizens would be a grievous injustice. Do you think it would be just to make everyone pay the same income tax regardless of his or her income?

Reasonable people do want differences of treatment between men and women based on their obvious factual differences, namely that women have babies (and men do not) and that women do not have the same physical strength as men. These differences vitally affect the draft, combat duty, family support, factory work, and manual labor. If ERA is permitted to deprive us of options to make the reasonable differences that reasonable men and women want, it will be the most grievous injustice ever perpetrated.

The ERA would be dead today if it were not for the unconstitutional White House pressure and illegal expenditure of Federal Funds used to try to force the state legislators to ratify ERA. Article V of the U.S. Constitution gives the ratification power exclusively to state legislatures, and it is shocking the way Big Brother in the Executive Branch of the Federal Government is telling state legislators how to vote.

Nevertheless, the momentum is all going against ERA, and nine states have already defeated it this year.

STATEMENT TO POPE JOHN PAUL II: BE MINDFUL OF THE INTENSE SUFFERING AND PAIN

Sister M. Theresa Kane, R.S.M.

Woman's liberation is not simply a matter of politics, as this and the remaining documents, demonstrate. Gender-based distinctions characterize the whole of life. And nowhere are they more clearly and insistently drawn than in religious matters. The Roman Catholic Church, like many other religious organizations, reserves its highest ministerial roles for men. Only they can be priests. Only priests can be bishops. And so on.

For centuries Catholic women religious, called sisters or nuns, accepted their role as handmaidens. But, the wave of change associated with the Second Vatican Council of the early 1960s—changes which included the abandoning of the Latin Mass and a much increased say in church affairs for the laity—caused many women religious to question the traditional restrictions placed on them.

Sister Kane claims to speak for those Catholic women who are torn between their devotion to the Church and their deep conviction that its treatment of them is unfair.

The following is the text of the remarks made by Sister M. Theresa Kane, R.S.M., to Pope John Paul II at the National Shrine of the Immaculate Conception in Washington, D.C., on October 7, 1979.

STATEMENT TO POPE JOHN PAUL II . . .   From: *Redbook*, April, 1980, Reprinted by permission of Redbook Magazine. Copyright © 1980 by The Hearst Corporation. All rights reserved, p. 151.

In the name of the women religious gathered in this shrine dedicated to Mary, I greet you, Your Holiness Pope John Paul the Second. It is an honor, a privilege and an awesome responsibility to express in a few moments the sentiments of women present at this shrine dedicated to Mary, the Patroness of the United States and the Mother of all humankind. It is appropriate that a woman's voice be heard in this shrine and I call upon Mary to direct what is in my heart and on my lips during these moments of greeting.

I welcome you sincerely; I extend greetings of profound respect, esteem and affection from women religious throughout this country. With the sentiments experienced by Elizabeth when visited by Mary, our hearts too leap with joy as we welcome you—you who have been called the Pope of the People. As I welcome you today, I am mindful of the countless number of women religious who have dedicated their lives to the Church in this country in the past. The lives of many valiant women who were catalysts of growth for the United States Church continue to serve as heroines of inspiration to us as we too struggle to be women of courage and hope during these times.

Women religious in the United States entered into the renewal efforts in an obedient response to the call of Vatican II. We have experienced both joy and suffering in our efforts. As a result of such renewal women religious approach the next decade with a renewed identity and a deep sense of our responsibilities to, with and in the Church.

Your Holiness, the women of this country have been inspired by your spirit of courage. We thank you for exemplifying such courage in speaking to us so directly about our responsibilities to the poor and the oppressed throughout the world. We who live in the United States, one of the wealthiest nations of the earth, need to become ever more conscious of the suffering that is present among so many of our brothers and sisters, recognizing that systemic injustices are serious moral and social issues that need to be confronted courageously. We pledge ourselves in solidarity with you in your efforts to respond to the cry of the poor.

As I share this privileged moment with you, Your Holiness, I urge you to be mindful of the intense suffering and pain that is part of the life of many women in these United States. I call upon you to listen with compassion and to hear the call of women, who comprise half of humankind. As women we have heard the powerful messages of our Church addressing the dignity and reverence for all persons. As women we have pondered upon these words. Our contemplation leads us to state that the Church, in its struggle to be faithful to its call for reverence and dignity for all persons, must respond by providing the possibility of women as persons being included in all ministries of our Church. I urge you, Your Holiness, to be open to and respond to the voices coming from the women of this country who are desirous of serving in and through the Church as fully participating members.

Finally I assure you, Pope John Paul, of the prayers, support and fidelity of the women religious in this country as you continue to challenge us to be of holiness for the sake of the Kingdom. With these few words from the joyous, hope-filled prayer, the Magnificat, we call upon Mary to be your continued source of inspiration, courage and hope: "May your whole being proclaim and magnify the Lord; may your spirit always rejoice in God your savior; the Lord who is mighty has done great things for you; holy is God's Name."

WOMEN OF "LA RAZA" UNITE!

Feminism has historically been largely a movement of white, middle, or upper-class women; but women of color and working-class women have always been active in the movement. And this has become more pronounced in recent years as minority women have formed committees and caucuses to advance their interests both in national woman's rights organizations like NOW and in minority group bodies like the NAACP.

The following platform, as excerpted in *Ms.*, was adopted by the *Chicana* caucus at the National *Chicano* Political Conference in San Jose, California in 1971. It set out the major concerns of women of Mexican-American descent. The *La Raza Unida* (the Party of the United People) referred to in the document was founded in 1970 to advance the interests of Mexican-American and other Spanish-speaking groups in the United States.

We, as *Chicanas*, are a vital part of the *Chicano* community. (We are workers, unemployed women, welfare recipients, housewives, students.) Therefore, we demand that we be heard and that the following resolutions be accepted.

Be it resolved that we, as *Chicanas*, will promote *la hermanidad* [sisterhood] concept in organizing *Chicanas*. As *hermanas*, we have a responsibility to help each other in problems that are common to all of us. We recognize that the oldest example of divide-and-conquer has been to promote competition and envy among our men and especially women. Therefore, in order to reduce rivalry, we must disseminate our knowledge and develop strong communications.

Be it also resolved, that we as *Raza* must not condone, accept, or transfer the oppression of *La Chicana*.

That all *La Raza* literature should include *Chicana* written articles, poems, and other writings to relate the *Chicana* perspective in the *Chicano* movement.

That *Chicanas* be represented in all levels of *La Raza Unida* party and be run as candidates in all general, primary, and local elections.

JOBS   *Whereas* the *Chicana* on the job is subject to unbearable inhumane conditions, be it resolved that:

Chicanas receive equal pay for equal work; working conditions, particularly in the garment-factory sweatshops, be improved; *Chicanas* join unions and hold leadership positions within these unions; *Chicanas* be given the opportunity for promotions and be given free training to improve skills; there be maternity leaves with pay.

PROSTITUTION   *Whereas* prostitution is used by a corrupt few to reap profits for themselves with no human consideration for the needs of *mujeres*, and *whereas* prostitutes are victims of an exploitative economic system and are not criminals, and *whereas* legalized prostitution is used as a means of employing poor women who are on welfare, be it resolved that:

(1)   those who reap profits from prostitution be given heavy prison sentences and be made to pay large fines;

WOMEN OF "LA RAZA" UNITE   From "The Bulletin Board," *Ms.*, December, 1972, pp. 128–29.

(2)   that *mujeres* who are forced to prostitution not be condemned to serve prison sentences;

(3)   that prostitution not be legalized.

ABORTIONS   *Whereas* we, as *Chicanas,* have been subjected to illegal, dehumanizing, and unsafe abortions, let it be resolved that we endorse legalized medical abortions in order to protect the human right of self-determination. Be it also resolved that *Chicanas* are to control the process to its completion. In addition, we feel that the sterilization process must *never* be administered without full knowledge and consent of the individual involved.

COMMUNITY-CONTROLLED CLINICS   We resolve that more *Chicano* clinics (self-supporting) be implemented to service the *Chicano* community:

(1)   for education about medical services available (birth control, abortion, etc.);

(2)   as a tool for further education of *Chicana* personnel into medical areas, returning to the *barrios;*

(3)   as political education for our people in view of the contracting *bandid* programs now in existence.

CHILD-CARE CENTERS   In order that women may leave their children in the hands of someone they trust and know will understand the cultural ways of their children, be it resolved that *Raza* child-care programs be established in *nuestros barrios.* This will allow time for women to become involved in the solving of our *Chicano* problems and time to solve some of their own personal problems. In order that she will not be deceived by these programs, be it further resolved that these programs should be run and controlled by *nuestra raza.*

DRUGS   *Whereas* drug administration and drug abuse is a big problem among our people, and *whereas Chicanos* and *Chicanas* are not presently adequately represented in drug-education programs, be it resolved that: this conference go on record as advising all local public health and public schools and *La Raza* that the possession of marijuana must be decriminalized; and that a study on *Chicanas* in prison on drug-abuse charges be made as soon as possible; and that *Chicanos* and *Chicanas* who are bilingual and relate to *La Raza* must be employed on a parity basis in all drug-abuse programs.

EDUCATION   *Whereas* we resolve that [legislation concerning sex discrimination in education] be supported and carried out by the *Chicano* community, we further resolve that a legislative clearinghouse be established to disseminate information pertaining to *Chicanas.*

That *Chicana* classes educating the *Chicana, Chicano,* and community in educational growth together be implemented on all campuses. That these classes be established, controlled, and taught by *Chicanas.* The classes should deal with existing problems faced by the *Chicana* as a wife, mother, worker, and as a member of *La Raza,* and historical research should also be done by the classes into the discrimination against *Chicana* women.

RESEARCH   *Whereas* we resolve that research information be gathered and disseminated on the *Chicana* in the following areas: (1) health, education, and welfare, (2) labor, (3) women's rights, (4) funding sources.

INTERPRETERS   *Whereas* many *La Raza* women do not speak English, and *whereas* this poses a problem in their support of their minor children, be it resolved that juvenile justice courts be petitioned to provide interpreters for Spanish-speaking mothers, and be it further resolved that *Chicanos* form a committee to offer time and moral support to mothers and children who have juvenile justice court actions.

VIETNAM   *Whereas* the Vietnam war has victimized and perpetuated the genocide of *La Raza,* and has been used as a vehicle of division within our community and *familia,* be it resolved that we as   *Chicanas* demand an immediate halt to the bombing and a withdrawal from Vietnam.

LESBIANS AND WOMEN'S LIBERATION:
"IN ANY TERMS SHE SHALL CHOOSE"
Vivian Gornick

Woman's rights advocates have always had to contend, as Elizabeth Cady Stanton, Susan B. Anthony, and other pioneers learned, with vituperative attacks not only on their ideas but on their personal lives as well. Historically, this has included accusations of lesbianism, a fact which helps explain why Stanton and other married suffragists always used the title Mrs. in referring to themselves.

The accusation is still heard today. But, today feminists no longer simply deny it as slander. This is because lesbians and male homosexuals have launched major campaigns to secure the right to live without discrimination or harassment. One result is that the woman's movement has had to attempt to come to terms with the gay liberation movement. Lesbian feminists have been outspoken in claiming the right to full participation in the woman's movement. And some, as Vivian Gornick's essay notes, have suggested that only a truly "woman-centered woman" can be a real feminist. Mainstream organizations like NOW have rejected that position, but they have included gay liberation as part of their overall set of demands.

Gornick, a frequent contributor to the *Village Voice* and other publications, is the co-editor of *Woman in Sexist Society: Studies in Power and Powerlessness* (1971) and author of *The Romance of American Communism* (1977).

LESBIANS AND WOMEN'S LIBERATION   From *Essays In Feminism*, NY: Harper & Row, 1978, pp. 69–75.

A month ago I spent a weekend in the company of a prominent feminist, a dedicated and intelligent woman who, in the course of the time we passed together, spoke out passionately against the open recognition of lesbianism in the movement, claiming—along with *Time* magazine— that the women's movement would destroy its credibility out there in "middle America" if it should publicly support lesbians as a legitimate element in feminism and in the movement. I found this position appalling, and I feel now that it raises an issue that must be argued more specifically than I had recently thought. For just as it seemed transparently certain to that feminist that open recognition of lesbianism in the women's movement would imperil the life of the movement, so it seems equally clear to me that denial of lesbianism in the women's movement will insure the death of the movement.

Hundreds of women in the feminist movement are lesbians. Many of them have worked in the women's movement from its earliest days of organized activity. They were in NOW three and four years ago, working steadily along with heterosexual women for the redress of grievances that affected them all; they are scattered today across the entire political board of women's organizations. They probably have more to gain from feminism than any other single category of women, both in the most superficial sense and in the more profound one. Certainly, they have more to *teach* feminists about feminism than has any other single category of human being—man or woman. And yet, until only this past year, lesbians have lived the same crypto-life in the movement that they live outside it. Sitting next to a heterosexual feminist who might rise in distress at a meeting to say, "Oh, let's not do *that*. They'll think we're a bunch of lesbians," the lesbian in the next seat could not rise and say, "But I *am* a lesbian," because her admission would have forced to the surface a wealth of fears only half understood, which would then quickly have been converted into panic and denunciation. It was an old, old story to the lesbians, one for which they could have written the script, and one which feminists should feel eternal shame for having played a part in.

It is the very essence of the lesbian's life that she leads an underground existence; that she cannot openly state the nature of her emotional-sexual attachments without thereafter enduring the mark of Cain; that in innumerable places and under all varieties of circumstances she experiences every manner of insult and injury to the soul that can be inflicted by the insensitive and the unperceiving; that in every real sense she is one of the invisible of the earth. It is this element almost alone, separated out from the multiple elements of her defining experience, that determines the character of the lesbian's life and often the shape of her soul. To live with the daily knowledge that what you are is so awful to the society around you that it cannot be revealed is to live with an extraordinary millstone slung from one's neck, one that weighs down the body and strangles the voice.

Imagine, then, the feeling of those lesbians who joined the feminist movement only to find themselves once more unable to be themselves. Here they were, women doubly cast out of society, both as women and as homosexuals, joined together in the feminist struggle for selfhood, being victimized by other women. For there's no mistaking it: the heterosexual feminist who disconnected herself, politically and spiritually, from the homosexual feminist sitting next to her (and did so most especially when she was saying, "Look, I don't care what *anybody* does in her private life, but there's no public place in the movement for that sort of thing") was disavowing that homosexual feminist, and thus victimizing her. The irony of it all was that in actuality the heterosexual feminist was victimizing herself even more, for that disavowal strikes at the bottommost roots of feminism, attacking the movement in its most vital parts, threatening its ideological life at the source.

Feminism, classically, has grown out of woman's conviction that she is "invisible" upon the earth; that the life she leads, the defining characteristics that are attributed to her, the destiny that is declared her natural one are not so much the truth of her real being and existence as they are a reflection of culture's willful *need* that she be as she is described. The feminist movement is a rebellious *no* to all that; it is a declaration of independence against false description of the self; it is a protest dedicated to the renunciation of that falsity and the courageous pursuit of honest self-discovery. The whole *point* of the feminist movement is that each and every woman shall recognize that the burden and the glory of her feminism lie with defining herself honestly *in any terms she shall choose.*

Sexual self-definition is primary to the feminist movement. After all, the movement's entire life is predicated on the idea that woman's experience has been stunted by society's falsifying views of the nature of her sexuality. Feminists are now saying to male civilization, "Your definition of my sexuality is false, and living inside that falsehood has now become intolerable to me. I may not know what I *am,* but I surely know what I am *not,* and it is offensive to my soul to continue to act what I am not." Thus, in essence, the feminist's course is really charted on the path of discovery of the sexual self. What *is* the actual nature of a woman's sexuality? What *are* its requirements? To what genuine extent does it exert pressure on her to fulfill herself through sexual love? To what extent will that miracle of force and energy—if diverted elsewhere—blossom into an altogether other and transformed kind of human being? Who knows? No one has the answers. We are only just beginning to formulate the questions.

Seen in this perspective, homosexuality in women represents only a variant of the fundamental search for the sexual self-understanding that is primary in the struggle to alter radically the position of women in this culture. In a word: some feminists are homosexual, and others are heterosexual; the point is not that it is wrong and frightening to be one or right and relieving to be the other; the point is that *whatever* a woman's sexual persuasion, it is compelling, and she must be allowed to follow her inclinations openly and honestly without fear of castigation in order to discover the genuine self at the center of her sexuality.

That, for me, is the true politics of the feminist movement. It is woman recognizing that she is a fully developed human being with the responsibility to discover and live with her own self, which means creating an emotional environment in which that self can not only act but be prepared to take the consequences for those acts as well. The determination of what the self is, or should be, is a matter of individual choice that must be honored by the movement, and acknowledged as a legitimate reference to the movement's ultimate aims.

What is most astonishing in all this is that the open flare-up last year between homosexual and heterosexual feminists is living proof of this deepest influence of the feminist movement on the need to be oneself. After enduring in silence for a number of years the movement's virtual denial of their existence, NOW's lesbians suddenly emerged a year ago as the Radicalesbians, demanding acknowledgment, and forming a consciousness-raising group of their own, thereby taking the movement at its word and using feminism's most valuable technique for support and definition as well. Most heterosexual feminists were initially startled by the lesbians' outburst, but many immediately grasped that the deepest principles of feminism were involved here and offered ready alliance. The lesbians were demonstrating for all those who had eyes to see that much of the movement's rhetoric had never been tested, that the issue of sexual liberation was an amazingly complex one, that at last the question of sexual fear was being turned on themselves. Many feminists did not see these things, however, and many, to this day, continue to see the open acknowledgment of lesbianism in the movement as irrelevant, or a threat to the movement's survival.

The claim that the question of lesbianism is irrelevant to the movement—that the struggle for recognition as a lesbian belongs properly to gay liberation and not to the women's movement—seems to me openly fallacious. The point is not that lesbians in the movement are homosexual; the point is that they are *feminists:* self-proclaimed, fully participating feminists who are being told, in a movement predicated on the notion that women are the victims of sexism, that the dominating principle of their sexuality is to be kept under wraps because the women out there in "middle America" simply wouldn't understand. This is the kind of emotional response masquerading as political analysis that panders to all our emotional and sexual fears. It encourages us to remain afraid of ourselves and to inflict injustice on each other in the name of our fears. And is that not what sexism is all about? If our emotional and sexual fears are not at the bottom of the condition that has brought us to feminism, what on earth is? Would we then not all profit immeasurably from the emotional daring involved in facing down the fear of lesbianism in the movement, and recognizing *it* for the true irrelevancy in the feminist struggle to reclaim our lives?

What I find more distressing than the charge of irrelevancy, however, is the aggressive talk from feminists that admission of lesbianism in the women's movement is a threat to the growth of the movement. From *Time* magazine I can take it, but from feminists it goes unbearably against the grain. If anything is a threat to the movement, it is the fear of taking just action in the name of political expediency. If anything will destroy this movement, it is losing sight of the fact that what feminism is genuinely all about is calling the shots as we see them. To be possessed of a bit of emotional truth, and then to go publicly against that truth because it is politically "wiser" to do so, is to totally misperceive the *real* politics of feminism—which has not to do with altering legislation or building a political party or taking over the government or uselessly increasing ranks. The real politics of feminism has to do with filling the social atmosphere with increased feminist consciousness and letting acculturation do its job. Nothing—absolutely nothing—is "wiser" than that, *Time* magazine and Kansas City housewives notwithstanding.

Really, the whole thing is so bewildering. Three years ago the women's movement was a renegade movement, willing to speak truths nobody wanted to hear. Suddenly, on this issue, it is being told it must speak *only* those truths middle-class America is willing to hear. And this is absurd, for in reality all the apprehension is groundless. When Ti-Grace first said, "Love is an institution of oppression," everybody panicked. Now, a year and a half later, the most respectable ladies in the movement don't bat an eyelash when the guilty phrase is invoked, and *Time* magazine nods knowingly. Clearly, then, if we stick to our guns, the rightness of our perceptions will obtain, and in two years' time lesbianism in the movement will be a fact of boring respectability in Omaha.

And that is all it should ever be. In radical circles in the movement there is now a rather alarming swing left toward the suddenly fashionable superiority of lesbianism, and the half-assed notion that the only "true" relationships for a feminist are with other women. One hears the silliness of the intellectual decision to become a lesbian because it's good for you, and worse, one hears a belligerent arrogance in some lesbians that amounts to angry revenge. One morning on Nanette Rainone's WBAI "Womankind" program I heard a lesbian assert that a woman couldn't really be considered a feminist unless she "related" to women in every way. Now that is power politics—nothing more, nothing less—and it is up to the straining honesty in both homosexual and heterosexual feminists to keep the central issue uncluttered and free of hysteria.

And the central issue is the question of self-definition for all women. What must be learned from the acceptance of lesbianism in the movement is that radically different truths inform different lives, and that as long as those truths are not antisocial they must—each and every one of them—be respected. If feminism is to have any historical significance, it certainly will be because it has taken an important place in this latest convulsion of the humanist movement to remind civilization that human lives become painful and useless when they cease to feel the truth of their own experience.

In the end, the feminist movement is of necessity the work of a radical feminist sensibility, and the fear of open recognition of lesbianism is the work of a liberal feminist sensibility. The falseness of the liberal's position is that while she apparently sorrows over the pain of the world, she offers only distant sympathy, when what is needed is partisan courage. By offering sympathy instead of courage, she increases rather than reduces the pain of this world.

A UNIQUE HISTORY

Charlotte Perkins Gilman

Belief in change presupposes the ability to imagine a different world. Hence feminists have long speculated on what a truly egalitarian social order might be like. One of the most entertaining as well as incisive of these musings is Charlotte Perkins Gilman's *Herland* (1915), a utopian fantasy about a society without men.

In the novel, three young adventurers, all male, hear rumors of a land where there are only women; despite their inability to believe such a place really exists, they set out to find it. Find it they do, although Herland's prosperous and efficient appearance only serves to strengthen their conviction that there *must* be men around somewhere. The three are captured by the women of Herland, and examined about the outside world. In return, in the excerpt reprinted here, the women tell how their country came to be.

Gilman, as her other writings included in this book show, was convinced that gender stereotyping warped both men and women. And she devoted much thought to the problem of identifying human, as opposed to male or female, characteristics. As a consequence, *Herland* is not so much about how women might get along without men as it is about how human beings might form a humane society.

And this is what happened, according to their records:

As to geography—at about the time of the Christian era this land had a free passage to the sea. I'm not saying where, for good reasons. But there was a fairly easy pass through that wall of mountains behind us, and there is no doubt in my mind that these people were of Aryan stock, and were once in contact with the best civilization of the old world. They were "white," but somewhat darker than our northern races because of their constant exposure to sun and air.

The country was far larger then, including much land beyond the pass, and a strip of coast. They had ships, commerce, an army, a king—for at that time they were what they so calmly called us—a bi-sexual race.

What happened to them first was merely a succession of historic misfortunes such as have befallen other nations often enough. They were decimated by war, driven up from their coastline till finally the reduced population, with many of the men killed in battle, occupied this hinterland, and defended it for years, in the mountain passes. Where it was open to any possible attack from below they strengthened the natural defenses so that it became unscalably secure, as we found it.

They were a polygamous people, and a slave-holding people, like all of their time; and during the generation or two of this struggle to defend their mountain home they built the fortresses, such as the one we were held in, and other of their oldest buildings, some still in use. Nothing but earthquakes could destroy such architecture—huge solid blocks, holding by their own weight. They must have had efficient workmen and enough of them in those days.

They made a brave fight for their existence, but no nation can stand up

A UNIQUE HISTORY   From *Herland*, New York, Pantheon Books, 1979. Originally published in *The Forerunner*, 1915, pp. 54–61.

against what the steamship companies call "an act of God." While the whole fighting force was doing its best to defend their mountain pathway, there occurred a volcanic outburst, with some local tremors, and the result was the complete filling up of the pass—their only outlet. Instead of a passage, a new ridge, sheer and high, stood between them and the sea; they were walled in, and beneath that wall lay their whole little army. Very few men were left alive, save the slaves; and these now seized their opportunity, rose in revolt, killed their remaining masters even to the youngest boy, killed the old women too, and the mothers, intending to take possession of the country with the remaining young women and girls.

But this succession of misfortunes was too much for those infuriated virgins. There were many of them, and but few of these would-be masters, so the young women, instead of submitting, rose in sheer desperation and slew their brutal conquerors.

This sounds like Titus Andronicus, I know, but that is their account. I suppose they were about crazy—can you blame them?

There was literally no one left on this beautiful high garden land but a bunch of hysterical girls and some older slave women.

That was about two thousand years ago.

At first there was a period of sheer despair. The mountains towered between them and their old enemies, but also between them and escape. There was no way up or down or out—they simply had to stay there. Some were for suicide, but not the majority. They must have been a plucky lot, as a whole, and they decided to live—as long as they did live. Of course they had hope, as youth must, that something would happen to change their fate.

So they set to work, to bury the dead, to plow and sow, to care for one another.

Speaking of burying the dead, I will set down while I think of it, that they had adopted cremation in about the thirteenth century, for the same reason that they had left off raising cattle—they could not spare the room. They were much surprised to learn that we were still burying—asked our reasons for it, and were much dissatisfied with what we gave. We told them of the belief in the resurrection of the body, and they asked if our God was not as well able to resurrect from ashes as from long corruption. We told them of how people thought it repugnant to have their loved ones burn, and they asked if it was less repugnant to have them decay. They were inconveniently reasonable, those women.

Well—that original bunch of girls set to work to clean up the place and make their living as best they could. Some of the remaining slave women rendered invaluable service, teaching such trades as they knew. They had such records as were then kept, all the tools and implements of the time, and a most fertile land to work in.

There were a handful of the younger matrons who had escaped slaughter, and a few babies were born after the cataclysm—but only two boys, and they both died.

For five or ten years they worked together, growing stronger and wiser and more and more mutually attached, and then the miracle happened—one of these young women bore a child. Of course they all thought there must be a man somewhere, but none was found. Then they decided it must be a direct gift from the gods, and placed the proud mother in the Temple of Maaia—

their Goddess of Motherhood—under strict watch. And there, as years passed, this wonder-woman bore child after child, five of them—all girls.

I did my best, keenly interested as I have always been in sociology and social psychology, to reconstruct in my mind the real position of these ancient women. There were some five or six hundred of them, and they were harem-bred; yet for the few preceding generations they had been reared in the atmosphere of such heroic struggle that the stock must have been toughened somewhat. Left alone in the terrific orphanhood, they had clung together, supporting one another and their little sisters, and developing unknown powers in the stress of new necessity. To this pain-hardened and work-strengthened group, who had lost not only the love and care of parents, but the hope of ever having children of their own, there now dawned the new hope.

Here at last was Motherhood, and though it was not for all of them personally, it might—if the power was inherited—found here a new race.

It may be imagined how those five Daughters of Maaia, Children of the Temple, Mothers of the Future—they had all the titles that love and hope and reverence could give—were reared. The whole little nation of women surrounded them with loving service, and waited, between a boundless hope and an equally boundless despair, to see if they, too, would be mothers.

And they were! As fast as they reached the age of twenty-five they began bearing. Each of them, like her mother, bore five daughters. Presently there were twenty-five New Women, Mothers in their own right, and the whole spirit of the country changed from mourning and mere courageous resignation to proud joy. The older women, those who remembered men, died off; the youngest of all the first lot of course died too, after a while, and by that time there were left one hundred and fifty-five parthenogenetic women, founding a new race.

They inherited all that the devoted care of that declining band of original ones could leave them. Their little country was quite safe. Their farms and gardens were all in full production. Such industries as they had were in careful order. The records of their past were all preserved, and for years the older women had spent their time in the best teaching they were capable of, that they might leave to the little group of sisters and mothers all they possessed of skill and knowledge.

There you have the start of Herland! One family, all descended from one mother! She lived to a hundred years old; lived to see her hundred and twenty-five great-granddaughters born; lived as Queen-Priestess-Mother of them all; and died with a nobler pride and a fuller joy than perhaps any human soul has ever known—she alone had founded a new race!

The first five daughters had grown up in an atmosphere of holy calm, of awed watchful waiting, of breathless prayer. To them the longed-for motherhood was not only a personal joy, but a nation's hope. Their twenty-five daughters in turn, with a stronger hope, a richer, wider outlook, with the devoted love and care of all the surviving population, grew up as a holy sisterhood, their whole ardent youth looking forward to their great office. And at last they were left alone; the white-haired First Mother was gone, and this one family, five sisters, twenty-five first cousins, and a hundred and twenty-five second cousins, began a new race.

Here you have human beings, unquestionably, but what we were slow in understanding was how these ultra-women, inheriting only from women, had eliminated not only certain masculine characteristics, which of course we did not look for, but so much of what we had always thought essentially feminine.

The tradition of men as guardians and protectors had quite died out. These stalwart virgins had no men to fear and therefore no need of protection. As to wild beasts—there were none in their sheltered land.

The power of mother-love, that maternal instinct we so highly laud, was theirs of course, raised to its highest power; and a sister-love which, even while recognizing the actual relationship, we found it hard to credit.

Terry, incredulous, even contemptuous, when we were alone, refused to believe the story. "A lot of traditions as old as Herodotus—and about as trustworthy!" he said. "It's likely women—just a pack of women—would have hung together like that! We all know women can't organize—that they scrap like anything—are frightfully jealous."

"But these New Ladies didn't have anyone to be jealous of, remember," drawled Jeff.

"That's a likely story," Terry sneered.

"Why don't you invent a likelier one?" I asked him. "Here *are* the women— nothing but women, and you yourself admit there's no trace of a man in the country." This was after we had been about a good deal.

"I'll admit that," he growled. "And it's a big miss, too. There's not only no fun without 'em—no real sport—no competition; but these women aren't *womanly.* You know they aren't."

That kind of talk always set Jeff going; and I gradually grew to side with him. "Then you don't call a breed of women whose one concern is mother-hood—womanly?" he asked.

"Indeed I don't," snapped Terry. "What does a man care for motherhood— when he hasn't a ghost of a chance at fatherhood? And besides—what's the good of talking sentiment when we are just men together? What a man wants of women is a good deal more than all this 'motherhood'!"

As to Terry's criticism, it was true. These women, whose essential distinction of motherhood was the dominant note of their whole culture, were strikingly deficient in what we call "femininity." This led me very promptly to the conviction that those "feminine charms" we are so fond of are not feminine at all, but mere reflected masculinity—developed to please us because they had to please us, and in no way essential to the real fulfillment of their great process.

To return to the history:

They began at once to plan and build for their children, all the strength and intelligence of the whole of them devoted to that one thing. Each girl, of course, was reared in full knowledge of her Crowning Office, and they had, even then, very high ideas of the molding powers of the mother, as well as those of education.

Such high ideals as they had! Beauty, Health, Strength, Intellect, Goodness— for these they prayed and worked.

They had no enemies; they themselves were all sisters and friends. The land was fair before them, and a great future began to form itself in their minds.

The religion they had to begin with was much like that of old Greece—a number of gods and goddesses; but they lost all interest in deities of war and plunder, and gradually centered on their Mother Goddess altogether. Then, as they grew more intelligent, this had turned into a sort of Maternal Pantheism.

Here was Mother Earth, bearing fruit. All that they ate was fruit of motherhood, from seed or egg or their product. By motherhood they were born and by motherhood they lived—life was, to them, just the long cycle of motherhood.

But very early they recognized the need of improvement as well as of mere repetition, and devoted their combined intelligence to that problem—how to make the best kind of people. First this was merely the hope of bearing better ones, and then they recognized that however the children differed at birth, the real growth lay later—through education.

Then things began to hum.

As I learned more and more to appreciate what these women had accomplished, the less proud I was of what we, with all our manhood, had done.

You see, they had had no wars. They had had no kings, and no priests and no aristocracies. They were sisters, and as they grew, they grew together—not by competition, but by united action.

We tried to put in a good word for competition, and they were keenly interested. Indeed, we soon found from their earnest questions of us that they were prepared to believe our world must be better than theirs. They were not sure; they wanted to know; but there was no such arrogance about them as might have been expected.

We rather spread ourselves, telling of the advantages of competition: how it developed fine qualities; that without it there would be "no stimulus to industry." Terry was very strong on that point.

"No stimulus to industry," they repeated, with that puzzled look we had learned to know so well. "*Stimulus? To Industry?* But don't you *like* to work?"

"No man would work unless he had to," Terry declared.

"Oh, no *man!* You mean that is one of your sex distinctions?"

"No, indeed!" he said hastily. "No one, I mean, man or woman, would work without incentive. Competition is the—the motor power, you see."

"It is not with us," they explained gently, "so it is hard for us to understand. Do you mean, for instance, that with you no mother would work for her children without the stimulus of competition?"

No, he admitted that he did not mean that. Mothers, he supposed, would of course work for their children in the home; but the world's work was different—that had to be done by men, and required the competitive element.

All our teachers were eagerly interested.

"We want so much to know—you have the whole world to tell us of, and we have only our little land! And there are two of you—the two sexes—to love and help one another. It must be a rich and wonderful world. Tell us—what is the work of the world, that men do—which we have not here?"

"Oh, everything," Terry said grandly. "The men do everything, with us." He squared his broad shoulders and lifted his chest. "We do not allow our women to work. Women are loved—idolized—honored—kept in the home to care for the children."

"What is 'the home'?" asked Somel a little wistfully.

But Zava begged: "Tell me first, do *no* women work, really?"

"Why, yes," Terry admitted. "Some have to, of the poorer sort."

"About how many—in your country?"

"About seven or eight million," said Jeff, as mischievous as ever.

WHAT IT WOULD BE LIKE IF WOMEN WIN

Gloria Steinem

Gloria Steinem, the founder and editor of *Ms.*, is one of the best known women in the United States. She is also, as this document illustrates, a long-time spokesperson for the woman's movement. In this *"Time* Essay" (a regular feature of that magazine) of 1970 she set out some of the major changes American society would undergo were the feminist cause to triumph. *Time* regarded these speculations as utopian dreams, and Steinem made use of the same terminology. Even so, it is clear that one of her major concerns in writing this piece was to reassure *Time* readers that the woman's movement was no threat to established institutions like the family. "The most radical goal of the movement," she wrote, "is egalitarianism." And it is striking how so many of her proposals, which seemed so far-fetched in 1970, could come to seem the essence of moderation well before the decade was over.

Any change is fearful, especially one affecting both politics and sex roles, so let me begin these utopian speculations with a fact. To break the ice.

Women don't want to exchange places with men. Male chauvinists, science-fiction writers and comedians may favor that idea for its shock value, but psychologists say it is a fantasy based on ruling-class ego and guilt. Men assume that women want to imitate them, which is just what white people assumed about blacks. An assumption so strong that it may convince the second-class group of the need to imitate, but for both women and blacks that stage has passed. Guilt produces the question: What if they could treat us as we have treated them?

That is not our goal. But we do want to change the economic system to one more based on merit. In Women's Lib Utopia, there will be free access to good jobs—and decent pay for the bad ones women have been performing all along, including housework. Increased skilled labor might lead to a four-hour work-day, and higher wages would encourage further mechanization of repetitive jobs now kept alive by cheap labor.

With women as half the country's elected representatives, and a woman President once in a while, the country's *machismo* problems would be greatly reduced. The old-fashioned idea that manhood depends on violence and victory is, after all, an important part of our troubles in the streets, and in Viet Nam. I'm not saying that women leaders would eliminate violence. We are not more moral than men; we are only uncorrupted by power so far. When we do acquire power, we might turn out to have an equal impulse toward aggression. Even now, Margaret Mead believes that women fight less often but more fiercely than men, because women are not taught the rules of the war game and fight only when cornered. But for the next 50 years or so, women in politics will be very valuable by tempering the idea of manhood into something less aggressive and better suited to this crowded, post-atomic planet. Consumer

---

WHAT IT WOULD BE LIKE IF WOMEN WIN From *Time*, August 31, 1970, pp. 22–23. Reprinted by permission of Gloria Steinem.

protection and children's rights, for instance, might get more legislative attention.

Men will have to give up ruling-class privileges, but in return they will no longer be the only ones to support the family, get drafted, bear the strain of power and responsibility. Freud to the contrary, anatomy is not destiny, at least not for more than nine months at a time. In Israel, women are drafted, and some have gone to war. In England, more men type and run switchboards. In India and Israel, a woman rules. In Sweden, both parents take care of the children. In this country, come Utopia, men and women won't reverse roles; they will be free to choose according to individual talents and preferences.

◇◇◇

If role reform sounds sexually unsettling, think how it will change the sexual hypocrisy we have now. No more sex arranged on the barter system, with women pretending interest, and men never sure whether they are loved for themselves or for the security few women can get any other way. (Married or not, for sexual reasons or social ones, most women still find it second nature to Uncle-Tom.) No more men who are encouraged to spend a lifetime living with inferiors; with housekeepers, or dependent creatures who are still children. No more domineering wives, emasculating women, and "Jewish mothers," all of whom are simply human beings with all their normal ambition and drive confined to the home. No more unequal partnerships that eventually doom love and sex.

In order to produce that kind of confidence and individuality, child rearing will train according to talent. Little girls will no longer be surrounded by air-tight, self-fulfilling prophecies of natural passivity, lack of ambition and objectivity, inability to exercise power, and dexterity (so long as special aptitude for jobs requiring patience and dexterity is confined to poorly paid jobs; brain surgery is for males).

Schools and universities will help to break down traditional sex roles, even when parents will not. Half the teachers will be men, a rarity now at preschool and elementary levels; girls will not necessarily serve cookies or boys hoist up the flag. Athletic teams will be picked only by strength and skill. Sexually segregated courses like auto mechanics and home economics will be taken by boys and girls together. New courses in sexual politics will explore female subjugation as the model for political oppression, and women's history will be an academic staple, along with black history, at least until the white-male-oriented textbooks are integrated and rewritten.

◇◇◇

As for the American child's classic problem—too much mother, too little father—that would be cured by an equalization of parental responsibility. Free nurseries, school lunches, family cafeterias built into every housing complex, service companies that will do household cleaning chores in a regular, businesslike way, and more responsibility by the entire community for the children: all these will make it possible for both mother and father to work, and to have equal leisure time with the children at home. For parents of very young children, however, a special job category, created by Government and unions, would allow such parents a shorter work day.

The revolution would not take away the option of being a housewife. A woman who prefers to be her husband's housekeeper and/or hostess would receive a percentage of his pay determined by the domestic relations courts. If divorced, she might be eligible for a pension fund, and for a job-training allowance. Or a divorce could be treated the same way that the dissolution of a business partnership is now.

If these proposals seem farfetched, consider Sweden, where most of them are already in effect. Sweden is not yet a working Women's Lib model; most of the role-reform programs began less than a decade ago, and are just beginning to take hold. But that country is so far ahead of us in recognizing the problem that Swedish statements on sex and equality sound like bulletins from the moon.

Our marriage laws, for instance, are so reactionary that Women's Lib groups want couples to take a compulsory written exam on the law, as for a driver's license, before going through with the wedding. A man has alimony and wifely debts to worry about, but a woman may lose so many of her civil rights that in the U.S. now, in important legal ways, she becomes a child again. In some states, she cannot sign credit agreements, use her maiden name, incorporate a business, or establish a legal residence of her own. Being a wife, according to most social and legal definitions, is still a 19th century thing.

Assuming, however, that these blatantly sexist laws are abolished or re-formed, that job discrimination is forbidden, that parents share financial responsibility for each other and the children, and that sexual relationships become partnerships of equal adults (some pretty big assumptions), then marriage will probably go right on. Men and women are, after all, physically complementary. When society stops encouraging men to be exploiters and women to be parasites, they may turn out to be more complementary in emotion as well. Women's Lib is not trying to destroy the American family. A look at the statistics on divorce—plus the way in which old people are farmed out with strangers and young people flee the home—shows the destruction that has already been done. Liberated women are just trying to point out the disaster, and build compassionate and practical alternatives from the ruins.

◆◆◆

What will exist is a variety of alternative life-styles. Since the population explosion dictates that childbearing be kept to a minimum, parents-and-children will be only one of many "families": couples, age groups, working groups, mixed communes, blood-related clans, class groups, creative groups. Single women will have the right to stay single without ridicule, without the attitudes now betrayed by "spinster" and "bachelor." Lesbians or homosexuals will no longer be denied legally binding marriages, complete with mutual-support agreements and inheritance rights. Paradoxically, the number of homosexuals may get smaller. With fewer overpossessive mothers and fewer fathers who hold up an impossibly cruel or perfectionist idea of manhood, boys will be less likely to be denied or reject their identity as males.

Changes that now seem small may get bigger:

MEN'S LIB. Men now suffer from more disease due to stress, heart attacks, ulcers, a higher suicide rate, greater difficulty living alone, less adaptability to change and, in general, a shorter life span than women. There is some scientific evidence that what produces physical problems is not work itself, but the inability to choose which work, and how much. With women bearing half the financial responsibility, and with the idea of "masculine" jobs gone, men might well feel freer and live longer.

RELIGION. Protestant women are already becoming ordained ministers; radical nuns are carrying out liturgical functions that were once the exclusive property of priests; Jewish women are rewriting prayers—particularly those that Orthodox Jews recite every morning thanking God they are not female. In the future, the church will become an area of equal participation by women. This means, of course, that organized religion will have to give up one of its great historical weapons: sexual repression. In most structured faiths, from Hinduism through Roman Catholicism, the status of women went down as the position of priests ascended. Male clergy implied, if they did not teach, that women were unclean, unworthy and sources of ungodly temptation, in order to remove them as rivals for the emotional forces of men. Full participation of women in ecclesiastical life might involve certain changes in theology, such as, for instance, a radical redefinition of sin.

LITERARY PROBLEMS. Revised sex roles will outdate more children's books than civil rights ever did. Only a few children had the problem of a *Little Black Sambo*, but most have the male-female stereotypes of "Dick and Jane." A boomlet of children's books about mothers who work has already begun, and liberated parents and editors are beginning to pressure for change in the textbook industry. Fiction writing will change more gradually, but romantic novels with wilting heroines and swashbuckling heroes will be reduced to historical value. Or perhaps to the sado-masochist trade. (*Marjorie Morningstar*, a romantic novel that took the '50s by storm, has already begun to seem as unreal as its '20s predecessor, *The Sheik*.) As for the literary plots that turn on forced marriages or horrific abortions, they will seem as dated as Prohibition stories. Free legal abortions and free birth control will force writers to give up pregnancy as the *deus ex machina*.

MANNERS AND FASHION. Dress will be more androgynous, with class symbols becoming more important than sexual ones. Pro- or anti-Establishment styles may already be more vital than who is wearing them. Hardhats are just as likely to rough up antiwar girls as antiwar men in the street, and police understand that women are just as likely to be pushers or bombers. Dances haven't required that one partner lead the other for years, anyway. Chivalry will transfer itself to those who need it, or deserve respect: old people, admired people, anyone with an armload of packages. Women with normal work identities will be less likely to attach their whole sense of self to youth and appearance; thus there will be fewer nervous breakdowns when the first wrinkles appear. Lighting cigarettes and other treasured niceties will become gestures of mutual affection. "I like to be helped on with my coat," says one Women's Lib worker, "but not if it costs me $2,000 a year in salary."

❖❖❖

For those with nostalgia for a simpler past, here is a word of comfort. Anthropologist Geoffrey Gorer studied the few peaceful human tribes and discovered one common characteristic: sex roles were not polarized. Differences of dress and occupation were at a minimum. Society, in other words, was not using sexual blackmail as a way of getting women to do cheap labor, or men to be aggressive.

Thus Women's Lib may achieve a more peaceful society on the way toward its other goals. That is why the Swedish government considers reform to bring about greater equality in the sex roles one of its most important concerns. As Prime Minister Olof Palme explained in a widely ignored speech delivered in Washington this spring: "It is *human beings* we shall emancipate. In Sweden today, if a politician should declare that the woman ought to have a different role from man's, he would be regarded as something from the Stone Age." In other words, the most radical goal of the movement is egalitarianism.

If Women's Lib wins, perhaps we all do.

ALTERNATIVES

Shulamith Firestone

However quickly Gloria Steinem's "utopian" speculations came to seem mild indeed, most of Shulamith Firestone's ideas are still as radical-sounding as when she first offered them in 1970. This is due, in no small measure, to her willingness to contemplate the end of marriage and the family. These are precisely the institutions which moderates like Steinem argue will actually be strengthened if women are freed from their second-class positions in society. Firestone, however, is no moderate; and she joined conservative critics of feminism on this one point of linking woman's liberation and the overthrow of the family.

The classic trap for any revolutionary is always, "What's your alternative?" But even if you *could* provide the interrogator with a blueprint, this does not mean he would use it: in most cases he is not sincere in wanting to know. In fact this is a common offensive, a technique to deflect revolutionary anger and turn it against itself. Moreover, the oppressed have no job to convince all people. All *they* need know is that the present system is destroying them.

But though any specific direction must arise organically out of the revolutionary action itself, still I feel tempted here to make some "dangerously utopian" concrete proposals—both in sympathy for my own pre-radical days when the Not-Responsible-For-Blueprint Line perplexed me, and also because I am aware of the political dangers in the peculiar failure of imagination concerning alternatives to the family. There are, as we have seen, several good reasons for this failure. First, there are no precedents in history for feminist revolution—there have been women revolutionaries, certainly, but they have been used by male revolutionaries, who seldom gave even lip service to equality for women, let alone to a radical feminist restructuring of society. Moreover, we haven't even a literary image of this future society; there is not even a *utopian* feminist literature in existence. Thirdly, the nature of the family unit is such that it penetrates the individual more deeply than any other social

ALTERNATIVES   From *The Dialectic of Sex: The Case for Feminist Revolution*, New York: William Morrow, 1970, 226–38, by Shulamith Firestone. Copyright © 1970 by Shulamith Firestone. Bantam edition, 1971. By permission of William Morrow & Company.

organization we have: it literally gets him "where he lives." I have shown how the family shapes his psyche to its structure—until ultimately, he imagines it absolute, talk of anything else striking him as perverted. Finally, most alternatives suggest a loss of even the little emotional warmth provided by the family, throwing him into a panic. The model that I shall now draw up is subject to the limitations of any plan laid out on paper by a solitary individual. Keep in mind that these are not meant as final answers, that in fact the reader could probably draw up another plan that would satisfy as well or better the four structural imperatives laid out above. The following proposals, then, will be sketchy, meant to stimulate thinking in fresh areas rather than to dictate the action.

◇◇◇

What is the alternative to 1984 if we could have our demands acted on in time?

The most important characteristic to be maintained in any revolution is *flexibility*. I will propose, then, a program of multiple options to exist simultaneously, interweaving with each other, some transitional, others far in the future. An individual may choose one "life style" for one decade, and prefer another at another period.

1)   *Single Professions*. A single life organized around the demands of a chosen profession, satisfying the individual's social and emotional needs through its own particular occupational structure, might be an appealing solution for many individuals, especially in the transitional period.

Single professions have practically vanished, despite the fact that the encouragement of reproduction is no longer a valid social concern. The old single roles, such as the celibate religous life, court roles—jester, musician, page, knight, and loyal squire—cowboys, sailors, firemen, cross-country truck drivers, detectives, pilots had a prestige all their own: there was no stigma attached to being professionally single. Unfortunately, these roles seldom were open to women. Most single female roles (such as spinster aunt, nun, or courtesan) were still defined by their sexual nature.

Many social scientists are now proposing as a solution to the population problem the encouragement of "deviant life styles" that by definition imply nonfertility. Richard Meier suggests that glamorous single professions previously assigned only to men should now be opened to women as well, for example, "astronaut." He notes that where these occupations exist for women, e.g., stewardess, they are based on the sex appeal of a young woman, and thus can be only limited way stations on the way to a better job or marriage. And, he adds, "so many limitations are imposed [on women's work outside the home] . . . that one suspects the existence of a culture-wide conspiracy which makes the occupational role sufficiently unpleasant that 90 percent or more would choose homemaking as a superior alternative." With the extension of whatever single roles still exist in our culture to include women, the creation of more such roles, and a program of incentives to make these professions rewarding, we could, painlessly, reduce the number of people interested in parenthood at all.

2)   *"Living Together."* Practiced at first only in Bohemian or intellectual circles and now increasingly in the population at large—especially by metropolitan youth—"living together" is becoming a common social practice. "Liv-

ing together" is the loose social form in which two or more partners, of whatever sex, enter a nonlegal sex/companionate arrangement the duration of which varies with the internal dynamics of the relationship. Their contract is only with each other; society has no interest, since neither reproduction nor production—dependencies of one party on the other—is involved. This flexible non-form could be expanded to become the standard unit in which most people would live for most of their lives.

At first, in the transitional period, sexual relationships would probably be monogamous (single standard, female-style, this time around), even if the couple chose to live with others. We might even see the continuation of strictly nonsexual group living arrangements ("roommates"). However, after several generations of nonfamily living, our psychosexual structures may become altered so radically that the monogamous couple, or the "aim-inhibited" relationship, would become obsolescent. We can only guess what might replace it—perhaps true "group marriages," transexual group marriages which also involved older children? We don't know.

The two options we have suggested so far—single professions and "living together"—already exist, but only outside the mainstream of our society, or for brief periods in the life of the normal individual. We want to *broaden* these options to include many more people for longer periods of their lives, to transfer here instead all the cultural incentives now supporting marriage—making these alternatives, finally, as common and acceptable as marriage is today.

But what about children? Doesn't everyone want children sometime in their lives? There is no denying that people now feel a genuine desire to have children. But we don't know how much of this is the product of an authentic liking for children, and how much is a displacement of other needs. We have seen that parental satisfaction is obtainable only through crippling the child: The attempted extension of ego through one's children—in the case of the man, the "immortalizing" of name, property, class, and ethnic identification, and in the case of the woman, motherhood as the justification of her existence, the resulting attempt to live through the child, child-as-project—in the end damages or destroys either the child or the parent, or both when neither wins, as the case may be. Perhaps when we strip parenthood of these other functions, we will find a real instinct for parenthood even on the part of men, a simple physical desire to associate with the young. But then we have lost nothing, for a basic demand of our alternative system is some form of intimate interaction with children. If a parenthood instinct does in fact exist, it will be allowed to operate even more freely, having shed the practical burdens of parenthood that now make it such an anguished hell.

But what, on the other hand, if we find that there is no parenthood instinct after all? Perhaps all this time society has persuaded the individual to have children only by imposing on parenthood ego concerns that had no proper outlet. This may have been unavoidable in the past—but perhaps it's now time to start more directly satisfying those ego needs. As long as natural reproduction is still necessary, we can devise less destructive cultural inducements. But it is likely that, once the ego investments in parenthood are removed, artificial reproduction will be developed and widely accepted.

3) *Households.* I shall now outline a system that I believe will satisfy any remaining needs for children after ego concerns are no longer part of our motivations. Suppose a person or a couple at some point in their lives desire to live around children in a family-size unit. While we will no longer have reproduction as the life goal of the normal individual—we have seen how single and group nonreproductive life styles could be enlarged to become satisfactory for many people for their whole lifetimes and for others, for good portions of their lifetime—certain people may still prefer community-style group living permanently, and other people may want to experience it at some time in their lives, especially during early childhood.

Thus at any given time a proportion of the population will want to live in reproductive social structures. Correspondingly, the society in general will still need reproduction, though reduced, if only to create a new generation.

The proportion of the population will be automatically a select group with a predictably higher rate of stability, because they will have had a freedom of choice now generally unavailable. Today those who do not marry and have children by a certain age are penalized: they find themselves alone, excluded, and miserable, on the margins of a society in which everyone else is compartmentalized into lifetime generational families, chauvinism and exclusiveness their chief characteristic. (Only in Manhattan is single living even tolerable, and that can be debated.) Most people are still forced into marriage by family pressure, the "shotgun," economic considerations, and other reasons that have nothing to do with choice of life style. In our new reproductive unit, however, with the limited contract (see below), childrearing so diffused as to be practically eliminated, economic considerations non-existent, and all participating members having entered only on the basis of personal preference, "unstable" reproductive social structures will have disappeared.

This unit I shall call a *household* rather than an extended family. The distinction is important: The word *family* implies biological reproduction and some degree of division of labor by sex, and thus the traditional dependencies and resulting power relations, extended over generations; though the size of the family—in this case, the larger numbers of the "extended" family—may affect the strength of this hierarchy, it does not change its structural definition. "Household," however, connotes only a large grouping of people living together for an unspecified time, and with no specified set of interpersonal relations. How would a "household" operate?

LIMITED CONTRACT. If the household replaced marriage perhaps we would at first legalize it in the same way—if this is necessary at all. A group of ten or so consenting adults of varying ages* could apply for a license as a group in much the same way as a young couple today applies for a marriage license, perhaps even undergoing some form of ritual ceremony, and then might proceed in the same way to set up house. The household license would, however, apply only for a given period, perhaps seven to ten years, or whatever was decided on as

---

*An added advantage of the household is that it allows older people past their fertile years to share fully in parenthood when they so desire.

the minimal time in which children needed a stable structure in which to grow up—but probably a much shorter period than we now imagine. If at the end of this period the group decided to stay together, it could always get a renewal. However, no single individual would be contracted to stay after this period, and perhaps some members of the unit might transfer out, or new members come in. Or, the unit could disband altogether.

There are many advantages to short-term households, stable compositional units lasting for only about a decade: the end of family chauvinism, built up over generations, of prejudices passed down from one generation to the next, the inclusion of people of all ages in the child rearing process, the integration of many age groups into one social unit, the breadth of personality that comes from exposure to many rather than to (the idiosyncrasies of) a few, and so on.

CHILDREN.   A regulated percentage of each household—say one-third—would be children. But whether, at first, genetic children created by couples within the household, or at some future time—after a few generations of household living had severed the special connection of adults with "their" children—children were produced artificially, or adopted, would not matter: (minimal) responsibility for the early physical dependence of children would be evenly diffused among all members of the household.

But though it would still be structurally sound, we must be aware that as long as we use natural childbirth methods, the "household" could never be a totally liberating social form. A mother who undergoes a nine-month pregnancy is likely to feel that the product of all that pain and discomfort "belongs" to her ("To think of what I went through to have you!"). But we want to destroy this possessiveness along with its cultural reinforcements so that no one child will be *a priori* favored over another, so that children will be loved for their own sake.

But what if there is an instinct for pregnancy? I doubt it. Once we have sloughed off cultural superstructures, we may uncover a sex instinct, the normal consequences of which *lead* to pregnancy. And perhaps there is also an instinct to care for the young once they arrive. But an instinct for pregnancy itself would be superfluous—could nature anticipate man's mastery of reproduction? And what if, once the false motivations for pregnancy had been shed, women no longer wanted to "have" children at all? Might this not be a disaster, given that artificial reproduction is not yet perfected? But women have no special reproductive *obligation* to the species. If they are no longer willing, then artificial methods will have to be developed hurriedly, or, at the very least, satisfactory compensations—other than destructive ego investments—would have to be supplied to make it worth their while.

Adults and older children would take care of babies for as long as they needed it, but since there would be many adults and older children sharing the responsibility—as in the extended family—no one person would ever be involuntarily stuck with it.

Adult/child relationships would develop just as do the best relationships today: some adults might prefer certain children over others, just as some children might prefer certain adults over others—these might become lifelong attachments in which the individuals concerned mutually agreed to stay together, perhaps to form some kind of non-reproductive unit. Thus all relationships would be based on love alone, uncorrupted by objective dependencies and the resulting class inequalities. Enduring relationships between people of widely divergent ages would become common.

LEGAL RIGHTS AND TRANSFERS.   With the weakening and severance of the blood ties, the power hierarchy of the family would break down. The legal structure—as long as it is still necessary—would reflect this democracy at the roots of our society. Women would be identical under the law with men. Children would no longer be "minors," under the patronage of "parents"—they would have full rights. Remaining physical inequalities could be legally compensated for: for example, if a child were beaten, perhaps he could report it to a special simplified "household" court where he would be granted instant legal redress.

Another special right of children would be the right of immediate transfer: if the child for any reason did not like the household into which he had been born so arbitrarily, he would be helped to transfer out. An adult on the other hand—one who had lived one span in a household (seven to ten years)—might have to present his case to the court, which would then decide, as do divorce courts today, whether he had adequate grounds for breaking his contract. A certain number of transfers within the seven-year period might be necessary for the smooth functioning of the household, and would not be injurious to its stability as a unit so long as a core remained. (In fact, new people now and then might be a refreshing change.) However, the unit, for its own best economy, might have to place a ceiling on the number of transfers in or out, to avoid depletion, excessive growth, and/or friction.

CHORES.   As for housework: The larger family-sized group (twelve to fifteen people) would be more practical—the waste and repetition of the duplicate nuclear family unit would be avoided, e.g., as in shopping or cooking for a small family, without the loss of intimacy of the larger communal experiment. In the interim, any housework would have to be rotated equitably; but eventually cybernation could automate out almost all domestic chores.

CITY PLANNING.   City planning, architecture, furnishings, all would be altered to reflect the new social structure. The trend toward mass-produced housing would probably continue, but the housing might be designed and even built (perhaps out of prefabricated components) by the people living there to suit their own needs and tastes. Privacy could be built in: either through private rooms in every household, or with "retreats" within the larger city to be shared by people of other households, or both. The whole might form a complex the size of a small town or a large campus. Perhaps campus is the clearer image: We could have small units of self-determined housing—prefabricated component parts set up or dismantled easily and quickly to suit the needs of the limited contract—as well as central permanent buildings to fill the needs of the community as a whole, i.e., perhaps the equivalent of a "student union" for socializing, restaurants, a large computer bank, a modern communications center, a computerized library and film center, "learning centers" devoted to various specialized interests, and whatever else might be necessary in a cybernetic community.

THE ECONOMY.   The end of the family structure would necessitate simultaneous changes in the larger economy. Not only would reproduction be qualitatively different, so would production: just as we have had to purify relations with children of all external considerations we would first have to have, to be entirely successful in our goals, socialism within a technetronic state, aiming first to redistribute drudgery equitably, and eventually to eliminate it altogether. With the further development and wise use of machines, people could be freed from toil, "work" divorced from wages and redefined: Now both adults and children could indulge in serious "play" as much as they wanted.

In the transition, as long as we still had a money economy, people might receive a guaranteed annual income from the state to take care of basic physical needs. These incomes, distributed equitably to men, women, and children, regardless of age, work, prestige, birth, would in themselves equalize in one blow the economic class system.

ACTIVITY.   What would people do in this utopia? I think that will not be a problem. If we truly had abolished all unpleasant work, people would have the time and the energy to develop healthy interests of their own. What is now found only among the elite, the pursuit of specialized interests for their own sake, would probably become the norm.

As for our educational institutions: The irrelevancy of the school system practically guarantees its breakdown in the near future. Perhaps we could replace it with noncompulsory "learning centers," which would combine both the minimally necessary functions of our lower educational institutions, the teaching of rudimentary skills, with those of the higher, the expansion of knowledge, including everyone of any age or level, children and adults.

Yes, but what about basic skills? How, for example, could a child with no formal sequential training enter an advanced curriculum like architecture? But traditional book learning, the memorizing of facts, which forms the most substantial portion of the curriculum of our elementary schools, will be radically altered under the impact of cybernation—a qualitative difference, to the apparatus of culture at least as significant a change as was the printing press, even as important as the alphabet. McLuhan pointed out the beginning of a reversal from literary to visual means of absorbing knowledge. We can expect the escalation of this and other effects in the development of modern media for the rapid transmittal of information. And the *amount* of rote knowledge necessary either for children or adults will itself be vastly reduced, for we shall have computer banks within easy reach. After all, why store facts in one's head when computer banks could supply quicker and broader information instantaneously? (Already today children wonder why they must learn multiplication tables rather than the operation of an adding machine.) Whatever mental storing of basic facts is still necessary can be quickly accomplished through new mechanical methods, teaching machines, records and tapes, and so on, which, when they become readily available, would allow the abolition of compulsory schooling for basic skills. Like foreign students in the pursuit of a specialized profession, the child can pick up any necessary basic "language" on the side, through these supplementary machine methods. But it is more likely that the fundamental skills and knowledge necessary will be the same for adults as for children: skill in operating new machines. Programming skills may become universally required, but rather than through years of nine-to-five schooling, it would have to be learned (rapidly) only in conjunction with the requirements of a specific discipline.

As for "career indecision": Those people today whose initial "hobby" has survived intact from childhood to become their adult "profession" will most often tell you they developed it before the age of nine.* As long as specialized professions still existed, they could be changed as often as adults change majors or professions today. But if choice of profession had no superimposed motives, if they were based only on interest in the subject itself, switches in mid-course would probably be far fewer. Inability to develop strong interests is today mostly the result of the corruption of culture and its institutions.

Thus our conception of work and education would be much closer to the medieval first-hand apprenticeship to a discipline, people of all ages participating at all levels. As in academia today, the internal dynamics of the various disciplines would foster their own social organization, providing a means for meeting other people of like interests, and of sharing the intellectual and aesthetic pursuits now available only to a select few, the intelligentsia. The kind of social environment now found only in the best departments of the best colleges might become the life style of the masses, freed to develop their potential from the start: Whereas now only the lucky or persevering ones ever arrive at (usually only professing to) "doing their thing," then everyone would have the opportunity to develop to his full potential.

Or not develop if he so chose—but this seems unlikely, since every child at first exhibits curiosity about people, things, the world in general and what makes it tick. It is only because unpleasant reality *dampens* his curiosity that the child learns to scale down his interests, thus becoming the average bland adult. But if we should remove these obstructions, then all people would develop as fully as only the greatest and wealthiest classes, and a few isolated "geniuses," have been able to. Each individual would contribute to the society as a whole, not for wages or other incentives of prestige and power, but because the work he chose to do interested him in itself, and perhaps only incidentally because it had a social value for others (as healthily selfish as is only Art today). Work that had only social value and no personal value would have been eliminated by the machine.

---

*If children today were given a realistic idea of the professions available—not just fireman/nurse—they might arrive at a special interest even sooner.

Supplementary Readings

ALMQUIST, ELIZABETH M. *Minorities, Gender, and Work*. Lexington, Mass.: Lexington Books, 1979.

ANDERSON, KAREN. *Wartime Women: Sex Roles, Family Relations, and the Status of Women During World War II*. Westport, Conn.: Greenwood Press, 1981.

ANGELOU, MAYA. *I Know Why the Caged Bird Sings*. New York: Random House, 1969.

BALDWIN, MONICA. *I Leapt Over the Wall: Contrasts and Impressions after Twenty-eight Years in a Convent*. New York: Rinehart, 1950.

BANNER, LOIS W. *American Beauty*. New York: Knopf, 1983.

————. *Women in Modern America: A Brief History*. New York: Harcourt, Brace, Jovanovich, 1974.

BARKER-BENFIELD, G. J. *The Horrors of the Half-known Life: Male Attitudes Toward Women and Sexuality in Nineteenth Century America*. New York: Harper and Row, 1976.

BAXANDALL, ROSALYN, LINDA GORDON, AND SUSAN REVERBY, eds. *America's Working Women: A Documentary History, 1600–Present*. New York: Vintage Books, 1976.

DE BEAUVOIR, SIMONE. *The Second Sex*. New York: Knopf, 1953.

BERCH, BETTINA. *The Endless Day: The Political Economy of Women and Work*. New York: Harcourt, Brace, Jovanovich, 1982.

BERG, BARBARA J. *The Remembered Gate: Origins of American Feminism: The Woman and the City, 1800–1860*. New York: Oxford University Press, 1978.

BERKIN, CAROL R., AND CLARA M. LOVETT. *Women, War, and Revolution*. New York: Holmes and Meier, 1980.

BERKIN, CAROL RUTH, AND MARY BETH NORTON. *Women of America: A History*. Boston: Houghton Mifflin Co., 1979.

BERNARD, JESSIE. *The Female World*. New York: The Free Press, 1981.

BERNIKOW, LOUISE. *Among Women*. New York: Crown Publishers, Inc., 1980.

BLAIR, KAREN J. *The Clubwoman as Feminist: True Womanhood Redefined, 1868–1914*. New York: Holmes and Meier, 1980.

BORDIN, RUTH. *Woman and Temperance: The Quest for Power and Liberty, 1873–1900.* Philadelphia: Temple University Press, 1981.

BROVERMAN, INGE K., et al. "Sex-Role Stereotypes and Clinical Judgments of Mental Health." *Journal of Consulting and Clinical Psychology,* 34 (1970), 1–7.

BROWNLEE, W. ELLIOT, AND MARY M. BROWNLEE, eds. *Women in the American Economy: A Documentary History, 1675–1929.* New Haven, Conn.: Yale University Press, 1976.

BRUCH, HILDE. *The Golden Cage: The Enigma of Anorexia Nervosa.* Cambridge, Mass.: Harvard University Press, 1978.

BUHLE, MARI JO. *Women and American Socialism, 1870–1920.* Urbana, Ill.: University of Illinois Press, 1981.

BULARZIK, MARY. "Sexual Harassment at the Workplace: Historical Notes." *Radical America,* 12 (1978), 25–43.

CHAFE, WILLIAM H. *The American Woman: Her Changing Social, Economic, and Political Roles, 1920–1970.* New York: Oxford University Press, 1972.

CHESLER, PHYLLIS. *Women and Madness.* New York: Avon Books, 1973.

CHODOROW, NANCY. *The Reproduction of Mothering: Psychoanalysis and the Sociology of Gender.* Berkeley, Calif.: University of California Press, 1978.

CHRIST, CAROL, AND JUDITH PLASKOW, eds. *Womanspirit Rising: A Feminist Reader in Religion.* New York: Harper and Row, 1979.

CHRISTIAN, BARBARA. *Black Women Novelists: The Development of a Tradition, 1892–1976.* Westport, Conn.: Greenwood Press, 1980.

CONRAD, SUSAN PHINNEY. *Perish the Thought: Intellectual Women in Romantic America, 1830–1860.* New York: Oxford University Press, 1976.

COTT, NANCY F. *The Bonds of Womanhood: "Woman's Sphere" in New England, 1780–1835.* New Haven, Conn.: Yale University Press, 1977.

COTT, NANCY F., AND ELIZABETH H. PLECK, eds. *A Heritage of Her Own: Toward a New Social History of American Women.* New York: Simon and Schuster, 1979.

COWAN, RUTH SCHWARTZ. "The 'Industrial Revolution' in the Home: Household Technology and Social Change in the Twentieth Century." *Technology and Culture,* 17 (1976), 1–23.

DALY, MARY. *Beyond God the Father: Toward a Philosophy of Women's Liberation.* Boston: Beacon Press, 1973.

DANCYGER IRENE. *A World of Women: An Illustrated History of Women's Magazines.* Dublin, Ireland: Gill and Macmillan, 1978.

DAVIDSON, CATHY N., AND E. M. BRONER, eds. *The Lost Tradition: Mothers and Daughters in Literature.* New York: F. Ungar, 1980.

DAVIES, MARGERY W. *Woman's Place Is at the Typewriter: Office Work and Office Workers, 1870–1930.* Philadelphia: Temple University Press, 1983.

DAVIS, ANGELA Y. *Women, Race, and Class.* New York: Random House, 1981.

DEGLER, CARL N. *At Odds: Woman and the Family in America from the Revolution to the Present.* New York: Oxford University Press, 1981.

———. "What Ought to Be and What Was: Women's Sexuality in the Nineteenth Century." *American Historical Review* 79 (1974), 1467–1490.

DELANEY, JANICE, MARY J. LUPTON, AND EMILY TOTH, eds. *The Curse: A Cultural History of Menstruation.* New York: Dutton, 1976.

DEXTER, ELISABETH ANTHONY. *Colonial Women of Affairs: A Study of Women in Business and the Professions in America before 1776.* Boston: Houghton Mifflin, 1931.

DINNERSTEIN, DOROTHY. *The Mermaid and the Minotaur: Sexual Arrangements and Human Malaise.* New York: Harper and Row, 1976.

DOUGLAS, ANN. *The Feminization of American Culture.* New York: Knopf, 1977.

DUBOIS, ELLEN CAROL. *Feminism and Suffrage: The Emergence of an Independent Women's Movement in America, 1848–1869.* Ithaca, N.Y.: Cornell University Press, 1978.

EHRENREICH, BARBARA, AND DEIRDRE ENGLISH. *For Her Own Good: 150 Years of the Experts' Advice to Women.* Garden City, N.Y.: Anchor Books, 1979.

———. *Witches, Midwives, and Nurses: A History of Women Healers.* Old Westbury, N.Y.: The Feminist Press, 1973.

EISLER, BENITA, ed. *The Lowell Offering: Writings by New England Mill Women.* Philadelphia: Lippincott, 1977.

EPSTEIN, BARBARA LESLIE. *The Politics of Domesticity: Women, Evangelism, and Temperance in Nineteenth-Century America.* Middletown, Conn.: Wesleyan University Press, 1981.

EVANS, SARAH. *Personal Politics: The Roots of Women's Liberation in the Civil Rights Movement and the New Left.* New York: Knopf, 1979.

FADERMAN, LILLIAN. *Surpassing the Love of Men: Romantic Friendship and Love Between Women from the Renaissance to the Present.* New York: Morrow, 1981.

FLEXNER, ELEANOR. *Century of Struggle: The Women's Rights Movement in the United States.* Rev. ed. Cambridge, Mass.: Belknap Press of Harvard University Press, 1975.

FONER, PHILIP, ed. *The Factory Girls: A Collection of Writings on Life and Struggles in the New England Factories of the 1840's.* Urbana, Ill.: University of Illinois Press, 1977.

FREEMAN, JO, ed. *Women: A Feminist Perspective.* Palo Alto, Calif.: Mayfield Publishing Co., 1979.

FRIEDAN, BETTY. *It Changed My Life: Writings on the Women's Movement.* New York: Random House, 1976.

———. *The Second Stage.* New York: Summit Books, 1982.

FRIEDMAN, LESLIE. *Sex Role Stereotyping in the Mass Media: An Annotated Bibliography.* New York: Garland, 1977.

FRIEZE IRENE H., et al. *Women and Sex Roles: A Social Psychological Perspective.* New York: Norton, 1978.

GARRISON, DEE. *Apostles of Culture: The Public Librarian and American Society, 1876–1920.* New York: Free Press, 1979.

GILBERT, SANDRA M., AND SUSAN GUBAR. *Shakespeare's Sisters: Feminist Essays on Women Poets.* Bloomington, Ind.: Indiana University Press, 1979.

GILLIGAN, CAROL. *In a Different Voice: Psychological Theory and Women's Development.* Cambridge, Mass.: Harvard University Press, 1982.

GILMAN, CHARLOTTE PERKINS. *Women and Economics.* New York: Harper and Row, rpt. 1966.

GOLDENBERG, NAOMI R. *Changing of the Gods: Feminism and the End of Traditional Religions.* Boston: Beacon Press, 1979.

GORDON, LINDA. *Woman's Body, Woman's Right: A Social History of Birth Control in America.* New York: Grossman, 1976.

GORNICK, VIVIAN, AND BARBARA K. MORAN, eds. *Woman in Sexist Society: Studies in Power and Powerlessness.* New York: Basic Books, 1971.

GREEN, RAYNA. *Native American Women: A Bibliography.* Bloomington, Ind.: Indiana University Press, 1983.

GREENWALD, MAURINE WEINER. *Women, War, and Work: The Impact of World War I on Women Workers in the United States.* Westport, Conn.: Greenwood Press, 1980.

GREER, GERMAINE. *The Female Eunuch.* New York: McGraw-Hill, 1972.

GRIFFIN, SUSAN. *Woman and Nature: The Roaring Inside Her.* New York: Harper and Row, 1978.

HALLER, JOHN, AND ROBIN HALLER. *The Physician and Sexuality in Victorian America.* Urbana, Ill.: University of Illinois Press, 1974.

HARRIS, BARBARA. *Beyond Her Sphere: Women and the Professions in American History.* Westport, Conn.: Greenwood Press, 1978.

HARTMANN, SUSAN M. *The Home Front and Beyond: American Women in the 1940's.* Boston: Twayne Publishers, 1982.

HASKELL, MOLLY. *From Reverence to Rape: The Treatment of Women in the Movies.* New York: Holt, Rinehart and Winston, 1974.

HAYDEN, DOLORES. *The Grand Domestic Revolution: A History of Feminist Designs for American Homes, Neighborhoods, and Cities.* Cambridge, Mass.: MIT Press, 1981.

HITE, SHERE. *The Hite Report: A Nationwide Study of Female Sexuality.* New York: Macmillan, 1976.

HOFFMAN, NANCY, ed. *Woman's "True" Profession: Voices from the History of Teaching.* Old Westbury, N.Y.: The Feminist Press, 1981.

HORNEY, KAREN. *Feminine Psychology.* New York: W. W. Norton, 1967.

HOWE, LOUISE KAPP. *Pink Collar Workers: Inside the World of Women's Work.* New York: Putnam, 1977.

HUBBARD, RUTH, MARY SUE HENIFEN, AND BARBARA FRIED, eds. *Women Looking at Biology Looking at Women: A Collection of Feminist Critiques.* Boston: G. K. Hall, 1979.

HULL, GLORIA T., PATRICIA BELL SCOTT, AND BARBARA SMITH, eds. *All the Women Are White, All the Blacks Are Men, But Some of Us Are Brave: Black Women's Studies.* Old Westbury, N.Y.: The Feminist Press, 1982.

JAGGAR, ALISON M., AND PAULA ROTHENBERG STRUHL, eds. *Feminist Frameworks: Alternative Theoretical Accounts of the Relations Between Women and Men.* New York: McGraw-Hill, 1978.

JANEWAY, ELIZABETH. *Man's World, Woman's Place: A Study in Social Mythology.* New York: Morrow, 1971.

JEFFREY, JULIE ROY. *Frontier Women: The Trans-Mississippi West, 1840–1880.* New York: Hill and Wang, 1979.

JELINEK, ESTELLE C., ed. *Women's Autobiography: Essays in Criticism.* Bloomington, Ind.: Indiana University Press, 1980.

JOHNSTON, JILL. *Lesbian Nation: The Feminist Solution.* New York: Simon and Schuster, 1974.

JOSEPH, GLORIA I., AND JILL LEWIS. *Common Differences: Conflicts in Black and White Feminist Perspectives.* New York: Anchor Press/Doubleday, 1981.

KAHN, KATHY. *Hillbilly Women.* New York: Avon, 1974.

KANTER, ROSABETH MOSS. *Men and Women of the Corporation.* New York: Basic Books, 1977.

KATZMAN, DAVID M. *Seven Days a Week: Women and Domestic Service in Industrializing America.* New York: Oxford University Press, 1978.

KELLEY, MARY. *Private Woman, Public Stage*. New York: Oxford University Press, 1984.

KENNEALLY, JAMES J. *Women and American Trade Unions*. 2nd ed. Montreal; St. Albans, Vt.: Eden Press Women's Publications, 1981.

KENNEDY, FLORYNCE, AND DIANE B. SCHULDER. *Abortion Rap*. New York: McGraw-Hill, 1971.

KERBER, LINDA K. *Women of the Republic: Intellect and Ideology in Revolutionary America*. Chapel Hill, N.C.: University of North Carolina Press, 1980.

KESSLER-HARRIS, ALICE. *Out to Work: A History of America's Wage-earning Women*. New York: Oxford University Press, 1982.

KINGSTON, MAXINE HONG. *The Woman Warrior: Memories of a Girlhood Among Ghosts*. New York: Vintage Books, 1977.

KINSEY, ALFRED C., et al. *Sexual Behavior in the Human Female*. Philadelphia: Saunders, 1953.

LADNER, JOYCE. *Tomorrow's Tomorrow: The Black Woman*. Garden City, N.Y.: Doubleday, 1971.

LAKOFF, ROBIN. *Language and Woman's Place*. New York: Harper and Row, 1975.

LASCH, CHRISTOPHER. *Haven in a Heartless World: The Family Besieged*. New York: Basic Books, 1977.

LAWS, JUDITH LANG, AND PEPPER SCHWARTZ. *Sexual Scripts: The Social Construction of Female Sexuality*. Hinsdale, Ill.: Dryden Press, 1977.

LEMONS, J. STANLEY. *The Woman Citizen: Social Feminism in the 1920's*. Urbana, Ill.: University of Illinois Press, 1973.

LERNER, GERDA. "The Lady and the Mill Girl: Changes in the Status of Women in the Age of Jackson." *Mid-Continental American Studies Journal*, 10 (1969): 5–15.

————. *The Majority Finds Its Past: Placing Women in History*. New York: Oxford University Press, 1979.

————., ed. *Black Women in White America: A Documentary History*. New York: Pantheon Books, 1972.

LIPPARD, LUCY R. *From the Center: Feminist Essays on Women's Art*. New York: Dutton, 1976.

LOEWENBERG, BERT JAMES, AND RUTH BOGIN, eds. *Black Women in Nineteenth-Century American Life: Their Words, Their Thoughts, Their Feelings*. University Park, Pa.: Pennsylvania State University Press, 1976.

MACDONALD, BARBARA, WITH CYNTHIA RICH. *Look Me in the Eye: Old Women, Aging, and Ageism*. San Francisco: Spinsters, Inc., 1984.

MACKINNON, CATHERINE A. *Sexual Harassment of Working Women: A Case of Sex Discrimination*. New Haven, Conn.: Yale University Press, 1979.

MACCOBY, ELEANOR E., AND C. N. JACKLIN. *The Psychology of Sex Differences*. Stanford, Calif.: Stanford University Press, 1974.

MARTIN, DEL, AND PHYLLIS LYON. *Lesbian/Woman*. New York: Bantam Books, 1972.

MASTERS, WILLIAM H., AND VIRGINIA E. JOHNSON. *Human Sexual Response*. Boston: Little, Brown, 1966.

MAY, ELAINE TYLER. *Great Expectations: Marriage and Divorce in Post-Victorian America*. Chicago: University of Chicago Press, 1980.

MEAD, MARGARET. *Blackberry Winter: My Earlier Years*. New York: William Morrow, 1972.

MELOSH, BARBARA. *"The Physician's Hand": Work, Culture, and Conflict in American Nursing*. Philadelphia: Temple University Press, 1982.

MILLER, JEAN BAKER. *Psychoanalysis and Women: Contributions to New Theory and Therapy.* New York: Brunner/Mazel, 1973.
———. *Toward a New Psychology of Women.* Boston: Beacon, 1976.
MILLET, KATE. *Sexual Politics.* Garden City, N.Y.: Doubleday, 1970.
DE MIRANDE, ALFREDO, AND EVANGELINA ENRIQUEZ. *La Chicana: The Mexican-American Woman.* Chicago: University of Chicago Press, 1979.
MOHR, JAMES C. *Abortion in America: The Origins and Evolution of National Policy, 1800–1900.* New York: Oxford University Press, 1978.
MONEY, JOHN W., AND ANKE EHRHARDT. *Man and Woman, Boy and Girl: The Differentiation and Dimorphism of Gender Identity from Conception to Maturity.* Baltimore: Johns Hopkins University Press, 1972.
MORGAN, ROBIN, ed. *Sisterhood Is Powerful: An Anthology of Writings from the Women's Liberation Movement.* New York: Random House, 1970.

NIETHAMMER, CAROLYN. *Daughters of the Earth: The Lives and Legends of American Indian Women.* New York: Collier Books, 1977.
NORTON, MARY BETH, ed. *Liberty's Daughters: The Revolutionary Experience of American Women, 1750–1800.* Boston: Little, Brown, 1980.

OGLESBY, CAROLE A. *Women and Sport: From Myth to Reality.* Philadelphia: Lea and Febiger, 1978.
OLSEN, TILLIE. *Silences.* New York: Delacorte, 1978.
O'NEILL, WILLIAM L. *Everyone Was Brave: The Rise and Fall of Feminism in America.* Chicago: Quadrangle Books, 1969.
ORBACH, SUSAN. *Fat Is a Feminist Issue.* New York: Paddington Press, 1978.

PEARSON, CAROL. "Women's Fantasies and Feminist Utopias." *Frontiers*, 2 (1977), 50–61.
PERUN, PAMELA, ed. *The Undergraduate Woman: Issues in Educational Equity.* Lexington, Mass.: Lexington Books, 1982.
PORTERFIELD, AMANDA. *Feminine Spirituality in America: From Sarah Edwards to Martha Graham.* Philadelphia: Temple University Press, 1980.

RICH, ADRIENNE. *Of Woman Born: Motherhood as Experience and Institution.* New York: Norton, 1976.
ROBINSON, PAUL A. *The Modernization of Sex: Havelock Ellis, Alfred Kinsey, William Masters, and Virginia Johnson.* New York: Harper and Row, 1976.
ROHRBAUGH, JOANNA BUNKER. *Women: Psychology's Puzzle.* New York: Basic Books, 1979.
ROSEN, MARJORIE. *Popcorn Venus: Women, Movies, and the American Dream.* New York: Coward, McCann, and Geoghegan, 1973.
ROSEN, RUTH. *The Lost Sisterhood: Prostitution in America, 1900–1918.* Baltimore: Johns Hopkins University Press, 1982.
ROSENBERG, CHARLES E. "Sexuality, Class and Role in 19th-Century America." *American Quarterly*, 25 (1973), 131–153.
ROSENBERG, CHARLES E., AND CARROLL SMITH-ROSENBERG. "The Female Animal: Medical and Biological Views of Woman and Her Role in Nineteenth-Century America." *Journal of American History*, 60 (1973), 332–356.
ROSENBERG, ROSALIND. *Beyond Separate Spheres: Intellectual Roots of Modern Feminism.* New Haven, Conn.: Yale University Press, 1982.

ROSSI, ALICE S., ed. *The Feminist Papers: From Adams to de Beauvoir.* New York: Columbia University Press, 1973.

ROUSMANIERE, JOHN P. "Cultural Hybrid in the Slums: The College Woman and the Settlement House, 1889–1894." *American Quarterly,* 22 (1970), 45–66.

RUBIN, LILLIAN. *Worlds of Pain: Life in the Working-Class Family.* New York: Basic Books, 1976.

RUDDICK, SARA, AND PAMELA DANIELS, eds. *Working It Out: 23 Women Writers, Artists, Scientists and Scholars Talk About Their Lives and Work.* New York: Pantheon, 1977.

RUETHER, ROSEMARY, AND R. S. KELLER, eds. *Women and Religion in America. Vol. 1: The 19th Century.* New York: Harper and Row, 1982.

RYAN, MARY P. *Cradle of the Middle Class: The Family in Oneida County, New York, 1790–1865.* New York: Cambridge University Press, 1981.

SADKER, MYRA POLLACK, AND DAVID MILLER SADKER. "Sexism in Teacher Education Texts." *Harvard Educational Review,* 50 (1980), 36–46.

SANGER, MARGARET. *Motherhood in Bondage.* New York: Brentano's, 1928.

SCHARF, LOIS. *To Work and to Wed: Female Employment, Feminism, and the Great Depression.* Westport, Conn.: Greenwood Press, 1980.

SCHLISSEL, LILLIAN. *Women's Diaries of the Westward Journey.* New York: Schocken Books, 1982.

SCHOEN, CAROL. *Anzia Yezierska.* Boston: Twayne, 1982.

SCOTT, ANNE FIROR. "The Ever-Widening Circle: The Diffusion of Feminist Values from the Troy Female Seminary, 1822–1872." *History of Education Quarterly,* 19 (1979), 3–25.

———. *The Southern Lady: From Pedestal to Politics, 1830–1930.* Chicago: University of Chicago Press, 1970.

SEIFER, NANCY, ed. *Nobody Speaks for Me!: Self-Portraits of American Working Class Women.* New York: Simon and Schuster, 1976.

SELLER, MAXINE S., ed. *Immigrant Women.* Philadelphia: Temple University Press, 1981.

SHERMAN, JULIA A., AND EVELYN TORTON BECK, eds. *The Prism of Sex: Essays in the Sociology of Knowledge.* Madison, Wis.: University of Wisconsin Press, 1979.

SKLAR, KATHERINE KISH. *Catharine Beecher: A Study in American Domesticity.* New Haven, Conn.: Yale University Press, 1973.

SMITH-ROSENBERG, CARROLL. "Beauty, the Beast, and the Militant Woman: A Case Study in Sex Roles and Social Stress in Jacksonian America." *American Quarterly,* 23 (1971), 562–584.

———. "The Female World of Love and Ritual." *Signs,* 1 (1975), 1–29.

SPENDER, DALE. *Man Made Language.* London, England: Routledge and Kegan Paul, 1980.

———, ed. *Men's Studies Modified: The Impact of Feminism on the Academic Disciplines.* Oxford, England: Pergamon Press, 1981.

STACEY, JUDITH, SUSAN BÉREAUD, AND JOAN DANIELS, eds. *And Jill Came Tumbling After: Sexism in American Education.* New York: Dell, 1974.

STAGE, SARAH. *Female Complaints: Lydia Pinkham and the Business of Women's Medicine.* New York: Norton, 1979.

STEINEM, GLORIA. *Outrageous Acts and Everyday Rebellions.* New York: Holt, Rinehart, and Winston, 1983.

STERNBURG, JANET, ed. *The Writer on Her Work.* New York: Norton, 1980.

STIEHM, JUDITH H. *Bring Me Men and Women: Mandated Change at the U.S. Air Force Academy.* Berkeley, Calif.: University of California Press, 1981.

STIMPSON, CATHARINE R., AND ETHEL SPECTOR PERSON. *Women—Sex and Sexuality*. Chicago: University of Chicago Press, 1980.

STOCK, PHYLLIS. *Better than Rubies: A History of Women's Education*. New York: Putnam, 1978.

STRASSER, SUSAN. *Never Done: A History of American Housework*. New York: Pantheon Books, 1982.

TEPPERMAN, JEAN. *Not Servants, Not Machines: Office Workers Speak Out!* Boston: Beacon Press, 1976.

THOMPSON, CLARA. *On Women*. New York: New American Library, 1964.

TILLY, LOUISE A., AND JOAN W. SCOTT. *Women, Work, and Family*. New York: Holt, Rinehart and Winston, 1978.

TODD, JANET, ed. *Gender and Literary Voice*. New York: Holmes and Meier, 1980.

TREIMAN, DONALD, AND HEIDI HARTMANN. *Women, Work, and Wages: Equal Pay for Jobs of Equal Value*. Washington, D.C.: National Academy Press, 1981.

TUCHMAN, GAYE, ARLENE KAPLAN DANIELS, AND JANE BENET. *Hearth and Home: Images of Women in the Mass Media*. New York: Oxford University Press, 1978.

TWIN, STEPHANIE L. *Out of the Bleachers: Writings on Women and Sport*. Old Westbury, N.Y.: The Feminist Press, 1979.

VETTERLING-BRAGGIN, MARY. *Sexist Language: A Modern Philosophical Analysis*. Totowa, N.J.: Rowman and Littlefield, 1981.

VICINUS, MARTHA. *Suffer and Be Still: Women in the Victorian Age*. Bloomington, Ind.: Indiana University Press, 1972.

WALSH, MARY ROTH. *"Doctors Wanted, No Women Need Apply": Sexual Barriers in the Medical Profession, 1835–1975*. New Haven, Conn.: Yale University Press, 1977.

WALTERS, RONALD G. *Primers for Prudery: Sexual Advice to Victorian America*. Englewood Cliffs, N.J.: Prentice-Hall, 1973.

WANDERSEE, WINIFRED D. *Women's Work and Family Values, 1920–1940*. Cambridge, Mass.: Harvard University Press, 1981.

WARE, SUSAN. *Beyond Suffrage: Women in the New Deal*. Cambridge, Mass.: Harvard University Press, 1981.

WATERS, JUDITH, AND FLORENCE L. DENMARK. "The Beauty Trap." *The Journal of Clinical Issues in Psychology*, 6 (1974), 10–15.

WELTER, BARBARA. *Dimity Convictions: The American Woman in the Nineteenth Century*. Athens, Ohio: Ohio University Press, 1976.

WERTHEIMER, BARBARA MAYER, AND ANNE H. NELSON. *Trade Union Women: A Study of Their Participation in New York City Locals*. New York: Praeger, 1975.

WOLOCH, NANCY. *Women and the American Experience*. New York: Knopf, 1984.

WOOD, ANN DOUGLAS. "The Scribbling Women and Fanny Fern: Why Women Wrote." *American Quarterly*, 2 (1971), 3–24.